HUMAN RELATIONS

A Game Plan for Improving Personal Adjustment

FOURTH EDITION

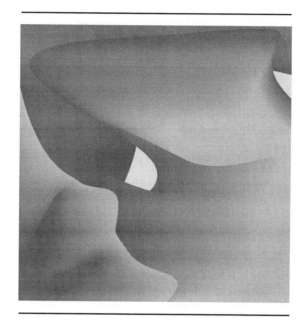

LOREN FORD

Clackamas Community College

PEARSON

Prentice Hall

Upper Saddle River,
New Jersey 07458

Library of Congress Cataloging-in-Publication Data

Ford, Loren.
   Human relations : a game plan for improving personal adjustment / Loren Ford. —4th ed.
     p. cm.
   Includes bibliographical references.
   ISBN 0-13-227563-5
  1. Adjustment (Psychology) 2. Interpersonal communication. 3. Interpersonal relations.
4. Self-perception. 5. Life change events. I. Title.
   BF335.F67 2006
   158—dc22

                                     2006015113

Executive Editor: Jeff Marshall
Editorial Director: Leah Jewell
Editorial Assistant: Jennifer Puma
Senior Marketing Manager: Jaanette Moyer
Assistant Managing Editor: Maureen Richardson
Production Liaison: Fran Russello
Manufacturing Buyer: Sherry Lewis
Cover Design: Kiwi Design
Cover Illustration/Photo:
Director, Image Resource Center: Melinda Patelli
Manager, Rights and Permission: Zina Arabia
Manager, Visual Research: Beth Brenzel
Manager, Cover Visual Research & Permission: Karan Sanatar
Image Permission Coordinator: Michelina Viscusi
Composition/Full-Service Project Management: Sarvesh Mehrotra/TechBooks
Printer/Binder: Bind-Rute Graphics

Credits and acknowledgments borrowed from other sources and reproduced, with permission, in this textbook appear on appropriate page within text (or on page XX).

Pearson Education LTD., London
Pearson Education Singapore, Pte. Ltd
Pearson Education Canada, Ltd
Pearson Education—Japan
Pearson Education Australia PTY, Limited

Pearson Education North Asia Ltd
Pearson Educación de Mexico, S.A. de C.V.
Pearson Education Malaysia, Pte. Ltd
Pearson Education, Upper Saddle River,
  New Jersey

10 9 8 7 6 5 4
ISBN 0-13-227563-5

C O N T E N T S

Preface vii

About the Author xiii

PART I
LAYING THE FOUNDATION

Chapter 1

Reaching Out 2

Basic Principles of Human Behavior 3
Diversity, Gender, and Multiculturalism 8
Verbal Communication 14
Nonverbal Communication 16
Gender and Communication 19
Self-Talk 21
Shyness 23
Overcoming Fear 25
Commitments 27
Setting Goals 28
Critical Thinking Skills 29
Action and Results 29
Personal Learning 31
Chapter Review 33
Sources and Suggested Readings 34
Reaction and Response—What Do You Think? 35

Chapter 2

Self-Awareness 36

Self-Concept 37
Importance of Self-Concept 38
Improving Self-Esteem 40
Locus of Control 44
Self-Disclosure 45

The Johari Window 47
The Shadow Self 48
Masks 51
Getting Attention 52
Physical Contact 55
Chapter Review 57
Sources and Suggested Readings 58
Reaction and Response—What Do You Think? 58

Chapter 3

Expanding Comfort Zones 59

Comfort Zones 60
Thinking Patterns 65
Attribution Theory 67
Assertiveness 67
Personality 72
Exploring Psychological Types 76
Developing Character 83
Accountability 86
Belief Systems 87
Chapter Review 89
Sources and Suggested Readings 90
Reaction and Response—What Do You Think? 91

PART II
BUILDING TOGETHER

Chapter 4

Family Influences 94

Family History 95
Family Structures 96
Race, Culture, and the Family 98

Family of Origin   99
Birth Order   101
Functional Families   108
Stepfamilies   109
Parenting   111
Dysfunctional Families   115
Chapter Review   124
Sources and Suggested Readings   125
Reaction and Response—What Do You Think?   126

Chapter 5

Dealing with Emotions   127

Understanding Emotions   127
Emotional Building Blocks   130
Emotional Intelligence   132
Emotional Control   134
Thought Distortion   138
Defense Mechanisms   139
Anger   140
Guilt   145
Sadness   146
Excitement and Joy   148
Chapter Review   149
Sources and Suggested Readings   150
Reaction and Response—What Do You Think?   151

Chapter 6

Developing Close Relationships   152

Theories of Attraction   153
Types of Love   157
Attachment Styles and Romantic Relationships   158
The Dance of Intimacy   159
Codependent Relationships   161
Marriage Myths   164
Why Marriages Succeed or Fail   166
Gay Marriage   170
Making Marriage Last   171
Friendships   174
Chapter Review   175
Sources and Suggested Readings   176
Reaction and Response—What Do You Think?   177

Chapter 7

Human Sexuality   178

Perspectives on Sexuality   179
Social and Cultural Influences   181
Sex Education   183
Sexual Harassment   188
Date Rape   189
Sexual Abuse   190
Homosexuality   196
Sexually Transmissible Infections   201
AIDS (Acquired Immunodeficiency Syndrome)   203
Chapter Review   206
Sources and Suggested Readings   207
Reaction and Response—What Do You Think?   208

PART III
MEETING THE WORLD

Chapter 8

Coping Skills   210

Self-Defeating Behavior   210
Coping Strategies   213
Psychological Disorders   216
Components of Change   218
A Model for Change   223
Stress Management   224
Conflict Management   228
Guidelines for Getting Professional Help   231
Chapter Review   233
Sources and Suggested Readings   233
Reaction and Response—What Do You Think?   235

Chapter 9

Life Changes   236

Life Span Development   236
Life Passages   241
Transitional Times   248
Health and Wellness   250

Pyramid Building 252

Lifestyle and Being Overweight 254

Death and Dying Issues 256

Chapter Review 261

Suggested Readings 262

Reaction and Response—What Do You
Think? 263

Chapter **10**

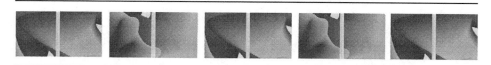

Positive Living 264

Values and Meaning 265

Decision Making 268

Work and Leisure 270

Life Satisfaction 276

Forgiveness and Love 279

Closure 281

Chapter Review 284

Sources and Suggested Readings 285

Reaction and Response—What Do You
Think? 286

Glossary 287

Bibliography 289

Index 295

CREDITS

Chapter 1
Page 3, Irene Springer/Pearson Education/PH College

Chapter 2
Page 52, Irene Springer/Pearson Education/PH College

Chapter 3
Page 63, Laima Druskis/Pearson Education/PH College

Chapter 4
Page 102, © Envision/CORBIS All Rights Reserved

Chapter 8
Page 229, Laimute E. Druskis/Pearson Education/PH College

Chapter 10
Page 266, Ken Karp/Pearson Education/PH College

In thinking about how to introduce this edition of the book, I recalled an amusing story from when I first got notice that the book was going to be published. I had written a couple of drafts that were self-published and used primarily for my own classes. My hope was that if I had more of a completed manuscript to offer to book representatives, they would have a better case when presenting it to the publishing companies for consideration. After the book was officially in production and I had been working for a while with the company whose offer I accepted, I asked the editor why they had chosen this book. The response was they had assigned the top three books being reviewed to the psychology editor, who took them home to read in the evening to make a decision. The next day the person reported that my book was the only one that didn't put them to sleep.

It has been more than 15 years since I first started work on this book. My initial effort was in many ways motivated by my desire to "walk the talk" and take on a personal challenge. In my course on human relations, I frequently ask students to expand their comfort zone and consider learning new behavior. I have always enjoyed telling stories and interacting with students in the classroom. Writing, though, was not an activity that I had a strong attraction to; however it represented an opportunity to take a risk, stretch my abilities, and gain self-discipline in the process. This book represents an area of growth for me.

My students were the ones who encouraged me to write down my stories and lectures. Over the years, I have continued to receive feedback on how they think it is an interesting book and how they often pass it on to family and friends. It was my goal originally to provide a text that would reach out and grab people and get them intrigued with the possibilities of personal exploration. I continue to take it as a compliment that many students say that this is one of the books they are going to keep at the end of the term.

With that encouragement, I am excited to be offering this fourth edition of *Human Relations: A Game Plan for Improving Personal Adjustment*. Although there have been some changes to the order of the content and new concepts added, the emphasis and focus of the book remain the same. While providing the academic subjects that are necessary for a greater understanding of human relations, the content is presented, as much as possible, in an informal and personal manner. It is important to learn how current research applies to human interactions, yet most of us are concerned with how that research will improve the quality of our lives and lead to more satisfying relations with the people we care about and are close to.

My intent is to make learning about and improving human relations enjoyable, yet there is also the reality that part of the journey of self-exploration requires presenting and dealing with concepts that include the more serious and significant aspects of life. This book offers the opportunity to look at some of the areas of life where self-examination and assessment of needed changes may not always be easy. I try to balance that seriousness by maintaining a sense of humor, even while dealing with subjects that are challenging. People often learn best when theory is combined with stories, examples, and humorous anecdotes from everyday life. Many people in the field of mental health believe that being well balanced means keeping things in perspective. As you explore the information offered, I hope you will keep the following in mind: *Blessed are those who can laugh at themselves, for they shall never cease to be amused.*

There is always the temptation to include as much academic research and theory as possible, but I feel it is important to balance that with the expectations and needs of the students. I have sat through enough psychology classes to know what it is like to have an instructor teach a course on human behavior as if there were no human beings in the classroom. Therefore, I have tried to balance relevant research and theoretical concepts with interesting anecdotes, case studies, and discussion opportunities to actively engage students.

And it is my students who have given me the opportunity to continue to grow and change. *Human Relations* is my attempt to remind myself what it is that I know and yet sometimes forget. We all can use reminders, at times, of the lessons that we need to learn—and relearn. It is my students and this course that remind me that often, "We teach best what we most need to learn."

Objectives of a Human Relations Course

A human relations course should teach practical skills for dealing with everyday situations. Because we tend to learn and remember things that require active participation, this book is designed for a course that encourages personal involvement in the quest for self-discovery.

Although covering a broad range of topics is an ambitious task, I think it is important to address as many pertinent topics as possible in an introductory course. This gives students and instructors flexibility in deciding which subjects to pursue in greater depth. Most human relations texts cover the areas of communication, self-concept, assertiveness, and conflict management, but it is also useful to include such topics as personality development, family relations, parenting, sexuality, and coping skills. This edition also includes new sections that incorporate material on critical thinking and goal setting, narcissism and perfectionism, attachment styles, guilt, sex education, and decision-making stategies.

During the past 30 years of teaching Human Relations 101, I have discovered particular rhythms and cycles to teaching in a college setting. This text presents topics in a manner consistent with the cycles within the term or semester, and it also incorporates the group dynamics of a classroom into the process and content of the course. Most texts put topics in a logical order that makes sense when reading the book independent of a class, but some topics can be introduced only after the class has reached a particular point of readiness. Over the years, I have developed a curriculum that is based, in part, on my feeling about how topics naturally overlap and build on previously presented material.

Pedagogical Features of the Text

Each chapter ends with a chapter review section, a list of resources, and suggested readings for additional information. This is followed by a reaction and response section of exercises and activities that give students the opportunity to apply the information from the text to personal situations. The questions and activities are divided into Level I, II, and III assignments. In this edition, Level I includes questions that pertain to the material presented in the chapters (*what* they learned), as well as general questions about class activities and discussions. Level II questions are intended to give students the opportunity to respond on a more personal level and to show *why and how* they might use and apply the information in their lives. Level III provides further opportunity for students to consider their behavior and think about the specific examples of *when and where* it would be important to begin to act on the new material being presented.

To further encourage active learning on the part of the students, numerous question-and-answer sections, now labeled "Questions for Critical Thinking," are included. These stopping points offer an opportunity to reflect on the information and are useful in beginning to take notes that will assisst in organizing thoughts and reactions for the different Level assignments. Various feature articles, poems, and anecdotes are highlighted throughout the text to create interest and promote introspective thinking. In this edition there are student stories and case studies to provide more concrete examples of the principles being presented.

Organization of the Text

There are a number of ways that the content of a book on human relations could be organized. Many of the topics could fit easily into several different chapters. The order in which the content of this book is presented is based mainly on what I have learned from my students about their level of readiness as a term progresses. Assertiveness is presented early on, in Chapter 3 of Part I, in order to connect that with expanding comfort zones. Various other coping skills are presented later in Part II, Chapter 8, in order to have covered the material that will provide ample personal stories and situations for which having new problem solving skills would be useful.

Also, the order of the chapters is designed so topics build on previously presented material. In particular, this edition returns to an earlier format of presenting the chapter on families before the chapter on emotions. Discussing family life and its influences is a natural bridge for discussion of the rest of the more in depth chapters in Part II that include emotions, close relationships, and sexuality. In general, I have found it useful to present material that has personal relevance in order to better explain behavioral patterns. Students often seem to prefer having an example before learning about a more complex, abstract theory.

Part I: Laying the Foundation

The first three chapters are designed to help people get to know themselves better, while building relationships with others in the class. The topics presented are general psychological concepts that apply to everyday life. The ideas presented also lay the foundation for how to explore and use the material presented in the rest of the text.

Chapter 1, "Reaching Out," deals with improving communication skills, using positive "self-talk", and overcoming shyness and fears. The chapter also discusses the importance of committing to the process of learning and taking action to get results. This is supported by the new material on critical thinking and goal settng.

This edition includes a greatly expanded section on diversity, gender, and multiculturalism. The material in the diversity section provides information about how to view the content of subsequent sections in a new light.

Critical thinking skills and goal setting are also presented, as those concepts will apply regarding most of the topics covered in the rest of the book.

Chapter 2, "Self-Awareness," is about self-concept and the importance of learning more about ourselves, including aspects of ourselves that we may avoid or keep hidden. The chapter includes information about self-disclosure, the shadow self, the masks people wear, and the importance of attention and physical contact. Information is provided about locus of control and its relationship to self-concept. A revised section on improving self-esteem has been added. New material is presented regarding cognitive restructuring as a part of increased self-esteem.

In the section on self-concept, this edition includes a discussion on whether there is such a thing as "too much" self-concept. This is explored by introducing narcissism and the effects of perfectionism.

Chapter 3, "Expanding Comfort Zones," provides the opportunity to learn about comfort zones, taking risks, understanding personality, developing character, challenging self-defeating behavior patterns and limiting beliefs, and developing character and accountability. Assertiveness is presented in this chapter; the topic is appropriate because the common theme of the chapter encourages expanding boundaries. The intention for introducing the topic in this chapter is to provide information that helps students express their opinions and define their own beliefs. New information has been added on the "Big Five" personality variables, exploring psychological types, and attribution theory.

Part II: Building Together

Part II moves the text discussion to a more personal level. These four chapters examine the origins of beliefs that affect behavior in a variety of different situations.

Chapter 4, "Family Influences," explores the influence of the family of origin, including the implications of birth order—and its limits—for the roles we play, and issues that arise in stepfamilies. The chapter also outlines the elements of a functional family and the complications of living in a dysfunctional family. The section on parenting has been expanded.

A new section has been added on the history of the family, with information based on the 2000 Census. New information is presented comparing beliefs about how families have operated in the past and what they will need in the future. Consideration is given to the changing face of the American family. Also, a new section has been added on race, culture, and the family.

Chapter 5, "Dealing with Emotions," presents a number of building blocks that help to develop greater emotional control and challenge thought patterns and irrational beliefs. Theories of emotion are presented, along with practical suggestions for greater emotional control. It is important to have the flexibility to know when to express your emotions and to what degree.

The chapter covers a range of emotional responses—anger, sadness, excitement, and joy—pointing out that much of our training in dealing with emotions takes place during the formative years in our family of origin. Understanding and dealing with feelings of guilt is included. There is a new section presented on defense mechanisms that explores the connection with the material on thought distortions.

Chapter 6, "Developing Close Relationships," studies attraction, mate selection, and marriage. More theories are offered about attraction in this edition. Information and discussions cover the difficulties in achieving intimacy, codependent relationships, and aspects of successful relationships. Information from John Gottman is included on how to create and maintain a successful marriage.

New material is presented from David Snarch on the importance of *differentiation* in establishing a healthy relationship. The importance of developing and maintaining friendships is also discussed. Attachment theory is also presented in this edition.

Chapter 7, "Human Sexuality," examines social and cultural influences on sexual behavior, highlighting the fact that many beliefs about sexuality are influenced by how the topic is approached within the family system. The subjects of sexual abuse, homosexuality, and sexually transmitted infections are also covered. An updated section has been added on the importance of understanding what constitutes sexual harassment, and updated information on AIDS has been added. New material has been added on sex education in the United States.

New material is presented in regard to the current approach to sex education and abstinence-only funding. The chapter also discusses the topic of date rape.

Part III: Meeting the World

The three chapters in this part explore specific issues that most people will have to confront at one time or another in everyday life. This part focuses more on the external variables in human relations. It deals with the specific skills needed to deal with issues that arise over the course of one's life.

Chapter 8, "Coping Skills," describes self-defeating behavior patterns and provides new coping strategies. The chapter also encourages students to consider changes that could be made as a result of having new choices.

A new model for change is offered in this edition. There is also a section on psychological disorders. Sections on stress management and conflict management have been updated in this edition, because both are important coping skills. Information on how to get professional help, and when it might be appropriate, is also included.

Chapter 9, "Life Changes," portrays the inevitability of change and loss as a developmental aspect of human relations and offers guidelines for dealing with life passages and transitions. Information is offered about the effects of our rapidly changing society, and means for dealing with the transitions that will occur in life are suggested. New topics related to health, the new Food Pyramid, lifestyle and well-being, and the increase in obesity are also included in this chapter.

Chapter 10, "Positive Living," starts with a new section on the importance of values clarification and the benefits of having meaning and purpose in life. This chapter also includes theories of career development and discusses the significance of having a balance between work and leisure. The chapter suggests ways to maintain the changes that have been accomplished as students have progressed through the course, emphasizing the fact that personal changes usually require a certain degree of commitment. A discussion of the components of good decision making is included.

The final sections focus on the importance of achieving life satisfaction, caring for yourself and others, and approaching the world with forgiveness and love.

Supplements

An Instructor's Manual with Tests is available, including course outlines, schedules, and suggestions for promoting class participation and discussion of the material in the text. The Instructor's Manual provides numerous activities and exercises that students can do in class, with information about group follow-up, and also includes a test bank of multiple-choice and true-false questions. The test bank is also available online at www.prenhall.com/psych:

MAC PH Custom Test

WIN PH Custom Test

Also, *Human Relations* is accessible at the Prentice Hall psychology site:
http://www.prenhall.com/~psychmap

Acknowledgments

I would like to thank all of the instructors, trainers, and supervisors I have studied with over the past 30 years. Much of the material presented in this book is a compilation of ideas from various sources of information. I am indebted to so many influential people from all the courses, training sessions, and workshops I have taken, that it would be impossible to name them all. Thank you, in general, to all who have assisted me in my own growth as a counselor and educator, and, in particular, to Lucille Bletcher, who was one of my first supervisors and therapists.

Michael Grinder is primarily responsible for helping me believe that this book was possible and for pointing me in the right direction. He has given me considerable time and energy that has been invaluable in completing this text. I greatly admire his skill, commitment, and integrity in working with people.

Thanks to my reviewers:

Tammy Ruff
Nashville State Community College
Dewitt Drinkard
Danville Community College
Lynn McKinley
Grossmont College
Gordon Fultz
Chemeketa Community College
Robert Beneckson
Miami-Dade College
Robert Brill
Moravian College
Dale Doty
Monroe Community College
Kathleen Felton
Indiana University East

I am deeply indebted to all of my students who have had the courage to share so much of themselves and to be involved in the process of personal growth. The interaction in the classroom has given me endless opportunities to learn and evolve as an instructor and counselor.

I thank my mother, Virginia Lewis Bradley, who always encouraged me to be a free spirit, and my father, Dr. Robert R. Ford, who taught me the importance of education and continued learning. Thanks also to my grandfather, William Hobart Lewis, who gave me unconditional love.

Most of all, my heartfelt appreciation goes to my wife and family. You are and will continue to be my greatest teachers. There is nothing like the warm support of people who also insist that you practice what you preach and give you ample opportunity to do so.

Last, I would like to give a special acknowledgment to Dorothy Juanita Woods. She has been an incredible source of inspiration and support. She is my teaching assistant and research assistant, and she has written the student stories and case studies for the book. My special *guardian angel*, who has walked many a dark valley, is a constant example of the power of optimism. Her energy, enthusiasm, and love for life is amazing. She is totally unique, a "giver" in life, and a true friend. And, it is to her—and to her incredible journey—that this book is dedicated.

Those readers who would like to contact me with comments or suggestions can reach me via e-mail at:

lorenf@clackamas.edu

Loren Ford
Clackamas Community College

Loren Ford earned his master's degree in psychology from California State University, Long Beach, in 1974 and did doctoral work in a clinical program during the 1980s. He is a Licensed Professional Counselor (LPC) in the state of Oregon and has a part-time private practice. Over the past 30 years, he has worked at several mental health facilities doing therapy with adolescents and families.

Since 1977, Loren has been on the faculty at Clackamas Community College in Oregon City. He teaches a number of classes on personal development, including human relations, college success, life-span human development, and introduction to counseling.

With an interest in the implications of mental health as played out on a larger stage, he began studying American history a number of years ago. In addition to teaching Oregon History and an occasional United States History course, he also has a class on Psychology and the Civil War.

With an eye toward retirement in the next five years, he is moving back to the country. This will allow for greater time with his horses, dogs, and family (not necessarily in that order). He will also continue with his passion for playing music. The front porch is a great place for pickin' and grinnin' with No Strings Attached, the band he has played with for the last 15 years.

Woodstock Photography

I

LAYING THE FOUNDATION

People wear masks—put up facades—for different reasons, such as avoiding disapproval or trying to gain approval
Photo: Roberta Hershenson/Photo Researchers, Inc.

1
C H A P T E R

REACHING OUT

One year, around Christmastime, I knew that I needed something new in my life. I had been going through some significant personal changes and thought that an adventure of a different type would help with the transition. I usually made the pilgrimage home to visit family at that time of year and wondered whether the trip might provide an opportunity to have a new experience. So I decided that a different mode of transportation might make the journey more enlightening. That's how I came to be on Amtrak for 28 hours, riding between Portland and Los Angeles. I wanted to spend some time with my kids, and this seemed like the perfect solution. There would be time to connect, time to think, and time for a shared adventure as well.

When we arrived at the train depot, the line of passengers already snaked from the platform all the way across the station. Each group of people had encircled itself with luggage, and everyone was careful not to invade anyone else's turf. The same mentality seemed to pervade the air as we boarded the train and people staked out their seats. We entered the first phase of the trip in the midst of people preoccupied with their own books, tapes, and private conversations. No one seemed interested in talking to strangers. After about three hours, though, it seemed that some were ready for a degree of interaction. People began to wander around the train exchanging stories about intended destinations as a way of making contact. The previous mood of eyeing each fellow traveler as if he or she were a potential mass murderer had begun to wane.

The next shift in attitudes and interactions came as the sun set and there was no longer a view of the passing scenery. The light from the dome on the train turned the window glass into a mirror, and the reflection made all of us more aware of being fellow travelers as we viewed ourselves in this capsule. As a result of reflecting on the situation, it seemed that everyone relaxed a bit more and began interacting in a friendlier manner. People opened up about their lives, sharing more than just destinations.

After a night of trying to sleep sitting up, there was a new level of interaction among the weary travelers. The neat, orderly scene at departure had been transformed into what the federal government might fund as a natural disaster area. People spent a good deal of time comparing various aches and pains of different parts of their anatomy. Throughout the day, everyone was much friendlier, seemingly as a result of having shared and endured a common ordeal. The whole train became more of a living room, and everyone on board seemed to be a member of a temporary family.

The energy and level of interaction continued to increase, until it peaked with the announcement that we were only three hours from Los Angeles. A tremendous roar went up as people began to act as if it were New Year's Eve. Everyone was now everyone else's long-lost buddy, and the last three hours of the trip flew by as we all partied our way into the station. The people getting off the train didn't seem to be the same people who had gotten on in Portland. Particular seat assignments had long since ceased being important, and all on board went about claiming possessions in a helpful and cheerful manner. As bodies spilled off the train, good feelings were conveyed with the "Good lucks" and "Take cares" sandwiched between the

exchanges of phone numbers and addresses. I wondered what the experience might have been like if everyone had acted in the same manner at the beginning of the trip as they did at the end.

I decided to try an experiment. Faced with the same 28-hour ride on the way home, I wondered if I could initiate interactions sooner. My children and I boarded the train for the trip home and allowed an appropriate amount of time for people to settle into their places. Then we thought about how to make the beginning of this trip back up to Portland more like the end of the trip down. I had my mandolin along and took it out. I play in a bluegrass band and like to practice when I'm traveling. We started by singing Christmas songs, and with a little help from the holiday spirit still lingering in the air, we soon had a number of kids singing along. The carefree attitude of the children eventually got the parents involved, too. Within a short period of time, we had quite a crowd laughing and having a good time.

While we were singing and telling stories in our end of the train car, people from other cars walked through the group on their way to and from the dining car, observation dome, or bathrooms. Most would smile and nod approval, and some even stopped for a song or two. When we had sung most of the songs we knew, and because another group had started up at the other end of the car, we decided to take a break.

We had no idea how successful our experiment had been until we took a walk to the dining car at the other end of the train. As we walked through the different train cars, we were pleasantly surprised to find a group of people singing in every one. Apparently, there was a chain reaction as people walking through our song group took the idea back to their cars. In each new group we passed, we noticed the faces of people who had stopped to sing with us. Perhaps encouraged by the children's uninhibited response to a good time in our original group, the adults

had decided not to worry about looking foolish. Some people had taken the risk of breaking the ice and carried the enjoyment and enthusiasm back to their cars.

It was exciting to walk the length of the train and find people relating and connecting in a manner similar to the last few hours of the trip down—and this was only three hours into the ride home. Needless to say, the journey home was much more comfortable and enjoyable. When people got over their initial reluctance to deal with each other, they got to do what they probably wanted to do all the time.

Basic Principles of Human Behavior

The following 10 concepts serve as a foundation for understanding principles that apply to many of the areas of human behavior that are covered in the rest of this text. These ideas and themes will be revisited throughout the text as we explore information about human relations.

The First-Day Morgue Syndrome

A number of people seem to think that the best response to a new or unusual situation is no response at all. Many of us feel somewhat uncomfortable when meeting new people or encountering a different situation for the first time. Unfortunately, some people become overly concerned about the right thing to do, so they freeze up and act as if they're dead. They would be better off using all of their senses to notice what is going on around them to better understand the situation.

It might be inappropriate to be too boisterous or outspoken in some places, but a college course on human relations is hardly one of those places. Have you ever noticed that some people lower their voices when they go into a bank? They act as if it is a funeral home or as if they don't want to disturb the money. It is fine to be quiet sometimes or to play it safe in new situations, but the question is: Do you have a choice, and can you be different when you want to? One of the goals of a human relations course is to help you be more connected to the world around you. So, to remain flexible and have choices, you might want to remember the following: *"When in doubt, don't check out."*

In a new or unusual situation, it may be useful to stay in the present moment and notice what is going on—both internally and externally.

> **"***Man's mind, once stretched by a new idea, never regains its original dimension.***"**
>
> *Oliver Wendell Holmes*

Check in instead of checking out. Then you can use that information to decide what course of action, if any, you wish to take.

Fears

There are many reasons for the first-day morgue syndrome, and most of them have to do with imagined responses to attempts to start a conversation. When asked what stops them from initiating conversations, people offer a variety of reasons for their fear of talking to someone or of communicating their thoughts and ideas. Most of those reasons have to do with the fear of being rejected, saying the wrong thing, or looking foolish. The amazing thing to me, though, is that out of fear of embarrassment or concern about looking foolish, people will sometimes do incredibly strange things.

For example, on the first day of one class, I found 30 people standing in the hall outside the classroom. I asked one student why everyone was waiting out there. He shrugged and looked at the ground. Someone else volunteered, "I think the door is locked." I went to the door, turned the handle, and walked into the room. (Where is *Candid Camera* when you need it?) After the class sheepishly filed into the room, I asked them why they had been standing out in the hall. It seems that the first person to arrive, afraid of looking foolish, had not wanted to be the first one in the room, so he sat down on a bench in the hall. The next person to arrive saw him sitting there and, not wanting to appear foolish, didn't bother to ask if he had tried the door. Each subsequent arrival, afraid of appearing foolish, failed to try the door or to ask why everyone was standing in the hall. Out of a fear of looking foolish, we can sometimes end up doing the very things that make us appear foolish.

So, even if you are afraid of looking foolish, it is sometimes better to think about the consequences of not taking action. When we let our fears get in the way of being how we would like to be, we sometimes contribute to the very situation we are trying to avoid.

Double Standards

Not only are our fears frequently unfounded, but also we may have a completely different set of rules for our own behavior than we have for others' behavior. This is a more general application of the concept of double standards. However, in our society and in many cultures, there are vastly different standards of behavior based on gender, and this may be a more common association with the concept. It is also important to understand, in a broader sense, that we all have a tendency toward judging our own and other people's behavior by different criteria and standards.

Did you ever have a bad day, when you walked around like a junkyard dog, growling and snarling at anyone who tried to talk to you? Didn't you expect everyone to understand, without words, that it was just you and that they shouldn't take it personally? Now think of a time when the situation was reversed. You probably took it to heart and ended up feeling bad because someone snapped at you.

At a party where you don't know many people, isn't it comforting to have someone approach you and start a conversation? Assuming that the other person acts appropriately, most people feel welcomed, included, and a little more relaxed when someone else starts a conversation. The double standard enters again when we think about initiating a conversation with another person, and suddenly the first-day morgue syndrome and the fear of looking foolish creeps up again. It is all right for someone else to start a conversation, but not for us.

Another example of the double standard in human relations is the notion that we all make sense to ourselves. Most of us behave in ways that we know don't make much sense at times, but we behave that way anyway. We may even be aware that to anyone who doesn't know the motivation behind the behavior, we may seem a little strange. Yet, we often expect everyone to know our motivation and to be patient, kind, and understanding. What happens when that situation is reversed? What happens when we see someone exhibiting behavior that we don't understand? Suddenly, most of us have a whole new set of standards. We expect others to make sense and to be consistent at all times. How dare anyone else do something that seems a little strange? It is important to remember that we all have idiosyncrasies that make sense if we know the underlying reasons for the behavior.

Don't use a bigger hammer if a little one didn't work. Sometimes the solution is to use the right tool for the job.

Paradox

Paradox is an important word for us to understand as we begin to study human nature. People's behavior is often counterproductive. It is a paradox that what makes sense is that we don't always make sense, and it makes sense that to understand human behavior, we sometimes have to stop trying to make sense of it. Human beings don't always operate logically, and it is therefore important to be able to adapt to a different level of thinking. Using only a logical, sequential approach to understand people is not always useful. There is a saying: *The heart has reasons that the mind knows nothing of.*

Although we try to rationalize our own behavior, people don't always make sense, even to themselves. At times, we are all experts at getting exactly what we don't want. How many people do you know who say they don't want X (some undesirable event) to happen, and yet every time they do Y (some behavior), X happens? The prior 20 times they did Y (behavior), they got X (unwanted result); still, they persist in doing Y over and over again, each time expecting something different to happen. One definition of insanity is doing the same thing over and over and expecting different results.

If every time you do Y, something bad happens, then why keep doing Y? Some people will stop doing Y for a while, and life starts getting better. Then they think, Well, I haven't done Y in a while, so I think I'll try once more just to see what happens. They try it, and when something goes wrong, they feel victimized by the world. That is paradoxical.

For example, recall the old Alka-Seltzer commercials: A man is sitting on the edge of the bed saying, "I ate too much, I ate too fast," over and over. He then proceeds to drop a couple of tablets in water and suddenly feels better. Have you ever wondered why it doesn't occur to him to just stop overeating and eating too fast? Some people feel bad if they eat or drink a particular item. They may say they don't want to feel bad, but they continue to do what will most likely cause them to feel bad. They may even temporarily quit the behavior (eating and/or drinking the wrong thing) that is causing them problems. After a while, though, they become curious about the connection between the behavior and the results and decide to find out if it is still true. It is a paradox that they do the same thing expecting different results and that they are surprised or upset when they get the same results.

There is another version of paradox in relationships. Some people have told me they felt so bad after the breakup of a relationship that they didn't go out with anyone for years. It was almost self-imprisonment. It is paradoxical to think that such behavior will make you feel better. There are even some people who hurt themselves just to make their ex feel bad. Wrong! It seldom works, and even if it does, it is the ultimate paradox: hurting yourself so you can hurt someone else so you can make yourself feel better.

It is also a paradox that in attempting to make something better, we sometimes make it worse. An example of this I call the *Bigger Hammer Theory.* People often try to solve a problem by doing *more* of the thing that isn't working. If a little tap from a little hammer doesn't fix it, then their solution is to get a bigger hammer and hit harder. But what if the solution is that you need a different tool? More of the same thing won't work and may even make things worse. That kind of thinking can be observed in many relationships. What each partner does to try to change or fix the other person may make the other resistant, with the end result that each gets less of what he or she wants. So remember the concept and don't fall into the trap of solving a problem by getting a bigger hammer. Use the right tool for the job. If what you are doing doesn't work, do something—anything—else.

Positive Double Bind

The original double bind (damned if you do, and damned if you don't) came from the novel *Catch-22* by Joseph Heller. The story takes place during World War II. Captain Yossarian decides it is hazardous to his health to continue flying bombing raids, so he goes to the Army psychiatrist and tells him of his concerns. The shrink decides that because Yossarian is afraid to fly, he is sane, and he therefore has to go ahead and fly. Yossarian then devises a scheme to prove he is crazy: He tells the shrink that he loves to fly bombing raids and go on dangerous missions. The shrink's response: Even though wanting to risk his life and continue to fly would normally prove he is crazy, he is in the Army; he has to fly anyway.

How does that apply to a human relations course? Let's consider how to use the double bind in a healthy way. Do you ever do something that you wish you wouldn't do? Or is there something that you wish you knew how to do, but you don't? When you are in a situation that provides an opportunity to acquire a new skill, do you find yourself running in the opposite direction? That is a paradox. The behaviors that we know how to do, even if they are negative, we keep on doing; the behaviors that we might benefit from learning, we frequently avoid or put off learning. That is what a human relations course is about: getting yourself to do more of what you know you should do and avoiding more of what you shouldn't do. From now on, your motto should be: ***If you want to, you don't have to; if you don't want to, you probably need to.*** That is the New Catch-22. All too often, we have a tendency to avoid the things we know we would benefit most from learning to do and resort to old habitual behavior whether it is useful or not. It would be useful to consider how to reverse that.

Risk Taking

Just as in life, the benefits you get from this book and this course are directly related to the level of risk you are willing to take. I am not talking about physical risk but about emotional and psychological risk: a willingness to try something new or to explore different aspects of your personality.

Consider the cliché, No pain, no gain. I want to be very clear about what that means in a human relations course. Emotional and physical

> **"** You see things as they are and ask, "Why?" But I dream things that never were and ask, "Why not?" **"**
>
> *George Bernard Shaw*

risk can mean many things to many people, and it has different meanings depending on the time and place in your life. If you have been cruising along for some time with few challenges and you are ready to shake things up a bit, it might be useful to stretch and make some changes. However, it is important to consider that if life has been handing you a considerable amount to deal with lately, you might want to take it easy on yourself.

There is a definite relationship between the amount of risk you are willing to take and the benefits you will gain. In general, the more you put out, the more you'll get back. But keep it in perspective, and remember that there is also a law of diminishing returns. Over the past 20 years there have been some well-intentioned programs that required too great a risk from people and created reactions and situations that weren't helpful or useful. Be firm but gentle with yourself in your requirements and expectations. In this class, as well as in life, take into account what is the optimal amount of risk for you to take. Consider what your challenge point is, the point at which you take the amount of risk that will result in the greatest benefit.

There are many ways to take risks; one is to initiate conversations and/or meet new people. This is important not only in a class setting, but also in social or work situations. Most of us wait for someone else to break the ice. Have you ever been to a party where everyone stood around twiddling their thumbs, waiting for the party to get started? It is paradoxical that you go to a party to meet new people and then talk only to the

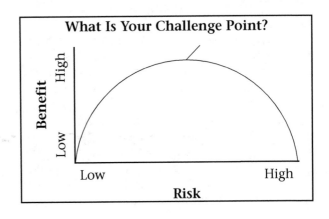

ones you already know. Some parties only get going when they are almost over, and then everyone says they wish things had started happening sooner. Keep this in mind; maybe you can be the icebreaker now that you know that most people are waiting for someone else to initiate contact.

Observing Yourself

The way to really benefit from a human relations course is to observe yourself. That means to suspend judgments for a while and just be curious about yourself. (It might be useful to think of class time as laboratory time.) Act as if there aren't any rights or wrongs, just opportunities to explore your reactions to new experiences. Life often gives us the opportunity to learn about our reactions in a given event. People react differently to the same circumstances. There have been times when I have presented material that provoked various responses in students. For example, in response to the same story, one student laughed, one got irritated, one got bored, and one thought it was so significant and touching that she almost cried. Our reactions tell a lot about us. When you do a class activity, you will have a chance to observe your own response. If you are observing only the instructor or other people, you are missing the best part of the course.

One principle in counseling theory is that the first step toward change is awareness of yourself and of the situation. To be where you want to be, you have to start with where you are, not where you wish you were. You can assess where you are by asking yourself these questions: What is my response to my response, and what are my reactions to my reactions?

If you have a particularly strong response to someone or some situation, stop and get curious about where that reaction came from and what it might mean about you. Becoming more introspective means being more observant about who you are, what you do, and what beliefs motivate you.

OBSERVE **YOURSELF**

AN EVENT IS SUBJECT TO INDIVIDUAL INTERPRETATION

The Ninety-Percent Rule

Anyone dealing with human beings and human nature can be right only for about 90 percent of the subject 90 percent of the time for 90 percent of the people. When discussing information that could be useful in improving human relations with a large group, it is often necessary to deal in generalities. Yet, attempting to include as many people as possible creates the likelihood that some people will not fit the guidelines being offered. For some, the information may not be important or may be useful only in the future. Human beings don't fit formulas and equations very well. So, as valuable as the information in this book might be, remember to use it in the right time and place. What works well for one person might not be useful at all to another.

Many human relations skills come from (1) knowing that there are many choices regarding how to be and (2) developing the perceptive ability to know how and when to use the information you have. Part of the task of a human relations course is being flexible enough to notice what is most likely to yield the desired result in a given situation. If you disagree with some of the information presented, feel free to just note it and move on. It is quite likely that not everything offered will be applicable at this time in your life. As much as possible, just pay more attention to what is useful and what does fit than to what doesn't.

Playing the Devil's Advocate

Most of us have been in a group where a few people dominated the conversation. Often, the people who talk the most are the ones who disagree the most with the points being discussed. My definition of a devil's advocate is someone who spends more time looking at the 10 percent that doesn't fit than the 90 percent that does. This can be a useful skill in some areas, and there are people who make a living troubleshooting; but remember that the people who most need to develop a devil's advocate part of themselves are the ones who too often accept things at face value.

How often do you have a tendency to play the devil's advocate? It's not that it is good or bad, so much as it is a matter of when you do it, how much you do it, and whether it is a choice. The following is a story my friend Michael Grinder told me that illustrates these points: There was a man who had a job at Pendleton Woolen Mills. All day long he watched fabric coming off weaving

DEVIL'S ADVOCATE

machines. He had a talent for noticing irregularities in fabric, so he was put in charge of quality control. Day after day he just looked for flaws. This was a valuable skill at work and greatly enhanced his career, but his friends and family were a bit dismayed when he began to look for flaws everywhere he went. Eventually, his life began to unravel, as he could only look for flaws and wasn't satisfied until he found them.

Needless to say, this ability didn't enhance his personal relationships. A stitch in time may save the fabric, but it seldom does much for mending a friendship. What started out as a useful skill became a detriment to living a well-balanced life. We all need to have the choice of when to point out errors and inconsistencies and when to just accept people and their imperfections.

Choice and Balance

The link between choice and balance is one of the most important concepts to be presented. I will refer to it throughout the text as we cover its application to a number of different topics.

Many aspects of life involve trade-offs and balances. There are many areas that require us to moderate between opposing needs and desires. For example, an increasing dilemma in two-income families in the new millennium is how to balance work and family. Good mental health is related to the ability to keep a sense of balance, and the factor that seems to relate most to that ability is having choices. Some people are out of balance because they have only one emotion, or they don't have much choice about how much of their emotions to experience. Others are out of balance because they aren't structured or disciplined enough to do what it takes to make a living. For example, if John is limited in his choices for emotional expression, he will probably be out of balance in his personal relationships. Or, if he is out of balance in his time and commitment to work and family, it may be due to a lack of choices, real or perceived.

Questions for Critical Thinking

What did you learn from these introductory concepts, and how can you apply them in your life? Which one was most significant for you?

_____

_____

_____

_____

_____

_____

_____

_____

_____

There is a reciprocal relationship between choice and balance. The more choices you have, the more likely you will be in balance. The more balanced you are, the more likely you will be able to develop more choices. One thing I hope to offer in this text is insight about opportunities for choices and balance in all aspects of your life.

Diversity, Gender, and Multiculturalism

Numerous sources indicate that we are living in an increasingly diverse culture in this country. Although projections based on statistics are fallible, some sources (*USA Today,* September 7, 1999) state that by mid-century the white population will be a minority—with no particular racial group being a majority. More recent reports (*Newsweek,* September 18, 2000) project that by 2050 whites will make up a slim majority—53 percent. Whatever the exact figure, the fact remains that a large portion of the country in the future will site a place of birth as somewhere other than Europe (Bucher, 2000, p. 210). The face of America is literally changing as more people from different races come to the United States. This is also due, in part, to the fact that there are more interracial marriages as the various groups living in the same community intermingle.

Evidence of the changes that are taking place in this country are apparent in the results of the last census. The U.S. Census Bureau states that 281.4 million people were counted in the last survey on April 1, 2000. This population growth of 32.7 million people between 1990 and 2000 represents the largest increase in American history. Although this figure may reflect changes in census coverage, as well as births, deaths, and net immigration, it is still a significant gain in population. In percentage terms, the population increase of 13.2 percent may not be as high as the percentage change during the 1950s and 1960s, but the gain of that era was fueled by the post–World War II baby boom. And, the aging baby boomers will also represent a rapidly increasing segment of the population—the elderly and aged.

The question of race for Census 2000 was different from that for Census 1990 in a number of ways. Most important, respondents were given the option of selecting one or more race categories to indicate their racial identities. Although caution must be used when interpreting changes in the racial composition of the United States population during that time, there are still some interesting implications. People were given the option of choosing one or more races from the following categories: white, black or African American, American Indian and Alaska Native, Asian, Native Hawaiian and Other Pacific Islander, and some other race. Therefore, each category could be reported alone or in combination with one or more races.

Although because of this option (being counted as alone or in combination with other races), a range of figures was reported for the increase of the population by race, all racial groups other than white increased faster than the 13.2 percent rate for the total population. The Hispanic population, as measured by the various options in the question Spanish/Hispanic/Latino, had increased more than 50 percent since 1990. The white population increased more slowly than the total population between 1990 and 2000. The term *white* refers to people having origins in any of the original peoples of Europe, the Middle East, or North Africa. Of the 216.9 million, or 77.1 percent, who reported white, 5.5 million people are included who reported white as well as one or more other races.

The changes in the survey and the increase in the number of people reporting more than one race seem to indicate that we are rethinking the concept of race in this country! A number of prominent people from all walks of life are starting to question the whole notion of racial categories. Tiger Woods is famous not only for his accomplishments in golf, but for having attempted to defy being defined by racial categories. He is reported to have coined the term "Cablinasian" (combination of Caucasian, Black, Indian, and Asian) to describe his race because of the varied racial background of both his mother and father.

Nearly 7 million Americans described themselves as multiracial in Census 2000. "The nation is much more diverse in the year 2000 than it was in 1990," said Jorge del Pinal, a Census Bureau official. "That diversity is much more complex than we've measured before." That diversity—which stems in part from a change in the way race is officially measured—is particularly true among children, mostly because multiracial couples have more than quadrupled (*DC Washington Post,* March 13, 2001).

The increased national focus on race, as is evident in all forms of the media, brings up the question of who is to be considered white these days. In a *Newsweek Special Edition* (September 18, 2000), Ellis Cose wrote an article entitled, "What's White, Anyway?" He states that the question is as old as America itself, and the answer has often changed. There was a time at the turn of the 20th century when various Eastern and Southern Europeans were considered to be "inferior" and a lesser grade of white racial stock. Cose also tells the story of how in 1922 the case of a Japanese national who had lived in America for two decades made its way to the Supreme Court. Takao Ozawa argued that the United States, in annexing Hawaii, had embraced peoples even darker than the Japanese—implicitly recognizing him as white.

Nationally, 2.4 percent of people described themselves as belonging to more than one race. The single largest multiracial category was "white and some other race," which census officials said was checked mainly by Hispanics. Considered an ethnic category, Hispanics can be of any race. Levonne Gaddy, of Tucson, Arizona, president of the Association of MultiEthnic Americans, said, "When I see the word *race*, I cringe, because I don't see there is much connected to the word. It's not about biological purity. I don't see the word race as really a valid word to express anything except about what we socially think about this concept" (*DC Washington Post,* March 13, 2001). These sentiments are also reflected in "The New Face of Race" (*Newsweek,* September 18, 2000), an article that gives numerous examples of young people who describe themselves as "mixed" and some who have begun to think it is "cool." Carlos Aguilar, living in Birmingham, Alabama, says that people see him for who he is, not where his parents came from. "They all know me, they know what I'm about," says Aguilar. "Everybody has their own respect for everybody." A voice from a young man that reflects, perhaps, an ideal for the nation.

America's cult of whiteness was never been just about skin color or physical traits, though. It was about who could, or could not, be admitted into the mainstream. "Those boundaries clearly are no longer where they once were. And even as the boundaries of whiteness have expanded, the specialness of whiteness has eroded. Being white, in other words, is no longer quite what it used to be" (*Newsweek*, September 18, 2000). Clearly the time has come when we need to acknowledge that diversity isn't something to accept; it is a fact.

Acculturation: Melting Pot Versus Salad Bowl

America has always been diverse. From the very beginning of the country's history to the present, there have been a great number of ethnic groups with different cultures that lived together. The term *melting pot* originated in 1910 and was used to describe the assimilating tendencies of the 1 million European immigrants who were entering the country each year. The current issue seems to be how to shift from the time when the melting pot theory of **assimilation** was embraced to developing a "salad bowl" theory that incorporates **pluralism.** Pluralism is a process through which cultural differences are acknowledged and preserved. The melting pot assailed the preservation of individual differences in the fact that the pot was dominated by a particular ingredient. This image differs from that of a tossed salad, which is symbolic of multiculturalism: Each ingredient is visible and not overcome or subsumed (Locke, 1998).

Although diversity represents positive aspects of human nature to some, there are others that are concerned for American culture. Allan Bloom, in his book entitled, ironically, *The Closing of the American Mind*, takes the position that we are losing something by trying to accommodate all the different cultures. He believes that we should go back to the educational model of teaching the classics and taking a "great books approach" to developing a common culture. Noted historian Ronald Takaki, author of *A Different Mirror: A History of Multicultural America* (1993), takes a different approach. He believes that we are made stronger by acknowledging all of the different ethnic backgrounds and cultures. Further, he believes that we have always been a diverse culture. It is just that the story of other cultures and ethnic

groups has never been told in much detail before. Actually, they have sometimes been omitted by the **dominant culture,** which is an example of how power is sometimes expressed.

There was a time when immigrants were expected to assimilate into the general population as quickly as possible. A biography of Henry Ford, shown on PBS, gave a visual example of that particular phenomenon. During the early 1900s Ford was instrumental in providing employment for a vast number of immigrants. As part of the training program for working on the assembly line in his factories, he had a graduation ceremony. People were dressed in a wide variety of costumes representing various ethnic backgrounds. They all walked across a stage showing their national dress and then proceeded backstage to a changing room. When the people emerged and walked across the stage again, they were all dressed in identical clothing and waving American flags. Perhaps it was analogous to the very production methods that Ford created, and there were certain benefits to uniformity. But, it was also a very visual demonstration of the beliefs of the dominant culture of the times. The process of becoming an American meant that you gave up your old customs and blended into the new culture.

There are a number of ways in which an ethnic group might attempt to adjust and adapt to a more dominant group. While some people believe that **acculturation** is a neutral term because changes may occur in both groups, usually the change occurs more in one group than the other (Berry and Sam, 1997). Berry and Sam discuss four acculturation strategies: (1) assimilation, (2) traditionality, (3) integration, and (4) marginality. *Assimilation* describes those people who do not desire to maintain their cultural identity and seek sustained contact with the culture other than their own. *Traditionality* describes the people who choose to hold on to their cultural connections and avoid contact with others. *Integration* is best described as being bicultural. This describes people who hold on to their own culture while simultaneously seeking interaction with the other cultures. *Marginality* is having little interest in maintaining one's own culture and limited desire to interact with those from different cultures.

America as a concept and a country has been diverse since its beginning. Perhaps we need to expand the definition of America by including more information in schools about the various ethnic groups that compose this country. Appreciating diversity is an alleged position of democracy. Popular sayings such as "different strokes for different folks" and "it takes all kinds to make the world go round" suggest an awareness and an acceptance of differences. Although certain differences may be valued, a multicultural society is still an ideal and not yet a reality (Robinson and Howard-Hamilton, 2000).

Dimensions of Diversity

Dimensions of diversity refer to specific traits viewed as distinguishing one person or group from another. Race, gender, and ethnicity are three examples. **Race** refers to a category of people who are perceived as physically distinctive on the basis of certain traits, such as skin color, hair texture, and facial features. Whereas race relates to physical differences, ethnicity focuses on cultural distinctiveness. **Ethnicity** is defined as the consciousness of a cultural heritage shared with other people. **Gender** has to do with the cultural differences that distinguish males from females. For instance, in any given culture, people raise males and females to act certain ways. Do not confuse the term *gender* with *sex*. *Sex* refers to biological differences, such as hormones and anatomy.

(Bucher, 2000)

Race and gender aside, there are ways in which we are like all people, ways in which we are like some people, and ways in which we are entirely unique as individuals. Just as there are no common cultural characteristics across American ethnic groups, there are no common cultural characteristics among African Americans, Asians, and Latinos. We all could benefit from learning about and developing a greater appreciation for our differences and similarities in this world.

Diversity is multidimensional and may or may not have anything to do with race or gender. Therefore, an important aspect of human relations is to become more aware of the similarities and differences between all people. Just as self-awareness is an important part of the educational process, so, too, is becoming more aware of the complexities of our differences. Concepts that are important to understand and areas to explore include:

Dimensions of diversity may be hidden or visible.
Dimensions of diversity are found within groups as well as within individuals.
Dimensions of diversity are in a constant state of flux.
Dimensions of diversity are not always clear-cut or easily defined. (*Bucher, 2000*)

Gender

Gender refers to the roles, behaviors, and attitudes that come to be expected of persons based of their biological sex. Scarcely more than a generation ago, traditional gender roles were accepted as natural, normal, and even inevitable. The basis for gender distinctions and the "nature/nurture" debate—whether or to what degree gendered behavior is controlled by biology or socialization—continues, but we all know the traditional definitions of masculinity and femininity. "Although lactation is a sex role that men tend to be biologically incapable of and penile ejaculation is a sex role genetically normal women are biologically incapable of, changing diapers and taking out the garbage are not sex roles. They are both socially constructed gender roles. There is no gene for changing a diaper or flying an airplane, yet the arbitrary divisions of labor that society has constructed based on biological sex are stringent and far too often attributed to biology" (Robinson and Howard-Hamilton, 2000).

The word **sexism** did not exist until the early 1960s. Many people assumed that women had the same rights as men but they were content with their domestic role, caring for their homes and families. "Sexism is the subordination of an individual woman or group of women and the assumption of the superiority of an individual man or group of men, based solely on sex. Like racism, sexism is reflected in both individual and institutional acts, decisions, habits, procedures, and policies that neglect, overlook, exploit, subjugate, or maintain the subordination of an individual woman or all women" (Cyrus, 2000).

The traditional division of labor with the man as breadwinner and the woman as homemaker was already being challenged by the economic realities of that time, though. In 1963, Betty Friedan published *The Feminine Mystique,* in which she investigated the general unhappiness that haunted the well-educated suburban housewife. Women began organizing **consciousness raising groups,** and problems previously perceived as personal were increasingly viewed as part of a larger web of social limitations (hence the slogan—*the personal is political*). The value of women and the advocacy of social, political, and economic equality for both women and men became the widely accepted and widely debated platform of modern **feminism.** Observing society through a feminist lens reveals fundamental gender inequality that is embedded in our social system. Although considerable gains have been accomplished in the past 30 years, there is more to do in achieving true equality. And, until society-ascribed gender roles are transformed, men and women alike will suffer from the constricting consequences of inequalities based on biological sex and socially constructed roles (Cyrus, 2000).

Developing Diversity Consciousness

One way to develop diversity consciousness is to begin to separate fiction from fact. What exactly is multiculturalism, and what is required in order to understand and become more accepting of our differences? Many people have a reaction to what they feel is the increased pressure to be politically correct. How do we as a country become more aware and accepting while striving for the balance that respects all cultures?

Diversity is a concept that means many things to different people. Richard Bucher, in *Diversity Consciousness,* offers the following information as a means of clarifying some **common myths:**

1. Diversity = women + minorities.
2. Diversity is a new phenomenon.
3. Diversity = deficiency.
4. Diversity = divisiveness.
5. Diversity is to be feared.

He also does an excellent job of describing what it is not. As Bucher aptly states, "Diversity consciousness cannot be manufactured during a one-hour TV talk show or a day-long training session." Diversity consciousness is not (1) simply common sense, (2) the result of good intentions, (3) the result of some simple formula or strategy, (4) important for just some of us, (5) simply ignoring differences and treating everybody the same, or (6) a passing fad.

We have long been somewhat confused as a nation about how to deal with the different people and cultures that inhabit our boundaries. We strongly support and encourage individuality, while at the same time we expect that everyone should blend in and not make waves. We seem to think that everyone should express their differences—as long as it is in an acceptable way. Perhaps we are guilty of having a double standard. There is the stereotype abroad of the "ugly American" who travels in other countries and refuses to acknowledge or behave according to local customs. Americans tend to take their culture with them and expect that everyone should act more American wherever they go. Yet, when other people come to this country, Americans tend to think that the visitor or immigrant should immediately begin to act as we do in this country.

Mara Hurwitt, in an article entitled "Cultural Diversity: Towards a Whole Society," states,

People may fear diversity simply because they are accustomed to the way things used to be and change makes them uncomfortable. Others may somehow feel threatened because they perceive increased participation by traditionally underrepresented groups in the workplace and political process as a challenge to their own power. If left unaddressed, these fears can lead to resentment and bigotry. However, these fears can often be countered through education.

The process of education can begin with understanding more about the diversity of our country. The development of diversity consciousness can be broken down into six areas:

- *Examining yourself and your world.* Before we begin to make sense of other cultures and cultural differences, we need to become aware of who we are. A major focus of this book is on how self-awareness helps to improve human relations.

- *Expanding your knowledge of others and their world.* While it is a good start, don't just focus on a few noteworthy people and events. Try to decrease the social distance between you and those groups or individuals about whom you know very little. Also, look for similarities as well as differences.

- *Stepping outside yourself.* One way to practice stepping outside yourself is to imagine putting yourself in someone else's place. The ability to "put yourself in somebody else's moccasins" increases your awareness, understanding, and diversity skills. How can you actually experience what someone else's life might be like to some degree?

- *Gauging the level of the playing field.* Social inequality refers to the unequal distribution of resources, such as wealth, power, and prestige. A social class is a category of people who share similar amounts of those. What is your experience with poverty or class discrimination? Are you assuming that if one person can succeed, anybody can?

- *Checking up on yourself.* How are your critical thinking skills? Can you freely question and evaluate ideas and information? Is your behavior consistent with you thinking?

- *Following through on new behavior.* We learn by doing. We can only develop and refine diversity skills through constant use and self-evaluation. (*Bucher, 2000*)

The following strategies, which revolve around education, self-examination, and networking, can help you move toward the goal of developing diversity consciousness:

- Expand your knowledge through reading. Articles, novels, and personal narratives can provide you with realistic and dramatic portrayals of diversity.

- Put yourself in a learning mode in any multicultural setting. Suspend judgments and adopt a childlike kind of inquisitiveness.
- Remember that your own life experiences are one of many important sources of knowledge. We all have experiences that could be useful or instructive if shared with someone else.
- Move beyond your comfort zone. Growth sometimes requires taking a risk, but doing something new and different can be rewarding.
- Don't be too hard on yourself if misunderstandings arise. The important thing is to acknowledge your mistakes and learn from them.
- Realize that you are not alone. There are other people out there who care about you and will support you. Surround yourself with these kind of people. (*Bucher, 2000*)

Diversity consciousness prepares you for life, empowers you and others, and changes the way you view differences. Many of these concepts will be discussed in other chapters throughout the book.

Developing Skills

We all have certain barriers that we have experienced in communicating with other people. Beginning to become more respectful and understanding of people from another culture or ethnic background requires a new set of skills. **Diversity skills** are those competencies that allow people to interact with one another in a way that respects and values differences. Diversity skills such as communication, teamwork, and self-evaluation are key components of diversity consciousness. As you read about the following skills, examine yourself. Which are your strengths? Which need a little more work? What might you do to improve certain skills?

Flexible Thinking   This is the ability to understand and adapt to a variety of perspectives, depending on the situation. One example that applies to many students in the classroom is learning styles. There are a number of methods of teaching, and some students learn better using one style than another. Many students have had the experience of needing their style of learning addressed so as to improve their performance in the course. Yet, expanding your abilities to learn in different styles also facilitates being able to learn more from a wide range of instructors.

Ability to Appreciate and Maintain Pride in One's Background and Culture   Research suggests that students are far more successful if they maintain pride in their culture (Nieto, 1992).

Ability to Network and Learn from Everyone and Anyone   We increase our chances for success, in school and at work, by expanding and diversifying our social network.

Ability to Deal Effectively with Barriers   Although expectations of others may act as barriers, it is just as important to examine one's own beliefs. When faced with a challenge, can you get in touch with your "I'll show you" part that gets more determined in the face of opposition?

Acknowledging and Overcoming Diversity Barriers

An important part of learning new skills is to understand the challenges that are inherent in developing new behavior. The following list may be useful in affecting behavior changes.

Barrier 1: Limited Perceptions Perceptions refer to the way in which we receive and interpret information from our senses. We have all had times when we experienced "seeing what we wanted to see," when we had high expectations that an event would turn out a certain way. This is also called *selective perception*. If we believe that certain people are going to act a particular way, we may only notice the things that support that belief.

Barrier 2: Ethnocentrism This refers to the assumption that our way of thinking and acting is naturally superior to any other. Sometimes culture envelops us so completely that it is difficult to realize that our perspective is one of many.

Barrier 3: Stereotypes Our social environment provides us with a set of images, many of which are stereotypes. These are unverified overgeneralizations that we associate with a group of people.

Barrier 4: Prejudice This is an irrational and inflexible opinion, formed on the basis of limited and insufficient knowledge. Stereotypes and prejudice often go hand-in-hand.

Barrier 5: Prejudice Plus Power When people in power show prejudice, the consequences can be that much more severe. The various "isms" are at work when we talk about prejudice plus power (ageism, sexism, racism, classism).

Although it is important to realize that there is no single strategy that is right for everyone or appropriate for all situations, the following suggestions could be useful:

- Recognize that barriers sometimes exist.
- Develop and maintain pride in yourself.
- Develop and maintain pride in your culture.

◗ If you encounter discrimination, whether it is directed at you or others, speak out if at all possible.

◗ Fine-tune your anger. Resist the urge to scapegoat.

◗ Try to keep focus on the offensive behavior rather than the person. Treat people as individuals.

◗ Seek support and work with others to find new and effective ways to address intolerance.

◗ Combat the prejudices, stereotypes, and ignorance that exist within each of us.

◗ Each of us has the power to choose our reactions and overcome barriers that get in the way. (*Bucher, 2000*)

Conclusions

The implications from this information are clear. We will be living in an increasingly diverse society and, for better or worse, will be working and playing together. Human relations skills will need to be expanded to encompass the ability to understand and communicate with people of all races and ethnic backgrounds. Learning to deal with people from diverse backgrounds is a requirement, not an option.

Along with learning new skills, beginning to embrace the inevitable changes in our national demographic gives us the opportunity to develop personally. And, isn't that what a good human relations course is all about?

Verbal Communication

When I ask people what they want to learn from a human relations class, invariably I get the response: I want to learn to communicate better. This section explores the concepts and behaviors that are important to understanding how to improve communication skills. Some people do well in one-on-one situations but are terrified of speaking in front of a group. Fear of public speaking is probably one of the most common fears, yet seldom in life do we talk to only one person at a time. Public speaking is a valuable skill well worth developing. On the other hand, there are people who enjoy talking in or to groups, yet some of those same people are intimidated by one-on-one conversations. To improve communication skills, it is important to have choices and abilities in both situations.

This text provides opportunities for communication choices: talking in large groups, debriefing activities in small groups, and working in dyads, or pairs. After reviewing quite a few communications books, I find that most theorists agree that dyads are the central element in conversational patterns. Even in groups, interactions usually take place between two people at a time. It is valuable to understand all the complexities of what occurs when people are talking. Communication experts also agree that we cannot *not* communicate. We are all communicating all the time, so let's explore the implications of what that means.

To understand the different levels of communication, we will explore four key elements:

1. Reasons for communicating.
2. The process of communication.
3. How to be a good message receiver (listener).
4. How to be a good message sender (speaker).

As you begin to learn more about each of these aspects of communication, keep in mind this concept: *Who you are speaks so loudly that people can't hear what you say!*

Various disciplines (psychology, sociology, speech) agree that the major part of communication happens on the nonverbal level. How you say something is as important as what is said. Most people are so concerned about saying the right thing that they miss this valuable point. This concern can be used in a positive way, though, as a reminder to relax and be less critical about the actual words you use. Being congruent (when your words and nonverbal communications match) is often more important than the words themselves. If you approach someone in a friendly manner, what you say may not matter so much. Focus on your intention, and others will usually get the message and react accordingly.

Reasons for Communicating

The benefits of connecting with other people are numerous. We can learn new and interesting things; we can play or be helpful. Sometimes we communicate to persuade or influence. (This is usually what happens in marriages when trying to decide where to go for dinner or what movie to see.) We communicate to relate to others. Perhaps you have heard John Donne's line, "No man is an island." The reasons for communication can be broken down into these categories: physical needs, identity needs, and social needs (inclusion, control, and affection). Entire books have been written just on these topics. Suffice it to say, then, that we are truly social animals. The importance of this concept can be seen in prisons where

> **❝***You are the same today that you will be five years from now except for two things: the people you meet and the books you read.***❞**
>
> *Benjamin Franklin*

solitary confinement is used as a method of punishment. If you have taken away almost everything a person has, the only further punishment is to take away the opportunity to communicate with others.

The Communication Process

When two people are having a conversation, there is an elaborate system of **encoding** and **decoding** messages that is constantly being influenced by each person's thoughts, feelings, and filters. Encoding and decoding is the process that gives meaning to the words we say and hear. The concept of filters is important because it explains why misunderstandings occur. Filters are all the beliefs that can cause distortion in the message we receive when listening to someone. Those filters come from the family in which we grew up, our past experiences, and the attitudes and beliefs that resulted from our interactions in those situations (Adler and Towne, 2003).

Our ability to understand and communicate effectively is influenced by our internal dialogues. How many times during a conversation have you been so busy talking to yourself about what you are going to say next that you haven't even heard what the other person has been saying for the past five minutes? Some communications experts call that *internal noise*. The noise that affects filters can be influenced by emotions, the situation, and your self-concept. Is it any wonder, then, that we all have days when we don't communicate very well? It should be obvious why it is extremely important to understand this communication process and to learn the skills that help eliminate the effects of your filters. There is a saying that illustrates this: **I know that you think you understand what I said, but do you also realize that what you heard is not what I meant to say?** Maybe you have even experienced this personally, which brings up a valuable lesson about flexibility. There are a number of barriers to effective communication that require

awareness of our own and other people's filters. One way to improve your ability to communicate is to be aware of the things you may do that contribute to complications. Accurate communication often depends on what you stop doing as much as what you may need to start doing. Consider times when you have done the following and what the consequences were.

Barriers to Communication

- ❯ Being critical or sarcastic: Seldom does it help a conversation if people feel that they are constantly being judged.
- ❯ Stereotyping: Generalizations are frequently incorrect and only add to the filters that keep us from hearing what is being said.
- ❯ Overreacting and/or interrupting: This usually leads to defensiveness and frustration on the part of the speaker.
- ❯ Having a hidden agenda: It is difficult enough to solve a problem when all the cards are on the table.
- ❯ Being overly anxious: Trying too hard or communicating when upset may cause difficulties.

Methods to Improve Communication

- ❯ Be more accepting: We usually want other people to be accepting of our ideas, even when they may not appear to make sense. Try to reciprocate and be accepting of other people's ideas, even when the logic may not be apparent.
- ❯ Be attentive: Most of us like to think that what we are talking about is important or meaningful, and paying attention to the person talking says we're listening.
- ❯ Wait for the big picture: When someone is talking and we only notice the details, we may miss the main point.
- ❯ Listen between the lines: If we pay attention to the nonverbals as well as the words, we may get the real meaning.
- ❯ Share responsibility for connecting: To improve communications, both parties need to be involved in making sure that they understand each other.

Finally, one of the most valuable tools I've received in my training over the years is to remember the following: ***The meaning of any communication is the response you get.*** It doesn't matter what you think you said; the response you get tells you how effective you were in communicating your message or what the receiver of the message heard. Have you ever given someone a compliment, after which he or she seemed to be irritated? Based on the results, even if you had the best intentions, he or she wasn't complimented. Have you ever expressed irritation with someone who responded by laughing? Maybe the person didn't understand that you were angry. It is up to you to be flexible enough to notice the response you are getting and to change your behavior to get the response you want. Most of us get annoyed when people don't hear what we think they should have heard, yet it is our responsibility to be flexible enough to change our approach if we don't think we were heard. There is a saying from Gestalt therapy that being responsible means that we are "response-able." That requires flexibility and creativity. As previously stated, if what you are doing doesn't work, do something else.

How to Be a Good Listener

- Make an appropriate amount of eye contact.
- Use body posture that indicates listening behavior.
- Provide verbal and nonverbal responses, such as head nodding and "uh-huhs."
- Use appropriate gestures or touching.
- Ask open-ended questions, such as, "Tell me more about Y."
- Paraphrase and feed back what you hear. (See box entitled, "Simple Listening Isn't an Easy Thing to Do.")
- Don't try to problem-solve unless asked to.
- Avoid distractions by working at listening for more than just the words.

How to Be a Good Speaker

- Be congruent by making your body language and words say the same thing. People are more likely to believe your actions than your words.
- Make "I" statements and own your message. It is usually better to state your own thoughts, feelings, and needs than to tell others what they should do or how they should think. Good "I" messages start with phrases such as the following: "I think . . . ," "I prefer . . . ," and "I have found. . . ." Phrases that are variations on that theme include "It appears to me that . . . ," "What I'm feeling is . . . ," and "In my opinion. . . ."
- Do an appropriate amount of self-disclosure. It is seldom useful or appropriate to tell the stranger at the bus stop your entire life history.
- Be specific and direct. Using generalities may cause confusion if the examples you offer have different meanings to your listeners.
- Repeat the message, if necessary, especially if it seems that people have not understood you, as indicated by their response.
- Make the message match the audience and context. There is a time and a place for certain interactions.

- Match the rhythm, volume, and inflection of the listener(s).
- Keep it simple. Sometimes less is more.

Human relations courses provide ample opportunity to practice the above concepts and skills. In discussion groups, keep in mind that you can observe the process of the communication as well as participate in the content. You might try thinking about one concept at a time and concentrate on practicing it. All of these skills take practice, and all of them will become easier with practice.

In everyday life, you have numerous opportunities to communicate and connect with other people. Think about your interactions as a building project. Are you contributing to a common goal? Is what you are offering creating something new? Concentrate on making an effort to work together. You may have had the experience of being in a conversation with someone who only seemed interested in tearing things down. Some people spend more time looking for how things don't fit than how they do. Not very pleasant, is it? If someone has an opinion different from yours, get curious: this could be an opportunity to learn something new. Learn to value those who have dissimilar points of view, and listen to them. There may come a time when you want someone who disagrees with your point of view to listen to you! Here is a message that might help make all of this information applicable: ***Nobody cares what you know until they know you care!***

Nonverbal Communication

Nonverbal communication refers to messages that are transmitted from one person to another by means other than linguistic. These other means include body language (facial expression, eye contact, gestures), space and distance, and paralanguage (various aspects of a person's voice). For example, I have seen couples in marriage counseling sitting in silence staring at each other, yet obviously communicating with each other. After a period of time, one person may clear his throat, making a particular sound, and then the other person may raise her eyebrow a quarter of an inch. That results in the first person's leaning forward in his chair and beginning to accuse his partner of horrible behavior in an angry tone of voice. The recipient of the accusation then may cross her arms and begin to complain about the unfairness of the attack. In this type of situation, many things are communicated other than verbal messages.

SIMPLE LISTENING ISN'T AN EASY THING TO DO

Unschooled at simple listening—without advising, fixing, judging, teaching, moralizing, or trivializing—many people are unable to respond helpfully to their friends or lovers, who end up feeling misunderstood or even invisible. So, people turn to professional listeners: therapists, analysts, psychologists. How can you help people who confide in you to feel that you've heard and understood them? Here are some tips from the experts:

❑ **Pauses and silence:** Therapists (and skillful interviewers) know the value of silence when a person finishes speaking. As Gerald Goodman, a psychology professor and author of *The Talk Book* (1988), points out, "Don't be afraid of dead air space in human relationships." "Allowing people a few seconds to think, to give them a sense you're not just thinking of what you've got on your mind, lets them feel less disregarded," Goodman said in a Portland interview. "We pay people to wait; in therapy it ranges from seventeen seconds to two minutes."

❑ **Mirroring:** This is known as "active listening." The listener attempts to reflect what the speaker is feeling by saying, "You're really angry"; "You're feeling frustrated about this"; "You feel unappreciated at work." The speaker feels validated—a prerequisite to clarifying and solving a problem.

❑ **Disclosing:** Want to have the other person "get real"? Then do so yourself. "The best way to get somebody to open up is to open up yourself," Goodman said. But premature disclosure—telling too much about yourself too soon—is inappropriate and may cause the other person to back off, he cautions.

❑ **Questioning:** "Good listening is not passive—it means taking over sometimes, saying, 'Say that again, I didn't get it,'" Goodman said. But beware of becoming an interrogator who isn't really seeking information, Goodman warns. Excessive questioning can be judgmental and hostile ("Are you still watching TV?") or an attempt to avoid disclosing yourself.

One way to help others become good listeners is to tell them what you need from them before you begin talking: "I don't need advice right now, I just need to sort this out for myself," or "Let me lay this out, then tell me what you think, OK?" or "I just need to dump this stuff."

The art of listening is illustrated in this anonymous poem:

Listen

When I ask you to listen
and you start giving advice,
you have not done what I have asked.
When I ask you to listen
and you begin to tell me why I shouldn't feel
the way I do,
you are trampling on my feelings.
When I ask you to listen
and you feel you have to do something to
solve my problem,
you have failed me, strange as that may seem.
Listen,
all I asked you to do was listen, not talk, or do.
Just hear me. I can do for myself;

I'm not helpless—perhaps discouraged or
faltering, but not helpless.
When you do something for me
that I need to do for myself,
you contribute to my fear and weakness.
But, when you accept as fact that I feel
what I feel, no matter how irrational,
then I can stop trying to convince you and
get on with understanding
what's behind that irrational feeling.
And, when that's clear,
the answers will be obvious,
and I won't need any advice.

Source: Article written by Jann Mitchell.

Further evidence of the effects of nonverbal communication appears when there is a discrepancy between words and actions. People often say one thing while their bodies contradict their words. If a person is red in the face, yelling, and pounding his fist, it may not make a difference that he is saying, "I am not angry." Which message would you be inclined to believe if you were getting those two opposing messages?

Part of the importance of understanding the various aspects of nonverbal communication is the realization that it is nearly impossible not to communicate. Our actions give out signals about our state of being, whether we intend them to or not. Even when we try to mask or control our nonverbal messages, we frequently have a difficult time doing so. When people make a very determined effort not to let their emotional underpinnings show through, their true feelings usually emerge spontaneously and leak past the attempt at control (Simons, Kalichman, and Santrock, 1994). Or, as Freud stated, "Self betrayal oozes from all our pores." Therefore, it might be useful to become more aware of how often and in what manner we communicate, in addition to the verbal messages we send.

Paralanguage   Paralanguage refers to the non-linguistic aspects of verbal communication that may carry additional information and meaning. Examples include the following:

> *Speed:* A rapid rate of speech may convey a different meaning than the same words spoken in a leisurely manner.

> *Pitch:* When someone raises his or her voice, it may indicate embarrassment or an emotional response. The importance of pitch is evident when talking to someone who speaks in a constant monotone and never varies the pitch.

> *Volume:* How loudly or softly words are being spoken gives additional meaning and emphasis to the message.

> *Rhythm and inflection:* Emphasis that is given to some words may change the whole meaning of a sentence or change it into a question. A classic example from an old vaudeville routine is to say, "What is this thing called Love?" and emphasize a different word each time you repeat it. That will demonstrate how rhythm and inflection can affect meaning. It is not what you say but how you say it that is often more important in learning better communication skills. Psychologists have studied for some time the effects of nonverbal cues on the communication process. Some have even suggested that it is by far the most important aspect of communicating. In a study of nonverbal communication,

Albert Mehrabian (1993) claimed that 55 percent of a communication was facial expression, 38 percent was vocal expression (volume and tone of voice), and only 7 percent was the verbal message. Those figures emphasize the need for understanding how what you don't say, but show, is of great importance. And, it's not what you say but how you say it that matters.

Body Language   The science of body language is called *kinesics,* and Julius Fast (1970) helped to popularize the notion that posture and movement convey meaning. However, a cautionary note is important: Not all gestures or body movements mean the same thing from one person to another. This is especially true when considering different cultures. In U.S. culture, when a person puts his or her thumb and first finger together in a circle, it means "OK." In another culture, that may mean the equivalent of raising the middle finger in an upright gesture in U.S. culture. More important than trying to ascribe universal meaning to a particular gesture or movement is the understanding of meanings for each individual. It could be useful to know that every time a friend feels defensive or feels criticized, he crosses his arms. That same movement might have different meaning for someone else. The point is that it is better to calibrate behavior for the individual than to generalize to all human beings. That said, let's look at the various aspects of what constitutes body language.

Facial expressions reveal a great deal of what a person is feeling. It is often possible to tell if a person is feeling sad, excited, angry, or bored, even without words. Facial expression may also convey judgments, intensity of emotion, and comprehension.

Eye contact, or the lack of it, is also a form of communication. We have an elaborate system of unspoken rules in our culture about whom it is permissible to have direct eye contact with and for how long. We have such sayings as, "The eyes are the windows to the soul" and "You can tell if a person is honest if he or she looks you in the eye." If a man stares at a woman, it may be a sign of attraction, whereas if he stares at another man for too long, it may be a sign of aggression or an

> ❝*Who you are speaks so loudly, that I cannot hear what you are saying.*❞
>
> *Ralph Waldo Emerson*

invitation to fight. In some cultures, direct eye contact may be interpreted as a sign of disrespect; in others, it means just the opposite.

Gestures and touching convey a great deal of meaning. Some people are very demonstrative and "talk with their hands." There are those who would be unable to communicate if they had to sit on their hands while talking. Pointing a finger at someone or shaking a fist communicates as much as words. Physical touch is another way to communicate with the hands. We place a good deal of importance on the ritual of handshaking in our culture, and much transpires unconsciously during that process. There are times when words just aren't enough, and a hug, a pat on the back, or a hand on the shoulder carries more meaning.

Space and Distance   Personal space and the distance between two people who are communicating also has meaning. We all have an invisible circle around us, and most people are aware of just how close to come to someone while interacting. Edward Hall (1969) described four distinct categories of space and distance:

- Intimate distance is the space from our skin to about 18 inches and is usually reserved for close friends and loved ones.
- Personal distance is from 18 inches to 4 feet and is usually the appropriate distance for normal conversations.
- Social distance is from 4 feet to 12 feet and is likely to occur when there is an impersonal or business relationship.
- Public distance is from 12 feet or more and is used for speaking to a large audience.

When having a conversation, notice how moving closer to or moving away from the other person can have an impact on the level of communication. Consider a time when someone invaded your personal space in a conversation.

Gender and Communication

Many people are familiar with the book that John Gray wrote about men and women being from different planets. He described stereotypical behavior of each sex, and then attributed differences in communication styles to those behaviors. Although it may be true that men and women differ in needs and reasons for communicating, the book is mainly based on speculation and informal observations. This doesn't mean that some of his observations weren't correct, but

there are far more variations in verbal communication patterns within each gender than between them. There are a number of studies (Santrock, 2006) that do find gender differences in communication, but perhaps it would be more useful to say that there are people from Mars and people from Venus.

Deborah Tannen (1990) wrote about gender differences and described some of the differences. Women, who seem to value relationships more, engage in **rapport talk.** This is intended to establish connections and develop relationships. Men tend to engage more in **report talk,** which is an opportunity to give information. Men tend to hold center stage by telling stories, jokes, or conveying information on their particular expertise.

Suggestions for Improving Communication
Hints for Men

1. Notice if you have a tendency to interrupt, especially when talking with women. If this is the case, make a goal of changing that habit.
2. Avoid responding in monosyllables. Give details about your experiences.
3. Learn the art of give and take. Ask women questions about themselves.
4. Make requests instead of commands. Ask women to do something rather than issuing demands and expecting immediate compliance.
5. Learn to open up about personal issues. Talk about your feelings, hopes, and interests.
6. Don't be afraid to ask for help if you need it. This can help to convey confidence in the relationship.

Hints for Women

1. When others interrupt, redirect the conversation back to you. It is permissible to declare that you haven't finished your point.
2. Look the person you are talking to in the eye. Direct communication doesn't have to be combative.
3. As much as possible, use a lower tone of voice. This gets more attention and respect.
4. Talk about yourself and your accomplishments. This is appropriate if others are doing the same.
5. Make a point of being aware of current events. This is an opportunity to contribute to a conversation.
6. Resist the temptation to be overly apologetic. Don't say "I'm sorry for everything" even when you aren't responsible.

GENDER-BASED COMMUNICATION: TALKING ACROSS TWO DIFFERENT CULTURES

Deborah Tannen, a professor of linguistics at Georgetown University, recently wrote a fascinating and widely praised book called *You Just Don't Understand: Women and Men in Conversation* (1990), which deals with the complexities of communication between the sexes. Drawing upon a distinguished research career, Tannen presents vivid examples of how women and men are socialized to relate and dialogue with others in such pronouncedly different ways that the two sexes often stumble in their efforts to connect. In various public lectures as well as in her book, which was a national best-seller, Tannen maintains that the sexes are, in a very real sense, communicating from the perspective of two different cultures.

Tannen contends that men use language to convey information, to achieve status in a group, to challenge others, and to keep from getting pushed around. Women, on the other hand, use language to achieve and share intimacy with others, to promote closeness and equality in a group, and to prevent others from pushing them away. Stated another way, men often grow up thinking that people will try to push them around if given a chance, and thus often enter into conversations concerned about who is one-up and who is one-down. From this perspective, communication becomes something of a contest in which a man endeavors to avoid being put in a one-down position. A man operating within this framework might be expected to be overly sensitive about asking advice or directions, being told to do something, or engaging in any other behavior or dialogue that even remotely resembled being in a one-down or pushed-around position. Tannen illustrates this point with the example of a man whose wife has requested that he do some specific task around the house: Rather than complying with her request immediately, he might wait and let some time pass before responding, so it will not appear that he is being told what to do. In contrast, women are not typically socialized to use language as a defensive weapon to avoid being dominated or controlled. Rather, their concern is often to use dialogue as a way to get close to another—and as a way to judge how close or distant they are from a valued partner.

Tannen has some particularly enlightening things to say about women and men engaging in what she calls troubles talk:

> Women and men are both frustrated by the other's way of responding to their expression of troubles. And they are further hurt by the other's frustration. If women resent men's tendency to offer solutions to problems, men complain about women's refusal to take action to solve the problems they complain about. Since many men see themselves as problem solvers, a complaint or a trouble is a challenge to their ability to think of a solution, just as a woman presenting a broken bicycle or stalling car poses a challenge to their ingenuity in fixing it. But whereas many women appreciate help in fixing mechanical equipment, few are inclined to appreciate help in "fixing" emotional troubles. (pp. 51–52)

A woman may talk about her problems to foster a sense of rapport and to achieve a feeling of "I am not alone." What she wants is a response that says, "I understand; I have been there too." For a woman, "trouble talk is intended to reinforce rapport by sending the message 'We're the same; you're not alone'" (p. 53). Such a response would put both communicators on an equal footing, thus allowing intimacy to be built around equality. However, when a man responds with advice when his partner is only looking for understanding, his response frames him "as more knowledgeable, more reasonable, more in control—in a word, one-up. And this contributes to the distancing effect" (p. 53). Tannen tells women to minimize this relationship-eroding influence by telling their male partners that when dealing with emotional troubles, they do not want solutions, just someone to listen.

Other key gender differences in communication styles discussed by Tannen include women's inclinations to think a relationship is working if both partners continue to talk about it, contrasted with men's tendencies to think things are okay if they do not need to keep talking about their relationship; women using face-to-face eye contact during dialogue more than men; and men's propensities to clam up at home, a place where they feel free not to talk (no need to keep their edge in a competitive, one-up world), as opposed to women's tendencies to open up in the comfort of home, where they feel free to talk.

Tannen stresses that the first step in improving communication is understanding and accepting that there are systematic gender differences in communication styles, and that it is not a question of one style being more right or wrong than the other. Tannen reports that many people have indicated to her that once they came to understand these differences in how the sexes use language, they were better able to put their problems of communication with the other sex in a manageable context—and often to arrive at solutions to seemingly unresolvable predicaments.

Self-Talk

No, you're not crazy if you talk to yourself. We all do it every day, whether we are aware of it or not. Actually, you're probably crazy if you don't talk to yourself. There is a great deal of evidence that positive self-talk can greatly improve your life in a number of ways. Most of the thinking we do during the course of the day is actually conversations we have with ourselves. How many times have you talked yourself into going back to bed because of the negative conversation you were having with yourself about the scheduled events of the day? By the same token, have you ever been physically ill but gotten yourself "psyched up," recovering for an exciting event that came up unexpectedly? These are examples of the power of self-talk.

Dennis Waitley, author of *The New Dynamics of Winning* (1993), has worked for more than 20 years in the field of human achievement. He has studied success, both as a researcher and as a therapist. In one of his studies, he showed that as Olympic runners imagined competing in races, small but measurable amounts of contractions took place in the muscles associated with running. Trainers working in the field of sports psychology believe not only that imagined activity produces associated muscle responses, but that the same pathways in the brain are stimulated when you are imagining an activity as when you are actually doing it. Waitley contends that it is the ongoing undercurrent conversation we have with ourselves that fuels the imagination. In other words, there is a direct relationship connecting self-talk, imagination, and actual performance.

Examine your self-talk and you will see how you are training yourself to respond. What percentage of the time are the things you think about and say to yourself positive? What percentage of the time are they negative? The way we think is likely to have a significant influence on the way we feel and what we do. The way we perceive a given situation, what we tell ourselves as we think about it, affects the feelings we experience and how our actions follow as a consequence. The process is likely to be as follows:

1. Stimulus event.
2. Self-talk about the event.
3. Consequences exhibited in feelings and actions.

The same stimulus event can produce quite different outcomes, depending on the thoughts that are introduced at the second stage. At some time, you have probably witnessed two people who had drastically different responses to the same situation. Most likely, the difference was due to the perceptions of the two people, and that was directly related to their internal dialogue describing the event.

One common element of successful people is that they have learned how to precede their actions with positive self-talk. You would do well to remember Shakespeare's line (*Hamlet*, Z. Z. 259): "There is nothing either good or bad, but thinking it makes it so." So why is it difficult to keep positive thoughts in mind? There are a number of reasons, according to John-Rodger and Peter McWilliams in their book *Life 101* (1990). They say it is not at all surprising that people have a difficult time thinking positive thoughts, because the deck seems to be stacked against us. It might even be considered a miracle that we have any positive thoughts at all.

General Negativity

Our parents, for the most part, raised us by pointing out what not to do. When we learned and adapted, our new behavior was accepted—and then expected—as normal. Often, we were trained to look for the bad so that we would not do it. Is it any wonder that we sometimes find ourselves unconsciously scanning the environment for bad things not to do? Also, the flight-or-fight response to danger served humans well for thousands of years when it was important to be alert at all times for the sake of self-preservation. It is counterproductive today, when it gets translated into focusing only on what is wrong. Some people are constantly wary and looking for the negative in the environment as if it were a life-or-death matter.

Further, what is on the news every evening? Bad news about how everything is falling apart. The law of entropy seems to be in effect: Anything left alone seems to deteriorate, and the things we try to fix get worse. And what is the favorite mode of conversation? Gossiping and complaining about people and situations. Have you ever noticed that people will give you about five minutes when you are really excited and happy about something, but if you're down in the dumps, you can always find someone to talk to for hours?

All of these things lead to negative thoughts. But that doesn't have to be the case. You are in control of your own thoughts, unless you think

> **"**It's a funny thing about life; if you refuse to accept anything but the best, you very often get it.**"**
>
> *Somerset Maugham*

your mind is being controlled by alien beings. When you are caught up in negative thinking, it often is best just to notice your thoughts and let them go. Don't resist them; just notice them and move on. Trying not to think a particular thought can make it more likely that you will think it. Daniel Wegner, author of *White Bears and Other Unwanted Thoughts* (1994), found that the very act of suppression creates a rebound effect, in which suppressed material pops back with more force than before. More effective is to pick a single distracting thought and stay with it. The good news is that the thing to be concerned with is your focus. In the big picture of things, where are you putting your attention? Pick a positive thought about yourself and concentrate on that.

Affirmations

One way to flip the switch on negative thinking is to use affirmations. This is a fairly common practice with people who are interested in personal growth or are in recovery from some type of addictive behavior. To *affirm* means to make firm, solid, and more real. Thoughts that are repeated over and over become more firm in our minds. They become feelings, behaviors, and experiences. Many sources suggest that what we think about, we truly become. Affirmations usually begin with "I am" and are stated in the present tense. Affirm as though you already have what you want, even though you don't yet have it. (The operative word is "yet.") You can write down your affirmations and then put them in places where you will see them. A powerful technique is to say your affirmation while looking yourself in the eyes in a mirror. As stated in *Life 101*, you can "learn to automatically turn all your wishes and wants into affirmations. Then start catching your negative thoughts, switching them around, and making affirmations out of them. By slightly revising the negative chatter, you can turn all those formerly limiting inner voices into a staff of in-house affirmation writers" (McWilliams and McWilliams, 1990, p. 97).

What have you noticed about your self-talk when you observe your internal dialogue? How often is it positive, and how often is it negative? What would be an appropriate affirmation for you that would increase positive thinking?

_____

_____

_____

_____

_____

_____

_____

_____

_____

Shyness

If you sometimes feel uncomfortable meeting new people, you're not alone. Most people suffer from shyness at one time or another. Shyness is not an emotional problem; it is simply an inability to communicate skillfully with others. It is a very common problem, according to a study of 10,000 U.S. adults by Phillip Zimbardo (1994), indicating that 40 percent of the respondents were troubled by shyness at the time of the survey. The survey also reported that 80 percent experienced being shy at some stage in their lives. Shyness is an anxiety reaction in social situations, a failure of confidence, and extreme discomfort when interacting with or confronting other people. Shy people are overly concerned with themselves: how they look, how they sound, how others view them. They are often afraid they will be regarded as foolish, unattractive, unintelligent, or unworthy. This attitude obviously impairs their ability to develop good human relations skills, and shy people find it hard to make friends. Further evidence of the importance of understanding and overcoming shyness is the reciprocal relationship between shyness and loneliness: shyness leads to loneliness and loneliness leads to shyness.

There are a number of other consequences of shyness that support the need for learning coping skills to overcome the negative effects of shy behavior. Some of those consequences, according to Zimbardo (1994), are as follows:

- *Reluctance to experience new situations:* Shyness prevents people from taking appropriate risks and therefore inhibits learning new skills.
- *Unassertiveness:* Shyness prevents people from standing up for their rights and expressing their own thoughts and feelings.
- *Limited ability to show personal strengths:* This prevents others from making positive evaluations and giving positive feedback.
- *Preoccupation with self:* This leads to further self-consciousness.

Various studies in recent years have identified three potential sources of shyness: heredity, lack of social skills, and improper social programming that fosters poor self-esteem instead of self-confidence (Weiten and Lloyd, 2003). One study, conducted by psychologists at Yale and Harvard universities, found that 10 to 15 percent of children are born with a propensity to shyness. We have all seen infants who turn away from strangers and toddlers who hide behind a parent when spoken to, even when by an adult they know. Of course, circumstances play a role in determining whether an inherited tendency to become shy is expressed. The Yale-Harvard study revealed that two-thirds of shy children had older siblings who perhaps bullied or belittled them, shaking their self-confidence. Parents can also seriously undermine a child's self-esteem through repeated negative comments about the child's ability or appearance or by failing to praise the child's accomplishments, however limited.

Another possible cause of shyness is our highly competitive society. We have a higher incidence of shyness than other cultures. From birth, we are constantly compared with others; this can lead to inferior feelings and set up another reciprocal relationship. If people think they are inferior, they may act shy and that can create a self-fulfilling prophecy—when people behave in a manner that supports their existing beliefs about who they are and what is possible for them. People can change, however. Even lifelong shyness behavior can be overcome, and many professionals conduct clinics and workshops to help people gain the self-confidence and social skills that will enable them to assert themselves in most situations.

PUSH THROUGH FEAR SO YOU CAN DO AND BE

Fear feels lonely. Things seem so much easier for all those other people. Because we're scared, we often feel inadequate, incompetent. The worse we feel about ourselves, the tougher it becomes to psyche ourselves up to do what's hard for us. Fear becomes a trap of our own making, holding at arm's length things we long to do, places we want to go, people we yearn to meet. We may tell ourselves we'll get to it when we're no longer afraid—the old "when/then" game. Sometimes, "when" never comes. That means that now may be the time to pick up *Feel the Fear and Do It Anyway,* by Susan Jeffers (1987). This isn't a new book, but it is worth reading for the basic and reassuring truth that it's normal to feel afraid, tackling something you've never done. Just like that first day of school, first date, first day on the job. Not so frightening now, huh?

- ❏ The fear will never go away as long as I continue to grow. Growing involves taking risks, doing things we've never tried. So we'll always feel some fear about the next new thing.
- ❏ The only way to get rid of fear of doing something is to go out and do it. There's nothing quite as exhilarating as conquering a fear; the pride you feel is like the little kid on his first two-wheeler—"Look! I can do it!"
- ❏ The only way to feel better about myself is to go out and do it. The longer I let fear keep me trapped, the worse I feel. Taking action is the way to spring the trap.
- ❏ Not only am I going to experience fear whenever I'm in unfamiliar territory, but so is everyone else. We don't have to feel like failures for being scared; it's natural.
- ❏ Pushing through fear is less frightening than living with the underlying fear that comes from a feeling of helplessness. When fear prevents us from acting, we wait for other people to give us what we want—just as small children must. Short-term fear of doing is easier to handle than long-term fear that we'll never be able to take care of ourselves.

Once we've accepted that fear is a normal part of being human, we can cope with it. Dr. Gerald Jampolsky, author of the popular *Love Is Letting Go of Fear* (1979), reduces life to two basic emotions: love and fear. We can act out of fear ("I better stay in this job/marriage/apartment even though I'm miserable") or out of love ("I care enough about myself to make a change for the better"). How can we tell which we're feeling? Kathleen Stone, a wise friend, gauges it this way: Fear asks "Why?" Love asks "Why not?"

Physician Charles Whitfield, author of *Healing the Child Within* (1988), notes that fear paralyzes, blocks the ability to heal, stifles creativity, and lowers our immunity to disease. He says fear can be disguised as worry, anxiety, panic attacks, nervousness, or insomnia. He suggests dealing with it in two ways. On a blank sheet of paper, make three headings: What I Am Afraid Of, What Could Happen, How I Would Handle It. Then write your fears down. Also, ask yourself: Does this fear belong to me or to someone else? (Is it really my father's fear of not making enough money? My mother's fear of gaining weight?) If you're carrying someone else's fear, Whitman says, "Let it go back to them with love and healing."

Motivational speaker James Melton, author of *Your Right to Fly* (1979), urges his audiences, "Don't tell yourself what you can't have, tell yourself what you can have." Thinking that you can't have what you want, he says, is "like standing by the Mississippi with your little cup in your hand saying, 'Oh—mine just went by!'"

Source: Article written by Jann Mitchell.

> **"** *No one can make you feel inferior without your consent.* **"**
>
> *Eleanor Roosevelt*

Components of Shyness

To overcome shyness, the following three components of shyness must be addressed:

1. *Feelings:* Feelings associated with shyness include anxiety, insecurity, tension, fear, and confusion.
2. *Physical reactions:* Physical reactions include shaking, perspiring, faint feeling, pounding heart, and blushing.
3. *Thoughts about self and others:* Thoughts about yourself might include: "I'm not as good as others," "I'm not very interesting," or "I can't deal with embarrassment." Thoughts about others might include: "They probably won't like me," "They're going to reject me," or "They are watching everything I do."

Most important to you are thoughts about yourself. The major difference between shy people and those who are not shy is self-evaluation. What you say to yourself has an impact on your feelings and physical reactions. You can change your "internal self-talk" and that can change your evaluation of yourself. Interrupt the internal conversation you have with yourself if you start to compare yourself to others. Then say positive things to yourself about your abilities.

Remember, the only person to compare yourself to is you. Ask yourself if you are doing the best you can at that moment, keeping in mind that you are just as valuable as any other person.

Dealing with Shyness

Overcoming shyness may not be easy at first, but it can be done. The following steps will help in the process of dealing with shyness:

1. *Identify your shyness:* Identify what situations and settings tend to elicit your reactions. Identify the causes in each situation and the thoughts that preceded your shyness. Ask for feedback from a friend on how you can improve.
2. *Build your self-esteem:* Set your own standards for how you want to be in life. Recognize that you really can control how you see yourself. Set realistic goals and don't demand too much of yourself. Talk to yourself in a positive manner and remember that you are a good person.
3. *Improve your social skills:* Find a role model and observe how he or she interacts; then imitate that behavior. Smile and make eye contact. Listen and really focus on the other person. Rehearse what you want to say and practice (with a tape recorder) how you want to sound. Remember, you aren't alone.

Experts in the field of counseling point out that there is tremendous power just in beginning to think of how you want things to be, rather than imagining what you don't want. In one case study, a man changed his behavior considerably by paying attention to his own thought patterns. He had previously thought things such as, "They probably won't like me" when being introduced to new people. He had never thought, "They just might like me." As simplistic as it sounds, it made a difference in his behavior and feelings.

Overcoming Fear

We all know what fear feels like. It is probably the most common limiting emotion. For some people, it is the most common feeling. One description of fear could be the acronym FEAR: *False Expectations Appearing Real.* For the most part, what we fear is not real; it is merely our mind imagining something awful that has not yet happened. Put another way, fear is interest paid on a debt you may not owe. Surprisingly, fear has a gift for us: It is called energy. If you think (or possibly feel) about it, fear and excitement have a very similar physiological reaction. When you are bored with life and start to think about the thing you have been avoiding that is a little scary, don't you feel your pulse quicken? Fear and boredom are incompatible. The trick is to use the fear to energize yourself and to get curious about how you can learn from the situation.

When we were growing up, our parents taught us to be afraid of things that they believed were dangerous. Usually with the best of intentions, they wanted us to feel fear and pay attention to it as a reason not to do harmful things. The problem is that many of us learned only to feel fear without noticing the lesson about using it to make good decisions. No one told us what a gift the state of arousal can be. We must persistently tell ourselves that fear is heightened energy and awareness, that it allows us to do our best and learn the most in new situations. As the saying goes: *"It's all right to have butterflies in your stomach. Just get them to fly in formation."*

CASE STUDIES AND STUDENT STORIES

Amy described her parents as good people, but they were very poor. Mice ran around at night eating crumbs of what little food they had. One of her first recollections of childhood was a mousetrap with a dead mouse in it falling off a shelf and landing on her head. It seemed to Amy that there just wasn't enough food to go around, but she remembered feeling somewhat happy as long as she wasn't around people outside the family.

Her dad was a struggling artist, and her mom stayed home to take care of the children. The family had cardboard in the windows of the house, and she remembered feeling so cold during the night that she thought she would freeze to death. While the family tried to make ends meet, they were all aware that they didn't have what others had.

Years passed, and Amy entered high school. She was so poorly dressed and so shy that the other kids taunted her and made fun of her. The thoughts of high school were like a nightmare to her, because there was no way she could image to make things any better.

As her senior year rolled around, though, something happened in Amy. She became so depressed that she sought out her school counselor. During one of her counseling sessions dealing with her feelings of inferiority, she said she felt something like an awakening. She realized she wanted her life to change for the better. Amy was tired of feeling out of place because of what she thought others' opinions were about her. Together with her counselor's help, she began to make plans.

As her counseling sessions continued, Amy found that a willingness to change took over as she explored her thoughts. She called it determination, and the will to focus on the future. Other people became less of the source of her belief about herself. She began to think that she could make friends if she made the effort. She said that her newfound belief in herself gave her power to believe that other things were also possible.

Following high school, she entered college to pursue an art degree. It was there that she found acceptance and friendship from her peers. Her artistic ability flourished, and she found happiness by believing in herself. Her artistic flair was well respected in her workplace, and her skills were sought after.

Today Amy is a successful businesswoman. She has learned to assert herself in her field of expertise and has become a source of inspiration to those that are around her. She is no longer the shy child from the poor part of town, but a woman of great courage who leads others to find their purpose.

Source: By D. Juanita Woods.

Part of doing our best in a new situation involves learning. There is so much to learn from a new experience, and it provides opportunities to learn about ourselves. Fear provides a good environment for learning—not ideal, but good nonetheless. Most people treat fear as a wall; it is really the edge of their comfort zone. Fear is not a wall; it is just an emotion. If you want to learn about fear, whatever it is you fear doing is the very next thing you need to do! Keep in mind, though, the appropriate amount of risk you are ready for at the time.

When you start doing the thing you fear, the fear is used for its true purpose: free energy. Hence the suggestion from Bertrand Russell: *"Feel the fear and do it anyway."* In her book of the same title, Susan Jeffers states: "If everybody feels fear when approaching something totally new in life, yet so many are out there doing it despite the fear, then we must conclude that fear is not the problem" (1987, p. 33).

When we know something is not physically dangerous, we can go ahead and do it. It may feel uncomfortable, but keep moving one step after another in the direction of doing it. As you move, the energy will transform itself from barrier to blessing. You will have energy, not limitation.

> *Courage is resistance to fear, mastery of fear, not the absence of fear.*
>
> Mark Twain

Commitments

Has anyone ever told you he or she was going to do something for you and then backed out without letting you know? How did you feel? How did you respond? You undoubtedly had some negative thoughts, including some expletives and rather colorful adjectives about the person. When someone disappoints us, we usually express some form of disapproval. Trying to avoid disapproval is what motivates most of us to keep our commitments to others. We don't want people to think badly of us. Think about what percentage of the time you keep commitments to other people. Is it fairly high? That is probably because you want to avoid the disapproval of other people. You don't want them to think the same bad thoughts about you as you thought about them when they broke a commitment.

Now we are going to use that line of reasoning but take another perspective. What percentage of the time do you keep commitments to yourself? Every term, I hear students say, "This is the term I'm going to go to all my classes," or "I'm going to finish all the units I start." This type of situation occurs in many contexts, not just in an academic setting. Many of us have a "New Year's Resolutions" approach to life, in which we make all kinds of promises to ourselves but never fulfill them. As a result, we soon begin to see ourselves as the kind of person who never follows through on commitments.

Be very careful about the commitments you make to yourself. What you think of yourself is just as important as what someone else thinks of you. It is interesting that we will go to great lengths, in most cases, to avoid others' disapproval. Yet, when it comes to our view of ourselves, we act as if what we think of our own dependability is irrelevant. Nothing could be further from the truth. Those who frequently make and then break agreements with themselves might benefit from reading that statement again. Remember that we keep commitments to others to avoid disapproval. Approval from yourself is just as important as, or more important than, approval from others.

There are people who make too many commitments, and keep them at whatever cost. Then others take advantage of them, knowing that they find it difficult to say no and that, once committed, they will do the job no matter what. Those who break agreements easily need to start keeping them! On the other hand, those who

sacrifice too much to others need to give a higher priority to keeping commitments they have made to themselves. For example, there are some people with codependent tendencies who will drop everything they are doing, no matter how important, if anyone asks a favor of them. Once they have agreed to help, they will go to great lengths to keep the commitment, regardless of the sacrifice in their own lives. For them, it might be beneficial to say no and negotiate whether they have the time and energy to give. Generally, a useful guideline and a good way to improve self-concept is to *make fewer commitments and keep them.*

In assessing behavior regarding commitments, there are a number of double standards that explain why some people have difficulty keeping their word. Understanding those double standards will help you to be more aware of your actions and to begin making any necessary changes. Most people say that they would rather hear the truth than a lie. Yet, how many times have you answered yes to a request even as a voice in your head was screaming no? This is the first level of self-deceit. We tell ourselves that we want the truth, but that others, well, they can handle the lie.

The second level of self-deceit is evident in the belief that we have a good nonsense detector but that others don't. Don't you feel a little insulted when someone tells you an obvious lie? The double standard comes into play when you tell others the same type of obvious lie, believing they will accept it as truth. Most of us, at some time, have given a lame excuse that was transparent. We act as if we are the only ones who have a functioning nonsense detector! We tell ourselves that we know the difference between a legitimate excuse and a manufactured one, but that other people can't tell at all.

The third level of self-deceit is the excuse we use for being less than honest in the first place. We tell ourselves that we do it to spare other

> **❝** *Most of us feel that others will not tolerate emotional honesty in communication. We would rather defend our dishonesty on the grounds that it might hurt others; and having rationalized our phoniness into mobility, we settle for superficial relationships.* **❞**
>
> *John Powell*

people's feelings. The reality is that we do it to protect our own feelings, which might be hurt from other people's disapproval. But it doesn't work that way. If Joe tells Sam he can't help him move because he will be out of town, what happens when they run into each other at the store? If you risk saying no when you need to, you may face some disapproval at that time. But, in the long run, if you tell the truth, you will usually earn some respect from that person for being honest. The other person will learn that you can be counted on when you do say yes. Remember: If you never say no, what does yes really mean?

There are a number of variables affecting the development of self-esteem, but one sure way to increase your self-esteem is to know that you can count on yourself to stick with a decision. Think about times when you took on a challenging project and saw it through to completion. There is usually a sense of satisfaction in doing something that requires real effort and ability. Life can be seen, at times, as a series of accomplishments. Self-esteem increases as you learn and grow from those accomplishments, and you are more likely to achieve goals when you determine your priorities and stick with your commitments to attain them. One other major accomplishment could be the commitment to develop greater honesty with yourself and others about what you truly will or will not do.

Questions for Critical Thinking

How often do you make commitments? What percentage of the time do you keep commitments to others? To yourself? What do you need to do to improve your relationship commitments with others?

_____

_____

_____

_____

_____

_____

_____

_____

_____

_____

Setting Goals

Many people make New Year's resolutions because there are things they want to accomplish, usually about personal behavior. Most of them are forgotten by the beginning of February! Why do we act as if our goals weren't important enough to take seriously? Goals are important because by setting some you can achieve more, improve your performance, and help to motivate yourself. Goals are also an important means for improving your self-confidence and increasing your satisfaction with your achievements (Corey and Corey, 2006).

Some people don't want to set goals because they don't like the process of making known their desires either to themselves or to others. They prefer to act as if they don't have any plans. That way, if they don't accomplish anything in life it won't seem like failure. The problem with that kind of thinking is that everyone has aspirations. Whether or not we let ourselves in on it, we all have hopes for the kind of life we would like to live.

Many young people engage in risky behaviors because they don't think much beyond next week, let alone years into the future. Long-range planning may be what they are going to do over the next break. Others think that nothing will ever happen to them and they will live forever, so why consider how their actions will influence tomorrow? But, life does go on, and an important part of human development is seeing the big picture. There is an old saying: "If you don't know where you are going, you will probably end up somewhere else."

Ask yourself where you would like to be in five, ten, or twenty years from now. How else are you going to get there if you don't have any plan? What do you want to accomplish in the world in regard to education, career, and family? How long you expect to live may influence attitude, personal health care, and physical activities. If only on an unconscious level, we all have things we would like to accomplish in life.

Effective Goal Setting

1. State the goal in a positive manner: what you want to do or accomplish, rather than what you don't want to have happen.
2. Be precise and specific. Make sure that achievement can be measured. What constitutes progress, and what are the target dates and/or times?
3. Prioritize. It will be much easier to get organized and work toward a goal if you first prioritize. That can give you direction and provide motivation.

4. Write your goals down. It is amazing how powerful it can be to take something out of your mind and put it down on paper. When you can see it and read it, the goal takes on a new dimension.

5. Keep your goals small and operational. If you have a large or long-term goal, it is important to be able to notice incremental changes. This also provides more opportunities to reward progress.

Evaluating Your Goals

1. If you base your goals on personal performance or skills or knowledge to be acquired, then you can keep control over the achievement of your goals and draw satisfaction from them.

2. Goals based on outcomes are extremely vulnerable to failure because of things beyond your control.

3. Are your goals set unrealistically high? Some people take on others' goals that may not be useful. Is this an opportunity to set yourself up for failure? Is your goal so high as to almost guarantee that it is unattainable? Some people who are concerned about taking risks and want an excuse to play it safe may use high goals as a chance to tell themselves, "I told you so."

4. Are your goals set too low? If you're not prepared to stretch yourself and work hard, then you are extremely unlikely to achieve anything of real worth.

5. Strive for the balance so you set goals that are slightly out of your immediate grasp, but not so far that there is no hope of achieving them.

If you revise your list of goals on a regular basis, you can greatly contribute to your accomplishments in life. And, it follows that achieving the things that you want in life will contribute to your overall happiness and satisfaction.

Critical Thinking Skills

An important part of being able to assimilate new information is learning the tools to evaluate the information being presented. Some people accept things at face value and don't question behavior or events enough. They put too much value on common-sense explanations, even though there are times when what seems obvious is not really an explanation for the event. In order to utilize this book/course to the fullest extent, it is important to know how to analyze new ideas and to think in a critical manner that is positive and useful.

The following guidelines have been adapted from Weiten and Lloyd (2006).

1. Ask questions and be willing to wonder. Rather than passing judgments about behavior—yours and others'—get curious. What does the behavior really accomplish?

2. Define the problem. It helps to think in concrete examples when changing behavior. Rather than thinking about how to be a better person, ask yourself what exactly could you do to become more of what you would like to be.

3. Examine the evidence. Is it someone's personal assertion or opinion? Does the evidence come from research that is valid and reliable?

4. Analyze biases and assumptions. Are you willing to consider evidence that contradicts your beliefs? Can you evaluate and recognize the bias of others?

5. Avoid emotional arguments—yours and others'. Feelings are important, but they should not substitute for careful appraisal of arguments and evidence.

6. Don't oversimplify. Look beyond the obvious. Reject simplistic either-or thinking. Be wary of anecdotal stories as the basis for new information.

7. Consider other interpretations. Before you leap to conclusions, think about the other explanations. Be especially careful about assertions of cause and effect.

8. Tolerate uncertainty. Be willing to accept some guiding ideas and beliefs, but also be willing to give them up when evidence and experience contradict them.

Although it is important to explore what your behavior and beliefs, sometimes it is just as valuable to think about *why* you have a certain belief, and what it is that your behavior accomplishes.

Action and Results

Seminars that deal with increasing human potential often refer to the importance of having "clear intention" in getting the results you want and/or being successful in life. Some seminar leaders say, "It's all a matter of intention, and you know your intention based on the results you get." If you really wanted to make something happen and had clear intentions of the results you were going to produce, then you would have attained your goal. But there is something missing in that. Every baseball player who comes to bat has a clear intention of getting a hit, but, according to this theory, based on results, they only intended to get a hit maybe 30 percent of the time! It is little consolation to tell someone who is going through a divorce that it must not have been their intention to stay married. *Intention* is a word that represents a generalization and covers a number of specific elements, including commitment. Let's take a closer look at those elements and their relationship to being successful and getting the results you want in life.

Limiting Beliefs

Norman Vincent Peale (1976) said, "What the mind of man can conceive and believe, he can achieve." Likewise, what we believe we can't do will be almost impossible to achieve. The most important element in achieving a goal is your belief about what is possible for you. Richard Bach, in his book *Illusions* (1974), states: ***"Argue for your limitations, and sure enough, they are yours."***

Self-defeating behaviors are often a result of negative beliefs about what is possible for you in your world. Your belief system is like a gate valve, and a number of those beliefs are subconscious. The more you become aware of and eliminate your limiting beliefs, the more likely you will be to reach your goals. Challenge that part of you that unnecessarily questions your potential.

Clear Objectives

There is a saying: "If you don't know where you are going, you'll probably end up somewhere else." It is valuable to have specific goals in mind and to make sure that they are realistic for you. Exploration in this area can help you assess whether or not the stated objective will in fact result in the experience you want.

Skill Development

Do you have the necessary skills to accomplish what you say you are after? Theoretically, we can do anything. Practically speaking, having the necessary skills is a key factor. Some people have the physique to become athletes; others do not. Some people have the capabilities to become musicians, and others do not. Whatever your innate talents and abilities are, it is important to also do what is necessary to acquire the skills to accomplish what you want.

> **"** *Even if you're on the right track, you'll get run over if you just sit there.* **"**
> *Will Rogers*

Desire

A great deal is said these days about the importance of "following your bliss." This means to listen carefully to what your inner voices tell you about what is truly important to you. Desire and will are the fuel for the engine of your accomplishments. There has to be a strong desire motivating you to keep on track.

Commitment and Self-discipline

It takes commitment to yourself and your goals to reach them. Dr. M. Scott Peck tells us that the most important contributor to a successful life is self-discipline. Commitment and self-discipline go hand-in-hand; each implies and depends on the other. In an interview with the magazine *Bottom Line/Personal*, Peck (p. 11, 1995) states:

> Without discipline, we can't improve ourselves, or solve problems, or be competent, or delay gratification, or assume responsibility. Without discipline we cannot find reality and truth—we never evolve from children into productive adults. Most people think that the point of life is to be happy. But life is really about self-improvement. We're not born perfect. It's our job to make ourselves as good as we can be. Those things that hurt, instruct. Yet the concept that life can be difficult is alien to most people. The only way we can improve ourselves is through discipline. Without it, we can't solve any problems. With some discipline, we can solve some problems. But with total discipline, we can solve all of our problems. Discipline makes us competent. The problem with competence is that there's a vacuum for it in the world. So as soon as people become more competent, either God or life gives them bigger problems to deal with. There is, however, a certain kind of joy that comes with knowing you're worrying about the big problems and that you're no longer getting bent out of shape about the little ones.

An equation using all of the above concepts might look like this: Absence of Limiting Beliefs + Clarity of Objectives + Skills + Desire + Commitment = Intention. You might think that *intention* would then equal definite results, right? Wrong. One essential ingredient remains before you have results, and that is *action*. All the good intentions in the world won't lead to much without action. What's the old saying about the road to hell?

As you think of the things that you would like to accomplish while exploring the ideas presented in this book, remember the importance of taking action. Life is a participatory event. The more you get involved and the more energy and effort you put in, the more valuable will be what you learn or get back.

Personal Learning

There are many different styles of learning, and the best educators try to incorporate as many approaches as possible to better serve the learner. A great deal has been gleaned from various sources regarding how people have different types of intelligence and learn through different modalities. Some people are more visual and need to see and be shown things in order to learn. Others are auditory and like to listen to and/or read instructions. Then there are those who need a "hands-on" experience and have to *do* things to fully understand. This information is valuable, and it is important to understand your own style; but perhaps there is another emphasis that is just as important. That area involves passive versus active learning.

Many of us have had an education that did not promote active learning. Some educators and school systems are more comfortable with students who do not question things, think for themselves, or try to direct their own learning. For many of us, it was expected that you took a passive stance by doing the work assigned, memorizing facts, and giving back information on tests. Learning that truly promotes personal growth takes much more of a holistic approach. Carl Rogers, a well-known humanistic psychologist, wrote the book *Freedom to Learn for the 80's* (1983). He emphasized that attitudes and values are just as important as factual knowledge. Some of elements of personal learning that he proposed follow:

> ▶ It is self-initiated, in that there is a sense of discovery, reaching out, and comprehending that comes from within the learner.
> ▶ It is pervasive, meaning that it makes a difference in the behavior, attitudes, and personality of the learner.
> ▶ The locus of evaluation is within the learner; that is, the learner determines whether what is being learned is meeting his or her needs.

> **❝** *Nothing in the world can take the place of persistence. Talent will not; nothing is more common than unsuccessful men with talent. Genius will not; unrewarded genius is almost a proverb. Education will not; the world is full of educated failures. Persistence and determination alone are omnipotent.* **❞**
> *Calvin Coolidge*

> ▶ It is significant and matters to the learner; that is, it is holistic in that it combines the logical and cognitive with the intuitive and feeling dimensions.

All of these elements make for a richer educational experience, but it takes active learning to accept the challenge of accomplishing them. Students need to put forth the effort necessary to take advantage of the system that is designed to better meet their needs.

Learning Goals

Some people have difficulty setting goals for themselves, and yet numerous authors in the field of human potential believe that having goals is the most important element for motivating yourself to self-improvement. Some people set their goals too high and set themselves up for disappointment. Others set their goals, if they have any at all, too low. This may be an attempt to avoid anything that might remotely look like failure. If you don't intend to accomplish anything, how can you be disappointed? Take a moment and think about your style. What might be reasonable goals for improving your human relations skills?

Many years ago I used the book *Being and Caring* (Daniels and Horowitz, 1998) in a course for interpersonal growth and awareness. I'm pleased to see that after a number of years, it is back in print. Here are some of the guidelines the authors of the book use to help students set goals for the course:

> ▶ Learn to appreciate and enjoy yourself, your life, and other people, rather than depreciate and judge all these.
> ▶ Live in a self-determining, authentic way that's based primarily on who you are rather than on what others want you to be.

▶ Develop the neglected sides of who you are and become a more fully integrated person.

▶ Increase your freedom and power by accepting responsibility for your behavior.

▶ Sharpen your ability to be aware of events both within and outside yourself.

Take time to consider these ideas as you think about your goals for the course, how best to make the learning process a valuable personal experience, and how you can actively participate in a manner that will promote personal learning.

Application

Now that you have considered the information offered in this chapter, and thought about what you would like to get out of your human relations course, it might be a good idea to review the table of contents and browse through the rest of the book. What topics are of particular interest to you? If you were to accomplish what you want by taking this course, what would be different in your life?

A healthy, balanced sense of self-discipline is a prerequisite for success in any area of human relations. Being able to focus on future goals and withstand the temptations of immediate gratification is essential for many important accomplishments in life. Take some time to consider what you might need to do more or less of to develop a balanced sense of self-discipline. What plan of action are you willing to commit to at this point to learn the information in this course?

This chapter introduced concepts that are useful in understanding human relations, regardless of the topic or subject being discussed. The information presented in this chapter is also useful in promoting group interaction while covering the information in the remainder of the text. To talk about human behavior, it is important to deal with breaking the ice, communication issues, shyness, confronting fears, and being committed to a course of action that will facilitate learning. In that sense, this chapter is the foundation on which the following chapters will build.

THE RULES FOR BEING HUMAN

1. You will receive a body. You may like it or hate it, but it will be yours for the entire period this time around. How you perceive it is your choice.

2. You will learn lessons. You are enrolled in a full-time informal school called life. Each day in this school you will have the opportunity to learn lessons. You may like the lessons or think them irrelevant and hence choose to ignore them—no matter, keep reading.

3. A lesson is repeated until learned. A lesson will be presented to you in various forms until you have learned it. When you have learned it, you can then go on to the next lesson.

(continued)

4. There are no mistakes, only lessons. Growth is a process of trial and error, of experimentation. The "failed" experiments are as much a part of the process as the experiments that ultimately "work."

5. Learning lessons does not end. There is no part of life that does not contain its lessons. If you are alive, there are lessons to be learned.

6. "There" is no better than "here." When your "there" has become a "here," you will simply obtain another "there" that will again look better than "here."

7. Your answers lie only inside you. The answers to life's questions lie only inside you. All you need to do is look, listen, and trust.

You will probably forget all of this.

CHAPTER REVIEW

Basic Principles of Human Behavior

Ten building blocks represent concepts that will be referred to throughout this text. They provide information for understanding human behavior in a number of contexts. Concepts such as double standards, paradox, catch-22, and playing the devil's advocate apply to topics and behaviors that are introduced in later chapters.

Diversity, Gender, and Multiculturalism

On a certain level, we all have entirely unique experiences of the world. Therefore, appreciating diversity is a concept important for everyone, regardless of race, gender, or culture. The goal of multicultural education is to recognize and appreciate that differences exist among people. It is important to learn more about how that affects our behavior and influences our interactions with other people.

Verbal Communication

Learning how to connect with people by improving your ability to listen as well as to speak will enhance communication. When discussing topics in small groups or large groups, think about building bridges rather than walls.

Nonverbal Communication

It is virtually impossible not to communicate. Body language and nonverbal communication are important. What we don't say may communicate as much as what we do say. How you say something is just as important as what you say.

Self-Talk

Negative internal dialogue limits your behavior. Numerous experts in the field of human potential suggest methods such as affirmations for increasing your positive thoughts. What you say to yourself about your abilities affects your behavior, so it is important to observe that internal process.

Shyness

Many people experience shyness in some situations. Fear of public speaking is particularly common. When you analyze the situation and are more aware of your self-talk, you can begin to improve your self-esteem as well as your social skills.

Overcoming Fear

Fear and excitement produce similar physical reactions. When you start an activity that is anxiety provoking, it often becomes easier to deal with. We are all afraid at times, but it is important to understand fear and then channel it in a manner that doesn't limit our behavior.

Commitments

We often keep commitments to others to avoid their disapproval. It is just as important, however, to be able to count on ourselves. What we think of ourselves should be as important as what others think of us. Therefore, it is important to honor the commitments we make to ourselves as well as those we make to others. The ability to be clear about commitments to yourself and others has valuable implications for any learning situation that requires self-discipline.

Action and Results

Some people think that having a clear intention will produce results. Actually, there are a number of elements that combine to accomplish the results you want. Those elements include absence of limiting beliefs, clear objectives, skill, desire, commitment, and self-discipline. Most important, none of these things will lead to what you want without your taking the necessary action.

Personal Learning

Now is the time to consider what you would like to get out of your human relations course. A balanced sense of self-discipline and the ability to focus on future goals are very important.

SOURCES AND SUGGESTED READINGS

Adler, Ron, and Neil Town. *Looking Out/Looking In.* New York: Holt, Rinehart and Winston, 2003.

Atwater, Eastwood. *Psychology for Living.* Englewood Cliffs, NJ: Prentice Hall, 1999.

Devito, Joseph A. *Messages: Building Interpersonal Communication Skills.* New York: Harper & Row, 1990.

Hanna, Sharon L. *Persons: Positive Relationships Don't Just Happen.* Englewood Cliffs, NJ: Prentice Hall, 2003.

Jeffers, Susan. *Feel the Fear and Do It Anyway.* New York: Fawcett Columbine, 1987.

Koester, Jolene, and Myron Lusting. *Intercultural Competence: Interpersonal Communication Across Cultures,* 4th edition. Boston: Allyn & Bacon, 2002.

LeBaron, Michelle. *Bridging Cultural Conflicts: New Approaches for a Changing World.* Francisco: Jossey-Bass, 2003.

Tannen, Deborah. *You Just Don't Understand.* New York: Ballantine, 1990.

Zimbardo, P. G. *Shyness.* New York: Jove, 1994.

Web Site Resources

American Self-help Clearinghouse Source Book
   http://www.cmhc.com/selfhelp

Deborah Tannen's Homepage
   http://www.georgetown.edu/tannen

Gender Talk: Provides explanations and challenges to conventional attitudes about gender issues and identity
   http://www.gendertalk.com

Time Management Hints
   http://www.briefings.com/cbTimeMgmt.html

The Shyness Institute: Offers network resources, including articles, associations, and agencies, for people seeking information and services for shyness
   http://www.shyness.com

REACTION AND RESPONSE—WHAT DO YOU THINK?

Chapter One   Level I Assignments

The Level I assignments are intended to encourage introspective thought. This is an opportunity to respond to the material presented in the chapters, the class activities, and the group discussions. Although the questions pertaining to class discussions and activities are the same for each chapter, your answers will vary greatly according to the content of the class. The following specific questions are provided as examples of how to use the chapter information in a creative manner. These are only guidelines, however, so feel free to include other information about your response to the chapter that is important to you.

In response to the information in the chapter:

1. Where, when, and in what circumstances have you experienced shyness? How would you look, sound, and feel if you were to act more in accord with your desires? What has been your objection to acting in that manner? What would need to change to enable you to act how you would like to be?

2. What did you learn from the section on diversity? What are some ways in which we are like all other people? What are ways in which we are all unique? What are some of the cultural barriers that keep people from getting to know one another? What are some of the diversity skills that you could practice

to improve your relations with people of different backgrounds?

3. What would you like to learn from your human relations class? What changes are you interested in making? What actions are you willing to take to accomplish those goals? If you were to learn what you hope for from the course, how would your life be different?

In response to the class activities, group discussions, and exercises:

1. What are your reactions and opinions?
2. What did you learn or rediscover?
3. How are you going to apply what you learned?

Chapter One   Level II Assignments

Level II assignments help you further evaluate and consider the personal application of the ideas and concepts presented in each chapter. Contemplate the implications of the chapter material and the meaning it has for your life. You may want to share your own examples of how the ideas presented have influenced your life. Feel free to write pertinent descriptions of how you plan to apply the information in everyday situations.

1. From the section on the Basic Building Block, what are some examples of how you have done things that made a situation worse rather than better? What are some double standards that you have? Do you have a tendency to play devil's advocate? What behaviors do you know you need to do more often, and which ones do you need to do less often?
2. What are your communication strengths? What skills should you practice? In what

ways could you improve, and what would it take to do that? How could you *build bridges rather than walls* in your group discussions?

3. What part of the chapter had the greatest impact on you? What did it remind you of regarding your experiences in interacting with other people? What stories could you share about how you intend to use the material in the chapter to improve your human relations skills?

Chapter One   Level III Assignments

After considering what you have written about the implications of the new information in Level I (**what** you have learned), and then exploring the personal applications of the material in Level II (**why and how** you can use it), this level is an opportunity to begin to imagine using those concepts when applying them in your everyday life situations (**where and when** it would be valuable to act on the new choices). Feel free to discuss personal history to the degree you are comfortable.

1. How do you really feel about being a student? What are your expectations of what an education will do for you? What change do you most need to address in order to be more successful?
2. How are you at setting goals? Do you sabotage yourself in some way so that you don't attain them? What would it mean to you to have some kind of future plan? What goal can you set for today?
3. How do you motivate yourself to take action when it is needed? What is a time when you have been excited about learning? How do you get yourself "psyched up" in a new situation?

2

C H A P T E R

SELF-AWARENESS

There are people in the world who probably shouldn't have been parents. Everyday you can read newspaper accounts of people who abuse and/or abandon their children. There was a case a number years ago of a mother and father who went on a vacation to Mexico and left their 9-year-old at home in charge of their 4-year-old. They were gone for two weeks and were surprised to be arrested upon returning. It is not uncommon to read of the latest drug bust where the authorities had to take children into custody who were living in a home where drugs were being manufactured and sold. Often, children are exposed to toxic chemicals in a situation where law enforcement agents wear complete protective covering. There are reports of mothers who have to leave home and seek assistance in a shelter for battered women. Often, this is done in the interest of protecting the children from being exposed to further violence or from becoming the direct target of escalating physical abuse.

All too many children have to grow up in an environment where there is violence, lack of proper caretaking, and drug or alcohol problems. Some of these children develop poor self-concept and, incredibly, even mistakenly believe that they might in some way be to blame for their situation.

How does such a thing occur? How can children who have grown up in a crazy situation ever come to think bad things about themselves as a result of living with parents who have numerous problems? It is a strange paradox that it might actually be reassuring for the children to think that in some way they are to blame for their circumstances—in a twisted form of logic, they might even feel a little more in control.

Consider the hypothetical case of a child who grows up in a home where the father is violent and abusive and the mother is a marginally functioning alcoholic or drug addict, or both. Frequently, when adults' lives are in turmoil, they have a tendency to take things out on their family and children. It is a fairly common scenario that adults, who are often stagnant in their own development, will direct their anger and insecurity toward children and treat them badly.

The child confronted with such a frightening and confusing situation is not very likely to assess the situation in an accurate manner. Depending on their age, children may have the awareness that they are living in a horrible situation and that things are not as they should be. But to see the situation for what it really is might be even more frightening.

Imagine that little Susie looks up at her parents and decides that they are really "crazy." She may be correct in assessing the situation, and the fact that she is being treated very badly may have nothing to do with her. Being mistreated may be more a reflection of the parents, in some cases. But, if she decides "I'm OK" and "they are the crazy ones," what then? She might have 10 more years that she has to live with "monsters." Thinking that the problem is with her parents may be more frightening because then there is no reason for why she is being treated badly—after all, she didn't do anything. And if there is no sense to how she is being treated, how can she do anything about it? It produces anxiety for a child to think that the people in charge are not in control.

Contrast that decision with blaming herself for how she is being treated and for the problems in the family. Although that is an incorrect assessment of the situation, it might be a less anxiety-provoking position. If Susie thinks that the reason she is being mistreated is because of something she has done, then at least the unpleasantness of her circumstances makes sense: "She gets treated badly because she is bad" has a certain kind of logic. And if she is the problem, then there is some hope: Maybe she can figure out what will get her parents to treat her better. She retains an element of control by thinking that, if she really tries hard, she might be able to get them to care about her.

This is one explanation of how a person might come to an incorrect assumption of self-worth: It might have served the function of self-preservation while growing up. The problem comes when the person forgets to reassess self-worth when finally out of the original situation. What had been an attempt at making sense of life in a crazy situation might become the source of difficulty in adulthood.

A number of people go through life thinking poorly of themselves because of this well-intentioned strategy of blaming oneself. What was once an attempt to make life bearable may make things more unpleasant at another point in life. It is important to explore the origins of one's self-concept, because there may be some incorrect assumptions. For many people, not liking themselves may be a case of mistaken identity.

Self-Concept

If asked to write three things that we like about ourselves, some of us will take a half-hour to do so, yet take only 10 minutes to list 10 things we don't like about ourselves. Why is that? Imagine how different life would be if we all had a ready list of our positive attributes, but had to take some time before coming up with a list of unproductive self-criticism and put-downs.

What happens during our development that makes it difficult to think of ourselves in a positive way? We seem to have a culturally conditioned opinion that people who think well of themselves are egomaniacs. Yet, the movers and shakers in the world, those who make things happen and accomplish great deeds, usually have positive attitudes about their abilities. Even in everyday situations, the people who are doing well in life seldom spend much time thinking negative thoughts about themselves. To lead a productive life, it is extremely important to regard ourselves

> **"** The unexamined life is not worth living. **"**
>
> *Socrates*

and our abilities in a positive way. We do need to distinguish people with good self-concepts from people with swelled heads, however. People with high self-esteem can enjoy their accomplishments and the attention from others, but they can also share the limelight. People who have a strong need to convince others of how great they are seldom truly feel that way.

Self-awareness can be increased by exploring the different aspects of your self-concept. This chapter deals with defining the elements of self-concept as well as providing specific methods for improving self-esteem. Many books have been written on the importance of feeling good about yourself, and just as important is the information on how to attain that goal. Essential to reaching that goal is learning about appropriate self-disclosure and developing the ability to look at the parts of yourself that you keep hidden. In looking behind the mask, you can begin to discover and appreciate the real you.

The Definition of Self-Concept

Self-concept is the set of perceptions you have about the different aspects of yourself and your abilities. It is your internal mental image of yourself and the collection of beliefs about what kind of person you are. **Self-concept** is your cognitive awareness of who you are and what you think about yourself. **Self-esteem** is how you feel about yourself based on those perceptions and is reflected in your belief about what is possible to accomplish in the world. Some of the aspects of self-concept include the following:

Your social self: The part of you that interacts with others in the world and determines your sense of belonging.

Your emotional self: The feelings you have, or allow yourself to have, and how you express those feelings. This includes your ability to control your emotions when it is appropriate.

Your mental self: Your cognitive abilities and capacities for logic and reason. How you feel about your ability to make decisions is part of your mental self.

Your physical self: Your degree of comfort about your body, appearance, and/or your athletic abilities.

Your spiritual self: The part of you that connects to something greater than yourself, the basis for your values and the meaning you assign to life. Whereas religion may be measured by denominational affiliation, spirituality is internally defined, transcends the tangible world, and serves to connect you to the greater universe. (*Baron, 1990*)

Your assessment of these aspects of yourself is part of your self-concept. We will explore these categories more throughout the text.

Dimensions of the Self

Each of the previously mentioned aspects of self-concept interacts and influences behavior in a number of different domains. Another method of exploring your self-concept is to consider the difference among your private, public, and ideal selves. This requires another level of introspection as you consider the person you are in public compared to the person you are in private. Who you really are may at times be quite different from who you are and how you act around other people. Many of us project a different image of ourselves depending on the social setting.

Many people carry around an image of how they would like to be or how they would change if they could be more like their ideal. We all would like to change some aspect of who we are, hopefully for the better. The image of how we could be if we were our best self is an ideal to strive for. Think about and imagine each of the following aspects of who you are:

Private self: How you perceive yourself to be with all your thoughts, fears, hopes, and dreams. These are what you express to yourself and may know about yourself, but they may differ from how others think of you.

Public self: The different parts of yourself that you present to the world, including the roles, images, and masks that you sometimes adopt. Social pressures and interactions influence a great deal of your behaviors.

Ideal self: How you would like to be and the changes you would like to make in yourself. Some people have very high standards and expectations for themselves, which may influence their behavior in public or private.

One way to develop an accurate self-appraisal is to imagine each self as a circle, and then imagine the three circles in relationship to each other. How big would each circle be, and how

> **❝** *The display of status symbols is usually the result of low self-esteem. The self-confident person can afford to project a modest image.* **❞**
>
> H. Jackson Browne

much would each one overlap with the others? Consider how you would like to be different and what it would take. Look at the accompanying diagram, and then draw the circles to represent what you have learned about yourself.

A number of psychologists, including Karen Horney, have done research using this method for determining an individual's self-concept. They have concluded that the degree of **congruence** (overlap and similarity) between the circles is related to positive self-concept. Carl Rogers, a humanistic psychologist, believed that adjustment is more likely to occur when the various aspects of the self are congruent. That means that how you are in public, how you are privately, and what your ideal self would be like are all fairly similar.

The Importance of Self-Concept

Why is self-concept so important? Low self-esteem is blamed for a number of societal ills these days. After years of working with people in the field of counseling and education, I can say that a major source of problems for many people is lack of belief in themselves and their basic self-worth. This idea is supported by Bernie Zilbergeld, who reviewed outcome studies on psychotherapy more than 20 years ago in *The Shrinking of America* (1983). He concluded that counseling does have a positive

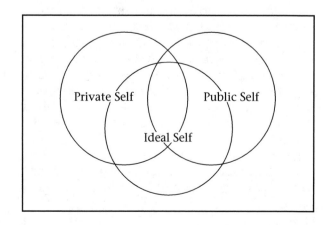

Questions for Critical Thinking

How much do the circles overlap in your self-assessment? What would it take to have them be more congruent? What did you learn from doing this exercise?

_____

_____

_____

_____

_____

_____

_____

_____

_____

“Not in time, place, or circumstance, but in the person lies success.**”**

Charles Rouce

influence on clients and that raising self-esteem may be the most important outcome. Increasing self-esteem can change many aspects of a client's experience.

Self-concept affects almost all aspects of life, including ability to communicate and communication style, willingness to learn and perform tasks, and ability to enter into and maintain healthy relationships. It is significant that so many divergent fields of study (psychology, sociology, education, counseling) refer to self-concept. Freud said a good sign of mental health is the ability to love and work. A healthy self-concept is a prerequisite for both.

Another example of the importance of self-concept is its influence on the "self-fulfilling prophecies" in our lives. Have you ever watched a friend create a difficult situation for himself that you, from the sidelines, could see was totally unnecessary? You knew something negative was going to happen, yet he seemed intent on carrying out an ill-conceived plan because he believed it to be his only possible option. When we think negative things about ourselves, we often cause negative things to happen, sometimes without even being aware of it. Never underestimate the power of beliefs! This is also closely related to the concept of **self-defeating behaviors.** When self-esteem is low, we are much more likely to do things to cause trouble for ourselves. A belief that we don't deserve to have good things happen to us will definitely affect our behavior. The cycle continues when adverse situations reinforce the belief that "this is the way life is" and we can't change it. But improved self-esteem can interrupt that process.

The Sources of Self-Concept

We aren't born with beliefs about who we are or what we deserve in life. Self-worth develops from interactions with our surrounding world. Well-researched studies of self-esteem (Weiten and Lloyd, 2003) conclude that the major portion of this foundation is laid during interactions between parent and child. A child who is wanted, loved, and appreciated will do much better in the world than one who is not. You don't have to be a psychologist to observe this principle in action—just visit a park or a grocery store and observe parent-child interactions.

For example, one day while sitting in a park with my family, I listened to a father yell at his toddler, who had taken off running and ignored his father's order to stop. When the father chased the child down, he began a tirade full of statements about the child's worth, such as, "You no-good brat, I'll teach you to listen," and, "You're a bad boy; I'm tired of you being such a problem." The sad part was that this child was probably new to walking and only had forward gear. It looked like he continued to run only because he couldn't stop and was actually trying to keep his balance. More than likely, the poor kid didn't understand half the words being said to him, but he got the message.

Self-concept develops primarily from the following three areas:

1. *Social information and interactions:* All the messages we receive while growing up—about who we are and what we are capable of doing—have an influence on our self-concept. Messages that say we are wonderful and talented are uppers while those that limit our belief in our potential abilities are downers.

2. *Social comparisons:* These happen when we look around us and make decisions based on how we think we compare to others. Sometimes, the evaluations are realistic and/or useful, but more often, we have judged ourselves unfairly because we have chosen impossible standards. When a person watches a basketball player who is 7 feet tall, and then decides he doesn't measure up because

ASSESS YOUR OWN LEVEL OF SELF-ESTEEM

1. Are you easily hurt by criticism?   yes ___ no ___
2. Are you very shy or overly aggressive?   yes ___ no ___
3. Do you try to hide your feelings from others?   yes ___ no ___
4. Are you able to laugh at (and learn from) your own mistakes?   yes ___ no ___
5. Do you fear close relationships?   yes ___ no ___
6. Do you find excuses for refusing to change?   yes ___ no ___
7. Do you look for and tackle new challenges?   yes ___ no ___
8. Do you wish you could change your physical appearance?   yes ___ no ___
9. Do you give yourself credit when credit is due?   yes ___ no ___
10. Are you happy for others when they succeed?   yes ___ no ___

he is only 5 feet, 6 inches tall, that is an unfair expectation. Seven-foot-tall people hardly represent a realistic basis for comparison. We sometimes impose equally absurd standards on ourselves regarding our abilities.

3. *Self-observation:* This is often a combination of and/or a reaction to the previous categories. Thoughts can have a major impact on behavior: "It's not what happens to us, but what we think about what happens to us." When some people encounter difficulties in life, they dig in and try harder; others seem to give up at the first sign of trouble. One person, on hearing a rude comment about herself, might think, "I wonder what's wrong with the person who said that?" Another might respond to that same comment with, "What's wrong with me?" It is useful to monitor the kinds of thoughts we have about ourselves because it is one way to begin to improve our self-esteem (*Hanna, 1999*).

Improving Self-Esteem

According to Nathaniel Brandon (1994), self-esteem is more than the innate sense of self-worth and the spark that therapists and educators try to nurture into flame. It is the full realization that we matter and are up to the challenges of life. Self-esteem is the evaluative and affective component of self-concept. It is a complex concept that may best be understood as a hierarchy: an indi-

vidual's overall self-concept is at the top, with specific perceptions about different areas below. Those areas include general competence, moral self-approval, power, and love worthiness (Epstein, 1973).

The importance of self-esteem has long been researched and discussed. But recently, there has been an increasing emphasis on the connection with action and behavior. William Damon, an education professor at Sanford University, said, "It is a classic case of putting the cart before the horse. We can't make kids feel good about themselves unless we give them something to feel good about." Evidence to support this is apparent in the lack of studies of how high self-esteem produces high achievement. Although it may be true that there is a link between high self-esteem and school success, the success has to come first. Self-esteem researcher Susan Harter (1990) believes that enhancement programs that targeted self-esteem itself—where individuals were simply encouraged to feel good about themselves—were often ineffective. Empty praise doesn't work because students see through it. Harter believes that interventions should target the sources of self-esteem. Praising a student's efforts and willingness to take on the challenge of learning something new might be more beneficial in the long run.

To that end, Nathaniel Brandon offers specific suggestions on how to increase self-esteem in his book *The Six Pillars of Self-Esteem* (1994). He believes that to gain the confidence necessary to feel worthy, deserving of success and happiness, and entitled to assert one's needs requires certain practices in everyday life. They are as follows:

1. *The practice of living consciously:* When you live consciously, you do not imagine that your feelings are an infallible guide to truth.

2. *The practice of self-acceptance:* Self-acceptance is the refusal to be in an adversarial relationship with yourself.

3. *The practice of responsibility:* No one owes you the fulfillment of your wishes.

4. *The practice of self-assertiveness:* Self-assertiveness means the willingness to stand up for yourself, to openly be who you are, to treat yourself with respect in all human encounters.

5. *The practice of living purposefully:* The root of your self-esteem is not your achievements but those internally generated practices that, among other things, make it possible for you to achieve.

6. *The practice of personal integrity:* When you behave in ways that conflict with your judgment of what is appropriate, you lose face in your own eyes.

Building Self-Esteem

Throughout your life, and during this course, you will have numerous opportunities to improve your self-concept and gain self-esteem. You will have opportunities to use new information to become more aware of how you can improve your interaction with others. The more you use situations as an opportunity for positive feedback, the better you will feel about yourself. When you learn something new, don't you feel better about yourself? Isn't it exciting to attempt a difficult task and succeed? And doesn't that success make the next attempt a little easier? It is true that taking risks can lead to setbacks or negative experiences, but these can be useful, too, if you build strength as you learn to deal with adversity.

The following general concepts are useful as guidelines for how to apply the material from Nathaniel Brandon:

▸ *To be how you want to be, start with where you are:* In *How to Raise Your Self-Esteem* (1987), Brandon states that the first step is to choose how you want to function and begin to live accordingly. Observe what you say to yourself. What are your beliefs about your self-concept? Where did they come from? How accurate or valid are they?

> **❝** *Self-reliance is the greatest gift a parent can give a child.* **❞**
>
> *Virginia Satir*

▸ *Concentrate on your strengths and demonstrate them:* Focus on how you can use those abilities more, and get involved in situations where your strengths can be an advantage in learning new skills. Look for areas where growth potential and talent overlap. Make a plan and start putting it into action.

▸ *Make positive changes in your lifestyle:* Feeling better physically will give you more energy, will, and desire to make emotional or psychological changes.

▸ *Watch your "self-talk":* What thoughts are affecting how you experience the world? Do the changes you want to make represent realistic expectations? Are your beliefs based on realistic perceptions? Do your self-talk words increase your self-esteem? Be cautious about trying to be too much of your ideal self if that creates some kind of perfectionist torture game. The objective is to feel better, not worse.

High Self-Esteem Versus Narcissism

Is there such a thing as having too high or too much self-esteem? Although feeling good about yourself is valuable, problems can arise when people have a view of themselves that is over-inflated and/or grandiose. People who feel good about themselves are usually confident, stable, and secure. They don't usually overreact to criticism. The people who truly have high self-esteem are not likely to become aggressive when their ego is threatened by someone else's evaluation of them.

For some time, the view that aggression stems from low self-esteem has been treated as common knowledge. People used to think bullies or violent aggressive people were really people with low self-esteem. Counselors, social workers, and teachers all over the country have been persuaded that improving the self-esteem of young people is the key to curbing violent behavior and academic success. Schools frequently have *feel-good* exercises designed to raise self-esteem. But is this really such a good thing to do? Should students feel good about themselves without having sufficient cause as evidenced by their accomplishments?

Recently researchers have begun to question some of those very assumptions. New research now supports the idea that it is more a case of threatened ego than low self-esteem. People with low self-esteem are not usually aggressive. People who have a negative view of themselves are typically muddling through life, trying to avoid embarrassment, and seldom have a need to prove their superiority. People with low self-esteem tend to avoid risks, and if they fail, they blame themselves, not others (Baumeister, Bushman, and Campbell, 2000).

As defined by clinical psychologists, narcissism is characterized by overinflated sense of self (too high self-esteem). Narcissistic people spend a great deal of time telling themselves how important they are and have a grandiose sense of their accomplishments. They are preoccupied with their needs and feel that they deserve special treatment. They have an unreasonable sense of entitlement. They lack empathy and are often seen as arrogant.

Criminals and gangsters who commit violent acts often have a sense of superiority. Baumeister speculates that they can become hostile and aggressive when they experience threats to their ego and their view of themselves. The key component is whether they feel provoked. Narcissists are no more aggressive than anyone else as long as no one insults or criticizes them (Baumeister, 1999).

"These findings have important practical implications. Most rehabilitation programs for spousal abusers, delinquents, and criminals are based on the faulty belief that these individuals suffer from low self-esteem. In opposition to this view, current research suggests that efforts to boost already inflated self-esteem are misguided; a better approach is to help such individuals develop more self-control and more realistic views of themselves" (Weiten and Lloyd, 2006).

Self-Esteem, Race, and Culture

For many years, research on self-concept indicated that many ethnic and racial groups had poor self-concept when compared to whites. More recently, research indicates that African Americans, Mexican Americans, and Puerto Ricans have equally positive self-concepts. This may be, in part, due to the movement that started during the 1960s emphasizing ethnic pride. This emphasis on the richness of various cultures appears to have improved the self-concept of ethnic minority groups (Walker and Brokaw, 1998). It appears that there has been a change from the "melting pot" philosophy—where everyone was expected to fit in—to the "salad bowl" analogy of

honoring the different elements of the whole. How can we best maintain positive identity while learning to live and work together in a world that is increasingly diverse?

Perfectionism

Perfectionism is not a healthy pursuit of excellence. There is a big difference between healthy achievers and perfectionists. Those who strive for excellence take genuine pleasure in trying to meet high standards. Perfectionists on the other hand are full of self-doubts and fears. There are some people who have a healthy drive to achieve, and others who are absolutely driven.

Perhaps you are one of those people who believes everything will be fine if you can just do everything right. You may become anxious if something isn't up to your standards. Do you have trouble accepting your human imperfections? Do you demand the same level of commitment from others around you? Perfectionists often don't realize that they are hurting themselves—and their relationships—by their own actions.

Healthy strivers enjoy the process as well as the outcome. They set high standards, but make them attainable. They keep normal anxiety and fear of disapproval within bounds, and they are able to see mistakes as opportunities for growth and learning.

Perfectionists never seem to be satisfied and may be overly depressed when faced with disappointment. Mistakes are evidence of unworthiness, and perfectionists become overly defensive when criticized. Although the intent is positive, misdirected energy can lead to being compulsive and obsessive. The paradox is that perfectionism usually ends up with the person being less efficient rather than more.

Further, there is a price to pay for perfectionism. This outlook on life can lead to anxiety in a number of settings: performance, test taking, and even social situations. Once again it is important to observe your self-talk because many of the beliefs about how to achieve are based on myths. The "perfect human" is appealing, and so there are a number of things people can say to themselves in an attempt to support that ideal.

Some of the **myths** that perfectionist have a tendency to believe are:

1. I wouldn't be the success I am today if I weren't a perfectionist. **Reality:** Perfectionists fail to realize that their success has been achieved despite their compulsive striving.

2. Perfectionists get things done, and they do them right. **Reality:** Perfectionist often have problems with procrastination and missed deadlines.

3. Perfectionists are determined to overcome all obstacles to success. **Reality:** Perfectionists are vulnerable to depression, writer's block, and social anxiety.

4. Perfectionists just have a strong desire to please others. **Reality:** Perfectionists are may be driven by low self-esteem, so their needs ultimately blind them to the needs and wishes of others.

Often, the self-inflicted pressure to be perfect is an attempt to improve. Here are several coping strategies that will help replace perfectionistic habits with healthier behavior.

1. Make a list of the advantages and disadvantages of trying to be perfect.

2. Increase your awareness of the self-critical nature of all-or-nothing thoughts, and how they extend to other people in your life.

3. Be realistic about what you can do. Set reasonable goals.

4. Set strict limits on each of your projects. When the time is up, move on to another activity.

5. Learn how to deal with criticism. Don't take it personally, even when it is.

Cognitive Restructuring

Building on the concept of "watch your self-talk" in the last section—as well as similar material presented in the first chapter—a good place to begin in making specific changes and improving self-esteem is to take a closer look at your own thought processes. It is sometimes difficult to begin to think positive thoughts until you have addressed the source of the negative ones. A therapeutic technique for beginning to address negative self-talk is to give a name to the inner critic. What would you call the part of you that is overly critical and/or demanding? Personifying the critic helps begin to externalize the self-accusing voice (McKay and Fanning, 1992).

Before coming up with an answer to the critic, it can be useful to consider if there is any positive function that it serves (more will be discussed about this in the section on the change process in Chapter 8). Sometimes the inner critic just needs to find a new way of accomplishing the positive function. When we are hassling ourselves about what we have or haven't done in life, it is often with the best of intentions. The problem

may be that legitimate concerns get overblown and begin to have the opposite effect in changing our behavior. Learning the critic's function sometimes requires extensive inquiry, but it is a good place to start in beginning to change behavior.

The other important concept to understand about the negative self-talk of the inner critic is that we sometimes get a reward from listening to that voice. If we don't believe that we can accomplish a certain goal, then there is no use even beginning to work toward it. Sometimes we believe things about our abilities—or lack thereof—in order to avoid any possibility of not doing well. If you don't ever try anything new, at least you won't fail . . . or at least it seems that way in the moment.

A number of great psychologists, counselors, and educators, including McKay and Fanning, have addressed the concept of identifying thought distortions. Distortions can be at the root of the difficulty in developing positive self-esteem. Part of any therapy or treatment program includes a component on examining troubling beliefs. The more you are aware of these types of thoughts, the more choices you have for beginning to change the thoughts that tend to contribute to negative feelings.

The following are some common thought processes that can cause problems:

All-or-nothing thinking: You look at things in absolute, black-and-white categories.

Overgeneralization: You view a negative event as a never-ending pattern of defeat.

Filtering: You dwell on the negatives and ignore the positives.

Discounting the positives: You insist that your accomplishments or positive qualities don't count.

Jumping to conclusions: You conclude things are bad without any definite evidence. You do this by (a) mind reading—assuming people are reacting negatively to you, and (b) fortune-telling—predicting that things will turn out badly.

Magnification or minimization: You blow things way out of proportion or you shrink their importance.

Emotional reasoning: You reason from how you feel: "I feel like an idiot, so I must be one."

Global labeling: Instead of saying, "I made a mistake," you tell yourself, "I'm a jerk" or "I'm a loser."

Blame: You blame yourself for something you weren't entirely responsible for, or you blame other people and overlook ways that you contributed to a problem (*Burns, 1999*).

Few of us haven't been guilty of one or more of these thought patterns. A point to consider is the degree to which these thought distortions affect our lives. Lapsing into one or two of these limiting ways of thinking is different from using a significant number to a great degree.

David Burns wrote an excellent book, *Ten Days to Self-Esteem* (1999), that provides specific exercises to begin to change your thought patterns. He strongly supports the notion that "you feel the way you think." One activity that he suggests throughout his book is to keep a daily mood log. You can improve your self-concept by monitoring your reactions to various events throughout the day. If you have an upsetting event, write down the negative thought and then consider the list above. Having done that, what would be an appropriate positive thought to replace the negative one? Practicing that process can lead to a more positive self-concept.

Identifying thought distortions is important because these distortions are often the weapon of choice of the inner critic. Beginning to refute the critic may mean questioning the very logic of the critical voice that is nagging at you. Another way to refute the critic is to develop a **healthy voice** that can counter any negative thinking. What is it that you want or need to think in order to feel better about yourself?

Sometimes the internal critic is so strong that there is little room for the healthy voice. In that case, it is important to employ **thought-stopping** procedures. McKay and Fanning (2000) have a technique they call Howitzer Mantras. They suggest that when you hear negative self-talk you respond with statements such as: "These are lies," "This is poison," "Shut up," "Screw you, asshole," "Stop this garbage," and "Get off my back." Screaming these type of statements internally (you may appear rather odd if you yell these things while standing on the street corner) can be an effective way of interrupting negative self-talk long enough to enable the healthy voice to counter with a more accurate statement. Reinforcing the healthy voice within yourself works hand-in-hand with developing and identifying your strengths.

Self-esteem is more than just recognizing your positive qualities, though; it is an attitude of acceptance and nonjudgment toward yourself and others. So, if you have difficulty identifying your strengths or developing an accurate self-assessment, try viewing yourself as friends or loved ones see you. What would someone who holds you in high regard have to say about your strengths or positive traits? What would be on their list?

It is important to have a list of things you like about yourself because this provides a means of coping with life's trials and tribulations. Most people don't function well when they are under pressure. When life is going along fine, it is easy to have lots of choices and to think good things about ourselves. Choices start to decrease under stress, however, and it becomes harder to remember positive things about our abilities. Therefore we all need to have a large supply of positive things to think about ourselves when life is going well, so as to have a reserve on hand for bad days. If we don't have a large supply of positives on the good days, how are we going to survive on the days when we're "down in the dumps"? We need to increase our number of positive beliefs so that, on down days, we can still have something with which to pull ourselves up.

Locus of Control

In ancient times, people thought they had no control over their environment. The world moved in mysterious ways, and there was little anyone could do to deal with the powerful forces that affected their lives. Many cultures developed superstitions as a means of making sense of life events and as an attempt to exert some control over their world. The carryover of that kind of thinking is evident today in people who think that everything is fate and that they have no control over their lives, but these people carry a rabbit's foot for good luck.

Psychologists have identified two sources of perceived control. One is an *internal locus of control,* where the individual believes he or she has control over life events. The other is an *external locus of control,* where the individual believes that some outside force such as fate, destiny, other people, or random circumstances controls life events. *Externals* believe that their efforts won't make any difference in the course of events, so, naturally, they seldom put forth much effort to change things. Some people go through life as though they just have to roll over and take it anytime something happens. *Internals* believe that their effort makes a difference, so they are more likely to take action and attempt to cope with the situation.

People who perceive an internal locus of control are less likely to blame others or past events for their limitations in life. The good news about believing in the responsibility for the outcome of your life is that even when you have created a bad situation, you still have the ability to do something about it. It also stands to reason that you can create your own joy and happiness.

Research has shown that the presence or absence of perceived control has important consequences in our lives over and above the actual control available to us in a given situation (Martin and Dixon, 1994). This gives credence to the familiar adage, "Whether you believe that you can or you can't, you are probably right." People who have a high degree of perceived control are more likely to seek knowledge and information about the events that affect their lives. This becomes a self-fulfilling prophecy, in that people who feel in control take actions that actually make them more in control of their lives. And, as you might expect, there is a strong positive relationship between perceived control and personal adjustment. People with an internal locus of control use more effective strategies for coping with stress, as well as take steps that will maximize their overall health and well-being.

The first step toward changing your locus of control is to change your self-talk. Externals need to rephrase "can't," "couldn't," and "shouldn't" thinking and begin to think about the possibilities of trying new behaviors. Some of those behaviors might include:

- *Changing aspects of your environment.* Ask yourself what type of people you spend time with and how they affect your belief in yourself. Being with others who support self-reliance could be useful. What is it about your school or work situation that could change to increase your feeling of being in control?
- *Trying new activities rather than the old familiar ways of doing things.* Examine old habits about clothes, food, and manner of transportation. How could you experiment with doing new things in general by trying fun activities that provide a different perspective on life? Taking charge in pleasant activities may make you feel better about yourself and help you to see that you are in control of your life.
- *Assuming more responsibility for tasks at home, work, and school.* Start slowly, but volunteer to do things that you usually don't do. Assume a leadership role and take charge of a situation that you know you can handle.

The most important element in all of these suggestions is taking action and trying to exert control over the areas of your life that are under your control. By starting slowly with small steps, you can begin to build up experiences that will support taking more appropriate risks when you are ready.

> **"** *What we have done for ourselves dies with us. What we have done for others remains and is immortal.* **"**
>
> Ignatius Joseph Firpo

Self-Disclosure

Self-disclosure is the process of intentionally revealing information about yourself that others would not normally know. It is the act of verbally sharing aspects of who you are, including thoughts, feelings, and reactions to people and events in your life. Some of the requirements for self-disclosure are that it is *deliberate, significant, and not already known to the other person.* It hardly qualifies as self-disclosure if you accidentally let something slip, share a trivial fact such as your preference for vanilla ice cream, or share an obvious fact that has been known to the other person for years. In this section, we explore the relationship between self-awareness and self-disclosure.

It is difficult to reveal information about your thoughts and feelings if you aren't aware of them yourself. Through self-disclosure, you can begin to clarify and confirm some of your thoughts and feelings. Sharing yourself can also help to build relationships. Sharing on a more personal level breaks the ice and gives the other person permission and reason to reciprocate. After all, real friends are the people who know your thoughts and feelings. Self-disclosure increases communication and the ability to discuss matters on a deeper level, as well as providing an opportunity to relieve stress by getting something off your chest.

Social Penetration

When learning about self-disclosure, it is important to understand the concept of social penetration. Social psychologists Irwin Altman and Dalmas Taylor (1973) describe two types of communication that can occur to differing degrees. The first concerns the **breadth** of disclosure. You may have relationships at work in which you discuss only things directly pertaining to the job. Or you may have friends with whom you share many interests but with whom you do not talk about any one thing to any significant degree. The next dimension of disclosure is the **depth** of the information being shared. With some people you may discuss very personal aspects of your life.

THE MONKEY TRAP

One way to catch a monkey is to use the rigidity of its own thinking patterns. All you have to do is put some kind of attractive food in a container or box with a hole just big enough for the monkey to squeeze its hand through the opening. After the monkey grabs onto the food and makes a fist, it is unable to withdraw its hand. Refusing to let go of the food and unaware that it is a prisoner by its own design, the monkey is easily trapped while struggling with the container that has been anchored down.

This parable has numerous applications to human behavior. People with rigid beliefs are unable to explore the possibility of new solutions. And, how often have you witnessed people trapped by their own beliefs when all they would have to do to get out of the situation is let go? There are a number of variations to this story, but they all seem to have the same message.

Depending on the breadth and depth of information being shared, a relationship can be defined as casual or intimate. In a casual relationship, the breadth may be great but not the depth. In a more intimate relationship, there is likely to be great depth of sharing in at least one area. The closest relationships usually involve both types of sharing to a great degree.

Developing close relationships requires sharing personal information, but doesn't mean you should tell perfect strangers your entire life history. You may have had the experience of sitting on a plane next to someone who insisted on telling you all the details of his or her life, whether you wanted to hear about it or not. There are certain times for sharing and certain people with whom you might want to share. It is difficult and not always useful to share yourself in large groups, but it is important to be able to share personal things in the appropriate context.

One way to determine the depth of disclosure is to look at the types of information we share. Self-disclosure usually proceeds through the following stages and can be indicative of increased friendship or closeness:

Stage 1: Clichés. These are the ritualized responses to social situations, such as "How are you doing?" or "Let's get together sometime." Clichés serve as a valuable shorthand to make things easier and to indicate the potential for future conversation.

Stage 2: Facts. These statements convey information about what you do, where you live, or what your interests are. They may also provide information about what is happening in your life. Disclosing important information in conversation suggests a level of trust in the other person that could signal a desire to move the relationship to a new level.

Stage 3: Opinions. This is a more revealing level of communication. Statements such as "I support abortion rights" or "I think John is doing a great job" are letting you know where that person stands. Such information lets you know how the relationship might develop. When people offer personal opinions, they are giving valuable information.

Stage 4: Feelings. The most revealing level of self-disclosure is the realm of feelings. There is a difference between opinions and feelings, which is evident in the following statements: "I don't think John is doing a good job, and I'm angry" is more revealing than "I don't think John is doing a good job."

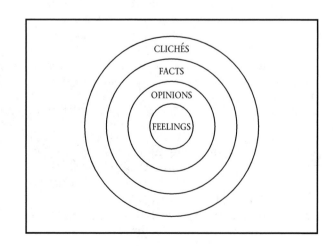

How often do you use each of the different stages? Who would you like to share opinions and feelings with more often?

_____

_____

_____

_____

_____

_____

_____

_____

_____

_____

The Johari Window

One way to increase awareness and sharing is to explore the Johari Window model. The name was derived from the first names of the two people who developed it, Joseph Luft and Harry Ingham (1969). For a relationship to develop into a quality relationship, there needs to be a mutual sharing of information and feelings. One definition of an open communicator is a person who is willing to accept feedback as well as to offer personal information and feelings. Let's explore the four different categories of self according to the Johari Window model:

The Open Self: This represents all the information that you and other people know about you. We all have ways of being that are obvious to us and those who know us. For some people, a large part of who they are is represented by this category, whereas for others this is not the case. Sometimes, not being open is by conscious choice; at other times, it is due to a lack of awareness. The relationship between this aspect of self and the other three that follow is that the more open you are, the more you will be available to connect and communicate with others.

The Blind Self: This is the part of you that others can see but you can't (sometimes called your "blind spots"). Do you have a friend who exhibits a particular behavior, yet swears that she doesn't? A clue to the fact that you have blind spots is how often you find yourself being defensive or not understanding feedback. There is an old saying that if one person calls you a jackass, forget it, but if 10 people call you that, get a saddle. People who have the largest part of themselves represented by this category are sometimes referred to as the "bull-in-the-china-shop type." This doesn't mean they are clumsy; but they seem to be unaware of the impact they have on their surroundings. If a considerable amount of yourself is represented by this category, you may be good at giving feedback, but not very good at receiving it.

The Hidden Self: All of us keep secrets about ourselves from other people. Most of us have done something of which we aren't proud; when we take the risk of sharing, often we find out we aren't alone. Keeping things hidden contributes to loneliness and the often erroneous belief that you are the only person to have ever done this thing. One of the benefits of sharing with others is finding out that maybe we're not so bad after all. Sometimes, the process of keeping a secret causes more distress than the original problem. People who hold back a lot of themselves while wanting or waiting for others to share are the interviewer types. They love to ask questions but prefer not to answer them.

The Unknown Self: How can you know what you don't know? Well, have you ever done something you later regretted? Was there a small part of you that had some idea of what the negative consequences would be? This is the part of you outside your conscious awareness that you don't know about, and, consequently, others don't know about either. We all have aspects of ourselves that nobody knows about, but that doesn't mean they don't affect our behavior. In some instances, what has been relegated to the unknown can be a major factor in what motivates or influences what we do in life. That is why it is important to observe your behavior when you do things without understanding why. People who have the largest part of themselves represented by this category and want to leave it that way are referred to as turtles.

After reading the descriptions of the different areas of the Johari Window, how would you rate yourself in each category? Although you are probably different at times, depending on the situation and the people present, what percentage of who you are, in general, would you put in each category? Write a number (a percentage) in each part of the Johari Window circle (total = 100 percent).

When you have completed that part of the self-rating, consider the assessment of yourself according to the chart below. This is an opportunity

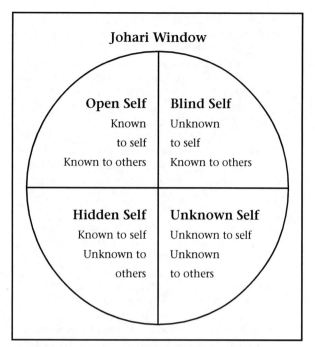

Johari Window

Open Self	Blind Self
Known to self	Unknown to self
Known to others	Known to others

Hidden Self	Unknown Self
Known to self	Unknown to self
Unknown to others	Unknown to others

Source: Adapted from Joseph Luft, *Of Human Interaction.* Palo Alto, CA: Mayfield Publishing Co., 1969.

to learn how you are in different contexts. In a more detailed exploration, how would you rate yourself in each of the contexts listed in the chart? For each context, enter a percentage in the appropriate Johari Window category. Do you notice a pattern?

You can increase your capacity for openness and improve communication with the following:

- ▶ *For the Blind Self:* Be willing to accept feedback. Open your eyes and ears and be more aware of your surroundings and your impact on others.
- ▶ *For the Hidden Self:* Be ready to share more about yourself. You may be pleasantly surprised by the closeness sharing confidences can create.
- ▶ *For the Unknown Self:* Explore your motivations and beliefs. Nobody does anything for nothing! There is always a reason, whether you recognize it or not. Use every opportunity to be more introspective.

Learning how and when to volunteer personal information is a skill that takes some practice. Considering the importance it has in your ability to be a better communicator, it is well worth it. Here are some guidelines that will help make the effort of self-disclosure rewarding for you and others. Ask yourself these questions:

- ▶ Is the other person important to you?
- ▶ Is the risk of disclosure reasonable?
- ▶ Are the amount and type of disclosure appropriate?

Questions for Critical Thinking

When you filled in the Johari Window circle, what process went into your decision? What would your Johari Window look like if you were how you would like to be? What would it take for that to happen? Are there any contexts in which you would like to be more open?

_____

_____

_____

_____

_____

_____

_____

_____

_____

- ▶ Is the disclosure relevant to the situation?
- ▶ Will the disclosure be reciprocated?
- ▶ Will the disclosure be constructive?
- ▶ Is the disclosure clear and understandable?

The Shadow Self

We all have parts of ourselves that we would prefer not to own. (Consider the classic example of *Dr. Jekyll and Mr. Hyde.*) Parts of our personality that we would like to avoid acknowledging get relegated to the shadow self; that which we try to deny gets pushed down into the dark recesses of our being, and we choose a more pleasant persona for everyday wear. Negative emotions and behaviors—rage, jealousy, shame, resentment, lust, greed, dishonesty, and suicidal and/or murderous tendencies—reside just beneath the surface, masked by our more proper selves. For many of us, this remains untamed and unexplored territory.

Although there are many theories about human motivation, it may be useful to consider the shadow self as a means of more fully understanding the power and influence of the unknown self in the Johari Window. People often do things without thinking, and later regret them and wonder what motivated their behavior in the first place. The concept of the shadow self is generally credited to C. G. Jung, who believed that our behavior is sometimes motivated by needs that are outside of our awareness. He also believed in the *collective unconscious,* which is the common reservoir of images derived from our early ancestors' universal experiences. Jung said that the collective unconscious explains why, for many people, spiritual concerns are deeply rooted and why people from different cultures share certain myths and images.

The real problem is not that the shadow self exists, but that it is ignored. That which you try to exclude from awareness does not cease to exist. In fact, it is more likely to affect your behavior— hence, the importance of becoming acquainted with and owning your shadow self.

For many children, the early years of life include frightening and painful experiences. Some children have parents who don't respond to their needs to be held and caressed. Others have parents who subject them to physical violence. Even children who have warm and loving parents sometimes have frightening experiences that are beyond anyone's control. Children do not have conceptual knowledge of their own needs, nor do they have the ability to comprehend their parents' or others' behavior. But they do understand pain and fear, which can become overwhelming. To protect themselves, they learn to deny their feelings. The fear and pain that are not permitted to be experienced become locked behind walls of physical and emotional tension. This establishes a pattern of reactions that tends to recur when individuals are threatened by feelings they don't want to experience. It is not only the negative feelings that are blocked; the ability to experience pleasure or to be excited and spontaneous can also be diminished. It must be recognized, of course, that emotional repression is a matter of degree; in some individuals it is far more profound and pervasive than in others. What remains true for everyone, though, is that to diminish one's capacity to experience pain is to diminish one's capacity to experience pleasure as well.

In *Meeting the Shadow* (1990), Zweig and Abrams suggest a number of ways we meet the shadow part of ourselves every day. These illustrate the importance of exploring our hidden selves for greater self-knowledge, which enables

> **"** *By becoming more aware, perhaps . . . perhaps we can also, in that way, refrain from adding our personal darkness to the shadow.* **"**
>
> *Zweig and Abrams*

us to learn new ways of being. Some of the ways we can meet the shadow self are as follows:

- In our exaggerated feelings about others.
- In negative feedback from others who can serve as our mirrors.
- In interactions in which we continually have the same troubling effect on several different people.
- In our impulsive and inadvertent acts.
- In our exaggerated anger over other people's faults.

It is important to know all the parts of who you are, because not knowing about your shadow doesn't prevent it from influencing your behavior. The aim of meeting the shadow is to develop an ongoing relationship with it, to expand your sense of self by balancing your conscious attitudes with your unconscious depths. An open relationship with the shadow offers us a great gift: a path back to our buried potentials.

Through *shadow work*—the continuing effort to develop a creative relationship with the shadow—we can do the following:

- Achieve a more genuine self-acceptance, based on a complete knowledge of who we are.
- Defuse the negative emotions that erupt unexpectedly in our daily lives.
- Feel more free of the guilt and shame associated with our negative feelings and actions.
- Recognize the projections that color our opinion of others.
- Heal our relationships through more honest self-examination and direct communication.
- Use creative imagination via dreams, drawing, writing, and rituals to own the disowned self.

> **"** *When you judge others, you are revealing your own fears.* **"**
>
> *C. G. Jung*

CASE STUDIES AND STUDENT STORIES

Sally always had a smile on her face, and to anyone that knew her well she seemed to be happiness personified. The sad fact, though, was that under the surface there was a frightened child wanting to hide in a closet at any sign of disapproval. Her fear was not without provocation, but holding onto her façade each day and trying to participate in her family and job activities was becoming impossible. The standards that her family and friends had for her were unrealistic, and she realized that if something didn't change soon, she would self-destruct.

In the fall of the year, that day came. While driving to school, she contemplated veering her car across traffic in front of a log truck. The pain of living life while keeping a part of herself hidden in the shadow had become unbearable. She felt as if she couldn't take one more day of pretending and not being herself.

Words like *hopeless* and *failure* clouded her mind as she made her way to work. As she pulled her car off the highway, she realized that she needed help. She also realized that her pretend life had to end, and she had to let someone see her real self. She recalled an old friend that she hadn't seen for some time. She turned the car around and found her way to the friend's house. When her friend answered the door she collapsed. With tears streaming down her face, she recounted how the fairy-tale world that she had set up for herself was all a pretense. She admitted her real feelings and about how hard it was to keep up a phony image. She then began to talk about her fears and needs. The veil that she finally lifted allowed her to seek help, and to begin work on the demons that tormented her mind.

Today, five years later, Sally is a different person. She no longer tries to juggle five things at once, allows time for herself, and sets realistic goals for each day. She lets those close to her see all the parts of her personality. Revealing her shadow self has given her freedom and a sense of reality that she has never felt.

In her final session she said, "You can run, but you can't hide from yourself. It is always right behind you. I am so thankful that I stopped long enough to let my real self catch up with me. My life is full and happy in my newfound world of reality. I can be who I am more fully, and I accept all the parts of me, even the ugly ones I used to hide."

Source: By D. Juanita Woods.

DON'T BE FOOLED BY ME

Don't be fooled by me.
Don't be fooled by the face I wear.
For I wear a thousand masks, masks that I'm
afraid to take off, and none of them are me.
Pretending is an art that's second nature with
me, but don't be fooled,
for God's sake, don't be fooled.
I give the impression that I'm secure, that all is
sunny and unruffled with me,
within as well as without, that confidence is
my name and coolness my game;
that the water's calm and I'm in command, and
that I need no one.
Please don't believe me.
Please.
My surface may seem smooth, but my surface is
my mask.
Beneath this lies no complacence.
Beneath dwells the real me in confusion, in
fear, and aloneness.
But I hide this. I don't want anybody to know it.

I panic at the thought of my weakness and fear of being exposed.

That's why I frantically create a mask to hide behind, a nonchalant, sophisticated façade, to help me pretend, to shield me from the glance that knows.

But such a glance is precisely my salvation. My only salvation.

And I know it. That is if it's followed by acceptance, if it's followed by love. It's the only thing that will assure me of what I can't assure myself, that I am worth something.

But I don't tell you this, I don't dare. I'm afraid to.

I'm afraid you'll think less of me, that you'll laugh at me, and your laugh would kill me. I'm afraid that deep-down I'm nothing, that I'm no good, and that you will see this and reject me.

So I play my game, my desperate game, with a façade of assurance without, and a trembling child within.

And so begins the parade of masks. And my life becomes a front.

I idly chatter to you in the suave tones of surface talk. I tell you everything that is really nothing, and nothing of what's everything, of what's crying within me; so when I'm going through my routine do not be fooled by what I'm saying. Please listen carefully and try to hear what I'm not saying, what I'd like to be able to say, what for survival I need to say, but what I can't say. I dislike hiding. Honestly!

I dislike the superficial game I'm playing, the phony game.

I'd really like to be genuine and spontaneous, and me, but you've got to help me.

You've got to hold out your hand, even when that's the last thing I seem to want.

Only you can wipe away from my eyes the blank stare of breathing death.

Only you can call me into aliveness. Each time you're kind and gentle, and encouraging, each time you try to understand because you really care, my heart begins to grow wings, very small wings, very feeble wings, but wings.

With your sensitivity and sympathy, and your power of understanding, you can breathe life into me. I want you to know that. I want you to know how important you are to me, how you can be the creator of the person that is me if you choose to.

Please choose to. You alone can break down the wall behind which I tremble, you alone can remove my mask. You alone can release me from my shadow-world of panic and uncertainty, from my lonely person.

Do not pass me by. Please—do not pass me by.

It will not be easy for you. A long conviction of worthlessness builds strong walls.

The nearer you approach me, the blinder I strike back.

I fight against the very thing I cry out for.

But I am told that love is stronger than walls, and in this lies my hope.

Please try to tear down those walls with firm hands, but with gentle hands, for a child is very sensitive.

Who am I, you may wonder. I am someone you know very well.

For I am every man you meet, and I am every woman you meet.

Source: Article written by Jann Mitchell.

Masks

If being more open yields so many benefits, then why do so many people wear a mask? This façade is a form of protection against what others might think of us. Sometimes we put on masks to avoid unpleasant experiences. That can be paradoxical because acting a certain way to protect yourself from other people's disapproval may cause you to disapprove of yourself. If you are not being your true self (or true to your real self), you may later regret not being how you wanted to be or not having said what you really wanted to say.

People also put on masks to gain approval. The problem with that is: If others like the mask, what do you do next? People who wear a mask for a long time—pretending to be the way they believe someone else wants them to be—often become confused as to who they really are.

If you put on a mask so someone will like you, how will the *real* you feel, knowing that what the other person likes is the mask? Wouldn't this make you feel a little sad or lonely? At least, when you take the risk of being genuine, you can give yourself approval for having done that. You can respect yourself regardless of whether another person likes you or not.

Being totally honest or adapting to a situation is a continuum. Keep in mind that this is not a matter of black and white, but rather many shades of gray. We all wear masks of one kind or another at times. What matters is how much and how often you feel you have to put up a façade and whether you have some choice and control over when you want to be seen a certain way. There are times when masks can help you get along in a social setting. You are probably a little different at work (at least when you're in the boss's office) from the way you are with friends and family.

Some people never wear a mask and insist on being exactly how they feel like being, wherever they are. In the extreme, the ones who pay no attention at all to what the rest of the world thinks about them are also the ones who frequently get locked up.

There is a distinction between wearing masks and having different roles in life. For example, I have a teacher role, a musician role, a counselor role, a parent role, and a number of other roles that I play at different times. The person I am when I'm playing with my band is different from the person I am when I'm teaching a class. Even if you play many different parts in life, you can still be genuine in each of them. In later chapters, we will discuss how that relates to personality.

Getting Attention

There are a number of theories about human motivation, and Maslow's hierarchy of needs will be discussed in another chapter. For our purpose here, considering human relations and life skills, we also need to consider everyday social interactions. If there were one phrase to describe what motivates most of human behavior, in that sense, it would probably be "getting attention." There are only a few basic drives in life, and this one seems to explain 90 percent of why we act as we do. Whether it is by getting approval or disapproval, we all want to be noticed and attended to on occasion.

Everyone needs and wants a certain type or amount of attention, even those who deny it. Newborn babies literally couldn't survive without enough attention. As we get older, though, various cultural influences seem to teach us that we are not supposed to need or want attention. We still do, but we learn to become more devious about getting it. It becomes more difficult for some of us to ask for what we need as we grow up. This was not the case with most of us when we were children. Ask any parent if you don't believe how creative children can be in getting attention. Most children have few inhibitions about asking for or receiving attention. Have you ever watched a mother trying to talk to another adult when her child wants something? I've seen children reach out and turn their parent's face to ensure getting complete, focused attention. That's how important and powerful the need for attention is.

How many parents have had to play the "watch me" game? When my son Riley was three years old, he reminded me constantly of the importance of getting attention by playing that game. "Watch me, Dad," he would say, as he prepared to demonstrate the amazing feat of jumping off the couch for the hundredth time. "Watch . . . no, you're not looking . . . watch, here I go . . . keep watching!" Then, after he completed the amazing feat, he asked, "Wasn't that great, Dad?" Most of us, we hope, grew up in families where it was acceptable to need, want, and ask for attention. Having wants and needs attended to should be part of every child's birthright.

In the process of growing up, something happens to our desire to be the center of attention. For most of us, the change occurred when we started school. What we had been used to getting or expecting had a whole new meaning in the classroom. At home, we could get plenty of individualized attention. When we finished drawing

SOME PEOPLE WEAR MASKS ALL YEAR 'ROUND—DO YOU?

Remember how as kids we discussed for weeks "What are you going to be for Halloween?" We debated between pirates and fairy princesses, monsters and mummies. We finally settled on one, carefully assembled a costume, and spent our allowance on a mask. Then we trekked far beyond our own neighborhoods in search of loot. We lugged it home and removed our masks, feasting on the goodies for weeks.

In childhood, we took our masks off. As adults, we frequently leave them on, long after the rotting Halloween pumpkins have been kicked off the porch. We continue wearing our masks to feel safe, a face we show to the world to avoid feeling vulnerable.

Wearing our masks has some rewards: a sense of identity, recognition of others, a set way of viewing the world without having to think things through. But these masks also are liabilities: they show only part of who we are. They keep us stuck. And worst of all, they prevent us from truly connecting with other people. Here are some popular adult masks:

The Joker: We make a joke out of anything and everything. Our spouse is often drawn to us because we're so fun and carefree, but the gags get old fast when we use humor to mask the need to deal with reality. If we're cracking jokes while our mate is crying and begging us to be serious for once in our lives, we've got a problem.

The Sexpot or Super Stud: Our dress is sexually flamboyant and our talk is too. We define our worth based on how attractive we are; if heads aren't turning, we don't feel alive. Often, we were sexually abused as children and are sexually aggressive in adulthood to avoid feeling like victims ("I'll get you before you get me"). We settle for the shallow attention and sex, but long for love and acceptance.

Lookin' Good: The rent's past due, our teenager's on drugs, and we feel like walking death, but ask how we are and our answer is always "Fine." We have the mistaken notion that we're not okay unless we're problem-free. We feel we have to handle it all ourselves, without asking for help. The harder we fight to maintain the impression of perfection, the more tired and lonely we get.

Ms. or Mr. Efficiency: We zip around the office, getting our tasks done ahead of deadline and volunteering for more. At home, we buzz around doing more than our share. As long as we are busy and productive like humming machines, we feel we are worthwhile people. We also don't have time to feel what's bothering us, or to share intimacy with others.

Poor Little Me: The boss hates us, our mates don't treat us right, and even the dog picks our shoes to chew on. We'll list our litany of complaints to anyone who will listen. As long as we can play the perpetual victim, we'll never have to take responsibility for the fix we're in.

The Know-It-All: For us, being right is about being all right. If we don't know the answer or have the last word, we feel stupid and worthless. We're constantly raining fun facts down on folks, and we hand out unsolicited advice like leafleting zealots. We'd do well to remember that we can be right—or we can be liked.

Mr. or Ms. Superior: Our house, vacation, children, job, and even our gas mileage are always better than yours. We're the masters of one-upmanship and don't know how to live without drawing comparisons in which we come out on top. That makes us snobs at best and bigots at our worst. Our need to look superior is a mask for our inferiority.

Do you spot your costume here? After Halloween, let's throw out these outmoded masks. Being a whole, human, vulnerable, and imperfect person is so much easier. And it's in season, all year long.

Source: Article written by Jann Mitchell.

> 66 *The range of what we think and do is limited by what we fail to notice. And because we fail to notice what we fail to notice, there is little we can do to change until we notice how failing to notice shapes our thoughts and deeds.* 99
>
> R. D. Laing

a picture, we ran up to a parent and said, "Look what I did—isn't it great?" But when we tried that at school, where there were 25 other kids, what happened? It was a whole new ball game.

This could be why the word *attention* began to acquire a negative connotation. When asked what they did to get attention as kids, most people assume that the question refers to negative behavior, such as breaking things, throwing fits, pouting, or doing something mean. They have forgotten the times when attention could mean something positive. They may not remember getting attention for being kind or cooperative or for asking to be held.

This could also be the origin of the *double bind* about getting attention as adults: We still need and want attention but think we have to disavow this fact. Have you ever witnessed an adult receiving some well-deserved honor, maybe even one she had been hoping to get? As soon as the spotlight was on her, she acted as if it was the last thing in the world she wanted, and tried to duck out, all the while smiling and really enjoying the attention. As adults, we don't necessarily need less attention, we just develop more creative methods of getting it, sometimes trying to disguise the fact that we are actually seeking attention.

The confusion about how to get what you want and whether it is all right to want it is very evident in families. I've had days when I've put out a great deal of energy teaching and counseling and then gone home expecting to be greeted warmly by my family. I may get a certain amount of attention from standing in front of a class all day, but the focus is usually on the students' needs. I still want someone to listen to my problems.

One day I walked through the door and Riley said, "Go away! I don't want Betty (the baby-sitter) to leave." He jumped off the couch, started for the back room, and ran right into the counter. Now he wanted me. As he was screaming in my ear, my

daughter Maegann came out of her room needing to talk. She was upset and needed attention because of the way some other kids at school had been treating her. Riley needed attention, Maegann needed attention, and I needed attention. Then I remembered that it was piano lesson day, and off we went. An hour later, we were back at home and I was fixing dinner, with my daughter protesting that I was going to poison the family. Then the phone rang. So there I was on the phone with someone who needed my attention about something important, Riley was hanging on my leg, and Maegann wanted me to sit on the couch with her so she would feel better. And then my wife came home and said, "I've sure had a hard day—I'm tired and I need some attention." (I know we have all had days like that. My wife calls it "the rich texture of family life.")

We all learned different things in our families about getting attention. It is interesting that most of us knew which button to push if we wanted to upset our parents. The problem was that some of us never learned which button gets the positive response. We all want to get something, which explains why some people do things that get a negative reaction from others. Positive and negative attention are not two ends of a continuum. They are actually two sides of a coin, and that coin is on one end of the continuum. The other end is getting nothing. Nobody wants to be totally ignored. Ask anyone who has worked at a child protection agency (agency names vary from state to state) about the effects of neglect and abandonment.

For some people, negative attention seems better than no attention. I'll bet you've seen a kid who was being ignored do something that resulted in punishment just to get attention. Well, imagine that person grown up, 20 years later. What do you think that person would be like if he or she never learned any alternative behavior? Have you ever been at a party where someone came into the room and within five minutes, everyone there knew who he was and didn't like him? That person could be referred to as a *power victim.* The power victim's motto seems to be, "You may not like me, but you'll never forget me." Some people are experts at getting negative reactions from others. (Some adolescents are considered to be masters in that area.)

It all comes back to what was available as you were growing up. If you never got acceptance, caring, or positive regard, how are you going to go out in the world and get what you never received?

We may not like power victims, but we'll know who they are and we won't forget them. They usually make sure of that by the kind of attention they demand. It is sometimes easier to help that kind of person make changes, though, than the person who has just given up and really doesn't want any attention. Usually, nobody wants to get no attention unless something traumatic has happened. In that case, it seems as though withdrawing is the only way to be safe from the attention they did get, which was probably extremely negative.

There are implications in this for relationships in adult life, some of which will be discussed in later chapters, especially in the area of marriage and couples relations. If you didn't feel loved by your parents as a child, you may not have an easy time forming a lasting intimate relationship. If you didn't get enough positive attention from your family, how are you going to accept it from a stranger? How do you accept that someone wants to be with you if the people you counted on when you were a child deserted you?

Consider what you learned from your family. Did positive attention exist in your family? Did you live in a family where Mom and Dad didn't say a kind word to each other for 30 years, not to mention what was or wasn't said to the kids? Did you know that positive attention existed, but felt that only your siblings could get it? (I've heard hundreds of stories such as, "My sister was the talented one" and "My brother was the smart one.") Maybe you learned how to get attention, but you didn't feel you really deserved it. This is how attention and self-concept are related.

Have you ever known someone who was uncomfortable getting attention or questioned when things were going well? For some people, getting too much positive attention can seem unusual if they have low self-esteem and don't think they deserve it. Our media frequently provide examples of this kind of situation. How many times have you read about some attractive, talented, rich, and famous person who seemed to have it all—and then committed suicide? There are many complex reasons for a person to take his or her life. Often, though, the stories about famous people who do commit suicide involve tales of early childhood deprivation or emotional neglect. Some people who appear to be successful by society's standards may still feel insecure. Obviously, having it all doesn't compensate for not feeling deserving.

Physical Contact

Although particular types of touching mean different things to different people, touch is one of the primary types of nonverbal communication. A great deal has been written about the importance of body language in nonverbal communication; tactile communication is one of the most powerful forms of nonverbal communication and important to understand.

Touch is one of the first means of consolation in our lives. Many times, the desperate cries of babies can't be quieted without the reassuring touch of another human being. Likewise, sometimes the pain and sadness of a traumatic life event can be soothed only by the healing touch of a friend or family member. Although everyone reacts differently to touch, depending on the person touching and the relationship involved, touch is basic to human existence.

Richard Hesler (1983) developed a classification system of the types of touch that correspond to the relationship of the interactants:

▶ *Functional-Professional:* This category refers to touching that is intentionally impersonal and is used to perform a specific activity unrelated to any interpersonal relationship between two people. Those who are touched generally know that the purpose of the touch is simply to perform a job, as with a doctor.

▶ *Social-Polite:* When we touch others to greet, congratulate, or otherwise recognize them in some way, we are engaging in social-polite touching. These behaviors are simply ways of carrying out social functions.

▶ *Friendship-Warmth:* This is physical touch that shows liking and nonintimate affection for another person. Back-patting and putting an arm around someone are examples.

▶ *Love-Intimacy:* Examples of this type of behavior include hugging, kissing, and caressing. These behaviors are used to communicate intimate affection and emotional attraction.

▶ *Sexual Arousal:* Touching behavior that involves sexual arousal may or may not occur within close, intimate relationships.

These categories are indicative of the wide range of touching behaviors and their implications. It is unfortunate that our culture tends to view physical contact that is meant as friendship as being in the love-intimacy or sexual arousal category. As a result, a number of people go through life feeling uncomfortable even with touching experiences in the functional-professional and social-polite categories. Very few of us are in

> **"** *There is no experience better for the heart than reaching down and lifting someone up.* **"**
>
> H. Jackson Browne

danger of being hugged too much; we might do well to remember that some physical contact (when it is appropriate) is just an expression of warmth.

The importance of becoming more comfortable with touch as a form of nonverbal communication is evident in the work of Jones and Yarbrough (1985). They indicate, in the extensive behavior categories they list, how frequently we use touch as a part of communication. Some of those behavior categories are as follows:

1. Support that serves to reassure ("You'll be all right").
2. Appreciation and expressions of gratitude.
3. Inclusion that draws attention to the act of being together.
4. Playful affection or playful aggression that serves to lighten the interaction ("Why are you being so serious?").
5. Compliance.
6. Attention-getting ("Look at that").
7. Greeting and departure rituals at the beginning and ending of an encounter.

All of these behaviors occur in interactions every day and all are forms of contact that are part of the communication process. Touch and physical contact are valuable options in learning to communicate more effectively.

Studies in the field of psychology (Spitz, 1945) have long supported the importance of touch in the raising of infants. Dating from World War II, research on infants in nursing homes has frequently demonstrated that physical contact is essential for survival. Children who were orphaned by the war and were in large institutions in England had a high mortality rate. Even though there were at least adequate food and blankets, there was often only one nurse for 30 or more babies. As a result, they received little physical contact and many failed to thrive.

In her book *A Natural History of the Senses* (1991), Diane Ackerman reaffirms the importance of touch with her accounts of the extensive work that is currently being done with premature infants in hospitals. She gives a number of examples of how preemies who are massaged regularly are much healthier than those who are not. Massaged babies gain weight much faster; they are also more active, alert, and responsive, and they tolerate noise better. As a result, many in the medical profession have taken to using volunteers to hold and caress infants. Earlier, the policy for premature babies was to not disturb them any more than necessary, and they lived in a kind of isolation booth. But now the evidence about touch is so plentiful that more hospitals are encouraging touching on a large scale. Ackerman concludes that without hugs and caresses, people of all ages can sicken and grow touch-starved. Perhaps there is more to the bumper sticker "Have you hugged your child today?" than we thought. As more children grow up nurtured and cared for, maybe there will be more adults who will be comfortable with expressions of warmth and caring.

Counselors often emphasize the importance of touch because of the people they see in counseling who tell them how much human contact is missing for them. Although it may not be the presenting problem (the problem described at first may not be what the client really needs or wants to talk about), counselors frequently hear about situations in which someone is distressed about the lack of contact with a significant person in his or her life. There are parents who talk about the loss when their children grow up and think they are "too big" to hug anymore. Couples frequently complain about the lack of physical expressions of caring between them. Once, a young man who was dealing with anger at his father told me that the only time his father ever touched him was when they shook hands on the day he left home. Obviously, we are not a society that is in danger of being too physically affectionate, even when it is appropriate. (Keep in mind that harassment and abuse are different matters entirely.)

How many times have you witnessed a scene at an airport or train station where relatives are saying good-bye, and they wait until the last moment and then give a hurried embrace? You can almost feel the confusion from 30 feet away. Part of them wants to hug and part is inhibited by years of restraint.

Consider that the other person may just be waiting for you to initiate contact. When it's appropriate, think about taking a risk. You may be pleasantly surprised.

Culture and Contact

There are vast differences among cultures when it comes to touch. The Japanese are known to have a strong taboo against touching strangers. Although the inhibition to touch when communicating is not as great in the United States, it is still far more so than in some countries. Latinos tend to touch far more when communicating than do European Americans (Halonen and Santrock, 1997). What have you observed about physical contact between people from other cultures or countries?

CHAPTER REVIEW

Self-Concept

Your self-concept is the set of perceptions about yourself, which includes thoughts about how you interact in social situations, your mental and physical abilities, and your ability to cope with feelings. Your self-concept originates from social information, social comparison, and self-observation. Learning methods for increasing self-esteem will improve your relationships with others.

Improving Self-Esteem

An important part of raising your self-esteem is monitoring your self-talk. Sometimes the inner critic needs to be challenged directly. It is useful to examine any thought distortions that you have that result in coming to erroneous conclusions about your worth or abilities. Cognitive restructuring is a useful method for changing beliefs that have prevented you from having higher self-regard.

Locus of Control

Part of self-concept is influenced by the degree of control that you experience in the world. Some people feel that the majority of factors that affect their lives have to do with external variables. Other people believe that they have a good deal of influence on the events that occur in life and rely more on internal variables.

Self-Disclosure

There are various levels of sharing about your personal beliefs and opinions. The Johari Window is one method for exploring the different aspects of yourself. You can bring more awareness into the open area of your window by examining the hidden, blind, and unknown parts.

The Shadow Self

It is important to explore all the aspects of who you are, even the parts of yourself that you wish didn't exist. What you don't know about yourself still influences your behavior. Negative traits that are relegated to the shadow may actually cause you more difficulty in the long run. Examining hidden or unconscious areas of your being enables you to make changes and increase your potential in other areas.

Masks

We all wear masks at times. Being aware of when you do and whether it is a matter of choice is important. People are sometimes less than genuine out of a need for approval. Being someone you aren't, whether it is to gain approval or avoid disapproval, seldom works in the long run. Your own approval is what is important.

Getting Attention

From the time we are born, we all need attention. We sometimes get conflicting messages from society about how to meet those needs as we grow up. What we learned in our families about how to get positive attention, and whether we deserved it, has consequences for relationships later in life.

Physical Contact

We are all "social animals," and physical contact is not only an important need, but also a method of communicating. A wide range of behaviors is associated with touching, and some people are more comfortable with contact than others. From a handshake to a pat on the back to an arm around someone's shoulder, touch is a valuable choice to have in communicating with others.

SOURCES AND SUGGESTED READINGS

Brandon, Nathaniel. *How to Raise Your Self-Esteem.* New York: Bantam Books, 1987.

Brandon, Nathaniel. *The Six Pillars of Self-Esteem.* New York: Bantam Books, 1994.

Dyer, Wayne. *Your Erroneous Zones.* New York: Avon Books, 1977.

Helsin, R., and T. Alper. "Touch: A Bonding Gesture." *Nonverbal Interaction.* Eds. J. M. Wiemann and R. P. Harrison. Beverly Hills, CA: Sage, 1991.

Jourard, S. M. *The Transparent Self,* 2nd edition. Princeton, NJ: Van Nostrand, 1971.

Luft, Joseph. *Of Human Interaction.* Palo Alto, CA: Mayfield, 1969.

Montague, Ashley. *Touching.* New York: Harper & Row, 1971.

Rogers, Carl. *On Becoming a Person.* Boston: Houghton Mifflin, 1961.

Satir, Virginia. *The New People Making.* Mountain View, CA: Science and Behavior Books, 1988.

Web Site Resources

Mental Help Net
   http://www.mentalhealth.net

American Psychological Association (APA)
   http://www.apa.org

A Psychological View of Motivation
   http://mentalhelp.net/psyhelp/chap4/chap4i.htm

Anxiety Disorders Association of America, Phone: (240) 485-1001

   http://www.adaa.org

REACTION AND RESPONSE—WHAT DO YOU THINK?

Chapter Two   Level I Assignments

In response to the information in the chapter:

1. What did you learn about your self-concept? How can you raise your self-esteem?

2. What did you learn from the Johari Window about what you need to do to be more open (when that is an appropriate choice)? What clues have you had as to how the unknown or unconscious parts of yourself have been affecting your life?

3. What was your reaction to the section on physical contact? How comfortable are you with giving people hugs? How often do people in your family have physical contact?

In response to the class activities, group discussions, and exercises:

1. What are your opinions and reactions?

2. What did you learn or rediscover?

3. How are you going to apply what you learned?

Chapter Two   Level II Assignments

1. What parts of you do you keep in the shadow? What would happen if you confronted those parts that you try to keep hidden? What effect does it have on you to try and avoid the parts of yourself that you would rather not acknowledge?

2. What was your reaction to the information and articles on masks? Where and when do you sometimes try to be someone that you are not? What would happen if you made the effort to be more genuine in those situations?

3. What did you do for positive and negative attention as you were growing up? How do those patterns influence your interactions and relationships with others today? Do you know anyone who has been a power victim at some time in his or her life?

Chapter Two   Level III Assignments

1. What people and events have you experienced as *uppers* in your life? Which ones have been *downers*? How have those experiences affected you?

2. How have you put those experiences in perspective, good and bad? What do you need to do to begin to put them in the proper perspective so that the *downers* don't liimit you?

3. In what situations—think of at least three—do you most need to remember what you learned in this chapter?

3

CHAPTER

EXPANDING COMFORT ZONES

I had always wanted to build my own home and live in the country. While living in California, I often fantasized about having a log house in the woods. It was a big change to leave where I had grown up, but the dream began to take shape when I moved to Oregon and bought 30 acres. The night before I signed the papers on the loan I was in near panic. I had managed to work my way through graduate school without being in debt. The amount of the loan seemed overwhelming, and the amount of time to pay it back seemed like forever. I constantly had to remind myself that other people had built houses, and that if I took it step by step I could too. Besides, hadn't I just finished graduate school, class by class and term by term? Maybe I could think about this as though I was just getting another degree. Find out the requirements and just plug along one class at a time. That strategy had worked before, and perhaps I could reach this goal in a similar manner.

I remember the combination of excitement and anxiety when my log home package kit arrived at the top of the driveway to my property. Having reached out to friends and neighbors, I had plenty of support. But, I still had to confront my inner demons that wondered what the hell I had gotten myself into. Youthful naivete and enthusiasm are sometimes a good thing; in this case, they kept me from knowing how much I didn't know. As we began to unload the logs and make plans for transporting them to the building site, I kept chanting my mantra from *The Little Engine That Could*—I think I can, I think I can, I think I can.

Anyone who has ever been in or involved with construction work probably knows that very little

happens on schedule or in the way you planned. My life of teaching college involved being in the right place at the right time and some part of me liked that things were predictable. Every day at the building site required a new kind of mental flexibility, though. I quickly began to think outside the box as complicated situations arose. When the bulldozer broke down and the gravel company postponed delivery, but the lumber company was all set to bring the flooring out anyway, I had to get creative or have a breakdown.

Some aspects of my personality suited me well for the job. After all, I was building a log house due, in part, to the fact that my idea of detail work was using a chain saw or a sledgehammer. Need a new window here, fire up the chain saw. Something doesn't quite fit, hand me the 12-pound micro-adjuster, and I'll take care of that. But, there were times when my usual style worked against me, and I had to begin to pay attention and learn from those who were more skilled in detail work and planning ahead. My concrete guy, who built the forms for the foundation, was off by 1/4 of an inch on a 52-foot run.

As work continued and I came in contact with various types of people with different personalities, I began to notice what they did and modeled some of their behavior. It wasn't always easy, but I knew that if I was going to reach my goal, I was going to have to stretch my usual style of doing things. It was difficult at times, but by adjusting my approach to the project, I found that some jobs moved along much more quickly.

Little did I know that when I finally did finish building the external structure, my real challenge would be in finding a bank that would lend me the money to finish the interior. Blind faith can be a good thing, but it is also important to check in with reality at times. Unbeknownst to me, by building my own house I had created a situation where I had three strikes against me. Log homes were considered unconventional structures at the time, the house was half-finished and the banks would be coming in at the middle of the project, and I had been my own contractor for the job. All of my assertiveness training was about to be put to the test.

I called more than 20 banks before I even got one that would consider a loan for completion of the house. The first half-dozen times that I heard the loan officer laugh at my request, I was able to bounce back and keep trying. After that, it became increasingly difficult to be optimistic. Each time I heard no I began to despair, but I kept on calling. Finally, my "I'll show you" part kicked in, and I became even more determined. Hadn't I been in a tight spot before where someone said I couldn't do something and then had pulled it off?

Finally I found a loan officer who may have heard the renewed determination in my voice. He agreed to lend me the money on the condition that I used a bank-approved contractor from one of their lists. I began the familiar process again as I called contractor after contractor who was less than interested in getting involved in my project. May there be a special place in Heaven for Lee Youst, the man who came to my rescue. He came to the building site and inspected the work that had been done. Perhaps he saw something of himself in me that reminded him of his days of just starting out. He agreed to be the supervising contractor and shepherded me through the remainder of the necessary work to finish the inside of the house.

When the new log home was finally completed, friends, neighbors, and everyone who had helped out along the way gathered for a housewarming. It was then that one of my friends, Curt, turned to me and said, "You know, Ford, when I first saw you swing a hammer, I didn't think you would ever finish this place." I knew just what he meant. I smiled and enjoyed the moment. It was the best compliment I had ever received.

Comfort Zones

Most of us have some routine and predictable behavior in our lives. This can be useful because it allows us to focus on what is important. On the other hand, there are many areas in which we develop a range of comfortable behaviors that may be limiting at times.

For example, we may have comfort zones that limit behaviors, such as taking the risk of speaking out in groups, developing friendships, expressing emotions, or taking the physical risks that may be required for certain adventurous activities. This doesn't mean that everyone needs to be more outgoing and self-revealing or that everyone should be a thrill seeker. It is perfectly fine to be a private person or to be cautious and reserved. (The section on personality emphasizes the importance of accepting and appreciating different personality styles.) This chapter is meant to help you explore what areas of your life may be unnecessarily restricted by your beliefs.

In my years of teaching and counseling, I have found that most people limit their options in life to some degree, usually out of fear of disapproval from themselves or from others. There are some people who may be too aggressive, overbearing, or reckless in their risk taking, but I have found them to be in the minority. Even for those people, the concept of comfort zones is important because it might be a real stretch for them to become more aware of or sensitive to others.

There are many ways to explore or challenge your comfort zone. Some people love to go river rafting through huge rapids. Others jump out of airplanes as a form of recreation. Obviously, these people's comfort zones are different from those whose idea of a good time is watching television, where the major risk is "channel surfing" with the remote control. (That activity has even replaced the "risk" of walking across the room to change the channel.) On the other hand, there are some people for whom constantly doing things right on the edge is normal. For them, "expanding their comfort zone" might mean doing something considered ordinary or mundane, then sticking with it even when they aren't excited all the time. (Being married, raising children, and having a career are worthwhile endeavors that are not exciting at every moment.) A useful expansion of the comfort zone of these adventurous types could be to learn the self-discipline necessary for long-term accomplishments. Regardless of what you want to learn to do, most new behavior entails some form of risk.

There may be a connection between learning to take some physical risks and the ability to alter thinking patterns to take psychological risks. There are currently many successful programs that help people expand their potential by challenging their beliefs regarding their physical abilities. A number of these programs

> **"** *Come to the edge," he said. They said,*
> *"We are afraid." "Come to the edge," he*
> *said. They came. He pushed them . . .*
> *and they flew.* **"**
>
> *Guillaume Appollinaire*

include rafting, mountain climbing, and wilderness survival. Most important, though, is the process of exploring psychological limitations due to beliefs that keep one in a comfort zone that restricts desired behavior.

It is important to keep in mind that these physical challenges are really only exercises. You don't have to travel or do something dangerous to look for adventure. In fact, the stakes are higher at home. It is easier to risk harm climbing a mountain than it is to risk being old and alone, or unloved and unneeded, or being thought stupid or insane. It is easier to die than to perhaps live as a failure.

For some, it takes real courage to go to a party, initiate a conversation, or talk in front of a group. Sometimes the real heroes are the ones for whom it takes tremendous strength and effort to stand up for their own beliefs and deal with the everyday situations of life.

Do you know people who always travel the same route wherever they go, always eat at the same restaurant, and generally avoid new people and places? Some people who choose to do that are perfectly happy. But there are many people who rarely try anything new out of fear rather than choice. They seem to have an approach to life that says, "This is what I know, and I had better stick with it. I don't want to do something I'm not sure about." To a certain degree, most of us have a comfort zone in our lifestyle. But there are many ways in which people unnecessarily limit what is available to them in life. We are going to talk about comfort zones and how they apply to taking risks and increasing potential. I am not suggesting that you go out and do something daring or dangerous, but we are going to discuss the beneficial effects of developing an attitude that allows you to expand your comfort zone. You will learn how to begin stretching your concept of what is possible by using the appropriate form of *comfort zone aerobics* for different situations.

Here is an anecdotal story that is an example of how the comfort zone concept operates. Years ago, during the 1970s, the business community

and field of psychology were becoming increasingly involved with cooperative ventures. Because companies wanted to increase profits, they were interested in developing screening methods and hiring procedures that would enable them to enlist the best people for sales positions. One large company hired researchers from a university to provide psychological services. The university did an investigation of the sales records of that particular company's personnel. At the time, those salespeople were making between $16,000 and $24,000 per year. The fact that they were working on commission indicated, to a degree, that the amount they made had a connection with how long or hard they were willing to work. The university was attempting to discover which personality traits were indicators of good salespeople so that the company could screen for those characteristics when hiring. Researchers started tracking performance and sales records of the best employees, and along the way, they discovered some interesting information that has implications for the importance of understanding comfort zones—and what limits them.

Fear of Success

After following the sales records of employees for a period of time, the researchers found that whenever a salesperson exceeded the salary range of most people in the company, that salesperson invariably went back down in sales the next year. The term *fear of success* generally applies to that reaction. Something about doing well and having an exceptional year seemed to affect some people adversely.

Although the above term had been around before, increased awareness of this principle came about in part because of the feminist movement. Around the time of the university study, more women had begun to move out into the business world, taking on tasks for which they were qualified but that were not traditionally considered women's jobs. Many women, while trying to change their beliefs about what was possible for them to achieve, ran into their own limitations and fears about what was acceptable. They would do exceptionally well for a time, and then, perhaps shocked by their success, sabotage their own efforts in some manner. Much of the information on self-defeating behavior came from studying women who were intelligent and capable, yet perhaps being held back by their own beliefs about what was acceptable for women to accomplish—an example of the fear of success.

THE COMFORT ZONE

I used to have a Comfort Zone
where I knew I couldn't fail.
The same four walls of busy work
were really more like jail.
I longed so much to do the things
I'd never done before,
but I stayed inside my Comfort Zone
and paced the same old floor.
I said it didn't matter
that I wasn't doing much.
I said I didn't care for things
like diamonds, furs, and such.
I claimed to be so busy
with the things inside my zone.
But deep inside I longed for
something special of my own.

I couldn't let my life go by,
just watching others win.
I held my breath and stepped outside
to let the change begin.
I took a step and with new strength
I'd never felt before,
I kissed my Comfort Zone "goodbye"
and closed and locked the door.
If you are in a Comfort Zone,
afraid to venture out,
Remember that all winners were
at one time filled with doubt.
A step or two and words of praise
can make your dreams come true.
Greet your future with a smile;
success is there for you!

The concept is equally applicable to men, as is evident from the number of men in high places who have undermined their own accomplishments. (The real problem of the *glass ceiling*—women being held back from advancement in business by sexist beliefs—is an entirely different story.) So it would appear that when people are outside their comfort zone, even in regard to positive accomplishments, they are susceptible to being limited by their beliefs about what is appropriate for them to accomplish.

Why do people return to their comfort zones? One reason has to do with expectations. Do you know people who do well and then feel uncomfortable because they feel pressured to maintain or exceed that level of accomplishment in the future? I have observed that phenomenon with students who are capable and get good grades on occasion, yet don't want to have to do it again. They could get As but would rather do B or C work so that others don't expect as much from them. A variation is that many people who slide along on C grades do so simply because that is what has been expected of them, and they don't want to have to deal with pressure. They know they are capable of achieving better grades, but they think that if they do it once, people might expect it of them all the time. This also applies to a number of settings other than academia. (Remember the concept of paradox? It doesn't have to be logical and it doesn't have to make sense.)

Peer pressure is also a factor of fear of success. There are some people who screw up just so they can be part of a group. You may recall that in high school, there were a lot of people who thought that acting stupid was cool. They pretended to be dumb when they really weren't. The problem with sleeping through classes and ignoring assignments to be cool and "in" with friends was that the next year, half of those people were no longer their friends anyway! They may have wasted a year because of what somebody else thought about doing well academically.

The type of situation previously described occurs in a number of settings. Coworkers at a certain level in a company, who have been associating socially with each other, may have difficulty when one of them gets offered a promotion. They may pressure that person not to leave the group. Have you ever had something good happen to you only to find that your friends were not happy for you? Sometimes, your success makes those who aren't doing well or those who are stuck in their comfort zone feel bad about themselves, and they can't be happy for you.

Here is a story that illustrates this type of thinking and behavior. In San Francisco on Fisherman's Wharf, a wide variety of seafood is sold by vendors in an open-air market. The places that sell live crabs often keep them out front in a box with low sides. It's not a very big box, but the crabs just sit there. They could crawl away, but they don't. One of the reasons they don't have to be put into a large box is that the crabs all get into a big pile and grab each other and hold on for security. Out of their element, all they want to do is hang on. If one of the crabs breaks away and starts to get out, the rest grab it and pull it back into the box. The crabs seem to be saying, "We are all in this together, and as we're on a one-way trip to the boiling pot, no one gets out alive."

Have you ever felt as if you were in a little box and decided, "I want to get out of this and go somewhere else"? Were there people who said, "No, stay here; stay with the rest of us—stay safe. We're all in this together"? Like the crabs, they told you, "If we're going into the boiling water, so are you." Sometimes, to be successful, you have to be willing to go against what other people think you are supposed to do or what they feel is right for you.

People who act "crablike" may believe the comfort zone limits are real. They may say, "You have to stay within these boundaries. You've got to stay in the box." If other people get out of their comfort zone, alter their lives, and do something new, then those still in the box are forced to look at their own lives and what has been limiting them. That might be upsetting. They have been saying to themselves, "I have to stay here. There's no way out." If someone does get out of the box and says, "Look at what I did," then the others can't use the "it's not possible" excuse anymore. So they say, "No, no—come back in the box with us. It's safe. It's comfortable. It may be terrible, but it's familiar. I know this town stinks, this job is lousy, and so on, but if I go out there, what then? It could be worse."

For this reason, many people who complain about their jobs or any other life situation usually complain while maintaining their comfort zone and staying in the situation. If they were to expand their comfort zone, they might have to move beyond their usual behavior and go outside their self-imposed limits. They might have to examine their limiting beliefs. That could be too scary! It might be easier for them to stop their behavior, however positive it is for them, than to examine what is keeping them from making changes that they want to make.

Another interesting aspect of the effects of comfort zones on behavior is that there is a benefit to going outside of them. Even though it may be uncomfortable at first, the rewards of having taken a risk and succeeded are significant. When people expand their comfort zone, they are more likely to go beyond it in the future, even if they temporarily succumb to the fear of success. Once they have had an experience of succeeding, they are more likely to try new things in the future.

Fear of Failure

Another reason people limit themselves is fear that they might not do well. According to the previous story about the university researchers, whenever a salesperson dropped below the lower level in the range of incomes, he or she either went back up the next year or left the company. Both alternatives maintained the comfort zone regarding salaries. The salespeople either took the necessary steps to ensure an increase or moved on to another job or company. Quitting allowed them to use the "sour grapes" perspective, which says, "If I can't have it or get it, it must not have been worthwhile

and I didn't want it anyway." Then they could get another job or not, which-ever was more likely to reestablish their comfort zone.

It may sound unusual to talk about expanding your comfort zone in the area of failure. Ironically, it is important to expand your comfort zone regarding the fear of failure, so you realize that not doing well doesn't mean the end of the world or that you can't ever try again. You need to have some experiences that don't turn out right to realize that you can still pull yourself back together and move on to new opportunities.

An often-quoted statistic from human potential seminars is that the average millionaire has made and lost a fortune 2.3 times. A curious fact, if it's true. Why were these people able to lose vast sums of money and still make a comeback? Probably because they weren't afraid of failure. Taking the kinds of risks necessary to make that kind of money means that you can't be too worried about failure. The fact that these people made it, lost it all, and then made it again enabled them to say, "I've been down, I've been broke. So what?"

Considering what actually constitutes failure is another important concept in understanding how not to limit yourself. What is a catastrophe to one person might only be a minor setback to someone else. Some people think that anything less than perfect equals failure, which is one sure way to limit what you attempt in life and to contribute to self-defeating behavior. It is important to remember that sometimes failure is helpful. For instance, have you ever had something happen to you that seemed terrible at the time, but after a period of time you could see that it was very useful or beneficial?

It is also important to separate failure from not doing well. Sometimes, people would like to learn a new game, skill, or hobby, but they limit themselves right from the beginning because they are afraid they won't do well immediately. Being a beginner and not doing well at a complicated task is to be expected, and it certainly isn't failure. If you have the tendency to think that way, try breaking down the behavior into smaller pieces or steps. Define success as making a good effort or as doing the appropriate practice for that task. You don't learn to play a musical instrument, become a competent athlete, or start a business overnight. Most things take time and a willingness to be a new learner before the skill is incorporated.

These are some of the reasons for expanding your comfort zone regarding the fear of failure. According to the human potential movement: "If you want to be more successful, double your

failures." The more you are out there trying new things, the more likely you are to succeed at what you want to do. If you don't try anything, you probably won't progress.

It is important to develop an attitude that allows you to expand your comfort zone to deal both with success and with what constitutes failure. Unless you are actively involved in periodically stretching yourself, both mentally and physically, life may begin to close in on you. It is almost like gravity. Unless you are doing your comfort zone aerobics by actually pushing against those boundaries, there is a temptation to take the course of least resistance. Most of us know people who haven't done anything new or different in their lives for 20 years. The longer they go without taking any kind of risk to achieve something new, the harder risk gets for them. There is a fine line between being in the groove and being in a rut.

Expanding your comfort zone requires taking risks. When you try something new and stretch your potential, you also learn more about your own style and how and when taking risks is appropriate for you. That can be useful information. Keep in mind that you need to have choice and balance to use that information. Sometimes, you should ignore the "crabs" in your life who want to stop you. At other times, it might be important to listen to the voice from within that cautions you about taking on too much. Once you expand your comfort zone in either direction, it won't have as much power over you. The more you take appropriate risks, the more you will have the choice and balance you will need for other situations later on in your life.

Finally, keep in mind that most people have comfort zones because they assume that they will be safe from unpleasant events. They seem to think, "If I only do what I know how to do,

RISKS

To laugh is to risk appearing the fool.
To weep is to risk appearing
sentimental.
To reach out for another is to risk involvement.
To expose feelings is to risk exposing your
true self.
To place your ideas, your dreams, before a
crowd is to risk their loss.
To love is to risk not being loved in return.
To live is to risk dying.
To hope is to risk failure.

But risks must be taken,
because the greatest hazard in life is to risk
nothing.
People who risk nothing, do nothing, have
nothing, and are nothing.
They may avoid suffering and sorrow,
but they cannot learn, feel, change, grow, love,
live.
Chained by their attitudes, they are slaves;
They have forfeited their freedom.
Only a person who risks is free.

nothing bad will happen to me. I can stay in control." Unfortunately, it doesn't work that way! Sometimes, bad things happen to good people no matter what they do. As Steve Goodman wrote in one of his songs: "Don't go looking for trouble, it will find you anyway." In reality, trying to always play it safe doesn't work. It probably only limits potential and positive accomplishments. In general, people with a narrow comfort zone don't necessarily feel less fear. More likely, they feel even more fear because they are afraid to feel afraid. They don't try anything that requires them to "rise to the challenge." In the book *Feel the Fear and Do It Anyway* (Jeffers, 1987) is very good advice. Remember that one of the benefits of increasing the ability to do new things is that it also increases self-esteem.

Thinking Patterns

Have you ever had a friend confide in you about a problem he was having, one for which he didn't see any solutions? You could tell, though, that the real problem was the fact that he was limiting himself to possible solutions. For example, John has a misunderstanding with his boss at work. He believes that he is being mistreated and, therefore, must either quit or get fired. The real problem in that situation may be any or all of the following: (a) his perception of the situation is distorted and his boss is not really that upset; (b) he believes that there are few or no choices; and (c) he sees the world only in

terms of black and white, which precludes considering choices and alternatives in the gray areas.

In most counseling situations, a prerequisite to addressing the presenting problem (what the client perceives the problem to be) is exploring current thought processes and limiting beliefs. Part of the problem may be how the person is perceiving the situation. Another part is how he or she is thinking about possible solutions. People experiencing difficulty in their lives frequently see the world in terms of black and white; they think that solutions can come from only one source or manner of behavior. Ironically, that source or manner of behavior is usually what they have already tried and found to be unsuccessful and inadequate to solving their problem. (Remember Chapter 1: If what you are doing doesn't work, do something else.) Solutions to problems often come from places we haven't looked before. People will often open their refrigerator 10 times, hoping that something will have materialized since they last looked, rather than open the cupboard or drawer where there is food. When they can't find their keys, they continue to stare at the empty spot where they thought they left them, rather than look for them in a new location.

You can expand your comfort zone on thinking patterns by examining your own thought processes. Just as solutions come from places you haven't looked, sometimes they emerge from changing your self-talk and becoming aware of your thought processes. Rigidity of thinking is just a form of having a narrow comfort zone in regard to mental activity. When did you last attempt some form of mental aerobics? People who tend to reduce the world to black and white are usually trying to establish a comfort zone of control over complex situations. This seldom works, especially in these ever-changing and increasingly confusing times.

What is needed is the latitude that exploring the vast gray areas of life provides. If you want to change certain behaviors and act in new ways, it is beneficial to begin to think differently. Beginning to understand that most of life is composed of shades of gray and that little of it is black or white is also a developmental issue. Part of changing from a child to an adolescent is acquiring enhanced cognitive abilities. Even with their increased understanding of the world around them, many adolescents still tend to experience the world in terms of black and white. Maturity requires both flexibility of thought and tolerance for the ambiguities and complexities of life. Those adults who continue to see things as black or white have a case of "arrested development." Modern times require the ability to hold two conflicting thoughts in mind at the same time. Some psychologists even consider that ability a sign of maturity.

Considering the following concepts will help you expand your mental comfort zone and allow for more gray areas in your life. That, in turn, should enable you to be more creative in your personal growth and problem solving as you encounter the many challenges life has to offer.

1. Think of a time when you knew something to be true, and later on you found out it wasn't true at all. Is it possible that some of the things you think now might prove to be untrue in the future?

2. Consider a time when you had beliefs that may have been true for that time but are no longer useful in your life today. Thinking like a 10-year-old is fine when you are 10. It does little good to apply those beliefs when you are 30 or 60.

3. When was the last time you had an opinion that was changed by gaining new information? Consider reading or listening to a point of view that you consider to be the opposite of yours. If you associate only with people who think like you, how will you ever think anything new?

4. Have you ever had the experience of beginning to think a thought that you never thought you would think? This will most certainly happen to you when you reach middle age, so you might as well get prepared, if you haven't already been through it. Doing so will prepare you for the future, regardless of age.

Another benefit of increased flexibility of thought is your greater acceptance of differences in others. When you have an increased tolerance for the gray areas in your own thinking, it becomes easier to accept differences of opinion with people from other lifestyles or cultures. It becomes easier to view these differences as differences in perspective. There are a vast number of personalities and styles in the world, and learning to look for similarities rather than focusing on differences will greatly enhance your human relations in a number of situations.

When thinking about sensitive ethnic, cultural, and gender issues, it is important for us to consider all sides of the issue. It is important that we remember that there are always many different points of view when discussing human behavior. Without examining our beliefs or making room for the possibility of new ways of thinking, we may be relying on inadequate information and come to incorrect conclusions. We fall prey to stereotypes and prejudice when we think that our beliefs and our own personal experiences are the only source for our conclusions about other people. Remember the saying "Walk a mile in another person's shoes before you judge him or her."

Questions for Critical Thinking

Think of a time when you tried something new that you weren't sure you would be able to do and you pulled it off! Wasn't that a great feeling? What was the last successful risk you took? What did you do that made it a success? What will be the next risk you take?

_____

_____

_____

_____

_____

_____

_____

_____

_____

_____

Attribution Theory

Attribution theory is about how people make causal explanations for behavior. We are social animals and are curious about why others do the things that they do. We want to make sense of the behavior of the people around us, and we look for reasons for bizarre behavior. It is the other person that we are concerned with because their behavior may seem odd. This goes back to the first chapter and how we all make sense to ourselves. To a large extent, much of what we notice around us has to do with our perceptions, our beliefs, and our expectations.

When you see garbage on your neighbor's lawn, do you think it is because of an incident that was beyond their control, or do you blame it on the "fact" that they must be sloppy people? We tend to attribute the best motives to our own behavior, but when someone else does something that doesn't appear to make sense, it is because they are flawed human beings.

Attributions (Weiten and Lloyd, 2006) are inferences that people draw about the causes of their own behavior, others' behavior, and events. People tend to locate the cause of behavior either within a person, attributing it to personal factors, or outside of a person, attributing it to environmental factors. *Internal attributions* ascribe the causes of behavior to personal dispositions, traits, abilities, and feelings. *External attributions* ascribe the causes of behavior to situational demands and environmental constraints.

A second dimension people use in making causal attributions is the stability of the causes underlying the behavior. A stable cause is one that is more or less permanent. An unstable cause might be a person's mood (internal) or something as unpredictable as the weather (external).

A third dimension in the attribution process acknowledges the fact that sometimes events are under one's control and sometimes they are not. If you are a gifted athlete, did you develop that skill (controllable), or if you are musical is it that you were born with that attribute and/or ability?

Self-attributions are inferences that people draw about the causes of their own behavior. Often, our explanations of our own behavior are designed to put us in the best light. Self-serving bias especially emerges when our self-esteem is threatened. We tend to attribute our successes to our own characteristics but to attribute our failures to external factors. We take credit for our success, but blame our failures on others or the situation.

Fundamental Attribution Error   The fundamental attribution error is the tendency to overestimate the importance of a person's traits and under estimate the importance of situations when they seek to explain someone else's behavior (Santrock, 2006). The types of attributions people make about others can have a tremendous impact on everyday interactions. Some aspects of the attribution process are logical, but often the process is illogical and unsystematic.

Assertiveness

During the course of reading the previous chapters and participating in the chapter activities, some of you may have started to make changes in your lives. Unfortunately, not all of the people in your circle of contacts will be pleased. If you begin to change, even if it is for the better, it may require others to examine their beliefs and behaviors. If they are reluctant to make changes of their own, they may discourage the advances that you have made. Being how you would like to be, whether others approve or not, often requires assertiveness. Learning to be assertive is key to standing up for your beliefs as well as making, and feeling confident about, positive changes in your life.

There are a number of books on assertiveness, and most give valuable advice on developing assertiveness skills and behavior. Three classics in the field are *Your Perfect Right: A Guide to Assertive Living* (Alberti and Emmons, 1986), *Asserting Yourself* (Bower and Bower, 1996), and *When I Say No, I Feel Guilty* (Smith, 1975). The last addresses what a number of books leave out: the power of the underlying beliefs about getting what you want. It doesn't matter how much information people are given if they don't believe they have permission to use it. As valuable as it may be to develop the skills necessary to become more assertive, a person has to believe that it is in his or her best interest to use those skills. Sometimes, that means challenging childhood beliefs about what it means to stand up for yourself.

Consider the implications in the following example:

One afternoon, the family was out for a drive— Mom and Dad in the front seat and the three children in the back. Suddenly, Sarah, the oldest, blurted out, "Dad, can we have some ice cream?" Dad, somewhat startled, replied, "I don't know; maybe, if you don't bug me about it." The three children exchanged glances, some more hopeful than others. John, the middle child, nudged Sarah and whispered, "Give him a chance to think about it." Mom, musing out loud to herself, commented on how nice the weather was. Allison, the youngest, just closed her eyes tight and crossed her fingers.

A little further down the road, Sarah couldn't contain her excitement any longer and again asked, "Please, Dad. We'll be good. Can we have some ice cream?" In an irritated voice, Dad snapped back, "I'm thinking about it! I told you not to keep bothering me!" Mom, staring straight ahead through the windshield, calmly stated, "We do have enough time, and dinner won't be for a while yet."

Just as the car rounded the next turn, an ice cream store came into view. The children all began bouncing up and down in the back seat. John had just put his hand on Sarah's arm, but it was too late. Sarah had already begun to call out, "There it is! There it is! Can we? Oh, please, let's stop."

At that point, Dad yelled, "There! Now you've done it! I told you not to keep bothering me. I'll be darned if I'm going to stop now, when you kids don't mind me. Maybe that will teach you a lesson." Mom, in a voice that was barely audible, stated, "I don't know what lesson that would be." Sarah began to seethe and mull over possible means of retaliation and crossed her arms while quietly plotting revenge. Allison began rummaging around in her little backpack looking for her favorite dolly and quietly wiped away a tear. John leaned forward slightly and said, "That's OK, I guess we can wait 'til later. There's always next weekend." The hum of the road and the squeaking of the car were the only noises to fill the familiar silence the rest of the drive home.

Some people believe that the more they ask for or try to get what they want, the less likelihood there is of getting it. Is it any wonder that some people have difficulty believing it is possible to gain new skills that will enable them to be more assertive? In their lives, that wouldn't make any sense. Why try to learn behaviors that would only make your situation worse?

For instance, take Sarah from the ice cream story and add 20 or 30 years. For her, that incident and many more like it may have been transformed into a belief that the more you ask for something, the less chance you have of getting it. If you believed that, what would you start doing? Not asking! That is what might have happened for one of the children in that car. At an early age, she decided that the more she let her dad know what she wanted, the less chance she had of getting it. So after a while, she stopped asking for what she wanted and just sort of hinted. (Don't ask, but let people know, somehow.) But it seemed to her that no matter how much she let

people know what she wanted, as soon as they knew what she wanted, she knew she wouldn't get it. As a grown woman (based on a composite), she not only stopped asking but also stopped letting people know about her needs and desires altogether. The problem then was that if she knew she wanted something, she always felt that she was going to be disappointed, so eventually she cut off her feelings and desires and stopped letting herself know what she wanted. This was her way of trying to protect herself from the pain of disappointment.

This woman, who is representative of many clients I have seen in counseling, was in her 30s when she came for help. She didn't know what she wanted, of course, but she knew that for at least 20 years she had felt a vague sense of uneasiness and dissatisfaction with life. No wonder she was depressed! If she didn't want anything, how could she have any sense of direction or purpose? She had decided early in life that it was better not to want anything. She finally decided to get help when she realized that 20 years of not wanting anything was worse than the disappointment that she was trying to avoid by not wanting anything. If you don't want anything, you'll never get anything.

Beliefs About Assertiveness

If people don't believe they deserve to get what they want, or don't believe that standing up for themselves is possible or useful, then learning new skills is not going to be of much help. I have known many people who undermined their ability to learn assertiveness skills because they believed that assertiveness contradicted their perception of the world. Some people just give up and decide that it's hopeless, that there is no sense in trying when life doesn't work out as they planned. They may give something a halfhearted try, but they passively accept the outcome of whatever happens next. When things don't go their way, they blame the world. They may even get angry or vindictive when the world doesn't pay off the way they believe it should.

Fortunately, not all people learn to give up in the face of adversity. There are those who get more tenacious and try harder when things aren't going their way, because they believe that they should be getting what they want in life. Those who are fortunate enough to have been taught that they are deserving will find a way to persevere. When dealing with disappointment, there is a huge difference between thinking, "This is what I expected, just par for the course," and "What's wrong here? What else do I need to do to get what I want?"

Assertiveness and persistence often go hand in hand. Some people learn to become the "squeaky wheel" and keep asking until they get what they want. They truly believe that if they keep trying, the world will respond. They have learned that assertiveness and persistence pay off. They have confidence that it is permissible to ask for what they want and to stand up for their needs. Assertiveness and persistence can be taken to extremes, however. Consider the kind of behavior that can be observed at the local grocery store. For example, some kids just keep making a scene until Mom surrenders and gives them whatever they want just to keep them quiet. That isn't assertive behavior—that is aggressive and obnoxious behavior!

Developing a sense of perspective about getting what you want from other people and the world in general is extremely valuable. It is important to have a balanced approach: to know when to try harder and when to accept life as it is.

Here are some examples of personal beliefs in action: I used to work in a halfway house for adolescents who had been in trouble at home, in school, or with the law (usually, a combination of all three). One girl I worked with, who had fairly low self-esteem, used to say at least six times an hour, "No matter what I do, there is no way on God's green earth that I'm ever going to get what I want." It wasn't surprising to learn that those words were almost verbatim what her mother had told her for years. Her mother, who had an impoverished background and was having a rough time in life, used to say that to herself. Whenever her daughter asked for something, that was what she said to her, too. As a result, resolving conflicts with the other girls in the halfway house was usually difficult for this girl. Being assertive was a skill she knew little about.

Contrast that with the will and assertiveness of the average four- or five-year-old who knows exactly what he or she wants. You may have witnessed child-parent interactions in a store where the child's persistence just wears the parents down until they give in. Although that may not be the best parental model for setting limits with a child, the point is that some kids just won't take no for an answer. Within certain limits, the belief that it is acceptable to get what you want in life can be useful. Part of what makes parenting some adolescents such a challenge is that when the children want something, they are incredibly creative about how to get it. Parents may limit themselves to a few choices of how to respond, but the assertive adolescent will try anything and everything in an attempt to achieve the desired goal.

ASSERTIVENESS BILL OF RIGHTS

I.   You have the right to judge your own behavior, thoughts, and emotions, and to take the responsibility for their initiation and consequences upon yourself.

II. You have the right to offer no reasons or excuses for justifying your behavior.

III. You have the right to judge if you are responsible for finding solutions to other people's problems.

IV. You have the right to change your mind.

V.   You have the right to make mistakes—and be responsible for them.

VI. You have the right to say, "I don't know."

VII. You have the right to be independent of the goodwill of others before coping with them.

VIII. You have the right to be illogical in making decisions.

IX. You have the right to say, "I don't understand."

X.   You have the right to say, "I don't care."

YOU HAVE THE RIGHT TO SAY NO, WITHOUT FEELING GUILTY.

> **❝**Accept human differences and limitations. Don't expect anyone to be perfect. Remember, the other person has a right to be different. And don't be a reformer.**❞**
>
> *David Schwartz*

Assertiveness Defined

There are a number of ways to describe assertive behavior, such as standing up for your own rights without depriving others of theirs, or standing on your own two feet without stepping on someone else's toes. Both statements show the need for balance. Assertiveness should be the middle point on the continuum between passive and aggressive behavior.

For example, a man named Rick recently had the misfortune of needing to stop near the freeway at one of those restaurants that stay open all night. He was on a trip that necessitated traveling at night, and he decided to stop to eat at 3 A.M. to stay awake for the rest of the journey. He ordered a grilled cheese sandwich. When the waitress brought him the sandwich, it looked as though it had never been acquainted with the grill. Passive behavior would have been to accept the sandwich as it was, and aggressive behavior would have been to become angry and combative with the waitress. Instead, he simply said, "I don't think this sandwich is done; the cheese isn't melted. Could you take this back to the kitchen, please?" The waitress took the sandwich back and placed it on the counter under the red warming lights. It apparently got no closer to the grill, because when she brought it back, the cheese still had the impressions of the plastic wrapper on it. The waitress then inquired, "How's the sandwich now?" Passive behavior would have been to just accept it; aggressive behavior would have been to become critical and judgmental, or to threaten the cook. Once again, he simply made his request: "Please take this back to the kitchen; the cheese still isn't melted." After once again letting the sandwich sit under the lamp for a while, the waitress returned the sandwich in the same unmelted condition. At that point he told the waitress, "I am sorry, but I can't accept this sandwich because it hasn't been cooked. I'm unhappy with the service. Thank you for the trouble, but I'm going to try another place." He then left the restaurant.

What do you think Rick should have done? There are many possible responses, but I believe that what he did was in the realm of assertiveness. He didn't think he should accept a grilled cheese sandwich that hadn't been grilled. Although it is open to interpretation, there are certain standards that most people have regarding how they expect to be treated as a customer. Some people might have just taken the sandwich on the last attempt, regardless of condition, for fear of upsetting or inconveniencing the staff. Others might have gotten angry and abusive over not getting the service they expected. Rick didn't accept something that wasn't up to standard and wasn't what he ordered. He didn't tell the restaurant staff what to do, but stated what he wanted and then said what he would do.

Some people have difficulties not because they lack certain skills and are nonassertive, but

D.E.S.C. MODEL OF CONFLICT RESOLUTION

D: DESCRIBE the behavior.
E: EXPRESS your feelings regarding the behavior, using "I" statements.
S: SPECIFY a more acceptable behavior, either with or without the input of the person that you have the conflict with.
C: CONSEQUENCES, both positive and negative, might need to be developed.

because they are actively engaged in behaviors that don't help them get what they want. Many people use the term *nonassertive* in place of passive; but I believe that, in some situations, passive is actually a better word to describe certain behaviors. Some people apologize to the very person who is taking advantage of them. That is more passive than nonassertive. For example, one time in a large crowd, I unintentionally stepped on someone's toes, and the person turned to me and said, "I'm sorry." I had stepped on his toes, but he was apologizing to me. I imagine that this person, having reacted in that way, has difficulty standing up for himself in other situations. For some people, difficulty in confronting situations when it is necessary seems to go beyond a lack of assertiveness.

In any event, what extremely passive and extremely aggressive behavior have in common is that both are likely to get a person less of what he or she wants. Those two ends of the continuum almost come full circle. Passive people almost give their power away, and people who are too aggressive are likely to have others react to them by trying to prevent them from getting what they want.

Passive (or nonassertive) behavior is not sharing your ideas, thoughts, or feelings when it would be beneficial to do so. Passivity is not responding to obvious provocation, not standing up for your rights. Being overly anxious of others' criticism or disapproval is passive. There is almost an element of dishonesty in passive behavior when you allow others to violate your right to be treated with respect and dignity and then fail to say anything about it.

Aggressive behavior involves expressing your feelings through insults, sarcasm, labels, put-downs, or hostile statements and actions. Whether it is direct or indirect, aggressive behavior involves expressing thoughts, feelings, and opinions in a way that violates others' right to be treated with basic respect.

Assertive behavior, on the other hand, involves describing feelings, thoughts, opinions, and preferences directly to another person in an honest and appropriate manner. The following are characteristics of assertive individuals:

1. They are open and express their feelings.
2. They are confident about expressing their opinions and beliefs.
3. They are capable of being contentious and will stand up for their rights even if it entails a degree of unpleasantness.

Non-assertive	Assertive	Aggressive
Self-denying	Self-enhancing	Self-enhancing at others expense
Hurt, anxious	Feels good about self	Hurtful, deprecates others
Allows others to choose	Chooses for self	Chooses for others

4. They act in a manner that shows self-respect and are aware of their own limitations.
5. They aren't easily persuaded or intimidated and will make up their own minds. (Bower and Bower, 1996)

The accompanying chart clarifies the differences among nonassertive (or passive), assertive, and aggressive behaviors.

Assertiveness Skills

There are a number of approaches to learning assertiveness skills, but almost all of them incorporate ideas from the following:

Identify negative self-talk: Are you putting too much pressure on yourself to be perfect? Perhaps your goal needs to be learning to improve, rather than having everyone respond to you differently immediately. Are you assuming catastrophe if you assert yourself, imagining that if you assert yourself and it doesn't work, something terrible will happen? Do you feel that if you assert yourself you're being selfish? Counter that self-talk with the knowledge that it is OK to get what you want in life as long as you don't deprive others of that same opportunity.

Use more "I" statements: Make a habit of saying "What I want is. . . ." and "What I'm feeling is. . . ." rather than telling people who you think they are ("you" statements) and what they should do. Adler and Towne (2003) state that "I" language describes the other person's behavior without making any judgments about its worth. A complete "I" statement has three parts: It describes (a) the other person's behavior, (b) your feelings, and (c) the consequences the other's behavior has for you. (Notice the use of these elements in the previous example of my trip to the restaurant: "I can't accept this sandwich because it hasn't been cooked [description of other's behavior]. I'm unhappy [description of feelings] with the service.

Thank you for the trouble, but I'm going to try another place [description of the consequences].")

Even the best "I" statement won't work unless it is delivered in the right way. If your words are nonjudgmental but your tone of voice, facial expression, and posture all send "you" messages, a defensive response is likely to follow. The best way to make your actions match your words is to remind yourself before speaking that your goal is to explain how the other's behavior affects you—not to act like a judge and jury (Adler and Towne, 2003). Some assertiveness therapy groups have a rule that no one can ask questions, only make statements. The means starting each sentence with the word "I." Although this is not how people usually talk, it helps people learn to use more "I" statements.

Put it in perspective: Much of what constitutes assertiveness has to do with who you are and who the person you are dealing with is. Many assertiveness training programs give instructions as if "one size fits all." Words spoken by one person may not carry the same meaning when spoken by someone else. The 6-foot, 6-inch man who is used to dealing only with other men may need to tone it down when talking to a woman who is 5 feet tall. He may be intimidating and perceived as aggressive because of his size and demeanor. Conversely, some people need to turn up the volume to be perceived as assertive. Notice the response you are getting: If you consistently put others on the defensive, you may be mistaking aggressive behavior for being assertive. For some people, learning assertiveness skills means learning how to control their temper and be more considerate of others' rights.

Other assertiveness tools require observation and analysis of behavior—yours and others'. These suggestions also build on a number of familiar topics, such as positive self-talk and cognitive restructuring. Becoming more assertive may include the following:

Observe the behavior of others: Notice people you consider to be assertive. What do they do? How do they look, sound, and act?

Observe your own behavior: How often do you use self-talk and "I" messages? What is the difference between the times you have been assertive and the times you haven't been?

Rehearse being assertive: Imagine being the way you would like to be in a particular situation. Practice what you would say and how you would say it.

Be assertive: To get better at assertiveness you have to practice. Start off with less-threatening people or events. To use the words of Jeffers's (1987) book title, "Feel the fear and do it anyway."

Everyone attempting self-improvement needs to have something to stick on the front of the refrigerator. The box, entitled "Assertiveness Bill of Rights" provides a list from Smith's book *When I Say No, I Feel Guilty,* (1975), which is intended to help you be more assertive. These pointers can be helpful in many circumstances.

Personality

Personality is the way you present yourself to the world. Your personality determines the way you think, feel, and behave—the qualities that make up how you are uniquely you. Personality influences your style of communication; it is your unique self-expression reflecting your attitudes and beliefs. Some theorists in the field of developmental psychology believe there is a solid core of attitudes and behaviors that remains constant throughout life, and that core gives us our identity. Personality refers to an individual's unique constellation of consistent traits. Although none of us is entirely consistent in the way we behave, the quality of consistency across situations lies at the core of the concept of personality.

Elements of Personality

Some degree of personality is innate. In newborns, this is referred to as temperament. Even though it isn't called *personality* at that age, it is the precursor to personality. In the study of developmental psychology, infants are rated on a scale of 1 to 10 regarding different observable behaviors (such as reaction to noise, level and amount of movement, and response to touch). The range of response to each behavior gives some evidence that there is considerable difference among infants even at birth. Some mothers report that differences in their children were evident even in the womb.

As we grow older, there is a reciprocal relationship between our perceptions and our personalities. We develop filters due to the influence of our personality on our perceptions and interpretations of life events. Those filters then influence our personality in subsequent events, and personality becomes a code of behavior telling us how to conduct ourselves. Personality is in some manner a code of conduct. It is a checklist of responses that are in accordance with the values and beliefs we have developed. It can even determine what type of reactions we are likely to fall back on in any given situation.

Personality is also an innate expression of our interpretation of life. Some people are born with an ability to see life through rose-colored glasses, as Taylor Hartman (1987) states, whereas others tend to see the world through dark glasses. Your personality determines whether you are easily depressed, casual, formal, careful, or carefree. It determines whether you are passive or assertive. Do you dash off at the last minute for an appointment or always arrive with time to spare? Do you prefer deep, meaningful conversations or would you rather party the night away? When considering the innate aspects of personality, it is valuable to keep in mind that some things are not as easily changed as glasses. Sometimes, it is more important to acknowledge and work with our views of life rather than try to alter them.

Have you ever wondered why people consult their horoscopes even though they don't necessarily believe in them? It has to do with a basic curiosity about personality traits and predicting behavior. For some people, personalities and individual differences are a mystery not worth pursuing. Others agree with Socrates: "The unexamined life is not worth living." Most of us want to understand ourselves better, and talking about different types of people and different points of view is one way of doing that. In ancient times, when the only known elements were earth, air, fire, and water, it was thought that there were only four related personality types, and people were described accordingly. Currently, there are many different methods and criteria for describing personality types. The commonality is that those differences are found in every culture in the world, in every age group, in every religion, in every race, and in each sex.

Trait theories (Allport, 1961; Cattell, 1966) state that personality consists of broad dispositions, called *traits*, that lead to characteristic responses. This means that people can be described in terms of the basic ways they behave, such as easygoing and reflective, or dominant and assertive. Although trait theorists differ on which traits make up personality, and how many there are, they all agree that traits are the fundamental building blocks of personality. A personality trait is a durable disposition to behave in a particular way in a variety of situations. Adjectives such as honest, dependable, moody, impulsive, anxious, domineering, and friendly describe dispositions that represent personality traits (Weiten and Lloyd, 2003).

In recent years, Robert McCrea and Paul Costa (1999) have stimulated a lively debate among psychologists by arguing that the vast majority of personality traits are derived from just five higher-order traits that have come to be known as the "Big Five." Let's take a look at those five traits:

Extraversion. People who score high in extraversion are characterized as outgoing, sociable, upbeat, friendly, assertive, and gregarious. Introverted people tend to be shy, retiring, and quiet.

Neuroticism. People who score high in neuroticism tend to be anxious, hostile, self-conscious, insecure, and vulnerable. Emotionally stable people are more calm and centered.

Openness to experience. Openness is associated with curiosity, flexibility, imaginativeness, and unconventional attitudes. People low on this dimension are sometimes shallow, plain, or simple.

Agreeableness. Those who score high in agreeableness tend to be sympathetic, trusting, cooperative, and straightforward. People low in this dimension are cold, quarrelsome, and unkind.

Conscientiousness. Conscientious people tend to be diligent, disciplined, well organized, punctual, and dependable. Impulsive people tend to be careless, disorderly, and undependable.

McCrea and Costa maintain that personality can be described adequately by measuring the five basic traits that they have identified. Their bold claim has been supported in many studies by other researchers, and the five-factor model has become the dominant conception of personality structure in contemporary psychology (Weiten and Lloyd, 2003).

Personality and Cultural Studies

Cross-cultural research further confirms the utility of five dimensions. If the Big Five dimensions were the result of some sort of biasing stereotypes, then they would not replicate in other cultures. But, so far at least, the scheme seems to work quite well throughout the world. But, research also yields some warnings about uncritical use of personality dimensions. Although many cultures recognize that people vary along such dimensions, cultures differ markedly in how much they value each trait.

A good example concerns pressures toward competition versus cooperation—striving independently for success versus helping others. Comparisons between Mexicans and Americans have shown some interesting differences. Americans (and Euro-Americans) are expected to compete, to dominate, to win. Mexican (and Mexican American) culture, on the other hand, prizes trust, cooperation, and helping one's peers. These preferential differences can have important implications, such as in the classroom. Should we continue to emphasize competition for grades, or should we foster an atmosphere of cooperation in the learning environment? Such issues remind us that individual differences in traits do not develop outside a specific cultural context; culture is always relevant (Friedman and Shustack, 1999).

Personality Theories

Although there are a number of significant theories of personality, there are essentially four basic schools: psychodynamic, social-cognitive, humanistic, and biological. Each perspective emphasizes certain aspects, but none provides the complete truth. The attempt to prove which is most correct is currently regarded, for the most part, as a waste of energy. Each perspective explains some aspects well while overlooking others. The psychodynamic approach calls attention to our unconscious needs and conflicts and discusses the influence of early childhood. The social-cognitive perspective focuses on the importance of learning and the environment, as well as offering practical strategies for changing behavior. Humanistic theories emphasize the potential for freedom and growth in each of us and belief in the lifelong process of self-actualization. The biological perspective reminds us of the importance of recent discoveries in the field of genetics and its influence on personality. Thus, by examining each perspective, we may develop a more inclusive and well-balanced understanding of personality.

Psychodynamic Perspective

Sigmund Freud was the original **psychoanalytic theorist** who proposed that most of what makes up personality is unconscious, or beyond awareness, and heavily influenced by emotions. The Freudian concept of personality states that who we are is mainly influenced by the internal struggle of the psychic forces that are mostly concerned with sexual and aggressive impulses. Psychoanalytic theorists believe that to truly understand a person's personality, we have to look at the symbolic meaning of behavior and the deep inner workings of the mind. Freud believed that personality was composed of three structures: the id, the ego, and the superego.

One way to understand the three structures, according to transactional analysis, is to consider them as the child, adult, and parent aspects of an individual (Berne, 1972). In Freud's view, the id is unconscious and can therefore work entirely from the pleasure principle. The id always

seeks immediate pleasure and the avoidance of pain. The childlike id wants to believe that it can have complete obedience. It is spoiled, willful, impatient, and self-centered. The id wants what it wants right now, not later. The id is the appetite of the self. The ego, as the adult, has the job of getting things done. It is more tuned into reality and is responsive to society's demands. The superego is concerned with right and wrong. Like the parent, it must tell the greedy id that there are purposes in life other than immediate gratification.

Freud was among the first theorists to explore many new and uncharted regions of personality. Some of his ideas have been updated, others revised, and some have been discarded. In particular, Freud's critics have said that his ideas about sexuality, early experience, social factors, and the unconscious mind were misguided. The following list is from *Human Adjustment* (Simons, Kalichman, and Santrock, 1994). Freud's critics emphasize the following:

- Sexuality is not the pervasive underlying force behind personality that Freud believed it to be.
- The first five years of life are not as powerful in shaping adult personality as Freud thought; later experiences deserve more attention.
- The ego and conscious thought processes play more dominant roles in our personality than Freud gave them credit for; we are not wed forever to the id and its instinctual, unconscious clutches. The ego has a line of development separate from the id; viewed in this way, achievement, thinking, and reasoning are not always tied to sexual impulses.
- Sociocultural factors are much more important than Freud believed. Freud placed more emphasis on the biological basis of personality by stressing the id's dominance.

It may be easy to ridicule Freud for some of his ideas, but it is important to keep in mind that he began to develop his theories over a century ago. It is not entirely fair to compare his theories to those of more recent times. Freud deserves credit for breaking new ground and developing ideas that have had a tremendous influence and impact on modern thought.

Social-Cognitive Perspective

The social-cognitive is a broad perspective that includes behavioral and social learning theory as well as cognitive psychology. Early behavioral psychologists relied on scientific methods to observe behavior and how it is learned; hence the term *learning theory*. Most learning theorists, including the pioneer B. F. Skinner, focused on the mechanics of behavior and reinforcement and excluded human consciousness. Many of their studies were based on animal studies. In recent years, there has been a shift toward understanding complex human behavior and real-life problems. As a result, learning concepts are being integrated with cognitive psychology. There is now more emphasis on the interaction between people and their environment and how thought processes affect learning and behavior (Atwater and Duffy, 1999).

Albert Bandura (1997) is one of the behaviorists who have assigned an important role to the cognitive processes. He points out that humans obviously are conscious, thinking, feeling beings. He also argues that, in overlooking cognitive processes, Skinner ignored the most distinctive feature of human behavior. Bandura and like-minded theorists call their brand of behaviorism **social learning theory.** According to social learning theory, models have a great impact on personality development. Children learn to be assertive, dependable, confident, easygoing, and so forth by observing others behaving in those ways. The foremost contribution Bandura has made is his description of observational learning. Observational learning occurs when an organism's responding is influenced by observing others, who are called models (Weiten and Lloyd, 2003).

In recent years, psychologists have begun to study the impact of cognition on behavior. Cognition, essentially, is the process of gathering information, paying attention to the environment, using memory, and developing self-motivation. Walter Mischel (1986) suggests that there are five basic categories of cognitive variables that influence our response to a given situation:

1. *Competencies:* These are our skills and abilities that influence our response to an event.
2. *Encoding strategies:* These are the filters that affect how we perceive and categorize experiences.
3. *Expectancies:* Different learning experiences lead to different expectations for future events.
4. *Personal values:* Our thoughts about priorities shape our decisions and actions.
5. *Self-regulatory systems:* These are the plans, goals, and strategies that influence our actions.

The continuum inherent in each of these variables has an important implication for personality. How we behave in a given situation has a great deal to do with our belief in being able to influence the world around us. Bandura (1997) believes that self-efficacy is a crucial element of personality. Self-efficacy is the belief about one's ability to perform behaviors that should lead to the expected and desired outcome. The cognitive variables mentioned above are useful in considering the reciprocal relationship between our thoughts and our personality.

Humanistic Perspective

Humanistic theory emerged during the 1950s and was somewhat of a response and a reaction to the psychodynamic and behavior theories. Many critics, concerned about technology's threat to human values, argued that both schools of thought viewed people as helpless pawns controlled by their environment or their past. Humanistic psychology developed as a group of related theories emphasizing the capacity for self-direction and became known as the "third force" in psychology. Humanistic psychologists are interested in issues important to human existence, such as love, creativity, and personal growth.

Humanistic theorists have an optimistic view of human nature. In contrast to most psychodynamic and behavioral theorists, humanistic theorists believe that (a) human nature includes an innate drive toward personal growth; (b) individuals have the freedom to chart their own course of action regardless of the environment; and (c) people are largely conscious and rational beings who are not dominated by unconscious motivations. The humanistic approach definitely provides a perspective on personality different from either the psychodynamic or behavioral approaches (Weiten and Lloyd, 2003).

Carl Rogers (1980), a leading humanistic psychologist, was one of the founders of the human potential movement. He based his work on extensive therapeutic work with his clients and believed that a person's perceived reality is more important than absolute reality. Hence, the emphasis on self-concept and how what a person believes is possible to accomplish is of utmost value. Essentially, human behavior is the goal-directed attempt by individuals to satisfy their needs as they experience them.

Rogers mainly saw personality in terms of one construct: the self. He believed that self-concept develops from interactions with the significant people in a child's environment while growing up. As children become aware of themselves, they automatically develop a need for positive regard and acceptance. Rogers stressed the subjective nature of the developing self-concept and concluded that many people have problems because their beliefs are not consistent with their actual experience. Rogers used the term *incongruence* to refer to that disparity. To put it more plainly, many people's self-concept is inaccurate. When someone has developed a poor self-concept, it may be a case of mistaken identity. Rogers, a proponent of unconditional positive regard in therapy, believed that unconditional love from parents fosters congruence and that conditional love fosters incongruence.

Biological Perspective

In the fifth century B.C., Hippocrates, the Greek physician considered to be the pioneer of modern medicine, described four temperaments that he believed were linked to various bodily fluids. The sanguine temperament was optimistic and energetic, the melancholic was moody and withdrawn, the choleric was irritable and impulsive, and the phlegmatic was calm and slow. However quaint this theory now seems, Hippocrates anticipated modern linkages of biochemistry with behavior and described types of people as familiar today as they were in ancient times.

Today, the rapid increase in knowledge about brain functioning and genes provides more substantial scientific evidence for the biological basis of personality. Numerous studies of twins reared together or apart have shown clear evidence that genetics plays a part in personality. There is considerable anecdotal evidence of twins reared apart who, meeting as adults, discover amazing similarities. According to a number of studies, overall genetic influences account for anywhere between 25 percent and 50 percent of the differences in personal characteristics in the general population.

But you may not want to jump to the conclusion that heredity is more important than environment. Consider that there are also studies of twins and others in adoptive families that have shown that people who grow up together do not strongly resemble one another in personality, whether they are biologically related or not. Perhaps children in the same home may be treated quite differently because of differences in gender and birth order, influencing parents' approaches to child rearing.

Why does the shared pool of genes together with a common environment have so little effect on siblings' personalities? It could be that each child experiences the same home environment somewhat differently. This tends to support that each child is unique. As a result, it makes more sense to speak of the nature-nurture issue as nature via (through) nurture rather than nature versus nurture (Atwater and Duffy, 1999).

Exploring Psychological Types

Whatever you believe about how you have been influenced by the theories discussed so far, it is valuable to be aware of them. Understanding the interaction of the forces these theories discuss is important because your personality has an impact on most of your life decisions. Personality is often the basis for making connections in our relationships and in choosing careers.

In this section, we explore the elements of personality and the psychological types that are the underlying indicators of personality. There are a number of paradigms (models) used to discuss types of people, depending on which book you consult, with various resulting categories. The different classifications represent numerous areas in the study of human behavior that have been found useful for exploring types of people. For example, Virginia Satir (1972) describes placaters, blamers, computers, and distracters in her counseling and family therapy. In the field of education, D. A. Kolb (1984) introduces the categories of accommodator, diverger, assimilator, and converger in discussing the different styles of learning. William Sheldon's somatotype theory (1954) states that each individual has a distinct body type—endomorph, mesomorph, or ectomorph—that is associated with specific personality characteristics. Think of types as a subset of personality. An awareness of types facilitates understanding how personality influences behavior. The main message, though, is that having information about personality types can enable you to be more accepting of the behavior of others and to become more flexible in your own.

Let's look at a few of the modern-day versions of different personality types. There are a variety of personality tests, but the Myers-Briggs Type Indicator (MBTI) is probably one of the most extensively known. It has been increasingly used in a number of settings. A "well-person" instrument, the MBTI is used for team building and conflict reduction in business and education. It is based on the theory of C. G. Jung's psychological types. Through the use of a psychometric questionnaire, one can determine a person's Jungian type.

The test is a composite of the scores on a continuum of four different dichotomies. (Portions of the following descriptions are indebted to *A Guide to the Development and Use of the Myers-Briggs Type Indicator,* Myers and Myers, 1985.)

Extroversion (E) Versus Introversion (I) People who prefer extroversion tend to focus on the outer world of people and the external environment. They need to experience the world to understand it and thus tend to like action. They communicate energy and enthusiasm and respond quickly without long pauses to think. They seek out groups and prefer face-to-face over written communication. At work, they are good at greeting people and they like variety and action. They like to learn a new task by talking it through with someone.

Introverts tend to be more interested and comfortable when their work requires a good deal of their activity to take place quietly inside their heads. They like to understand the world before experiencing it, and so they often think before acting. They like quiet for concentration and can work on one project for a long time without interruption. They are interested in the idea behind the job and may prefer to learn by reading rather than talking or experiencing.

Sensing (S) Versus Intuition (N) One way to learn things is to use your eyes, ears, and other senses to tell you what is happening. If you are a sensing type, you like to use and work with facts. Sensing types tend to accept and work with what is given and therefore are realistic and practical. They like established ways of doing things and reach a conclusion step-by-step. They like to work steadily with a realistic idea of how long it will take to do the job.

The other way to learn is through intuition, which shows you the meanings, relationships, and possibilities that extend beyond the facts. If you like using intuition, you are good at seeing the big picture, new possibilities, and new ways of doing things. Intuitive types value imagination and inspiration. At work, they tend to focus on how things could be improved. They work in bursts of energy powered by enthusiasm, with slack periods in between.

Thinking (T) Versus Feeling (F) One way to make decisions is through your thinking. People with a preference for thinking seek an objective standard of truth. They predict the logical consequences of any particular choice or action. They

are frequently good at analyzing what is wrong with something. In communication, they prefer to be brief and concise, and they consider emotions and feelings only as cognitive data to weigh in the formula. At work, they tend to be firm and tough-minded and are able to reprimand or fire people when necessary.

The other way to decide is through your feelings. This means making decisions based on values, not necessarily emotions. When making a decision for yourself, you ask how much you care, or how much personal investment you have, for each of the alternatives. Those with a preference for feeling like dealing with people and tend to be sympathetic, appreciative, and tactful. When communicating, they prefer to be sociable and friendly and are convinced by personal information. They like harmony on the job and will work to get it.

Judgment (J) Versus Perception (P) Those with a judging attitude tend to live in a planned, orderly way, wanting to regulate life and control it. Judging doesn't mean being judgmental, but refers to the fact that you like to make decisions, come to closure, and then carry on. People with a preference for judging usually are structured and organized. They dislike surprises and want advance warning. They communicate results and achievements and like to talk about purpose and directions. They work best when they can plan the job and follow the plan.

Those who prefer a perceptive process when dealing with the outer world like to live in a flexible, spontaneous way. People with a preference for perceiving seek to understand life rather than control it. They prefer to stay open to experience, enjoying and trusting their ability to adapt to the moment. In communicating, they present their views as tentative and modifiable and they talk about options and opportunities. At work, they start too many projects and have difficulty finishing them, although they get a lot accomplished at the last minute under pressure of a deadline.

In her book *Gifts Differing* (1989), Isabel Myers-Briggs discusses the benefits of understanding that each personality type has something valuable to offer. The more you can appreciate the fact that each person's style of being is useful in some context, the more you can be accepting of yourself and others. Each of us has a vastly different way of experiencing the world at times, and the more you learn about those differences, the better you will be able to communicate. Realizing that each person's type has a gift with it can also help you become more willing to be flexible in learning to stretch your own style of being.

Personality Style: Self-Assessment

The personality matrix (see diagram) will help you further assess your personality and explore your style and preferences. The purpose of working with this matrix is to better understand your own behavior, appreciate individual differences, learn about the style of others, and learn where further development would be useful. Taking the full Myers-Briggs test may be valuable at some point in your life, and you may want to take advantage of the opportunity if it is available. But, since it might not be an option for some people, here is a diagram/form that is a simple and easy-to-use method for doing a self-assessment. There are a number of different characteristics that could be used in developing a personality chart or assessment tool. Over the years, I have seen numerous variations of personality self-tests. Some use symbols (different colors) and/or metaphors (different animals). The diagram presented here is a composite of some of those variations. These categories provide a basis for discussion and further exploration of the implications of personality for human relations.

How to Determine Your Style   The horizontal axis represents the continuum of behavior between dominant/assertive (1.00) and easygoing/reflective (4.00). In assessing where you are on that continuum, consider the point you choose will indicate how you are, **in general,** across all situations. Let 1.00 or 4.00 indicate the extremes of the continuum of your most preferred/consistent style. The various degrees of representation of each style are then indicated by a number along that axis between 1.00 and 4.00. You may act differently at times—depending on the context and the situation—but you probably have a pretty good idea of which style you prefer. Do you tend to be more outgoing or more reserved? Where would you place yourself on the continuum? Put an **X** on that spot that represents your self-assessment and put it on one side or the other of the midpoint. Even if you are fairly well balanced in your approach to others and the world, it is necessary

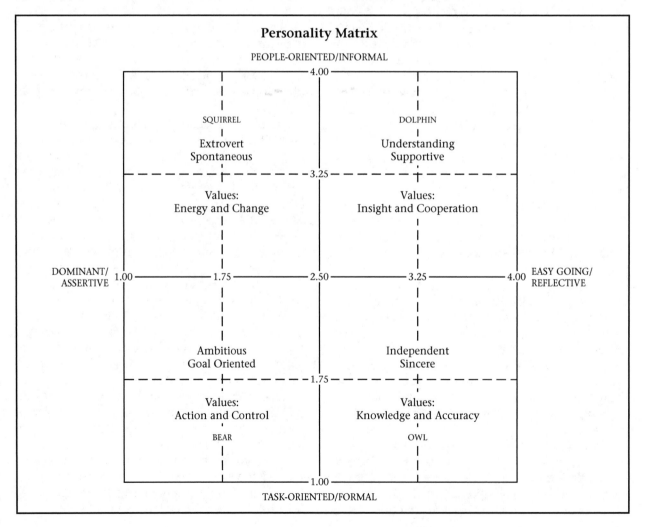

Personality Matrix

PEOPLE-ORIENTED/INFORMAL

	4.00	
SQUIRREL		DOLPHIN
Extrovert Spontaneous		Understanding Supportive
	3.25	
Values: Energy and Change		Values: Insight and Cooperation

DOMINANT/ASSERTIVE   1.00 —— 1.75 —— 2.50 —— 3.25 —— 4.00   EASY GOING/REFLECTIVE

Ambitious Goal Oriented		Independent Sincere
	1.75	
Values: Action and Control		Values: Knowledge and Accuracy
BEAR		OWL
	1.00	

TASK-ORIENTED/FORMAL

for the using this assessment tool to put the mark on one side or the other of the vertical axis.

Now do the same for the people-oriented/informal and task-oriented/formal continuum. On the vertical axis line, place an **X** representing your usual style of relating. Do you tend to be more people-oriented or more task oriented? Remember, the informal/formal continuum has little to do with actual dress . . . although it might influence overall appearance. People with a tendency to favor a more formal style are usually interested in structure, organization, and having a plan. Informal style people are more comfortable with being spontaneous, enjoy the unpredictable nature of relationships, and group things in a "pile." Where would you place yourself on that axis/continuum? Having placed an **X** on each axis, you can now determine which quadrant you are in by the point at which they intersect.

Each personality style is a combination of the traits from one end of each of the two continuums. For example, the ***Promoting/Emotive Style*** is a combination of people-oriented/informal characteristics and dominant/assertive characteristics. How well do the words listed for your style describe you? Another method of using the

STYLISTIC DIFFERENCES

	Promoting/Emotive Squirrels	Controlling/Directive Bears	Supportive/Responsive Dolphins	Analytic/Precisive Owls
Measure progress by...	applause—active, dominant feedback from their audience	results; they are goal-oriented	attention; they like to have others stroke them	activity; they keep busy so results will fall into place
Will ask...	"who?" (the personal, dominant question)	"what?" (the results-oriented question)	"why?" (the personal, non-goal question)	"how?" (the technical, analytic question)
Try to save...	effort; they like to take the easy way	time; they are busy and efficient	relationships; friendship means a lot	face; they hate to look bad
Take endorsement from...	social skills; they like to be good at winning people	getting the job done well and on time	friends ("If they still like me, I must be doing it right")	knowledge; they relate to others via information
Rely on the power of...	feeling; they expect their winning ways to carry them	personality; they hope they are strong enough to wing it	acceptance; they rely on their ability to stroke others	expertise; when in doubt, they bring more data
Must be allowed to...	get ahead quickly with a fast-moving challenge	get into competitive situations and try to win	relax and feel good about the people around them	be let off the hook and not feel cornered or pressured
Need leadership that...	inspires them to bigger and better accomplishments	allows them freedom to do things their own way	details specific plans and activities	structures a framework to follow
Need to be given...	some structure within which to reach goals	a position that requires them to rely on cooperation	structure for the goal and methods for the task	some methods for dealing with other people
Need to learn to...	pause, check themselves, count to ten (discipline)	listen to feelings as well as words (humility)	reach for goals (determination)	make decisions without waiting for more data (initiation)
Respond as adults by...	giving personal endorsement and minimizing task problems	expanding task possibilities, clarifying and reasoning out problems	becoming open personally, combining the task with the relationship	giving task endorsement and minimizing interpersonal problems

matrix is to consult the stylistic differences box on the various behavioral preferences and then place an **X** in the appropriate quadrant. You may also want to read ahead and check the more detailed description of the style you selected as being most representative of you.

Promoting/Emotive Style   People with a promoting/emotive style tend to get involved with people in active, rapidly moving situations. They generally like exciting activities of an inspirational nature. Not given to detail analysis, they can make easy generalizations without sufficient pause to gather information. They are usually stimulating people to be with, lively and personable. Socially outgoing and friendly, they tend to be fun-loving and informal people who enjoy being with others. Some people see squirrels as impulsive. Because of their somewhat dramatic nature, they may think aloud in a manner convincing to others, but they may only temporarily convince themselves. Their vigor and excitement can come across as egotism.

In a job setting, people with a promoting/emotive style of behavior generally are eager to please others, especially those who respond to their outgoing ways. They attach themselves to people they admire and want recognition from them. They tend to be imaginative and respond to incentives, wanting to be measured by their personal contribution. They tend to get personally involved with others and sometimes will settle for less than the best to get on to something else, because they frequently like to move rapidly from task to task. Although they may not always like it, they work best in a setting that provides some structure where they can be helped with planning and follow-through, which is unnatural to them.

These people may be seen as trying to sell themselves and their point of view to others. They are viewed as socially outgoing and forceful and may even be perceived as manipulative and as using people. They are aware of and concerned about others' feelings, however, not just their ideas, and they try to include others in their plans and activities. They tend to be open with their feelings and try to be helpful in interpersonal situations. They may try to achieve status and prestige by attaching themselves to people who they believe have those qualities.

People with the promoting/emotive style usually lack concern for details and may move forward too rapidly before completing a task. They may jump to conclusions too rapidly. A more organized approach could make their enthusiasm more effective, because they may appear careless.

Their changeable decisions may have a disrupting effect on those around them. They can be highly competitive, to the point that, if they are thwarted in their efforts, they can chew out other people quite dramatically. They need to learn to work with and through others.

Controlling/Directive Style   People with a controlling/directive style tend to be active, independent, and ambitious, giving an appearance of self-confidence. They tend to take the initiative with other individuals and in groups and enjoy running things, which they do with a "take charge" attitude. They generally are strong-willed and forceful and are willing to confront others about their ideas and attitudes. They usually make decisions easily and sometimes rapidly, having about them a sense of urgency. Because it may be difficult for them to show much feeling, they appear to others to be businesslike and concerned with efficiency. They may resent other people having power over them; they want to run their own lives.

In a job setting, people with a controlling/directive style generally respond to a fast-moving challenge and tend to get bored if they find the pace too slow. They are task oriented and sometimes offend others with their eagerness to get the job done. They want to know what's going on around them, to be "in-the-know," and to help direct the course of the work group. Not having the situation under control makes them tense. They tend to set their objectives and then work toward them without delay. Because they direct their energy toward task results, others tend to accept their authority and leadership.

Others look to them for results but probably not for encouragement, inspiration, or support. They can be demanding at times and may work to meet their own objectives without realizing that their behavior might be irritating to others. They are seen as competent and determined, but at times they push too hard and are critical of others for not responding. They are likely to want to get the job done first before taking time to work on interpersonal relationships.

People with a controlling/directive style tend to lack patience and may not find it rewarding to work with the same problems over a long period of time. They may need to strengthen their ability to listen to others and recognize the importance of feelings and attitudes as well as logic. Their need for personal success may limit their ability to cooperate with others to accomplish organizational objectives. They will be more effective if they remember that they can come on strong with others and that their behavior can be overwhelming at times.

Supportive/Responsive Style People with a supportive/responsive style tend to be perceived as casual and likable people who try to minimize interpersonal conflict. Though they are responsive to people, they generally let others take the initiative in social situations. They find it difficult to turn down a request because they want to be helpful, even if they must subordinate their interest to the interests of others. Their understanding and friendly approach to people make them nonthreatening and easy to be with. Usually not highly competitive people, they don't impose themselves on others to try to convince others of their point of view. They tend to be more concerned about the feelings of others and their relationship with them than they are about logic. Because they are unpretentious people, they tend to be permissive with others.

In a job setting, people with a supportive/responsive style of behavior are generally cooperative and willing to be of service to others. They tend to work through a structure to prevent interpersonal misunderstandings and, therefore, accept supervision readily. They try to please others by doing what is expected of them. They like reassurance that they are doing well and respond to the personal attention they get from superiors. Because they don't like to hurt others or be disliked, they sometimes withhold unpleasant information. They frequently welcome direction from others to overcome their natural desire to continue to work with what is familiar to them. If they believe that their ideas can benefit others, they will put them forth in a nonthreatening manner.

They will probably be seen as people who seek close, warm, and lasting relationships. They are good listeners who take time with people and help them relax and be at ease. They extend themselves to others and are accepting of different styles of people, partly because they need to be liked by them. Responsive to praise, they may be too eager to please, pretending to consent to and agree with people even though they disagree and don't intend to comply. They usually are sensitive to others' feelings and try to keep from hurting them.

People with the supportive/responsive style tend to lack interest in planning and goal setting and may need structuring and specific descriptions of the activity expected of them. They expend effort to be liked, but they will be more effective as they apply open and honest feedback to the job to be done. There are probably times when more

open and honest feedback to others would benefit themselves and others. They may need to learn to stand up for their ideas, although their likable style will undoubtedly be a benefit to them.

Analytic/Precise Style People with an analytic/precise style tend to take a problem-solving approach to situations, oriented more toward ideas and concepts than toward feelings. They prefer study and analysis to immediate action and appear to be thoughtful, perhaps even hesitant. With their restrained and unassuming ways, they tend to be a steadying influence in a group setting. Deliberate and nonaggressive, they usually wait for others to come to them rather than offering their opinion. They typically want to collect a great many facts and opinions before making a decision. Consulting with others seems to suit their serious and precise manner. Others may perceive them as academic and as taking themselves very seriously.

In a job setting, people with an analytic/precise style generally take an orderly, systematic approach. Detailed and thorough people, they usually like things to be rational and well organized. They are likely to pause until they are sure the task is clear, then work at it with persistence, conscientiousness, and industriousness. Well-established rules and procedures create an environment in which these people's methodical effort will be most effective. They may become tense when surrounded by confusion or ambiguity and perhaps even become immobilized. Because they are not likely to thrive on hard competition, they more naturally move to an advisory role. Their steady and quiet manner will probably cause others to look to them for advice.

These people are probably seen as hesitant in relationships, not readily taking risks or trusting others. Though they tend not to initiate relationships, others seek them out because they are good listeners, quiet, and nonthreatening. They tend not to seek personal recognition, but instead use their ability as problem solvers to establish and build relationships. They usually wait until they are sure of their ground before they offer opinions. Though they appear calm and reasonable, they can be tough and arbitrary when tensions are high. But they probably prefer to avoid interpersonal confrontations and conflict.

People with the analytic/precise style tend to be unable to be casual in interpersonal situations and therefore may be perceived as aloof or stuffy. They can get too involved with analysis, seeking more data when it may be time for action. They sometimes need to look more at the forest and less at the trees by establishing overall priorities and not getting distracted by details. They could probably be more effective if they learned to be less critical and loosen up.

How to Use the Information

As an analogy, think of the different personality styles as representing whole departments in a corporation or company. This is a generalization, but imagine Supportive/Responsives as the staff or personnel office, Promoting/Emotives as the advertising or public relations department, Controlling/Directives as management and supervisors, and Analytic/Precisives as the accountants, data processing unit, or quality control department. Which personality style would run the company? The usual response is the Controlling/Directives, but that isn't necessarily so. Although Controlling/Directives might be good at getting results in some areas, the people who are more likely to be effective in the long run are those who have the greatest flexibility in their style and who can communicate effectively in a number of areas with different types of people. The real leaders of a business are probably the people who can walk among the different departments and speak the language of each. If the Controlling/Directives speak only their own language (results) when talking to the Supportive/Responsives (relationships and cooperation), there might be a breakdown in communication. Likewise, if the Promoting/Emotives (action) go to the Analytic/Precisives (deliberation) and start yelling, "Hurry up and decide," they may not get much response. It is useful in human relations to *learn to speak the language of groups other than your own.*

This type of reasoning is perhaps even more important on the home front when considering

DIFFERENT DRUMS AND DIFFERENT DRUMMERS

If I do not want what you want,
please do not tell me that my want is wrong.
Or if I believe other than you, at least pause before you correct my view.
Or if my emotion is less than yours, or more, given the same circumstances,
try not to ask me to feel more strongly or weakly.
Or yet if I act, or fail to act, in the manner of your design for action, let me be.
I do not, for the moment at least, ask you to understand me.
That will come only when you are willing to give up
changing me into a copy of you.
I may be your spouse, your parent, your offspring,
your friend, or your colleague.

If you will allow me any of my own wants, or emotions,
or beliefs, or actions, then you open yourself,
so that some day these ways of mine might not seem so wrong,
and might finally appear to you as right— for me.
Not that you embrace my ways as right for you,
but that you are no longer irritated or disappointed with me
for my seeming waywardness.
And in understanding me you might come to prize
my differences from you, and, far from seeking to change me,
preserve and even nurture those differences.

Source: David Keirsey and Marilyn Bates, *Please Understand Me: Character and Temperament Types.* P.O. Box 2748, Del Mar, CA, 92014: PN Book Co. Reprinted by permission.

family interactions and domestic relationships. For example, all too often, the stereotypical Controlling/Directive father has kids who represent various styles, none of whom are Controlling/Directive. The father who wants to maintain a caring, loving relationship with his children may need to learn how to communicate in a number of different styles. Likewise, the prudent offspring will practice the necessary skills of putting on their Controlling/Directive suit and speaking the appropriate language (logical, businesslike, goal-oriented) when entering Controlling/Directive country. The very nature of families and the potential for conflict with people who share close living quarters suggest the importance of learning about, appreciating, and adjusting to different personality styles.

Developing Character

Understanding personality and your own personality style is useful in numerous ways. If you always follow your tendencies, however, you may be adversely affected by the limitations of your style. You develop character when you develop the ability to override the tendencies of your personality when necessary. Character

Questions for Critical Thinking

Now that you know about the different personality styles, what is your preferred style, what is your secondary style, and which style do you avoid the most?

Knowing your own style, what would you need to do to be more flexible in connecting with other styles? What approach would you use to communicate with each of the other styles more effectively?

----

development means developing the ability to behave in the manner that is most appropriate to the context, rather than taking the path of least resistance and following your tendencies. There are times when your preferred way of doing things will be disadvantageous. Individuals develop character strengths and limitations just as they have innate personality strengths and limitations. As Taylor Hartman (1987), in his book *The Color Code*, offers: "Character, not personality, is the predominant factor in ultimately determining the quality of our lives. Character is essentially anything we learn to think, feel, or do that is initially unnatural and requires effort to develop. Character is reflected with the changes we make in our values and beliefs throughout our lives" (p. 90).

Regardless of your personality type, your ability to grow and change is directly related to your ability to get yourself to do things that are difficult: usually anything that isn't your preferred way of being!

Given the benefits of developing strength of character, it is important to have some idea of how to go about accomplishing that in a conscious manner. There are a number of factors affecting character development. What follows are the components of character development and some suggestions from Hartman (1987).

Identify Positive Life Principles: There are universal truths that affect all people, such as the importance of being honest, being able to love and be loved, and having a sense of purpose and meaning in life. Many of us have our own truths, which may or may not be useful, that have nothing to do with universal truths and are not necessarily applicable to all people. It is essential to incorporate universal truths in developing positive life principles.

Accept the Concept of Free Will: If free will were not at the core of our very existence, we would be subject to the limitations of our innate personality from birth. Developing character is the process whereby we can balance our personality.

Pay Attention to the Influence of Others: We have all heard about the importance of being a good model for those whom we are trying to influence. Actions do speak louder than words. We also need to notice whom we choose to be with and who our role models are. We are all affected by our family and friends, and influence can be bidirectional. Choose to be with people who will help you to be the person you want to be.

After considering the factors involved in character development, it is time to apply the steps that lead to greater strength and ability. The character-building process requires us to do the following:

1. Identify healthy life principles.
2. Accept them into our lives.
3. Commit to consistently living them.
4. Share them with others.

This information can be useful in beginning to develop your own guidelines for how to build greater strength of character. You may know someone you admire for her ability to do what is necessary, even when that requires doing something that is difficult or unpleasant. More than likely, she didn't become that way overnight. Developing character requires awareness, dedication, and commitment to an ongoing process. The benefits are worth it, though. When you, as well as others, know that you can be counted on to hang in there and do the right thing when the chips are down, your self-concept and human relations will improve.

Principle-Centered Lives

Stephen R. Covey has written an excellent book entitled *The Seven Habits of Highly Effective People* (1989). It is a valuable resource for learning

> ## ▶ Questions for Critical Thinking
>
> *What could you do to develop greater strength of character? What principles or habits do you most need to apply? What would be different if you did?*
>
> _____
>
> _____
>
> _____
>
> _____
>
> _____
>
> _____
>
> _____
>
> _____
>
> _____
>
> _____
>
> _____

strategies for putting your life in order and living by principles that can guide you through any number of situations. Putting the principles into effect requires a commitment to developing character. Part of that incorporates the strength to examine your beliefs and make a paradigm shift when necessary. A *paradigm* is a map or mental representation through which we understand the world. Paradigms are assumptions about how things work that are usually not questioned, whether they work or not. For example, some people think that blaming others is the way to get them to change.

All the effort or attitude adjustment in the world won't make a difference if your original paradigm is incorrect, which is why it is important to know when there is a need for a paradigm shift. Remember how long it took for some people to accept the fact that the Sun was the center of the universe or that the Earth actually was round?

The *Seven Habits* that Covey writes about have their origin in years of teaching and consulting, as well as a 1976 research study conducted by Covey as he reviewed the success literature of our country's 200-year history. Covey's purpose was to identify the major determinants of success as viewed by the important writers of the day. I am indebted to the *Teacher's Guide from the Covey Leadership Center* (1991) for the following information.

During the first 150 years of the nation's history, the focus in the success literature was almost exclusively on character. Character in this context meant such traditional traits as industry, thrift, commitment, courage, service to others, honesty, consideration, and patience.

Then, a marked shift occurred. The focus for the next 50 years changed from character to personality. The personality ethic teaches that techniques can be mastered quickly and will lead to immediate results. Skill mastery is seen as the key to success with others. People end up trying to talk themselves out of problems they've behaved themselves into. Covey concluded that efforts to develop the personality component are neither good nor bad in theory. The main factor is whether the personality is firmly connected to a character base. If not, people who attempt to improve in the personality department will become adept only at manipulating others.

This concept can be visualized as an iceberg. The character of an individual, the great unseen mass below the surface, is the base or foundation on which one then builds one's social skills.

However, attempting a quick fix in the personality department is analogous to cutting off the tip of the iceberg and setting it adrift. That makes one susceptible to the ever-changing currents of society's fads.

This research led Covey to the underlying premise on which the *Seven Habits* are based: that, in the course of human development, some things must come before other things. We can't run before we can walk. A house isn't framed until the foundation is laid. It is difficult, if not impossible, to work successfully with others if one has not achieved a certain level of self-mastery.

The maturity continuum that is necessary for development is characterized by three distinct stages: dependence, independence, and finally, interdependence. The lowest level of maturity, dependence, means you need others to get what you want. The independent state means a person is basically self-reliant. The highest form of maturity, interdependence, means you have the capacity to work cooperatively with others, particularly when stress and pressure are present.

The Seven Habits of Highly Effective People is divided into three parts. The first three habits develop independence or self-mastery. To succeed in this area, a person must achieve a private victory over old habits and old patterns. The person can then choose to achieve a public victory, which is developed by the next three habits. A public victory enables a person to overcome a previous habit pattern when confronted with a difficult circumstance, such as lashing out at others under stress. Keep in mind that public victory does not mean a victory over others. It means a victory in achieving a mutually beneficial solution that represents a win-win outcome for both parties. The seventh habit is the habit of self-renewal and continuous improvement, and maintains the other six habits over time.

Habit 1: Be Proactive. When we are proactive, we accept responsibility for who we are, what we have, and what we do. When we are proactive, we focus our energy on what we can influence rather than what we

> **"***Character is what you are; reputation is what others think you are. Reputation is from other people; character is in you.***"**
>
> *Thomas Jefferson*

can't. Proactive choices are guided by values. Think about taking action rather than just reacting to the events that occur in life.

Habit 2: Begin with the End in Mind. All things are created twice: first mentally, then physically. Beginning with the end in mind is a process of rescripting. A personal mission statement aids in rescripting and sets an overall purpose for our lives. Be clear about what you want to accomplish before you start out.

Habit 3: Put First Things First. We gain control of time and events by seeing how they relate to our mission. The first principle of organization is scheduling. Keep things prioritized and don't get distracted by the things that seem urgent but really aren't important in reaching your true goals.

Habit 4: Think Win-Win. The most mature attitude in a relationship is "win-win or no deal." Maturity may be defined as courage balanced with consideration. Helping the other person to accomplish his or her objectives will benefit you in the long run.

Habit 5: Seek First to Understand, Then Be Understood. To understand another person, we must be willing to be influenced. By seeking to understand, we gain influence in a relationship. Empathy is listening with the eyes and the heart. When someone truly feels listened to, he or she is much more inclined to be receptive to new ideas.

Habit 6: Synergize. Synergy means one plus one equals something more than two. Synergy is the process that reveals the third alternative. The first step in taking advantage of differences is to respect them and appreciate them.

Habit 7: Sharpen the Saw. Take care of your tools and practice using them. We sharpen the saw in four areas: physical, mental, spiritual, and social-emotional. The key to sharpening the saw is doing little things consistently. Private victories precede public victories. This is the habit of using and improving the other habits.

ATTITUDE

Watch your thoughts; they become words.
Watch your words; they become actions.
Watch your actions; they become habit.

Watch your habits; they become character.
Watch your character; it becomes your destiny.

Accountability

There are some people who seem to be forever having unfortunate things happen to them. They go through life with a "poor me" attitude and wonder why bad things keep happening. We all have unavoidable difficulties at times, but some people seem to drive miles out of their way to find troubles that they might have avoided. Even though they ignored at least three detour signs, seldom do they accept any responsibility for the problems they run into. It is usually someone or something else that is to blame for their having run into a ditch.

One way to improve ourselves and help life go more smoothly is to explore what contributes to our self-defeating behaviors. We can interrupt old patterns by paying attention to ways we may be creating situations. Do you have a little voice in your head that occasionally says, "No, stop. Don't do that. Go back"? When you hear that voice, do you tell it to shut up? (You may later recognize that voice as the same one that comes back and says, "I told you so.") Interrupting the cycle of being a victim is sometimes simply a matter of noticing what you are pretending not to know!

Playing the Victim Role

Here are some examples of how people set themselves up for unfortunate situations. Have you ever played the "Let's see how far I can drive on fumes" game? The needle on your fuel gauge has been on empty for days, but when you run out of gas, who gets blamed? Isn't it always the fault of the car, the gas station, or whoever drove the car last? There are a number of variations on the theme of "what you are pretending not to know." These can be situations in which you were ignoring the obvious outcome of a preventable situation. You wouldn't go out and stand in the middle of the street, even if you were in the crosswalk, and then blame the car if you got run over. Some people do the equivalent of that by standing in the way of oncoming trouble and not doing anything to get out of the way.

Have you ever tried to carry too many things at once, knowing full well that you were likely to drop something? When that happened, did you feel like a victim and try to plead "poor me"? Sometimes, people truly are victims, such as during floods, hurricanes, or earthquakes. However, most of the problems we face are more like trying to carry an extra bag of groceries into the house even though we suspect, from the ripping sound, that it will tear and cause an accident.

ELEPHANT IN THE BOTTLE

Given that information, imagine a circle representing all the accidents that happen to you in life. About 90 percent of that circle would be accidents to which you contributed in some degree while playing the victim game; only about 10 percent would involve being a real victim. People continue playing the victim role by denying any accountability for their predicaments. This continues the cycle of self-defeating behavior. It is what I call the *Elephant-in-the-Bottle Technique.* Trying to take all of the negative events that you had some part in and cram them into the area that constitutes being a real victim is like trying to put an elephant in a bottle. You'll notice that 90 percent doesn't readily fit into 10 percent. It takes a great deal of effort to ignore your own contribution to unpleasant events. Rather than disavow any knowledge or understanding of the process, one way to begin being less of a victim in life is to become more accountable for your actions.

It is important to make the distinction between responsibility and accountability. Just because something bad happens to you doesn't mean that you are responsible for that event or that you caused it to occur. But if you are in the wrong place at the wrong time, you are most certainly accountable for the outcome of saying the wrong thing in that situation. You don't go into a Hell's Angels bar and yell nasty things about bikers. You aren't responsible for getting beaten up—you didn't make them do it to you—but you certainly are accountable for what you yelled.

Why do people play the victim game? There are a number of payoffs. The biggest is getting to be right! It is amazing how far people will go to be right. Some people push things so far they get to be dead right. Have you observed the absurd behavior of some motorists on the highway who

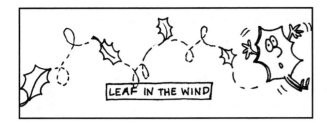

LEAF IN THE WIND

risk having a traffic accident because they would rather be right than safe? Other payoffs include sympathy, attention, and denial of any accountability. If you didn't have anything to do with what happened, how can you do anything about it? This is what I call the *Leaf-in-the-Wind Theory.*

Some people act as if they have to go through life just being blown about by the winds of change. They act as if they aren't in control of their own lives. If you think that way, you prevent yourself from learning anything about how incidents occur. While avoiding accountability, you also limit your ability to change or grow. If you don't admit having anything to do with repeatedly ending up in problem situations, then how are you ever going to avoid them in the future? That's part of what contributes to the ongoing pattern of self-defeating behavior. On the other hand, playing the victim game prevents you from taking credit for your successes because, you rationalize, they may have just been something that happened to you.

Playing the 100 Percent Accountable Game

What if you decided to act as if you were accountable for everything that happened to you? If you accept that there are no accidents, whether that's true or not, you can ask yourself a different set of questions when life's little bummers come along. The victim asks "Why me?" and then gets the usual payoffs. Playing the accountable game means you might ask yourself, "What did I do that might have made this situation happen, and what can I learn about myself?" The payoffs are entirely different now. You can learn about possible mistakes, and you can be responsible and gain more self-respect. For instance, have you ever had a friend who made a mistake but said, "No, it wasn't me. I didn't have anything to do with it. It's not my fault"? If you know your friend did have something to do with what occurred, how do you feel about him? Compare him to the friend who says, "It was me, and I messed up. I'm sorry. What can I do to make it up to you?" You may be angry with her, but don't you also feel more respect for her because she took responsibility?

This is what I call the *Captain-of-Your-Ship Theory.* You may end up on the rocks or get beached sometimes because you didn't read the charts right, but if you had something to do with getting there, the good news is that you can do something about avoiding that situation in the future. You can ask yourself, "How did I contribute to this happening? What was I pretending not to know? What was the payoff and how can I change that to something positive?" Only use this concept if it is useful, though. Don't turn it into another version of being a victim. Being accountable doesn't mean beating yourself up every time something unfortunate happens. The message is about paying attention to what you can learn so that you can avoid the situation in the future.

Belief Systems

There are some situations in which the accountable game isn't appropriate. There are stories in the newspaper every day about incidents in which there were victims of violent crimes. There are national disasters that leave large numbers of people homeless. In those situations, it would not be useful to ask yourself how you might have contributed to the event's happening. This is especially true in the case of children who come from homes where there was abuse. Children don't choose to be mistreated, and they usually have nothing to do with their situations.

Therefore, it is important to examine your beliefs about why bad things happen. There are people who have been truly victimized. Yet, when traumatic things happen, they still need to allow themselves to heal at some point. Over the years, I've learned some valuable information about how people do that. It seems to come down to a few basic ideas. Whether working from a background in philosophy, psychology, or religion, almost all healing agents help people who have experienced trauma to "reframe" the event by giving it different meaning and less emphasis.

There are a number of ways to reframe a given event, but the common element seems to be helping the person regain some sense of personal power and control. One method for accomplishing that is for the person who has experienced a traumatic event to ask himself or herself the following questions:

What is the lesson for me from this event?
How can I give this situation meaning?

CASE STUDIES AND STUDENT STORIES

Nancy and Emily were sisters, and even though they were very different in personality, they were close and hung around together. Nancy was a couple of years younger than Emily, but it was more than age difference that seemed to define them. Growing up in their family they experienced many of the same life events, but they always seemed to have their own way of interpreting those experiences.

When Nancy and Emily were entering adolescence, a series of unfortunate events struck their family. Their older sister, who was years apart from them, died of a sudden illness. Their mother developed a stomach ulcer from the stress, and their father had what some called a mental breakdown.

The trauma that was caused by these events was more than Nancy could handle, and she began to withdraw. She blamed her mother for everything as a way of dealing with her sadness. Nothing made any sense.

Emily, on the other hand, seemed to be able to realize that there was nothing her mother could have done to prevent their sister's death. She was deeply saddened that her mother had an ulcer, and she knew that her father's breakdown was due to his own inability to deal with the loss and sadness.

Both girls had the same parents and were raised in the same family, but each saw the unfolding life circumstances in a totally different way. Eventually, their versions of life stories took on different meanings, and each carried these stories into her marital relationship.

Every time Nancy would enter into a relationship, she would find it necessary to demean her mother to her future mate. In her mind, the story was bonding for the couple, and sharing her pain made her feel like they were closer. Blaming others seemed to be comforting.

This dysfunctional dynamic continued for nearly 20 years until the day came that she heard her daughter blaming her for the fact that she didn't make it into a particular college. She stopped short when she realized that history was repeating itself. She was devastated by the blame that was being laid on her, and as she worried she began to think about what she could do to change things in the future.

Emily, on the other hand, always introduced her prospective mates to her mother by describing fond memories and paying her loving compliments. Emily eventually married and had two children. She was thrilled when one day she heard her son telling a friend about how proud he was of his mom. She sometimes wondered about how she and her sister had come to such different places in life. (*by D. Juanita Woods*)

These questions require people to think about things on a different level and perhaps to discover a deeper meaning for the events in their lives. They also provide the opportunity to clarify values and to consider one's purpose in life.

For those people who have been fortunate enough not to have had any traumatic events in their lives, or who have not had any major problems to deal with so far, this information may not seem relevant now. Just remember, it is almost inevitable that, as you grow older, you will have to deal with loss or disappointment on some level. For that reason, it is important to learn how to deal with difficult times as well as how to appreciate the good in life.

According to figures from a number of sources, including the National Institute of Mental Health, in any class of 25 or more students, there are likely to be three or four people who have been sexually abused in some manner or who have been traumatized because of incest or rape. There will also be people dealing firsthand with the effects of drug or alcohol abuse. There will be even more people dealing with the impact of having grown up in homes where there were such problems. Therefore, the information on healing is important not only from the standpoint of personal application, but also for developing understanding and empathy for those with whom you may be acquainted who have to deal with those types of problems.

Remember that there are real victims, and these people didn't have anything to do with what happened to them. Even with traumatic events, however, there may be a chance for you to learn, grow, and change by asking yourself how you can give some meaning to what happened.

What lesson can you learn from the event? The woman who started MADD (Mothers Against Drunk Driving) is an example of someone who took a tragedy—her child was killed by a drunk driver—and said, "I've got to give this some meaning." She channeled all the energy from her anger and pain into doing something constructive. At times, you will need to consider the question of how you are going to give meaning to something that makes no sense at all. How are you going to derive some valuable or positive lesson from something that may have been really traumatic?

To use this concept, it is important to think about your beliefs and life philosophy in general. Why do you believe what you believe about birth, death, and life? Why do bad things happen to people? For some, considering why any particular event occurs may border on religious or spiritual beliefs. At this point, I want to make it clear that I'm not going to take a particular position. That is mainly because I think considering how to give meaning to a traumatic event can be useful

regardless of your beliefs. It may even be complementary. The main question to consider about any of your beliefs is: Does it work for you, and is it useful for helping yourself or someone else in the healing process? It is also interesting to consider that your religious beliefs, or lack of them, are some of the most important factors determining how you live and how you give meaning to life. People have been trying to make sense of the unknown for centuries, and we all need ways of thinking that will help us feel better about traumatic events.

Finally, however you decide to heal from painful events in life, it is important to remember that one way to prevent becoming a victim in situations where things might have been avoided is to explore your beliefs about accountability. When you take charge of your life and pay attention to what you previously pretended not to know, you can eliminate some unpleasant events. An added benefit is that being more accountable for your actions allows you to take credit for the positive events that occur in your life.

CHAPTER REVIEW

Comfort Zones

We sometimes limit ourselves in what we think we can accomplish. Playing it safe and restricting ourselves may be due to either a fear of success or a fear of failure. Some people might feel threatened by our attempts to change and grow. The "crabs" may attempt to discourage any expansion of our comfort zone. Taking risks by taking on new challenges is an important part of the comfort zone aerobics that are necessary to confront fears and increase self-esteem.

Thinking Patterns

Some people see the world only in terms of black and white. Personal growth and development requires that you begin to see more of the gray areas. Seldom are the answers to life's problems on one end of the continuum or the other. Increased tolerance for ambiguity in your own thinking leads to greater flexibility in dealing with others who have different views.

Assertiveness

Before learning assertiveness skills, it is important to examine your beliefs about what it means to

get what you want, what you think will happen if you are assertive, and whether you feel deserving. Some people believe that the squeaky wheel gets the grease; others think that the more they ask, the less they get. Being assertive means standing up for yourself without taking away others' rights. Part of learning appropriate new behaviors comes from understanding the balance between being aggressive and being passive. To be more assertive, you can analyze the behavior of others, analyze your own behavior, rehearse being assertive, and start to practice assertiveness. All are easier when you watch your self-talk and use more "I" statements to describe your desires and needs.

Personality

A number of preferences and tendencies contribute to and make up your personality style. The preferences you have, some innate and some developed, greatly influence the filters through which you experience the world. Each personality type has strengths and weaknesses. Understanding all the variables enhances your ability to improve relationships and communication with others. Understanding and being aware of personality types increases flexibility in your own behavior.

Developing Character

It is important to be able to override your personality style and preference at times. Character is the strength and courage you need to develop to behave in the manner that is most appropriate to the context. Character also means having a set of principles that you adhere to even when it is difficult.

Accountability

Some people play the victim role more than others. One method for decreasing self-defeating behavior is to be more accountable for the outcome of your behavior. There are various ways for you to change your approach in life from one of "Leaf-in-the-Wind" to being "Captain-of-Your-Ship."

Belief Systems

There are real victims, and it is important to understand some of the healing processes necessary for those who have experienced traumatic events. Whether that applies to you or not, understanding these processes will be useful, given the likelihood that someone you know during the course of your lifetime will have to contend with a tragic event. Understanding your own belief system can assist in that process.

SOURCES AND SUGGESTED READINGS

Dyer, Wayne. *You'll See It When You Believe It*. New York: Avon, 1989.

Hartman, Taylor Don. *The Color Code: A New Way to See Yourself, Your Relationships, and Life*. Trabuco Canyon, CA: Taylor Don Hartman, 1987.

James, Muriel, and Dorothy Jongeward. *Born to Win*. New York: Nass Addison Wesley, 1973.

Jeffers, Susan. *Feel the Fear and Do It Anyway*. New York: Ballantine, 1987.

Kroeger, Otto, and Janet Thuiesen. *Type Talk*. New York: Delacorte, 1988.

Maslow, Abraham H. *The Healthy Personality*. New York: Van Nostrand Reinhold, 1969.

Myers-Briggs, Isabel. *Gifts Differing*. Palo Alto, CA: Consulting Psychologists Press, 1989.

Satir, Virginia. *Your Many Faces*. Berkeley, CA: Celestial Arts, 1978.

Viscott, David. *Risking*. New York: Pocket, 1977.

Web Site Resources

Kiersey Temperament Sorter
http://www.ibiblio.org/personality

Psychological Types Profile
http://www.ibilio.org/pub/academic

An excellent Web site that has lots of free personality tests that you can take and score online
http://www.queendom.com/tests

Dedicated to education about human personality, personality differences, and the dynamics of personality development
http://www.members.tripod.com/PersonalityInstitute/Personality I. htm

Reaction and Response—What Do You Think?

Chapter Three   Level I Assignments

In response to the information in the chapter:

1. Who have been the "crabs" in your life? How will you deal with them in the future? What are specific ways that you can challenge your fear of success and your fear of failure? How and in what area of your life will you expand your comfort zone?

2. What did you learn about personality and your particular style? What did you learn from your mother and father about personality style and preference? How do you think your personality developed? What did you learn about the relationship between personality and character?

3. What did you learn about thinking patterns? When have you thought of things in black or white terms? Give an example of a time when you began to realize that the world is more shades of gray. How can you expand your comfort zone by thinking new thoughts?

In response to the class activities, group discussions, and exercises:

1. What are your opinions and reactions?
2. What did you learn or rediscover?
3. How are you going to apply what you learned?

Chapter Three   Level II Assignments

1. To be more assertive, what do you need to do more and what do you need to do less? What are your beliefs about being assertive, and are any of them limiting in some ways? What did you learn about how to be assertive in the appropriate situation?

2. What did you learn from the section on being accountable, as opposed to being a victim? How can you take responsibility for your actions more? What would it take to be more like the captain of your ship? How did this section apply to your life, and what are you going to do in the future?

3. What self-defeating behaviors would you like to stop? What would be different if you did? What would it take to accomplish that? How was the information in this chapter helpful?

Chapter Three   Level III Assignments

1. What are some of the ways in which your perceptions are influenced by attribution theory? Do you have a tendency to excuse your own behavior while holding others accountable?

2. When have you been guilty of the "fatal attribution error"? Where did you get the underlying belief that may have influenced you in the situation?

3. Where (in what situations) could you begin to practice developing the *character* that you would like to build in your relations with others?

II

P A R T

BUILDING TOGETHER

Our relationships with others are affected by how we learn to interact within our family circle.
Photo: David Aronson/Stock Boston

CHAPTER 4

FAMILY INFLUENCES

It had been about 10 years since Rick left home and moved out of state. He was the middle child who had struck out on his own. His older brother, after a stint in the Navy, had returned home to look for a stable job. If he hadn't landed a job with the fire department, he would have made a good cop. Rick's younger brother, the athletic one who had played on all the teams in high school, headed out to Hawaii as soon as possible after graduation. But, after a few years as a surf bum, he returned to the area to successfully take up a job as a salesman. His younger sister, the only girl, was the last one to leave the nest. She was the one most caught in the crossfire when their parents' marriage went south and they decided to split the sheets. She had attended a community college dental assistant program, with hopes of some day becoming a hygienist in order to have a flexible work schedule. The rest of the family, though, still lived in or around their hometown.

Rick's parents had divorced after about 25 years of marriage. Each had remarried and acquired adult stepchildren. His father had moved out, but his mother remained in the house he had grown up in. Over the course of those years, Rick had always been the one who traveled to stay in touch with the family and to visit for the holidays. It was often quite a chore to get around to all the relatives and in-laws during the course of a visit back "home." This was the first time that his father, Roy, had reciprocated and traveled out-of-state to come and see him on his own turf.

Within minutes of arriving, Roy was making the usual comments about how Rick needed a haircut and how much better he would look if he shaved off his beard. Rick ignored the invitation to take up the old pattern of verbal jousting and led his father on a tour of the new house he had recently built. It was a log cabin home kit that was suitably nestled into the slope of a partially wooded valley. It was a far cry from the neat, orderly neighborhood he had grown up in.

Situated on five acres with a view to the south, it provided privacy but with a sense of warmth and openness. With a full basement and garage under the two-story structure, it was an impressive sight. Rick was proud of his accomplishment, the fulfillment of his dream to escape from Southern California and live in the country. He and his dad made the expected small talk about the construction process as they toured the house. They stood on the deck admiring the view when they had finished. It was then that Rick's dad had turned to him with a quizzical expression and asked, "Tell me, son, how does someone like you get something like this?"

Though it was true that Rick had done his share of acting out during adolescence, he was still taken aback by the comment. The 12 years of maturity he had gained since being booted out of the house enabled Rick to resist the urge to say something snide in return. He had hoped that even if his father hadn't changed during those 12 years, at least he could be different. It was because he wore wire-rimmed glasses—an obvious indication of 1960s "communist tendencies"—that he had been instructed to leave. He didn't want to repeat his father's pattern of intolerance and had invested considerable effort in resolving his own inner conflicts. Years of studying and working as a counselor had paid off, to some degree. Yet, it was still a struggle to hear the intended compliment rather than the actual words his father had spoken. His dad was an expert at conveying the belief that he had expected Rick to be dead or in jail by the time he was 30 years old. Finally, Rick decided to respond to the unspoken message. He turned and simply said, "Thanks, Dad, I'm glad you like it."

Family History

In 1992, Stephanie Coontz wrote *The Way We Never Were,* a book that examined the last two centuries of family life. In her assessment of the last half of the 20th century, she states that the *Ozzie and Harriet* and *Leave It to Beaver* households not only were a thing of the past, but may have never really existed. Many of the television programs of the 1950s were nothing more than advertisements for the way people wished they could be. The media projected fragments of the white middle-class experience onto the general public. Many of those myths distorted the diverse experiences of other groups in America, and they didn't accurately reflect the group they were supposedly portraying.

In 2000, Coontz wrote a new introduction to her book and updated the material while continuing to support many of the conclusions of earlier work. In her original work, Coontz argued against the prevailing attitudes of the early 1990s and countered the notion that all of America's social ills stemmed from abandonment of "traditional" family forms. She suggested that family dilemmas were due to financial inequality and the resulting crisis of caregiving. Also, that simply encouraging everyone to get married was not going to meet the challenges that people faced. In the new introduction, Coontz continues to emphasize the importance of economic factors in considering personal dysfunction rather than family structure.

Coontz provides evidence that social and economic inequality have contributed to the various problems that have had a detrimental effect on the quality of family and community life. She finds hope for the families of today, though, when problems are viewed as one symptom of a larger societal predicament. Although she may tend to focus on economics as the root problem, this is in some ways encouraging, for it means that people have not suddenly and inexplicably "gone bad." They are struggling with serious dilemmas, and although many people make poor choices or don't live up to their highest ideals, they are generally trying to do their best (Coontz, 1992).

Disappointed about the persistence of the myths described in her earlier work, she continues to argue for understanding what is really happening with families because of the necessity of educating our political leaders. Part of the reason for the positive developments in the family of the 1950s was economic and political support rather than family practices. Loans, financial aid, and the G.I. Bill all contributed to the stability of the family. Knowing that there was no golden age of family life could help politicians to deal more effectively with today's problems rather than romanticizing about the "good old days." Families have seldom been economically or socially self-sufficient and have frequently relied on assistance from the government. Contemporary research demonstrates that there is nothing inherently ennobling about *not* receiving aid.

Coontz also counters a number of the present-day beliefs about our problems and their sources. The United States has had the highest homicide rate in the industrial world for almost 150 years, long before the advent of violent video games. Although the murder rate declined by 20 percent between 1990 and 1998, the number of murders covered by network news broadcasts increased by 600 percent. We have a tendency to unfairly blame the latest spate of violent events in our society on divorce, poor parenting, or lack of parental attention. "Similarly, drug abuse was more widespread at the end of the 1890s than at the end of the 1990s, and the rate of alcohol consumption was almost three times higher in the nineteenth century than it is currently. Prostitution and serious sexually transmitted diseases were also more prevalent in America one hundred years ago than they are today" (Coontz, 1997).

Many of the conclusions drawn in the media about the status of marriage and the family are based on distortions of the data. Coontz points this out in a discussion of how the marriage rate is calculated. The rate is based on how many single women over the age of 15 get married each year. But, the median age for marriage has risen from age 20 to almost 25 since the original study was done in 1960. There are many social and cultural consequences of a rising age of marriage, but we can't evaluate these trends realistically if we exaggerate them to suggest that marriage is on the verge of extinction.

Pessimists claim that current trends and alternative lifestyles indicate the collapse of the family system. Optimists believe that we are merely diversifying and creating new types of families. In either case, there has been an idealization of a past that may never have occurred. To say that no easy answers are to be found in the past is not to close off further discussion of family problems but to open it up. To find effective answers to the dilemmas facing modern families, we must reject attempts to recapture family traditions that either never existed or existed in a totally different context. Only when we have a realistic idea of how families have and have not worked in the past can we make informed decisions about how to support families in the present or improve their future prospects (Coontz, 1992, p. 5).

In response to the considerable historical information in *The Way We Never Were*, Coontz had numerous requests to appear on radio and television, and her work was quoted frequently in magazines. As a result, she had the opportunity to discuss a wide variety of topics about family with people from all walks of life. People wanted to know more regarding what history and sociology had to teach about where they had been before, as well as where they had never been. And they wanted to know more about where to go from here. To that end, Coontz followed up with *The Way We Really Are* in 1997. She reiterated that "there never was a golden age of family life, a time when all families were capable of meeting the needs of their members and protecting them from poverty, violence, or sexual exploitation" (p. 57). But, in her follow-up book, she attempted to offer more concrete suggestions about what would be useful in strengthening American families.

The Way We Never Were came out just as the presidential election of 1992 was heating up and "family values" was a hot topic of debate. Each political party spent a great deal of time developing its own definition of the problems society faced due to the perceived decline in the traditional family. In her latest book, Coontz takes the politicians to task for reducing a number of complex issues to a series of sound bites. Each side had its slogans, but spent more time blaming than looking for solutions to what would help families. She doesn't believe the alleged "new consensus" that there has been a collapse in family values. It isn't useful to reduce the problems facing families today to a one-dimensional approach, and Coontz believes that the American public understands the complexity and diversity of family life. She states that what we need is to get down to individual cases, let go of the generalities, build on the strengths that each family has, and offer concrete help to those in need.

Coontz makes it clear that it is time to stop arguing about the relative merits of ideal family types and have a serious discussion about how to build the support systems that modern families need. Some of her suggestions for what would help families, and society in general, are (a) affordable child care, (b) a tax allowance for children that keeps up with inflation, (c) family-friendly work policies that include family leave, (d) job training, (e) stiffer child support enforcement, and (f) a national health insurance program. These types of programs need to be expanded rather than cut back to provide the help that today's families really need (Coontz, 1997).

Many of these suggestions are for programs that are preventative, but we also know how to help families and children who are already in trouble. Coontz takes a balanced approach in declaring that neither the conservative rhetoric of stricter laws and more prisons nor the liberal emphasis on workshops for self-esteem contain all the answers. The first factor in assisting families that are in trouble is to provide another chance to succeed at something that a person has failed at in the past. This could mean receiving education and training, an opportunity to correct a wrong rather than just being punished, and/or concrete aid with the chance to reciprocate. The second factor, strongly supported by developmental psychology, is having just one caring person outside the family willing to get involved in a person's life. Polarized debates over whether to set high standards or foster self-esteem miss the point. What will help families and benefit society is a combination of both (Coontz, 1997).

The problem with the campaign to restore the traditional family is that it keeps people focused on grieving for the past rather than looking for new possibilities in the present. It is also time to plan more effectively for the future. We need to do more of what does work and less of what doesn't. While supporting the programs that increase self-reliance for families, we need to curtail red tape and stop fragmenting services, overloading caseworkers, and hiring bureaucrats or consultants rather than people who will pitch in and really help.

Family Structures

According to the U.S. Census Bureau report entitled *America's Families and Living Arrangements*, family households have traditionally accounted for the majority of all households. In 1970, 81 percent of households were family households.

By 2000, that number had dropped to 69 percent. Another noticeable trend is the decline in the proportion of married-couple households with their own children, from 40 percent of all households in 1970 to 24 percent in 2000. In contrast, the proportion of households that were made up of married couples without children remained relatively stable. An overall trend for the 30 years between 1970 and 2000 was that nonfamily households (a person living alone or one who shares the housing unit with a nonrelative) became more common and family households became less common (U.S. Census Bureau, 2000).

Married couples made up a smaller portion of family households in 2000 than in 1970. Households and families have become smaller, and one-parent families numbered 12 million in 2000. Households with their own children made up only a third of all households, a drop from 45 percent in 1970.

According to the Census Bureau, changes in the number and types of households depend on population growth, shifts in the age and composition of the population, and the decisions individuals make about their living arrangements. Demographic trends in marriage, cohabitation, divorce, fertility, and mortality also influence family and household composition. Additionally, changes in norms, values, laws, and the economy and improvements in the health of the elderly over time can influence people's decisions about how they organize their lives (U.S. Census Bureau, 2000).

Given the changes that society is going through regarding perceptions of the family, how do we reconcile the needs of today's society with the values that the traditional family represented? What do we really think about the family system and structure? What is it that we are looking for in our society that we want the family to provide?

A survey of 400 adults, reported in the *Oregonian* (May 24, 1992), revealed an increased acceptance of new notions of what constitutes a family and what comprises a realistic set of needs and expectations. Three-fourths of respondents said that one family arrangement is as good as another as long as the children are taken care of properly. Nearly two-thirds agreed that the father going to work and the mother staying home with the children is no longer realistic. Three-fourths said that husbands and wives shouldn't stay together just for the sake of the children. Paradoxically, people want the traditional family structure while simultaneously embracing the need for new family systems. And, although the survey is more than 10 years old, the work of Stephanie

Coontz suggests that these trends are accurate today (see the introduction to the 2000 edition of *The Way We Never Were*).

By a wide margin, the survey indicated that people embrace the notion of family. Most would take in an aging parent or an adult child who was experiencing difficulties. Four out of five said their extended family gathers for major holidays and events. In an age when better than half of marriages end in divorce, we still favor two parents raising their children together. This is in direct contrast to the majority of those who work outside the home, who said that they would continue to work even if finances weren't an issue.

With the rise in the number of single-parent and two-career households, almost half of the respondents in the Mass Mutual American Family Values Study done in 1992 said they do not spend enough time with their families. In naming the most important reason for the decline in family values, 35 percent selected "parents having less time to spend with their families." When asked what measures would be "extremely effective" in strengthening family values, 54 percent picked "spending more time with the family." As parents have less time to instill family values, children are left with less desirable models, including television and their peers. Unfortunately, some 79 percent surveyed agree that it takes two paychecks to support a family, and only 27 percent would favor a return to one parent staying home to raise the children. People are united in their perception of the major family problem, but there is no clear solution in sight.

If we are so devoted to the notion of family life, why are we having such difficulty with our ideals? It is an unusual family that hasn't been touched by separation or divorce. Many families have dealt with situations that could only be whispered about a few decades ago. Now people have to openly contend with adultery, homosexuality, cohabitation, babies out of wedlock, and multiple marriages. "It is as if an earthquake shuddered through the American family," says Arlene Skolnick, a research psychologist and professor of human development at the University of California, Berkeley. The traditional family has been buffeted by many changes and challenges over the past three decades. Some of the most significant are:

- Prevalence of divorce and the resulting stepfamilies.
- Entry of women into the workforce and the changing economic picture.

- Decline in fertility rate and subsequent smaller households.
- Increase in single parents.
- Epidemic of child abuse.
- Acceptability of new emotional and sexual bonds of partnership.

In her book *Brave New Families*, sociologist Judith Stacy (1991) reframes the current transformations in a kinder light by stating that today's families are *crafting multiplicity,* a term that indicates the need to handle the chaos of increasingly complex situations involving many variables. Perhaps the time for generalities about good or bad family structures and correct or incorrect parental roles is past. How a family functions is more important than its structure or its formal role.

So what happened? A tremendous wave of change in values and attitudes, for one thing. Americans are, in some ways, far more tolerant of difference today. For example, they marry later and consider parenthood an option rather than an obligation, and they are more egalitarian in their attitudes toward sex roles. Researchers detect more introspection and a greater attentiveness to the emotional quality of relationships.

One change that seems beneficial in response to all of the transitions in society is that we are redefining the term *family.* Family Service America, a network of 300 counseling agencies and educational programs, recently revamped its definition to go beyond blood ties, reflecting how varied households have become. They define family in terms of function, not form. A well-functioning family, they say, provides emotional, physical, and mutual aid to its members. It is intense, intimate, and committed. Apparently, Americans appear to be as deeply committed to marriage and family as ever. A number of different surveys and research sources indicate that *family* is still the deepest single source of satisfaction and meaning in life.

So what does the future hold for the family unit? Based on current trends, the Department of Human Development and Family Sciences at Oregon State University makes the following predictions:

- Couples will be faced with pursuing careers in different geographic locations, and commuter marriages will grow.
- Society will become more accepting of childless marriages.
- Nearly half of all marriages will continue to end in divorce.

> **"***Happiness is a large, close-knit family in another city.***"**
>
> *George Burns*

- More workers will demand family leave to care for newborns and newly adopted children, as well as elderly and ill family members.
- The declining fertility rate combined with increased life expectancy means that the average married couple will have more parents than children.
- Most people can expect to spend more years caring for an aging parent than for dependent children.
- The majority of children will continue to be reared in nontraditional families. This will include single-parent and stepparent families, and families led by grandparents, by lesbians and gays, or by single women who have adopted a child or been artificially inseminated.

Whatever form the family takes in the next few decades, we all will continue to be greatly influenced by the family system. Families have always been important, and throughout history, people have experimented with different types of extended families to meet their needs. To some degree, we are all shaped by our earliest experiences with the people we are closest to. And, regardless of the structure, our families will continue to affect how we relate to others as we connect with the larger family of humanity.

Race, Culture, and the Family

A common theme in describing families from racial or cultural minorities is emphasis on the importance of the concept of extended family. Whether due to racism, oppression, or the interaction with the dominant culture, many groups within America have a strong need to rely on more than just the immediate family for support.

No discussion of African American family structure would be complete without some attention to the extended family. "The basic family unit is the multigenerational informal extended family, wherein, in addition to one or both parents and their biological children, true kin, fictive kin (long-time friends or informal adoptions), and visiting relatives may be included" (Locke, 1998, p. 34).

Strengths found in African American communities are evident in the form of informal day care services, informal foster care, services to unwed mothers, and services to the elderly. The meaning of the term *parents* includes natural parents and grandparents as well as others who, at different times, assume parental roles and responsibilities.

Some descriptions of the traditional extended family of Native American Indians also describe the *clan* as the basic unit. A clan consists of a "group of families or households which traces its descent through the head of the house from a common ancestor." Although exact genealogy may not be important, many clans trace their ancestry through matrilineal descent. In these clans, the female has traditionally been responsible for the duties necessary to preserve the "social organization." Unlike the dominant culture of the United States, which emphasizes youth, Native American culture values and respects the wisdom and experience of age (Locke, 1998).

Consistent with the value of respect for authority and elders, one finds among Japanese Americans values of allegiance to the family and dependency versus individualism and self-reliance. Japanese Americans find themselves duty-bound and obligated to the family.

Related to the concept of shame, or the avoidance of bringing disgrace to the family name, is the idea that the individual is of minimal importance. To reach for self-fulfillment would be to display attributes of selfishness and exaggerated self-importance. Love and affection between parent and child is combined with a strong sense of reciprocal obligation and dependence.

Among many Mexican Americans, the family is the core and center from which the view of the world extends. Even with respect to identification, the Mexican American self-identity is likely to take second place to the family. A Mexican American in need of emotional support, guidance, or money expects and is expected to turn to family first.

Because of the patriarchal nature of the culture, relatives on the father's side of the family may be considered more important than those on the mother's side. Among extended family members there is often much communication, visiting, sharing, and closeness.

Mexican American extended family structure also includes godparents, who ensure the welfare and religious education of the children. Like the traditional family, though, the choosing of godparents has been declining, particularly in cities where pressures to acculturate are greater and urban life dilutes traditional practices (Locke, 1998).

Although the characteristics of the various groups described here may suggest homogeneity, it is also important to remember that there is considerable diversity within each group described.

Family of Origin

Recently, I was watching a program on PBS about violence and teenage gangs. A teenager was being interviewed about his reasons for joining a gang, a decision that seemed to be dangerous given the incidence of violence among gang members. At one point in the program, the person being interviewed looked right into the camera and said, "They are my family. The gang is the only ones that watch out for me. We take care of each other." This was an interesting comment on the risks the person was willing to take to be a part of the group. It appears that, regardless of whether a person has a biological family, there is a strong need for belonging to a group that one considers family. Behavior is greatly influenced by the groups that we are connected to, and what we learn in those group systems has implications for interactions with others and the world in general.

Dr. Murray Bowen, one of the early explorers of the powerful influence that family systems have on the behavior of individuals, hypothesizes, "Human beings' perceptions of self and others are more strongly influenced by the quality of their emotional dependency in family relationships than by any other social or environmental factor" (Bowen, 1978, p. 132). Bowen realizes that you can't translate individual psychoanalytic concepts into the language of families; the family is a natural structure in itself, with its own wiring. For Bowen, the submerged ebb and flow of family life, the simultaneous push and pull among family members for both distance and togetherness, is the force underlying all human behavior. Although Bowen did not invent systems thinking, he was the first to conceptualize the family as a *natural system,* one that was more like an ant colony or an elephant herd than most people cared to admit. It could be fully understood only in terms of the fluid but predictable processes among members. Furthermore, Bowen introduced a highly novel form of family therapy based on one family member's researching and coming to terms with his or her own family of origin. Unlike most family or individual therapists, Bowen (1991) conceived personal growth and family interaction as part of an indivisible whole, creating a therapy that involved both the self of the individual and the multiple relations in the family.

Bowen's theory suggests several benefits in resisting the pressure of the family by changing functioning positions in the relationship systems. That seems to be a key point: how people extricate themselves from the pressure to function in a certain manner or fill a particular role and still be part of the family unit. The challenge of that endeavor may be best met by understanding the forces at work within the family system. Eight major concepts have been developed from Bowen's initial conceptualization of the family unit:

1. *Differentiation of Self:* This is the ability to see yourself as an individual, separate from the family identity, while still being able to maintain connections with the family.
2. *Triangles:* When the anxiety in a two-person relationship reaches a certain level, a third person is predictably drawn into the emotional field of the twosome.
3. *Nuclear Family Emotional System:* Three methods are used in most families when the anxiety amasses in the system. The adaptive mechanisms are marital conflict, dysfunction of a spouse, and projection to a child.
4. *Family Projection Process:* Parents stabilize their relationship with each other and lower the anxiety in the twosome by viewing a child as their shared "problem."
5. *Emotional Cut-Off:* Cut-offs are particularly frequent between the parent and grand parent generations of a family. One direct consequence of emotional cut-off is the burdening of the nuclear system with an equivalent overinvestment of feelings and expectations.
6. *Multigenerational Transmission Process:* There is a strong tendency to repeat limiting patterns of emotional behavior in successive generations. Unless conscious efforts to modify these impaired patterns are made, such behavior is usually repeated automatically in the next generation.
7. *Sibling Position:* Seniority and sex distribution among siblings in the same and related generations have a strong influence on behavior.
8. *Emotional Process in Society:* The strength of the emotional forces in society, such as destructive political leadership, may make it difficult or impossible to differentiate from the family.

This list raises questions about how family influence affects behavior in various situations outside of the home environment. The Bowen theory suggests specific ways in which family and nonfamily behavior may be linked. Some of these linkages may be described in terms of family systems concepts:

1. A person who acts in accordance with others' expectations for a particular chronological or assumed sibling position tends to repeat the same behavior patterns in various social settings.
2. A person who is the object of a family projection is more vulnerable to projection or scapegoating processes in other social settings.
3. A person who is triangled into a family system tends to be easily caught up in the emotional interdependencies of other relationships and social groups.
4. An individual's differentiation of self in a social group depends on the effectiveness of that person's differentiation of self in the family.

These assumptions can be used to explore the extent to which family processes are primary determinants of behavior. To what extent does your family influence how you act in situations outside the family? The general concept of the emotional system can also be used to draw parallels between family and nonfamily behavior. This can be done by observing the shared characteristics of families and other groups and the shared behavior patterns of their respective members. Patterns of family interaction and family programming influence past, present, and future behavior. Family systems theory has far-reaching implications, to the extent that social groups such as work, friendship, religious, and political systems manifest relationship characteristics similar to those of families (Hall, 1991).

One practical application of this information is to explore the sibling relationship, a topic that is being explored by an increasing number of popular books (e.g., *The Sibling Bond* by Banks, *Mom Loved You Best* by Hapworth and Heilman). Sibling relationships—80 percent of Americans have at least one—outlast marriages, survive the death of parents, and resurface after quarrels that would sink any friendship. In a world of shifting social realities, working couples, disintegrating marriages, "blended" households, disappearing grandparents, and families spread across a continent, this validation of the importance of sibling influences comes none too soon. And for the

═══ Questions for Critical Thinking

How does this information on families affect you? What do you believe are the implications for your future? How have changes on the family system influenced your behavior?

_____

_____

_____

_____

_____

_____

_____

_____

_____

_____

baby boomers, a generation in which late marriages and fewer children are the norm, old age may become for many a time when siblings—not devoted sons and daughters—sit by the bedside. Rivalry between siblings often wanes after adolescence, allowing for connecting on a more adult level. The importance of understanding the richness of that possibility has many implications. Says author Judith Viorst, who has written of sibling ties, "There is no one else on Earth with whom you share so much personal history" (Goode, 1994, p. 57).

Birth Order

Alfred Adler (1927) was one of the first to focus attention on the possible influence of birth order. As one of the inner circle of Freud's psychoanalytic society, he argued that the foremost human drive was not sexuality, but a striving for superiority. He believed that young children naturally feel less competent when compared to older siblings or adults. These early inferiority feelings supposedly motivate individuals to acquire new skills and develop talents. We all have some degree of feelings of inferiority, and therefore learn to compensate. The particular form that compensation takes and the skills that are developed are related, in part, to the position one occupies in the family.

In recent years, prominent scholars have argued that the impact of birth order on behavior is a myth. "Birth order influence is a disappointment," said Jules Angst, a psychologist from Zurich. Angst arrived at this conclusion after he and his colleague, Cecile Ernst, surveyed birth order research from 1946 to 1980. In their book *Birth Order* (Ernst and Angst, 1983), they concluded that birth order didn't consistently predict personality traits or behavior. According to Toni Falbo (1994), an educational psychologist at the University of Texas, most serious researchers have stopped talking about birth order.

But perhaps the problem with assessing birth order is the almost impossible task of getting a clear focus on what is being studied. Even Adler recognized that classifying people by birth order was simplistic. A family is an incredibly complex and dynamic system. There are so many variables that would make untangling the interwoven factors a difficult task, at best. And yet, considerable anecdotal evidence persists in declaring that there are common traits for certain birth positions. More recent studies may indicate in increasing interest in the connection between birth order and behavior.

Lawrence Lyman (1995), from the Department of Psychology at the City College of New York recently published a study indicating a consensus about the nature of each birth position independent of the subject's own birth position. Subjects were asked to list three words that described the characteristics of each birth position. If suitable, words could be used to describe more than one birth position. After all of the categories had been completed, the subjects were instructed to rate each descriptive word in terms of positive or negative connotation on a scale ranging from most negative (25) to most positive (15). It seems that participants held a shared image of the negative and positive qualities of each birth position, whether the view was from the top or the bottom of the family hierarchy.

One of the latest contributors to the discussion of birth order is Frank Sulloway, a science historian at MIT. His findings, in *Born to Rebel* (1996), suggest that the most significant factor of historical change is not the church, state, or economy, but family structure. He says that *people with the same birth rank have more in common with each other than they do with their own siblings.* For all its intuitive appeal, Sulloway is aware that birth order research has had a reputation for flakiness. Therefore, he came up with an ingenious method for testing his hypotheses. By sifting through the 2,000 studies that Ernst and Angst discarded in 1983, he found a number of studies that factored out differences in social class and family size before looking for birth order effects. Those studies, which included nearly 121,000 participants, supported his predictions about each of the five personality dimensions that psychological tests look for.

Sulloway then took a different approach and focused on the world of science, and the sole issue he measured was willingness to challenge established opinions. There was a clear pattern when he examined 28 scientific controversies over the past 400 years. Those least likely to accept new theories were firstborns with younger siblings. Later-borns were five times more likely than firstborns to support the Copernican and Darwinian revolutions. In case after case, the influence of birth order was remarkable.

Sulloway's theory (1996) is that firstborn children identify more readily with parental authority because they are often put in charge of younger siblings. Through this identification, firstborns adopt the norms and values of their parents, and society, in ways that subsequent children do not. The older child gets the responsibility, and the younger ones test the limits and try to see what they can get away with. The oldest is the first in line and is born to be boss. In the world of the family, sibling rivalry is a case of dog-eat-dog, and the oldest seldom goes to bed hungry. The later-born children are literally born to rebel. They seem to believe that if you can't beat 'em, don't join 'em. Therefore, later-born siblings often excel by choosing different paths.

This isn't to say that birth order is all that counts, for there are always exceptions. Sulloway devotes much of his book to showing ways in which different influences interact. For instance, gender has a huge obvious impact on personality. But studies have found that firstborn girls are typically more confident, assertive, and verbally aggressive than their younger brothers and sisters. Also, conflict with a parent may offset a firstborn's conformist ways. Once estranged from the status quo and relegated to the underdog role, anyone becomes more radical. Sulloway doesn't claim to have solved any ultimate question, but he has certainly shed light on evidence that supports the notion that our families greatly influence the way we interact with the world.

Re-creating Our Families

The roles we play in the family while growing up can have a significant impact on the type of relationship we have with other people later in life. There are a number of different situations in which our earliest training can have a profound influence on our behavior. Have you ever wondered why you were born into your particular family or how your sex and birth order have affected your personality? Has your family makeup forced you to deal with particular issues? Although the conclusions aren't entirely consistent, recent research indicates that family birth order influences the roles we play in life. If you want to know about differences in family due to birth order, talk to a mother of three or more children, or ask a middle child whether he stirred things up or played the mediator in the family.

There is a saying: "If you change any part of a system, you change the whole system." This applies to families and underlines the importance of understanding birth order. For each child who joins the family, the whole family shifts and changes to a degree. The arrival of a younger sibling may cause distress to an older child accustomed to parents' exclusive attention, but it also stirs enormous interest, presenting both children with the opportunity to learn crucial social and cognitive skills: how to comfort and empathize with another person, how to make a joke, how to resolve arguments, even how to irritate.

If two children who grew up in the same family are vastly different, and genetics accounts for only part of these differences, what else is going on? The answer may be that brothers and sisters don't really share the same family at all. Rather, each child grows up in a unique family, each one shaped by the way he or she perceives other people and events, by the chance happenings he or she alone experiences, and by how

> **"***Children despise their parents until age forty, when they suddenly become just like them—thus preserving the system.***"**
>
> Onetin Crewe

other people—parents, siblings, and teachers—perceive and act toward him or her. In that respect, each person in a family unit may have a totally different perspective on the dynamics of the family. If you interview all the members of a family about their experience of being a part of that unit, you might get as many different responses as there are respondents. Each person may have a part of the truth, with no one really having the whole picture. Inevitably, though, each child will have part of his or her perspective influenced by the order in which he or she joined the family.

The family is where we learn the most about who we are, what we can do, and what to expect from the world. As adults, we tend to replicate our original families as we interact in a variety of social arenas.

Birth Order Roles

Birth order is typically described in terms of oldest, middle, youngest, and only, the last case being an increasing phenomenon in our society as more people have children later in life. As an introduction to the influence of birth order roles, see if you find any pattern in the following illustrations. Remember back in high school when you went out cruising on Friday night? One person in the car always wanted to hang bare-ended out the side window, throw bottles, or do something else disruptive. Another person usually tried to keep everybody together and out of jail: "Sit down, we're not doing anything weird; we're going to the dance, and we're not going to get drunk." Then there was the person who said, "I don't care what we do, just as long as I get to come along."

At work, some people always tell everyone else what to do, how to do it, and when to do it, even though doing so is not their responsibility. Others channel their creative energy into avoiding actual work by hiding out in the bathroom, hanging over the counter visiting with drop-in friends, or taking lots of coffee breaks. And then there are the ones just standing around waiting to

be told exactly what to do. Is a pattern beginning to emerge that tells us something about families and birth order?

Have you ever noticed that there seems to be a powerful and unusual force influencing whom people select as a partner in life? Maybe that influence is birth order. Consider a woman, the oldest of 10 kids, who has been in charge of unruly siblings since she was 12 years old. Do you think she marries someone who is going to tell her what to do? Fat chance! She goes out and finds some guy who is the youngest of eight kids and had seven mother figures who fed him, dressed him, and told him what, where, and how to do everything while he was growing up. This guy wanders around the world saying, "What do I do now?" until along comes this woman who tells him, "Come here, do this, sit here, eat this." People accustomed to certain family roles often go out in the world and re-create that same setup. It is a way of going back to the familiarity of the role they had when growing up. Just as the role may have been adopted in an unconscious manner, so too is the influence on behavior as an adult often unconscious.

The following are just some examples of how birth order can influence life. They represent the general tendencies of the stereotypical oldest, middle, youngest, and only children.

The oldest is most likely to be the protector of the family system, carrying on the standards of the family. He or she is more responsible because he or she often has more responsibilities. The oldest gets a certain amount of attention just for being the oldest. In English aristocracy, major considerations are given the firstborn in terms of inheritance and title. The oldest also experiences considerable pressure from the expectations of parents. The firstborn is often the guinea pig for nervous new moms and dads.

Oldest children, having been only children for some period of time, want to stay in first place. They may feel dethroned when a sibling is born. They may seek undue attention, which can be constructive if they channel that energy into positive accomplishments. The flip side is that this can become a problem if they don't feel they have received the attention they deserve. Oldest children tend to be steady, dependable, and conscientious. They get along well with authority figures. They are often high achievers who are concerned with their own prestige. Some feel that they have to please others and tend to be perfectionistic.

The middle child is more likely to stir things up, challenge authority, and question the family system. Middle children tend to elbow their way through life. Middle children are usually creative about getting attention because they are in competition with the oldest and/or the youngest, who get attention simply by being in their respective roles. They have the privileges of neither the oldest nor the youngest. They are always running to catch up to the oldest, but are frequently the opposite of the oldest. They may feel unloved and squeezed out. They may believe that adults are unfair and struggle against that unfairness.

Depending on the level of conflict in the family, middle children may act as either social coordinator or mediator, but they are usually in the "middle" of it all. They are adaptable and social. They are also sensitive to injustices. Middle kids, however, have to be a little bit more outgoing, outlandish, and/or creative to get attention. If they become discouraged, they can become the problem child in the family. They are often rebels.

The youngest, like the oldest, doesn't have to do a lot to get a certain amount of attention—it's there, it's guaranteed. All the baby has to do is look cute, burp, drool, or whatever, and the world says, "Isn't that wonderful? Look at that; isn't he cute?" Parents usually have completely different expectations for the youngest than for the oldest. Parents may be more affluent during the years that the youngest is growing up, so they may have a tendency to spoil the youngest.

The youngest child, like the only child, is never displaced by a newborn. They have a special spot and may get a lot of attention because others in the family feel a sense of responsibility for them. They are often indulged, but that doesn't mean that they are spoiled in a negative way. They just learn to expect good things from life, so they usually end up being great optimists. Youngest children who have been treated well are usually sociable, easygoing, and popular. If they were treated unkindly or teased, they may be shy and irritable with others (Richardson, 2000).

Youngest children have siblings to serve as models for what to do and what not to do. They also have the opportunity to find out what they can get away with. They may not be taken seriously because of their size and may lack self-confidence and seek to have others do things for them. The may retain childish behavior into adulthood.

The only child often has a combination of oldest and youngest tendencies. Depending on the orientation of the parents, only children may, to a large degree, adapt to the role expected—either youngest or oldest. Some people who are

only children report being treated just like junior adults from the time they were born. Some parents with one child expect the child to fit into the adult world and emulate their behavior. The child may grow up having the choice of playing by himself or herself or learning to interact with adults. If that is a positive experience, the only child may become quite precocious. The other possibility is that the only child may be overprotected and pampered. Some people in that position report having been focused on with such intense energy that they were limited in their ability to learn to do things for themselves.

Children with no siblings may feel incompetent because they are always around more competent adults, yet they feel more comfortable around adults than with their peers. Because they have no rivals, they may become the center of their parents' interest. These children have less opportunity to learn how to share and settle disputes. They also tend to be creative and have better relations with peers as adults than as children.

These descriptions may hold true in many families, but certainly not all. Remember the 90 percent rule: There are exceptions to everything in discussing human behavior. Throughout the chapter, more information will be provided to help you discover how your position may affect you, including the many other variables that can affect these roles.

The following is a good example of birth order and roles. A friend of mine has three daughters. The oldest, age 11, will walk into the room at a gathering and pull up a chair, sit down at the table with the adults, and join in the conversation. This oldest kid is mature beyond her years and wants to be part of the adult group. When we try to gently say, "Hey, you're a kid. Go be one. Get out of here and go play," she feels hurt. The middle kid, by contrast, will run in and say, "Hey, I'm doing gymnastics—want to see?" She'll start doing flips down the middle of the living room floor while we say, "Wait! Would you please do that outside?" She will run outside, find out where everyone is sitting, and yell in through the big picture window, "Hey, look!" and start doing more flips and handstands out in the yard. The youngest, the baby, will just come up and grab your leg, wrap herself around it, and stand on your foot so that everywhere you go you carry her wrapped around your leg. She is wonderful about being cute and adorable; she just sort of drools and looks at you as if to say, "I wanna sit with you." She gets loads of attention for being the sweet, nice little kid. The way my friend's kids fall

into the stereotypical patterns based on birth order is remarkable.

Buying or Rejecting the Role

Although we are born into a particular position, we may or may not assume the role. This is called buying or rejecting the role. For example, the oldest child has the second lieutenant role and quite often is in charge of maintaining the family system. An oldest child may decide to do this by fitting into some pattern established by the parents. Oldest children are often commissioned to take charge of the siblings and enforce the rules. Because of this role, they may say to themselves, "Well, OK, I think I can be smart, be in student government, be whatever Mom and Dad want for me. There is a lot of pressure, but I can handle it and I'll stick with the role."

On the other hand, an oldest may not conform to the stereotype. There may be too much pressure, too many expectations, too much responsibility. Some parents are so tough on their first kid, determined that this one will be perfect, that the child says, "No, I'm rejecting this. I don't know if I want to be the leader or role model. I don't think I can hack it. I don't want it, so I'm rejecting it." That's why some oldest children seem to go in the opposite direction and act more like a middle rebellious child or a whiny baby. But keep in mind that the role influences the person's behaviors whether he or she buys it or not.

The same type of thing can happen with middle children. This is the in-between role. Middle kids aren't sure which direction to go in. Should they be more like the oldest or the youngest? To get attention, middle children may buy the role of the social coordinator for the family. They are the ones who are lively and entertaining, jokers

or clowns; they keep things moving in the family. They are very outgoing if they buy the role. If they decide that there isn't enough attention in the family, they may rebel and act out the "black sheep" role, perhaps even electing to live at someone else's house, join the Hell's Angels, or do something else outrageous to get attention. Another variation is that they might go in the opposite direction and become very withdrawn, staying in their room for two or three years because they aren't sure whether they fit in. They don't know if they want to fill the middle kid role, but the other roles are taken, so they don't know what to do. They may feel left out, as though there is no room for them.

The same thing is true with the youngest. The brat's role also has its good and bad aspects. Some people who were the youngest of several kids may go out into the world and say, "I've never had to think for myself. I was treated like a little toy, carried around, dressed, and fed. They told me what to do, where to stand, and where to sit. I had four mothers growing up. Why should I make a decision? It'll never happen. No matter what I said or did while growing up, nobody ever listened to me." These people continue that role as adults. Sometimes, though, they almost seem to be the opposite; if they rejected the role, they act more like an oldest child than a youngest child. They've decided, "That's it. I'm tired of people telling me what to do. I've had someone spoonfeeding me my entire life, and as soon as I get out of here, I'm going to take care of myself. That is the last time anybody will ever tell me what to do." They may end up being in charge and telling others what to do, because for 18 years they had to listen to everybody else. These examples give an indication of why a person born into a particular position may not fit the stereotypical description of his or her birth order.

The Independently Existing Role

In almost any family of more than three children, birth order roles exist even if the person born into a position doesn't fill that particular role. If a role isn't being held down by one sibling, there may be a shifting of roles. For example, if the oldest decides "I don't like this role, don't want it, can't do it," someone else in the family will move in and fill the oldest role. The middle child may say, "Well, I think I'll take over that turf." If that leaves the middle child role empty, the youngest may move up to fill that one. The specific people may shift around, but the roles exist regardless of who fills them.

My personal family experience might serve as an example of this concept. My older brother and I were close in age, about 18 months apart. Then there was an eight-year gap between me and my younger brother and sister. (From what I can remember overhearing, I'm not sure my parents wanted any more kids after having me.) For eight years, my older brother, Larry, got certain things for being the oldest, and I got certain things for being the youngest, and it worked out fair and even. He got certain privileges sometimes, but I got certain benefits, too, and everything was OK.

Then a new youngest came along, and suddenly I was a middle child, and I started looking around for turf. This was the beginning of the attention war. I was in the in-between position, and part of me said, "I used to be the youngest. I still want to be that, but I've been ripped off. My younger brother can play this role better than I can. He's cuter, and I'm 8." Each of my brothers seemed to have a position that got them certain benefits. I remember one day when my older brother got a BB gun, and immediately I wanted one just like it. I was told I wasn't old enough or responsible enough. A few hours later, my younger brother came home with a new Roy Rogers lunchbox, and suddenly I wanted one of those, too. I didn't even have to be told that I was a little old for that. Should I try to act more mature, or should I try to regress? I didn't know which direction I wanted to go. Hence, the in-between role.

When I did start acting a little more like my older brother, I think he felt a lot of pressure because I was looking around for a new role to fill and I might choose his. He decided there was already enough pressure from Mom and Dad about how and what to be. Then here comes this smart-alec little brother breathing down his neck, saying, "Hey, you. If you don't do this right, I'm here. If you don't protect your turf, I'm going to pick up whatever is left."

Another family role that is sometimes needed for a family to function is that of the identified patient, or black sheep. If the black sheep leaves the family for any reason, someone else may pick up that person's role. The role exists independent of the person. In some families, it defuses or redirects the attention from the real problem to have someone else having difficulties. If the family system operates only when there is someone to focus on as the problem, then that role may even be passed around within the family.

In large families with six or seven kids, sometimes two or three band together to fill each role. In a family of eight, it may take a deputy to help the oldest maintain order. Or, the youngest three may band together for mutual protection. Another option in large families is to split each role into a dichotomy of internal and external relations. One person may be the oldest in the family (internal), but another is the responsible one in the community (external).

A final example of this concept is what happens when the oldest gets married, gets a job, and moves out. If a role is vacated, usually there is someone else in the family who will straighten up and get his or her act together to assume the role of the oldest. Without the competition, he or she may think it feasible to take on that role. Now that the responsible second lieutenant role is empty, there is room for him or her in that position. Over the course of time, people may try new ways of being and rotate through all the different roles. More than likely, though, there will be one role that has been your primary influence.

Gender-Influenced Roles

How does your gender affect the role you decide to play? Fair or not, in our society we do have some culturally conditioned sexist beliefs. If you were the only female in an all-male family, most likely you were treated as the baby. You represented the "rose among the thorns." The only girl in the family gets to be special because she's the only one wearing dresses. She gets all sorts of new things, as opposed to hand-me-downs, because there is no one she has to share with.

If you were the only male in an all-female family, you may have been treated as the oldest regardless of your birth order position. Dad may have said, "This is my son and he is going to be the second lieutenant." In a number of cultures, the male is groomed for a particular role regardless of birth order. This is not an equitable situation, but it does occur frequently.

Career and Job Choices

The role that you played most in your family (although you may have played more than one) may influence your choice of career. If they bought the role, oldest children usually feel more comfortable in a structured setting. They might like to work for a company in a management position where they can either be the second lieutenant or work for one. The firstborn of this country are disproportionately represented in *Who's Who of America* compared to total population. I've read that 90 percent of all astronauts are firstborn. Oldest siblings who strike out into new territory do it in a much different fashion than middle children.

The middle child's role is generally that of the entrepreneur. Middle children will probably find work that allows a great deal of freedom and provides an outlet for their creativity. The oldest may become rich and powerful through conventional means, but it will be the middle kid who "invents" the pet rock and makes a fortune.

The youngest children may work well in sales or personnel, where they can rely on their charm and winning ways. They may even make good "politicians," as they expect to be rewarded for doing very little if they were the ones who were spoiled. Depending on their particular family, some youngest feel comfortable with specific guidelines and structure in the workplace. Or, if they rejected their role, they might go in the opposite direction by starting their own company so that no one will tell them what to do.

Relationships

We are all affected by how we learned to interact in our families. Anytime a group of people gets together, there are interactional patterns that are reminiscent of sibling relationships. If the group is task-oriented, family dynamics as well as personality types spring into action.

In marriages, an oldest will probably look for a middle or youngest. Why? When two oldest marry, sparks fly over who rules the roost. If cooperation existed among the siblings in the original family, the oldest may look for a youngest to marry. However, if there was conflict in the family, he or she may marry a rebellious middle child to re-create the old familiar scene.

Depending on whether they bought or rejected the role, youngest children may look for a person who will guide them or choose a partner they can dominate. Sometimes, a person will swing back and forth between wanting to be cared for and wanting to be in charge if his or her needs weren't met in the family of origin. This situation can be frustrating for the spouse, to say the least.

Influence on Parenting

The oldest of several children will be a much different parent than the youngest of the family.

Often, the oldest was in charge from the age of 12 or 14. Contrast that with the youngest, who may still live at home at 24, with Mom doing the laundry. Some parents try to be peers of their own children, which is usually detrimental to both. It's fine to be friends with your children, but don't try to be their peers. It's the youngest who is more apt to adopt that parenting style because they were never in charge while growing up. Middle kids may have a tendency to have a laissez-faire attitude toward parenting, in which they may set guidelines but will be likely to foster independence.

Limits of Birth Order Influence

You probably know several firstborns who are typical of their birth order: organized, high achieving, somewhat conventional. But you probably know others who share similar characteristics but were born second, third, or possibly fifth. By the same token, although you may recognize many of the typical "middle-child" traits (never feeling noticed or recognized, for instance) among middle-born friends, it's unlikely that they all fit this mold. And there are sure to be some last-borns in your acquaintance to whom you would never apply the label "baby."

On the other hand, the fact that there are exceptions to the rules doesn't make birth order meaningless. Some exceptions can be explained by looking at birth order in more detail. For example, in many families, a firstborn *son* might be accorded the usual firstborn privileges and subjected to the usual firstborn pressures, even though he has an older sister. Other ways that a later-born child might grow up being treated like a firstborn (and therefore exhibit many of the typical firstborn traits) include being born after a gap of several years so that the parents are in some senses starting over; when the actual firstborn child has a chronic illness or developmental disability so that the parents attach their highest aspirations and pressures to the later-born child; or when by temperament the firstborn is particularly easygoing or relaxed, and therefore not inclined to fill the typical firstborn role.

These exceptions highlight the fact that birth order is just one of many influences that come to bear in shaping a child's personality. Here are some other key factors:

1. Parents' age and station in life at the time the child is born. A first child born to an unwed teen

mother, for example, may have a very different experience growing up than does the next child, born when the mother has completed her schooling and perhaps has married.

2. Parent and child temperament or behavioral style. Famous research by the child psychiatrists Stella Chess and Alexander Thomas has shown that a child's psychological well-being depends on the appropriateness of the fit between the child's temperament and his parents'. For example, children who are very active do well with parents who themselves have a lot of physical energy; paired with parents who are more sedate, the same children are more likely to develop behavioral and perhaps emotional problems.

3. Sibling sexes. A youngest boy with four older sisters has a different family position than a youngest boy with four older brothers. A boy who falls in the middle of two sisters may have a different experience than a girl in the middle of two brothers, particularly if the parents harbor traditional (that is, sexist) views of the relative importance of boys and girls.

4. Parents' personality (which is likely to have been influence by birth order itself). Parents who were first born and grew up following the rules and succeeding often impose similar expectations on their children—particularly their firstborns. If their firstborns are inclined by temperament to be persistent and self-directed (some might put this less kindly and call it "stubborn"), the family may be in for many years of discord.

Of course, there are many other factors that play important roles in the formation of a child's personality. To name just a few: family ethnicity; economic hardship or plenty; political and cultural events in the larger world (for example, the generation of children whose outlook on life was shaped by the Vietnam War or the Cold War), losses of important people and emotional traumas, and so on. Factoring birth order into the mix can often help explain how some of these other variables may be operating. Birth order alone is not destiny, but it does offer a powerful lens that can help bring development into focus.

(*Source:* Adapted from "Birth Order Is Not Destiny," by Robert Needlman, M.D., APA Online).

Functional Families

A prerequisite to having a healthy, functioning family is having healthy, functioning parents. The degree to which a couple has a good, solid, mutually respectful relationship is usually the degree to which they can model the types of behavior they want their children to exhibit. When two people in a healthy relationship become parents,

they can model self-discipline and self-love for their children. In fact, the more stable and secure the parental relationship is, the more the children are free to establish their own identities. That process is a necessary component of a healthy family.

In my work with adolescents at various treatment centers, I often encountered parents who wanted someone to "fix" their child but were unwilling to explore the possibility that their relationship might be a contributing factor to the family difficulties. Fortunately, some parents come to realize that change often occurs "from the top down." If the parents aren't willing to look at their own behavior and entertain the idea that there might be some changes they could make, it is usually difficult for the children to change. When the parents are willing to learn, it gives the children permission to make changes in their behavior.

Functional parents will also be able to model maturity and autonomy for their children. Their strong identity lessens the possibility of unresolved issues being repressed and unconscious. Therefore, the children don't have to take on elements of their parents' problems. The children are then free to grow in their own self-awareness and develop a separate identity. Family therapist Virginia Satir (1972) calls this endowment "the five freedoms":

1. The freedom to see and hear what is here and now, rather than what was, will be, or should be.
2. The freedom to think what one thinks, rather than what one should think.
3. The freedom to feel what one feels, rather than what one should feel.
4. The freedom to want and choose what one wants, rather than what one should want.
5. The freedom to imagine one's own self-actualization, rather than playing a rigid role or always playing it safe.

When these ideas are accepted and incorporated into the family unit, communication improves. It is permissible to express one's thoughts, feelings, and desires. With that ability to communicate in a healthy manner comes an increase in the sense of personal power for each of the family members. They can then use those powers to cooperate, individuate, and get their collective and individual needs met. As John Bradshaw (1988a) says, "A functional family is the healthy soil out of which individuals can become mature human beings" (p. 48). Beliefs common to

FIFTEEN TRAITS OF A SKILLED FAMILY

1. Communicates and listens.
2. Affirms and supports one another.
3. Teaches respect for others.
4. Develops a sense of trust.
5. Has a sense of play and humor.
6. Exhibits a sense of shared responsibility.
7. Teaches a sense of right and wrong.
8. Has a strong sense of family in which rituals and traditions abound.
9. Has a shared core of religious or spiritual beliefs.
10. Has a balance of interaction among members.
11. Respects the privacy of one another.
12. Values service to others.
13. Fosters family table time and conversation.
14. Shares leisure time.
15. Admits to and seeks help with problems.

Source: Dolores Curran, *Traits of a Healthy Family.*

functional families, according to Bradshaw, are as follows:

1. The family is a survival and growth unit.
2. The family is the soil that provides the emotional needs of the various members. These needs include a balance between autonomy and dependency, and social and sexual training.
3. A healthy family provides for the growth and development of each member, including the parents.
4. The family is the place where the development of self-esteem takes place.
5. The family is a major unit in socializing and it is crucial for a society if it is to endure.

Stepfamilies

Stepfamilies are an increasingly common family form, especially given the current divorce statistics. Divorce rates are highest in California, New York, and Texas. Approximately half of divorces involve children. Remarriage of parents with children has given rise to the new Brady Bunch phe-nomenon, in which there are not only "his kids" and "her kids," but also "our kids." Second marriages in which one partner already has children have an even greater chance of ending in divorce. This is because stepfamily life can be very complex and problematic, with few guidelines and role models to rely on.

Part of the difficulty of blended families is that they challenge established roles. Birth order and position in the family are up for grabs when the parents remarry and there are children involved. There are a number of differences between the stepfamily and the original family, but one of the most significant is that the stepfamily is born of loss. Therefore, as parents and children come together to form new families, there will be times when there are tremendous loyalty conflicts for both children and parents.

Some other examples of stepfamily differences, according to Cecile Currier (1982), in *Learning to Step Together,* include the following:

1. The parent-child bond predates the couple bond.
2. There is a biological parent elsewhere who has influence on the stepfamily.

COMMON STEPFAMILY MYTHS

Stepfamilies Are the Same as Nuclear Families. This myth might be what people wish for and try to create, but it also often contributes to problems in forming a new family. Given all of the dynamics and interactions with new people added to the system, it is unrealistic to expect that things will be the same as in the original nuclear family.

Stepchildren Are Easier to Manage When They Are Not Living in the Home. Often, families are harder to manage when stepchildren do not live in the home, because when stepchildren visit, it can be difficult to establish a routine and basic rules. When stepchildren live in the home, it is possible to establish expectations that enhance adjustment.

In the Event of Death of a Spouse, Rather Than Divorce, Stepparenting Is Easier. Actually, it is hard for a stepparent to compete with the idealized image of a dead parent. Whatever the stepparent does may be judged deficient.

Love Will Happen Instantly in the New Family. Stepmothers especially expect love to happen instantly, which sets up expectations that hamper adjustment. Many stepmothers feel that they should love and care about their stepchildren as they would their own. But love takes time to develop and grow.

3. Children may spend time in two households, each with different rules and expectations.
4. The values and lifestyles of the adults and children living in step relationship may be very different and often in conflict.

Part of the difficulty of readjusting to a new family system is that there frequently are unrealistic expectations. Everyone wants to recapture what was lost and attempts to establish things as they were before, which is seldom possible. It helps to recognize and understand some of the myths that surround blended families in order to better cope with the changes that are necessary.

A more realistic approach to adjusting to the stepfamily system comes from understanding that all families go through stages of development. The stages of development in a stepfamily encompass common issues that must be resolved for the family to become a mature, stable system that supports its members. In the first stage, the issues are recovery from loss and dealing with entering a new relationship. It is important to acknowledge feelings and to mourn the previous relationship. Children will need help in talking about their feelings of loss, jealousy, and guilt about divided time with parents.

In the second stage, conceptualizing and planning for the new marriage requires talking about fears and insecurities. It is important to discuss doubts about second marriages with your prospective spouse, as well as discussing ways in which your changed attitudes and behaviors will make this marriage different from the previous one. It is during this phase that parents need to regard potential family members as a primary source of emotional gratification. The couple needs to establish a strong emotional bond to provide security for the children, even though it may be difficult for the children after having a primary bond with one of the parents. It is during this stage that the stepfamily needs to resolve feelings about the former family system and give up the fantasy that they will re-create the original family. In this phase, they need to begin investing emotional energy in the current relationships.

The third stage is the actual formation of the new family system by restructuring roles of discipline and nurturing. This incorporates the need to accept the stepparent's right to function in both areas. Another task in this phase is establishing generational boundaries. Children need to know that there are special times for just them alone, and there are times when the parents need to be a couple. Accomplishing this will reduce the competitiveness children feel toward the stepparent. Children also need to come to terms with and define their relationship with their other

TIPS FOR STEPPARENTS

Tips for Stepmothers

1. Accept the role of stepmother.
2. Don't be a nonparent.
3. Clarify your role with your spouse.
4. Learn to live with the reality of exspouses.
5. Don't blame yourself for every misbehavior of your stepchildren.
6. You don't have to love your stepchildren—like and respect them, yes.
7. Save time for your own activities.
8. Make yourself available.
9. Be patient—relationships take time to develop.
10. Be discreet with physical attention.

Tips for Stepfathers

1. Develop a relationship before attempting discipline.
2. Help your partner establish rules, but don't enforce them too soon.
3. Take the side of the stepchild if Mom is being unreasonable.
4. Remind children that they continue to be loved by their mother.
5. Get chore issues out into the open and negotiate.
6. Talk to your wife if you feel undermined.
7. It's OK to ask for thanks from your stepchildren.
8. Discuss appropriate dress, privacy, and modesty standards for teenage stepchildren.
9. Share yourself; spend time with each stepchild.
10. Be discreet with physical attention.

Source: Cecile Currier, *Learning to Step Together.* Baltimore, MD: Stepfamily Association of America, Inc., 1982.

biological parent. They will need help discussing feelings of anger, jealousy, and abandonment. This won't be easy, but it is important in the formation of the stepfamily for the children to remain connected to both biological parents if at all possible. Counselors often recommend that stepfamilies have regular family meetings to discuss such topics. During that time, the family can problem solve as well as talk about the positive things that they are experiencing in their new situation.

To conclude this section, it is appropriate to share a quote from a course that goes with the book called *Learning to Step Together:* "Time passes, kids grow out of their insecurities, troublesome ex's marry, move away, or otherwise loosen their hold. Couples grow closer through their crisis and

stepparents become an accepted part of family history. In stepparenting your greatest ally is time. May you use it well" (Currier, 1982, p. 111).

Parenting

Volumes have been written on various aspects of parenting, and it is not in the scope of this book to delve into the particulars. What can be offered are some pointers on the adoption of attitudes necessary for becoming a better parent at any stage of the game. The previous information on functional families supports the notion that it is important to have good parenting skills. The following information (used by permission) is from

> **Questions for Critical Thinking**
>
> *What are your experiences with blended families? How have people you know been affected by the role of stepparent or stepchild? What do you believe would help relationships in a stepfamily?*
>
> _____
>
> _____
>
> _____
>
> _____
>
> _____
>
> _____
>
> _____
>
> _____
>
> _____

the Cline-Fay Institute, which has developed the program and numerous books on love and logic. The following excerpt from the introduction to *Parenting with Love and Logic* (Cline and Fay, 1990) explains their approach.

> Ours may be the first generation of parents who cannot even ponder parenting the way our parents did, and be successful at it. For hundreds of years, rookie parents learned the fine points of child-rearing by example; they took the techniques their parents had used on them and applied them to their children.
>
> Today, this approach is more apt to bomb than to boom. Many of us, when we meet failure, throw up our hands in frustration and say, "I can't understand it. It worked for my dad!" Yes, it did. But things have changed. The human rights revolution, the communication explosion, changes in the family—these, and many other factors, have radically changed how our children view life. Kids are forced to grow up quicker these days, so they need to learn sooner how to cope with the tremendous challenges and pressures of contemporary life. The impact of divorce and other changes in the family have been dramatic.
>
> Effective parents must learn to use different techniques with kids who live in today's complex, rapidly changing world. That's where parenting with love and logic comes in. Why the terms love and logic? Effective parenting centers around love: love that is not permissive, love that doesn't tolerate disrespect, but also love that is powerful enough to

allow kids to make mistakes and permit them to live with the consequences of those mistakes. The logic is centered in the consequences themselves. Most mistakes do have logical consequences. And those consequences, when accompanied by empathy—our compassionate understanding of the child's disappointment, frustration, and pain—hit home with mind-changing power. It's never too late to begin parenting with love and logic.

> Parenting with love and logic is not a foolproof system that works every time. In fact, it is not a comprehensive system at all. Our approach is more an attitude that, when carried out in the context of a healthy, loving relationship with our children, will allow them to grow in maturity as they grow in years. It will teach them to think, to decide, and to live with their decisions. In short, it will teach them responsibility, and that's what parenting is all about. If we can teach our kids responsibility, we've accomplished a great share of our parental task. (p. 12)

Ineffective Parenting

Helicopter Parents   Some parents think love means rotating their lives around their children. They are helicopter parents. They hover over and rescue their children whenever trouble arises. They're forever running lunches and permission slips and homework assignments to school; they're always pulling their children out of jams; not a day goes by when they're not protecting little junior from something—usually from a learning experience the child needs or deserves. As soon as their children send up an SOS flare, helicopter parents, who are hovering nearby, swoop in and shield the children from teachers, playmates, and other elements that appear hostile.

Although today these "loving" parents may feel they are easing their children's path into adulthood, tomorrow the same children will be leaving home and wasting the first 18 months of their adult life, flunking out of college or meandering about "getting their heads together." Such children are unequipped for the challenges of life. Their learning opportunities were stolen from them in the name of love.

The irony is that helicopter parents are often viewed by others as model parents. They feel uncomfortable imposing consequences, though. When they see their children hurting, they hurt too. So they bail them out.

But the real world does not run on the bail-out principle. Traffic tickets, overdue bills, irresponsible people, crippling diseases, taxes—these and other normal events of adult life usually do not disappear because a loving benefactor bails us out. Helicopter parents fail to prepare their kids to meet that kind of world.

Drill Sergeant Parents Some parents are like drill sergeants. They, too, love their children. They feel that the more they bark and the more they control, the better their kids will be in the long run. "These kids will be disciplined," the drill sergeant says. "They'll know how to act right." Indeed, they are constantly told what to do.

When drill sergeant parents talk to children, their words are often filled with put-downs and I-told-you-sos. These parents are into power! If children don't do what they're told, drill sergeant parents are going to make them do it.

Kids of drill sergeant parents, when given the chance to think for themselves, often make horrendous decisions—to the complete consternation and disappointment of their parents. But it makes sense. These kids are rookies in the world of decisions. They've never had to think—the drill sergeant took care of that. The kids have been ordered around all of their lives. They are as dependent on their parents when they enter the real world as the kids of helicopter parents.

Both of these types of parents send messages to their children—all in the name of love—about what they think their kids are capable of. The message the helicopter parent sends to the child is, "You are fragile and can't make it without me." The drill sergeant's message is, "You can't think for yourself, so I'll do it for you."

Although both of these parental types may successfully control the children in the early years, they have thrown major obstacles into the kids' path once they hit the "puberty trail." Helicopter children become adolescents unable to cope with outside forces, unable to think for themselves or handle their own problems. Drill sergeant kids, who did a lot of saluting when they were young, will do a lot of saluting when teenagers. But the salute is different: now it's a raised fist or a crude gesture involving the middle finger.

Effective Parenting

Consultants Consultants in the business world are always available to give suggestions and offer options. They also know when to zip their lips and let their clients make the final decision. Consultant parents know how to zip their lips, too. They are willing to share alternative solutions to problems. They are willing to describe how they would solve the problem—if it were their problem. The consultant parents say, "It's

your life. You get to decide. Good luck!" And then they zip their lip.

The hardest job in parenting is zipping the lip. That's why we have helicopters and drill sergeants in homes. It is easier to make a racket than to keep quiet. One crucial difference between consultant parents and helicopters and drill sergeants is ownership of a problem. Helicopters and drill sergeants both claim ownership of a child's problem. Consultant parents let the child retain ownership (as long as the child can learn the lesson at an affordable price—you don't let kids play on the freeway so they can learn that cars are a problem).

When Johnny droops over the kitchen table of a consultant parent and announces he's friendless, a consultant parent responds, "No friends! That's sad for you. What are you going to do about it?" When Johnny shrugs his shoulders, Mom says, "You don't know? That's even sadder—having a big problem and not knowing what you're going to do about it. I've watched other people with problems like that, and I could share with you some of the things they've tried. It might give you some ideas. If you ever want to hear what they tried, let me know—I sure hope you can work it out." Then she zips her lip—until Johnny asks to hear what others have tried.

Allowing a child to keep ownership of a problem sends an implied message, too. That message is: "You are wise enough to make good decisions. I trust you to know how to handle this." That implied message builds him or her up instead of putting him or her down.

A child who has no control over his or her life is a child who will spend nearly 100 percent of the time trying to take control of adults and manipulate the system. A child who has some control over his or her life will spend very little time trying to control adults or manipulate the system. It's like magic!

Here are three rules for being a consultant parent (especially important for single parents who are often doing double duty) that should become easier with practice:

1. Rule 1: Take good care of yourself.
2. Rule 2: Provide your child with choices you can live with.
3. Rule 3: Take the appropriate action.

Used regularly, these three simple rules can prevent power struggles and silence the racket of helicopters and drill sergeants. (For further information, call The Love and Logic Institute at 1-800-338-4065. They will be happy to provide a catalogue of books available.)

Influence of Parenting Styles

Developmental psychologists have been interested in how parents influence the development of various aspects of children's competence, and their level of self-esteem. One of the approaches to this area of study has been to examine what is usually called "parenting style." This section defines parenting style, explores four types, and discusses the consequences of the different styles for children.

Parenting is a complex activity that includes many specific behaviors that work individually and together to influence child outcomes. Although specific parenting behaviors, such as spanking or reading aloud, may influence child development, looking at any specific behavior in isolation may be misleading. Many writers have noted that specific parenting practices are less important in predicting child well-being than is the broad pattern of parenting. Most researchers who attempt to describe this broad parental milieu rely on Diana Baumrind's concept of parenting style. The construct of parenting style is used to capture normal variations in parents' attempts to control and socialize their children (Baumrind, 1991). Two points are critical in understanding this definition. First, parenting style is meant to describe *normal* variations in parenting. The parenting style typology developed does not include deviant parenting, such as might be observed in abusive or neglectful homes. Second, Baumrind assumes that normal parenting revolves around issues of control. Although parents may differ in how they try to control or socialize their children and the extent to which they do so, it is assumed that the primary role of all parents is to influence, teach, and *control* their children.

Parenting style captures two important elements of parenting: parental *responsiveness* and parental *demandingness* (Maccoby and Martin, 1983). Parental responsiveness (also referred to as parental warmth or supportiveness) refers to "the extent to which parents intentionally foster individuality, self-regulation, and self-assertion by being attuned, supportive, and acquiescent to children's special needs and demands." Parental demandingness (also referred to as behavioral control) refers to "the claims parents make on children to become integrated into the family whole, by their maturity demands, supervision, disciplinary efforts and willingness to confront the child who disobeys" (Baumrind, 1991).

Four Parenting Styles

Categorizing parents according to whether they are high or low on parental demandingness and responsiveness creates a typology of four parenting styles: indulgent, authoritarian, authoritative, and uninvolved (Maccoby and Martin, 1983). Each of these parenting styles reflects different naturally occurring patterns of parental values, practices, and behaviors (Baumrind, 1991) and a distinct balance of responsiveness and demandingness.

> *Indulgent parents* (also referred to as "permissive" or "nondirective") "are more responsive than they are demanding. They are nontraditional and lenient, do not require mature behavior, allow considerable self-regulation, and avoid confrontation." Indulgent parents may be further divided into two types: democratic parents, who, though lenient, are more conscientious, engaged, and committed to the child, and nondirective parents.
>
> *Authoritarian parents* are highly demanding and directive, but not responsive. "They are obedience- and status-oriented, and expect their orders to be obeyed without explanation." These parents provide well-ordered and structured environments with clearly stated rules.
>
> *Authoritative parents* are both demanding and responsive. "They monitor and impart clear standards for their children's conduct. They are assertive, but not intrusive and restrictive. Their disciplinary methods are supportive, rather than punitive. They want their children to be assertive as well as socially responsible, and self-regulated as well as cooperative."
>
> *Uninvolved parents* are low in both responsiveness and demandingness. In extreme cases, this parenting style might encompass both rejecting–neglecting and neglectful parents, although most parents of this type fall within the normal range.

In addition to differing on responsiveness and demandingness, the parenting styles also differ in the extent to which they are characterized by a third dimension: psychological control. Psychological control "refers to control attempts that intrude into the psychological and emotional development of the child" (Barber, 1996) through use of parenting practices such as guilt induction, withdrawal of love, or shaming. One key difference between authoritarian and authoritative parenting is in the dimension of psychological control. Both authoritarian and authoritative parents place high demands on their children and expect their children to behave appropriately and obey parental rules. Authoritarian parents, however, also expect their children to accept their judgments, values, and goals without questioning.

In contrast, authoritative parents are more open to give and take with their children and make greater use of explanations.

Consequences for Children

Parenting style has been found to predict child well-being in the domains of social competence, academic performance, psychosocial development, and problem behavior. Research based on parent interviews, child reports, and parent observations (Baumrind, 1991) consistently finds the following:

1. Children and adolescents whose parents are *authoritative* rate themselves and are rated by objective measures as more socially and instrumentally competent than those whose parents are nonauthoritative.

2. Children and adolescents from *authoritarian* families (high in demandingness, but low in responsiveness) tend to perform moderately well in school and be uninvolved in problem behavior, but they have poorer social skills, lower self-esteem, and higher levels of depression.

3. Children and adolescents from *indulgent* homes (high in responsiveness, low in demandingness) are more likely to be involved in problem behavior and perform less well in school, but they have higher self-esteem, better social skills, and lower levels of depression.

4. Children and adolescents whose parents are *uninvolved* perform most poorly in all domains.

In regard to parenting style, one is struck by the consistency with which authoritative upbringing is associated with both instrumental and social competence and lower levels of problem behavior in both boys and girls at all developmental stages. The benefits of authoritative parenting and the detrimental effects of uninvolved parenting are evident as early as the preschool years and continue throughout adolescence and into early adulthood. Although specific differences can be found in the competence evidenced by each group, the largest differences are found between children whose parents are unengaged and their peers with more involved parents. Authoritative parents appear to be able to balance their conformity demands with their respect for their children's individuality. Children from authoritative homes appear to be able to balance the external conformity and achievement demands with their need for individuation and autonomy.

Parenting style provides important indicators of parental functioning that predict child well-being across a wide spectrum of environ-ments. Both parental responsiveness and parental demandingness are important components of good parenting. Authoritative parenting, which balances clear, high parental demands with emotional responsiveness and recognition of child autonomy, is one of the most consistent family predictors of competence from early childhood through adolescence. However, despite the long tradition of research into parenting style, a number of issues remain outstanding.

Source: Adapted from an article by Nancy Darling, Ph.D.

Influence of Sex, Ethnicity, or Family Type

It is important to distinguish between differences in the distribution and the correlates of parenting style in different subpopulations. Although in the United States authoritative parenting is most common among intact, middle-class families of European descent, the relationship between authoritativeness and child outcomes is quite similar across groups. There are some exceptions to this general statement, however: (a) demandingness appears to be less critical to girls' than to boys' well-being (Weiss and Schwarz, 1996), and (b) authoritative parenting predicts good psychosocial outcomes and problem behaviors for adolescents in all ethnic groups studied (African, Asian, European, and Hispanic Americans), but it is associated with academic performance only among European Americans and, to a lesser extent, Hispanic Americans.

Dysfunctional Families

There are those who feel that the term *dysfunctional* has become overused. What were once the secrets in the closet of the national psyche are now the latest topics for television programs. Every week a new celebrity comes forward with tales about how his or her problems are a result of the past. Possibly as an outcome of having so many people relate their personal stories on various talk shows, we seem to be experiencing a reactionary swing. Some feel that perhaps it is time to explore a balanced approach to healing rather than focusing only on blame.

This is not to say that there aren't people who lived in abusive homes as children. Imagine how devastating it would be to grow up in a family in which multiple levels of abuse exist. Every day, newspapers report incidents of family violence. Most women who are admitted to hospital

BLENDING FAMILIES IS NOT AN EASY CHORE

So you're getting married again! Congratulations. But if you already have children—and especially if you plan on blending your families—you've got some work cut out for you. Subsequent marriages have a high divorce rate, and problems with the children are a big factor. Every parent knows there are days when you have trouble liking your own child. But someone else's?

As adults, we go into a second marriage feeling older and wiser. And we may be. But that doesn't mean our children are. They may still be mourning the divorce or resenting us for leaving. Or perhaps we've finally succeeded in healing their confusion and anger, only to have them feel abandoned all over again as we clasp a new love (and perhaps other children) to our hearts.

How children receive the big news depends on their age, the circumstances of the divorce, the length of the separation, and our closeness to them. Tiny tots may be thrilled to have a daddy in the house again; teens used to their autonomy may resent a new authority figure on the scene. A child who has felt responsible for either parent's welfare may feel relieved at sharing the responsibility—or jealous at being displaced. In our own excitement about a second chance at happily-ever-after, we may forget that we each bring old baggage into this new union. We not only have the image of marriage we got from our parents, but also the one we developed with our first mates. And we're likely to continue playing out our old roles unless we consciously break them through working on ourselves or seeking couples counseling (many modern couples do this before marrying). Here are some suggestions for creating happy stepfamilies:

- ❑ Move to a different home, which is new to you both. Give the kids some choices, such as what colors their rooms will be painted.
- ❑ Consider including the children in the ceremony so they feel a part of this new union. Family medallions to present to children—as well as a written ceremony that includes them—are available from Clergy Services, 706 W. 42nd St., Kansas City, MO, 64111, or call (800) 237-1922.
- ❑ For the first year or two, have the child's own parent handle discipline. Trying to shape up your mate's children will only foster resentment.
- ❑ Realize that many children will be torn in their loyalties between the stepparent and the original parent. Help the children know that to love one doesn't mean they must stop loving the other. Parents can help by not bad-mouthing the other parent to the child.
- ❑ To foster equality among his kids and her kids, periodically rotate chores and even bedrooms, so that no one is stuck with the dirtiest job or the smallest room.
- ❑ Learn about each family's history by sharing old home movies and photo albums.
- ❑ Try to incorporate the customs of both families for holidays and birthdays. Gradually, you'll add new traditions.
- ❑ Consider holding weekly or monthly meetings where it is safe for everyone to express feelings and discuss problems without reprisal.
- ❑ Don't let the children divide you as a couple. They may try, through manipulation and guilt. Make time for yourselves alone.
- ❑ Get to know a stepchild better or maintain closeness with your own child with periodic times alone doing something you both enjoy.
- ❑ Ex-spouses can be threatened by your remarriage. Now is the time to be kind but firm. Focus on what's best for the children.
- ❑ Eventually having a new child between you may create a firm bond among stepsiblings, as they will have something in common. But having a child too soon may create problems; make sure your marriage is stable first.
- ❑ Avoid treating the kids as a crowd. They are each individuals with their own special needs, talents, and feelings.

Source: Article written by Jann Mitchell.

> *"Nobody, as long as they move about among the chaotic currents of life, is without trouble."*
>
> C. G. Jung

emergency rooms were battered by their spouses. Although the statistic that one in three admissions are due to domestic violence has been challenged by Christina Hoff Sommers (1994) in *Who Stole Feminism?*, the debate over the frequency of battering should not overshadow the fact that, when it occurs, violence has a devastating impact on the family. The children who witness those events in their families are often irreparably damaged. The survivors of such incidents will likely need assistance and counseling at some time. As sordid as some of the talk shows are, they do serve some valuable purpose in getting certain topics out in the open. It is only then that adequate solutions can be explored.

We do need to keep things in perspective, however, as not all adult behavior is attributable to something that happened to the inner child while growing up. We have all had some degree of difficulty while learning to cope with unrealistic expectations and various forms of negative family dynamics. There is a saying in the mental health field that ACOA (Adult Children of Alcoholics) really stands for Adult Children of Anybody. This is not meant to diminish the trauma or the difficulties that come from growing up in the family of an alcoholic. Rather, it is meant to point out that we all have been affected to differing degrees by the families in which we grew up. Even the effects of a normal, neurotic middle-class American family (few of us grew up in a *Leave-It-to-Beaver*-type home) can have an impact on our life well into our adult years.

It seems odd that, while our country continues its claim of support for the family, most of the programs that deal with family dysfunction have to struggle for funding. Numerous experts in the field of child development agree that the most critical time in a person's life, in terms of implications for future adjustment, is the first three years. As a society, we wait until after the effects of neglect, poor health, and abuse have taken their toll on a person. Then, after the fact, we attempt to correct the problems by committing vast amounts of financial resources to dubious solutions. It appears that we would rather pay $30,000 a year to keep someone in prison than spend $3,000 a year to help prevent a child from becoming a delinquent. It might make more sense to provide families with medical and mental health assistance before problems arise.

LIFE IS FOR LEARNING

You were born to live life to the fullest and to grow from each of your experiences. With each new situation you encounter, first ask yourself, "What did I learn? Am I a wiser and more compassionate person because of what I experienced?" Through your struggle to answer this question, you will slowly grow in knowledge and wisdom.

Often, pain will be your greatest teacher. Whereas comfort puts us to sleep (when things are going our way, we rarely ask "What am I learning from this situation?"), discomfort forces us to question our assumptions and consider new ways of looking at life.

Second, ask yourself, "How much did I love?" Those who have gone through the near-death experience report that at the moment of death they focused on the love or lack of it in their lives. Material achievements, on the other hand, paled in significance. Nobody ever said at that critical moment, "I regret that I didn't spend more time at the office."

Thus, your most important teachings will involve matters of the heart. If life is for learning, all of your experiences can be reduced to a single lesson: the lesson of learning to love.

Abuse and Its Effects

There are a number of different types of abuse that contribute to and define a dysfunctional family. Usually, there are three main categories:

1. Physical and emotional abuse.
2. Drug and alcohol abuse.
3. Sexual abuse (dealt with in Chapter 7).

People who grew up in homes in which any of the above categories or combinations thereof occurred share similar characteristics. It is important to understand the characteristics and patterns that people develop in those situations because those characteristics and patterns may affect their relationships with other people in the future. For some people, the effects of having grown up in a home where there was violence, alcoholism, or sexual abuse can last long into adulthood. Many people from such homes experience low self-esteem, poor communication skills, inability to cope with stress, poor decision-making ability, lack of trust, and apprehension about close relationships.

Education and information help to alter the unhealthy coping mechanisms that might have been learned earlier in life. It is important to evaluate past behavior, even those patterns that seemed to be working at one time. We all do the best we know how to do in a given situation, but it is valuable to continue to update our abilities in coping with life's difficulties. That is the whole point of exploring the traumas of the past: to understand what happened, to learn new methods for coping, and to change old patterns into new ones that are more useful for getting on with life. In this section, we cover the topics related to domestic violence and substance abuse; sexual abuse is addressed in the chapter on human sexuality.

Physical Abuse American women have far more to fear from the men they know and once loved than from any stranger on the street. Domestic violence is the leading cause of injury and death to American women, causing more harm than vehicular accidents, rapes, and muggings combined. "Thirty-four percent of all female homicide victims older than fifteen years are killed by their husbands or intimate partners," said a report by Associated Press editor Teri Randall, citing FBI data from 1976 to 1987. Each year, an estimated four million women are beaten by the men they live with, and even when they are believed, they are often blamed

for staying with their abuser (*Chicago Tribune,* Feb. 10, 1992). What has become known as the *battered wife syndrome* may be somewhat of a misnomer, because, according to the University of New Hampshire's Family Research Laboratory, 60 percent of abused wives report that the physical violence started before marriage, while they were still dating their future husbands. About one-third of all young women under age 20, researchers report, experience some violence in dating relationships.

Domestic violence sometimes continues in cases where doctors largely ignore the situation. Of women who visit emergency rooms, 22 to 35 percent have abuse-related symptoms, according to a report in the *Journal of the American Medical Association* (August 1990): "While most clinicians wouldn't consider discharging a patient with a life-threatening condition, data from emergency department records show that a majority of women who are victims of domestic abuse are discharged without any arrangements being made for their safety, to return to the same abusive relationships that caused their injuries."

Why don't women leave abusive relationships? The answer is a combination of complex variables that involve lack of self-esteem, beliefs about what is normal or acceptable, and the high degree of likelihood that the victim was physically abused in the home while growing up. Sarah Buel was once herself the victim of an abusive spouse. She eventually went to Harvard Law School and is now an assistant district attorney for Norfolk County, Massachusetts. As a leading advocate for battered women and someone concerned with court reform, she lists some of the problems of women who try to leave:

▶ Most do not have enough money to live on: They can't support themselves or their children, particularly if they require day care.

▶ Most have trouble finding a place to live: Five women are turned away for every one who seeks shelter, and 95 percent of shelters will not accept women with children.

▶ Leaving an abusive spouse doesn't necessarily bring safety: It often triggers more serious violence.

▶ Women who leave are afraid they will lose their children: Men, who usually control the money, are often able to hire good lawyers and fight for custody of the children.

More often than not, the law fails to protect battered women. Abusive men, instead of being prosecuted and jailed for committing acts of criminal violence, either are not arrested or are released by disbelieving judges. That situation is being addressed nationally and, we can hope, is being rectified, as many states take a different stance and begin to adopt new laws. Oregon protects the victims of domestic violence with laws that have become a model for the nation. They include the following:

- *Mandatory Arrest:* A police officer at the scene of a domestic disturbance who believes an assault has occurred or that one person has placed the other in fear of serious injury shall arrest the suspected abuser. Arrest is no longer at the victim's discretion.
- *Restraining Orders:* This order says that a person can be arrested if he contacts his victim again. Women don't have to have a lawyer to get such an order. They can ask for the Petition for Restraining Order to Prevent Abuse from their county courthouse.
- *Marital Rape Laws:* Marriage or cohabitation is no defense for any crime of violence, including sexual assault against a spouse or partner or child. Husbands and boyfriends have been prosecuted for forcing sex on their partners.

The long-term effects of physical abuse include an increased tendency to act aggressively. A study of young children finds that physical abuse at home is more strongly linked to later aggressive behavior than are such factors as poverty, divorce, or marital violence. John Bates, a psychology professor at Indiana University, stated for the Associated Press that his study of 309 children followed from age 4 until kindergarten showed that those who were physically abused by an adult at home were more likely to be aggressive or even violent in difficult social situations. As a result of living in an unpredictable setting where they were mistreated, many people grow up lacking the needed social skills to deal with life's everyday problems.

Substance Abuse A commonality between those who were physically abused and those who grew up in homes where there was alcohol and/or drug abuse is that both groups become overly fearful of unpredictable events in life. A dysfunctional aspect of life in a home where

---

The Oregon Committee for the Prevention of Child Abuse lists these 10 reasons not to spank:

Spanking Teaches Children:

1. That they don't have control over their behavior, leading to a lack of inner control.
2. To rely on others for control of their behavior.
3. That hitting is acceptable; that violence is a way to channel anger or solve problems.
4. That it is OK to hit someone you love, which can perpetuate domestic violence.
5. To seek revenge; it teaches children to hate, fear, and/or avoid the punisher.

Spanking Also:

6. Models an imbalance of power, based on size.
7. Is not effective; the effects of spanking are immediate but usually short term.
8. Is useless as children get older; the degree of intensity would have to increase as the child grows.
9. Tells children what not to do, but does not teach them appropriate behavior.
10. Encourages violence and frustrates the child.

Source: Article written by Jann Mitchell.

CASE STUDIES AND STUDENT STORIES

Maxine's recollection of childhood was the smell of alcohol and garlic. It took her years to make a connection between the memory and the reality of her youth. One morning, as an adult, she woke up with a start realizing that the smell that she recalled was that of her stepfather coming into her bedroom when she was 6 years old. The details of being molested came slowly at first, but as time passed the picture became clearer.

She was in the first grade when her mother married her stepdad. He appeared to be an average blue-collar worker. He had lost his former wife to cancer and seemed to be happy marrying again. From outside appearances all looked normal, but things soon changed.

Maxine was shocked the first time her stepdad entered her bedroom in the middle of the night. He explained to her that now that he was her dad he would need to teach her things that she needed to know as an adult. As she shared her story tears welled up in her eyes and she recounted the graphic details. She was told that it would be "their little secret" and if she told anyone, harm would come to her mother.

The first few nights he talked to her and held her, but as time progressed he went from gentle fondling to raping her. She had no one to talk to, and a paralyzing fear gripped her as she lived each day. Finally she decided to run away from home. She packed her bag and headed for the railroad tracks, hoping to catch a freight train. Her freedom lasted a few precious hours before she was caught and taken back home. The next few years were a constant nightmare to this young child.

Although it has been a long road back, she has learned to cope with what happened and is healing from the *horrible dream*. Today Maxine is in charge of security for a large Northwest company. Countless therapy sessions and an understanding mate have helped her to conquer her demons and simply live life again. Maxine said the advice she would give to anyone who is being abused is to simply tell a "safe person." And, find refuge in knowing that others have shared that nightmare. You are not alone.

Source: Written By D. Juanita Woods.

there is substance abuse is the frightening lack of structure or predictability. The child never knows when a parent might become irrational or abusive. One day, a parent might act as if nothing is wrong, and the next day he or she might be passed out on the floor. One moment, the parent might be friendly and caring, and the next, screaming and violent. There is often a great deal of confusion about what is expected and how to please the parents in those kinds of situations. Those from the Alcoholics Anonymous background frequently refer to the following three rules that children, unfortunately, learn while growing up in those families:

1. Don't talk.
2. Don't feel.
3. Don't trust.

Obviously, there are a number of problems that arise from living in an environment where one learns these rules. Frequently, families with problems deny that any difficulty exists. Therefore, a child is seldom permitted to express his or her feel-

ings about living in such conditions. As a result, the child learns not only to distrust his or her own experience, but also to distrust authority figures. And if children can't trust themselves or anyone else, is it any wonder that they have difficulty forming relationships and having a family of their own?

Indicators of Chemical Dependency

Dependence on alcohol or other drugs is a widespread problem. Chemical dependency is simply the inability to control the use of some physical substance—not being able to quit and not being able to limit how much is used. If you have a dependency problem, recognizing it can help you move toward a happier and healthier life. You might think of a chemically dependent person as someone who can't live without his or her drink or drugs, who is often drunk or stoned, who uses every day, or who is irresponsible, immoral, and weak-willed. The fact is, a person can be chemically dependent without showing such obvious signs, and dependency can cause serious problems in a person's life. We are gradually beginning to realize that a person's genetic makeup may affect his or her chances of becoming dependent, and that dependency is often a physical condition that cannot be cured by willpower alone.

Here are some of the signs that might indicate a chemical dependency problem in yourself or someone you love:

Job Performance

- Absenteeism.
- "On-the-job absenteeism," lack of productivity.
- High accident rate.
- Difficulty in concentration.
- Confusion.
- Spasmodic work patterns.
- Inflexibility with work—doesn't change easily.
- Coming to or returning to work in an obviously abnormal condition.
- Generally lowered job efficiency.
- Poor employee relations.

Social Interactions

- More or less social (opposite of his or her normal pattern).
- Changes of friends, social circles.
- Changes in reaction of others to him or her.
- Showing more anger.
- More manipulative of others.
- Changes in speech: disconnected thoughts, rapid speech, unfinished sentences.
- Voicing more complaints.
- General negative change in attitude.
- Increased financial problems.
- More problems in family and/or other relationships.
- Borrowing more money from friends.

Personal Health

- Uses alcohol or drugs differently.
- Unusual and/or frequent illness.
- Energy level changed from normal patterns.
- Daily living or work routine changes.
- Change in general appearance: personal hygiene, clothing style.
- Facial changes.
- Changes in body: pronounced weight gain or loss.
- Increasing complaints regarding sleep patterns.

Emotional Health

- Signs of "nerves" or irritability.
- Grandiose thinking or delusions.
- Excessive sharing of personal problems.
- Unwillingness to talk at all about problems or denial that any problems exist.
- Erratic mood swings.

Chemically dependent people often act unwisely or inappropriately while under the influence of their drug. They may act in ways that will embarrass them later, when they learn of what they have done. They may endanger their health, their lives, and the lives of others by having unsafe sex or by driving while intoxicated. They may lose their jobs or families as people around them are hurt by their actions.

Recognizing that there is a problem is the first step toward recovering from chemical dependency. If you think you might have a problem of this type, here are some steps you can take:

1. Acknowledge the problem openly and limit time spent with people who encourage drug use.
2. Seek professional help from doctors or therapists who deal with chemical dependency and recovery. You might benefit from counseling or a recovery program at a hospital or private clinic.
3. Seek out the support of people who are recovering themselves. Many 12-step programs, such as Alcoholics Anonymous, are available for various types of dependencies.

If you grew up with an alcoholic parent, try the following:

1. Find out more about alcoholism and its effects on family members of alcoholics. Contact Al-Anon for information on special groups for Adult Children of Alcoholics, or ask your employee assistance program for referrals to other helpful programs.
2. Talk about your feelings and experiences with friends, relatives, people in 12-step programs, or health professionals.
3. Remember, you didn't cause your parent's drinking, and no one but the parent had any chance of controlling it or curing it.

Coping and Recovery

People who have grown up in dysfunctional families learn different roles and coping mechanisms. In addition to the usual birth order roles, children from troubled families add another level of complexity to their behavior: they adopt roles they think may help in dealing with the family dynamics. Literature on alcoholics and their families lists the following as some of the ways that children attempt to cope with the situation. As

HOW TO GET HELP

If you know a child living in an alcoholic home, try doing these things:

1. Gently encourage the child to talk about life, and listen well.
2. Invite the child to an outing, or offer a quiet place to do homework.
3. Encourage the child to think of people who would be understanding and helpful in hard times—perhaps a teacher, friend, relative, or neighbor.
4. If the parent drinks and drives, give the child your phone number and offer to come pick him or her up.
5. Suggest checking the library for books about alcoholism, or attending Alateen. Give the child the phone number and offer a ride to the first meeting.
6. Tell the child that he or she cannot cause, control, or cure his or her parent's drinking.
7. Tell the child that alcoholism is a disease, and it's OK to love the parent but hate the disease.

> **"**Men stumble over the truth from time to time, but most pick themselves up and hurry off as if nothing happened.**"**
> *Sir Winston Churchill*

with birth order roles, these roles are often adopted unconsciously. They represent the child's attempts at coping with difficult situations and constitute a form of defense mechanism.

The Superhero: Superheroes are the children who hope that if they try hard enough, are good enough, or take care of everyone just right, everything will turn out okay. They often appear outwardly to be strong and competent, but inside may feel inadequate, lonely, and guilty.

The Scapegoat: Scapegoat children think that serving as the lightning rod for family emotions and conflict will somehow diminish the problem. They are frequently the ones acting out the family's pain and calling attention to what others don't want to deal with.

The Lost Child: Lost children hope that being invisible will lessen the pain. They withdraw, spending considerable time alone in their rooms, the backyard, or inside their heads. They may hope that by being good and quiet, they will contribute to the family's getting better. It may be

useful at the time, but is seldom beneficial for the person later on in life.

The Mascot or Distractor: Children who are mascots or distractors learn to be funny and entertaining, hoping they will interrupt the argument or prevent people from noticing the size of the problem. Their behavior is an attempt to divert attention away from the painful reality of the family system.

Chief Enabler: Enabler children try desperately to smooth things out or to get everyone to go along and not make waves. Frequently, they try to protect the chemically dependent family member at almost any cost. They spend a great deal of energy trying to cover up and make things right.

The negative aspects of adopting one of these roles is part of the focus for people in recovery. Patterns that were learned in childhood have a way of cropping up and repeating themselves when people become adults. The term *inner child* refers to that part in all of us that still remembers and retains elements of being a child. Some people have been damaged by the experiences of severe abuse and have psychic wounds that have been internalized. As a result, there are those who would qualify as cases of arrested development. The positive and useful aspects of the recovery movement are that they address the need to heal wounds from the past and develop new methods of coping with problems in the present.

ADULT CHILDREN OF ALCOHOLICS

The following list is indicative of the extent of the problems that some people face as a result of living in dysfunctional families. It can also help us understand the depth of the healing that must take place in order to have better human relations:

Adult Children of Alcoholics:

1. Guess at what normal behavior is.
2. Have difficulty following a project through from beginning to end.
3. Lie when it would be just as easy to tell the truth.
4. Judge themselves without mercy.
5. Have difficulty having fun.
6. Take themselves very seriously.
7. Have difficulty with intimate relationships.
8. Overreact to changes over which they have no control.
9. Constantly seek approval and affirmation.
10. Usually feel they are different from other people.
11. Are super responsible or super irresponsible.
12. Are extremely loyal, even when evident the loyalty is undeserved.
13. Are impulsive. They tend to lock themselves into a course of action without giving serious consideration to alternative behaviors or possible consequences. This impulsivity leads to confusion, self-loathing, and loss of control over their environment. In addition, they spend an excessive amount of energy cleaning up the mess.

Source: Janet G. Woititz, *Adult Children of Alcoholics.* Deerfield Beach, FL: Health Communications, Inc., 1983.

There are a number of programs and approaches that essentially do inner child work. Both John Bradshaw (1988a), author of *Bradshaw: on the Family,* and Melody Beattie (1987), author of *Codependent No More,* lead people back through childhood to discover the origins of troublesome behavior.

Bradshaw contends that when a child comes from a dysfunctional family, he or she internalizes the guilt and shame that is felt about the situation. The result is that a great many people end up feeling bad about themselves due to what was really a very bad set of circumstances. Unfortunately, these people may end up blaming themselves, rather than the perpetrators, for something that wasn't their fault. Hence, Bradshaw's term *toxic shame.* The elements of doing inner child work include asking yourself how old that child is, and allowing yourself to remember what was painful. It is usually at the point of some traumatic event that people feel stuck. The defenses learned and used in that situation are frequently the source of difficulty in adult life. People often create negative situations, however inadvertently, when looking for others to act as the parent who denied them what was missing earlier in their lives. An aspect of recovery that is helpful is learning to avoid codependent behavior by developing alternative ways of meeting your own needs. It is possible to reparent yourself using some of the following methods:

Stop the internal criticism: Treat yourself as you would your own children when you are acting at your best.

Give yourself now what you didn't get while growing up: That could mean a wide range of things, such as a chance to play, permission to say no, respect, or an opportunity to explore more about who you are and what you like.

Read and gather information: Find out about what others have been through and how they have learned to cope. Seek therapy and attend support groups to have a place to express the feelings that you weren't allowed to have or talk about.

Stop the denial: Don't deny to yourself or to others what happened.

Apologize to your inner child: Apologize, if it is appropriate, for not having protected the inner child in the past from abusive people, and try not to let it happen again.

Even the most strident critics of the recovery movement accept that during the course of the past decade, much has been accomplished that is of value. Many people have benefited from counseling, support groups, Alcoholics Anonymous, and workshop presentations that include processes similar to those presented in this chapter. However, there is currently a reaction to what has become an overuse of the term *adult child* and the overgeneralization of the word *abuse*. With all the self-help books that have been written recently, it seems that nearly everyone is an adult child of something, due to a negative situation in his or her childhood. The problem with that is that you can't go around putting parental nagging on a par with sex abuse. There really is a dif-

ference between not getting help with your homework and being molested by your father.

That type of thinking reflects the notion that there may be a downside to the recovery movement. Although there have been benefits, it is important to listen to those who raise a cautionary note. Some counselors point to books such as *Toxic Parents* (Foward, 1990) as evidence that valid information may at times be misinterpreted. There are self-help books that go too far and, to some degree, sanction blame-shifting and erode personal responsibility. Although there are some parents who have done harm to their children, it is important not to overindulge in blaming parents for all of one's problems. There is some legitimacy to the criticism that too much "You did this to me" and "Don't blame me, blame my parents" is just another form of being a victim. Critics of the movement say that subscribing to the adult-children theory creates children, not adults. They say that obsessing about damage itself is damaging, because it blocks out more affirmative thinking. That idea is reflected in a joke that even people in the recovery movement tell: Once someone gets involved in Alcoholics Anonymous, they just "Al-Anon-An-On-An-On." Perhaps there can be a balance of healing the wounds of the past and learning to develop skills that can help us face the challenges of the future without living in the past.

CHAPTER REVIEW

Family History

Many of our beliefs about the family structure of the 1950s were based on myths. There never was a golden age of the family. Some of our ideals were reflected from the media and its portrayal of how we wished we were. There are many programs that can truly help struggling families of today.

Family Structures

There have been many changes in the nuclear family, and we need to adapt to new rules and roles. Most people still believe in the traditional family unit, especially when it comes to raising children; but economic factors increasingly require two incomes. That makes it necessary to become more creative about providing child care. The current divorce rate means that more

people will grow up in blended families with stepparents.

Race, Culture, and the Family

While many families share common traits, there are some differences due to race and/or culture. Many minority families have a greater emphasis on extended family. Some cultures place more emphasis on cooperation and support rather than competition.

Family of Origin

The family that you grew up in has a tremendous influence on how you view yourself and your role in the world. Families operate as a system, and if you change any part of the system, you change the whole system to a certain degree. There is a constant push-pull for closeness and distance. Part of the maturational process is to differentiate oneself from the family while still maintaining contact and connection.

Birth Order

Your position in the family influences your behavior in a number of ways, including mate selection and parenting style. Birth order has also been related to career choice. Although you may have played more than one role during the time you grew up, one position most likely influenced how you gain attention. Competition for the various roles in the family has significance for how siblings interact.

Functional Families

There are a number of characteristics that are common to healthy families. It is important for members to feel free to be who they are and to express themselves, and for the parents to have a strong, healthy couple relationship to model the types of behavior that are beneficial for the family. It is useful for parents to adopt a consultant style of parenting to help their children develop personal responsibility.

Stepfamilies

More people are forming families in which there are children that are "his," "hers," and "ours."

There are three stages that the stepfamily system needs to go through. The first concerns dealing with issues of loss and entering a new relationship. The second is about conceptualizing and planning the new marriage while learning to share fears and insecurities. The third stage is the formation of the new family system through the restructuring of discipline and nurturing roles.

Parenting

There are a wide range of parenting styles, but effective methods have universal commonalities. Being involved and setting limits is important. Young people need a certain amount of structure, but with enough freedom to develop autonomy. It would appear from the research that the most detrimental style for children is neglectful.

Dysfunctional Families

A common characteristic of those who were physically abused or who lived in families where there was physical abuse or substance abuse is the insecurity and lack of trust that develops due to the unpredictability of the situation. Many people learn the three rules—don't talk, don't feel, and don't trust—as a means of coping. Others take on a role that will help them deal with the family system.

SOURCES AND SUGGESTED READINGS

Baumrind, D. (1991). "The Influence of Parenting Style on Adolescent Competence and Substance Use." *Journal of Early Adolescence, 11*(1), 56–95.

Beattie, Melody. *Codependent No More.* New York: Harper/Hazeldon, 1987.

Black, Claudia. *It Will Never Happen to Me.* Denver, CO: M.A.C., 1982.

Bloomfield, H. H., with L. Felder. *Making Peace With Your Parents.* New York: Ballantine, 1983.

Bowen, Murray. *Family Therapy in Clinical Practice.* New York: Jason Aronson, 1978.

Bradshaw, John. *Healing the Shame That Binds You.* Pompano Beach, FL: Health Communications, 1988.

Cline, Foster, and Jim Fay. *Parenting With Love and Logic.* Denver, CO: Pinon Press, 1990.

Fay, Jim. *Helicopters, Drill Sergeants, and Consultants: Parenting Styles and the Messages That They Send.* Golden, CO: Love and Logic Press, 1994.

Leman, Kevin. *The Birth Order Book.* New York: Dell, 1985.

Whitfield, Charles L. *Healing the Child Within: Discovery and Recovery for Adult Children of Dysfunctional Families.* New York: Ballantine, 1989.

Wholey, Dennis. *Becoming Your Own Parent.* New York: Doubleday, 1991.

Woititz, Janet G. *Adult Children of Alcoholics.* Deerfield Beach, FL: Health Communications, 1983.

Wyckoff, Jerry. *Discipline Without Shouting or Spanking.* New York: Meadowbrook, 1984.

Web Site Resources

Divorce help for children and teens
http://www.childrenanddivorce.com

Family Service America 1-800-221-2681
http://www.fsanet.org

National Institute on Alcohol Abuse and Alcoholism
http://www.niaaa.nih.gov

Stepfamily Association of America, Inc. 1-800-735-0329
http://www.stepfam.org

WholeFamily: Extensive information and resources on family life
http://www.wholefamily.com/

National Center for Assault Prevention
http://www.ncap.org/aboutncap.htm

National Committee for the Prevention of Child Abuse
http://www.preventchildabuse.org

REACTION AND RESPONSE—WHAT DO YOU THINK?

Chapter Four   Level I Assignments

In response to the information in the chapter:

1. How accurate was the information on birth order in describing your general characteristics? Where and when have you observed the interactions described in that section? How have you *re-created* your family in other situations in life?

2. How did your gender influence how you were treated as you were growing up? Did birth order or gender influence your decisions about education and career?

3. Ask your parents about their families and what their parents were like. What themes or messages have been passed down through the generations? Make a genealogy chart (family tree or genogram) that includes significant events and life circumstances. Try to include grandparents and great-grandparents.

In response to the class activities, group discussions, and exercises:

1. What are your opinions and reactions?
2. What did you learn or rediscover?
3. How are you going to apply what you learned?

Chapter Four   Level II Assignments

1. What were the positive and negative aspects of the family that you grew up in? What do you want for the family that you create? How will you contribute to the possibility of that happening?

2. What did you learn for the sections on functional and dysfunctional families? What did you learn about coping skills?

3. Make a timeline of your life. Include commentary on the high and low periods of your life. What contributed to things getting better or worse?

Chapter Four   Level III Assignments

1. Were there problems with drugs and/or alcohol in the family? How did that affect you?

2. What style of parenting do you think your parents used? What style would you like to use, and what would it take to do that?

3. What do you believe about spanking? Do you believe it is necessary? Do you think it is effective?

5
CHAPTER

DEALING WITH EMOTIONS

A few years ago, I was on a vacation in the San Juan Islands and was taking the ferry back to Seattle with my wife, mother-in-law, and kids. I had gotten out of the car and was standing on the deck of the ferryboat when a man, visibly angry and upset, walked up to me. He said, "Hey, do you own a yellow Volvo?" I replied that I did. "Well," he said, "you dented my car and you're going to pay for it. I want you to come down and take a look at it." I had no idea what this was all about. Now, I could have gotten irritated, which would only have escalated his anger. But I didn't. I said, "Well, I don't know what you're talking about, but if that happened, we sure would need to take care of it." Immediately, the guy cooled off. I added, "Could you tell me more about what happened here?" I was asking for information, not resisting. He replied, "I'm parked on the passenger side of your car, and someone dented my car when they opened the door." I explained that because I had gotten out on the other side of the car, I hadn't noticed anything.

We went to my wife, and I said, "This guy says one of us dented his car. Do you know anything about it?" She said, "Well, I don't, but let's take care of it, because if somebody dented his car, we really want to do right by him." My wife, who also works in the mental health field, knew what to say to lessen the conflict. We acknowledged that if something had happened, it needed to be taken care of. As soon as he felt he had been heard, the man relaxed and was much less aggressive.

When we got to the cars, the guy's wife was there and still in a huff, even though he had calmed down considerably by then. I looked the situation over and said, "Well, my mother-in-law was in the back seat, and she might have done this; I don't know." By now, the guy was almost ready to establish some basis for discussing what happened. He had a chrome strip around the rear wheel well of his car. There was only a tiny dent in it, but I guess his wife had gotten upset and it was important to her. He decided to assess whether it might have been someone in our car by lining up the dent with our car door. The dent and the car door didn't match by about an inch.

I realized, however, that they didn't match because of the weight of the people who had been in the cars. When everyone got out of the two cars, each car adjusted to a different height. With the cars empty, the dent and the door didn't match, but it was close enough that I could see they probably had at one time. I think that my mother-in-law may very well have dented his car. He assessed the situation, though, and said, "Ah, no. It doesn't match. It wasn't you. Just forget it." The fact that I hadn't hassled him but instead had acknowledged his point of view made it possible for him to finally say "Forget it." I know people who would have gotten into a fight about this up on the main deck without ever seeing the cars.

Understanding Emotions

Emotions affect behavior in a number of ways. Our reactions to situations influence our ability to perceive what is happening around us. Emotions create filters that affect our communications. Our physiological condition is also greatly influenced by the manner in which we deal with our feelings. And our emotional responses give us a good deal of satisfaction and enjoyment in life.

It is crucial to keep things in perspective and strive for balance when dealing with emotions. Some people suppress their feelings to the extent that the suppression yields negative results. People who initially *overcontrol* their emotions may finally overreact to situations and behave in an inappropriate manner. Lack of appropriate emotional expression may contribute to poor communication skills and affect the ability to have close relationships. Unexpressed feelings may even exhibit themselves in physiological ailments and illness.

On the other hand, people who *undercontrol* their feelings may experience difficulty in their relationships due to poor impulse control. When emotions are given too much emphasis, they cloud our ability to process cognitive information. Feelings can motivate us to do wonderful things and accomplish great deeds, but strong emotions can also make us act in ways that we later regret.

We have all been overwhelmed or confused by our own emotions at times. A greater understanding of the complexity of feelings can lead to better comprehension of our behavior. That, in turn, can lead to increased flexibility in dealing with others.

A number of theories over the years have attempted to explain the relationships among emotions, physical response, and behavior. The *common sense* approach says that if we see a bear, we have an emotional feeling—fear, most likely. This leads to arousal and an increase in heart rate, and leads to a behavior—running, for instance. However, the James-Lange theory of emotions stated that bodily arousal does not follow a feeling such as fear. Instead, James and Lange argued, emotional feelings follow bodily arousal. Thus, we see a bear, run, are aroused, and then feel fear as we become aware of our bodily reactions. This theory may explain an interesting effect that you may have observed in yourself or others. When you are feeling down but force yourself to get up and do something, or even just try to smile, you sometimes feel an actual improvement in your mood. A counseling axiom is: *If you change the physiology, you can change the emotion.* This is true for some people, but neither the common sense approach nor the James-Lange theory adequately explain the complexities of human emotional responses.

In reviewing the historical background on emotion, it is important to note the Cannon-Bard theory (1927). Agreeing that the body becomes aroused during an emotion, Cannon and Bard noted that there are only slight differences in the physiology of various emotions. These differences are not enough to allow for the rich and varied emotional life that humans experience. Cannon and Bard also pointed out that the viscera and internal organs are relatively insensitive, which casts doubt on the idea that emotional feelings come mainly from the body. In their theory, seeing a bear activates the thalamus, which in turn alerts both the cortex and the hypothalamus for action. (The brain may be thought of as having three layers: the brain stem or reptilian core, the limbic system or old mammalian brain, and the cerebral cortex, which is the most recent brain evolution.) The cortex is responsible for emotional behavior, the hypothalamus is responsible for arousing the body, and the brain stem is in charge of autonomic functions. Thus, if the bear is seen as dangerous, bodily arousal, running, and feelings of fear will all be generated at the same time by brain activity.

Stanley Schachter (Schachter and Singer, 1962) believes that cognitive and mental factors also contribute to certain feelings. According to Schachter, emotion occurs when a particular *label* is applied to general physical *arousal*. When we are aroused, most of us have a need to interpret and label our feelings. The label—fear, anger, or happiness—applied to bodily arousal is influenced by past experience, the situation, and the reactions of others. If we see a bear, our reaction is determined by the label we give the arousal. A bear in the zoo creates a different reaction from a bear in the woods. A further extension of the cognitive influence on emotions is the concept of internal dialogue. We feel differently because we say different things to ourselves about the two bears. The topic of how self-talk applies to different emotions will be explored later in the chapter.

The latest research on emotions is attempting to map the anatomical ties between the cognitive and emotional centers in the brain. Findings suggest that emotions not only shape what we perceive but also sift out what we remember. Research on animals is generating some intriguing explanations of why certain phobias can't be erased, and why some individuals tend to be more emotional than others. New information may explain why emotionally laden events that happen to individuals before they reach their third birthday can have a strong influence on the rest of their lives.

Application of Theory

In general, there are three components of emotions: physiological changes, subjective cognitive states, and expressive behaviors. The component of physiological arousal has to do with the biological reactions of the nervous system, various glands and organs within the body, and activity in the previously mentioned brain structures. The second component, our subjective cognitive state, is what we are aware of and how we appraise and label our emotions. Physical arousal may be given any number of different labels depending on the context of the situation. The sensation we feel when the airplane hits an air pocket and drops suddenly is fairly similar to the sensation of riding a roller coaster over a big drop. One experience may be called "fear," whereas the other might be labeled "fun and excitement." The third component is expressive behavior. People have many ways of expressing similar feelings. Some people are reserved about showing any type of emotion, but that doesn't mean that they don't feel it. Other people are highly demonstrative regardless of the emotion being experienced and give little thought to the time, place, or circumstance in which it occurs.

As valuable as this type of information is, most people are more interested in what to do with their feelings than what anatomical conditions caused them. Although at times, there may be a direct connection between physical behavior and emotional states, in most situations, the mind plays an important role in determining how we feel.

Our thoughts and self-talk influence our feelings. And our feelings, along with bodily arousal, influence our cognitive processes. A greater understanding of the connection between thoughts and emotions can help us learn to handle feelings better and to cope with emotional situations with others in a more productive manner.

It is useful to learn about beliefs, reactions, and how feelings are created in order to have more emotional control. Have you ever responded to a situation or a person without knowing what brought about your emotional reaction? Have you ever wanted to experience an emotion, but been unable to define exactly what or how it was you were feeling? We all have difficulty in dealing with our emotions at times. Two people experiencing the same event may react emotionally in very different ways. The fact that we feel anger about something one day but laugh about the same thing another day indicates that we have more emotional control than we realize.

Understanding emotions is important because they play a major role in everyday behavior and in human relations in general. This chapter lays a foundation for understanding emotions, having appropriate control in different situations, and learning how feelings affect relations with others.

Types of Emotions

There are hundreds of words in the English language for emotions, but most psychologists handle the problem of classifying emotions by looking for clusters. There are certain feelings that people tend to identify as being combinations of several emotions. Some psychologists use wheel diagrams to classify our emotions. Robert Plutchik (1980) has identified eight primary emotions, which are inside the perimeter of the wheel. He suggests that these primary feelings can be combined to form other mixed emotions, which are listed on the outside of the wheel. Plutchik believes that emotions are like colors on an artist's palette. The various hues of emotional feelings can be produced by mixing the primary colors. His model proposes that emotions have four dimensions: (a) they are positive or negative; (b) they are primary or mixed; (c) they vary in intensity; and (d) many are polar opposites, but you can't feel opposites simultaneously.

A more simplistic approach has been offered by Emery and Campbell (1986). They believe that

Questions for Critical Thinking

What did you learn about emotions? What is the connection between physiology and cognition? How do emotions influence your behavior?

_____

_____

_____

_____

_____

_____

_____

_____

_____

there are only four basic emotions: mad, sad, glad, and scared (fear). They suggest that all emotions that we experience are just derivatives of these basic four. These categories are explored more fully in this chapter. Guilt, which may be an expression of anger or sadness, is also discussed.

Emotional Building Blocks

The following 10 concepts will help you understand more about your emotions. These concepts provide a foundation to build on as we discuss dealing with emotions and having more emotional control.

1. *Emotions Aren't Right or Wrong.* Feelings are indicators that something is happening inside you; you are having a reaction to an event, real or imagined. Our society tends to classify emotions as good (e.g., happy) and bad (e.g., angry or depressed). Emotions aren't necessarily right or wrong; they just are. Suspending judgment on feelings allows a person to concentrate instead on the internal message the feeling is sending and to consider what caused the reaction and what can be learned from the experience.

You should accept an emotion before attempting to change it. For example, refusing to acknowledge anger doesn't help you change that feeling. Telling yourself you aren't angry when you are won't help you learn to control or express that emotion in an appropriate manner. However, accepting your various emotional responses doesn't automatically justify any type of behavior.

2. *Context Makes a Difference.* Some people are good at cutting their feelings off immediately. Others have an emotional reaction at almost any time or place. Each of these styles can be useful in certain situations. Stopping or starting feelings is not as important as the context in which it happens. An emergency room doctor must be able to detach emotionally in order to function effectively, but that same detachment might be detrimental when interacting with family members at home. The person who easily experiences a full range of emotional responses may do well in personal relationships but have difficulty functioning in problem-solving or task-oriented situations. The context of the situation dictates which response is most useful.

3. *Family Beliefs Affect Emotions.* In some families, any and all feelings are given expression. In contrast are families where emotions may not be tolerated or expressed. The Wild Wilsons and the Silent Smiths are illustrations of the extremes on the continuum of emotional response. In the Wild Wilson home, all emotions are freely expressed, usually at maximum volume. They have loud parties and regular Friday night fights. People and objects fly out the windows during their recreational arguments. On the other end of the spectrum is the Silent Smith home, in which no one has raised a

WILD WILSON   **SILENT SMITH**

Family influence on emotions.

voice in anger in 20 years, and they pride themselves on never having had an argument. Unpleasant feelings cause a cold, dark, brooding atmosphere reminiscent of a late-night horror movie.

Members of these two families obviously have different beliefs about emotional expression. The importance of understanding family background becomes clear when imagining people from these two families marrying each other. When they have relationship problems, the situation will be compounded by their emotional differences. Most likely, they will argue about the problem, about how to express emotions about the problem, and about what constitutes problem solving. Some of the worst fights that couples have are about how they are fighting!

4. *Repressing Feelings May Make Them More Intense.* Children often express the full range of emotions available to them between getting up in the morning and eating breakfast. They don't have hang-ups about emotional situations; they simply express what they are feeling at the moment. An early morning "I hate you and will never speak to you again, ever" argument between two children will be resolved and forgotten by afternoon of the same day, whereas adults will refuse to talk to each other for a week after such an argument. Many adults create more problems for themselves by ignoring or suppressing their feelings. As we grow up, we learn to censor certain emotions as unacceptable, probably because of family training and societal pressure.

Our culture seems to condition adults to repress any emotions that are less than neutral. The acceptable adult response to "How are you doing?" is "Fine," even when that is untrue. Trying to suppress anger or irritation usually increases the intensity of the emotion. In some cases, the difficulties that arise from trying to avoid an emotional situation may be more of a problem than the original one. Most of the time, it is better to deal with the feelings and the situation causing them than to try to cover them up.

5. *Limiting One Feeling May Limit Them All.* Some people think it is possible to limit their feelings of sadness or anger yet experience all the happiness they want. It doesn't work that way! The control valve is not on individual feelings but on the main emotional output channel.

Trying to limit certain emotions to a particular degree actually limits them all to the same degree. Have you noticed that people who don't express sadness or anger also have difficulty expressing joy or happiness? These are the *Spocks* of the world, who have an extremely narrow emotional comfort zone. After all, they believe that emotions are illogical! Counseling theories suggest that to have more happiness, a person must experience all emotions. That includes those considered to be other than positive or neutral. How do you feel today?

6. *We Have Feelings About Feelings.* Emotions are complex because they are seldom experienced in a pure form. You may feel a range of emotions, from pensiveness to sadness to depression. You may feel anger and sadness at the same time. In addition, each of those primary emotions can be experienced on a continuum from mild to intense.

Often, we have a reaction to an emotion itself, which may then cause additional feelings. Some people get scared after they have felt and expressed anger. The reverse is also true. For many people, the original feeling was fear, but it then got expressed as anger. Other people actually feel scared when they are very happy because they fear that something negative will soon happen.

Our society finds it more acceptable for men to feel anger than to feel sadness. As a result, men have different feelings about being mad than about being sad. For women, the reverse is true: they get more acceptance for being sad than for being mad. Is it any wonder that men and women have different reactions to those feelings? An example of that type of reaction for males is evident in the stereotypical cowboy, as presented by the general media. He walks into the White Horse Tavern and he's feeling sad, maybe because he's lost his wife, job, dog, or all three. He feels sad and close to tears and that scares him because he's not supposed to cry. So then he gets angry because he feels scared about feeling sad, and instead of feeling any of that he tries to scare someone else. He may attempt to discharge the emotions by provoking another person. If he gets angry and gets into a fight and is thrown into jail, he may feel better temporarily because he no longer feels so scared at feeling sad. Except now, the cycle starts over again because he has feelings about the feeling of being in jail!

7. *The Way Out Is the Way In.* Sometimes, the only way to get over an event is to go through it. There are some situations in life that only get worse if ignored, such as pretending a toothache doesn't exist. It may eventually get better by itself, but only after a long time of being in pain and only then because, eventually, the tooth falls out. The original problem may have gone away, but there is a new one: How are you going to eat corn on the cob? Some people ignore their problems for years, hoping they will just disappear, but some changes in life only come about when people are willing to endure the short-term discomfort involved in doing the needed work. Only then are they free to get on with their lives without worrying about the long-term difficulties.

8. *Know How to Get In and Get Out.* Some people have no problem getting into their feelings. They dive right in, but then they go to the bottom and stay there. If they have a bad experience, they rehearse it in their minds a hundred times and continue talking about problems that should have been forgotten months ago. They know how to get into their feelings but are stuck when it comes to getting out.

Other people are the opposite. Their feelings happen so fast that they don't even realize that anything has happened. They may have cut the feeling off before they were even conscious of having it. For them, getting out of emotions is easy, but they don't know how to really experience an emotion when it is appropriate. It is important to have both choices and to know how and when to use each one.

9. *Use a Dimmer Switch on Emotions.* People have methods of emotional control analogous to the electrical switches in a house. Some people are "hard-wired," with no switch at all; they are either permanently on or permanently off. These people respond to everything with one emotion or don't respond at all. Others have an on/off switch, but it doesn't allow for any intermediate responses; it's either dead calm or a volcano exploding.

The best option is using a dimmer switch. In your house, this is called a *rheostat.* It is a switch that allows the use of 10 watts or 110 watts of electrical power. This metaphor is useful if you think of an emotional dimmer switch that allows the use of 10 to 110 watts of emotional power, depending on the mood or situation. For most of us, the use of this dimmer switch would give us more choice in our emotional responses.

10. *Remember to Remember.* We all have times when we handle emotional situations well and times when we handle them poorly. Think about situations in which you have handled your emotions in a useful and suitable way. What elements of the situation enabled you to be that way? Now think of a time when you were less resourceful. What specific actions on your part made the situation turn out the way it did? The key seems to be remembering what needs to be done in a particular context before the occasion arises. What signal alerts you to the fact that you have reached a point where your choice of actions will determine the outcome? How can you ensure that you will remember the signal in the future? To use your abilities to deal with feelings to your own advantage,

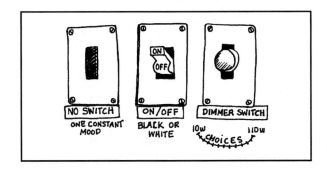

Questions for Critical Thinking

Think of an example of a time when you handled your emotions well and a time when you didn't. What was the difference between the two situations and your behavior in each? What was the "difference that made the difference," and how will you remember that in the future?

_____

_____

_____

_____

_____

_____

_____

_____

_____

you need to remember to remember before you need the information. It doesn't do much good to recognize a better way of handling a situation half an hour after you've blown it with an inappropriate emotional response.

Emotional Intelligence

Considerable attention has been given to emotional intelligence recently. Reports and articles have appeared in numerous sources across the nation, from *Reader's Digest* to an alternative media source, the *Utne Reader. USA Today* has run a self-test for assessing one's EQ (emotional quotient). *Time* magazine has discussed the implications of possible controversy regarding the application of the information.

The phrase *emotional intelligence* was coined by Yale psychologist Peter Salovey and the University of New Hampshire's John Mayer. The term describes such qualities as understanding one's own feelings, empathy for the feelings of others, and "the regulation of emotion in a way that enhances living." These concepts are entering into everyday conversation because of the book *Emotional Intelligence* by Daniel Goleman (1995).

Goleman, a Harvard psychology Ph.D. and a *New York Times* science writer, has brought together a decade's worth of behavioral research into how the mind processes feelings. His thesis: When it comes to predicting people's success, brainpower as measured by IQ and standardized achievement tests may actually matter less than the qualities of mind once thought of as *character* before the word began to sound quaint (*Time*, October 2, 1995).

EQ is not the opposite of IQ. Some people are blessed with a lot of both, and others seem to have very little of either. Researchers have been trying to understand how EQ and IQ complement each other. What is the relationship between the ability to handle stress and the ability to concentrate and use one's intelligence? Researchers generally agree, regarding the ingredients for success, that IQ counts for only about 20 percent; the rest is due to numerous other factors. That's where EQ comes in.

Some people think that measuring emotional intelligence may be restrictive. Attempts at establishing what is "right" to feel may be detrimental. Other critics see emphasis on emotional awareness as an effort to reinvent the encounter group. But educators can point to all sorts of data to support this new direction. Students who are angry or depressed have a difficult time learning. The business world is also responding to the importance of people skills. Karen Boylston, from the Center for Creative Leadership, reports that customers are telling businesses, "I don't care if every member of your staff graduated with honors from Harvard or Stanford. I will take my business where I am understood and respected." Goleman (1995) feels that, given the number of social problems we face in this country, there should be a demand for remedial emotional education. He offers information that he feels could be valuable for restoring "civility to our streets and caring to our communal life" (p. 137).

*A New Form of Intelligence**

It has always been thought that IQ is the best indicator of how well you will do in life. But a more critical factor influencing success at work and in personal relationships can be how emotionally smart you are.

**Source:* Interview with Daniel Goleman. Reprinted by permission from *Bottom Line/Personal*, Vol. 16, no. 24, December 15, 1995.

Emotional intelligence reflects the functioning of your emotional brain—the part that generates and regulates feeling and fear, mood and anger—just as IQ shows how well the thinking part of your brain is working. Emotional intelligence is a key tool for getting along with others, taking control of your life, thinking clearly, and making decisions.

The Power of Feelings Emotional intelligence is made up of five closely related factors:

- *Self-awareness:* Feelings have a major influence on all our decisions. When making a decision, your brain doesn't unemotionally tally up the pros and cons to produce a neat printout. Instead, it processes all the relevant data, which in turn help you produce a feeling about what you should do. When your emotional brain is working well, this feeling is shaped by your entire life's wisdom and experience. If you're not in touch with your feelings, you won't hear the emotional message.

- *Mood management:* Depression, anxiety, and anger interfere with working memory—your brain's ability to integrate facts and ideas. This prevents you from thinking straight or working smart. Emotional intelligence allows you to manage your moods by cheering yourself up when you're down—calming yourself when you're anxious—and helping you to express anger effectively when you are upset.

- *Motivation:* The ability to maintain hope and optimism—even when you encounter setbacks—is crucial in working effectively toward your goals.

- *Empathy:* Sensitivity to other people's feelings is a key to understanding their needs and modifying your behavior. In marriage, empathy means fewer fights and less stress. At work, it's a key management skill.

- *Social skill:* The ability to deal with the emotions of others—to harmonize, persuade, and lead—draws on all aspects of emotional intelligence; for example, a study conducted at Bell Laboratory found that the most trusted, valued employees don't stand out because of their IQs or academic backgrounds, but because of their ability to get along with others. Emotional intelligence is the key to being a team player, and it is perhaps the most critical tool available in the workplace today.

Being More Sensitive

Like IQ, emotional intelligence is partially predetermined by the brain with which you were born. But emotional intelligence can be shaped constantly—much more so than IQ—by learning from repeated experiences of life. Here's how to boost your emotional intelligence:

- *Make a habit of self-awareness:* You can dramatically improve your emotional intelligence by listening to yourself and observing your own behavior. It is helpful to remind yourself to think about your feelings as you're talking to coworkers, spending time with friends, or pondering decisions.

- *Learn skills to calm anxious feelings:* When you're nervous or worried, activities such as exercise, listening to music, or a hobby will distract you. Such activities are also effective at banishing anxious thoughts. Another strategy is to practice a relaxation exercise for fifteen or twenty minutes a day, and you will be able to call on it when you feel anxiety building up. Sit quietly and focus on your breathing, saying to yourself the words *in* and *out*. When your mind wanders, simply refocus on your breathing.

- *Find ways to lift your mood when you're down:* Intense feelings of anxiety are important, provided they are not prolonged. When they are, however, such feelings can distract you and cloud your judgment and perspective. One strategy: a brisk walk, which works for many people—or completing a long-postponed household chore.

- *Fine-tune your empathy by discussing your spouse's or close friend's feelings:* Trying to understand the feelings of others helps heighten your emotional sensitivity. One way to do this is to compare your reading of someone's emotional state with what he or she is actually feeling.

- *Increase motivation by nurturing hope:* When your confidence dips, set a new goal immediately, determine what it will take to reach it, and resolve to use your energy and persistence to pursue those steps. Every time you evaluate what appears to be a hopeless situation, form a plan, and turn the situation around, you move toward a more optimistic mind-set.

- *Improve specific social skills:* Heighten harmony at home by listening and speaking to others nondefensively. Resist the urge to defend yourself against criticism. Try to separate the criticism or the anger from the emotional message that is behind it. For example, someone who says, "You're always so selfish," may actually mean, "I feel so hurt."

- *Tune in to the feelings that complicate your relationships:* Feelings of self-righteousness or the feeling that you are an "innocent victim" can become a toxic habit. They are really excuses. When you find yourself thinking this way, stop and challenge these thoughts. For example, in an argument, recognize when strong emotions threaten to overwhelm reason. Agree to call a twenty minute time out so you can cool down with your self-management skills. Be frugal with your criticism—and generous with praise—at work. When you must criticize an employee or coworker, try to do it artfully—and do it in private. Empathy for the feelings of the person who is receiving the comments gets results, while an insensitive put-down creates resentment and bitterness between you.

Emotional Control

Have you ever been in the middle of an argument and suddenly seen the situation from outside yourself and found it incredibly funny? Maybe imagining how you looked to the other person changed your whole feeling about the situation. Most of us, at times, are able to actually step outside ourselves and view the situation from another perspective. That distance, artificially created, offers a different experience and changes the feeling of the original situation.

Most of us, on the other hand, have also created unnecessary emotions about an incident that never materialized. Have you ever experienced sitting calmly in a pleasant situation and starting to feel bad as you began imagining some future event about which you were worried? That occurred because you imaginatively put yourself into a situation and acted as if it were really happening.

These are examples of how your mind works and clues as to how you can better control your emotions. The mind is an incredible tool, and it is beneficial to know and understand the relationship between thoughts and feelings. Remember that having feelings or not isn't the main emphasis; the context and whether it is useful to have the feelings is more important. Learning an individual strategy for increasing and decreasing your emotions can give you some degree of control and can be beneficial in a variety of situations.

The following two sets of instructions for how to recall the same memory might help you more fully comprehend the principles on which we will be building.

First, imagine sitting in your living room getting ready to watch old home movies. As you look at the blank screen, remember a time in the past when you were getting ready to take a roller coaster ride. Can you see yourself on the screen as you got into the roller car? Watch as you and the other people sit down and get strapped into the seats. Can you see all the cars of the roller coaster as it approaches the top of the big drop? From your living room, watch that old movie of a past time when you rode a roller coaster. Watch the ups and downs of the ride as if someone else had taken pictures from the ground while you were on it. As it comes to an end, what do you look like getting off the ride? Now, as you assess that, notice the level of feeling that you had while recalling that memory.

Now let's try an entirely different way of remembering that roller coaster experience. In this second perspective, step into that movie at the beginning. Imagine you are there now and can see and hear everything going on around you as you get into the car for the ride. As you feel the seat underneath you, you can hear the sound of the bar coming down across your lap. What does the bar feel like as you reach out and grip it? As the ride starts and you are pressed back in the seat, what do you see ahead of you? Can you hear the clicking of the wheels on the track as you look up into the sky while making the first ascent? After that brief pause at the top, what do you hear, see, and feel as you race down that big drop—all the way to the bottom—and start the rush up the other side? Continue to experience the ride in this manner all the way through to the end. As you get off the ride, how are you feeling? What are the people around you saying? What does the world look like to you as you walk away from the ride? Now assess your feelings and reactions to this way of remembering your roller coaster ride.

For most people, the first experience decreases emotional response and the second increases it. If you think about an event as though it were happening in the present, you will probably experience a greater degree of feelings than if you think about it as though it happened long ago. Whether or not you have been consciously aware of the effects of this type of thinking and remembering, understanding the process is the key to emotional control.

Your memory and how you use it has a major influence on your emotions. What you remember

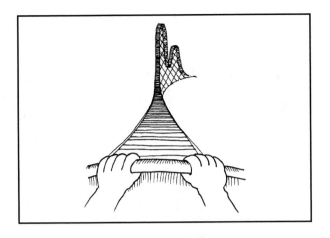

ago. An excellent example comes from the film *Bullitt*, starring Steve McQueen. In that 1970s movie, moviemakers strapped the camera on the shoulder of one of the drivers in a car chase scene and literally put the viewer in the driver's seat, instead of showing the chase from the perspective of a bystander as two cars race past. The technique was quite effective in increasing audience response as well as industry profits. Today, getting the audience to be totally associated with the experiences in movies has become standard procedure.

Decreasing Feelings: Dissociated

In situations where it would be useful to control or diminish your emotional response, the following steps will be helpful:

1. Imagine the event as having already happened in the past, or imagine another event that will take you into the future. Remember the example of watching the roller coaster ride as an old home movie. The other method for stepping out of the situation is to think of another time and place. Have you ever been so involved in a daydream that you were completely oblivious to what was happening in the present?

2. Step out of yourself. Imagining yourself in some other time and space automatically generates a different perspective. Some people have a part of themselves that is constantly outside, watching, assessing, and commenting on their behavior.

3. Watch yourself and others involved in the situation. Whether the event is a memory or is currently taking place, see your interactions from the perspective of watching a movie about what was or is happening. The ability to dissociate is valuable for anyone who is or will be a parent, because children seem to have an innate talent for knowing which buttons to push to get a reaction. Most parents can tell when a child wants to play "gotcha." When someone is trying to get you and you don't want to get "got," it can be helpful to dissociate. We are usually more patient and resourceful if we can remember to step out and not take the behavior of others personally.

and how you remember it can have a significant impact on your feelings about a given situation. Keep in mind that we all have selective memories and that reality is a relative term. For example, have you ever had others relate a childhood story about you so often that you began to have a memory about the incident even though it happened when you were much too young to remember it yourself? Have you ever retold an event as you wish it had happened rather than as it actually did happen? After a while, did you begin to believe in the story rather than the reality? Other evidence of selective memory becomes obvious when members of the same family begin to talk about the family and the past. Two different people can have vastly divergent descriptions of family members and events. These are important concepts to think about as we move on to the specific components of learning to increase or decrease feelings.

Increasing Feelings: Associated

In situations where it would be appropriate to experience and express your feelings, the following steps will be helpful.

1. Experience the event fully in the present. Your capacity for emotional response will increase when you focus on the moment that your feelings are happening.

2. Step into the experience and stay in your body. Watch the event unfolding as you look out of your own eyes. See the event or the others involved from inside the movie as it is happening to you.

3. Be aware of your self-talk. Describe the feelings you are having and give yourself permission to experience your feelings.

The movie industry, being in the business of creating experiences, discovered these steps long

Here is an example of how to use these principles. There are days when I can tell from the sound of her footsteps on the stairs that my daughter has had a bad day at school. On one occasion, she proceeded to make sure that I had a bad day, too. I dissociated and watched the interaction as if it were happening to someone else. As I imagined watching myself, I thought about how I would behave if I were demonstrating intervention techniques to use with children. (It is amazing how different you can be if you think that others are watching you.) Pretending that I was doing a demonstration for a psychology class kept me focused on how to be resourceful. By watching the interaction as if it were a movie, I was able to keep things in perspective. I became curious about her needs and thought about how to connect with her on a meaningful level.

Another interesting phenomenon happens if I imagine that someone else's child is doing the behavior. When my son spills his milk for the second time at the same meal, I can feel myself start to approach the breaking point. If I dissociate, though, and think of him as the neighbor's child, it is amazing how much more patient and understanding I am. It's strange how we yell at our own children yet wouldn't think of doing that to someone else's children. By dissociating, we can relate to our own children in a detached yet caring way. One last note to parents: *Remember that a child acting like a child is much different from a parent reacting like a child. It is the parent's responsibility to develop and maintain more choices than the child and to have a greater degree of emotional control.*

Most people have both choices, to associate or to dissociate, but often they aren't aware of how or when they do each one. As an example of the need to have a balanced approach to each method, consider the following situation demonstrating gender differences. Men and women frequently have dissimilar emotional responses to the same event. The following is a hypothetical example (and an exaggerated stereotype) of both options, associating and dissociating, operating in the same situation: Imagine that a man and a woman are watching a movie on television. When the movie gets to the sad, emotional, or romantic scene, what does the woman do? She steps into the movie and becomes fully associated with the experience. She doesn't just watch it, she lives it! She sees, hears, and feels everything she would experience in that same situation as if it were actually happening to her. Meanwhile, what is the man doing? He has dissociated himself from the scene. He sees it as being about someone else and not in the here and now. It's just a movie about some event that he is reluctantly watching. He may observe from an analytical position and think about what the scene has to do with the story.

The positions reverse during the action parts of the movie. The man now steps into the movie and fully experiences the situation. He isn't just watching Rambo; he is Rambo! Being associated, he can see, hear, and feel the explosions in the shoot-'em-up parts of the movie. Where is the woman? To her, it has to be just a movie. She is most likely keeping the experience at a distance. She experiences it from a dissociated state as much as possible.

These may be gender stereotypes, but the scenario is a fairly accurate description of how we create different emotional states. In addition, it reflects our culturally based gender training, which dictates who cries during soap operas and who gets excited and yells at the TV screen during sporting events. Probably, we could all do with a little more balance in the emotions department.

Application

Some people have both choices, to increase or decrease feelings, but have difficulty being flexible in the application of those choices. Do you know people who have feelings even when they wish they didn't and yet can't turn them on in situations where they want to express them? They may be exercising both associative and dissociative options in dealing with their emotions, but they seem to have the appropriate context reversed.

There is also a difference between our ability to empathize with other people's feelings (incoming emotions) and to experience or express our own feelings (outgoing emotions). Some people are very aware of their own feelings and have no trouble expressing them, but are oblivious to the feelings of other people and what they might be experiencing. For others, that is reversed: they downplay their own emotional response while being overly focused on what others might be feeling.

There are four different combinations of the previously stated variables based on the incoming and outgoing continuum of emotional expression and the associated or dissociated mode of experience. Here are some of the characteristics of the four combinations:

1. *Feelers:* Feelers are the people who are associated when it comes to experiencing others' feelings as well as their own. They step into what they perceive others to be feeling and experience the emotions as though they were their own. This may or may not be useful, depending on the context. Empathy can sometimes turn them into "Red Cross nurses," trying to save everyone else at their own expense. They are also very in touch with their own feelings and are comfortable with the outgoing expression of them.

2. *Sponges:* Sponges are people who experience everyone else's pain but ignore their own. They increase awareness of incoming emotions but dissociate from their own. They soak up everything around them, further masking their own feelings, which they may already object to expressing. These people frequently benefit from diminishing their concern for others' feelings and increasing their awareness of their own.

3. *Blamers:* Some people easily step into their own feelings and increase them, and then vent them on others because it is easier to deal with outgoing feelings. It's ironic, though, that these same people then put up a stone wall against incoming emotions and acknowledging the feelings of others. They know how to dissociate, but might benefit from reversing the situations when they do that—stepping out of their own feelings but being available when others express their emotions.

4. *Spocks:* Spocks are constantly dissociated. They downplay their own emotions as well as other people's. These overintellectualizing types don't understand that logic doesn't always solve the problem. They could benefit from realizing that the world doesn't always make sense. The heart has a logic that the mind can't comprehend. Decreasing emotions can be useful in some circumstances, but constant dissociation is tough on personal relationships and family life.

As you consider this information, keep in mind the choice and balance concept. We all have these abilities, and we all have some part of us represented by these different types. We need to be aware of what we have a tendency to do, and use the option to act differently at times. It is useful to know more of how we contribute to the

Questions for Critical Thinking

What type do you tend to be most like? What do you need to do more of, and less of, regarding emotions? How can you be more balanced?

_____

_____

_____

_____

_____

_____

_____

_____

_____

experiences that we have and how our tendencies create certain kinds of situations. With this information, it is possible to consider the context of the situation and choose the most appropriate response.

In-Coming Emotions (Feelings Expressed by Others to You)		
	Experience	**Do Not Experience**
Experience	Feeler	Blamer
Do Not Experience	Sponge	Spock

Out-Going Emotions (Your Feelings Expressed to Others)

CASE STUDIES AND STUDENT STORIES

As a small child, James remembered tearing apart vacuum cleaners or burying his toys in the park to express his anger. Whenever something made him mad, he either broke it or buried it. The strategy seemed to work for awhile. But, as an adult, neither one of these methods seemed to contain his anger.

He found that beating the sides of his car or breaking out windows in his house was not accomplishing anything, and the pain that he endured was maddening. But, whenever he got angry he had no idea how to deal with it, so he continued the unhealthy pattern.

Following one of his outbursts, with sweat running down his back and with his heart racing, he realized he had to make a change. He sat down outside on his back steps and screamed as loud as he could. The only word that he could yell was WHY?

Each day James resolved that he was going to end his violent outbursts of anger, and each evening he felt guilty for the things that he had done during the day. From kicking the cat to screaming at someone who had pulled out in front of him, his anger continued to plague him.

One morning James woke up feeling like he was consumed with rage. He cussed out the garbage man for accidentally spilling garbage, yelled at his neighbor for waking him up to give him his morning paper, and when the doorbell rang for the fourth time in an hour he opened it with anger all over his face.

Looking straight ahead he could not see the little boy standing at the door. As he growled and began to shut the door, a frightened scream emerged from the boy: "Please don't hurt me." As the child ran down the street, James sat down on his front porch and began to cry.

He realized that if he didn't do something about managing his anger, he was going to hurt someone or himself. It was with this resolve that he found an anger management class, and the process of James's healing began.

He met other people who suffered from the same emotional problem that he did, and he was willing to try anything that was suggested. It wasn't an easy road for James, but things started to get better. He learned to vent his frustrations in a more appropriate manner in his therapy group. He also acquired a number of methods for controlling and dealing with his anger before it led to an angry outburst. James also realized that he had to control his thought, and that his imagination was controlling his life. Through countless therapy sessions, often with two steps forward and one step back, James started on a path to a new life.

James no longer takes apart his *toys* or breaks windows, and he has found new ways to vent his anger. On any given night, if you are in the vicinity of the local park, you just might hear him howling at the moon. He says the sound soothes his anger and enables him to feel better without making someone else feel bad.

Source: Written by D. Juanita Woods.

Thought Distortion

Emotions have a cognitive component: your feelings are affected to a significant degree by the thoughts that you have about a given situation. When you overreact to something or someone, it is usually due to playing an old tape every time you have been in a similar situation. When the words in your internal dialogue describe the situation as being worse than it really is, you often have a stronger emotional response than might be appropriate. Stress is usually the result of being overwhelmed by intense feelings and the resulting physiological effects. The negative aspects of stress are frequently brought on by your beliefs about what should or shouldn't be happening to you. (The topic of stress management will be covered in Chapter 8.) Thus, stress and difficulty in coping with emotions frequently share the common element of distorted thought processes. It is not so much what happens to you in life, it's the way you think about it that determines how you feel.

According to David Burns (1989), in his book *The Feeling Good Handbook,* certain kinds of negative thoughts make people unhappy. Burns believes that unhealthy negative emotions such as depression, anxiety, excessive anger, and inappropriate guilt are always caused by illogical, distorted thoughts. This includes the thoughts that seem valid at the time of an event. Burns suggests learning to look at things more realistically by getting rid of your distorted thinking patterns (review the list in the section on cognitive restructuring in Chapter 2). He believes one can break out of depression or a bad mood, often in a short period of time, without having to rely on medication or prolonged psychotherapy.

There are a number of methods for coping with your emotions in a healthy manner. Keep in mind that just because you are having strong feelings, that doesn't necessarily mean you need to modify your behavior. If it would be useful for you to change how you deal with some situations, you can use the following basic steps:

1. Identify the situation that is upsetting you.
2. Identify the distortions in your thoughts from the prior list. Interrupt negative thoughts that are intrusive and create more of a problem.
3. Imagine how you could think differently and how you would act if you did.
4. Make sure that your change in thinking is not just an intellectual exercise and that you have effected a change on the gut level by devising a test for your beliefs. It is important to put your new way of thinking, and the resulting behavior, into action.
5. Change your physiology. Some people get stuck in a particular emotional response because they freeze their body posture in the manner they have in the past when they were having that emotion. To change your mood, sometimes you have to move your body. Get up and move around.
6. Make sure that you continue to breathe in as normal a pattern as possible, because oxygen is a prerequisite to all other activities, and you will think better if you aren't holding your breath.

Whether it is in regard to your self-concept, stress management, or dealing more effectively with your emotions, it is always useful to be aware of and to monitor your thoughts. The content of your self-talk can have far-reaching implications in a number of areas of your life. Changing your thoughts in a positive manner will improve your relationships with others.

Defense Mechanisms

Closely related to thought distortions is the self-deception that is often necessary in order to employ any particular defense mechanism. Few of us like to think bad things about ourselves, and it is difficult to stay with any emotion that is troubling to experience. Anxiety is distressing for most people, so they often try to rid themselves of unpleasant emotions any way that they can. This effort to ward off anxiety often involves the use of defense mechanisms. These are unconscious reactions that protect a person from painful emotions. Typically, they are mental maneuvers that work through self-deception (Weiten and Lloyd, 2006).

A common example is rationalization, which involves creating false but plausible excuses to justify unacceptable behavior. If you cheat or steal and try to reduce your guilt by telling yourself that "everyone does it," then you are rationalizing. Most of us would like to think of ourselves as rational beings, but closer to the truth is that we are more likely to be "rationalizing" beings. The following is a partial list of the many defense mechanisms (Weiten and Lloyd, 2006):

Projection involves attributing one's own thoughts, feelings, and motives to another. People who are angry and hostile may see the world as a dangerous place where other people want to hurt them.

Displacement involves diverting emotional feelings (usually anger) from their original source to a substitute target. This is the age-old story of the man who is mad at his boss but takes it out on his wife, who then takes it out on the kids, who in turn mistreat the family dog.

Repression involves keeping distressing thoughts and feelings buried in the unconscious. Repression in a kind of "motivated forgetting." That dental appointment you really did not want to keep wasn't all that important anyway, now was it?

Reaction formation involves behaving in a way that is exactly the opposite of one's true feelings. There are news accounts from time to time about zealots who lead movements against immoral behavior, only to be found visiting prostitutes.

Regression involves a reversion to immature patterns of behavior. How many of you know people who are over 40 but can be reduced to the level of a two-year-old having a tantrum when they don't get their way?

Intellectualization involves cutting off emotion from hurtful situation or separating incompatible

IRRATIONAL BELIEFS

1. It is essential that one be loved or approved by virtually everyone in one's community.
2. One must be perfectly competent and achieving to consider oneself worthwhile.
3. Some people are wicked or villainous, and therefore should be blamed and punished.
4. It is a terrible catastrophe when things are not as one wants them to be.
5. Unhappiness is caused by outside circumstances; the individual has no control over it.
6. Dangerous or fearsome things are causes for great concern, and their possibility must be continually dwelt upon.
7. One should be dependent on others and must have someone stronger on whom to rely.
8. One should be quite upset over people's problems and disturbances.
9. There is always a right or perfect solution to every problem, and it must be found or the results will be catastrophic.

Source: Albert Ellis, 1984. *Reason and Emotion in Psychotherapy.* Seacacus, NJ: Lyle Stuart.

attitudes in logic-tight compartments. People who want to avoid emotions are often experts at developing their own peculiar logic. One way to avoid feelings is to spend all your time trying to think your way out of the box.

Overcompensation involves covering up feelings of weakness by emphasizing some desirable characteristic or making up for frustration in one area by overgratification in another.

Above all else, defense mechanisms shield the individual from the emotional discomfort elicited by stress. Their main purpose is to ward off unwelcome emotions or to reduce their intensity. People are especially defensive when the anxiety is due to some threat to their self-esteem. They also use defenses to prevent dangerous feelings of anger from exploding into acts of aggression (Weiten and Lloyd, 2006).

Anger

Do you boil over, or do the slow burn? Anger and its various forms of expression are part of everyone's life. Recent research shows that women get angry as often as men, as intensely as men, and for many of the same reasons. And what they get in return for expressing their anger like a man is a bad bill of health. Just like men. According to an interview with Sandra Thomas, R.N., Ph.D. (1997), director at the Center for Nursing Research at the University of Tennessee, extreme anger, whether vented or suppressed, creates problems for everyone. Given the current state of scientific research, though, the best advice is to get rid of your anger and reflect on the triggers that create it. Instead of letting problems fester, says Thomas, address anger-causing problems right away. If it's a person and you can't approach the instigator, then at least discuss it with a trusted friend or relative.

Remember, emotions themselves are neither right nor wrong—they simply are. However, it is important to consider the context and/or outcome of these emotions. People who are taken advantage of because they are always nice to everyone, or those who bottle up their anger for 20 years and then develop ulcers, would probably benefit from expressing their anger. Unfortunately, those who need help in dealing with their anger because they have violent outbursts and/or become physically abusive are seldom the ones who seek help. They may believe that anger is a powerful tool for getting what they want because it frightens people. They don't notice that how they express themselves relates directly to how much and what type of assistance they receive from others. That, in turn, leads to a cycle of frustration because the more angry they get, the less they get what they want. The paradox is that the people who need to moderate their expression of anger and become more aware of its effects on others seldom do so, whereas those who could benefit from expressing their anger and speaking up have difficulty letting go of their concern about how their anger will affect other people.

Early Training

Let's look at where those reactions to anger originate. Why do some people fly off the handle, while others are patient to a fault? It goes back to families like the Wild Wilsons and the Silent Smiths. We all grow up with messages about what to do with anger, such as "Don't you raise your voice to me" and "You had better get control of yourself right now." It's true that actions speak louder than words, and often the most powerful messages are the ones that aren't spoken out loud. Have you ever seen a parent screaming, "It's wrong to hit someone" while spanking a child? Powerful messages are being conveyed in that situation about what to do with angry feelings. Is it any wonder that some of us grow up confused?

One method of exploring dealing with anger is to look to your parents. How did they express anger with each other, with their children, and with the world? Were they similar in their actions, or was one a Wilson and the other a Smith? What did you learn from them about handling angry feelings? Are you a reflection of either parent or a composite of their styles? Whether you modeled their behavior or went in the opposite direction, you were influenced by how your parents handled their anger.

Gaining Control

People who lose control when angry begin to change when they realize that they do have more control than they were aware of. When gaining that information, they begin to notice how that knowledge can be the key to acting differently in the future. For example, people who throw things in anger usually go through a whole series of decisions before actually breaking anything. Some little voice says, "Something of theirs, not mine," or "The $5 vase, not the $500 one," or "Not through the window, you'll have to fix it. Yes, the fireplace. It'll look great when it smashes." People who can step out of themselves long enough to make those decisions already have the key to learning to dissociate long enough to consider other options as well.

Have you ever been in the middle of an argument when the phone rings? Isn't it incredible how cultural conditioning brings everything to a stop when the phone rings? One of the participants walks over and answers the phone with a pleasant, "Hello. Oh, just fine. How are you doing?" By the time the phone call has ended, some people have forgotten what the fight was about; others go back and pick up the argument at the exact point at which the telephone call interrupted it. If you can push the pause button long enough to answer a phone call, why not use that same strategy to step out and consider other options, or at least to notice if the argument is getting the desired results? We all have more control than we realize.

Can you remember a time when you were really upset but knew that it would be detrimental to express those feelings? Compare that incident to a time when you did lose control. What was the difference? Becoming more aware of how you act when coping with anger in a constructive way is the first step to having more choices in other areas of your life. People who are working on being more assertive usually need to give themselves greater latitude in expressing anger. Others need to learn to tone it down some and to step out and observe themselves more often. In either case, it is beneficial to know more about how and when you lose control compared to when you maintain it. Make sure you remember to use that information in the proper context.

The Nature of Anger

Anger is a completely normal, usually healthy, human emotion. But when it gets out of control and turns destructive, it can lead to problems—problems at work, in your personal relationships, and in the overall quality of your life. And it can make you feel as though you're at the mercy of an unpredictable and powerful emotion.

Anger is "an emotional state that varies in intensity from mild irritation to intense fury and rage," according to Charles Spielberger, Ph.D., a psychologist who specializes in the study of anger. Like other emotions, it is accompanied by physiological and biological changes; when you get angry, your heart rate and blood pressure go up, as do the levels of your energy hormones, adrenaline, and noradrenaline.

Anger can be caused by both external and internal events. You could be angry at a specific person (such as a coworker or supervisor) or event (a traffic jam, a canceled flight), or your anger could be caused by worrying or brooding about your personal problems. Memories of traumatic or enraging events can also trigger angry feelings.

KEEPING YOUR COOL

Reappraise the Situation: When you are provoked by someone, consider the source. Maybe it means more about them than it does about you. Rather than saying something negative to yourself about the other person, try to empathize or find justification for his or her actions.

The Old Standard Count to Ten: Then use a technique the experts call reflective coping, which means trying to solve the underlying problem or source of anger.

Keep an Anger Diary: Become an expert on your own anger. Write down each episode and all the particulars of the situation. This helps to demystify the emotion and shows that it isn't an uncontrollable force.

Sweat It Out: Vigorous exercise is an excellent outlet for powerful emotions, including anger.

Cut Your Losses: If there's no possibility of effecting a change, then remove yourself from the anger-provoking situation.

Source: Carol Tavris, *Anger: The Misunderstood Emotion.* New York: Simon & Schuster, 1989.

Expressing Anger

The instinctive way to express anger is to respond aggressively. Anger is a natural, adaptive response to threats that allows us to fight and to defend ourselves when we are attacked. A certain amount of anger, therefore, is necessary to our survival. On the other hand, we can't physically lash out at every person or object that irritates or annoys us; laws, social norms, and common sense place limits on how far our anger can take us.

Anger can be suppressed, and then converted or redirected. This happens when you hold in your anger, stop thinking about it, and focus on something positive. The aim is to inhibit or suppress your anger and convert it into more constructive behavior. The danger in this type of response is that if it isn't allowed outward expression, your anger can turn inward—on yourself. Anger turned inward may cause hypertension, high blood pressure, or depression.

Unexpressed anger can create other problems. It can lead to pathological expressions of anger, such as passive-aggressive behavior (getting back at people indirectly, without telling them why, rather than confronting them head-on) or a personality that seems perpetually cynical and hostile. People who are constantly putting others down, criticizing everything, and making cynical comments haven't learned how to constructively express their anger. Not surprisingly, they aren't likely to have many successful relationships.

Finally, you can calm down inside. This means not just controlling your outward behavior, but also controlling your internal responses, taking steps to lower your heart rate, calm yourself down, and let the feelings subside.

The goal of anger management is to reduce both your emotional feelings and the physiological arousal that anger causes. You can't get rid of, or avoid, the things or the people that enrage you, nor can you change them, but you can learn to control your reactions.

Why Are Some People More Angry Than Others?

According to Jerry Deffenbacher, a psychologist who specializes in anger management, some people really are more "hotheaded" than others are; they get angry more easily and more intensely than the average person does. There are also those who don't show their anger in loud spectacular ways but are chronically irritable and grumpy. Easily angered people don't always curse and throw things; sometimes they withdraw socially, sulk, or get physically ill.

People who are easily angered generally have what some psychologists call a low tolerance for frustration, meaning simply that they feel that they should not have to be subjected to frustration, inconvenience, or annoyance. They can't take things in stride, and they're particularly infuriated if the situation seems somehow unjust: for example, being corrected for a minor mistake.

What makes these people this way? A number of things. One cause may be genetic or physiological: There is evidence that some children are born irritable, touchy, and easily angered, and that these signs are present from a very early age. Another may be socio-cultural. Anger is often regarded as negative; we're taught that it's all right to express anxiety, depression, or other emotions but not to express anger. As a result, we don't learn how to handle it or channel it constructively.

Is It Good To "Let It All Hang Out?"

Psychologists now say that this is a dangerous myth. Some people use this theory as a license to hurt others. Research has found that "letting it rip" with anger actually escalates anger and aggression and does nothing to help you (or the person you're angry with) resolve the situation. It's best to find out what it is that triggers your anger, and then to develop strategies to keep those triggers from tipping you over the edge.

Relaxation   Simple relaxation tools, such as deep breathing and relaxing imagery, can help calm down angry feelings. There are books and courses that can teach you relaxation techniques, and once you learn the techniques, you can call on them in any situation. If you are involved in a relationship where both partners are hot-tempered, it might be a good idea for both of you to learn these techniques.

Some simple steps you can try:

Breathe deeply, from your diaphragm; breathing from your chest won't relax you. Picture your breath coming up from your "gut."

Slowly repeat a calm word or phrase such as "relax," "take it easy." Repeat it to yourself while breathing deeply.

Use imagery; visualize a relaxing experience, from either your memory or your imagination.

Nonstrenuous, slow yoga-like exercises can relax your muscles and make you feel much calmer.

Practice these techniques, and learn to use them automatically when you're in a tense situation.

Changing Your Environment   Sometimes it's our immediate surroundings that give us cause for irritation and fury. Problems and responsibilities can weigh on you and make you feel angry at the "trap" you seem to have fallen into and all the people and things that form that trap.

Give yourself a break. Make sure you have some "personal time" scheduled for times of the day that you know are particularly stressful. One example is the working mother who has a standing rule that when she comes home from work, for the first 15 minutes "nobody talks to Mom unless the house is on fire." After this brief quiet time, she feels better prepared to handle demands from her kids without blowing up at them.

If you and your spouse tend to fight when you discuss things at night—perhaps you're tired, or distracted, or maybe it's just habit—try changing the times when you talk about important matters so these talks don't turn into arguments. Or, if your child's chaotic room makes you furious every time you walk by it, shut the door. Don't make yourself look at what infuriates you. Don't say, "Well, my child should clean up the room so I won't have to be angry!" That's not the point. The point is to keep yourself calm.

Cognitive Restructuring   Simply put, this means changing the way you think. Angry people tend to curse, swear, or speak in highly colorful terms that reflect their inner thoughts. When you're angry, your thinking can get very exaggerated and overly dramatic. Try replacing these thoughts with more rational ones. For instance, instead of telling yourself, "Oh, it's awful, it's terrible, everything's ruined," tell yourself, "It's frustrating, and it's understandable that I'm upset about it, but it's not the end of the world and getting angry is not going to fix it anyhow."

Be careful of words like *never* or *always* when talking about yourself or someone else. They also alienate and humiliate people who might otherwise be willing to work with you on a solution. Remind yourself that getting angry is not going to fix anything, and that it won't make you feel better (and may actually make you feel worse).

Two other concepts can be helpful in dealing with anger. The first is to consider whether the anger is based on an irrational belief. Albert Ellis, a proponent of **rational-emotive therapy** (RET), says that, frequently, disappointment and its subsequent anger are due to unrealistic expectations of the world in general. Life is not fair or equal and probably never will be. That's a tough one to handle because many of us continue to be upset when the world doesn't play according to our rules. Most of us know that not everyone is going to like us, and yet we get upset if we encounter a person who doesn't. Part of the human condition is dealing with disappointments; it is useful to accept some events in life as par for the course rather than as reasons for anger.

When working with people experiencing difficulty, Ellis abbreviated the therapy process into the letters A, B, C, D, E. Therapy usually starts at C, the individual's upsetting emotional Consequence; this might involve anger, depression, or anxiety. The individual usually says that C was

ANGER IS A FRIGHTENING, PAINFUL FEELING FOR SOME

Anger is a scary subject for people who never learned how to express it appropriately or recognize it as a healthy, normal feeling. You may have a problem with anger if:

❏ You're frightened around angry people.

❏ You swallow your anger instead of saying how you feel.

❏ You avoid conflict at any cost.

❏ You hurt people or things when you're angry.

❏ You're afraid that if you ever let yourself get good and mad, you'd kill someone.

❏ Others complain about or seem uncomfortable with your so-called teasing.

❏ You don't feel angry, but you get sick a lot and suffer assorted bodily aches.

❏ You fear the consequences of expressing anger (e.g., your partner may leave, you could get fired, your children may not love you, etc.).

❏ You say things like "There's not an angry bone in my body" and "I don't get angry—I get even!"

❏ You don't feel angry—but people say you seem angry.

"People who are afraid of anger learned early that anger isn't safe," said John Lee, a specialist in male psychology. Lee is director of the Austin (Texas) Men's Center and author of *The Flying Boy—Healing the Wounded Man.* What he said about anger at a recent San Francisco conference on dysfunctional families applies to men and women. As children, Lee said, many people see that anger equals pain: If Dad gets angry, he punishes the kids. When Mom gets mad, she may grow silent and withdrawn. Angry children are sent to their rooms. So people learn to suppress anger—and get plenty of help: "You're not really mad at your brother." "If you can't say something nice, don't say anything at all." "Go to your room until you're through being angry."

After a few years of this, Lee said, people learn not to act angry—not even to feel angry. They become numb and might even be proud of the fact that people could do anything to them, and they don't feel a thing. "Anger is a healthy, positive emotion—but we weren't taught that it was," Lee said. "We confuse it with rage, and we're scared of it." Anger is an energy that has to be discharged. Like a good cry, Lee said, anger needs to be experienced and expressed. If it's not, repressed anger can fester and burst out as rage. All the anger of a lifetime can boil over in reaction to some incident. It's scary, and angry people feel out of control. And they are. Anger isn't safe. The ultimate example of rage is the person—usually described as a "nice, quiet fellow"—who takes a rifle and shoots coworkers or even strangers.

People experience rage when they overreact to a situation. Sometimes it's not just a particular incident they're reacting to, but scores of incidents from childhood on, where anger was choked down instead of appropriately expressed. Think of it this way: Instead of making your house payments as they fall due, you ignore them and are finally forced to write one huge, painful check. Ouch!

When people react more strongly than the situation warrants, therapists urge them to ask, "What am I really angry about?" "Nine times out of ten," Lee said, "whatever you thought it was that was making you angry—it wasn't. You either had too many expectations or were replaying an old scene."

This happens frequently in relationships. It may not be what this man or woman is doing that makes someone furious, but what other men or women—or Dad or Mom—did that they never got angry about. "Most of us spend more time trying to repress anger and sadness than it takes to feel it," Lee said.

Source: Article written by Jann Mitchell.

caused by A, the *Activating* experience, such as a marital blowup, loss of job, or problems in school. The therapist works with the individual to show that an intervening factor, B, the individual's *Belief* system, is actually the reason he or she moved from A to C. Then the therapist goes on to D, *Disputation,* the point at which the irrational beliefs are disputed or contested by the therapist. Finally, E is reached, *Effects* or outcomes of RET, when individuals put their new beliefs to work (Ellis and Yeager, 1989).

Another concept is getting in touch with what is beneath the anger, which quite often is sadness. People frequently react to pain or sadness by being angry. This behavior derives from the mistaken notion that one can gain some measure of control over sadness by ranting and raving at someone else. When you allow yourself your true feelings, the need to overreact in other areas will diminish. If you are feeling sad and allow yourself to experience sadness, you won't need to feel as much anger!

Guilt

Guilt is feelings of responsibility for negative circumstances that have befallen yourself or others. It is feelings of regret for your real or imagined misdeeds, both past and present. It can be a sense of remorse for thoughts, feelings, or attitudes that were or are negative, uncomplimentary, or nonaccepting concerning yourself or others. Guilt is a complex emotion that can incorporate feelings of obligation for not pleasing or not helping another. It can be feelings of loss and shame for not having done or said something to someone when you wish you had.

Guilt can be, and often is, anger turned inward. When we're angry at someone the gun is aimed at *them.* When we're feeling guilty, *you* are under the gun. No one can achieve perfection. Yet many of us insist that we must never make mistakes or do any-

thing wrong. What's underneath this striving for perfection? We're trying to prove our worth, to ourselves and to the world. We strive mightily to avoid making any errors, to maintain a good rating.

Guilt can lock us in, though. If every time we catch ourselves at some wrongdoing we begin to attack ourselves, soon we're going to be feeling pretty hopeless about our ability to change. A person should be careful to limit feelings of regret over wrongdoing. We all have bad habits, and it will take time to change them. You may need to learn first to be more patient with yourself.

Remember that the minute we become more aware of our mistakes, they are no longer failures. They become steps in the process of becoming better as a person. **Good judgment comes from experience, and experience comes from poor judgment.** So we can profit from our mistakes, rather than criticize ourselves for them.

Guilt usually comes in two varieties. There is the regret and remorse which arise from actual wrongdoing. This is **constructive** guilt. It is part of the process of behavior correction, which has three steps: (1) admitting that we've done wrong, (2) expressing remorse and regret over the wrong, (3) resolving to avoid repetition. The guilt we're talking about here, though, is of the **destructive** sort. It, too, begins with an admission of wrongdoing. But now, instead of appropriate regret and a firm resolve to avoid repetition, we viciously attack ourselves and end up feeling spent and miserable. Destructive guilt can:

- Make you become overly responsible, striving to make life "right." You overwork. You overgive of yourself. You are willing to do anything in your attempt to make everyone happy.
- Make you overly conscientious. You fret over every action you take as to its possible negative consequence to others, even if this means that you must ignore your needs and wants.

SUGGESTED STEPS TO OVERCOME UNNECESSARY GUILT

Step 1: You can recognize the role guilt is playing in your life by choosing a current problem and answering the following questions:

What problem is currently troubling me?

Who is responsible for the problem?

How much guilt do I feel about this problem?

If I felt no more guilt, what would my problem look like then?

Step 2: Redefine your problem with the absence of guilt as an issue. In answering the questions in Step 1 you recognized that guilt was preventing resolution of the problem. To redefining your problem, answer the following questions:

How insurmountable is the problem?

Is this problem an interpersonal or intrapersonal problem?

If it is interpersonal: Can I help the other person and myself to set aside guilt and resolve this problem?

If it is intrapersonal: Can I set aside guilt or the fear of it and resolve this problem?

Is it my problem or another's? Am I taking on another's responsibility?

Step 3: If the problem is really someone else's, give the problem back to the person(s) to solve and to deal with. If the problem is yours, go to Step 4.

Step 4: You must confront the real or imagined guilt or fear of guilt preventing you either from handing the problem back to the person(s) whose problem it really is (Step 3) or from handling the problem on your own. Consider the following:

❑ What fears are blocking me at this moment from taking the steps I need to resolve this problem?

❑ What are the irrational beliefs behind these fears?

❑ Refute the irrational beliefs.

❑ Initiate a program of self-affirmation

Step 5: If your guilt is not resolved after completing Steps 3 and/or 4, return to Step 1 and begin again.

Affirm for yourself that:

You deserve to solve this problem.

You deserve to be good to yourself.

You deserve to have others be good to you, too!

▶ Make you overly sensitive. You see decisions about right and wrong in every aspect of your life and become obsessed with the tenuous nature of all of your personal actions, words, and decisions.

▶ Immobilize you. You can become so overcome by the fear of doing, acting, saying, or being "wrong" that you eventually collapse, give in, and choose inactivity, silence, and the status quo.

▶ Interfere in your decision making. It is so important to always be "right" in your

decisions that you become unable to make a decision lest it be a wrong one.

▶ Be hidden by the mask of self-denial. Because it is less guilt inducing to take care of others first, instead of yourself, you hide behind the mask of self-denial. You honestly believe it is better to serve others first, unaware that "guilt" is the motivator for such "generous" behavior.

▶ Make you ignore the full array of emotions and feelings available to you. Overcome by guilt or the fear of it, you can become emotionally blocked or closed off. You are able neither to enjoy the positive fruits of life nor to experience the negative aspects.

▶ Be a motivator to change. Because you feel guilt and the discomfort it brings, you can use it as a barometer of the need to change things in your life and rid yourself of the guilt.

Sadness

There seems to be a national conspiracy to avoid being anything less than fine. "How are you doing?" The answer is "Fine!" We are all fine, and we are supposed to be fine all the time. Perhaps that is due to media hype that portrays people as continually having the time of their lives. It is imperative that we be having a "Bud" moment at all times. Even feeling neutral is seen as a violation of the natural order of things. Have you ever had a day when you were just feeling middle-of-the-road, neither up nor down, and had people ask you, "What's wrong?" We all have down times and even need some neutral moments to balance out the cycles of life. There are experts in the counseling field who suggest that being able to experience joy and happiness in life is connected with the willingness to also experience sadness. To feel alive and exuberant, we must also surrender to our pain and sadness at times. This is the concept *Limit one feeling, limit them all.* To explore your beliefs about sadness, answer the following questions: How often do people need to cry, or how often should they cry? How often would people cry if they let themselves?

If you answered, "Whenever they need to," how often would that be: once a day, once a week, once a month, once a year? When was the last time you cried?

Some people think that you could cry once a week if you let yourself, and yet haven't let themselves cry in a year. What does that say? Do you have different sets of rules for yourself and for other people? Most people inhibit themselves when it comes to expressing sadness. And yet,

paradoxically, they report feeling much better after having a good cry. Why do we have objections to feeling sad? The answer, in part, goes back to families and how you were treated as a child when you cried. What was the response of parents and siblings to crying? That early training can affect you well into adulthood.

This is especially true for men in our society. From a very young age, boys are expected to cope with pain and sadness without crying. This message is delivered in various ways. The 6-year-old boy who cries at being left at school on the first day is called a sissy. The 9-year-old boy who gets hit between the eyes while playing baseball is expected to shake it off and act like a man; then he is given a round of applause for managing to stay on his feet and stagger to first base. By adolescence, most males have been thoroughly versed in the notion that the only acceptable way to deal with pain is to inflict it on others. Hence, the teenage boy who has been jilted goes out and gets in a fight or destroys property; 30 years later, this man may be in therapy because he hasn't learned any other method of coping.

An example is a man who said he hadn't cried in 25 years. That didn't seem like a problem to him until his father died, and he couldn't cry at the funeral even though he wanted to and thought he should. Over the next few years, he came to understand that he vented this unexpressed sadness on those around him in a hostile way. After his wife left him, his kids refused to talk to him, and his boss fired him for having a bad attitude, he finally cried. He cried for three days and thought he was having a nervous breakdown. Well, he wasn't having a breakdown, he was having a breakthrough!

In counseling, he learned that most of his problems were due to his inability to experience or share his sadness. As he learned to be in touch with his feelings in the present, he could stay with them long enough to express them. Then he could go back to some earlier events in his life and allow himself to have the feelings he had cut off before. By stepping into a situation, being associated, and imagining it as the present, he could have the feelings he had needed to have for so

> **"**It hurts to lose something important.
> It hurts worse to pretend otherwise.
> To expect more than reality can offer
> only sets you up to hurt badly
> and needlessly.**"**
>
> *David Viscott*

> **"**Life is like an onion. You peel it back
> one layer at a time, and sometimes you
> cry.**"**
>
> *Carl Sandburg*

long. He came to realize that in trying to avoid pain, he had only caused himself more. It was only through grieving for the losses in his life that he was able to pick up the pieces and move on.

On the other end of the continuum are people who need to learn how to step out, turn it off, and let go of the emotion. Some people experience their feelings readily but then keep replaying the tape long after it has any use or value, as the following example illustrates. An 18-year-old girl came into my office in tears, talking about a lost love and broken romance. Had the relationship just ended? Well, it had ended about six months ago. Had they known each other for a long time? Oh, yes, about three weeks. It seemed that each time she heard "their song," she relived the moment of the breakup. She didn't need to get into her feelings, she needed to get out of them. I think it's fair to say that six months is an adequate length of time to get over a three-week romance, even at 18.

Some people need to experience their feelings more, and some need to do it less. If you need to let go of an event in your life, remember to see it as an old movie from long ago. See yourself from the position of the director of that scene and tell yourself, "Thank goodness that's over." Before putting something in the past, though, be sure to check out your objection to letting it go. If you are still feeling sad about some long-ago event, it may be serving some unconscious purpose for you.

A woman still mourning the death of her husband after 10 years knew it was time to put it to rest, yet some part of her objected to letting go of being sad. By exploring her motives for continuing to feel sad, she discovered that she believed she was being a good wife by honoring and keeping alive the memory of her late husband. After redefining the meaning of being a good wife, she was free to find new options for honoring and preserving the memory of her husband. It was important for her to take care of that need and make that change before she could feel good about getting on with her life. *Never take away someone's pain before he or she is ready to give it up.* It may be serving some purpose.

Excitement and Joy

Many factors are involved in appraising life satisfaction. One component is the ability to enjoy the moment as well as the anticipation of future events. The following information describes how to have more excitement in life. It is a concept that may be useful in enhancing your enjoyment in any number of given situations.

The Two-for-One Principle

First, think about the excitement that comes from anticipating an event as one element, and the pleasure of the actual event as another. Then assume that there exists an artificial dichotomy where half of life's potential events happen and half of them do not. Let's explore the relationship between these two components. People raised with the adage "Don't count your chickens before they hatch" seldom get excited in advance about possibly pleasant events. They may have been told that by someone who had the best intentions and thought only of protecting them from disappointment. Therefore, people with the *Don't Count Your Chickens* approach don't usually get excited at the prospect of an upcoming opportunity or event, ostensibly to avoid disappointment. When the anticipated event really doesn't happen, they experience zero units of happiness. If the potential event does happen, they may feel happy then, but for every two events they get only one unit of happiness. Further, people who don't allow themselves to feel excited over an anticipated event may actually keep themselves from being happy when something good does happen. They seem to diminish their enjoyment by anticipating that something is going to go wrong eventually.

Contrast that line of thinking with people who **do** get excited in advance about a possible event. The "Go for the gusto" approach is represented by people who are always looking for the next big thing and approach life with the *Just Do It* attitude. As an example of the importance of joyful anticipation, consider the *big vacation.* Have you ever had a vacation for which the planning was the best part? Thank goodness for the three weeks spent in a euphoric daydream during the planning stage, because it rained every day of the actual vacation. There are many instances in life when the preparation for an event may be the best part.

With the *Go for the Gusto* approach, people get excited in advance, and then even when the event doesn't occur, they still get one unit of happiness. If the event does happen, they get a two-for-one: excitement at the possibility of the event and excitement when it actually happens. Hence, the Two-for-One Principle. So for every two life events, they get three units of happiness. Perhaps this helps to explain why some people seem to get three times as much enjoyment out of life as others.

The *Go for the Gusto* approach may seem unrealistic. Some may ask, "What about the disappointment when you count your chickens and

	Anticipated Event		
	Doesn't Happen	Does Happen	Units of Happiness
Don't Get Excited	0	1	= 1 (Don't Count Your Chickens)
Do Get Excited	1	2	= 3 (John Denver)

(row header: Emotional Experience)

they don't hatch?" But no one can control life by trying to avoid disappointment. Some things happen the way you want them to, and some don't. What can be controlled is the degree of disappointment felt when a hoped-for event doesn't take place. That is the secret of the *Go for the Gusto* approach: to get excited anticipating an event but not get too disappointed if it doesn't happen. Even if you take away half of the *Go for the Gusto* units of happiness for disappointment over events that don't happen, you are still ahead of those using the *Don't Count Your Chickens* approach.

Here is an explanation for that: People using the *Don't Count Your Chickens* approach are so concerned with disappointment that even when they get what they want, they may not get too excited. They have practiced inhibiting their enjoyment for so long that they have trouble feeling enjoyment. Some people can wonder what is wrong even when an event is positive. Hence the saying, "Don't look a gift horse in the mouth." Here is a gift for you, and it's free. Some people want to know what the catch is in a free gift, even when there isn't one. Because they give up half of their enjoyment by distrusting the gift, for every two hypothetical events they may experience only half a unit of happiness.

I once had a student who was very excited about attending an upcoming Rolling Stones concert and about the possibility that he might get a backstage pass. He was on cloud nine for weeks before the concert and listened to their music constantly. He wasn't just going to hear Mick Jagger; he was Mick Jagger—and he experienced a great deal of joy at the anticipation of the event as he danced and sang around campus. Unfortunately, he got so involved with the preconcert revelry that he missed the bus and the entire concert. When he returned to class after the weekend of the show and others learned of what happened, many fellow students thought that he must be terribly disappointed. His response, though, was, "Yeah, I was bummed at first. But, hey, I had the best three weeks of my life before the concert. And besides, next week the . . . are coming to town!"

Which camp is preferable? Each may be useful depending on the situation or the context. The choice may be easier if you remember how the two groups handle life situations. The *Gusto* people associate with excitement and dissociate from disappointment. This effectively increases their enjoyment in life. The student just mentioned was fully present in the moment while experiencing the anticipated event. He detached and viewed the event as something from the past when it didn't work out. The *Chickens* people do the reverse; they view an anticipated event with detachment and then exaggerate the disappointment by reviewing it over and over.

These ideas do not invalidate the importance of being cautious at times. The ramifications of a situation must be considered when making a decision that will have a lasting effect. But when all that is being risked is the degree of enjoyment to be derived from an event, I suggest you try this approach. You may be pleasantly surprised. On a final note, keep in mind that all of the ideas and concepts presented in this chapter may require a good deal of practice.

CHAPTER REVIEW

Understanding Emotions

Many theories attempt to explain emotions, and most include physiological and cognitive components. Research suggests that there are specific areas of the brain that are related to emotions.

Emotional Building Blocks

Feelings aren't right or wrong, but context is important. Repressing emotions can cause problems. Limiting one feeling leads to limiting them all. Your feelings about feelings originate in your family. Using the "dimmer switch" to control your emotions helps if you use it at the right time.

Emotional Intelligence

Emotional intelligence describes qualities such as understanding one's own feelings, empathy for the feelings of others, and the regulation of emotion in a way that enhances living.

Emotional Control

Knowing how to increase or decrease your feelings can be valuable. Being associated by stepping into the situation and staying in the present while describing the emotion will increase feelings. Being dissociated by stepping out, experiencing the situation as if at another time, and making directive comments will decrease your feelings.

Thought Distortion

Sometimes you can modify your moods by examining your beliefs. Many people have unrealistic expectations that predispose them to having unnecessary emotional reactions at times. Monitoring your thoughts and self-talk can be useful.

Defense Mechanisms

Another form of thought distortion is the defense mechanisms that we use to lessen our anxiety. When people feel scared, threatened, or have their ego damaged, they often rely on beliefs that will enable them to believe that everything is all right. Although this process is normal and rather common, it can also cause further problems.

Anger

We have more control of emotions than we think. Dissociating can be useful in a context where getting angry would be inappropriate. Coping with anger can be aided by examining your assumptions and considering what is beneath the anger.

Guilt

Guilt is often anger turned inward. If you have done something that you feel bad about, you might feel mad at yourself. There are two kinds of guilt: constructive and destructive. One comes from recognizing mistakes and doing what is necessary to remedy the situation. The other is often irrational or unnecessary. There are methods for dealing with constructive guilt in a useful manner.

Sadness

Sometimes you must allow yourself to feel sadness, and sometimes you must let go of sadness. It helps to consider your beliefs about expressing sadness. There are gender differences in expressing sadness. Be aware of your objections to the resolution of sadness; there may be a significant reason for them.

Excitement and Joy

Traits that foster joy are positive self-esteem, personal control, sociability, and optimism. The Two-for-One concept can help increase joy. We should consider all the implications of a decision, but too many people take the *Don't Count Your Chickens* approach. The *Go for the Gusto* approach increases joy by incorporating the excitement of anticipating an event.

SOURCES AND SUGGESTED READINGS

Adler, Ronald, and Neil Towne. *Looking Out/ Looking In.* New York: Harcourt, Brace, Jovanovich, 2003.

Atwater, Eastwood. *Psychology of Adjustment.* Englewood Cliffs, NJ: Prentice Hall, 1999.

Burns, David D. *The Feeling Good Handbook.* New York: Penguin, 1989.

Buscaglia, Leo. *Living, Loving, and Learning.* New York: Holt, Rinehart & Winston, 1982.

Goleman, Daniel. *Emotional Intelligence.* New York: Bantam, 1995.

Lerner, Harriet Goldhor. *The Dance of Anger,* revised ed. New York: Harper Perennial. 1997.

Real, T. *I Don't Want to Talk About It: Overcoming the Secret Legacy of Male Depression.* New York: Simon & Schuster, 1998.

Selye, Hans. *Stress Without Distress.* New York: Lippincott, 1974.

Tavris, Carol. *Anger: The Misunderstood Emotion.* New York: Simon & Schuster, 1989.

Web Site Resources

Exploring cool-down strategies for dealing with anger
   http://www.re.com/anger

Emotions and Emotional Intelligence Studies
   http://www.trochim.human.cornell.edu/

REACTION AND RESPONSE – WHAT DO YOU THINK?

Chapter Five   Level I Assignments

In response to the information in the chapter:

1. How will you apply the information about emotional intelligence? What was important for you about the material in that section? How will that influence how you deal with anger and sadness?

2. What do you think about getting excited in advance about an upcoming event? How much excitement is acceptable for you to experience, and do you have any fears about being too out-of-control? How will you use the Two-for-One Principle? What are the common elements of times and places where you have possibly sabotaged your own enjoyment?

3. What did you learn about defense mechanisms? Where and when have you noticed yourself using one of them? What might you think and do differently in the future?

In response to the class activities, group discussions, and exercises:

1. What are your opinions and reactions?
2. What did you learn or rediscover?
3. How are you going to apply what you learned?

Chapter Five   Level II Assignments

1. What did you learn about how to associate or dissociate regarding your emotions? Which do you have a preference for, and how can you develop a more balanced approach? Where and when will you apply this information?

2. What did your family teach you about expressing anger? What did you learn about coping with your own anger? How can you apply the information in the chapter about handling anger in a constructive manner?

3. What are your beliefs about sadness and its expression? Some people believe that you should cry as often as you need to; how often would that be for you? Do you have a different set of standards for yourself than for other people?

Chapter Five   Level III Assignments

1. When have you felt guilty? Was is legitimate guilt or unrealistic? Whom do you owe and apology?

2. Where, and in what specific situations, do you think you most need to use your EQ ? What gets you hooked? What pushes your buttons? What are your plans for beginning to practice new skills so you don't "get got"?

3. What are some of your irrational beliefs, and how do those lead to thought distortions? How do thought distortions and defense mechanisms overlap?

6

CHAPTER

DEVELOPING CLOSE RELATIONSHIPS

They were just finishing their dinner at the cozy little restaurant that they had been wanting to try out for some time. Mary was arranging the silverware that hadn't been used while John wiped up the last of the main course of his meal. He had been doing most of the talking that evening because he was happy just to be feeling good again. They hadn't been arguing as much lately and it was nice to have their lives taking a more normal turn with time for each other. It had been a while since they had gotten out together without the children, and it had been exhilarating to have an uninterrupted conversation. They could even laugh at themselves sometimes about how disgustingly conventional and commonplace were their yuppie concerns and problems. Yet, the tension and pressure on the relationship were all too real. Balancing schedules for a two-income family, with their small child and a prepubescent daughter from his former marriage at home, had proven to be more of a tight-rope act than either of them had expected. The past three years had been more than a little rocky.

"You haven't finished your broccoli," she said.

"Yep," he stated flatly in an attempt to practice what he had learned in their counseling sessions about not getting hooked.

"But it's good for you and you need to eat better."

"I'm full. Thanks for caring." A tinge of sarcasm was evident in his voice.

"It has lots of vitamins and you're in training. You need to eat right if you're going to be running more."

"I take care of myself just fine, and besides, I'm full."

"You're the biggest garbage pit I know. You're always eating junk."

John could feel his face start to flush as he looked at his out-of-shape wife and considered eating habits. "I do just fine."

"You cook the heck out of things at home . . . that is, when you cook," she corrected him. "This is how broccoli should be done . . . just lightly steamed so it still has the nutrients in it. You should eat the rest of yours."

"In a minute, you're going to eat my broccoli."

"You're so hostile. Why are you such an angry man?" It was more of an indictment than a question.

"Do you want to go to this party tonight or not?" he asked.

"Of course. I don't know why we can't have a little fun."

"I'll go pay the bill." He left the table abruptly and walked out to the car ahead of her to have a few moments alone.

Sitting in the car, he began to ruminate about the relationship and wondered what had brought them together in the first place. They were introduced by friends, who thought they would be a good match and seemed to have so much in common. But, the similarity of their backgrounds didn't compensate for their difference in personality. He had a greater need for closeness and contact and was more often the "pursuer" in the relationship. She was the "pursued" and only switched roles when he seemed ready to quit the chase. He was deep in thought, fiddling with the gearshift, and was considering how to change the pattern.

Just then Mary opened the car door and tossed her purse on the floor as she climbed in. As they drove off into the night, Mary put her hand on his arm and said, "Let's just try to have a good time tonight."

"I'd sure like that," he said as he gently squeezed her hand.

Theories of Attraction

In previous chapters, we covered various aspects of emotions and family relations, but we didn't talk about love. Possibly the most complex of emotions, love is inextricably intertwined with marriage and relationships and will be discussed in conjunction with these topics. We will discuss attraction and partner selection and explore the interactions that take place as people deal with similarities and differences in personal relationships.

Love seems to incorporate an incredibly wide range of emotions. Everyone wants and needs to feel loved, yet many people don't know how to handle the situation when they find it. As wonderful as a close relationship feels, some people sabotage themselves or the relationship just when things are going well. People have varying capacities and/or abilities for intimacy, and perhaps, as some psychologists suggest, we expect too much of marriage these days. Whatever the expectations, the dance that takes place in relationships is about resolving the issues involved with love and intimacy.

How we perceive others and their abilities to meet our needs frequently dictates our choice of partner. The fact that the need for a good relationship is powerful is evident from the number of people continuing to marry in spite of the national divorce statistics. Research shows that love is still the number one reason given for getting married, at least in our North American culture. The difficulty lies in defining exactly what love means. The possibilities of understanding love and having a good relationship are enhanced through awareness of the factors that influence the choice of partner. Being with the right person is a wonderful and fulfilling experience. So with that in mind, let's explore the elements of couples' relationships.

Have you ever looked at a couple and wondered, "What are those two doing together?" As unfathomable as it may sometimes appear, there are always reasons for two people being attracted to each other. To a significant degree, it has to do with our perceptions about ourselves and the potential satisfying of needs. There are two basic reasons for attraction: **social comparison** and **social exchange** (Franzoi, 2003). According to social comparison theory, a good deal of our desire to be with others is due to our need to have an accurate view of self and an accurate worldview. We are more likely to gain such knowledge by comparing our reactions with those of others. In contrast, social exchange theory contends that we are attracted to others because of the social rewards that are exchanged in various interactions. These relationships are sought out and maintained if the *rewards* received in the interaction exceed the costs. The following are some key factors for attraction discussed by Stephen Franzoi in *Social Psychology:*

Proximity: Proximity is physical and/or geographical closeness. We tend to like people with whom we come into frequent contact. That might mean passing his or her desk at work often or seeing him or her around town a great deal. Being in close proximity to someone on a regular basis increases the likelihood of making social contacts.

Familiarity: Familiarity may make someone seem safer, and it lessens the risk in initiating conversation. We tend to like people who are similar to us and who enjoy the same things we do. Common interests build relationships. An important force in attraction is agreement, and sharing the same views may be interpreted to mean that the other person is sensible and worthy. Being alike could also mean there will be fewer conflicts.

Reciprocity: Reciprocity means liking people who return the feeling. It is the "I like you because you like me" phenomenon. If someone thinks highly of us and that matches our self-assessment, then we have a tendency to concur and to like that person in return. The psychological costs are lower when you are involved with someone you know likes you.

Attractiveness: Although we say, "Don't judge a book by its cover," unfortunately, we seem to do just that. We tend to like people who meet our society's definition of attractiveness. Research indicates (Aronson, 1988) that if someone is good-looking, we attribute certain positive traits to the person. The physical attractiveness stereotype contributes to the belief that attractive people possess socially desirable personality traits and lead happier lives than less attractive people.

After considering the factors involved in initial attraction, it is important to examine the reasons for continuing to develop a relationship.

> *"By all means marry; if you get a good partner, you'll be happy. If you get a bad one, you'll become a philosopher."*
> Socrates (paraphrased)

Partner Selection

Deciding on a relationship is largely an unconscious filtering process for many people. A number of factors influence our assessment of a potential partner. Some people report that within minutes of arriving at a party they know whether anyone there interests them. Similarly, when two people begin to share more personal information, some people are very quick to judge based on information about the other person's background.

Initially, physical characteristics and proximity play a large part in mate selection. As a relationship develops and two people get to know each other, social characteristics and personality may determine whether they think of each other as potential partners. We also may decide to pursue or eliminate someone as a partner when we discover important aspects of his or her beliefs. We tend to get closer to people with whom we share common interests. Education, social class, race, and religion play a dominant part in this stage of a relationship.

The dichotomy *birds of a feather flock together* versus *opposites attract* has been around for some time. Many people have a definite idea of whom they should be with and what characteristics that person should possess. Sometimes, however, one person is attracted to another because he or she represents opposite values. Many people marry someone just because he or she represents everything parents or friends don't want for them in a partner.

The *complementary needs theory* also explains why some people are interested in their opposites. According to this theory, we are attracted to someone with personal characteristics that we lack. Someone who is more how we would like to be may provide an opportunity to gain certain social rewards. Regarding appearance, Franzoi (2003) calls this the *looks-for-status exchange*. Someone who is attractive by society's standards might be attracted to someone considered less attractive if that person is rich, famous, powerful, or from a different social class. In general, though, the contradiction seems to be that we want a partner whose personality traits complement ours, but at the same time we need to share similarities to increase understanding and agreement.

How do we find a balance between these two notions? It appears that similarities are more important for maintaining successful long-term relationships. Having opposite superficial characteristics may provide the spice of life, but when dealing with major life issues such as religion, philosophy, politics, family, work, and money, having common ground is best. That doesn't mean there can't be some differences, but people who differ too greatly in one area will probably need more similarities in other areas to balance that. For the most part, people who have similar values and backgrounds are more likely to work at resolving differences when opposite tendencies create difficulties in the relationship. As we explore how opposites attract and what happens when they do, consider this: The qualities that make someone attractive now are often the very things that will drive you crazy a year later! Most married people, or anyone involved in a long-term live-in arrangement, will immediately identify with that statement. When attraction is based on the belief that someone's traits can make up for our own deficiencies, there is potential difficulty.

Bricks and Balloons

What happens to couples looking to balance their needs while in an ongoing relationship? It is amazing how often opposites seem to connect. The classic example is what I call the "brick-and-balloon" combination. One of them talks all the time; the other one hardly says a word. One of them is spontaneous and energetic; the other is methodical and slow moving. One of them is orderly and organized; the other is casual and sloppy. All of these are combinations of very different people who are somewhat complementary.

So what are the bricks and balloons doing for each other? They are balancing each other! Here is an example of that type of relationship: The stereotypical man is authoritarian and needs things to be done just right. He wants order, structure, and logic. The stereotypical woman may be more of a free spirit, inclined to follow the whims of the moment. The more the man tries to lay down the rules for the house, the more the woman tries to balance things by going in the other direction. She may say things like, "Relax a little. You're too hard on the kids. Let's not make a big deal out of everything." To which he replies, "Somebody has to lay down the rules around here. If it were up to you, the house would be destroyed and the kids would be running naked in the streets." Simplistic and stereotypical, but the idea is clear.

Some people have maintained that type of relationship for many years. That is an example of external balance. The more rigid or heavy one becomes, the more the other tries to balance things by lightening them up. In the previous example, the farther he goes in one direction, the farther she goes in the other. When a brick and a balloon are tied together, a great deal of stress is put on the string. That is one of the problems with external balance. Too much of a person's behavior is based on reacting to what the other has done. The constant need to balance each other puts tension in the relationship. Sometimes, the string breaks.

The problem comes from attempting to find balance by looking for an external source. A person who looks to someone else to provide what is missing eventually becomes resentful of the other person's ability to fill that need. The very traits or abilities that were attractive during the courtship are the same ones that can become restrictive in a relationship. He was so brilliant and such a dazzling conversationalist that she couldn't help being awed at how he filled the gaps when she was shy in social situations. A year later, she resents it when she can't get a word in edgewise. How will she ever learn to speak up if she has to compete with someone who does it so much better?

Another variation is the woman who marries a man because he is lively, fun, and spontaneous, and then resents him because she feels she has to take on all the responsibilities of the household. How can she have fun when that's all he ever does, and how can she relax when he never notices what needs to be done? The free-spirited balloon who is adventurous, creative, and spontaneous can later be perceived as being irresponsible and flaky. The dependable brick who is reliable, predictable, and conscientious can later be seen as rigid and boring.

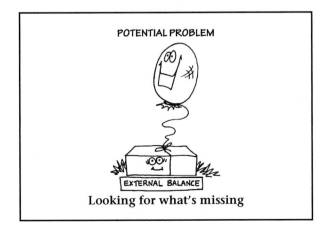

POTENTIAL PROBLEM

Looking for what's missing

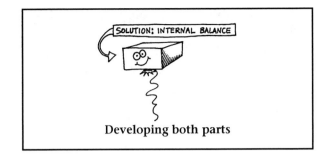

Developing both parts

The traits that originally seemed so wonderful have a flip side—which is why it is difficult, in most cases, to maintain a relationship based on the attraction of opposites. A better relationship develops when each person involved is capable of internal balance. Everyone needs to have some brick and some balloon parts to his or her identity.

More important than similarities or differences in partners is the concept of compatibility. This occurs when each partner has the choice of sometimes being a brick and sometimes being a balloon—being able to trade roles. Compatibility enables partners to take turns at filling a role when the circumstances are appropriate. She may be the brick when it comes to finances, and he may be the balloon in the role of social coordinator for the couple. They may reverse those roles in different situations so that sometimes she makes the dinner plans and he thinks about where to go that will save them money. Or she may be the brick with the finances for half the year, and he then takes over that role for the other half. However it works, the more each person in the relationship is internally balanced, the greater the potential for compatibility between the two.

People often wonder how to get their partners to be different, which usually means to be more like them. There is something that can be done to enhance the likelihood of that happening: The more Person A acts like Person B, the more Person B will act like Person A. A balloon wanting a brick to lighten up will never achieve that objective by telling the brick that he or she is wrong for being brickish. But if the balloon slows down and pays attention to what is important to the brick, the balloon may discover what needs to be done to make the brick feel like having fun. If one partner thinks that he or she has to do all the worrying, then the other one will have to demonstrate an ability to be more responsible before the worrier will relax. By the same token, a brick wanting a balloon to be less flighty may need to lighten up a little so the balloon doesn't think that becoming responsible means that both partners will be

Questions for Critical Thinking

Which is more important: Birds of a feather flock together or opposites attract? What are the implications of each? What have you learned about attraction, and how does that apply to you?

_____

_____

_____

_____

_____

_____

_____

_____

_____

_____

boring. This negotiation is best accomplished if both parties keep in mind that each choice is useful in some context.

The New Golden Rule

Most people have heard the saying, "Do unto others as you would have done unto you." This advice is useful in some situations, but it can cause problems when one person assumes that what he or she wants is also what the other person wants. This isn't always the case. Have you ever gotten a present that was what the other person wanted, not what you wanted? People do this with their feelings, too, when they project their needs and wishes onto others.

This projection is evident when people in relationships have different ways of demonstrating affection. If at the end of the day, John meets Mary at the door with a glass of wine and an invitation to snuggle on the couch and talk about the day, he may be doing what he would like from Mary if the situation were reversed. This may backfire if Mary's belief about what constitutes a show of affection is something totally different. She may want the house to be clean and orderly and the tasks for that day to have been completed. Mary, thinking she is showing her affection for John, may put her energy into making

> **"** *Expect what is reasonable in others, not what is perfect.* **"**
>
> *Anonymous*

sure that the house and their lives are neat and orderly, and that things that need to be done have been attended to. John will most likely be disappointed if his idea of being cared for includes playful contact, talking, and being hugged.

Perhaps we need to establish a new Golden Rule that ensures that people receive what they want rather than what someone thinks they want. The old rule implies that it is important to be nice to people and consider their feelings. This might be done best by adopting the new rule: **Do unto others as they would have done unto them!**

Marriage and Society

A frequent response to the question, "Why did you get married?" is "Because it was time." There is a social clock that runs continuously and yet affects people differently. (The social clock has always been relative. In Shakespeare's day, the age of marriage was approximately 13.) Our society is geared toward getting married; it's not *if*, it's *when*. Although the average age of first marriage currently is 23 or 24, according to numerous surveys, some people still feel pressure to get married right after high school. Others wait until after they turn 21 and have experienced the bar scene—a cultural phenomenon in which getting drunk and passing out in the parking lot of the local bar is supposed to be a sign of adulthood. Those who have postponed marriage to go to college or start a career begin to feel the pressure to settle down at about age 25. This frequently coincides with parental inquiries, such as "Have you found anyone yet?" At about 30, the question changes to "When are we going to have grandchildren?" and those still unmarried begin to feel the "over-the-hill" pressure.

The biological clock ticks even louder at 35, especially for women. Both women and men are influenced by the question of parenthood. There has been a trend of people having children later in life; this is especially true for the baby boom generation. As a result, there are people looking for partners, after years of being single, because they want to start families at an age that was previously thought of as the time to be taking care of grandchildren. Most people have some vague age in mind as to when they will be married. When that age arrives, it exerts an unconscious influence on people's decisions. Many couples who are dating suddenly feel that the time is right, even if they aren't entirely sure about each other. Marriage is one of those decisions that is affected by life's transitions and their timing.

Parents influence the *who* as well as the *when* of marriage, although parental influence may be less important today than in the past. For many people, there are those you date and those you take home to the family. Some people know exactly what type of person they are expected to marry, and they comply; others marry a particular partner just to spite their parents, and some even elope, knowing that will get a negative response. Parents pass on many beliefs about what marriage is, who is a good partner, and even what faith a couple should adopt. Those values influence us on many levels when choosing a partner, regardless of whether or not we choose to accept them.

Peer pressure is important also, but to a lesser degree. After dating someone for a while, most people go back to their friends and ask, "Well, what do you think?" A positive response usually raises that prospective mate's stature, just as a negative response will lower it or cause a person to at least take a closer look. A relationship is less likely to continue if the friends of one of the partners continue to ask, "What are you doing with someone like that?" Peer groups can exert more than just subtle pressure. Sometimes, people get involved in a relationship as a way of joining a group or maintaining a connection with one. As friends start to couple up, one way to remain a part of the old gang is to marry a person familiar to the group.

Types of Love

A number of psychologists have attempted to explain love and have examined the components that make up this complex emotion. Hatfield (1988) believes that there are two types of love: companionate and passionate. The first is the type of love for those with whom our lives are deeply entwined; the later is the head-over-heels romantic notion of what love is when we are first attracted to someone. Rubin (1973) believes that love has three components: attachment, caring, and intimacy. For all of the different theories and types of love, most believe that it is a combination of the various components that creates the different styles of love and relationships.

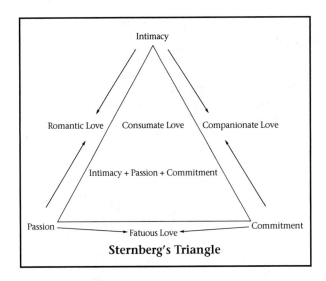

Sternberg's Triangle

Sternberg's Triangle Sternberg (1986) proposes a triangular theory of love and suggests that it has three components. After studying what differentiates romantic relationships from other types of love, he developed a theory built around the components of intimacy, passion, and commitment (see chart).

Intimacy is the emotional aspect of love and includes sharing, knowledge of each other, communication, caring, and closeness. Some people mistakenly believe that sex and intimacy are one and the same, or that one leads to the other. True intimacy has more to do with trusting your partner and being willing and able to communicate deep inner feelings and beliefs. It also implies a great deal of vulnerability and openness. Intimacy tends to develop more slowly than passion.

Passion is the motivational aspect of love and involves the physiological arousal and strong desire to be with the loved one. Passionate feelings may develop quickly and continue for the first few years of a relationship, but most couples experience a decline in passionate feelings after a while. Perhaps that is why there are so many self-help books offering advice about how to keep the passion in your relationship. It takes concerted effort and focus to maintain passion over the long haul. For most people, it is a process of transitioning from the high peaks of passion to the deeper and broader feelings involved with intimacy.

Commitment is the cognitive component of love and develops in a more straightforward manner than intimacy or passion. In long-lasting relationships, commitment begins gradually at first and then rapidly increases as the relationship intensifies. It may level off at some point in the relationship. If commitment begins to weaken, it is often a signal that the relationship is in decline and/or is ending.

Each of these components may be experienced alone or in combination with the others. This helps to explain why there are so many types of relationships possible. Intimacy alone indicates strong ties of friendship. Intimacy with passion is romantic love, and intimacy with commitment is companionate love.

Passion alone is usually considered to be infatuation. Passion with commitment is fatuous love, as evidenced in whirlwind romances where people get married without actually knowing the other person. Commitment alone usually is indicative of an empty marriage where the couple decide to stay together without intimacy or passion. Although difficult to attain, Sternberg considers love that involves all three components to be consummate love. This is the most idea relationship, and the one many people hope to develop.

Expressions of Love

People often have different ways of expressing love for their partner. As with learning to communicate better in any situation, it is an important skill to notice if the message being transmitted is coded in the way that it is most likely to be received. Even with the best of intentions, your expression of love may not be perceived or felt if it doesn't register on the other person's radar.

A good number of people believe that they should always feel like they did when they were in the "in love" stage of the relationship. Even though that experience usually transforms after a few years for most couples, sometimes the lack of feeling loved is due to forgetting how to tell the other that you care in the ways that they feel it.

Dr. Gary Chapman has concluded, after many years of counseling, that there are five "Love Languages" (1996). Dissatisfaction in marriage may have a simple root cause: We speak different love languages, he believes. Some husbands or wives may crave focused attention, whereas others might need regular praise. Gifts of any kind are highly important to one spouse, while another could see fixing a leaky faucet, ironing a shirt, or cooking a meal as filling their "love tank." Some partners might find physical touch makes them feel valued as in holding hands, giving back rubs, or sexual contact. Keeping in mind that none of these needs are gender specific, here are the languages Chapman describes:

1. *Words of Affirmation.* Some people need to hear expressions of love in order to feel it

and believe it. And, that is expressed not just in those words but by reassurances that their partner finds qualities about them attractive.

2. *Quality Time.* Love is experienced by some people when the other person in the relationship sets aside specific time to spend with them. It doesn't have to be talking, but just the act of being together.

3. *Receiving Gifts.* This is more than remembering birthdays and anniversaries, little "gifts" can be given on a daily basis. Some feel loved by getting a phone call. For others, the gift isn't as important as the experience of feeling that someone was thinking of you and knows you well enough to give you a present that shows that they care.

4. *Acts of Service.* Performing a task, of almost any kind, that is helpful to the other person can be perceived as an expression of love.

5. *Physical Contact.* We all know people who are "touchers" who only feel attended to by physical connections. They know they are loved and cared for through touch.

How you express love can be a choice, and learning to speak your spouse's language can make your marriage richer and more fulfilling. It may take effort to learn how to speak the language your partner will respond to best, but in doing so, your life together may be more satisfying.

Attachment Styles and Romantic Relationships

Attachment was first studied in animals, then in human infants, and later in human adults. A line of animal research that might be relevant to human attachment is **Harlow's experiments** showing that infant monkeys prefer a soft terry-cloth mother surrogate to a wire one, even when only the wire one dispenses milk. Also, severely deprived infant monkeys often come to behave differently from their normally reared peers (Novak and Harlow, 1975).

When a human or nonhuman primate infant is separated from its parent, the infant goes through a series of three stages of emotional reactions. First is **protest,** in which the infant cries and refuses to be consoled by others. Second is **despair,** in which the infant is sad and passive. Third is **detachment,** in which the infant actively disregards and avoids the parent if the parent returns (Hazan and Shaver, 1987).

The fundamental assumption in attachment research on human infants is that sensitive responding by the parent to the infant's needs results in an infant who demonstrates **secure** attachment, whereas lack of such sensitive responding results in **insecure** attachment. Other theorists have postulated several varieties of insecure attachment, including **resistant/ambivalent.** The three main styles of secure, avoidant, and resistant attachment were developed as a way of classifying infant behavior in the "**strange situation,**" a study of the interaction between parent and child (Ainsworth, Blehar, Waters, and Wall, 1978).

> **Secure attachment style:** Securely attached infants trust their caretaker, don't fear abandonment, and explore their world.
>
> **Avoidant attachment style:** The caregiver is distant or rejecting, and the infants avoid the parent or suppress the desire to be close.
>
> **Resistant/ambivalent attachment style:** Inconsistent caregivers are unpredictable and the infant may cling anxiously to them and then fight against the closeness by pushing away.

Attachment theory provides not only a framework for understanding emotional reactions in infants, but also a framework for understanding love, loneliness, and grief in adults. Attachment styles in adults are thought to stem directly from the mental models (attitudes and beliefs) of oneself and others that were developed during infancy and childhood. Ainsworth's description of attachment styles has been translated into terms of adult romantic relationships as follows (Hazan and Shaver, 1987).

> **Secure** adults find it relatively easy to get close to others and are comfortable depending on others and having others depend on them. Secure adults don't often worry about being abandoned or about someone getting too close to them.
>
> **Avoidant** adults are somewhat uncomfortable being close to others; they find it difficult to trust others completely, difficult to allow themselves to depend on others. Avoidant adults are nervous when anyone gets too close, and often, romantic partners want them to be more intimate than they feel comfortable being.
>
> **Anxious/ambivalent** adults find that others are reluctant to get as close as they would like. Anxious/ambivalent adults often worry that their partner doesn't really love them or won't want to stay with them. Anxious/ambivalent adults want to merge completely with another person, and this desire sometimes scares people away.

Keep in mind, though, that attachment styles aren't cast in stone. Because of life experiences, attachment styles can change. Stressful or traumatic events may lessen the ability to form attachments, and positive experiences may strengthen the ability to form relationships. Some individuals revise their attachment styles as they experience relationships in their adult years (Santrock, 2006).

The Dance of Intimacy

Most couples want intimacy in their relationship. Unfortunately, many are not capable of sustaining it. How often have you seen couples who seem to start arguments whenever things have been going too well for too long? We all want someone to be open and honest with, someone with whom we can be real and share our vulnerabilities. Yet that kind of intimacy also makes some people fearful, afraid of being hurt. Some guard against closeness because they fear that they will be controlled or lose their identity. Others think that intimacy will mean too many sacrifices and that they will lose their freedom.

Whatever the reasons, many relationships go through an on-again–off-again cycle as each person tries to change the other in hopes of establishing the level of closeness necessary to feel safe. We all have comfort zones for the level of closeness we can tolerate. This leads to a "dance of intimacy" (Lerner, 1989) that couples do while each person tries to attain the optimal position on the closeness-distance continuum. This is seldom a conscious negotiation, but each tries to get the other to behave in a way that meets his or her needs. Some couples adopt a style of relating to each other in which they are cast into the roles of pursuer and pursued. This allows each one to believe that the reason for not getting closer is the other person's fault. In reality, both may be equally responsible for maintaining a relationship based on a certain amount of distance. Here is a personal example:

Beginning when I was 19, I dated a girl I'll call "Jane" for almost five years. During that time, I did something to put distance in the relationship about every three or four months. Sometimes, it would be "forgetting" that we were going steady and asking her best girlfriend for a date. That's a sure way to get some distance! At other times, it would be as simple as not phoning her for a few weeks. If she got tired of the routine and decided the relationship was over, I always did or said whatever was necessary to reestablish it. Things would start improving, and we would get along great and become close again. We would become so close, in fact, that she would start to talk about marriage. Wham! I was off like a bolt of lightning again. I'd never let go entirely, though. I might have been straining to get away, but I was always holding on at the same time. Back and forth, moving apart and coming together. That's what I call the three-quarter waltz. What was Jane doing with a guy like me? One possible payoff for her was that every time I acted like a jerk, she got a tremendous amount of support from her friends, all of whom told her how great she was and how she deserved someone better (i.e., she got positive attention). No one does anything without a reason, so there may have been unconscious motives for her behavior, too.

When I tell that story to women, they usually say that if any man had ever done to them as I did to Jane, they wouldn't have given him a second chance, let alone a dozen. So, why did Jane stay? In retrospect, it seems that not having to deal with real intimacy served her needs, too. She may have had a greater capacity for closeness than I did at that time, but she could still count on the fact that I would reach the limits of my comfort zone before she reached hers. She could safely say she wanted to get married, knowing that it was highly unlikely to happen because every time I heard the word *marriage,* I took off running the other way.

People who really want to get married don't usually hang around with someone wearing a sign saying "No way in hell." Or do they? One young man gave me the opportunity to talk to the ghost of myself from 25 years ago. His was the familiar story of the girlfriend who had been wanting to get married for years. He confessed to having treated her shabbily at times but said that now, after having been through a number of maturing life experiences and some personal counseling, he was ready to make the commitment. He asked her to marry him and, within two weeks, she was saying that she thought maybe they should date other people for a while just to be

sure. Can you guess the rest of the story? As soon as he wanted her, she was no longer interested.

In her book *The Dance of Intimacy,* Harriet Lerner (1989) points out that the pursuer and the pursued, the one allegedly wanting distance, are often accomplishing the same goal and are more alike than different in some respects. Each takes on a particular role that fulfills his or her psychological needs and proceeds to play out the drama. The important element that keeps the game going is that each person has to believe that he or she is not getting what he or she wants because the other person is denying it. The couple gets caught up in the various story lines of each episode and fails to notice the repetition. To be aware of it might mean examining their own fears, needs, and behaviors.

Another variation of the dance of intimacy takes place when a person is attracted only to people who aren't interested or aren't available. There are people who make a game of seeing whom they can interest in a relationship, only to change their minds after achieving their goal and move on to the next pursuit. There are relationships based on exchanging the roles of pursuer and pursued, which I call the "Scotty Dog Tag," named after the prize in Cracker Jacks. This prize had black-and-white Scotty dogs with magnets on the bottom that would push each other back and forth, depending on which way one of the dogs was turned. There are couples who take turns creating distance as they chase each other back and forth. For some people, the excitement of a relationship is mainly in the looking, not in the finding.

Positive, healthy relationships do exist, though. One way to increase the likelihood of having one is to be aware of the factors that influence couples' interactions. The information presented here may help you avoid some of the pitfalls of unhealthy relationships. Successful marriages are more common for people who are relatively well-adjusted. The well-rounded and internally balanced person will be better able to find someone who is similarly well-adjusted. People with high self-esteem tend to attract others who have high self-esteem. The rewards of good relationships are more readily available to those who want one than to those who need one. We all have needs we want to have met, but there is a difference between wanting those needs met and needing to have those needs met at all times by someone else. Two whole people will be able to reciprocate and experience the positive aspects of a relationship better than people who are looking for what is "missing."

> **❝***Men always want to be a woman's first love; women have a more subtle instinct; what they like is to be a man's last romance.***❞**
>
> *Rick Lewis*

What concerns do you have about intimacy? Have you ever played the Scotty Dog Tag in a relationship? What is your closeness comfort zone, and how do you try to maintain it?

_____

_____

_____

_____

_____

_____

_____

_____

_____

Codependent Relationships

Although the subject of codependent relationships is a serious one, it is also important to approach it with a sense of humor. The term *codependency* has been bantered about so much lately that it is approaching *psychobabble,* in that it is used to describe so many types of relationships. As a result, even the people in those situations start to make up jokes about themselves. Perhaps you have heard: "First there was Advil, and now there is Co-Advil for codependents. When they hurt, you hurt, so take something for their pain." Or: "You know you are codependent when you are drowning and someone else's life flashes before your eyes!"

A codependent relationship can be one in which one person has a problem, and the partner has as much psychological investment in the problem as the person who actually has the problem. Both partners may be getting their needs met by being in a system where one person isn't functioning very well. People in that type of situation frequently develop a self-perpetuating cycle that keeps both locked in a limiting pattern of beliefs and behaviors.

I first encountered a truly codependent relationship years ago as a junior shrink in graduate school. I was hired one summer to do light construction work by a man I'll call "Art," who did remodeling and built decks on people's homes. The first few days on the job went well, although Art spent a lot of time complaining about his wife of 30 years. Then one morning, he showed up at 7:30 A.M. drinking 100-proof vodka with his orange juice. By noon, he was unable to work, and he sat in the shade calling out instructions to me. At the end of the day, he was so smashed that I had to drive him home. We didn't work the next day. On the third day, he showed up with a tale of woe about having been kicked out of the house and sleeping in the car. He spent the next night at a friend's house. On the following day, he said that he had apologized to his wife and asked for her forgiveness, so he was allowed to return home. Things went fine for a few days, and then one morning he showed up drinking again, and the whole process started over.

When this cycle was repeated for the third time, I knew this was a pretty crazy situation. It was unhealthy for me as well, and I began to feel that I had been roped into his routine. I was contributing to the situation by listening to him complain all day while doing his work for him and then driving him home when he was drunk. When I began to figure out the pattern and could see how destructive it was, I quit the job.

Although it was obvious that he had a problem, even back then I began to wonder about his wife. It drove me crazy in the three weeks that I dealt with the situation, and I began to wonder what it was like for his wife. I know now that they had a classic Saints and Sinners routine going. She was very religious, and when he came home drunk, she gave him "hellfire and damnation" and righteously kicked him out of the house. He then did penance by sleeping in the car. After a cooling-off period, he crawled home and begged for forgiveness, at which point she read him the Bible and pounded the pulpit. And eventually, being a good Christian, she forgave him. After a short time, the whole drama would be replayed. She needed him to have a problem as much as he did. Because they had been married for over 30 years, playing a part in that routine obviously met some of her needs.

There are many forms of codependence, but most incorporate one person with a problem and another person needing him or her to have that problem. In some cases, the codependent partner may unconsciously encourage the behavior in the partner with the problem. Another variation is when one or both partners feel so inadequate and incomplete that they have to have someone else from whom they can derive their identity. Their unspoken contract may be agreeing

CASE STUDIES AND STUDENT STORIES

Katherine grew up in a family where it was commonplace to see her mom being physically or verbally abused. One of her earliest memories of her family is her mother frantically running around the dining room while her stepdad chased her with an axe.

But, no matter how frightening things got, she learned at a very young age to hide her feelings and not to tell anyone. She survived her rough neighborhood by walking tall and talking tough. In the eighth grade she could arm-wrestle any boy in her class and take him down.

Years passed, and Katherine's life started a downhill spiral. She married twice, both times to abusive husbands. She began to believe what her second husband said when he told her she was worthless and no one would want her. She endured countless beatings and daily ridicule, and her life was totally focused on trying to please her husband.

On December 27, 1997, Katherine's life came to abrupt halt. She came home from a church-related gathering and found her estranged husband lying on her couch. He told her to get out of her own house, even though they had been separated for months. When she said no, he began beating her with an iron rod. As she lay in a pool of blood with thoughts that she might be dying, she strangely remembered a TV show she had seen regarding survival in abusive situations. In the show it stated that a victim should do anything to get the abuser to focus on something else. She asked her husband if she could confess something. For a moment he was so startled that he backed off and sat down. It was then she was able to escape down the stairs.

Doctors at the hospital were astounded that she had been able to run away. She suffered a brain injury, a broken eardrum, and a fractured rotator cuff. She did not walk again unaided for several months. Adrenaline had compensated for the impairment of all her injuries.

As a result of the attack, Katherine began to see a counselor. Week after week she poured her heart out and began to realize how her childhood had affected her adult life. On her counselor's advice she entered college to retrain for a profession and to get help for her brain injury.

The first few weeks were almost impossible. Without the aid of one of her teachers, she would never have even found her classrooms. An even worse situation occurred one day when Katherine could not find her car. If it were not for the aid of a fellow student, she may never have found it.

Going to college was the best thing that could have happened to her. She enrolled in self-help classes and continued to see a college counselor on a regular basis. When her first report card came out, she received all A's. Something in her spirit began to awaken, and the old tapes began to fade away.

She continued to seek her counselor's help, and over the weeks she slowly began to believe in herself again. In almost every therapy session, she explored the reasons why she chose abusive relationships. She learned warning signs that would help her make the right choices in the future. Her journey was long and often heart-wrenching, but in the end it was worth it all.

Today Katherine still calls herself a work in progress. She is an independent woman who attends college full time, enjoys the companionship of a best friend, and has developed zero tolerance for abuse.

Changing from a codependent person to an independent person has been the challenge of her life. She attributes her success to having the will to change, and a counselor who supported that will. Her daily mantra is to give back to the world what has been given to her, but to do so when and how she chooses.

Source: Written by D. Juanita Woods.

to live one person's life. Then there are the people for whom it is such a dire necessity to be in a relationship, no matter how detrimental, that the need borders on addiction. Most people know that it is important to spend some time on their own when one relationship ends before jumping into another one, but for some people, that time might be only one day. People in all of the previously described types of relationships encounter the problems that are inherent in looking to others to supply what is missing in themselves.

Looking for What's Missing

Two incomplete people looking for the other half are like pieces of a jigsaw puzzle. The two pieces can fit together but still not provide the whole picture. People looking for what is missing in themselves may find a partner who provides the missing piece, but there is a price to pay. Partners locked together in a mutually unhealthy dependence usually start to resent each other. If each is allowed to be only his or her piece of the puzzle, neither can grow or change. The illusion is that two halves can make a whole relationship.

There are relationships in which one partner never does anything without the other. They both cling to their respective roles and to each other, fearing what might happen otherwise. That kind of situation usually ends up stifling both parties. The best relationships are those that allow some degree of freedom in behavior and interests. Those who have been married know that, no matter how much you love someone or how good the relationship is, there are times when you wake up and don't want to see your partner's ugly mug. To maintain or revitalize a relationship, there are times when the partners need to be apart. It can be healthy for the relationship when each partner has some outside interests. This is only possible if both partners are secure in their own identities and can allow each other to have some separate time and space.

In some cases, people in a relationship will begin to be dissatisfied with the limitations of their arrangement. What happens, though, when just one person decides to change and become more well-rounded? Usually, one of three things will happen. The person not initiating the change will do one of the following:

1. Attempt to stop the other from changing with threats, put-downs, or sabotage.
2. Leave the relationship or threaten to do so in an attempt to stop the other from changing.
3. Begin to make changes and come to the realization that growth and change can be in his or her best interests, too.

Searching for the other half?

If one partner wants to attain more selfhood by developing a stronger sense of identity, the other partner may respond with one of these three actions. Family systems theory states that if one element of the system changes, the whole system changes. That may explain why the person not choosing or initiating the change will be reactionary. If one partner changes, inevitably, the other will have to change also. That invariably raises the anxiety of the person least interested in changing the system.

Power Differential

The following is an example of a codependent relationship. Although either sex can play either role, for the sake of discussion, let's use the stereotypical example of the woman as *Bambi* and the man as *Godzilla*. She is kind, considerate, and generous to a fault. She would never think of doing anything that would make someone else feel bad and usually sacrifices her own needs for others. He, on the other hand, breathes fire and smoke, stomps on people, and causes a great deal of damage without even being aware of it. This pattern is played out frequently in our society. There are women who report that they aren't allowed to leave the house without permission and aren't even allowed to drive. Some husbands even dismantle the car to maintain more control over their wives. There are husbands who feel threatened if their wives make any kind of advancement, whether it is educational, vocational, or personal. As a result, some of these Godzilla types stomp term papers into the mud, sabotage their wives' careers, have an affair, go on a binge, or physically abuse the family.

Often, Bambi is afraid of confronting Godzilla. What if he gets worse and starts breathing fire? What if he decides to leave? Interestingly enough, in a number of cases, Godzilla begins to calm down when Bambi decides that she has had enough. Relationships frequently get turned around when one of the partners decides to leave. The crisis point is the time when everything is up in the air. Ironically, it is precisely at that point that the potential for redefining the roles exists. It takes a lot of assertiveness for Bambi to stand up for herself, but what is really amazing is how often she is reluctant to do so for fear of hurting Godzilla. This is the ultimate form of codependence. She doesn't want to hurt his feelings about how much he hurts her feelings. Of course, Godzilla has feelings, too. But if he were as sensitive as Bambi, he would never have become Godzilla in the first place. It is an incredible paradox that the people who are the

Do you have an even playing field?

least likely to hurt someone else are the most concerned about doing just that. Bambi needs to let go of the illusion that Godzilla experiences things in the same way she does. It may be true that there is a sensitive person inside that fire-breathing dragon, but Bambi doesn't need to worry about hurting someone with skin three feet thick.

Another way of understanding the Bambi-Godzilla type of relationship is to use the analogy of an unregulated football game. Some people seem to believe that the 20-yard line is the 50, and they spend most of their lives playing on only one end of the field. They may have the notion that it's OK for one person to have 80 percent of the turf and the other to have 20 percent. It is difficult to help people change when they have been taken advantage of for some time. They feel that moving play from the 20-yard line to the 30-yard line is the same as going all the way to the other end of the field. Usually, they believe that they must stop well short of the 50-yard line because they don't want to take up more than their share of space. Fearing that they will become like the people who take more than their share, they make sure they never do that.

They also think that if they ever moved the game to the other end of the field, however temporarily, it might hurt the other person. They need to learn to look at the game from the grandstand. It may not always be possible to tell what the play was or exactly where the ball went from that perspective, but most people can tell the 20-yard line from the 50. Sometimes, the task is to realize that the best games are played using the entire field and involve moving back and forth with the give and take of the game.

Intimate Partners

In her book *Intimate Partners: Patterns in Love and Marriages,* Maggie Scarf (1987) discusses some important aspects of understanding what happens in close personal relationships. She says that almost all relationships are a reflection of our "first family." Getting married is the start of a family, whether or not there are children. A great deal of what gets acted out in the new family is a re-creation of the first family—the family of origin. What was learned from parents about being a couple will have an effect on relationships in the future. Problems in a marriage are often attempts to resolve issues from the family of origin.

Scarf points out that all problems serve a purpose and that the relationship is the "proving ground" for resolving old issues. When there is no unconscious motive or underlying issue, most problems get worked out. When problems persist, it is usually because the couple as a unit has a need that is being addressed by having the problem. Both people bring their own baggage with them when they enter a relationship. Their life stories are enacted in the process of becoming a couple. Therefore, the more each person understands about his or her own story, the more the couple will be able to productively address the issues that come up between them.

A common scenario in relationships is when one person with a problem is seen as *underfunctioning.* The other person, sometimes in an attempt to compensate, will then begin to *overfunction.* The problem the couple is focused on isn't always the main issue, though. Many arguments between couples have little to do with the real or underlying issues. Whether overfunctioning or underfunctioning, people are trying to reduce anxiety about the issues of being a couple. The methods of coping may appear to be opposite, but both attempt to protect the individual self-concept. Perhaps the old saying that we have to love ourselves before we can love anyone else really is true!

Marriage Myths*

Ah, June! The month when beaming brides and gussied-up grooms amble down the aisle, confident about their future because the candy mints match the bridesmaids' shoes. What would happen to America's divorce rate if engaged couples spent as much time in marriage counseling before the big day as they take careening from florist to

*Source: Adapted from an article written by Jann Mitchell.

jeweler to printer? Many smart couples are doing just that. Marriage and family counselors report that men and women are investing in preventive medicine (especially those marrying again). Here's a little quiz couples may want to consider:

1. Are you constantly seeking approval from your partner?
2. Do you feel responsible for your loved one's feelings?
3. Do you sometimes feel depressed for seemingly no reason?
4. Are there times you fear intimacy and yet fear being alone?
5. Do you set up expectations and don't tell your partner, but expect him or her to know?
6. Is it hard for you to say what you want when it may not be what he or she wants?
7. Do you find yourself going to any lengths to try to keep the peace?
8. When you're feeling hurt by something your loved one says, do you fear discussing it with him or her?

If your answer is yes to any of these questions, you may have relationship problems that need working on, says Ann Kafoury, therapist at Cedar Hills Hospital and director of the hospital's code-pendency service. It's easy to view marriage as a panacea for our problems, to expect someone else to make life better for us. It doesn't work that way. Let's look at a few marital myths:

I have some doubts about this, but it's probably just wedding jitters: It's scary to pay attention to that nagging little voice inside that raises doubts about what we're doing. So most of us just ignore it, dismissing what our hunch is telling us. And we go ahead and marry, shoving those doubts to the back of our minds as we will our wedding shoes to the rear of the closet. Invariably, those doubts—those truths—return to haunt us. Even as I write this, a tearful young divorced woman just wailed to me over the phone, "Why didn't I listen to myself? I knew he drank beer for breakfast. . . ." Just as I knew, at 18, that I had nothing in common with the man I was marrying. Even as she adjusted my veil, my mother said, "It's not too late. You don't have to do this." After all, the people were waiting. Eight years and three children later, I was divorced. That little voice is inside us for a reason. We rarely make a mistake heeding it.

When I'm married, my problems will be solved: Ever heard the saying, "Wherever you go, there you are?" It means that we always take our-selves—our attitudes, behaviors, values—into every circumstance. There's nothing magic about a circumstance (or another person) that automatically changes who we essentially are. We don't lose our problems in marriage. In fact, we get a whole new set: dealing with in-laws, compromising, coordinating two schedules, running a home, becoming parents. Problems don't disappear; they merely take on a new face.

After the wedding, he or she will change: Not true. People don't change unless they have a reason to, usually when they are prompted by emotional pain. If you don't like what your partner is now, don't expect him or her to be any different after marriage. This is especially true of violence; abusiveness accelerates if it's tolerated. If we permit someone to insult us, boss us around, or physically hurt us, we're teaching that person that it is all right. A Miami University (Oxford, Ohio) study of teenagers showed that 12 percent had experienced violence with a dating partner. Older people show higher rates of violence. Yet up to a third of those in abusive relationships felt that violence was a sign of love. "It's twisted logic, but they felt their partner wouldn't get upset or angry if he didn't really care," said researcher Sally Lloyd.

Being married makes me an official grown-up: Young couples are susceptible to this trap. We may believe that if we have all the trappings of a home and family, we are adults and everything is fine. We may work hard to decorate our homes just so, stage the perfect Christmas, or throw a barbecue with the man grilling the burgers. If it looks right, it must be right. Although the trappings can be comforting, we have to be careful not to rely on them. Just because a marriage looks good doesn't mean it is good. If we spend more time basting the turkey or edging the lawn than we do talking with our mates, we eventually will be in trouble.

If my spouse really loves me, he or she will know what I want without having to ask: Marriage doesn't make us mind-readers. When people are extra-attentive during courtship, it may seem that they do anticipate our needs and read our minds. As we settle into a routine, that second sense usually diminishes. That doesn't mean we aren't loved. It means we have to be clear about saying what we want, whether we're planning a menu or making love. Expecting a partner to know what we want (when sometimes even we don't know) only sets us both up for failure. We feel resentful and spouses feel like they have failed us. We do our relationship a favor by speaking up.

If problems arise, we'll just kiss and make up: When we try to make up without resolving a dispute, our pucker is likely to be powered by fear—fear that our partner will withdraw, leave, stop loving us. Women, especially, find it difficult to make love when they're not feeling emotionally close. To go ahead and do so may make us feel used, alienating us even further. Sex while feuding is premature, but touch is healing. Try holding hands while discussing a problem. This can keep us physically connected and remind the other of our love—even though we're not feeling particularly loving. Some couples find that lovemaking during or just after a quarrel is especially exciting. Some may even pick a fight for the adrenaline rush. Marriage counselors caution that this isn't a healthy pattern. It can be a cover-up for unresolved problems in the relationship.

I'll always have someone to do things with; I'll never be lonely again: Kahlil Gibran said, "Let there be spaces in your togetherness." Marriage doesn't automatically confer the same interests and enthusiasms or even concurrent moods on husband and wife. To expect it is the height of naivete and sets us up for disappointment. When we're dating, we often go along with what the other person wants to do because we're so anxious to please and to spend time together. When we live together, that wears off, and we're less likely to go along just for the heck of it. Instead of expecting a mate to want to do whatever we want (and when we want to), it makes more sense to invite a friend or family member to join us at the parade or for a day of shopping or fishing. If we cajole our mate into going along, he or she will do so reluctantly and we won't have a good time. If we guilt-trip a spouse for not going, resentments build on both sides.

Why Marriages Succeed or Fail

For more than 16 years, John Gottman (Gottman and Silver, 1999) has studied marriage and divorce at the University of Seattle in Washington. In what has become referred to as the "Love Lab" (an apartment where couples stay for a weekend while cameras and various kinds of equipment record their interactions and physiological responses), he has observed, studied, and quantified the type and quality of interactions of married couples. For privacy, he only records them from 9 A.M. to 9 P.M., and never in the bathroom. In 1994, he published the book *Why Marriages Succeed or Fail* in which he listed the factors that are most likely to lead to divorce. Based on the data he accumulated, he states that he can predict with over 90 percent accuracy whether a marriage will succeed or end in divorce.

Having observed so many couples' interactions, quarrels, and attempts at resolution, Gottman believes that often, he can tell within the first five minutes of an argument whether a couple's relationship will last. The signs that he looks for in predicting divorce are:

1. *Harsh Startup:* When couples have a disagreement, they often start with criticism, sarcasm, and/or contempt. Conversations that begin in this manner inevitably end with negative consequences. If things aren't going well in the first three minutes, it might be just as well to pull the plug and take a breather.

2. *The Four Horsemen:* These are the concepts that have to do with the effects of criticism, contempt, defensiveness, and stonewalling. These behaviors and reactions often enter the marriage in that order, and when they are present, things usually go in a negative cycle that leads to greater difficulty.

3. *Flooding:* When the negative interactions reach a certain level and/or come so suddenly, some people feel overwhelmed by the intensity. This frequently leads to being hypervigilant, and the person can think only about how to protect himself or herself.

4. *Body Language:* One of the consequences of flooding is extreme physical responses. When a pounding heart and other stress reactions happen in the middle of a discussion, the ability to process information goes out the window.

5. *Failed Repair Attempts:* Repair attempts are efforts the couple makes to deescalate the tension during a touchy discussion. These can be attempts at humor or such simple statements as, "Let's take a break" or "I need some time to calm down." These can be useful in putting on the brakes so that flooding is prevented.

6. *Bad Memories:* When a relationship is consumed by negative cycles, it is not just the present and future that are affected, it is also the past. If the marriage is not going well, over time, people tend to rewrite history. They begin to remember things as having been worse than they actually were.

When Gottman first figured out how to predict divorce, he thought that he had figured out the key to saving marriages. He presumed that all that was necessary was to teach people how to argue without being overridden by the four horsemen and without getting flooded. Gottman felt that if couples' repair attempts could succeed, they could work out their differences. Although the information about what creates the likelihood of divorce is important, he has since stated that this approach was misguided!

It now seems that Gottman fell prey to a myth that many marital therapists subscribe to: that learning to communicate and resolve conflicts is the road to romance and a happy marriage. Certainly, communication skills are important, but they alone are not going to solve most marital problems. David Snarch (1996) echoes this belief by stating that just teaching people how to communicate may make things worse, because "all they do is tell each other what they already know the other person has been thinking about them" (p. 121). Besides, it is one thing to listen as someone makes "I" statements about complaints and dislikes, and another to be the implied target of those statements. "Active listening" may be a worthy goal, but few married couples in the heat of an argument are capable of maintaining that stance.

After continued research and studies, Gottman now believes that successful conflict resolution isn't what makes marriage succeed. After studying 650 couples and tracking the fate of their marriages for up to 14 years, he has now concluded that there are a variety of methods for dealing with conflict, as well as maintaining a successful marriage. Part of what changed was that he began to analyze what went *right* in happy marriages. Some couples argue loudly and often; others tend to smooth things over as quickly as possible. But most successful marriages share certain commonalities. In his latest work, Gottman (Gottman and Silver, 1999) emphasizes how to make marriage better and states, "I now know that the key to reviving or divorce-proofing a relationship is not in how you handle disagreements but in how you are with each other when you're not fighting."

In *The Seven Principles for Making Marriage Work* (Gottman and Silver, 1999), Gottman builds on his previous studies and provides readers with a first-rate practical guide to improving relationships. Stressing that he is one of the few marital advisors who bases his ideas on facts and data rather than opinions, he offers down-to-earth, concrete suggestions and questionnaires in a highly usable workbook format. At the heart of his program is the common-sense belief that the simple truth of happy marriages is that they are based on deep friendship. Friendship fuels the flames of romance, and it also provides the best protection against feeling adversarial toward your spouse. It also increases the likelihood that "repair attempts" will be effective in preventing negativity from escalating out of control. In the strongest marriages, couples share a deep sense of meaning and provide support for each other.

One of the most surprising truths about marriage, paradoxically, is that most marriage arguments can't be resolved. Couples spend years trying to change each other, and often this not only doesn't work, it make things worse. This doesn't mean that there is nothing you can do if your marriage is constantly in conflict. Instead, it emphasizes the need to understand the bottom-line differences between you and your partner and the importance of learning how to live with those differences while honoring and respecting each other.

Whatever the current state of your relationship, Gottman believes that following the seven principles can lead to dramatic and positive changes. Those principles are:

1. *Enhance your love maps:* This concept is about really getting to know your partner. Many people think they know whom they are marrying, but find out that the person is different after marriage. It is important to continually update the information about who your partner is, what is important to him or her, what his or her concerns are, and what his or her dreams are for the future.

2. *Nurture your fondness and admiration:* What strengthens and supports a happy marriage is the expression of caring and respect for each other. Many people need to be reminded of how important this is, as well as how to do it.

3. *Turn toward each other instead of away:* It is important to continually invest in the emotional bank account of the relationship. That is, make sure to stay connected with everyday interactions about even the smallest things. Gottman gives numerous accounts of how love is expressed every day, not in the overblown Hollywood portrayal, but in the little exchanges that keep a couple connected.

4. *Let your partner influence you:* This idea has shown up in numerous newspaper and magazine articles, when it was reported as one of the findings most likely to predict marital success. When each spouse feels that his or her ideas, wants, and needs are important, and also that there is a good chance that those will influence his or her partner, there is a great deal of marital satisfaction.

5. *Solve your solvable problems:* There are perpetual problems and situational problems. As previously stated, some problems are just not going to go away, and the best thing is to develop a strategy for coping with them. These situations often have to do with religious differences, parenting, in-laws, and need for order and cleanliness. For the problems that are solvable, Gottman suggests using a "soft startup," learning to make and

receive "repair attempts," practicing soothing yourself and the other, being tolerant of each other's faults, and compromise.

6. *Overcome gridlock:* Some couples have the same argument over and over with practically the same dialogue taking place. It is important to remember that if there is a perpetual problem, the goal should be to move from gridlock to discussion, not necessarily looking for an immediate solution. To do that, it is useful to remember that arguments often represent repressed dreams and desires. Get curious about what is underneath the conflict and what dream needs an outlet for expression.

7. *Create shared meaning:* Couples need shared rituals in the relationship. Creating meaning can incorporate spiritual values as well as shared convictions and goals. Developing long-range plans can assist in creating shared meaning.

Though concluding that no book can solve all marital problems, Gottman believes that his approach will help put couples back on track. Once there, he has some ideas for how to stay on course. He and many other therapists recommend that couples have a 5-to-1 ratio for positive to negative comments and interactions. After following up on couples that attended workshops, he discovered another magic number: The couples that seemed to make the most progress in continuing to improve their marriage spent five hours more per week on the relationship practicing the seven principles they had learned. Gottman has come to refer to that time as the "Magic Five Hours."

In addition to spending more time on the relationship, it is also important to develop a detector for when the marital relationship is deteriorating and needs attention. Some psychologists and marital therapists believe that one source of unhappiness is when couples have overblown expectations of marriage, yet Gottman quotes studies that have found that people with the highest expectations for their marriage wind up with a higher-quality marriage. Those newlyweds who refused to put up with lots of negativity and noticed when things were not going well were more likely to be happy and satisfied years later. Perhaps it is important to educate people about the difference between unreal expectations and having high standards for their marriage.

Marriage Requires Healthy Differentiation

David Snarch (1996), in his book *Passionate Marriage,* dedicates an entire chapter to the concept

that nobody is ready for marriage—only marriage makes you ready for marriage. Marriage is a "people growing process" that requires each partner to develop and maintain their own integrity if they are going to have a truly intimate relationship. And, Snarch believes that integrity and integration are one and the same. Integration is the process of self-acceptance that comes when *who you are* and *who you think you should be* become one. It is necessary to have a developed sense of personal integration in order to be able to differentiate from the other person. Snarch gives numerous examples of the paradox that closeness is only possible when each person can stand alone.

People are living longer and remaining physically and mentally fit, but what's the point if you are living in a "dead marriage"? Too often people confuse love with fusion, but healthy relationships allow for each partner to have their own identity. Differentiation requires balancing the two life forces: the drive for individuality and the drive for togetherness. In an undifferentiated relationship, your spouse can always force you to choose between keeping your integrity and staying married, between "holding on to yourself" and holding on to your partner.

Differentiation is the ability to maintain your sense of self when your partner is away or when you are not in a primary love relationship. You value contact, but you don't fall apart when you're alone. The differentiated self is solid but permeable. Snarch (1996) states:

> Differentiation is the process by which we become more uniquely ourselves by maintaining ourselves in the relationship with those we love.
>
> It's the process of grinding off our rough edges through the normal abrasions of long-term intimate relationships. Differentiation is the key to not holding grudges and recovering quickly from arguments, to tolerating intense intimacy and maintaining your priorities in the midst of daily life. It lets you expand your sexual relationship and rekindle desire and passion in marriages that have grown cold. It is the pathway to the hottest and most living sex you'll ever have with your spouse. Differentiation brings tenderness, generosity, and compassion—all the traits of good marriages.

This should make the paradox of differentiation clear. It allows us to set ourselves apart from others while opening up the space for true togetherness. It's about getting closer and more distinct rather than more distant.

FINDING THE RIGHT LOVE MATE TAKES HONESTY, COMMUNICATION

Life is a process of learning from our mistakes. With love, that can be hard to see. It's far easier to keep blaming a man or a woman rather than accepting responsibility for the choices we make. And when we're nursing a broken heart, it's difficult to see that this fractured relationship is a growth opportunity. Hundreds of books are written about this, and here's a good one: *Are You the One for Me? Knowing Who's Right and Avoiding Who's Wrong* by Barbara DeAngelis. This savvy Los Angeles psychologist knows her stuff and says it succinctly. You can open the book to any page, read the highlighted portions, and learn something valuable. She weaves her own experience liberally throughout, sharing the mistakes she's made and the lessons she's learned.

The biggest mistake DeAngelis sees women make in a relationship is failing to honor their own wants and needs and communicate them, compromising too much when the needs go unfulfilled—and not giving men the chance to experience all this. The biggest mistake she sees men making is not putting enough time, energy, and feeling into their relationships—instead valuing performance and accomplishment.

"Men need as much love and intimacy as we do, but they're more afraid of it because they're not as good at it—and men don't like to do things they're not good at," says DeAngelis. "Women need to say to them, 'This is what I need. I know it's scary and a stretch for you. I'll be patient; all I want is the effort.' When a man knows you understand his processes, his stretches, he's much more willing to do it. I don't think men have any idea how little of the right stuff it really takes to make a woman happy. Five minutes of focused attention will keep her happy for five days."

The recovery movement, she says, has helped people understand how we're affected in adulthood by what happened in childhood. Unless we resolve old issues, we'll keep looking for Mom or Dad in our mates—and walk away disappointed. We project our unfinished business onto our partners and blame them for what is really our own problem. If we're both in touch with our issues and work on them, we can laughingly point them out to each other when we lapse into Mom and Dad stuff.

Here are DeAngelis's Ten Types of Relationships That Won't Work:

1. You care more about your partner than he or she does about you.
2. Your partner cares more about you than you care about him or her.
3. You are in love with your partner's potential.
4. You are on a rescue mission.
5. You look up to your partner as a role model.
6. You are infatuated with your partner for external reasons.
7. You have partial compatibility—a lot in common in one area—but you ignore the rest of the relationship.
8. You choose a partner to be rebellious.
9. You choose a partner as a reaction to your previous partner.
10. Your partner is unavailable (married or living with someone).

But don't despair. Change—and happiness—are possible.

Source: Article written by Jann Mitchell.

Gay Marriage

In the United States, the push to obtain the legal protections of civil marriage such as health insurance, hospital visitation, and social security survivor benefits for same-sex families has been taking shape since the early 1970s. The movement is supported by an assortment of groups such as the Human Rights Campaign. This effort did not reach widespread national attention until the 1990s after a series of court rulings, legislative votes, and political actions encouraged supporters.

The same political and legal events also gave rise to a counter movement to freeze the status quo by legally defining traditional marriage, the marriage of one woman to one man. This would have the effect of excluding nonheterosexual families from the legal protections of marriage. This counter movement was widely credited (or blamed) in some quarters for motivating voter turnout in the 2004 elections to support the Republican Party.

As of April 2005 in the United States, the state of Massachusetts recognizes same-sex marriage, whereas California, Connecticut, the District of Columbia, Hawaii, Maine, New Jersey and Vermont grant persons in same-sex unions a similar legal status to those in a civil marriage by domestic partnership, civil union, or reciprocal beneficiary laws.

Sixteen states have constitutional amendments explicitly barring the recognition of same-sex marriage, confining civil marriage to a legal union between a man and a woman. Twenty-seven states have legal statutes defining marriage to two persons of the opposite sex. A small number of states ban any legal recognition of same-sex unions that would be equivalent to civil marriage.

Popular Opinion

Advocates of same-sex marriage generally hold that lawful marriage and its benefits should not be denied to same-sex couples, and that such a denial infringes one or more of their rights as American citizens.

Critics of same-sex marriage reject this position and generally hold that lawful marriage should be defined as only consisting of a union of one man and one woman, a so-called "traditional marriage," and that no rights exist that should compel a state to recognize any relationships to the contrary of that definition.

A national poll by CBS in 2004 found that only 22 percent favored legal recognition of same-sex marriages, while 73 percent were in opposition to legal recognition of these marriages. Many people make a distinction between same-sex marriage and civil unions, which would provide same-sex couples some legal rights. Although fewer than one-fourth of Americans think gay and lesbian people should be allowed to marry, there is larger support for permitting civil unions. All in all, over half of Americans support some type of legal status for same-sex couples who wish to make a long-term commitment. Forty percent think same-sex couples' relationships ought to have no legal recognition.

Civil Unions

Outside of Massachusetts, where same-sex marriage is now legal, Vermont, California, New Jersey, the District of Columbia, and Connecticut are the only U.S. states and entities to offer same-sex couples all of the state-level rights and benefits of heterosexual couples. They do not use the word *marriage,* however, but call such unions *civil unions* and *domestic partnerships*. These arrangements do not, however, provide the federal-level rights, benefits, and protections that come with a civil marriage license, nor will they necessarily be recognized in states that have no such laws.

Hawaii and Maine's domestic partnership and reciprocal benefit laws provide similar benefits, but both stop short of full equality on a state level, much less marriage.

There are also bills in both chambers of the New York State legislature that would extend marriage rights to same-sex couples. These bills were introduced in early 2003 and are currently still in committee.

International Issues

The 2003–2004 interim legalization of same-sex marriages in seven Canadian provinces and one territory, and 2005 legalization of same sex-marriages across all of Canada has raised questions about U.S. law. Because of Canada's proximity to the United States and the fact that Canada has no citizenship or residency requirement to receive a marriage certificate, there could be future complications. Canada and the United States have a history of respecting marriages contracted in either country.

Immediately after the June 2003 ruling legalizing same-sex marriage in Ontario, a number of American couples headed or planned to head to the province in order to get married. A coalition

THINKING ABOUT DIVERSITY

One benefit of beginning to accept and appreciate cultural differences among individuals is that the process will be highly valuable in an intimate relationship. Whomever you decide to live with, there will be a time in your relationship when you will swear that the other person is from another country . . . if not another planet.

Where did this person get those beliefs about mealtime rituals? How could such different standards about what constitutes cleanliness exist? Why can't he or she understand the value of a dollar? Why doesn't he or she want to splurge on the same items that you find so necessary for your happiness? Doesn't he or she know which items you should throw out and which you should save? It is amazing how much you find out about a person's "culture" after you are married.

Perhaps the cultures that believe in arranged marriages aren't so strange after all. Is it possible that your parents really are good judges of whom you are compatible with? It would seem, given the current divorce rates, that they couldn't do much worse than those that choose their partner for love. At least in the "olden days" the parents were happy with the arrangement.

of American national gay rights groups issued a statement asking couples to contact them before attempting legal challenges, so that they might be coordinated as part of the same-sex marriage movement in the United States.

Making Marriage Last

Lifelong marriage is still the ideal, but marriage has become a conditional contract, according to Frank Furstenberg (1994) of the University of Pennsylvania. For some time, numerous sources have quoted the divorce rate at about 50 percent. The number of remarriages in the country has increased by 63 percent since 1970 to more than one million a year today. In fact, the National Center for Health Statistics reported that nearly half of all recent marriages are remarriages for one or both partners. And some of these remarriages are not second marriages, but third and fourth marriages.

The social forces that led to the rise in the divorce rate since the 1970s—including the growing economic independence of women and the growing acceptance of divorce—have created a pool of nearly 13 million eligible divorced people under 65. Although the chances of remarrying vary greatly with age and sex, more than 70 percent

of divorced men and women do eventually find new partners. The net result is that only about four of 10 adults are now married to their first spouses. The rest are either single, cohabiting, or remarried.

Fortunately, current trends indicate that the divorce rate is slowing down. Couples who have difficulties in their marriage are increasingly attempting to create a better relationship rather than heading for divorce court. This may be due in part to the current information about the problems that children of divorce encounter. Judith Wallerstein's work, including *Second Chances: Men, Women, and Children a Decade After Divorce* (Wallerstein and Blakeslee, 1989), has contributed to a reversal in the trend of how marriage problems have been handled during the past 10 to 15 years. Although there is current research that counters some of her predictions—there are some instances where divorce may have

> **"** A good marriage is not so much finding the right person as being the right person. **"**
>
> *Scott Rowley*

benefits for the children—we seem to realize that divorce itself has clear disadvantages. Some of these are as follows:

Divorce rarely solves the problem that it was intended to solve: People often repeat old patterns or end up with someone similar to the spouse in the previous marriage.

Divorce often creates a whole new set of problems: There are many changes that everyone in the family must contend with, not the least of which is the pain involved, which many people still feel years later.

Divorce is a tremendous adjustment for children: Most children report that they would rather have had their parents stay together. General consensus of various statistics indicates that there is currently a 50 percent divorce rate for first marriages, 60 to 70 percent divorce rate for second marriages, and an even slimmer chance of success for third and fourth marriages. It appears that the marriage you are in is the marriage that has the best chance for success.

The good news is that as you age, the likelihood of divorce goes down. Dr. Fisher, an anthropologist for the American Museum of Natural History, states that from an anthropological point of view, divorce is more natural than maintaining a lifelong partnership during your reproductive years. Even so, a long-term relationship seems to be what most people are striving for. Although a lifelong marriage is possible, those who work with couples universally agree that it takes effort from both partners. When Judith Wallerstein told Margaret Mead, a famous anthropologist, how upset she was over her early findings on children of divorce, Mead reportedly said, "There is no society in the world where people have stayed married without enormous community pressure to do so" (Wallerstein and Blakeslee, 1989). When that pressure is off, you can take it as an omen—or a challenge. Fisher offers the following suggestions for how to make marriage last:

Keep infatuation alive: Schedule time alone together often, and if you get a babysitter, don't talk about work or the children. Also, cultivate independent interests and friends. This enables you to bring new knowledge and experiences to the relationship.

Approach your marriage as you would a friendship: We keep our friendships alive by appreciating our friends, doing nice things for them, and being thoughtful of their feelings. Partners need just as much consideration as friends.

Allow for the differences between men and women: Fisher speculates that differences between men and women might be a result of the years when men were the hunters—and hunted in silence—while women raised the children and gathered the food—and talked while they worked. One result is that women create intimacy by talking, and men do so by doing things silently, side by side. Partners must understand these differences and integrate them into the relationship. Although these approaches to intimacy may not come naturally, they can be learned. John Gray (1992) has written a book, *Men Are From Mars, Women Are From Venus*. In the interests of improving communication, he describes the differences between men and women and how to understand and overcome those differences. Some of his critics contend that his information is based on rather loosely interpreted scientific research and tends to support gender stereotypes. It might be a more useful approach to think of *people* from Mars and *people* from Venus. People's needs and communication styles transcend gender.

Don't try to force your partner to change: In most instances, it is better to change yourself. Sometimes, the best way to influence your partner is to become more like him or her when possible. As you become more well-balanced yourself, it puts less pressure on the other person to change. People are more inclined to make changes when they feel there is an element of choice.

Communicate: Most Americans are great talkers but lousy listeners. Ask questions and pay more attention. Learn how to argue and fight fair. Sharing thoughts and feelings is essential to an ongoing relationship. Pay more attention to your own experiences and where your beliefs and values came from. Challenge your own irrational expectations. And most important, ask for what you want in the relationship—don't tell the other person how to be and what to do.

Be faithful: Faithfulness is the triumph of culture over human nature. Adultery doesn't work. It creates distance, destroys trust, and fails to solve the underlying problems that led to the adultery in the first place.

Zig Ziglar (1977), prominent speaker and author of numerous books, has come up with a novel approach to developing guidelines to help couples. For years at his seminars, he would ask how many people had been married for more than 25 years—and would marry the same person again. He then asked these people to fill out an extensive questionnaire about what kept their marriages going. Not necessarily approved scientific methodology, but the participants in the survey represented a broad cross-section of America. He says that many of the principles that he learned about are the same ones that he and his wife have been following for 45 years. What those people had to say about marriage and how to have a successful long-term one follows:

❧ Start with commitment.

❧ Treat your mate more like a friend.

❧ Start every day by saying, "I love you."

❧ Do something every day that shows caring.

❧ Hug each other a lot.

❧ Don't tell demeaning jokes.

❧ Go along to get along.

❧ Develop empathy and understanding.

❧ Remember nonspecial occasions.

❧ Don't put yourself in a position where you can be sexually tempted by others.

Harville Hendrix, director of the Institute for Relationship Therapy and author of *Getting the Love You Want* (1990), is one of the many counselors and therapists who have written books offering advice for people who want to improve their relationship. There are recurring themes and topics for what constitutes a good marriage. This is what Hendrix and other experts in the field say are the important factors in a lasting relationship:

Self-knowledge and high self-esteem are vital: The better you know yourself and your needs in a relationship, the more likely you are to be satisfied with the relationship. Love and accept yourself; define your own values and convictions.

Communication means learning to listen: Be honest with yourself and your partner. Express your wants rather than just giving criticism. Conflict can be useful when interpreted as "growth trying to happen."

Spend time together and apart: The trick is finding the balance. Have daily routines that allow for time together and time for play, as well as time to pursue separate interests. Have friends outside the relationship, and remember that no one person can meet all your needs.

Satisfying sex can be learned: Only your partner can tell you the most important things you need to know about your partner. So relate to each other rather than perform for each other. Ask questions and communicate your wishes. Schedule time for sex and share your fantasies. Remember that sex and romance aren't just what happens in bed; it is the touch and contact throughout the day.

Learn to fight fair: Don't sweep things under the carpet in hopes that they will go away. When you bring up problems, don't hit below the belt. Make sure that the problem you're fighting about is the real one. Deal with your anger before it builds into resentment. Most of all, learn to tell the difference between reacting and responding.

It is also important to remember that a relationship can't satisfy all of your needs. There are some things marriage can do and some it cannot. On some level, all of us want to be known and understood completely. We cling to the ideal that we can be connected and intimate and have someone take care of us all the time. But only in infancy is that need realized.

Psychologist Daniel Gottlieb (1991) states that you can demand, beg, or cry about it, but true love begins when you finally realize "you'll never find complete intimacy in your marriage." Perhaps it is from that point that intimacy and a relationship truly begin to grow. From his own experience, he

MARITAL "BOOT CAMPS"

If couples only had a way to divorce-proof their marriages. Marriage therapy doesn't always work because most people are on their way to divorce court when they start. Much more effective are the increasingly popular marital "boot camps" that offer basic training in relationship skills. The information is best used when taken as a preventive inoculation before marriage, or during the first year, when motivation to learn marriage-saving skills is high and destructive patterns have not yet formed. In Relationship Enhancement (RE), a nonprofit program, couples work on learning skills under the tutelage of an expert coach. To find out about workshops at locations around the country, call the National Institute of Relationship Enhancement at 1-800-843-6473.

describes how "I struggled with that notion for a long time. And when I could finally give up my delusions about the person with whom I was most intimate, only then could I face my wife differently. I was able to see her not as a caretaker or mother or some kind of ideal being that could fully know me—I saw her as just a woman with the same human flaws and frailties that I had."

Friendships

Shifts in the social order of the 1990s have produced a nation of people who now more than ever need their pals. Marriage, the hoped-for solution to our isolation, is taking up less of our lives than it used to. We are pairing up later, splitting up faster, and increasingly deciding to avoid the whole quagmire by staying permanently single. In other words, we're a society of people who increasingly need more than a little help from our friends.

A friend is a person one knows, likes, and trusts. We have best friends, close friends, good friends, and just friends. There are many types of friendships. There are friendships based on activities, social groups, and work—a category that is becoming increasingly important. There are crossroads friends that we connect with during transitional times in life, and there are the friends that come at 3:00 A.M. when you need them.

Many of us long for a broader web of friends to support us in times of need. However, unlike ties with our kin, our connections to friends can be exceedingly fragile. Friendship is an elective bond. There are no formalized rituals. According to Lillian Rubin, author of *Just Friends: The Role of Friendships in Our Lives* (1985), kinship falls into the realm of the sacred, but friendship remains in the secular. Even though it may be the friend, not the relative, who takes you to the airport or brings you food when you are sick, our society still seems to operate on the notion that kin is forever—but friends come and go.

Yet, the notion that family is more important than friends may be illusory. With fully a quarter of the nation's households now composed of a single person, we are fast becoming a society that is literally home alone. Even for those who enjoy or even prefer solo living, sneak attacks of loneliness can raise that panicky 3:00 A.M. question: Who really cares? When the other pillow on the bed is empty, when siblings and other kin are scattered across the continent and steeped in the minutiae of their own lives, one's best hope may be a good friend (Sandmaier, 1995).

Friends are especially important for children. The difference between no friends and two good friends is like the difference between a pitch-black room and one lit by birthday candles. Think back to your childhood, to the time when you first liked somebody outside your family and he or she liked you back; it was almost like a gift from heaven. It meant that somebody who was not from your family, who owed you nothing, simply cared for you. Children who don't have friends spend a huge portion of their day asking themselves, "Who will I play with? Who will I sit with?" These are questions reflecting the basic desire to know "Who will not leave me?" (Greene, 1993).

Rubin (1985) writes that in a best friendship, there is "a promise of mutual love, concern, protection, understanding and, not least of all, stability and durability" (p. 76). Best friendships embody the best of all the important relationships in our lives—kin, mate, and friend—along with the problems of all three. They bring us our greatest joys and our sorriest disappointments. "Do you have a best friend?" is a question Rubin asked 300 men and women (ages 25–55, working class and middle class) whom she interviewed for her research on friendship. More than three-fourths of the single women named a best friend, almost always a woman. In sharp contrast, fewer than one-third of the single men could identify a best friend, and those who were identified were much more likely to be a woman than another man. Rubin's results showed that, at every age between 25 and 55, women had more friendships than men did, and the differences in quality were considerable. Women's friendships with each other rested on shared intimacies and emotional support. In contrast, friendships between men were based on shared activities and were much more emotionally constrained.

One of the marks of a true friend is that he is there when there is every reason for him not to be, when to be there is costly.

As we begin to separate ourselves and grow away from our families in adolescence, friendships become even more important to us as sources of support. However, in late adolescence and early adulthood, friendships can take a back seat to romantic relationships. Marriage can disrupt friendships: Our interests change, and we begin to form relationships with other couples. In the same way, divorce can disrupt the friendships we formed as couples.

By the time people reach adulthood, most have learned the rudiments of friend making:

how to ask somebody to lunch, share a more or less retouched version of their life story, woo a new pal with humor or intellect or a talent for listening. After the initial connection is made, however, people often turn their attention elsewhere. Many of us still buy into the fiction that friendship simply happens, that it requires no special effort or consciousness to keep it alive and whole. There is also the embarrassment factor: Because friendship is not deemed a primary relationship in our culture and the expectations friends hold for each other are so rarely voiced, we may feel uncertain of our rights to go deeper, to make our needs known, even to directly express our feelings for our friends.

Like all important relationships, intimate friendships take work. They require us to open ourselves up, to trust, to share, to compromise, even to sacrifice. They involve caring enough for another person that his or her welfare becomes as important to us as our own, and caring enough to go far out of our way to render help when it is needed.

Friendships also take time. Some friendships can be measured in how much coffee (or other beverage) has been shared together. Time and opportunity to truly communicate are necessary ingredients in a friendship. Some conversations take place when there are just the two of you and there isn't a clock running. Priority needs to be given to the contact that is necessary to sustain the relationship. The effort is usually rewarded and well worthwhile in an era when it is more important than ever to have those connections (Arkoff, 1995).

CHAPTER REVIEW

Theories of Attraction

There are many reasons we are attracted to certain people. Some of the factors affecting attraction are proximity, similarity, reciprocity, and physical attractiveness. Some people adopt a "birds-of-a-feather" approach to partner selection; others subscribe to the "opposites attract" theory. The cultural time clock influences when people get married. All of us are influenced to some degree by our parents and peers when it comes to mate selection.

Types of Love

There are a number of different aspects to a loving relationship. Sternberg explores some the various ways in which people can experience love in a relationship.

Attachment Styles and Romantic Relationships

From early childhood people learn about closeness and intimacy. The degree of connection with parents has implications for later relationships. Trust, caring, and the ability to give are all connected with degree of attachment learned from different responses from parents.

The Dance of Intimacy

Many people simultaneously want and avoid intimacy. Many of the on-again–off-again cycles that couples go through are due to their need to establish the amount of distance that is within their comfort zone. The pursuer and the pursued have more in common than most people realize, and often, they will reverse roles.

Codependent Relationships

When you look for what is missing in yourself in someone else, you set up the basis for a restrictive relationship. Two halves looking for completion do not compensate for what is lacking and don't make a whole relationship. When one part of a couple decides to change and become more well-rounded, the other may not respond enthusiastically. Many people want to maintain their imbalanced relationship because it provides some benefits to them. People often re-create their family of origin in their marriages. Marriage issues can be an attempt to resolve conflicts from the family of origin.

Marriage Myths

There are a vast number of beliefs and expectations that influence an intimate relationship. Expectations for marriage and for a partner have changed in recent times. Sorting out false or unrealistic expectations can have positive results in a marriage.

Why Marriages Succeed or Fail

John Gottman has spent many years studying how couples interact. Originally focused on how to predict which marriages would fail, depending on their style of conflict resolution, he has recently published a book offering specific information on how to help marriages succeed. Although communication is still important, he emphasizes that it is more important to develop a relationship based on respect and friendship.

Much of the information about how to make marriage work has to do with what not to do. Most of the important concepts about what helps are common knowledge—the trick is remembering and applying them. Marriages improve and/or last when you communicate, have a good self-concept, fight fair, allow for differences, don't try to force changes, keep infatuation alive, and treat your marriage as you would a friendship.

Gay Marriage

There is considerable controversy in the country about who should be allow the rights of legally sanctioned marriage. Some feel that allowing gays to officially marry would change the nature

and status of the institution. Others believe that civil unions are one manner in which civil rights issues can be addressed.

Making Marriage Last

Much of the information about how to make marriage work has to do with what not to do. Most of the important concepts about what helps are common knowledge—the trick is remembering and applying them. Marriages improve and/or last when you communicate, have a good self-concept, fight fair, allow for differences, don't try to force changes, keep infatuation alive, and treat your marriage as you would a friendship.

Friendships

The ability to make friends is an important aspect of social development that most people learn while growing up. There is evidence that the importance of friendships is increasing in a society where marital partners may come and go and family members may live anywhere in the country. We all need people we can connect with and depend on. Women tend to have more close friends than do men, and men often state that their best friend is a woman. Friendships, just as any relationship, need to be nurtured and tended to.

SOURCES AND SUGGESTED READINGS

Gottlieb, Daniel. *Family Matters.* New York: Penguin, 1991.

Gottman, John. *The Seven Principles for Making Marriage Work.* New York: Crown, 1999.

Hendrix, Harville. *Getting the Love You Want: A Guide for Couples.* New York: Holt, 1990.

Lerner, Harriet. *The Dance of Intimacy.* New York: Harper & Row, 1990.

Pittman, J. F., and S. A. Lloyd. (1988). "Quality of Family Life, Social Support, and Stress." *Journal of Marriage and the Family, 50,* 53–67.

Rosellini, Gayle, and Mark Worden. *Barriers to Intimacy.* New York: Ballantine, 1989.

Scarf, Maggie. *Intimate Partners: Patterns in Love and Marriages.* New York: Random House, 1987.

Sternberg, Robert J. (1986). "A Triangular Theory of Love." *Psychological Review, 93,* 119–135.

Wallerstein, Judith S., and Sandra Blakeslee. *Second Chances: Men, Women, and Children: A Decade of Divorce.* New York: Basic Books, 1989.

Woititz, Janet G. *Struggle for Intimacy.* Boston: Health Communications, 1985.

Web Site Resources

Divorce Central
    http://www.divorcecentral.com

Relationships: The Counseling Center, University of Buffalo
    http://ub-counseling.buffalo.edu/Relationships

Whole Family: Extensive information on marriage and the family
    http://www.wholefamily.com

REACTION AND RESPONSE—WHAT DO YOU THINK?

Chapter Six   Level I Assignments

In response to the information in the chapter:

1. Are you more a brick or a balloon? What percentage of each are you, and how does that change when you are in a relationship? In which situations are you most likely to be one or the other? What, specifically, can you do to be more balanced? How might that affect your relationships in the future?

2. In what ways have you been "looking for what's missing" in your relationships? What is it that you hope to find, and how can you begin to develop that trait in yourself?

3. How many close friends do you have? Do you have different types of friends? How do you develop and nurture your friendships? What could you do to broaden your base of supportive friends?

In response to the class activities, group discussions, and exercises:

1. What are your opinions and reactions?
2. What did you learn or rediscover
3. How are you going to apply what you learned?

Chapter Six   Level II Assignments

1. Have you ever sabotaged a relationship just when things seemed to be going well? Do you think that you have any "codependent" tendencies? Are there any patterns that are evident in the type of person that you are attracted to?

2. Have you been involved in a relationship where there was a considerable power differential? What have you learned from the chapter that would be useful in changing that type of situation?

3. What have you learned about making marriage last? What is it that you want to avoid doing, and what is it that you want to make sure that you do more of?

Chapter Six   Level III Assignments

1. What are your reactions to the section on gay marriage? Where did your values and beliefs originate?

2. What did you learn from the information on attachment? What style do you think you had? How has that influenced your behavior in relationships?

3. Where could you use the information in the section on Expressions of Love from the Five Love Languages? What is important to you? How do you express love to someone who receives it in a different style?

C H A P T E R

HUMAN SEXUALITY

In the past, when I taught a course on human sexuality, I was always glad to be able to bring in speakers from outside agencies. One woman, who was from the Cascade AIDS Project, was particularly powerful and had quite an impact on my students. Her life story, and resulting work, left a mark on me, also. I think it is a fitting tribute that I share her story and the information that she passed on here.

Lynn D. grew up in a large Catholic family on the East Coast. Most of her early memories revolved around dealing with her father's drinking problem. Her parents offered little guidance, and for sure the topic of sex was not brought up. It was just understood that sex was bad and sinful, and something she shouldn't do.

For a number of years she, and other family members, tried to appease her father and protect him from himself. As time went on he became increasingly angry and violent. He began to physically abuse Lynn's mother and the children. Eventually, her mother moved out and obtained a divorce. Lynn had little recollection of her father after that and always felt somewhat abandoned.

Her mother remarried after a time, and at first her stepfather seemed like a blessing. He was attentive and gave her the affection that she was longing for. Then things turned dark. As an adolescent, her stepfather began molesting her, and eventually she ran away.

Sexual experiences with men her own age mostly occurred when she had been drinking. While living in various places with men she had met, she started a string of relationships that were most often characterized by aggressive behavior and sexual exploitation. When she became

pregnant, she married the child's father, but the relationship didn't last long.

The pressures of being a single mother and the haunting memories from her past contributed to increased use of drugs and alcohol. But, drowning her sorrows only ended up with her being committed to a rehabilitation program. It was after she got out and began to look at life through sober eyes that she began to realize how much she had missed growing up and how many of life's lessons about how to have a normal relationship she hadn't learned.

As Lynn struggled to deal with her past and develop self-respect, she began to explore the possibility of having a relationship that didn't begin with sex. She shared about how much she depended on her therapist to find out about how to get to know someone first and then gradually develop an intimate relationship. In her thirties, she began a relationship with a man who had also been in recovery, and they both worked on improving their communication with the opposite sex.

They talked about the implications of starting a sexual relationship, birth control, and the need for having a blood test. Lynn was elated when both tests came back negative, and they began to develop their relationship. But, it was not to last for long.

In yet another tragic twist of fate, it turned out that the man she was involved with had lied to her about having the test done. He had been an intravenous drug user in the past and had contracted HIV. Lynn eventually found out that she had it too, and her long journey in learning to live with the disease began.

It was with this background that Lynn began to talk about HIV and AIDS. She described all the particulars about blood count and T-cells and clarified the progression that occurs if the disease becomes classified as AIDS. Her presentation on the various treatments and drug combinations used was excellent. She described how her health went up and down over the years. Happily, she was also able to report that she was in remission and that her current treatment had allowed her to begin to think of herself as living with AIDS rather than dying from it. Hence she was able to become a part of the Cascade AIDS Project volunteer organization. It was an amazing transformation for her to begin to think about what she wanted to do with the rest of her life.

Happily, the story ends on a positive note. I write about her in the past tense only because the last time I called and requested she give her presentation for my class, I found out she had moved to Florida. She had found a partner who was incredibly caring and understanding and was going back to school to further her education. Her success with the speakers' bureau had added to her belief that she had something to offer the world, and she wanted to be able to do more to return what others had given her in support.

Lynn gave a human face to the disease and shared so much more than just information and statistics with my students. I'm sure that many of them will remember the other lessons as well: People who are mistreated often repeat the patterns; you have to respect yourself before others will; sex doesn't equal intimacy; trust and intimacy take time to develop; believe in yourself; and if you reach out, there are people who will help you if you let them.

Perspectives on Sexuality

This chapter deals with the social and emotional aspects of sexuality. Although the medical and anatomical information is important, it is necessary to limit the scope of the content to fit the context of this course. Therefore, the part that sexuality plays in social and personal interaction and its impact on our emotions and behavior are emphasized.

Even in today's society, there are myths and beliefs that have a strong influence on how we act with one another. Some people believe that all touch is sexual, which limits people's ability to express caring, concern, or friendship. Others believe that sex equals intimacy, which is a complex issue in relationships. Actually, sex can be used at times to avoid real closeness and intimacy. It is wonderful when the two go together, but that isn't always the case. Both of these beliefs are examples of ideas and values learned while growing up.

Why talk about human sexuality? Mainly because there are still people who don't think it's necessary to talk about it! There are even some who think that sex has nothing to do with human relations. Yet the need for information is becoming more important as the realm of sexuality becomes increasingly complex.

We are bombarded by conflicting messages in our society. Magazines and newspapers warn of the spread of AIDS and other sexually transmitted diseases (STDs). Yet the media—from billboards to movies to MTV—continue to reflect and support the notion that sex sells. Apparently, we all are expected to be great lovers, constantly involved in erotic relationships, living the carefree "Hollywood dream." In reality, people have as many concerns and fears about sexuality as ever.

There is considerable interest in the subject of sexuality, evidenced by the number of talk shows that discuss sexual topics. All it takes is a trip to the supermarket to notice the number of magazines that have articles offering explicit information about sexual behavior. Academic institutions might do well to provide the opportunity to discuss information about sexuality to the same degree as the media, for although there is increased support and awareness of sex education in schools, it would appear that much is being left unsaid in educational settings.

Even with all the information about contraception and its availability, the teenage pregnancy rate is alarming; the apparent lack of impact of sex education in this area needs to be examined. Young people need more resources for information and more people with whom they can talk about sex.

Legal and political issues complicate sexuality, issues such as test-tube babies and surrogate mothers. Recently, there was a case in which an egg was fertilized in vitro, implanted in a surrogate mother, and carried to term. After the child was born, the surrogate mother refused to release the child to the people for whom she had carried it. The judge's ruling that the surrogate mother was not entitled to keep the child created the legal question: Whom does this child belong to? Debate on this issue will continue for a long time.

Acquired immunodeficiency syndrome (AIDS) is another topic regarding sexual behavior that has legal and political significance. A lack of forthright discussion undoubtedly contributed to the panic reaction to AIDS when this disease was first reported in the newspapers. Reluctant to describe specific sexual behaviors, the media frequently used such euphemisms as "exchange of bodily fluids" to describe how the disease was transmitted. This use of euphemisms reinforced the mistaken idea that AIDS could be contracted by any physical contact and led to unfair and unnecessary discrimination against people suffering from the disease.

Only recently has it become acceptable to talk about and deal with sexual abuse in our society, and the silence that previously surrounded this issue undoubtedly was a factor in the prevalence and continuation of such abuse. The issue received national attention during the 1984 case involving the McMartin Day Care Center in California, in which hundreds of allegations of sexual abuse were made involving many children. The trial, lasting more than five years and costing millions of dollars, yielded ambiguous results. Few, if any, convictions were ultimately upheld. There were many legal complications due to the inexperience of those involved in taking the children's statements and testimonies. Further problems were created by what may have been premature conclusions on the part of the public as well as the legal system. The topic of sexual abuse was, and is, so volatile that there may have been some subsequent cases of overreaction. The pendulum has swung from one extreme to the other. For years, such incidents were underreported or denied. Then there was a reaction that fostered a public response that seemed to find abuse everywhere. A great number of day care centers were investigated after the McMartin case brought the issue to national awareness. By the end of 1995, a number of convictions in cases of abuse were reversed. It appears that our society is attempting to establish a balance between victims' rights and the rights of the accused.

One positive aspect of the McMartin trial was the development of better guidelines for dealing with child victims of sexual abuse. The negative side is that the need to use those guidelines has increased. After the McMartin case, similar situations were reported across the nation and the issue was finally out in the open, but the prevalence of abuse continues to be astonishing. National Institute of Mental Health reports estimate that as many as 1 in 5 girls will be subjected to some degree of abuse or molestation by the time they reach 18. The rate for boys is 1 in 10, which is higher than previously believed. Mental health facilities are diagnosing and treating more victims of such incidents as they begin to understand how often sexual abuse is the underlying issue for many other presenting problems. People from dysfunctional families in which rape, incest, and violence have taken place have many difficulties in their adult lives.

Because sexuality as a topic incorporates diverse elements of philosophy, psychology, politics, and the law, it is important to talk about sexuality and personal values. We need to explore where beliefs come from, why we think and believe the way we do, and how all these elements affect us in our interactions with others.

Beliefs and Values

Most parents feel responsible for imparting sexual information and values to their children. Their hope is that they are the primary source of information, followed by school educational programs, and only then followed by peers. Ironically, it is much more likely to be the other way around. As soon as children start school, one of their top priorities is telling dirty jokes during recess. There are a number of variations on the story of how "Daddy put his gun in Mommy's holster," or "The train went into the long tunnel." These kids are doing a reality check with one another. In effect, they are saying, "You know all that stuff about Santa Claus, the Easter Bunny, and the Tooth Fairy? Well, let me tell you about the Stork." They are saying to each other, "I know how babies got here; do you?"

Some schools have excellent sex education programs, but often, it is still a case of closing the barn door after the horse is gone. The majority of students have had some type of sex education by fifth or sixth grade. Unfortunately, at that point, most kids have already been talking to each other about sex for a couple of years.

Studies indicate that menarche, the onset of a girl's menstrual cycle, has been occurring at an earlier age over the past three or four generations. The average age of onset is 12 (Crooks and Baur, 1999), but some girls are starting their periods at 10 or 11. If one of those early-maturing girls starts her period in the fourth grade, how long is it before the whole school knows about it? What happens when the school doesn't have a formal program dealing with the topic until the sixth grade? Children are going to be sharing information, which may or may not be accurate, with each other before the school system begins to deal with the situation.

This is part of how beliefs are formed. Children are influenced by their peers and by the media. Drive past an elementary school and notice the number of children trying to emulate the latest media sex symbol. These children are being inundated with images of sexual behavior from billboards, television, magazines, and movies, and if schools come along with any educational information it is usually too little, too late.

Beliefs and values, then, are shaped by peers, the media, and the school system before some parents even begin to talk about sexuality with their children. When asked when their parents first talked with them about sex, it is not uncommon to have nearly half my students reply, "Never." It seems that the parents from the liberated generation of the 1960s have been having as hard a time as previous generations discussing sex with their children. What parents don't say about sex says a lot!

Parental Influences

Whether parents talk with children about sex or not, they are still imparting beliefs to them. Remember that actions speak louder than words. Children learn about values by what their parents say and do, just as those parents learned from their parents. Some people report that, as children, they didn't think their parents had sex; they thought of their parents as asexual. One person recalled that when he was young, he knew how babies were made, but decided that he must have been adopted because he simply couldn't imagine his parents doing that. Why do we have difficulty imagining our parents as sexual beings? It's confusing, to say the least, if parents tell children that sex is a normal, healthy aspect of life but never touch each other in an affectionate way in front of the kids.

If children believe it is all right to talk about sex, they will ask questions about issues when they are ready to deal with them. Daily life offers many opportunities to talk about sex. In many families, the opportunity arises when the second child is born. Even in families where there is only one child, many opportunities arise. The family pet having offspring could lead to an educational talk. If children feel that sexuality is a part of life and it is discussed on a level appropriate for their age, they will be more likely to ask questions about what they need to know.

Our family once had a bird that laid an egg, and my daughter, who was about 4 or 5, wanted to know why it didn't hatch. That provided a good opportunity to talk about fertilization. I told her, "The mamma bird laid an egg, but there wasn't a daddy bird around and there are certain things that a dad does that contribute to whether that egg turns into a little bird or not." We literally had a "birds and bees" talk. There are many opportunities, but parents need to be comfortable talking about sexuality because kids are going to ask some interesting questions at times!

Questions for Critical Thinking

What did your parents teach you about sexuality? What did they talk about, and what didn't they talk about? What messages did you get from the media and society? How did these things influence your values and beliefs?

_____

_____

_____

_____

_____

_____

_____

_____

_____

_____

Parents can teach their children healthy attitudes about sexuality by what they say and don't say and what they do and don't do. Children need information (books, discussion, and sex education classes) *before* physiological changes occur. They need to have accurate information and opportunities to talk about social and emotional issues with a source other than their peer group.

The values and beliefs conveyed in adolescent circles rarely help develop positive attitudes about the opposite sex. This is evident in the adult relationships that are formed later. As adolescents start dating, peers influence each other about what constitutes appropriate sexual behavior. By high school—and probably junior high, these days—the chaos of adolescent hormonal confusion has already affected some of their values. The residual effects are evident in some of the problems adults have many years later.

Social and Cultural Influences

One effect of peer influence is evident in the different names for girls and boys who are sexually active in high school. It is easy to detect a double standard in values in these names, which are used all across the country and have affected people for generations. In almost every high school, there are names for the girls who are sexually active and names for the ones who aren't. Some terms that are used for girls include *slut* (top of the list for at least 20 to 30 years), *whore, sleaze, nympho, easy,* and *cheap.* These words are all negative and derogatory. I found evidence that these terms are still in use while perusing my daughter's copy of *Seventeen* magazine. In an article about reputation, Peggy Orenstein (1994), author of *School Girls: Young Women, Self-Esteem, and the Confidence Gap,* states that she spent almost a year in junior high while doing research for her book. She made three points in her article: First, *slut* is still a commonly used term for a young woman, and the term can be applied indiscriminately to a wide range of behaviors. Second, there doesn't seem to be an equivalent term for males. Third, the term is often used as much by girls as it is by boys. The term is bantered about among girls and often used as a weapon against other girls for any number of reasons.

The terms used for girls who don't engage in sex aren't much better. They include *prude, frigid, bitch, dyke, goody-goody,* and *virgin.* For many females in our society, this perception is the origin of the double bind regarding sexuality. This attitude of "damned if you do, and damned if you don't" is inequitable and contributes to the reports that women feel more than a little confused at times about their sexual choices and behavior. However, one small DMZ (demilitarized zone) does exist in which a high school girl can be sexually active with impunity, providing certain conditions are met: She must be in love and/or going steady. If she has been going out with a guy for two or three years, most of the couple's peers will assume that they are having sex, but few will give her a bad time about it.

The difficulty for some young women occurs after high school, when they opt for education or career in lieu of marriage and have to consider the prospect of being single for a number of years. Currently, the average age of first sexual intercourse is just under 16 for females, and the average age of marriage is 23 (and increasing). The trend toward postponing marriage and family until later in life can cause confusion for women who have been taught that if they are going to be sexually active, they must be in love. Sometimes, women feel like having sexual relations even when the relationship they are in may not lead to marriage. If a woman is single for seven years and has no intention of getting married during that time, how does she reconcile those beliefs with having her sexual needs met? Many women are confused by the time they want to marry because every time they've had sex for the past seven years they have had to convince themselves, "This must be the real thing. I'm in love, and I'm probably going to get married." For some women, that might mean having to fall in love a number of times before getting married.

Some women come to counseling just to talk about the conflict regarding sexual activity and its relationships to labels, love, and marriage. There are women who are in their 30s, have been divorced, and are still trying to deal with the aftereffects of some of those beliefs from high school. They say, "I'm 32 years old, and when I go out with a guy I'm still struggling with those old ideas—if I go to bed with him, I'm a whore, and if I don't, I'm a prude. I have certain sexual drives. I'm healthy but I don't intend to settle down again right away. Maybe I'd like to have a relationship some day, but every time I think about being sexual with somebody, I go through this incredible confusion. I feel that I have to be in love to have a sexual relationship." As a result, they become confused about what love is and how to know when they really are in love. These are just some of the difficulties that stem from growing up female in our society.

Let's go back to the values imparted in high school and examine how boys are affected. It is a much different scenario. What are the terms used in reference to guys who are sexually active? Some of them are *stud* (top of the list), *macho, stallion, user, hunk, playboy,* and *gigolo.* Some of these terms may appear to be derogatory, but they are actually all positive. A young male in our society usually doesn't care which name is used as long as it refers to his sexual knowledge or abilities. Contrast that list with the ones for boys who aren't sexually active or at least expressing an interest in being so: *fag, homo, wimp, mamma's boy, queer,* and *nerd.* What kind of words are those? No guy wants to be on that negative list. Although girls can always get some support from friends, parents, and teachers for a decision not to be sexually active, boys very seldom get the same response to saying that they aren't interested in sexual relations yet. Consequently, guys learn fairly early to lie about it if they aren't doing it. There doesn't seem to be any DMZ for them. They are on either one side of the line or the other.

When I was growing up, if a guy didn't want to talk about a girl or what he had done on a date, other guys automatically assumed he had done

Questions for Critical Thinking

How were you affected by peer pressure in high school? How were your values and beliefs influenced? How have you changed since then, and what has made the difference?

_____

_____

_____

_____

_____

_____

_____

_____

_____

something. Then his so-called friends would make up stories and rumors about what he had "gotten off her." The message was, "Either you make up stories, or we will." This often had unfortunate outcomes for both parties involved in the stories that were circulated. The cultural expectation for young males was to try to have sex or at least to make up a story about what you think you were supposed to have done.

Thus, the high school culture seems to require adopting some negative perceptions about sex for both males and females. Boys feel a great deal of pressure about their sexual performance and knowledge and often learn to exaggerate to bolster their self-image. Girls must deal with the double bind and double standards that often leave them feeling somewhat crazy or confused. These typical high school attitudes combined with the absence of any information or discussion increases the impact and lasting effect of early training on people. As adults, some gain insight into the fallacies of these early notions, but many never do.

Sex Education

A visitor to the United States today might think that we have a completely open society with regard to sexuality. We are surrounded and bombarded by sexual information and materials. Sexual behavior and relationships are portrayed on soap operas, in the news, in magazines, and on television. And then there is explicit pornography, the largest single category on the Internet. Many of the programs and articles focus on the dangers of sexual behavior such as unwanted pregnancy and sexually transmitted diseases. But, if we are so open about sexuality, why does the United States remain the nation with the highest rates of virtually every sexual problem: teen pregnancy, rape, child sexual abuse, and AIDS (Davidson and Moore, 2001)?

Americans talk about sex all the time. Some conservative media pundits criticize our culture for its overemphasis on sex and suggest that the government has gone too far in allowing the free expression of sexuality. Some liberal commentators say exactly the opposite. They claim that our culture is downright puritanical. They cite as examples our lack of uniform standards for sex education in the schools, attempts to prohibit RU486 (the "abortion pill"), prohibition of gay marriages, and the current conservative agenda to just teach abstinence. Mostly, our culture gives mixed messages that are often confusing. We use sex to market and sell everything, but many schools are not allowed to teach a comprehensive course on all the important topics regarding sexuality (Blonna and Levitan, 2000).

Anke Ehrhardt, a psychiatry professor at Columbia University, says "In other countries, sex education is put in a positive context of loving relationships, but here we spread fear. And it hasn't worked. We have a much higher rate of teen pregnancy." Sex education programs became more common in the 1970s and 1980s. By the early 1990s, about 6 in 10 teenagers received some form of sex education in the schools. Few of these programs discuss relationships and the social/emotional aspects of sexuality, though. At the turn of the century, some estimate that only 10 percent of American children receive a comprehensive sex education in school (Rathus, Nevid, and Fichner-Rathus, 2000).

Today, nearly all states mandate or recommend sex education programs of some kind. But the content and length of programs vary widely. Most emphasize the biological aspects of puberty and reproduction. Few focus on controversial topics such as abortion, masturbation, or sexual orientation. Sexual pleasure is rarely mentioned. Sex educators face the challenge of being honest and open about sexual pleasure while also emphasizing the importance of mature decision making. But teenagers are often suspicious of sex education that ignores or minimizes the place of pleasure in sexual behavior (Westheimer and Lopater, 2002).

Why the emphasis on the importance of sex education? Because data suggest that the real alternatives are peers and the newsstand, which sell more copies of "adult" magazines than bookstores do of textbooks. Studies have consistently shown that peers are the main source of sexual information for both genders. When asked where teenagers today learn about sex, 5 of 6 (83 percent) said they had learned from friends (Rathus, Nevid, and Fichner-Rathus, 2000).

> The reality is that both government and society have limited influence on our sexuality. Our sexuality evolves and grows regardless of official sanctions or restrictions. We learn about sex whether we do or do not have sex education in our schools. It is not a question of whether we learn. It's more a matter of the *quality* of what we learn. Quality sexuality programs result from well thought out curricula, with goals and objectives for student learning. Curricula are based on accurate information, in which pursuit of knowledge is encouraged rather than restricted.
>
> (Blonna and Levitan, 2000)

The positive influence of sex education on behavior has been verified in many studies. It has been reported that education programs do not hasten the onset of sexual intercourse and may increase the use of contraception in general (Rathus, Nevid, and Fichner-Rathus, 2000). They indicate that specific programs increase the use of protection against pregnancy or STDs and HIV and/or reduce the number of sexual partners. Students' risk-taking behaviors have been altered by using appropriate behavioral change methods. Unfortunately, evaluations of comprehensive sex education programs indicate that many focus on whether they have helped young people delay sexual activity and prevent pregnancy. Other goals, such as helping young people develop an awareness of their bodies or learning to communicate effectively with peers and partners, are often overlooked (Haffner, 1998).

Sex education across the United States varies greatly regarding content, quality, and quantity of information. However, three surveys of sex education teachers and state and local education officials by the Alan Guttmacher Institute provide valuable insights into current teaching policies and practices for students in grades 7 through 12. One survey included more that 4,200 secondary

public schoolteachers in the disciplines most likely to teach sex education. Five key findings emerged:

1. The vast majority of sex education instructors are teaching their students about abstinence from intercourse, birth control methods, use of condoms, sexual decision making, and transmission of AIDS and other sexually transmitted diseases. In other words, these instructors are teaching those topics that can help students avoid unintended pregnancies and sexually transmitted diseases.

2. Almost all teachers think sex education is important, and they also believe that certain topics—such as birth control, AIDS, abstinence, gender identification, and sexual orientation—should be taught in earlier grades than the current norms.

3. Eighty percent indicate they need more help in teaching about prevention of pregnancy and STIs, in the form of more and better factual information, instructional materials, and teaching strategies.

4. Sex education instructors frequently feel they lack the support of parents, the community, or their school administration, especially when they teach such topics as homosexuality, condom use, abortion, and "safer sex" practices.

5. State agencies and large school districts generally place greater emphasis on education about STIs and AIDS than they do on instruction about prevention of unwanted pregnancies or on sex education generally. Curricula, particularly at the state level, often do not cover issues related to teenage sexual activity.

Much has changed in the past 40 years; it used to be that talking about sex was called *health studies*. In 1964, Carl, the football coach and physical education instructor, came off the football field and taught sex education. I was a junior, and the class was supposed to be "advanced" sex education, because there had also been a program in eighth-grade health class. Everyone was nervous but ready to hear about the real thing. However, what we learned about was strictly anatomy and physiology and was mainly a repeat of previous material. Any student who could spell "fallopian tube" got an A for the course. We covered the reproductive cycle and followed "Sammy Sperm" on the path to "Ethel Egg" to become "Zelda Zygote." Then we watched some films on the horrors of venereal disease. The discussion on contraception consisted of prophylactics (which no one could pronounce) and abstinence (which no one was interested in). That was it, and most of us felt that something was missing.

What was missing was any discussion of the personal implications of becoming sexual. Very little was said about the emotions involved and the importance of communication about sexual behavior. What needed to be discussed, and are even more crucial in today's society, are the following topics:

1. Emotional implications of a sexual relationship and discussion of fears and anxieties.
2. Communication about whether each party involved is ready for a sexual relationship.
3. What constitutes a good sexual relationship, and mutual respect of each other's boundaries.
4. Values, beliefs, and ramifications of becoming sexual.
5. Contraception and being responsible for your behavior.

When people become sexual, complex emotional reactions are involved. Many young people don't have the emotional maturity to cope with sexual relationships. When young people take the risk to be vulnerable, which is inextricably involved with becoming sexual, there are many potential complications. I have heard countless stories about the girl who has sex with a guy, only to be totally ignored by him the following day at school. A number of young women report that they felt used or taken advantage of after being sexual. And that doesn't apply only to the girls.

One male student described how devastated he was as a result of his first sexual experience. He had a crush on a girl for an entire year before they began dating. One night at a high school party, they drank too much, one thing led to another, and they had sexual intercourse. He thought it was incredible, and that because she had done that with him, it meant they were in love. It had tremendous importance and meaning for him. When he called her the next day, she answered the phone and pretended to be someone else and told him that his friend couldn't see him any more. He was deeply upset and confused. Now, she may have been regretting what they had done or may have been feeling guilty about it. Unfortunately, she wasn't able to say anything about that, possibly because of lack of self-knowledge. As a result, he went through a great deal of distress, wondering what he had done wrong and what her response meant about him. Those kinds of complications and the resulting emotional responses need to be discussed as a part of sex education classes.

The need for good communication skills is very important in a sexual relationship. Many young

ARE YOU READY FOR SEX?

You are ready for sex if:

1. You feel guiltless and comfortable about your current level of involvement.
2. You are confident that you will not be humiliated and that your reputation will not be hurt.
3. The partner is not pressuring you for sex and you are not pressuring him or her.
4. You are not trying to prove your love for the other person, increase your self-worth, prove that you are mature, show that you can attract a sexual partner, get attention, affection, or love, or rebel against parents or society.
5. It will be an expression of your current feelings rather than an attempt to improve a poor relationship or one that is growing cold.
6. You can discuss and agree on an effective method of contraception and share the details, responsibilities, and costs of the use of the method.
7. You can discuss the potential of contracting or transmitting sexually transmitted diseases.
8. You have discussed and agreed on what both of you will do if conception occurs, because no contraceptive method is 100 percent effective.

people don't know how to talk to each other with their clothes on, let alone with them off. That applies to some adults as well. Some couples have been married for five or 10 years and have never discussed their sexual relations. Discussing sexual relations is becoming even more critical today as the need for knowing a potential partner's sexual history increases. With the increase in STIs, the need for honesty has become absolute. If coed classes included discussing the implications of sexual behavior as well as values and beliefs, people might become more comfortable about talking on a personal level when it is appropriate.

Another area seldom covered in sex education classes is what constitutes a good sexual relationship: the ways and means of being a good sexual partner. Most schools seem to be concerned that parents will think introducing that kind of information encourages sexual activity. Yet, possibly, the lack of information will encourage exploration and experimentation. Frequently, the unknown prompts more curiosity than the known. Trust Dr. Ruth Westheimer to provide parents and teens with a middle ground. She has published *Dr. Ruth Talks to Kids* (1998), in which she writes for ages up to 14. Her thesis: Teach kids everything, and then encourage them to wait. "Make sure even the first kiss is a memorable experience, is what I tell kids," she says. "I don't think kids should be engaging in sex too early, not even necking and petting. I generally think age fourteen and fifteen is too early, in spite of the fact that by then girls are menstruating and boys may have nocturnal emissions." Above all, she says, kids need to have their questions addressed. Learning and talking about sex does not have to mean giving permission, she insists: "On the contrary, I think that a child knowing about his or her body will be able to deal with the pressure to have sex. This child can say no, I'll wait." In fact, Westheimer is a big advocate of waiting. "I say to teenagers, 'What's the rush?'" (Westheimer, 1998).

By the time young people are in high school, their values and beliefs are already shaped, for the most part. Those who have decided to postpone sexual activity are not going to suddenly change because they have been given information about the how-to of sexuality. Those who are already sexually active might benefit from knowing how to be more caring, sensitive, and communicative partners. All the books on techniques and positions may not be as important as each partner's being able to express his or her wants, needs, and desires. Once again, it is unfortunate that so much of the information on this topic is gained outside an educational setting.

ADVICE ON HOW TO HAVE A GOOD SEX LIFE

1. Build your self-esteem and accept your body.
2. Communicate with your partner about what you want, what feels good, and what turns you on. Share fears, difficulties, and sensitive areas. Stop during sex if you need to talk.
3. Get rid of resentments and anger.
4. Be willing to receive. Take turns receiving.
5. Be willing to please and pleasure yourself as well as your partner.
6. Follow your breath during sex—keep releasing deeper.
7. Stay focused in the present. Keep your mind on the area of your body that is being touched or stroked.
8. You're responsible for your own orgasm. It's not just your technique—it is the loving energy that does it.
9. Examine and change any personal beliefs that restrict your enjoyment. Gain information from books, workshops, or counseling.
10. Have fun and enjoy humor during sex.

ABSTINENCE-ONLY EDUCATION: THE COSTS—SOCIAL AND FINANCIAL

Since 1996, nearly $1 billion in federal and state matching funds has been committed to abstinence-only education (Boonstra, 2004). Because of the requirement that states match federal funds for abstinence-only programs, state dollars that previously supported comprehensive, medically accurate sexuality education—which includes but is not limited to abstinence-education—have been diverted to abstinence-*only* programs (Schemo, 2000).

The vast majority of Americans and parents support comprehensive, medically accurate sexuality education. Eighty-one percent of Americans and seventy-five percent of parents want their children to receive a variety of information on subjects including contraception and condom use, sexually transmitted infection, sexual orientation, safer sex practices, abortion, communications and coping skills, and the emotional aspects of sexual relationships. Fifty-six percent of Americans do not believe that abstinence-only education prevents sexually transmitted infections or unintended pregnancies. Given the choice, only one to five percent of parents remove their children from responsible sexuality education courses (Albert, 2004; Research! America and APHA, 2004; AGI, 2003a; AGI, 2003b; KFF, 2000; Kirby, 1999).

Fewer than half of public schools in the U.S. now offer information on how to obtain birth control, and only a third include discussion of abortion and sexual orientation in their curricula. A large, nationally representative survey of middle school and high school teachers published in *Family Planning Perspectives* reported that 23 percent of teachers in 1999 taught abstinence as the only means of reducing the risk of sexually transmitted infections and pregnancy, compared with two percent in 1988. The study's authors attributed the change to the heavy promotion of abstinence—not sound educational principles (Darroch, et al., 2000; Wilgoren, 1999). Currently, 35 percent of public school districts require abstinence to be taught as the only option for unmarried people and either prohibit the discussion of contraception or limit discussion to its ineffectiveness (AGI, 2003a).

Abstinence-only sexuality education doesn't work. There is little evidence that teens who participate in abstinence-only programs abstain from intercourse longer than others. It is known, however that when they do become sexually active, teens who received abstinence-only education often fail to use condoms or other contraceptives. In fact, 88 percent of students who pledged virginity in middle school and high school still engage in premarital sex. The students who break this pledge are less likely to use contraception at first intercourse, *and* they have similar rates of sexually transmitted infections as non-pledgers (Walters, 2005; Bearman and Brueckner, 2001). Meanwhile, students in comprehensive sexuality education classes do not engage in sexual activity more often or earlier, but do use contraception and practice safer sex more consistently when they become sexually active (AGI, 2003a; Jemmott, et al., 1998; Kirby, 1999; Kirby, 2000; NARAL, 1998).

The U.S. has the highest rate of teen pregnancy in the developed world, and American adolescents are contracting HIV faster than almost any other demographic group. The teen pregnancy rate in the U.S. is at least twice that in Canada, England, France, and Sweden, and 10 times that in the Netherlands. Experts cite restrictions on teens' access to comprehensive sexuality education, contraception, and condoms in the U.S., along with the widespread American attitude that a healthy adolescence should exclude sex. By contrast, the "European approach to teenage sexual activity, expressed in the form of widespread provision of confidential and accessible contraceptive services to adolescents, is . . . a central factor in explaining the more rapid declines in teenage childbearing in northern and western European countries" (Singh and Darroch, 2000). California, the only state that has not accepted federal abstinence-only money, has seen declines in teenage pregnancy similar to those seen in European countries. Over the last decade, the teenage pregnancy rate in California has dropped more than 40 percent ("California reduces . . . ," 2004).

Every reputable sexuality education organization in the U.S., as well as prominent health organizations including the American Medical Association, have denounced abstinence-only sexuality education. And a 1997 consensus statement from the National Institutes of Health concluded that legislation discouraging condom use on the grounds that condoms are ineffective "places policy in direct conflict with science because it ignores overwhelming evidence. . . . Abstinence-only programs cannot be justified in the face of effective programs and given the fact that we face an international emergency in the AIDS epidemic" (NIH, 1997).

For a complete list of the references contact the website listed at the end of the chapter.

Public Policy Contact Washington, DC: 202-785-3351

For medical questions, or to schedule an appointment with the nearest Planned Parenthood health center, call toll-free **1-800-230-PLAN** or **1-800-230-7526**.

The First Sexual Experience

There are many reasons for exploring the impact of your first sexual experience. (We'll assume, for the sake of discussion, that "first sexual experience" means sexual intercourse.) One reason is that such a big deal is made about it that it is almost impossible for it not to have an effect. All through adolescence the emphasis is on, Have you, Will you, or When are you going to "go all the way"? Such a fuss is made about it that it simply can't be ignored. It is also a major demarcation in the life span. Once people have had intercourse, several areas of their lives will be different. They can't go back to playing games and being children anymore. Some people perceive it, correctly or not, as a passage into adulthood. Becoming sexual is a significant change that affects how a person relates to his or her own gender, the opposite sex, and parents.

Informal classroom surveys over the years about first sexual experiences show that about one-third were positive, one-third were neutral, and one-third were negative. (If you were one of the people for whom it was positive, congratulations. For the rest, remember that you are not alone.) If the first experience was negative, you might want to consider your own best interests at this point. It may be healing to consider the experience and its effects.

Sexual Harassment

In 1980, the Equal Employment Opportunity Commission (EEOC) issued regulations defining sexual harassment, stating it was a form of sex discrimination prohibited by the Civil Rights Act, which had been originally passed in 1964. In 1986, the U.S. Supreme Court first ruled that sexual harassment was a form of job discrimination and held it to be illegal.

In 1992, this issue was thrust into the national consciousness with the much publicized Clarence Thomas/Anita Hill sexual harassment hearings that were held by the U.S. Congress. Ms. Hill came forward with her story around the same time that Thomas was nominated to the Supreme Court. The case received a lot of attention from the media, especially from television and newspapers. There is a certain irony in that the claims of harassment centered around a time when Thomas was Hill's boss at the Equal Employment Opportunity Commission, the same organization that previously defined what constitutes harassment.

The hearings brought the issue of sexual harassment out of the closet and have forced many organizations, businesses, and academic settings to take a look at how to deal with various behaviors. Since the hearings, the number of complaints to the EEOC has risen dramatically. Further, the U.S. Supreme Court has made it easier to sue in sexual harassment cases because the victims no longer have to prove psychological harm, just that sexually inappropriate behavior took place. Most people have come to understand that there are laws that prohibit sexual harassment on the job; however, it is still not always clear when bad behavior crosses the line into illegal behavior, and just who can be held liable for it.

Presently, new and more complicated harassment issues are being considered: The Supreme Court has now recognized that illegal harassment can occur between people of the same sex. Prior to this determination, lower courts concluded that men could not sexually harass other men, nor could women harass women; many dismissed same-sex harassment, blaming the person's gender, rather than looking at the offensive behavior. Currently, the court system acknowledges that same-sex harassment is in fact possible, based on the definition of sexual harassment, and have ruled that unwanted sexual behavior by one coworker toward another is illegal, regardless of gender (Repa, 1999).

According to the EEOC, sexual harassment consists of unwelcome sexual advances, requests for sexual favors, and other verbal or physical conduct of a sexual nature. These constitute sexual harassment when (1) submission of such conduct is made explicitly, or implicitly, a term or condition of an individual's employment or academic advancement, (2) submission or rejection of such conduct by an individual is used as the basis for academic or employment decisions, or (3) such conduct has the purpose or effect of unreasonably interfering with an individual's work or academic performance and creating a hostile environment.

Therefore, sexual harassment has two facets: unwanted sexual attention; or conduct on the job that creates an intimidating, hostile, or offensive working environment, where the individual faces daily stress and oppression. Although the two often go together, they can occur independently.

A hallmark of sexual harassment is the use and abuse of power to secure sexual favors. Sexual harassment has three attributes beyond the individual's perceptions that frequently characterize the situation:

1. A power differential in the relationship.
2. Inappropriate approach.
3. Pressure after expression of disinterest.

The boss, supervisor, and professor have power over workers and students by the nature of their roles and authority and should be more aware of the possible effects of their behavior. Awakened by the prospects of costly lawsuits, the public and private sectors alike have gone on the defensive. Sexual harassment training is becoming common. Formal policies are the rule now rather than the exception in the workplace.

The following guidelines may be helpful if you think that you have been the victim of sexual harassment on campus or at work:

1. If the harassment includes rape or attempted rape, file criminal charges against the perpetrator.
2. If it does not include rape, write a letter to the offender. Describe exactly what happened, your feelings about the incidents, and how you reacted. Include a short statement indicating your desire for the harasser to stop. Sign and date the letter, and make duplicate copies. Send a copy to the perpetrator, and indicate that if the behavior doesn't stop immediately, you will press charges using the letter as evidence.
3. When the harassment takes a lesser but still annoying form of off-color jokes, inappropriate cartoons or pictures, requests for dates, and comments about how you look, many experts recommend confronting the person directly and telling him or her to stop. According to these experts, this is effective about 90 percent of the time, when the harassment is at a lower level, as just described. When you clearly and assertively tell a harasser to stop, it lets the person know the behavior is unwelcome. If the person continues, you have taken the first step in making a formal complaint or even a legal case against the person.
4. Document the inappropriate behavior by writing down the date, time, and incident in a diary or journal; this can be important information if you need to take the problem to a supervisor, or even a lawyer.
5. Seek support. Don't hide what happened. Talk to coworkers, fellow students, and people identified with the issue. Relate your incidents to your significant other.
6. If the behavior doesn't stop, meet with the offender's supervisor. In a college setting, the place to file a report may be with the department chairperson, the student center, the sexual harassment panel, or the dean of students.
7. Know your rights. Sexual harassment is against the law, and you don't have to put up with it. Obtain the company/school sexual harassment policy. Read it thoroughly, and make sure that you follow its guidelines for handling your case.

Although it may seem frightening, it's better to act quickly than to wait and see what happens. Harassers seldom stop their activities if they are not challenged (Blonna and Levitan, 2000, p. 530).

Last, an ongoing and prevalent trend has to do with the need of employers to educate personnel regarding the definition and laws of sexual harassment. To this end, employers are developing their own policy regarding harassment, and many are producing manuals or films, or buying prefabricated media productions on sexual harassment. These may include online tutorials, virtual vignettes, and other Internet training aids. By providing the employee with this information, employers can often demonstrate to the courts that they are making a sincere effort to prevent, or promptly correct, sexual harassment by any employee (Robert, 2000).

Date Rape*

An important part of growing up is meeting new people, developing friendships, going out on dates. Getting to know others is an exciting part of life. Most friendships, acquaintances, and dates never lead to violence. But, sadly, sometimes it happens. When forced sex occurs between two people who already know each other, it is known as *date* or *acquaintance rape*. Even if the two people know each other well, and even if they were intimate before, no one has the right to force a sexual act on another against his or her will.

When people think of rape, they might think of a stranger jumping out of a shadowy place and sexually attacking someone. But it's not only strangers who rape. Actually, many people who have been raped already knew the person who attacked them. Even though rape involves forced sex, rape is not about sex or passion. Rape has nothing to do with love. Rape is an act of aggression and violence.

*Source: The previous section is adapted from http://kidshealth.org/teen/. Reviewed by: D'Arcy Lyness, Ph.D., and Neil Izenberg, M.D. Date reviewed: December 2002.

Healthy relationships involve respect—including respect for the other person's feelings. If a date, friend, or boyfriend is pressuring a girl to be more intimate than she wants to be, that's not a healthy relationship. Sex is not something that one person owes to another. Someone who really cares will respect a girl's wishes and not apply force or pressure about sex.

Alcohol use is involved in many date rapes. Drinking can loosen people's inhibitions, dull common sense, and—for some—bring out sexually aggressive behavior. A teen using alcohol will find many situations when it becomes harder to use good judgment, to be cautious, or to protect herself.

A recent trend, especially on college campuses, has been the illegal use of the drug **Rohypnol** (a trade name for flunitrazepam), sometimes called the *date rape drug*. Also called *roofies* or the *forget pill*, this drug may be prescribed to help people sleep. When Rohypnol and alcohol are mixed, however, the effects can be devastating.

Girls who have been given Rohypnol and alcohol may report feeling paralyzed, having blurred vision, and temporarily experiencing memory impairment. They can black out and forget things that happen to them while they are in this state. Because Rohypnol may be slipped into girls' beverages at a party or at other times without their knowledge, some experts suggest that girls should always handle their own beverages.

Protecting Yourself Against Date Rape

The best defense against date rape is to try to prevent it whenever possible. A girl or woman can help to protect herself from possible date rape by:

- Avoiding secluded places with someone until she knows him well and he has earned her trust.
- Not spending time alone with someone who makes her feel uneasy or uncomfortable. This means following her instincts and removing herself from situations that she doesn't feel good about.
- Staying sober. Many date rapes involve drugs or alcohol, and sometimes a date might slip drugs like Rohypnol into a drink to make a person more vulnerable.
- Learning to say "no" in a definite way. Girls should say it clearly when they need to, and guys should understand that "no" means "no"—it is not an invitation to try to persuade someone to have sex.

- Taking self-defense courses. These can build confidence and teach valuable physical techniques a person can use to get away from an attacker. And of course, even if a girl does use poor judgment, has a drink, gets herself into an uncomfortable situation, or doesn't yell "NO" loudly enough, a guy still never has the right to use force or coercion.

Getting Help

Unfortunately, even if someone takes every precaution, date rape can still happen. If a date or acquaintance rape does occur, the best thing to do is to get help and advice as soon as possible—from a parent, a doctor, a counselor, or another trusted, responsible adult. Local Yellow Pages have listing under Rape Crisis Centers or Human Services, and rape hotlines are staffed with counselors trained to help.

Sexual Abuse

Sexual abuse occurs whenever one person sexually dominates and exploits another—whether by means of activity or suggestion. The abuse can be explicit, as in rape, intercourse with a child, or fondling, but it can also be indirect, such as when a man (or boy) pressures a woman (or girl) to go further with him than she wants to. Abuse can also occur—and cause sexual harm—when no touching is involved. A person who has been forced to pose for pornographic pictures has suffered sexual abuse even though his or her body may never have been touched by the offender (Maltz, 2001). Moreover, when an adult shows a child or adolescent pornographic movies or explicit pictures, or comments inappropriately about the child's developing body, this too constitutes sexual abuse.

Expanding the definition of sexual abuse has helped many survivors identify their experiences more accurately and better convey the damage of their experience to others, which often helps the person cope with his or her misplaced guilt and self-reproach, and heal. "In the beginning of my marriage I told my husband about a sexual relationship I had with my stepfather," says Andrea, one survivor. "The term *sexual abuse* was not used in 1969, and rape and incest didn't seem accurate enough to be honest." Sadly, for many years this language gap prevented both her and her husband from realizing that her stepfather's sexual touching was abuse and kept them from understanding the extent of the damage the abuse had caused her (Maltz, 1991).

For many survivors, acknowledging sexual abuse is a difficult step. To help you understand the meaning of sexual abuse, and to identify whether you have been sexually abused, consider these four questions. If you answer yes to any of them, you have been sexually abused. (Questions and selected text excerpts are from Wendy Maltz, *The Sexual Healing Journey.* Copyright © 2001 by Wendy Maltz. Reprinted by permission of Harper-Collins Publishers, Inc.)

1. Were you unable to give your full consent to the sexual activity? If you were harassed, intimidated, manipulated, or forced into the sexual activity, you were not able to give full consent. If you were under the influence of drugs, alcohol, or medication, you were not able to give full consent. If you were a child, made to participate in sexual activity with an adult or older child, you were not able to give full consent.

2. Did the sexual activity involve the betrayal of a trusted relationship? If a person in a caretaking or authority role (such as a relative, teacher, religious leader, therapist, or employer) used his or her position to force or encourage you to engage in sexual activity, you were sexually exploited and thus sexually abused.

3. Was the sexual activity characterized by force or violence? Any sexual situation in which you were restrained or bound against your will, physically forced, or harmed constitutes abuse.

4. Do you feel that you were abused? For purposes of sexual healing, what matters most is whether you feel you were sexually abused. If an experience made you feel uneasy or exploited—regardless of how others perceive it—it has had an effect on you. You need to acknowledge the experience and its impact in order to be able to grow beyond it.

While the last is controversial, probably the most detrimental aspect of sexual abuse is the violation of basic trust. How does someone feel safe going through life, let alone dealing with sexual situations, when his or her boundaries have been violated in such a way? This is especially true in the case of incest. Being abused by the very people who are supposed to nurture you, and whom a child should be able to trust, takes an emotional toll on the person that often causes trust issues in later relationships, such as in a marriage. It is little wonder victims often have difficulties in many aspects of their lives, since abuse affects trust, self-concept, emotions, the ability to communicate, and the capacity for developing and maintaining relationships, and causes seriously blurred boundaries. The following are some of the common problems, difficulties, and life patterns for adults molested as children (A.M.A.C., a term that is frequently used in therapy or support groups):

General mistrust and expectation of betrayal: Lacking faith that people will be there when you need them.

Denial of pain and hurt: Inability to cope with emotions; confusion about feelings; showing one feeling on the outside while having a different feeling on the inside.

Self-destructive behavior: Attempting to cope through drug and/or alcohol use; creating chaos in your life as a diversion from the real problem.

Powerlessness: Being passive-aggressive and/or unassertive; playing the martyr role or being a perfectionist; feeling unnecessary guilt.

Disrupted family of origin: Strained relationship with various family members.

Disruptions in current family relationships: Tolerating spousal abuse; feeling unable to be a good parent; alternately seeking emotional closeness and withdrawing; seeking support and approval.

Public awareness of the frequency of sexual abuse has increased, and fortunately there are now more counseling programs and therapy groups to help victims deal with the resulting issues. Sometimes, because of denial of the original event, abuse victims become conscious of what happened only when some other crisis occurs later in their lives. Ellen Bass and Laura Davis (1994), in their book *The Courage to Heal,* give some excellent information about resolving problems that arise from abuse. In their workbook on healing, they cover the following steps that are important for that process:

1. Building a support system and dealing with crisis.
2. Assessing the impact of the abuse and learning about coping mechanisms.
3. Believing it happened and breaking silence.
4. Understanding it wasn't your fault and learning to trust yourself.
5. Dealing with the emotions of grief and anger.
6. Confronting and/or dealing with family.
7. Resolving and moving on in life.

The process is complex and requires effort, but there is hope for *survivors* (a term preferred over *victims*) to heal, and it usually begins with a willingness to acknowledge and confront the situation. There are a number of reasons why talking about what happened is an important step in the healing process and why "telling is transformative." The following information from Bass and Davis explains the values of letting others know what happened to you:

▶ You move through the shame and secrecy that keeps you isolated.

▶ You move through denial and acknowledge the truth of your abuse.

▶ You make it possible to get understanding and help.

▶ You get more in touch with your feelings.

▶ You make space in relationships for the kind of intimacy that comes from honesty.

▶ You help end child sexual abuse by breaking the silence in which it thrives.

▶ You establish yourself as a person in the present who is dealing with the abuse from the past.

▶ You become a model for other survivors.

▶ You (eventually) feel proud and strong.

Whether you are a victim of abuse or not, it is important to understand the stages that someone might go through in the process of healing. The statistics on abuse are controversial because of differences in definition, methodology, and survey techniques. Even so, given the incidence of sexual abuse for women (1 in 6 to 1 in 3, depending on the source), nearly everyone has or will have contact with another person who is a survivor of some form of childhood sexual abuse. Although most of the following stages are necessary for survivors, some are not applicable for everyone. (The following information comes from Ellen Bass and Laura Davis, "Stages of Healing," in *The Courage to Heal*, 3rd ed. Copyright © 1994 by Ellen Bass and Laura S. Davis. Reprinted by permission of HarperCollins Publishers, Inc.)

1. *The decision to heal:* After you recognize the effects of sexual abuse in your life, you need to make an active commitment to heal. Deep healing happens only when you choose it and are willing to change yourself.

2. *The emergency stage:* Beginning to deal with memories and suppressed feelings can throw your life into utter turmoil. Remember, this is only a stage. It won't last.

3. *Remembering:* Many survivors suppress all memories of what happened to them as children. Those who do not forget the actual incidents often forget how it felt at the time. Remembering is the process of getting back both memory and feeling.

4. *Breaking silence:* Most adult survivors kept the abuse a secret in childhood. Telling another person about what happened to you is a powerful healing force that can dispel the shame of being a victim.

5. *Understanding it wasn't your fault:* Children usually believe the abuse is their fault. Adult survivors must place the blame where it belongs—directly on the shoulders of the abusers.

6. *Making contact with the child within:* Many survivors have lost touch with their own vulnerability. Getting in touch with the child within can help you feel compassion for yourself, more anger at your abuser, and greater intimacy with others.

7. *Trusting yourself:* The best guide for healing is your inner voice. Learning to trust your own perceptions, feelings, and intuitions forms a new basis for action in the world.

8. *Grieving and mourning:* As children being abused, and later as adults struggling to survive, most survivors haven't felt their losses. Grieving is a way to honor your pain, let go, and move into the present.

9. *Anger—the backbone of healing:* Anger is a powerful and liberating force. Whether you need to get in touch with it or have always had plenty to spare, directing your rage squarely at your abuser, and at those who didn't protect you, is pivotal to healing.

10. *Disclosures and confrontations:* Directly confronting your abuser and/or your family is not for every survivor, but it can be a dramatic, cleansing tool.

11. *Forgiveness:* Forgiveness of the abuser is not an essential part of the healing process, although it tends to be the one most recommended. The idea is that forgiving someone frees you up to receive healing for yourself.

12. *Spirituality:* Having a sense of a power greater than yourself can be a real asset in the healing process. Spirituality is a uniquely personal experience. You might find it through traditional religion, meditation, nature, or your support group.

13. *Resolution and moving on:* As you move through these stages again and again, you will reach a point of integration. Your feelings and perspectives will stabilize. You will come to terms with your abuser and other family members. While you won't erase your history, you will make deep and lasting changes in your life. Having gained awareness, compassion, and power through healing, you will have the opportunity to work toward a better world.

Knowing Your Sexual Rights

Wendy Maltz (2001) has identified eight sexual rights that protect and enable each of us to develop positive sexuality:

1. The right to develop healthy attitudes about sex.
2. The right to sexual privacy.
3. The right to protection from bodily harassment and harm.
4. The right to say "no" to sexual behavior.
5. The right to control touch and sexual contact.
6. The right to stop sexual arousal that feels inappropriate or uncomfortable.
7. The right to develop our sexuality according to our sexual preferences and orientation.
8. The right to enjoy healthy sexual pleasure and satisfaction.

Sexual abusers can confuse their victims about many of these rights. Although offenders may try to convince themselves and their victims otherwise, sexual abuse does not occur by accident. Abusers either intentionally harm or take actions that they know could cause harm. Either way, they rob victims of their sexual rights.

In an article by Nancy Faulkner, Ph.D. (2002), posted on the *Pandora's Box* Web site, she disputed a *New York Times* article by reporter Frank Brunni (1997), where he called for society to hold the child responsible in adult-child sexual behavior. He further suggested that the words *child abuse* be changed to *misuse.* Faulkner stated, in her rebuttal to this article, that society, mental health professionals, juvenile justice workers, and the courts must continue to use the word *abuse,* as well as hold the adult in an adult-child sexual act both responsible and accountable. Moreover, she suggested that if society, the justice system, and professionals dismiss abuse as misuse, the wrong message is sent to offenders, and an even more destructive message is given to abuse victims and children in general.

AUTOBIOGRAPHY IN FIVE SHORT CHAPTERS

I

I walk down the street.
There is a deep hole in the sidewalk.
I fall in
I am lost . . . I am helpless
It isn't my fault.
It takes forever to find a way out.

II

I walk down the same street.
There is a deep hole in the sidewalk.
I pretend I don't see it.
I fall in again.
I can't believe I am in the same place.
But, it isn't my fault.
It still takes a long time to get out.

III

I walk down the same street.
There is a deep hole in the sidewalk.
I see it is there.
I still fall in . . . it's a habit.
my eyes are open.
I know where I am.
It is my fault.
I get out immediately.

IV

I walk down the same street.
There is a deep hole in the sidewalk.
I walk around it.

V

I walk down another street.

Source: Portia Nelson.

CASE STUDIES AND STUDENT STORIES

Tiffany stepped on the scales and was horrified when she viewed the reading. She weighed 312 pounds. Unhappily married and horribly depressed, she couldn't even begin to figure out how she had come to be in such a situation.

When exploring her childhood through pictures of the family, she recalled some of the events of the past. When she was around 8 years old, her father went on a business trip and her uncle Jake was left to care for her and a younger sister. After he left, Tiffany began to have strange dreams. She dreamed that a man, who resembled her father's brother, came into her room. The dream continued to haunt her for years. In the dream her uncle bathed her, something her dad had long since quit doing. The bathing escalated into fondling. But, as her uncle carried her to the bedroom, she usually awakened from the dream.

It was during this time that food became her solace. She could eat unspeakable amounts and had contests with her cousin over who could eat the most and the fastest.

Because of the recurring dream and her compulsive eating, Tiffany decided to seek counseling. Over the course of several months of therapy, she began to recall that her uncle had indeed raped her at the age of 8. The abuse had continued for some time.

When recalling her story as an adult, she realized that her weight gain had been an attempt to put a barrier between her and those around her—especially the uncle. She ate for comfort and protection, and any type of food made her feel better.

She also remembered that as a teenager she had suffered ridicule and taunting when she walked down the halls at her high school. She had finally quit school and then got married to a man older than herself in an attempt to be taken care of and to escape her problems.

Considering the patterns in her life, she began to realize that she had to do something. Somehow she wanted to shed her barrier of protection, so she could be a healthier, happier person.

Her counselor suggested Weight Watchers and Curves, and new patterns of behavior began to emerge. With time in counseling and new ideas of how to achieve weight loss, Tiffany began to slim down.

At this point, Tiffany has lost 60 pounds. She has a long way to go, but she realizes the motive for her weight gain. She is feeling more confident in the process of healing. Her husband is thrilled with her appearance, and her children have agreed to send her on a cruise when she loses another 40 pounds. Her barrier is crumbling ever so slowly along with the nightmares of the past.

Source: By D. Juanita Woods.

The False Memory Debate

With the increase in reports of sexual abuse over the years, there has been an increase in the number of people who have recovered memories of abuse from the past. Some memories are even based on incidents that may have occurred decades ago. Currently, there is considerable controversy over the possibility that some of the recollections of abuse are false. Many in the legal profession have seen a rise in the number of divorce cases where sexual abuse of the children is used as a weapon in custody battles. Some people in the general population think that perhaps the pendulum has swung too far in the direction of the everybody-is-a-victim syndrome. However, a few therapists and counselors have stated, "The client should always be believed."

It is in this context that families got together for the first meeting of the False Memory Syndrome Foundation (FMSF), a support and advocacy organization formed in March 1992 comprising the parents of 4,000 families who say they have been falsely accused of sexually abusing their children. Some stand accused of committing even more heinous and sadistic acts. As a result of these charges, many parents have lost all contact, not only with their accusing children but also with their grandchildren. The costs are not only social and emotional, however, as many now find themselves waging expensive battles against criminal and/or civil charges for abuses they are accused of committing a decade or two earlier, which their adult daughters or sons have only recently remembered. That these parents can be sued or prosecuted at all reflects the astonishing impact of the incest-recovery movement on the law itself (Wail, 1993).

Much of the current debate, due in part to the challenges brought forth by the FMSF, centers on traumatic memories. How trustworthy are memories 20 or 30 years old? Are traumatic memories stored differently than ordinary memories? Can people be influenced to remember things that didn't happen or to remember vastly distorted versions of what happened? Why is it that some people can't forget what happened to them (even when they wish they could), and others can repress the memory for years? According to Jim Hopper, Ph.D. (2002), amnesia for childhood sexual abuse is a bonafide condition, and the existence of this condition is beyond dispute. Dr. Hopper conservatively estimates that at least 10 percent of those sexually abused in childhood will have "complete amnesia" of the abusive events, followed by delayed recall. This estimate is based on 13 years of research and investigation, as well as his experience as a therapist.

Dr. Hopper used the words *extremely controversial* to describe the repressed memory/delayed recall debate. He stated that research statistics, and the interpretations of these findings, are often disputed by the experts. Some of the disagreement surrounds the use of certain research techniques, which according to some experts render the research inconclusive. This in turn casts doubt on the entire theory of repressed memory, according to the author. Beyond the problems inherent in this type of research, there are those who simply do not believe in the existence of this type of amnesia. Those experts who share this opinion believe that forgotten memories of abuse are fabricated by a patient and/or are encouraged by a zealous therapist looking for any clue to their client's dysfunctional behavior.

If the foregoing issues are not enough to complicate the clinical picture regarding abusive memories, experts also take issue with the "motivation behind the forgetting"; that is, do people "simply forget" because of the unpleasant nature of the abuse, and if so, is this forgetting active or passive? In addition, is there a brain mechanism or process involved in the forgetting, or is it purely psychological and defensive in nature? Although significant findings have occurred through research and clinical observation, there are still more questions than answers.

The following two authorities (excerpts from "The Shadow of Doubt") provide illuminating information about this controversy.

> Christine A. Courtois, clinical director of the Center for Abuse Recovery and Empowerment at the Psychiatric Institute in Washington, DC, psychologist in private practice, and author of *Healing the Incest Wound,* says that the controversy over "false memories" is part of a backlash against the long-delayed acknowledgment of sexual abuse, and that the "wholesale degradation of psychotherapy by some delayed memory critics" represents "displaced rage" at therapists for bringing the issue to public attention. She is also skeptical about the relevance of cognitive memory research to clinical practice with abuse survivors. "There is data to suggest that traumatic memory is physiologically encoded differently than normal memory," she says. "I think we have to be very careful about drawing conclusions about trauma memory from lab studies of ordinary memory, conducted on nontraumatized volunteers, usually college students who might be doing it for class credit or getting paid. We really cannot apply these experiments wholesale to the issue of traumatic memory."
>
> Elizabeth Loftus, a professor of psychology and law at the University of Washington and eminent authority on cognitive processes and eyewitness memory, has spent 20 years "trying to dispel the myth that human memory is infallible and immune from distortion." Citing extensive research—her own and others'—that demonstrate how memory is subject to inaccuracy, fabrication, confusion, and alteration, she argues that "repressed" memories of childhood sexual abuse—the sole source of criminal and civil charges against many parents—may well be false, the product of the therapist's suggestion and the client's imagination. "At this point, nobody can distinguish between false and real memories without external corroboration," says Loftus. Accepting all repressed memories as literally true, "no matter how dubious . . . is bound to lead to an increased likelihood that society in general will disbelieve the genuine cases of childhood sexual abuse that truly deserve our sustained attention."
>
> (Wail, 1993)

Ground Lost: The False Memory/Recovered Memory Therapy Debate

Until recently, the false memory/recovered memory controversy has been defined by zealots from both ends of the spectrum. Because the squeakiest wheel gets the most grease, the courts, legislators, public, and professionals have heard, and acted on, more diatribe than dialogue. To quiet this cacophony, we must make one fundamental observation: There is a crucial difference between opinion and belief on the one hand and science on the other. It is only by separating them that we can hope to understand and benefit from this unquiet controversy.

Those who do not believe in the validity of repressed memory have argued that most people do not forget trauma. Their point is accurate, but it hardly refutes the argument that some percentage of people do not consciously remember severe trauma. Some of these critics have appeared in court with citations for almost five dozen articles on remembered traumatization. But again, the fact that most people remember trauma is not relevant to the point that some do not.

Although people may continue to believe that repressed memory does not exist, there is no scientific support for that proposition. Expert testimony that repressed memory does not exist should, therefore, be subject to ethical sanctions.

Are repressed memories accurate? Both those who argue that repressed memories are always false and those who argue that repressed memories are always true appear to be mistaken. Although the science is limited on this issue, the only three relevant studies conclude that repressed memories are no more and no less accurate than continuous memories (Dalenberg, 1996; Widom and Morris, 1997; Williams, 1995). Thus, courts and therapists should consider repressed memories no differently than they consider ordinary memories.

The science clearly directs us away from the distracting issue of the existence of repressed memories, and toward the psychologically and legally significant issue of the validity of particular memories. The therapy room and the courtroom both benefit from distinguishing true and false memories (Scheflin, 1998). The science of memory shows that (1) memory is remarkably accurate for the gist of events, and less accurate for peripheral details; (2) all memories, repressed or continually remembered, may be influenced by later events or by the method of retrieval; and (3) all memories, whether implicit or explicit, may exert an influence on behavior (Schacter, 1999). With a renewed concentration on how memories are retrieved or influenced, therapists and lawyers might again be able to work as associates, not adversaries.

The fit between law and science has suffered a two-stage assault with regard to memory. In the 1980s, courts were told by many experts that hypnosis and related techniques inevitably contaminate memory. In the 1990s, courts were told that repressed memory does not exist and that memory is easily contaminated by even a hint of suggestion. In both decades, courts were told that memory is fundamentally untrustworthy. These views are wrong, and judicial reliance on science to support them has brought injustice to countless litigants. When the courts looked to experts for guidance, the experts failed to deliver with accuracy what the science said. Some experts have remained resistant to updating their opinions even in light of new studies.

Source: Adapted from Alan W. Scheflin, Psychiatric Times, November 1999, Vol. XVI, Issue 11.

Homosexuality

Some people think of homosexuality primarily as sexual contact between individuals of the same sex, but this definition is limiting. The word *homosexual* can be an objective or subjective appraisal of sexual behavior, emotional affiliation, and/or self-definition. Typically, a homosexual person's gender identity agrees with his or her biological sex. That is, a homosexual person perceives himself or herself as male or female respectively, and feels attraction toward a same-sex person.

A common synonym for *homosexual* is *gay*. This word was initially used as a code word among homosexuals, and it has moved into popular usage to describe homosexual men and women, as well as social and political concerns related to homosexual orientation. Cross-cultural attitudes toward homosexuality vary from condemnation to acceptance. However, in our society, negative attitudes toward homosexuality still predominate.

Homophobia is defined as irrational fear of homosexuality in others, fear of homosexual feelings within oneself, or self-loathing because of one's homosexuality. One indicator that our society has a homophobic segment is the persistent belief that homosexuals are deviant. But consider this: Pick up a newspaper any day of the week and read about rape and other violence. A frequent reason for a woman's being admitted to the emergency room of a hospital is battering by her spouse, a heterosexual male. It is an alarming comment on our society when a father drowning his child in the toilet (pick any article on violence toward children from the daily papers) receives less attention and causes less concern than what two consenting adults of the same sex do in the privacy of their home. Perhaps it is time to reconsider what is *deviant* in our society.

Attitudes toward homosexuality continue to change, possibly due in part to the role of activists and the number of people who have been *coming*

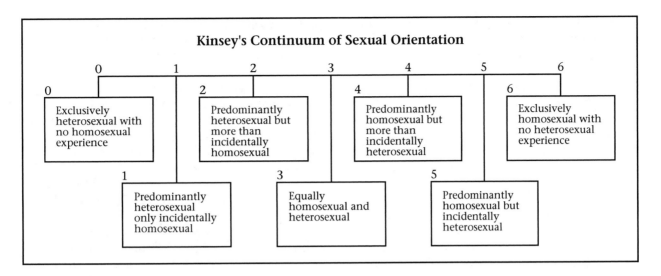

Kinsey's Continuum of Sexual Orientation

| 0 | 1 | 2 | 3 | 4 | 5 | 6 |

0 Exclusively heterosexual with no homosexual experience

1 Predominantly heterosexual only incidentally homosexual

2 Predominantly heterosexual but more than incidentally homosexual

3 Equally homosexual and heterosexual

4 Predominantly homosexual but more than incidentally heterosexual

5 Predominantly homosexual but incidentally heterosexual

6 Exclusively homosexual with no heterosexual experience

out. As more people realize that sexual orientation is only a part of who a person is, society as a whole may become more accepting. The American Psychiatric Association removed homosexuality from the category of mental disorders only in 1973, which shows that we have a way to go in learning to be more tolerant of differences.

Sexual Orientation

In our society, we tend to make clear-cut distinctions between homosexuality and heterosexuality. Actually, the delineation is not so precise. A relatively small percentage of people consider themselves to be exclusively homosexual; a greater number think of themselves as exclusively heterosexual. These groups represent the opposite ends of a broad spectrum. Individuals between the ends of the spectrum exhibit varying mixtures of preferences and/or experiences, which may also change over time. Sexual orientation is best evaluated by observing patterns over a life span rather than at any given time (Fox and Joyce, 1991). Sexual orientation—that is, the sex to which one is attracted—can best be thought of as on a continuum. (Orientation and sexual behavior may be inconsistent, as in the case of a person's being in a heterosexual marriage while being attracted to members of his or her own sex.) Some people are exclusively heterosexual, others are exclusively homosexual, and there is a wide range of responses in-between.

Alfred Kinsey (Kinsey, Pomeroy, and Martins, 1948) and others devised a seven-point scale from his surveys and research, using 0 to represent heterosexuality, 6 to indicate homosexuality, and 3 to represent equal attraction or bisexuality. According to the Kinsey data, the ex-

clusively homosexual category comprised 2 percent of women and 4 percent of men. Although this percentage of people who identified themselves as having had exclusively homosexual experiences appears small, 3 percent of the 250 million people in the United States is more than 7.5 million people. The number of predominantly homosexual people may be 10 percent of the population. Accurate statistics are hard to obtain because social pressures cause many homosexual people to conceal their orientation and/or activity (a behavior known as "being in the closet"). Social pressure for heterosexual conformity often results in homosexual people dating, having sexual experiences with, and even marrying partners of the other sex (Crooks and Baur, 2005). The importance of this information is that it demonstrates that sexuality isn't an either/or question. Although there are far more people on the heterosexual end of the scale, the range of responses is still a continuum, and that creates part of the confusion about just who is or isn't homosexual.

Development of Sexual Orientation

The controversy over the cause of homosexuality continues to receive extensive media coverage. For years, people have argued over the nature/nurture interaction: Are homosexuals a product of biologically inherited factors, or of their environment? Is it genetics that dictates orientation, or home life and family? There are a number of psychosocial and biological theories that attempt to explain the development of homosexuality. The psychosocial theories purport that homosexuality is the result of nurturing. For example, some of the psychosocial theories relate to parenting patterns, life experiences, and the psychological attributes of the person.

The biological theories, on the other hand, contend that homosexuality has a genetic basis. Theories of biological causation look to prenatal or adult hormone differences. Various "treatments" have been used to attempt to change homosexual orientation to heterosexual. Such attempts in the past have not been successful, and much controversy surrounds current therapy designed to develop heterosexual functioning in homosexually oriented individuals. Sexual orientation, regardless of where it falls on the continuum, seems to be formed from a composite of inconsistent and, to date, undetermined elements. Crooks and Baur (1999) state in *Our Sexuality,* "In conclusion, more research is beginning to suggest that there is a biological predisposition to exclusive homosexuality."

However, the causes of sexual orientation in general, and homosexuality specifically, remain speculative at this point. It appears to be more appropriate to think of the continuum of sexual orientation as influenced by a variety of psychosocial and biological factors that may be unique for each person, rather than thinking in terms of a single causative factor for sexual orientation.

A 1991 *Newsweek* article reported that the cause of homosexuality may be linked to the hypothalamus, the part of the brain that regulates heart rate, hunger, sex drive, and sleep. This study fits the emerging theory that sexual orientation is determined more by nature than nurture. The article also quoted a psychiatrist from the Medical College of Virginia: "I don't think we'll ever find a single cause of homosexuality." A follow-up article (*Newsweek*, 1992) about the original work of Simon Levay, a neuroscientist at the Salk Institute in La Jolla, California, presented further evidence regarding the biological influence on sexual orientation. Michael Bailey of Northwestern University and psychiatrist Richard Pillard of the Boston University School of Medicine have done a study of homosexuality in twins. The results show that if one identical twin is gay, the other is almost three times more likely to be gay than if the twins are fraternal, suggesting that something in the identical twins' shared genetic makeup affects their sexual orientation.

In both studies, the implications are significant. If it turns out that homosexuals are born that way, it could undercut the animosity gays have had to contend with for centuries. "It would reduce being gay to something like being left-handed, which is in fact all that it is," said gay San Francisco journalist and author Randy Shilts. Although the studies may intensify the debate rather than resolve it, the gay community may welcome the indication that gayness begins in the chromosomes. Theoretically, this could gain them the civil rights granted any other minority. And for some, it would be beneficial to lift the burden of blame from their parents. "A genetic component in sexual orientation says, 'This is not a fault, and it's not your fault,'" says Pillard. In the scope of human relations, it could be useful to focus more on acceptance and understanding of a different lifestyle.

Although the studies cited previously are now almost 15 years old, the controversy and latest research findings appear to be relatively the same. In *Speaking of Sexuality,* Davidson and Moore (2001) offer contrasting points of view in articles by Pillard and Bailey (1998) and William Byne (1999). In "Human Sexual Orientation Has a Heritable Component," Pillard, a psychiatrist, and Bailey, a psychologist, team up to explore the heritability component of human sexual orientation. They provide an overview of behavioral research on heterosexual and homosexual orientation. Against a backdrop of data about female and male sexual orientation, they impose recent research findings that suggest that sexual orientation is, at least in part, genetically based. In the article "Why We Cannot Conclude Sexual Orientation Is a Biological Phenomenon," Byne states, "In closing, we are a long way from understanding the factors that contribute to sexual orientation." Even if the size of certain brain structures does turn out to be correlated with sexual orientation, current understanding of the brain is inadequate to explain how such quantitative differences could produce qualitative differences in a psychological phenomenon as complex as sexual orientation (Davidson and Moore, 2001).

More important than the differences in the articles is the fact that they both seem to agree that perhaps we are placing too much emphasis on the answer, or that we are possibly asking the wrong question.

As research into the biology of sexual orientation proceeds, we should ask why we as a society are so emotionally invested in its outcome. Will it—or should it—make any difference in the way we perceive ourselves and others or in the way we live our lives and allow other to live theirs? Perhaps the answers to the most salient questions in this debate reside not in the biology of human brains, but within the cultures those brains have created.

(Davidson and Moore, 2001)

UNDERSTANDING TRANSGENDER

What Does Transgendered Mean?

A Transgendered (TG) person is someone whose gender identity (man or woman) does not match their biological sex (male or female). For most people, there is no incongruity between their biological sex and their internal gender identification. For TG people, their gender identity is in conflict with their biological sex.

Are There Different Types of Transgendered Individuals?

Yes! The term Transgendered (TG) is an umbrella term used for many kinds of people with differing gender expression:

Transgendered—The TG term is also used for someone who feels more comfortable as the other gender. TG individuals live part or full-time as the other gender.

Transsexual—Seeks to permanently change body to match her or his personal gender definition through gender reassignment surgery (GRS). "Non-op" refers to a person who has all the hormonal/surgical treatment except the GRS because s/he has no desire to proceed with the surgery, or cannot financially afford it.

Transvestite—Wears clothing of a gender opposite their birth sex for emotional or sexual purposes.

Two Spirited—Having both female and male spirits (Native American culture). Often viewed with respect because they were able to hold both gender spirits in their bodies.

Intersexed or Hermaphrodite—Rare medical condition where babies are born with both male and female sexual organs. Sex is assigned at birth.

Can People Stop Being Transgendered?

No. People cannot change their gender identity. Gender identity is believed to be related to neuroanatomy, hormones, and/or genetics. Although some people will "give it up," they typically return to cross dressing and recognize that they cannot fight their true nature.

Gender identity is NOT the same as sexual orientation.

Gender identity refers to how a person identifies as a man or a woman.

Sexual orientation refers to a romantic and sexual connection to a particular gender or genders (lesbian, gay, bisexual, or heterosexual).

A person's sexual orientation does not change after hormonal therapy or GRS. For example, when a genetic male, who is attracted to women undergoes the GRS (thereby becoming a woman), she would call herself a lesbian. She now identifies as a woman (gender identity) who is attracted to other women (sexual orientation).

If You Think You Are Transgendered

You may feel that you feel confused or don't know how to talk to your friends about this topic. It is important to explore your gender identity and seek help, whether that be through friends, family, counseling, support groups, or on-line chat rooms. Books, magazines, and web pages can help normalize your experience. Support from others will be important as you accept yourself.

Where can you get support for being Transgendered?

Counseling can be beneficial as you learn to accept this part of yourself and tell friends and/or family.

Support groups with other TG individuals will offer a community as you explore your gender identity.

Gender specialists can assist you in the fine details of how to act in your new gender (e.g., voice training).

Consultation with someone who is familiar with Transgendered issues can help guide you through medical and legal procedures.

Brochure Author: Jennifer Sager, M.Ed. **Series Editor:** Jaquelyn Liss Resnick, Ph.D.
Published by: University of Florida Counseling Center 301 Peabody Hall, Gainesville FL 32611 (352) 392-1575
© 2003.

Culture and Sexual Orientation

Pillard and Bailey in their article on the search for a possible "gay gene" state that should such a gene be found, one question that begs for an answer is the transcultural nature of homosexuality. Herdt (1994) and others have described "third gender" members in various societies—shamans, priests, berdaches, and celibates. Some of these individuals are described as having crossgender attributes and homosexual behaviors possibly analogous to gay and lesbian behavior in Western societies. One hypothesis is that there is a "gay genotype" of ancient origin, now widely dispersed in human societies, the phenotype expression of which takes the many forms of third genderness described by social scientists (Davidson and Moore, 2001).

A number of cultures permit sexual relations of some sort between individuals of the same sex. The very few studies that address the subject in a cultural context mainly focus on homosexual relationships between men. Because crosscultural studies of homosexual relationships are limited in number, it is difficult to know with certainty what percentage of societies accept, tolerate, or even support same-sex relationships. Nonetheless, Bolton (1994) concludes from a review of anthropological studies that male homosexual relations are common in 41 to 64 percent of societies studied (Gardiner and Kosmitski, 2002).

Although those figures should be viewed critically, given the wide range of percentage, the study still provides an interesting backdrop to looking at attitudes in our culture. If there are societies that are more accepting of homosexual relationships, what is it that influences beliefs in our society? Why do we believe as we do, and what might we learn from societies that are possibly more accepting?

A recent Associated Press poll reports that more than half of Americans say that gay/lesbian couples should not be allowed to marry, but more that one-half indicate that gay/lesbian partners should have some of the same legal rights as married couples: inheritance, social security benefits, and health insurance. Who are the minority sanctioning same-sex marriages? According to this poll, supporters include women rather than men, Democrats rather than Republicans, young rather than old, and more of those who feel that gays are born with their sexual orientation than those who see it as a choice (Davidson and Moore, 2001).

Answers About Homosexuality

The information presented here is taken from a review of research findings on sexual orientation by Gregory Herek, Ph.D. The review, entitled "Myths About Sexual Orientation: A Lawyer's Guide to Social Science Research," was published in *Law and Sexuality* (1991). This information was prepared by Sandra Moreland, Robinann Cogburn, and Maryka Biaggio for the Oregon Psychological Association (reprinted by permission).

What Is Sexual Orientation?   Sexual orientation is a way of classifying individuals according to the gender of the people they are attracted to. Attraction includes all the feelings you experience when you fall in love: emotional, romantic, affectionate, and sexual feelings of wanting to be with and share with another person. Heterosexuals are people whose deep feelings of attraction or romantic love are directed toward members of the opposite gender; homosexuals are people who feel these same feelings toward members of their own gender; bisexuals are people who experience these feelings toward persons of both genders.

Is Homosexuality a Mental Illness or Emotional Problem?   The answer is no. Psychiatrists, psychologists, and other mental health professionals agree that homosexuality is not an illness, mental disorder, or emotional problem. Much objective scientific research over the past 35 years shows us that homosexuals have no more emotional or social problems than heterosexuals. In fact, the only proven difference between the two is that of sexual orientation. Homosexuality was thought to be a mental illness in the past because mental health professionals lacked objective information about homosexuality and based their theories on assumptions, including false stereotypes and prejudice. When they examined the objective data, they had to change their views. In the early 1970s the term *homosexuality* was removed from the official manual that lists all mental and emotional disorders.

What Causes a Person to Have a Homosexual Orientation?   Sexual orientation develops early in life and appears to be affected both by heredity and by life experiences.

Is Homosexual Orientation a Choice?   Research indicates that sexual orientation is not a choice and cannot be changed for most people. Sexual orientation involves much more than performing sexual acts: It involves powerful inner feelings, self-concept, and social identity. Research shows that most homosexual individuals begin to experience homosexual feelings by early adolescence, and that homosexual behavior occurs an average of three years later. For some individuals, homosexual behavior (such as romantic relationships) is delayed until well into adulthood. Thus, sexual orientation develops before most people are able even to understand such complex matters, but expressions of sexual orientation may develop at any age. Psychologists generally agree that people who accept and integrate their sexual orientation (accept and act in accordance with their inner feelings) are psychologically better adjusted than those who don't. Thus, homosexually oriented people can refrain from acting on their feelings and from letting others know of their sexual orientation, but only at a substantial cost to their personal well-being.

Can Sexual Orientation Be Changed?   Sexual orientation usually cannot be changed, and attempts to change it can be harmful. Changing one's sexual orientation is not simply a matter of changing one's sexual behavior: It requires altering one's emotional, romantic, and sexual feelings, and restructuring one's self-concept and social identity. Some practitioners have developed so-called conversion therapies intended to change homosexual orientation to heterosexual. These therapies do not generally work. Some researchers claim success with conversion therapy, but the methods they use to determine if conversion was successful are questionable. Some religious groups also claim success in converting homosexual orientation to heterosexual, but these claims are not documented in a way that can be scientifically evaluated. Conversion therapies can result in serious psychological damage. Rather than creating heterosexual feelings, conversion therapies can deprive lesbians and gay men of the ability to feel significant romantic or sexual attraction toward anyone.

Should Homosexual Orientation Be Changed? There is no objective or scientific reason to attempt conversion of lesbians or gay men to heterosexual orientation. Homosexuality in and of itself is not harmful to society. Attempts at conversion can be harmful, however, and may encourage attitudes of prejudice. Such attitudes are harmful to society. Rather than trying to change the orientation of homosexuals, most mental health professionals work to help persons of all sexual orientations accept and integrate their inner feelings and overcome their prejudices and false beliefs about one another.

Does a Homosexual Orientation Affect a Person's Ability to Contribute to Society?   The answer is no. Objective data show that homosexual and heterosexual people lead equally stable and productive lives.

Are There Negative Effects on Children Raised by a Homosexual Parent?   The answer is no. Studies comparing groups of children raised by homosexual and heterosexual parents find no differences between the two groups in their intelligence, psychological adjustment, social adjustment, popularity with friends, development of sex role identity (that is, acting and feeling feminine for girls or acting and feeling masculine for boys), or development of sexual orientation.

Do Homosexuals Molest Children?   No, not any more than heterosexuals or bisexuals. A nationally recognized expert on child sexual abuse, Nicholas Groth, Ph.D., stated that in his 25 years of work with child abusers, he has never encountered an instance in which a gay person with a same-sex adult partner abandoned that partner to molest a child (*Oregonian*, Sept. 18, 1992). Researcher Paul Cameron published some studies that claim homosexuals molest children more often than heterosexuals. However, his methods are questioned by many psychologists and psychiatrists. The studies give no accurate information about the sexual orientation of the child molesters. Moreover, Cameron and his work have been criticized by a number of professional organizations, including the Nebraska Psychological Association, which disassociated itself from his statements on sexuality, and the American Sociological Association, which complained that he consistently misinterpreted sociological work on sexuality (*Oregonian*, Oct. 1, 1992).

Sexually Transmissible Infections

The terminology used in this section is different from past editions. The older term, *venereal disease* (VD), was replaced by *sexually transmitted disease* (STD) because it was imprecise. The current trend, noted in a number of textbooks on human sexuality, is to use the term *sexually transmissible infections* (STIs). The word *infections* more accurately characterizes these conditions, which are all acquired via invasion of the body by infectious agents, through sexual contact or other means.

You may be at least somewhat familiar with names of the most common STIs, but it may surprise you to know that there are more than 50 organisms and syndromes. There is considerable concern for public health, both worldwide and in the United States. Although the human immunodeficiency virus is the most threatening of the STIs, all STIs can be a source of physical and emotional discomfort. In addition, a person's health can be harmed through the indirect effects of STIs, such as infertility, ectopic pregnancy, miscarriage, and cancer.

Many STIs are epidemic, particularly among younger Americans, the vast majority of whom are poorly informed. Few Americans know that the two most rapidly spreading STIs are genital warts, caused by the human papilloma virus (HPV), and trichomoniasis, caused by a bacterium. Especially young people tend to grossly underestimate the prevalence of STIs and their personal risk of contracting one (McAnulty and Burnette, 2003).

Despite tremendous advances in research on STIs and the implementation of large-scale screening programs, health education, and behavioral interventions for their prevention, the United States continues to lead the industrialized world in the prevalence of these diseases. Each year, approximately 15.3 million Americans acquire an STI, and one in three sexually active Americans will have contracted one by age 24 (Kaiser Family Foundation/American Social Health Association, 1998).

Adolescents (10 to 19 years of age), young adults (20 to 24), women, and minorities are disproportionately affected by STIs. Adolescents and young adults run the greatest risk of acquiring an STI, largely because they tend to have multiple sexual partners and engage in more risk-taking behavior. If you are a college student, now is the time to pay particular attention! Adolescents tend to deny being at risk, to have more spontaneous sex, and to use fewer preventative measures. They are also likely to be involved with the use of alcohol, which seldom increases the likelihood of paying attention to "safer" sex practices. But it is women and infants who suffer the most from STIs in the long term. These diseases are associated with complications such as spontaneous abortions, fetal and neonatal infections, premature labor, and gynecological cancer (McAnulty and Burnette, 2003).

It is not entirely clear why the incidence of STIs is so high. Undoubtedly, a number of factors are operating in what many writers and health authorities have labeled an epidemic. Increasing sexual activity among young people has commonly been advanced as a prime reason for the accelerating rate of STIs. A contributory effect of "sexual liberation" has been a tendency to have multiple sexual partners, particularly during one's youth, when the incidence of STIs is the highest. It is also believed that increased use of birth control pills has contributed to the rising incidence rates by reducing the use of vaginal spermicides and the condom, contraceptive methods known to offer some protection against STIs.

It is possible that the effects of these factors could be counterbalanced through general public understanding of STIs and their prevention. Unfortunately, this has not happened. It is hoped that the present widespread ignorance will be overcome by more effective sex education at all levels of society (Crooks and Baur, 2005).

Although AIDS has received most of the attention lately, there are other STIs that are more prevalent. Herpes is caused by the *Herpes simplex virus* (HSV). Current estimates indicate that over 100 million Americans are afflicted with oral herpes (HSV-1) and 10 to 20 million have genital herpes (HSV-2). Current estimates also suggest that there are approximately 500,000 new cases of genital herpes annually in the United States (Crooks and Baur, 2005). Genital herpes appears to be transmitted primarily by penile-vaginal, oral-genital, or genital-anal contact. Oral herpes may be transmitted by kissing, sharing towels, drinking from the same cup, and so on. A person who has oral sex performed on him or her by a partner who has a cold sore or fever blister in the mouth region may develop genital herpes of either the type-1 or type-2 variety.

Chlamydia trachomatis infections are among the most prevalent and most damaging of all STDs. An estimated three to five million American men, women, and infants develop a chlamydial infection each year. Sexually active teenagers have higher infection rates than any other age group. Young women who use oral contraceptives seem to be at particularly high risk for developing a chlamydial infection if they are exposed. Chlamydial disease in the United States is transmitted primarily through sexual contact. It may also be spread by fingers from one body site to another, such as from the genitals to the eyes (Crooks and Baur, 2005).

STI Facts

The following is general information about STIs: their causes, effects, and symptoms:

▶ Sexually transmitted diseases affect more than 12 million Americans each year, many of whom are teenagers or young adults.

- Using drugs and alcohol increases your chances of getting STIs because these substances can interfere with your judgment and your ability to use a condom properly.

- Intravenous (IV) drug use puts a person at higher risk for HIV and hepatitis B because IV drug users often share needles.

- The more partners you have, the higher your chance of being exposed to STIs. This is because it is difficult to know whether a person is infected or has had sex with people who are more likely to be infected due to intravenous drug use or other risk factors.

- Sometimes, early in infection, there may be no symptoms, or symptoms may be confused with other illnesses.

- You cannot tell by looking at someone whether he or she is infected with an STI.

STIs can cause:

- Pelvic inflammatory disease (PID), which can damage a woman's fallopian tubes and result in pelvic pain and sterility.

- Tubal pregnancies (in which the fetus grows in the fallopian tube instead of the womb), sometimes fatal to the mother and always fatal to the fetus.

- Cancer of the cervix in women.

- Sterility—the inability to have children—in both men and women.

- Damage to major organs, such as the heart, kidney, and brain, if STIs go untreated.

- Death, especially with HIV infection.

See a doctor if you have any of these STI symptoms:

- Discharge from vagina, penis, or rectum.

- Pain or burning during urination or intercourse.

- Pain in the abdomen (women), testicles (men), or buttocks and legs (both).

- Blisters, open sores, warts, rash, or swelling in the genital or anal areas or mouth.

- Persistent flulike symptoms—including fever, headache, aching muscles, or swollen glands—which may precede STI symptoms.

(Willis, 1993, pp. 33–35)

The National Sexually Transmitted Disease Hotline can be dialed toll-free from 8:00 A.M. to 8:00 P.M. weekdays and from 10:00 A.M. to 6:00 P.M. weekends, Pacific time. The number is (800) 227-8922, or in California (800) 982-5883.

Barrier-Method Contraception

Many birth control choices are available for men and women. For more information, call the national number for Planned Parenthood (800) 230-PLAN. To prevent STIs, barrier methods of contraception are usually recommended.

Now that both men and women are encouraged to carry condoms, it is important to have the following information: Male condoms sold in the United States are made of either latex (rubber) or natural membrane, commonly called "lambskin" (but actually made of sheep intestine). Natural skin condoms are not as effective as latex condoms in reducing the risk of STIs because natural skin condoms have naturally occurring tiny holes or pores that viruses may be able to get through. Only latex condoms labeled for protection against STIs should be used for disease protection.

Lubrication may help prevent condoms from breaking and help prevent irritation. But lubricants do not give any added disease protection. If an unlubricated condom is used, a water-based lubricant can be used but is not required for the proper use of the condom.

Do not use petroleum-based jelly, baby oils, lotions, cooking oils, or cold creams, because these products can weaken latex and cause the condom to tear easily.

Condoms should be stored in a cool, dry place out of direct sunlight. Closets and drawers usually make good storage places. Because of possible exposure to extreme heat and cold, glove compartments of cars are not good places to store condoms. For the same reason, condoms should not be kept in a pocket, wallet, or purse for more than a few hours at a time.

AIDS (Acquired Immunodeficiency Syndrome)

Most likely, you have had discussions with your friends about AIDS and how to protect yourself from contracting it. By now you are probably aware that the disease has to do with the most intimate aspect of your life, namely, your sexual behavior. Although AIDS is tied closely to the sexual aspects of your life, it is also related to drug use, blood transfusions, pregnancy, and birth. Because there are no effective vaccines against AIDS, your best protection against this disease is information. AIDS is a complicated and life-threatening health problem that everyone faces.

The following information will give you a current overview of what AIDS is, who has the disease, and how to prevent it, as well as a brief history of the disease in this country. (The information comes from various excerpts from Frank D. Cox, *The AIDS Booklet,* 6th ed. Copyright © 2000 McGraw-Hill. Reprinted by permission of Times Mirror Higher Education Group, Inc. Dubuque, IA. All rights reserved.)

What Is AIDS?   The acronym *AIDS* is used to identify a deadly group of diseases caused by newly discovered viruses. The acronym stands for *acquired immunodeficiency syndrome. Acquired* means that the conditions are not inherited but are acquired from environmental factors, such as viral infections. *Immunodeficiency* means that AIDS causes deficient immunity, often reflected in poor nutrition and in low resistance to infections and cancer. *Syndrome* means that AIDS causes several kinds of diseases, each with characteristic clusters of signs and symptoms.

Each day you come in contact with many kinds of infectious diseases, but your immune system protects you from getting sick. When you do get an infection, such as chicken pox, the immune system manufactures antibodies that help fight the infection. When you get well, your body usually becomes immune to that particular infection. This is called *acquired immunity.* It means that you will normally not get the disease again. Unfortunately, people do not develop effective acquired immunity to HIV.

If the lymphocytes—which feed other cells, control cell growth, and guard against infection—in your immune system are damaged or destroyed, as with AIDS, the immune system does not respond properly. You are then more susceptible to some of the many infections and diseases that exist within the environment. You would also be likely to develop cancerous growth cells in your body. A damaged immune system fails to battle cancers, which often invade people with AIDS. It should be emphasized that people do not die directly of AIDS, but rather of one of the many diseases, infections, or cancers that are contracted because of a weakened immune system.

The virus that causes AIDS has different names, but the term preferred by most scientists is *HIV* (human immunodeficiency virus). Although people speak of one AIDS virus, there seem to be several viruses that can cause AIDS, its related conditions, and cancers in human beings. HIV-1 is still the most common cause of AIDS worldwide, except in West Africa, where HIV-2 is relatively common.

People afflicted with AIDS usually suffer from various combinations of severe weight loss, many different types of infections, and many different kinds of cancer. They go through long, miserable illnesses that end in death one to two years after the initial diagnosis of full-blown AIDS. However, this general description does not apply to every person with AIDS. Some people with AIDS alternate between periods of sickness and periods of fairly good health, at least early after diagnosis. Other people die within a few months, although a very few have now lived eight or more years after the initial diagnosis of full-blown AIDS. Having the AIDS (HIV) virus in one's blood is not the same as having the full-blown disease. Most people carrying HIV in their blood remain symptom-free for several years, during which time they can infect others. Although most people carrying the AIDS virus in their blood will sooner or later develop full-blown AIDS, it is unclear at this time whether all carriers will go on to develop AIDS.

Contracting the Disease   You hear about many different ways people get AIDS. Some of the stories are true, but many are false. It is unfortunate that you may be afraid of contracting AIDS when you need not be. It is even more unfortunate if you are not afraid of contracting AIDS when you should be. AIDS is a disease that you need to understand and think about clearly. It is vital to your health to know the actual ways by which AIDS is transmitted, as well as the ways by which AIDS is not transmitted.

Studies of high-risk groups in the United States tell us that engaging in sexual activities with multiple partners and without discrimination is particularly dangerous because HIV is primarily spread through the sharing of virus-infected lymphocytes in semen and blood. Another source of infection results from IV drug sharing. AIDS is spread in a few other ways, such as through HIV-infected lymphocytes in mother's milk and occasionally through transfusion of blood or blood products. Even if you personally do not engage in homosexual behavior or use IV drugs, AIDS can still be transmitted to you by partners who engage in these activities. Fundamentally, it is a disease of sharing sex, sharing needles, and mixing blood.

However, you cannot get AIDS from donating blood, and it cannot be transmitted through casual contact, such as shaking hands or eating with an infected person. For most men and women who enjoy regular vaginal intercourse, practice mutually monogamous patterns of sexual relationships, and refrain from intravenous drug use, there is little danger of contracting AIDS.

Origins of AIDS   Persuasive evidence that HIV was introduced to humans from chimpanzees was obtained by an international team of scientists who traced the roots of HIV to a related virus in a subspecies of chimpanzees that reside in central and southwest Africa. Humans may have contracted a form of the disease through exposure to chimpanzee blood from hunting or handling the meat during food preparation. Evidence suggests that the current disease evolved from the form in chimpanzees. The fact that AIDS has existed in humans for some time is supported by frozen blood samples of an adult male that were discovered in 1959. The disease, therefore, existed long before its identification in 1983. The disease spread globally with the increase in the amount of international travel. Thus, it now appears likely that HIV originated early in the 20th century, by means of cross-species transmission from a subspecies of chimpanzee to humans, and then was spread worldwide much later when Africa became less isolated (Crooks and Bauer, 2005).

WHO HAS AIDS?

The Centers for Disease Control reported approximately 900,000 total cases in the United States by January 1, 2004, and more than 500,000 have died from the disease since it was first diagnosed in 1981. The number of new AIDS cases reported annually in the United States grew rapidly throughout the early 1980s and reached a peak rate in the middle of the decade. The rate of new AIDS diagnoses slowed in the late 1980s. Since the early 1990s an estimated 40,000 new HIV infections have occurred annually in the United States. Although the overall incidence of new HIV infections in the U.S. population has been stable for a number of years, the number of new cases among teenagers, women, and racial minorities continues to rise.

Many young people were probably infected during their adolescent years. The growing problem of HIV infection among adolescents has been attributed to a number of factors, including the following:

 ▶ Many teenagers have multiple sexual partners.
 ▶ Many adolescents engage in sexual activity without using a condom.
 ▶ Access is generally more difficult for adolescents.
 ▶ Teenagers have higher rates of other STDs.
 ▶ Substance abuse, which often increases with risky behavior.
 ▶ Teenagers tend to be likely as a group to feel invulnerable.

In the United States, AIDS cases attributable to heterosexual transmission are accelerating. Heterosexual contact has always been the primary form of HIV transmission worldwide, especially in Africa and Asia. Each year about five million new HIV infections occur globally, and by January 2003 an estimated 42 million people worldwide were infected. The disease claims more than three million lives in the world community each year. Unless health professionals succeed in mounting a drastically expanded global prevention effort, experts project that an additional 45 million people will become infected with HIV by 2010.

Source: Adapted from Crooks and Bauer, 2005.

Preventing AIDS   The future of the AIDS epidemic in the United States depends largely on all of us. Each of us must assume responsibility for our own behavior, especially sexual and drug-related behavior. The following precautions (Cox, 2000) will help prevent contracting or spreading AIDS and other STIs:

 ▶ Sexual abstinence, especially when a caring relationship is not involved.
 ▶ Sexual fidelity.
 ▶ Use of barriers shown to prevent pregnancy as well as STDs, such as FDA-approved latex condoms that can protect a woman and a man from sharing semen and vaginal secretions during conventional vaginal intercourse, and spermicides such as nonoxynol-9, which paralyze sperm and migrant lymphocytes that may have gotten past the barrier (a few people will have allergic reactions to specific spermicides).
 ▶ Use of barriers strictly in accordance with recommendations supplied by the FDA, as well as inserts supplied by the manufacturers.
 ▶ Avoidance of anal intercourse with or without a condom (this is the most dangerous way to share semen, and condoms are not well designed for this means of sexual expression).
 ▶ Avoidance of sexual relations with persons at great risk for having AIDS or other transmissible viruses, such as homosexual or bisexual persons who "shoot" drugs, or persons who sell or buy sex.
 ▶ Avoidance of alcohol or drugs, which interfere with your caring for yourself as well as for other persons.
 ▶ Avoidance of drugs that are injected into the veins.
 ▶ Avoidance of sharing needles used for injecting drugs into the veins or handling sharp instruments contaminated with the blood of other persons.

Although AIDS seems destined to become one of the most deadly epidemics humans have faced, do not be afraid. Your chances of becoming infected are near zero if you apply the foregoing precautions.

Do not pay attention to rumors about AIDS. Whenever you have questions about AIDS or behavior that increases the chances of exposure, seek out answers from health profession-als, medical clinics, teachers, counselors, and other knowledgeable adults. Last but not least, it is important that you not be lulled into a sense of complacency or apathy, encouraged by the conflicting reports on AIDS in the news media. Although significant breakthroughs are often reported, you must do all you can to protect yourself from acquiring the virus, for all real and permanent cures still remain in the distant future.

CHAPTER REVIEW

Perspectives on Sexuality

There are many complex issues regarding sexuality in our society today. We are bombarded with images and messages about sex from the media at the same time that it is becoming increasingly important to be cautious about indiscriminate sexual behavior. Many of our beliefs and values are shaped by the media and our peer groups long before our parents begin to share information about sex. What parents don't say to their children speaks as loudly as what they do say.

Social and Cultural Influences

The impact of adolescent peer pressure during high school can linger long into adulthood for some people. In response to the need for more and better sex education at an earlier age, schools have broadened the curriculum. First sexual experiences carry a great deal of significance for many people and represent a major life transition.

Sex Education

The style and content of sex education programs vary widely across the United States. The topic continues to be controversial even though the "sexual revolution" of the 1960s was over 40 years ago. Contrary to the belief of some people, sex education does not necessarily lead to greater promiscuity. Further, there is evidence that students who have not had adequate sex education may be at greater risk regarding their health.

Sexual Harassment

It is important to understand the definition of harassment and what constitutes inappropriate behavior. There are legal implications that are of the utmost importance, especially regarding behavior in the workplace. There are guidelines that are useful for knowing your rights and how to address certain situations.

Date Rape

The incidence of rape when the victim and the assailant are known to each other is higher than previously believed. Rape is not just a stranger attacking someone on the street. It is important to know what constitute rape and learn how to protect yourself.

Sexual Abuse

There is a national trend toward the acknowledgment and treatment of sexual abuse. It is far more prevalent than previously believed. Victims of abuse frequently have difficulty adjusting and coping. Friends and family of sexual abuse victims should understand the healing process in order to provide support.

Homosexuality

Sexual orientation is on a continuum. Although the causes of sexual orientation remain speculative at this point, there is increasing scientific evidence that there is a biological predisposition to exclusive homosexuality. There are many misconceptions about homosexuals that often lead to discrimination.

Sexually Transmissible Infections

Although AIDS receives the most media coverage, there are a number of other diseases that can be contracted through sexual behavior. Regarding AIDS, general information is as follows: AIDS is caused by infection with the HIV virus that destroys the immune system, leaving the body vulnerable to a variety of cancers and opportunistic infections. Blood and semen are the major vehicles for transmitting the virus, which appears to be passed primarily through sexual contact and through needle sharing among IV drug users. People may significantly reduce their risk of becoming infected with HIV by following safer-sex strategies such as using latex condoms and virus-killing spermicides and by avoiding sex with multiple partners or high-risk people.

SOURCES AND SUGGESTED READINGS

Bass, Ellen, and Laura Davis. *The Courage to Heal.* 3rd edition. New York: HarperCollins, 1994.

Boenke, M. (Ed.). *Trans Forming Families: Real Stories About Transgendered Loved Ones.* New Castle, DE: Oak Knoll Press, 2003.

Carroll, J.L. *Sexuality Now: Embracing Diversity.* Belmont, CA: Thomson Brooks/Cole, 2005.

Cox, Frank D. *The AIDS Booklet.* 6th edition. New York: McGraw-Hill, 2000.

Crooks, Robert, and Karla Baur. *Our Sexuality.* Menlo Park, CA: Benjamin-Cummings, 2005.

Dobritch, Wanda, and Stephen Dranoff. *The First Line of Defense: A Guide to Protecting Yourself Against Sexual Harassment.* New York: Wiley, 2000.

Francoeur, Robert, editor. *Taking Sides: Clashing Views on Controversial Issues in Human Sexuality.* Guilford, CT: Duskin, 2002.

Gil, Eleana. *Outgrowing the Pain.* San Francisco: Launch Press, 1988.

Johnson, Earvin "Magic." *What You Can Do to Avoid AIDS.* New York: Random House, 1992.

Maltz, Wendy. *The Sexual Healing Journey.* New York: HarperCollins, 1991.

Masters, William H., Virginia Johnson, and Robert C. Kolodny. *Human Sexuality.* New York: HarperCollins, 1992.

Web Site Resources

Centers for Disease Control and Prevention
http://www.cdc.gov

International Federation for Gender Education (IFGE)
http://www.ifge.org

Parents and Friends of Lesbians and Gays (PFLAG)
http://www.pflag.org

Planned Parenthood Federation of America: The Reality-based Education And Learning for Life (R.E.A.L. Life) kit, a collection of 17 documents that can be used by professionals, parents, and other community members to advocate for responsible sexuality education; can be purchased for $10
http://store.yahoo.com/ppfastore/reallifkitre.html

Sexual Orientation: Science, Education, and Policy
http://www.psychology.ucdavis.edu/rainbow

Go Ask Alice: Offers answers to questions about relationships, sexuality, sexual health, emotional health, fitness, nutrition, alcohol, nicotine, and other drugs
http://www.goaskalice.columbia.edu

National Center for HIV, STD, and TB Prevention
http://www.cdc.gov/hiv/dhap.htm

Advocates for Youth
http://www.advocatesforyouth.org

Rape Abuse and Incest National Network
http://www.rainn.org

Recovered Memories of Sexual Abuse: Scientific Research and Scholarly Resources by Jim Hopper, Ph.D.
http://www.jimhopper.com/memory

Queer Resources Directory (QRD)
http://www.qrd.org/QRD

Sexual Assault Information Page
http://www.cs.utk.edu/~bartley/saInfoPage.html

SIECUS (Sexuality Information and Education Council of the United States)
http://www.siecus.org

Society for the Second Self (Tri-Ess)
http://www.tri-ess.org

REACTION AND RESPONSE—WHAT DO YOU THINK?

Chapter Seven   Level I Assignments

In response to the information in the chapter:

1. What do you think about the sex education you received in school? What do you think needs to be included in sex education classes today? What was missing in the information you received? How early should that information be introduced?

2. When did your parents give you the "birds and the bees" talk? What did your parents convey to you about their attitudes toward sex? How did they impart their values and beliefs to you?

3. What is your response to the information in the chapter about homosexuality? Where did your beliefs about sexual orientation originate?

In response to the class activities, group discussions, and exercises:

1. What are your opinions and reactions?
2. What did you learn or rediscover?
3. How are you going to apply what you learned?

Chapter Seven   Level II Assignments

1. How can you protect yourself from date rape?
2. What did you learn about the legal aspects of sexual harrassment?
3. What did you learn about STIs? How does that change your behavior and beliefs? What can you do to practice safer sex in the future?

Chapter Seven   Level III Assignments

1. What did you learn in the chapter about sexual abuse? Has anyone that you know been abused? How was the information on healing useful for you?

2. If you have had sexual intercourse, what was your experience the first time? Without going into specifics, how did you react and what did you think afterward? What did you decide about yourself, the other person, and sex in general?

3. What did you learn about transgendered people?

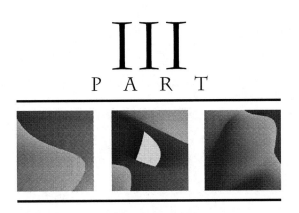

PART III

MEETING THE WORLD

Special relationships with people who know us and care about us are an important part of a strong support system.
Photo: Jim Whitmer/Stock Boston

8
C H A P T E R

COPING SKILLS

Sally is tired of being treated like a doormat and would like to change her behavior. When asked why she doesn't stand up for herself, she replies, "If I were to say what I want and what I am feeling, I might hurt someone else's feelings." Sally often feels responsible for everyone around her, whether she actually is or not. Whenever she thinks someone is in need or has hurt feelings, she feels duty bound to help that person. She has a self-imposed agenda of taking care of everyone's feelings except her own. There is a contradiction inherent in her lack of care for herself. When confronted with that, she says, "If I weren't taking care of other people and trying to protect them from having any bad feelings, then that would be proof that I was selfish—and people wouldn't like me." Apparently, part of being a doormat is avoiding disapproval from anyone at all costs.

When it is pointed out to Sally that it may not be possible to be how she would like to be and still avoid the disapproval of others at all times, she gets confused. She wants to make changes to stop being a doormat, but, because she thinks she must not upset anyone while making those changes, she is in a quandary. She even gets confused about being confused, because she knows that she wants to change yet doesn't think she can. After thinking about what being confused does for her, she realizes that it keeps her from having to take action. If she is confused, then no one will blame her or disapprove if she continues to do nothing. How can she be expected to act if she doesn't know what to do?

When asked what it does for her to not have to take action to deal with the problem of how she is treated, she says, "I don't have to deal with any conflicts." It is very important not to have any conflict so as to avoid the possibility of dealing with someone's anger. Paradoxically, by avoiding conflict and the possibility of any expression of anger, she gets mad at herself. The anger that she feels toward others gets directed inward.

The more she blames herself for her situation in life and the way others treat her, the more depressed she becomes. The more depressed she becomes, the more she feels she deserves to be treated like a doormat. And the more she feels that way, the more people in the world perceive her belief about herself and treat her accordingly.

Sally is caught in a cycle of self-defeating behaviors. Each part of the cycle is supported by the beliefs and subsequent behavior of the previous step. To interrupt the vicious cycle that is limiting her life, Sally needs to learn new coping skills. It would benefit her to learn new methods of coping with anxiety, emotions, conflict, and the fear of rejection or disapproval.

Self-Defeating Behavior

The previous case study demonstrates the power of self-defeating behavior. It shows how limiting beliefs can affect problem-solving ability. It also shows the need to eliminate self-defeating behavior to make behavioral changes and achieve goals.

People are often experts at getting exactly what they say they don't want. We all at times contribute to our own unhappiness. In this chapter, we will learn how to identify and minimize self-defeating behavior patterns, learned helplessness, and limiting beliefs—a prerequisite to learning coping skills and making changes. When dealing with the complexities of life, there are two general approaches for making life go more smoothly: Stop doing what doesn't work, and start doing what does!

After exploring self-defeating behavior and alternative coping skills, we will outline a process for making changes. A critical element in using coping skills and making changes is having the energy to apply those new abilities. Finally, information on what problems are most likely to benefit from professional help and how to select a counselor or therapist is included.

Limiting Beliefs

Self-defeating behavior is saying you want something and then proceeding to do everything possible to make sure it doesn't happen. Rebecca C. Curtis, a psychologist at Adelphi University and editor of *Self-Defeating Behaviors,* believes such behavior is often rooted in negative beliefs and expectations. "People bring these preconceived notions, sometimes deeply buried, about who they are and what they can have in life into new situations. Then they act in ways that make them come true," Curtis contends. Steve Berglas, a psychologist at Harvard Medical School and author of *The Success Syndrome* (1991), calls one strategy for limiting one's abilities *self-handicapping*. When people fear failure or the inability to sustain success, they create an impediment, or handicap, that makes success less likely. Then, if they do fail, they can blame it on the external impediment rather than some internal flaw of character or ability. If they succeed, then all the better, because they have done it despite the obstacle. This strategy is attractive because of its apparent win-win aspect.

The unconscious intention of self-handicapping is to shift the blame for an anticipated negative outcome from something more central to one's sense of self-esteem to something less central. Thus, no matter what happens, a person can protect his or her sense of self-esteem. Unfortunately, that pattern may work only in the immediate situation. In the long run, continually creating obstacles in one's life may have the opposite effect and lower self-esteem.

Passive Self-Defeat Not all self-defeating behavior is as dramatic as the case study at the beginning of the chapter. According to Berglas (1991), most people are more subtle. Withdrawing, dropping out, procrastinating, indecisiveness, obsessive planning but never getting to the act itself—all may be tactics for passive self-defeat. The most commonly used method of all, guaran-

teed as a self-defeating ploy, is just not trying very hard in the first place. People who coast along through life with a mediocre existence can always reassure themselves that they have been inadequately judged. After all, they never really gave it their all. Berglas feels that many of these behaviors may be due in part to faulty early feedback. In some families, parental praise is inconsistent, indiscriminate, or inadequate. In such families, a person is left with high expectations but little understanding of how to replicate the rewards he or she already received. Consequently, he or she may withdraw and put forth less effort.

High-Anxiety Avoidance The amount of anxiety generated by the possibility of failure or success greatly influences a person's willingness to try. In some families, it is risky to attempt new activities for fear of being criticized or humiliated. It may seem safer to not make decisions rather than risk doing or saying the wrong thing. Some children get the message, correctly or not, that they will be loved only if they are successful. The resulting fear of losing love contributes to their lack of ability or willingness to attempt the very behaviors that could make them more successful.

Fear of Change Underlying many of these styles of self-defeating behavior may be the fear of change itself. That is true even when the change is for the better. Many people become so attached to their particular way of being that they even mourn the loss of unhealthy patterns. It is a case of "old chains become familiar friends." This is evident in a common problem in psychotherapy: overcoming the client's fear of the unknown. Studies show that psychiatric patients nearing release sometimes develop new symptoms that may delay their release. Often, these symptoms are an expression of the fear and uncertainty they feel about the impending change. This phenomenon is not unique to the hospitalized patient. There are many people in the general population who would rather continue doing something that doesn't work well than risk trying something new.

Berglas suggests practicing risk taking in relatively safe settings, perhaps those that aren't so public or aren't in critical areas of life. She emphasizes seeking honest feedback from friends about trying new behaviors and the potential outcomes. We all could do with a little *reality testing* at times. Perhaps new information or a different perspective will be useful in reassessing one's abilities. Friends can also be supportive of the need to stretch oneself. There are often rewards for doing so. Positive self-esteem results from personal recognition that one is competent, and that feeling is derived from actually

> **"** I gain strength, courage, and confidence by every experience in which I stop and look fear in the face. . . . I say to myself, I've lived through this and can take the next thing that comes along. . . . We must do the thing we think we cannot do. **"**
>
> *Eleanor Roosevelt*

behaving in a more skilled manner. By taking risks to overcome old patterns of behavior, even when the intended outcome isn't accomplished, one can develop more of the "I can do it" attitude. That feeling may be one of the keys to breaking the self-defeating cycle. It is even possible to give oneself positive feedback and rewards for just taking a risk, regardless of outcome, because that in itself is a change and constitutes new behavior.

Learned Helplessness

Many patterns of self-defeating behavior are the result of past experiences that made people feel as though they have little control over aversive situations. For years, Martin Seligman (1975) has done considerable research in the area of **learned helplessness.** The following example was presented in *Innovations Abstracts* (Vol. II, No. 25), a publication of the National Institute for Staff and Organizational Development at the University of Texas at Austin. It was written by John Rouche, the director of the Program in Community College Education:

> A dog is placed in a large experimental box. A current of electricity, painful but not physically harmful, jolts the animal. He moves about frantically for about thirty seconds then lies down, whines, and passively accepts the shock. He does not look for the escape route that is available. After a full minute, the shock is over. A second dog is placed in the same box. He, too, frantically tries to escape the shock but he keeps looking until he discovers the escape route and crosses the barrier to the shock-free side of the box.
>
> The difference? Before he was placed in the experimental box, the first dog had been strapped in a hammock and given shock that he couldn't control or avoid. The second dog was what researchers term naive. He had received no previous shock. The experiment suggested that it was the inability to control the shock that produced passivity. The lesson of

the learned helplessness findings, demonstrated in similar laboratory experiments, is that when an organism experiences trauma it can't control, its motivation to respond in the face of later trauma wanes.

This debilitation has been shown in various animals, as well as human beings. Later, when Seligman tried to rehabilitate the passive, helpless dog, a whole series of persuasive maneuvers failed. For example, they removed the barrier between compartments, making it easy for the dog to reach safety. The dog did not move. One experimenter stood on the box's safe side and called and coaxed the dog. He did not come. Food was placed on the safe side to tantalize him to safety, over and over again. Finally, after dragging the dog to the safe side as many as one hundred times, the dog began to respond. Fortunately, the animal's recovery was complete.

Applications for Human Behavior For people who have developed patterns of learned helplessness, the motivation to respond, especially in a new situation, is diminished to the point that they may no longer be willing to try. Even if there is a positive response to effort, the person who has learned to be helpless doesn't associate that response with a sense of relief. The ability to learn is disrupted because the person cannot determine if or when he or she has successfully responded to the environment. The emotions of the person are unnaturally heightened; he or she frequently loses touch with time and shows unhealthy forms of anxiety. Further attributes of learned helplessness are as follows:

▶ Passivity becomes characteristic behavior.
▶ Fatigue and isolation may accelerate feelings of helplessness.
▶ A feeling of lack of control in one situation is generalized to other situations, usually of lesser importance.
▶ If a task's importance is stressed, helplessness will increase (anxiety) when an uncontrollable element is introduced (pressure).

Solutions Having some sense of control over one's environment will counter the effects of learned helplessness. Therefore, anything that contributes to increasing a person's ability and belief that he or she can have an impact on his or her circumstances will be beneficial. Based on the curative methods Seligman and other therapists employed, useful suggestions for changing the effects of learned helplessness include some of the following:

▶ Attempt to make the learning environment different from the one where helplessness was learned.

> ❝Whatever you think you can do or believe you can do, begin it. Action has magic, grace, and power in it.❞
>
> *Goethe*

▶ Provide early successful learning experiences when trying out new behavior, but make sure they are not too easy: it is important to make the connection between effort and results.

▶ Get involved in settings with people who have a sense of control over their activities. Remember that time can dissipate the effects of past experiences. Visualize a different scenario from the one that has typically brought feelings of helplessness in the past.

Scientists believe that what gives us self-esteem, makes us feel competent, and protects us against depression is our perception that we can have some control over experiences. Anything that supports the notion that effort can lead to achievement helps to fight against the debilitating effects of learned helplessness.

Coping Strategies

Coping is the effort we make to manage a situation we have appraised as potentially harmful or stressful. This definition of coping (Lazarus and Folkman, 1984) has three main features:

1. It implies that coping involves active planning and effort.
2. The definition does not necessarily imply a positive outcome. Some responses may work, others may not.
3. The definition emphasizes coping as a process.

There are differences in how individuals cope, but learning coping skills is important for everyone. Coping is the process of managing difficult situations, working to solve personal problems, and learning to minimize, reduce, or tolerate stress. Distressful situations can be rendered less stressful when we cope with them.

There are two general forms of coping, according to Lazarus and Folkman: *problem-focused coping* and *emotion-focused coping*. Problem-focused coping strategies have to do with facing the trouble squarely and trying to change the situation. That may be accomplished by altering the situation, by influencing the behavior of others, or by changing attitudes, self-talk, and cognitive perceptions of the situation. Emotion-focused coping is oriented toward managing emotional distress. Positive aspects of emotion-focused coping strategies include expressing feelings, seeking support, using relaxation techniques, and doing physical exercise. The negative aspects include the typical patterns of avoidance, denial, and rationalization.

People are more likely to use problem-focused coping when they feel there is something they can do about the problem. When a problem seems beyond control, they are more inclined to rely on emotion-focused coping. In most distressful situations, it is probably best to use a combination of the two strategies.

For example, if a conflict occurs with someone at work, it might be important to consider problem-solving techniques and plans for compromise, such as finding out what the rules and guidelines are in the area of dispute, as well as using emotion-focused coping such as sharing feelings with your spouse or a friend. You might also need to be less defensive and focus on staying relaxed while discussing the problem.

Coping strategies can be categorized as *active-cognitive strategies*, *active-behavioral strategies*, and *avoidance strategies*. Active-cognitive strategies are coping responses in which individuals actively think about a situation in an effort to adjust more effectively. It means using logical reasoning for what has happened and what might need to be done to improve the situation. Active-behavioral strategies are coping responses in which individuals take some type of action to improve their problem. That means seeking help, gaining more information, or taking a different course of action entirely when the problem arises in the future. Both of these strategies are preferred over avoidance strategies, which often create new problems or make the original one worse (Simons, Kalichman, and Santrock, 1997).

> ❝Rather than being the illness, the symptoms are the beginning of its cure. The fact that they are unwanted makes them all the more a phenomenon of grace, a message to initiate self-examination and repair.❞
>
> *M. Scott Peck*

Specific Coping Skills

There are many coping skills that are applicable to a variety of stressful situations. The following general descriptions of coping skills (Kleinke, 1998) will be useful additions to your coping arsenal.

Use Support Systems A coping skill overlooked by many is the constructive use of a support system. Research shows that people with a good social support system are less depressed and anxious and more optimistic than those with a poor social support system. A social support system satisfies our needs for nurturance and attachment, relieves stress, and bolsters our sense of self-worth. It also provides emotional support (someone to confide in), tangible support (help with a job or a loan), and informational support (advice or feedback about a problem).

Having a strong support system has little to do with how many people you know and a lot to do with developing special relationships in which someone knows you and cares about you. Having a good support system is not related to being sociable and having many acquaintances. People who like to spend time alone can have an effective support system to use when they need it. Building a good support system is a coping skill because it requires personal effort. It is not very effective to wait until others figure out you need their support. You must be willing to take the initiative.

If friends and family are unable to provide the support you need, it is wise to seek help from a health care professional. Health care professionals are in a position to provide support without being emotionally drained. Unfortunately, many people don't appreciate the fact that getting support from health care professionals is a coping skill and not a sign of weakness.

Problem Solving Problem solving is the procedure we follow when developing plans for responding to a challenge. It is a practical coping skill, but it is also useful psychologically. The practice of good problem solving builds confidence. The following steps describe a problem-solving approach to a situation that requires coping skills:

1. *Self-perception:* Develop a self-perception that includes the ability to problem solve. This means saying to yourself, "I know that I have the ability to remain calm and rely on my problem-solving skills to decide on the best possible course of action."

2. *Defining the problem:* Take some time to figure out the critical issues and conflicts. Then make a list of goals.

3. *Listing options:* Write down every possible plan and allow yourself to be creative. Support people can help brainstorm and prevent your getting stuck on one track.

4. *Decision making:* If you have defined the problem and generated many alternatives, you are ready to decide on a course of action. Run through the possible responses. Which are the most feasible? Which are most likely to get you what you want without causing other problems? Remember, in most situations, there is not just one correct course of action.

5. *Testing:* If your first course of action achieves success, that is great. If not, it is time to work through the stages of problem solving again. Have you defined the problem correctly? Did you consider all possible alternatives? You need to open yourself to all options.

Self-Relaxation The relaxation response is made up of three components: environment, body, and mind (Benson, 1984):

1. *Environment:* The relaxation response is easiest to learn in a quiet environment. Place yourself in a comfortable posture in a place where there aren't too many distractions. As you improve your relaxation skills, you will find that you can relax in other places as well.

2. *Body:* When you practice relaxation, your body slows down. Start with slowing your breathing. Breathe deeply and slowly, hold, and exhale. Repeat this process for five minutes. After a few minutes of deep slow breathing, you will begin to feel more relaxed. Next, teach your body to relax by getting in touch with different muscle groups, and then systematically focus your attention on that part of your body and let go of any tension.

3. *Mind:* The relaxation response is enhanced when you distract yourself from daily thoughts and move into a relaxing frame of mind. As you do deep breathing and muscle relaxation, imagine you are in a special place, such as by a cool waterfall, on a warm beach near the ocean, or in a peaceful meadow. Use your mind power to enhance your feelings of peacefulness.

Talk Yourself Through It Many cognitive therapists believe that **cognitive restructuring** (changing thought processes) can get people to think more positively and optimistically. Self-talk is often helpful in cognitive restructuring. Because self-talk often becomes a **self-fulfilling prophecy,** unchecked negative thinking can spell trouble. That's why it is so important to monitor your self-talk and replace negative self-statements with positive ones. *Thought-stopping* is a specific self-control and cognitive restructuring strategy in which the individual says, "Stop!" when an unwanted thought occurs and then replaces it with a substitute thought that is more positive or useful. Make a list of things that would be useful to say to yourself during times of stress and that could help remind you to think positively. In preparing for a challenge, you might say to yourself: "I can handle this, I've been through tough times before"; "This, too, will pass—it's only temporary"; or "I don't need to upset myself, and it won't help to worry." When actually confronting a challenge or dealing with a stressful situation, you might tell yourself: "I won't let anger and anxiety get the best of me"; "If I act as if I'm in control, I'll feel that way"; or "Relax and concentrate on what you have to do." Remember to be easy on yourself as you learn new skills. Use challenges as opportunities to test your coping skills. Be willing to make mistakes. Don't force yourself to be perfect.

Reward Your Accomplishments   If you are making progress in dealing with difficult situations, make sure you acknowledge that to yourself. People are often too hard on themselves. If the world has presented you with a number of stressful situations to deal with, you certainly do not need to add to the load. In fact, you may be able to lighten the load some if you recognize that you are improving, and reward yourself. It is amazing how reluctant many people are to give themselves credit when they do something worthwhile that has required considerable effort. Of course, it is always nice to be acknowledged by others. But positive feedback from others is not always reliable. If you want to accomplish anything with consistency, you may need to reward yourself. The reward may take many forms. Remember, though, that you are the one who knows best what that reward should be.

Keep a Sense of Humor   Perhaps you can think of a time when you were having a problem, yet, a year later, that same situation seemed funny. What would you need to do to keep that perspective in the present when encountering a difficult situation? Looking at things in a slightly different manner may make it possible to see the humor in the situation. Humor helps us avoid jumping to conclusions and blowing things out of proportion. A sense of humor allows us to make more balanced and objective appraisals of a situation. It also has a favorable impact on the people around us. We receive a lot more cooperation and support from others when we are

> **"**Give a man a fish, and you feed him for a day. Teach a man to fish, and you feed him for a lifetime.**"**
>
> *Japanese proverb*

perceived as pleasant instead of as a grouch. Developing a sense of humor also boosts feelings of self-efficacy. A sense of humor encourages a creative rather than passive attitude toward life challenges.

Developing Self-Efficacy

Self-efficacy means that our responses to life challenges can have a meaningful effect and that we are confident about our ability to solve problems. It is helpful to have a good sense of internal control to use the previously listed coping skills. People with a strong sense of efficacy face the difficulties that life presents with energy and persistence. They keep trying new alternatives until they succeed or at least survive the situation. The people who cope the best often have the greatest number of skills available to them and believe that they can effectively implement those skills. We develop self-efficacy, in part, by having role models. We do it by observing how other people deal successfully with challenges and by the kinds of teaching and support we received as we were growing up. Self-efficacy is built up by responding to life challenges with action, flexibility, and persistence. Action is essential because we learn best by doing. Flexibility encourages us to try new alternatives and to avoid getting stuck. We might not always succeed, but persistence will give us an attitude of survival (Kleinke, 1998). The following suggestions (Bandura, 1977) are useful in developing a more confident approach to life:

1. Live a life of goals: Make it a practice to have goals and to give yourself credit when you achieve them.
2. Set goals with reasonable standards: They should be challenging enough to provide a feeling of satisfaction, but also realistic so you can reach them.
3. Talk to yourself in a positive manner: What you say to yourself really is important. It can influence your behavior.
4. Seek out good role models: Role models don't have to be people we know personally, but

they should be people who inspire a life attitude of competence and mastery.

5. Remember that success in reaching goals and overcoming life challenges depends on our willingness to expend the required energy and effort.

A coping attitude provides people with a heightened sense of competence and self-efficacy. And it requires personal energy. A coping attitude is a philosophy that says life will not always be the way we want it to be, but our coping skills will allow us to make the best of the situation.

Psychological Disorders

Numerous studies suggest that a great number of people will have some type of mental disorder to some degree. According to various estimates, between 30 and 45 percent of people will seek help with psychological problems at some time in their life. Although the most common psychological and behavioral problems originate with drug and alcohol addiction, that is beyond the scope of this chapter. But, it is important to understand and be able to identify certain disorders to better help yourself and/or others in times of need.

Anxiety Disorders: The anxiety disorders include generalized anxiety disorder, phobic disorder, panic disorder, and obsessive-compulsive disorder (OCD). These disorders have been linked to genetic predisposition, temperament, anxiety sensitivity, and neurochemical abnormalities in the brain.

Many anxiety responses, especially phobias, may be caused by classical conditioning and maintained by operant conditioning. Cognitive theorists maintain that some people are vulnerable to anxiety disorders because they see threat everywhere. Stress may also contribute to the onset of these disorders.

Mood Disorders: The principal mood disorders are major depressive disorder and bipolar disorder. People vary in their genetic vulnerability to mood disorders, which are accompanied by changes in neurochemical activity in the brain. Cognitive models suggest that a pessimistic explanatory style, rumination, and other types of negative thinking contribute to depression. Depression is often rooted in interpersonal inadequacies, as people who lack social finesse often have difficulty acquiring life's rewards. Mood disorders are sometimes stress related.

Eating Disorders: The principal eating disorders are anorexia nervosa and bulimia. Both reflect a morbid fear of gaining weight. Anorexia and bulimia are both associated with other psychological

problems, and both lead to a variety of medical problems. Eating disorders appear to be a product of modern, affluent, Westernized culture.

Schizophrenic Disorders: These disorders are characterized by deterioration of adaptive behavior, irrational thought, distorted perception, and disturbed mood. Schizophrenic disorders are classified as paranoid, catatonic, disorganized, or undifferentiated. Research has linked schizophrenia to genetic vulnerability, changes in neurotransmitter activity, and enlarged ventricles in the brain.

Attention Deficit Disorder

Attention deficit disorder (ADD/ADHD) is a common behavioral disorder. The acronym ADD is normally used whether or not hyperactivity is present. It is estimated that between 3 percent and 8 percent of all children have ADD. Boys are diagnosed with ADD more often than girls, although ADD is considered to be as prevalent in girls as it is in boys. One theory for this is that ADD (inattentive type) may be more prevalent in girls and is harder to diagnose than ADD with hyperactivity.

ADD is characterized by symptoms such as hyperactivity, impulsiveness, distractibility, and difficulty sustaining attention for periods of time. Symptoms may be different in each person with ADD. Some may have more of a problem with inability to focus, whereas others may have the most difficult time with impulsiveness. Still others may struggle with hyperactivity. All symptoms of ADD need not be present in order to have a diagnosis of ADD.

Children with ADD are often diagnosed after beginning school. This occurs because school may be the first environment where a child is expected to sit still for extended periods of time and sustain attention and focus. This does not mean that ADD occurs when a child reaches school age. ADD is present at birth and continues into adulthood. However, at home, or in environments where there is more flexibility, the symptoms of ADD may not be as prevalent, or they may be accepted by caregivers and therefore are not seen as impairment. Most parents of children with ADD, however, have noticed differences in their child from a very early age, even if ADD was not diagnosed until later.

A primary physician most often completes diagnosis of ADD. The physician will gather information from parents, teachers, and caregivers as well as an evaluation of the child to determine if ADD is present. There are a number of physical illnesses that can cause similar symptoms. The physician should rule these out as a cause of symptoms, as well as determine if behaviors are a result of psychological factors such as a move or a divorce in the family. There are currently no medical tests that will show whether ADD is present or not. The diagnosis is made based on the information the physician gathers, as well as the physician's personal evaluation.

Although the biological origins of ADD have not yet been determined, there is a strong suggestion of heredity. A great many children with ADD have a close family member with ADD as well. There are theories that link smoking during pregnancy, low birth weight, and premature birth to ADD, but there has been no definitive proof to substantiate these theories. Research on the brain has shown that some areas of the brain can be up to 10 percent smaller in individuals with ADD; however, ADD does not affect intelligence.

Once a diagnosis is made, your doctor should work with you on developing a treatment plan. ADD is not curable, but with treatment those with ADD can live productive lives. Treatment usually involves behavioral therapy and, if needed, medications. Your doctor will help you determine what course of treatment is best for you.

Help for the Newly Diagnosed ADD Adult A diagnosis of ADD/ADHD in adulthood can be confusing. There are often periods of denial, confusion and not knowing what to do or where to turn. Some people have been compensating in numerous ways, often quite successfully, and are surprised that they get feedback that they may need help. For adults, and especially students, sometimes the limiting aspects of ADD are only apparent when the challenge or task is so difficult that the need for being organized and methodical becomes imperative.

Steps for Dealing with ADD

Step 1: Identify and accept your diagnosis. Get past years of not knowing what is wrong . . . the hurtful feelings. . . . the hole in your spirit that is filled with remorse/pity/shame of not measuring up to others' expectations. Start to put this behind you as you move forward to a new life. Realize that you have built an identity of yourself based on these negative feelings and your belief in your inadequacies. Without them you have no foundation for your identity.

Step 2: Accept that a diagnosis does not "fix" anything. Accept that once you have isolated ADD, you must work at corrections. A diagnosis is simply that, a diagnosis; it does not make anything better, nor does it make anything worse. It is the first step in a long journey toward creating a more positive life for yourself.

Step 3: Make a list of what your good traits are. You will need this for perceptive balance. If you come up short, get some help from those people close to you who *are* supportive. Make several copies of this list and keep one with you to read often. Tape a copy on your mirror. Once you have entered a journey to change your self-image, you will need to continually remind yourself of the positive aspects of your personality.

Step 4: Make the list of those things you are painfully aware of. These are the things that you have always been unable to do to your or others' satisfaction. When are the times when the difficulty of paying attention to details, staying with it until completion, being methodical and systematic have been a problem for you?

Step 5: Notice some of the things on both lists are the same human trait. They are just "two sides of the coin."

Step 6: Begin with those traits that appear on both lists. Understand that each one has both positive and negative qualities and benefits. Some may have negative outcomes in some situations, yet have positive outcomes in other situations.

Step 7: Start putting yourself in situations where you can increase your chance of success. Note that you must show that you believe in yourself, before you can expect anyone else to believe in you. Play to your strengths. There are numerous jobs where having high energy and the ability to deal with a number of things at once would be considered skills.

Step 8: Accept that those exposed to your past may not be willing to accept that you have changed at first. Some of your negative habits may have created difficulty for those around you, and it may take some time until they see results. Be patient, but do not allow their negativity to bring you down or stop you from moving forward.

Step 9: Use these small incremental victories. Go back to your list of positive traits and add some more from the perspective of the better, more balanced footing you have now.

Step 10: Realize that you cannot completely eliminate ADD. However, you can keep it in check, keep a balanced emotional footing, and manage symptoms of ADD so you can have a enjoyable life.

Step 11: Chart/take note of your progress. Feel good about this improvement. Stay focused: Years of negative feelings and not understanding or accepting yourself will not be improved overnight. Give yourself time, stay focused, and watch your self-image improve. Only with more effort can negativity be reduced to a manageable level.

Step 12: Do whatever it takes to enjoy your life. Don't try to live up to others' expectations or your perception of their expectations. Only your realistic goals based on this newfound realization of your situation are important. Over time those people who matter to you will come around to understanding you, if they are worth being with.

Components of Change

There are many ways to explore the process of change and many methods for accomplishing change. Self-help books often give information that is useful in thinking about what to do to make changes in your life. But if information alone did the trick, there would probably be fewer counselors and therapists. Other books offer guidelines for using the relevant information about the changes that you might want to make. Yet, even with the appropriate information and suggestions on how to implement it, many people find it difficult to accomplish their goals for behavioral change. What is needed, perhaps, is the next level of instruction on how to use or implement the guidelines—how to motivate yourself, how to develop a plan of action, and how to eliminate self-defeating behavior. I have developed the following formula, which should be helpful in accomplishing those objectives.

Let's take that formula step by step and explore its usefulness in accomplishing the change you would like to make. First, to have a goal for change to use in this formula, consider the following questions:

1. Is there something you do that you wish you didn't do? What do you need to start doing to stop that behavior? Considering the next question will help you find a goal that can be stated in the positive (what you want rather than what you don't want).
2. Is there something that you wish you knew how to do? What do you need to start doing to be able to learn that behavior?

Whether the change that you want to make is to start or stop some behavior, in both instances, you can develop a goal that can be stated in the positive. With the answers to these questions, you can begin to formulate a goal while considering the following explanation.

Goal (A)

What do you want? The first step in accomplishing a change is to determine your goal and clarify what you want. This may sound rather simplistic, but often people underestimate the complexities of selecting the right goal to work toward. The goal needs to be one that actually accomplishes the desired outcome. I frequently have worked with people who have a goal that doesn't really get them what they want and may in fact prevent them from getting it.

I once had a client who said he wanted to stop smoking. On further exploration of the problem, it became apparent that the real problem was that he was lonely. The only way he knew of making friends was to hang out with the group of people who smoked outside the building at work. It was a risk-free situation where the only requirement for being accepted into the group was to have a cigarette. Once his real goals were addressed—increasing self-esteem, developing social skills, becoming more assertive, and developing interests and hobbies—he began to make more friends and got what he wanted. Subsequently, he stopped smoking with minimal effort.

The goal must also be something that can be maintained by the person desiring the change. It is not an appropriate goal to get your ex-spouse to be different. It might be very useful—with past or present spouses—to have a goal of maintaining emotional control, being patient and forgiving, or not getting into useless arguments. Those are all behaviors that you have some control over.

Most goals that are appropriate for change are specific behaviors that can be observed and/or measured to some degree. It is better to have a specific behavior in mind than to try to change a general state of being. For instance, it is better to think of an action that can be taken, one that will increase the likelihood of our being happier, than to just have a general goal of enjoying life more.

Goal		Resources		Motivation		Objections	Self-Defeating Behavior		Positive Intention		Purpose		
[A	+	B	+	C]	−	[D	+	E]	+	F	+	G	=	Change
What you want		What it takes		What drives you		Fear of attaining goal	Payoff for sidetracking		Provide safety		Provide reason			

Questions for Critical Thinking

What would you like to start doing? What would you like to stop doing? Or, what would you need to start doing to stop a particular behavior? What is your goal for making a change in behavior?

A _____

_____

_____

_____

_____

_____

_____

_____

_____

Questions for Critical Thinking

What would it take to accomplish your goal for change that you wrote about in the last response?

B _____

_____

_____

_____

_____

_____

_____

_____

_____

The goal needs to be realistic and established at an attainable level. Some people set themselves up for failure by deciding they want to be a brain surgeon when they have just returned to college after 10 years away from school. Other people set goals so low that accomplishing them provides little satisfaction or real change.

Resources (B)

What does it take to get what you want? Developing the resources necessary for accomplishing the change you want to make means gathering information, developing support, and beginning to imagine how you would have to be different to accomplish the intended change. Most people have actually had some experience being how they would like to be, but want to increase how often they behave in that desired manner. For example, the person who wants to control her temper has most likely had times when she behaved in an appropriate manner. The goal may be to remember to be that way more often. Some people need to have a particular skill that they may never have demonstrated, at least not to their knowledge. In that case, one might develop a resource by noticing who the people are who have that skill or ability. It is even useful at times to draw on any and all models for a particular behavior—alive,

dead, or imaginary. Many people have an imaginary source that they can draw on at times for power and inspiration.

Motivation (C)

What drives you? In other words, what does it take to get yourself to do what is needed to get what you want? Why is it that sometimes you can get yourself to use the resources you know you have and other times you can't? Many people report that they know what they want, know what it takes to get it, and even have experiences of being self-motivated enough to take action—about half the time.

When working with people making changes, I often hear the question, "If I know what I want and how to get it, why do I still screw up so often? Why can't I be the way I want all the time?" The answer often lies in the unexplored beliefs of the person, where there are objections to making a change. Before exploring that idea, reflect on how you have motivated yourself in the past.

Sometimes it is helpful to remember that *nobody does anything for nothing.* That means there is usually a reason for not doing something that you say you want to do, especially when you know what it takes and have even done the behavior before. There is usually a payoff for most behaviors, but that doesn't necessarily mean that it is positive. The implication of the term *payoff* is that there is usually some side benefit, even to apparently negative behavior. Some people believe that messing up in some way may even prevent something worse from happening. In that way, messing up has the *payoff* of protection and safety.

I often see examples of that type of behavior in the college setting. A student says that she wants to get good grades. Maybe she has a goal of getting an A in a certain class. The real goal, then, is doing the particular behaviors that would accomplish that goal, namely, studying and preparing for tests. Yet, the student reports frequently procrastinating at study time, skipping classes, and partying the night before an exam. The student may be receiving any number of payoffs for her behavior. Perhaps she can lower others' expectations and relieve the pressure she puts on herself if she doesn't get an A for the course. Maybe, depending on her beliefs, others will like her more if she doesn't act like a bookworm. Some students even sabotage their own efforts, thinking that it will provide an excuse to drop out or get back at their parents for making them enroll in the first place.

The way to increase motivation often comes from exploring the part of you that doesn't want to accomplish a task, as well as looking at the part that does want to do it. In the previous case, the person needed to find out what part of her objected to getting good grades before being able to make the change to being a better student.

People invest large amounts of money and spend countless hours in seminars, workshops, and counseling and still have difficulty making changes. They have the ABCs and still haven't accomplished the desired results. Sometimes, the answer lies in their fears about the intended change in behavior. For some people, no amount of information is going to make a difference until they get rid of their objections to the change. Therefore, let's examine how to eliminate (subtract) the objections, and the resulting self-defeating behaviors, in the formula presented.

Objections (D)

What part of you doesn't want to change? Most of us have some degree of reservation when it comes to accomplishing a goal that requires a level of personal change. If an intended change creates too much fear, we may express that by exhibiting self-defeating behaviors. We are never more creative than when trying to find ways to avoid what we expect will be unpleasant experiences. If

Questions for Critical Thinking

What do you do to motivate yourself to use the resources you have when making a change? How have you been successful in the past?

C _____

_____

_____

_____

_____

_____

_____

_____

_____

_____

you seem to be shooting yourself in the foot while trying to accomplish something that you want, perhaps it is time to look more closely at the underlying fear and determine what the payoff might be for the self-defeating behavior.

Think of a time when you made a change without much difficulty. When there really are no concerns or objections to making a change, don't you just go ahead and do it? I have heard countless stories of people who reached a point when they were just tired and fed up with their old patterns and made significant changes without much fuss. We usually have to get rid of the objections first, though, to limit any further sabotage of the original goal. This may be more readily accomplished by attending to the concerns or fears rather than ignoring them.

Self-Defeating Behavior (E)

What is it that you don't have to do if you sabotage your efforts toward your goal? What is it that you are afraid will happen if you did reach it? These questions are useful in exploring what would need to change to accomplish the original goal (A) or behavioral change. I often hear in counseling sessions that people are afraid of change itself. Some think that, by sabotaging their efforts to change, they can maintain some aspect of their belief system and, therefore,

Questions for Critical Thinking

What are your fears, and resulting objections, about making the proposed change?

D_____

_____

_____

_____

_____

_____

_____

_____

Questions for Critical Thinking

What self-defeating behaviors interfere with accomplishing your goal for change? What is the payoff for sabotaging the process?

E_____

_____

_____

_____

_____

_____

_____

_____

_____

maintain their comfort zone. People will go to incredible lengths, at times, to avoid challenging some perception about the world. Never underestimate the power of beliefs! The paradox is that there is usually a positive intention behind the payoff that comes from the self-defeating behavior. Many people feel that by not having to change, they are actually providing some degree of safety from whatever negative things might occur if they were to act differently.

For example, a woman came to counseling for help with losing weight. She said she knew what she wanted, knew how to accomplish it, and had done so many times in the past. Real change for her occurred only when she began to explore what part of her didn't want to lose weight. She had many reasons for changing, but had never thought to explore the part of her that had objections to doing so. As she thought about what would happen if she were to attain her desired appearance, she got in touch with the part of herself that was afraid of having to date and deal with relationships with men. Her self-defeating behaviors surrounding weight loss provided the payoff of not having to deal with the perceived complications and resulting fears about dating. She also believed that if she stayed overweight, she could protect herself from any rejection that might come after a relationship had started. And, if she never even got into a relationship, she could also avoid having to deal with sexuality.

Therefore, her objections (to attaining the goal of weight loss) were due to fear of having to deal with men, dating, and possible sexual relations. That set of concerns led to self-defeating behavior (weight gain) for the payoff of avoiding relationships and sexuality. And that was accomplished with the positive intention, on a previously unconscious level, of providing a sense of comfort and safety. Incidentally, that whole cycle served to maintain her belief system about men, sex, relationships, and her own position in the world.

Positive Intention (F)

While thinking about the objections and self-defeating behavior (D and E) that need to be subtracted from the process, consider what you might want to keep. Is there anything useful about what you are doing? Do you believe what you are doing might protect you from consequences that could be worse if you were to proceed toward your goal? It is ironic that so many negative behaviors and patterns are actually done with the best of intentions.

Many people do things they might know aren't in their best interest, but they feel that, on another level, those behaviors may be ensuring their very survival. The person who gets angry and keeps people at a distance may think that he is protecting himself from being rejected. The person who does harm to herself by never speaking up or taking care of her own needs may believe that she is protecting herself from harm by someone else. The person who denies that a problem even exists may believe that the problem will just go away and life will get better. Many people involved in all forms of addictive behavior are trying to relieve some type of pain. What they are doing usually doesn't work, and may even make things worse, but their behavior is often directed toward accomplishing a positive intention.

The trick, then, is to develop alternatives that will accomplish the same positive intention as the behavior that may be creating difficulty and that needs to be replaced. When people have new choices that will work as well as, or better than, what they have been trying in the past, they are usually more inclined to change. The process of change frequently begins when people become fully aware that what they are doing, even with the best of intentions, doesn't work. At that point, after identifying what the negative behavior was meant to accomplish, they are free to explore and develop alternative means of accomplishing the same ends in a different manner. While subtracting the objections and self-defeating behavior (D and E) from the equation, it is important to keep the positive intention of those patterns.

People usually need new choices to be willing to change. People who have alternatives of their own design for handling unpleasant emotions or situations are less inclined toward addictive or self-destructive behavior. Often, the new choices necessary to accomplish the positive intention of negative behavior patterns become a goal to replace the original one.

For example, consider the following scenario: John had been feeling depressed and had withdrawn and become numb to the world. He wanted to change that situation, and he came to counseling with the goal of feeling better. He stated that he had been under pressure at home and at work. As we began to explore the various situations and how he was coping with the problems, John discovered that he knew what he wanted and had a goal (A) of being more engaged in life—his phrase for being happier and more connected and actively solving problems. He also had the resources (B) and knew what it would take to move in the direction of his goal. There were times in his past when he had been in similar situations, and he had been able to do what was necessary to get motivated (C) and take action. Before he could change, though, he needed to explore his objections (D) to changing and do something new. In John's case, part of him was afraid that if he started to deal with other people in the

problem situations, he would be "sucked dry" and left depleted of what little energy he had.

Therefore, the self-defeating behavior (E) that he used was to become numb in an attempt to avoid any further drain on his energy. This behavior was an attempt at self-preservation and had the payoff of having people leave him alone. The difficulty was that the strategy wasn't taking care of any of the problems. John had been reluctant to try to accomplish his goal because of his belief that being numb was protecting him from being overwhelmed and further drained of energy. Once he became aware of that, he could begin exploring other means of accomplishing that positive intention (F) of protection that was behind the behavior of being numb. At that point, his original goal began to change. His new goal became developing a means of providing protection for his limited energy supply. After addressing (D) and (E) to reduce (subtract) those behaviors, he was able to generate new alternatives for accomplishing (F), which included asking for what he needed in order to provide more energy in his life, setting limits on the time he was available to other people for problem solving, and giving

---

Questions for Critical Thinking

What are three new methods of fulfilling the positive intention of the objections and self-defeating behavior (D and E)? Imagine what you would look like, how you would sound, and how you would feel in each of the three choices. Make sure that each choice will work equally well, or better, in fulfilling the positive intention of the objections and self-defeating behavior (D and E).

*F*_____

_____

_____

_____

_____

_____

_____

_____

_____

himself permission not to act immediately on any given solution to a problem. He acknowledged that all of these choices were better than what he had been doing in the past. As he began to take care of himself in appropriate ways, he found that he had energy to solve many problems without having to withdraw.

Purpose (G)

The last part of the formula for change incorporates the importance of a reason for making the effort to be different. Many people need a reason beyond the scope of their own needs to encounter the challenge of changing some aspect of their lives. It may be useful to consider how others (family, friends, coworkers, or people in the community) would benefit from the change that you would like to make. Also, keep in mind that if you are changing to meet someone else's approval, you may be undermining your efforts. If you are changing because some part of you has been hounding you about what you should do, you may be reactivating the objections to changing. This formula is fairly complex, but well worth understanding. It provides an opportunity to explore self-generated solutions to any number of situations that a person may want to change. It might be beneficial to read this section again, now that you have covered all the steps, with

---

Questions for Critical Thinking

What is the big picture for your proposed change? What is the reason for changing, and how can that change give meaning to your life?

G _____

_____

_____

_____

_____

_____

_____

_____

_____

_____

---

another specific change in mind. Plug in content for each step of the formula that is applicable to your life. Using a pertinent topic should facilitate greater understanding of how the steps progress.

A Model for Change

James Prochaska and Carlo Diclemente (1995) developed a model of change that is unique in many ways. First, it is empirically driven. In other words, it is based on the researchers' scientific investigation of change in humans. Second, the model conceptualizes change as entailing a number of stages that all require alterations in attitude in order to progress. Third, the model depicts change as a cycle—as opposed to an all-or-nothing step. The authors contend that it is quite normal for people to require several trips through the stages to make lasting change. So in this sense relapse is viewed as a normal part of the change process, as opposed to a complete failure. This does not mean that relapse is desirable or even invariably expected. It simply means that change is difficult, and it is unreasonable to expect everyone to be able to modify a habit perfectly with out any slips.

A study by behavioral scientists on how people change to improve their behavior resulted in the concept that there are six definite stages in behavior modification. These observed stages of change in a person are:

1. Precontemplation.
2. Contemplation.
3. Preparation.
4. Action.
5. Maintenance.
6. Termination.

Understanding these stages and using the appropriate change process is considered a highly effective technique to help solve problems and improve a person's behavior.

Various psychotherapies can be used to modify or improve the behavior of people with problems. Most are mildly effective. Of these psychotherapy strategies, specific ones can be used in the various stages to more effectively improve the behavior of an individual.

1. *Precontemplation stage:* Precontemplation is a situation where the person can't see a problem, so he or she doesn't consider the need for a solution. People in this stage have no intention of changing their behavior and even deny having a problem, even though

SIX STAGES FOR IMPROVING HUMAN BEHAVIOR: MINIQUIZ TO CHECK YOUR UNDERSTANDING*

1. What is an example of a person in the preparation stage of change?

   I'm fine, but you have problems coping with me.
   I give myself a treat when see an improvement.
   I'm planning on quitting smoking soon.

2. Why is a public commitment more powerful than the private decision?

   There is social pressure to prove yourself.
   It is the other way around.
   You will get rewards from your friends for good intentions.

3. What environmental control can be used to help you stay on your diet?

   Reduce pollution caused by excess eating.
   A warning sign on the refrigerator.
   Environmental controls are only used in the pre-contemplation stage.

If you got all three correct, you are on your way to becoming a champion in understanding behavior. If you had problems, you had better look over the material again.

Source: Ron Kurtus, Internet posting, May 8, 2005.

others may complain about it. They resist change and would rather have those around them change.

An example is an alcoholic who would rather lose his family than stop drinking. Another situation is where peers may encourage cheating or stealing, causing the person to believe that is the correct way to behave.

2. *Contemplation stage:* People in the contemplation stage admit they have a problem and would like to change, but they aren't ready to make a commitment. They think about it but don't act.

Emotional arousal and giving a strong argument for the need to change can sometimes help move these people.

3. *Preparation stage:* People in the preparation stage are planning on taking action soon. They are committed to action, but they still may need to convince themselves that taking action is the best for them. They may have already started changing their behavior with small steps, but they still need some careful planning before taking full action.

Some preparation changes that can be made are that of improving the level of awareness, emotions, self-image, and thinking. These will lead up to changing the behavior.

4. *Action stage:* In the action stage, people modify their behavior and their surroundings. This is the most visible and requires the most commitment of time and energy.

5. *Maintenance stage:* There is a struggle to maintain the gains made in the action stage to prevent lapses. Maintenance is a long and ongoing process, and there is a fight not to give in to temptation to go back to the old ways.

6. *Termination stage:* The behavior is completely changed and the person has confidence that he or she is not threatened by temptation. In such a situation, a person may no longer crave cigarettes or have uncontrollable anger fits.

Source: Adapted from Robert Westermeyer. See above.

Stress Management

There is a saying: "If the world gives you lemons, make lemonade." Actually, that's pretty good advice. But how do you do it? Some people seem to have the recipe, but others don't have a clue. One of the ingredients is found in the definition of stress and how to cope with it. Some people define *anxiety* as fear, whereas others experience it as motivation. People who can make lemonade are usually able to think under pressure and become very resourceful when the lemons start piling up. This section deals with the following topics:

1. Identifying and utilizing anxiety.
2. Identifying internal strategies that produce pleasant or unpleasant experiences.
3. Developing strengths and resources.

These three elements can combine to help you maintain balance in your life.

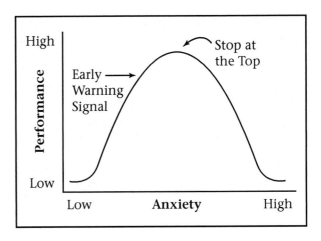

Anxiety

Anxiety is necessary in life. If people didn't have any worries, they probably would never get out of bed. A little anxiety can produce motivation and enhance performance; too much can be immobilizing. Students who feel no anxiety about taking a midterm exam without having opened a textbook might benefit from a little anxiety. Other students study so hard that they walk in and forget half of what they know because they are so concerned. Anxiety itself isn't the culprit; it is more a matter of how much you have and how you use it.

A frequent topic of research is the relationship between anxiety and performance when applied to particular tasks. There is a point that produces an optimal level of performance, and if stress increases beyond that point, the performance level drops (this is called the *Yerkes-Dodson law*). This is the basis for the concept that I call "Stop at the Top." It means being concerned enough to put forth your best effort, while being aware that any more pressure will result in a decrease of abilities. It is crucial to be able to tell when you are at that point of optimal performance and when pushing harder will end only in decreased results. Most of us at some time have pushed ourselves to the point of working twice as hard but getting only half the results.

It is important to know when you reach or pass that point. For example, if you are sitting in your car at the stop sign, it may be beneficial to put your foot to the floor to get moving. The same behavior that helped you accelerate may create difficulties, though, if at some point you don't modify it. If you still have your foot to the floor and you are doing 90 mph, even on the freeway you will probably be in big trouble.

One way of recognizing that point of diminishing returns is to pay attention to early warning signals that serve to alert you that you are on

overload and that it is time to back off a bit and slow down. Just as anxiety can be useful as a motivator, pain can be useful as an early warning signal. Pain can be a friend if you recognize it as a warning to relax and lower your stress level. Some people get overstressed and burn out because they don't pay attention to the signs. Your body usually sends out numerous signals when you are reaching the Stop at the Top point, the place where you should begin to slow down. Those signals can come as physical tension in the body, little internal voices warning of the outcome of continuing a current lifestyle, or brief mental glimpses of what might really be happening to you. Honor your body and pay attention to the signals. There is ample medical evidence about people who ignored their pain for years and paid a high price for it. So, to Stop at the Top, you need to pay attention to your early warning signals and stay in the range of optimal performance.

Internal Strategies

Whoever said "It's not what happens to you that counts, but what you think about what happens" made an accurate statement about how we create stress. What you think when using your internal voices and mental images plays a large part in how you feel. What you feel affects the level of stress experienced in any given situation, and the level of stress experienced influences behavior. Your behavior and its consequences then have a bearing on your thoughts. At that point, the cycle becomes self-perpetuating. One way to interrupt that cycle is to change your thought patterns. Changing what you hear and see, and even your interpretation of the situation, can change your feelings, thereby lessening the degree of stress you feel.

As an example of how thinking about a situation affects the amount of stress experienced, consider the following: Have you ever gotten totally upset over some insignificant event, yet stayed calm when a major crisis took place in your life? You have probably had one of those days when you became extremely distraught and more emotional than necessary at not being able to find the car keys. Yet, on another day when you didn't have the luxury of emotional indulgence, you set your feelings aside and coped with the situation to resolve a crisis. Did the difference in reactions have anything to do with your emotional state at the time of each event? How were your emotions affected by your thoughts before and during each of the events? A person who is thinking negative thoughts or is in a bad mood is more likely to become stressed out at one of life's little irritants, whereas a person facing a major problem may focus on handling the immediate needs and then talk to himself or herself about generally making things better in the future.

Now, let's connect the idea of thought processes with the concept of associating and dissociating. Some people replay an unfortunate incident a hundred times in their minds, stepping into it and intensifying the feelings each time. Those feelings then influence their images of future happenings, which are usually visualized as being even worse. That kind of thinking, sometimes called *catastrophic thinking*, influences behavior and usually reduces our capacity to deal with the stress head-on as well as our overall level of functioning. This can leave us feeling immobilized, which in turn leads to a cycle of self-fulfilling prophecies.

Contrast that with those who step out of a situation and look for what they need to learn from the situation. They imagine what they need to do in the future to make things better, step into that situation, and then become fully associated with the experience of doing what will correct that old event from the past. What you step into and what you step out of will make a major difference in the amount of stress in your life.

Replaying a stressful event over and over in your mind, whether it has actually happened or not, is usually counterproductive and only increases worry and anxiety. Focusing on the future and what needs to occur for things to work out better usually leads to a reduction in stress; it also empowers the person to deal with stress as it arises, rather than avoiding it. The people who are overstressed and who burn out are usually the ones who are associated while experiencing difficulty and dissociated from the solution. A better coping strategy is to dissociate from the difficult situations and then fully experience acting on the future solutions.

Strengths and Resources

The next step in the process of managing stress is creating and maintaining a state of resourcefulness in the proper context. This means (a) paying attention to your early warning signals so that you can Stop at the Top and use your energy to be productive and (b) increasing positive feelings by being associated with the desired end result or solution. When you reach the crossroad in life representing a choice between an old behavior that doesn't work and a new behavior that might, you need to be able to remember these two points. Doing so will require energy and being resourceful.

Here is an opportunity to practice. To begin creating the experience of making good decisions, think of a time when you were at that choice point and did the right thing. Now think of a time when you went down the same old road that wasn't productive. What was the difference in those two situations? That difference can be a clue to creating the mental attitude that will help in the future.

Building on that idea, think of a time when you were feeling strong and competent. Remember all the details of what you were seeing, hearing, and feeling in that situation. What signal will trigger remembering all of that when you need it? Now remember an exciting moment when you were feeling especially alive and creative. Stack both of those memories on top of each other and allow yourself to fully incorporate the experience. Do you feel some of the energy that may be useful in dealing with future situations? What will be your signal—a feeling or sensation, something you say to yourself, or a visual image—to remember what you just did? Call this your "competence cue."

Practice the application of that by imagining a time in the future when you might be under stress. Pay attention to the signal that will remind you to be how you want to be in that situation. Call up your competence cue, and take the right road at the choice point and fully experience the situation as you go through it in a manner that makes you feel satisfied with the results. Notice what you learned from that experience, and repeat the situation as often as needed to feel confident that you will remain resourceful in the future.

Physiology of Stress

Hans Selye (1974) was a physician who made the observation that patients who were under prolonged psychological stress all developed a similar cluster of symptoms. It did not seem to matter whether they were male or female, child or adult, physically well or ill; these patients experienced a loss of appetite, muscular weakness, and decreased interest in the rest of the world. Selye concluded that any number of environmental events can produce this stress response in the body.

The general adaptation syndrome (GAS) is Selye's theory for describing the common effects on the body when demands are placed on it. The GAS consists of three stages: alarm, resistance, and exhaustion. In the alarm stage, the body enters a temporary state of shock, a time when resistance to stress is below normal. The body detects the stress and tries to eliminate it. The body loses muscle tone, temperature decreases, and blood pressure drops. Then, a rebound called *countershock* occurs, in which resistance to stress begins to pick up; the adrenal cortex enlarges, and hormone release increases. After a short alarm stage, the individual enters the resistance stage, which is an all-out effort to combat stress. Hormones flood the body; blood pressure, heart rate, temperature, and respiration all skyrocket, but the body can only sustain this level of internal activity for so long. If the all-out effort fails and the stress persists, the individual moves into the exhaustion stage. Now the wear and tear on the body takes its toll. The person may collapse in a state of exhaustion, and vulnerability to disease increases (Simons, Kalichman, and Santrock, 1997).

Researchers now believe that the link between chronic stress and the onset of illness is a weakened immune system. This susceptibility to disease has been proven experimentally. In one study individuals undergoing prolonged stress (i.e., greater than one month) were deliberately exposed to a virus, as was a control group of subjects who had not experienced chronic stress. The researchers found that those subjects in the "prolonged stress group" not only became infected with the virus more often than the control group of "nonstressers," but they also took longer to recover (Cohen, 1998). This same phenomenon has been observed in rats with cancer. Visintainer (1982) found that when stress is chronic, and perceived as inescapable, the mortality rate from cancer was much higher than in nonstress control groups.

The GAS applies to both short-term and long-term stressors, although as just shown, long-term stressors have a more deleterious effect on the body. Our GAS can effectively get us through stressors for quite a long time, but it has its limits. Eventually, extended stress breaks down the body—which in turn affects behavior. To understand the human response to stress, a person's physical reactions to the stress, their personality, their physical makeup, their perceptions, and the context in which the stressors occurs must be taken in account.

Type A Behavior   Some people seem to create much of the stress they experience by their beliefs, self-talk, and behavior. Friedman and Rosenman (1974) studied the personality of the people, which they call **Type A,** whose behavior leads to a stressful lifestyle with the possible increase in coronary disease. Researcher are now implicating stress as a possible factor in diseases such as cancer, multiple sclerosis, several chronic gastrointestinal disorders, and many autoimmune disorders. The primary characteristics of the Type A personality are time urgency, a preoccupation with productivity and achievement, perfection, a chronic activation, and a competitive drive. These people seem to be constantly in a hurry, are frequently trying to do several things at a time, and are impatient. Typically, people with the Type A behavior pattern overschedule activities and then become tense when they don't complete the unrealistic tasks they have set for themselves. By assuming too many responsibilities, they become trapped in several stressful situations at once and do not know how to get out of them, which only further contributes to their sense of being overwhelmed.

Recently, research has begun to suggest that it is not just the behaviors alone that cause the increase in physical problems. Many people are highly driven and/or need to be involved in a number of activities at once. The difficulty in coping with that type of lifestyle seems to come into play when a great deal of suppressed and/or unexpressed anger is also present. Some researchers say it is the hostility aspect of anger that is the problem (Miller et al., 1996; Siegman and Smith, 1994). In fact, Siegman went so far to say that the combination of anger and hostility "can be lethal," possibly causing cardiovascular disease.

Type B Behavior   The best long-range way to deal constructively with stress is to make substantial changes in your way of living. In many ways, the **Type B** personality is the opposite of the Type A orientation. Type Bs are not slaves of

FIVE WAYS TO FACE DOWN STRESS

Discipline may be the key to developing greater stamina in the face of stress. The following five disciplines are a way to face down the effects of stress:

1. *Discipline of accepting incompleteness:* Work on accepting life with its loose ends. Don't be obsessed with perfection.
2. *Discipline of falling forward:* Rather than retreat in the face of failure, try to grow in response to it.
3. *Discipline of serving others:* Do something for someone else, and you'll quickly feel restored.
4. *Discipline of patience:* You can only conquer your problems one at a time. Don't overwhelm yourself.
5. *Discipline of giving yourself to what's at hand:* Work on what's in front of you today. It's vital to laying a solid foundation for your work tomorrow.

Source: Ralph LaForge, *Executive Health Report.*

time and are not preoccupied with achievements and aggressive competition. When they work, they do so in a calm and unhurried manner. They are able to relax and have fun without feeling guilty. They are able to play without the need to win at any cost. Transforming yourself from a Type A personality entails learning a balance in life, especially a balance between work and play. It involves changing attitudes and beliefs so that you do not react so intensely to situations and thus cause stress. Most of all, it requires that you accept full responsibility for how you are living.

Type C Behavior   Although a fairly new concept, Type C behavior may begin to receive as much attention as Type A behavior. **Type C** refers to people with a cancer-prone personality, which consists of being inhibited, uptight, emotionally inexpressive, and otherwise constrained. This type of individual is more likely to develop cancer than are emotionally expressive people (Temoshok and Dresher, 1992). The concept of Type C behavior fits with the discussion about different aspects of Type A behavior. Many people who are highly competitive and driven don't develop heart disease. Current research seems to support the notion that hostility may be a more precise link with coronary risk for Type A behavior. Likewise, the concept of Type C behavior fits with stress and health researchers'

findings that being inhibited and unwilling to talk about problems can be an impairment to health.

Conflict Management

Notice that this section is entitled *conflict management,* not *conflict avoidance* or *conflict resolution.* Conflict is a part of life; it will show up at work, with your friends, and most certainly in domestic relations with your spouse and children. Conflict is not always negative. It can be useful at times, because it can raise issues that need to be dealt with for things to run smoothly.

The fact that a couple hasn't argued in 10 years doesn't necessarily mean that they have a good relationship. Sometimes, a relationship evolves in a healthy manner only when all the cards are laid on the table. Some businesses have failed because the partners didn't want to upset each other by bringing up details they thought were being overlooked. Government is fraught with examples of **group think**—when people go along with a bad decision because it is politically expedient and they want to cover their rears. Being nice isn't always helpful. (Where are the devil's advocates when you need them?)

Assertiveness (covered previously) is an essential part of conflict management skills. Acquiescing

doesn't mean that the problem has been taken care of; most likely, it will surface again. For two parties to negotiate, both have to be willing to state their goals and objectives.

Here is an example: John and Mary are having a heated argument about whose turn it is to take out the garbage. Each one escalates the argument and points out flaws in the other's mental capacities and memory. Suddenly, John (it could as easily be Mary) has a blinding flash of insight as he remembers a piece of the puzzle and realizes that he is the one who is wrong. What does he do then? He argues even harder or louder. Or, if need be, he changes direction in the middle of it all and tries to shift the argument to a subject he is right about. Sound familiar? It's called *kitchen sink fighting* because the object is not to resolve anything but to throw in whatever you need so you can be right.

What was really going on in this example? Perhaps the argument was really about needing attention or being appreciated. Perhaps one or the other was feeling resentful about a perceived inequity in the workload of domestic chores. Maybe the argument was really a smoke screen for issues about money, sex, or dealing with relatives. The point is, it is difficult to resolve a conflict if the real issues aren't on the table. Another complicating factor has to do with what happens when one person realizes that perhaps he or she contributed to the problem more than he or she had previously thought. If John realizes that he made an error of some type but covers that by escalating the argument and creating more confusion, the problem is compounded. Perhaps the first step in learning how to manage conflict is examining the attitudes and behaviors that allow one to practice new skills.

Attitude Adjustment

The following principles are part of specific negotiating skills. The example of John and Mary shows the importance of the first point:

Let go of the need to be right: If you are interested only in proving your point and/or proving someone else wrong, resolution will be difficult. If your need to be right is greater than your need to resolve the conflict, then additional skills won't mean much! Some people argue for the sake of argument; if you run up against one of these people, you're better off in the long run if you let it go. If you keep arguing and it seems to be going nowhere, perhaps that is what one of you wants.

Don't offer resistance: It really does take two to tango. If someone is trying to start an argument and you don't fight back with the "I'm right" routine, it really is difficult for the other person to keep going. Some people need to let off steam before they can discuss the problem. If their behavior isn't too severe (remember that it is important to have boundaries and not let anyone abuse you), then it might be useful to just listen. In the John and Mary example, what do you think would have happened if John hadn't offered resistance? At the point when he realized that he was wrong, saying so to Mary would have immediately lessened the conflict. (That is, assuming that he had any intention of doing so.)

Acknowledge the other person's position: I've often heard people say, "I don't care if you agree with me; I just want to be understood." Many arguments are over miscommunication and misunderstandings. Some fights continue because one person wants to have his or her beliefs validated, to know that the other person doesn't think that he or she is crazy. It is amazing how effective it can be to say something like "I understand how you might feel that way, given your perception of the situation."

Offer your point of view: When stating your own beliefs, desires, and opinions, it is important to impart, by word and behavior, that you are sharing your point of view about the situation. Nothing disrupts an attempt to negotiate like someone speaking as if his or her words are carved in stone. Express what is true for you. State your beliefs, ideas, and suggestions, but make it clear that you are only offering an opinion.

Agree to disagree: If all else fails, you can always agree to disagree. If both parties let go of being right, offer no resistance, and acknowledge the other's point of view, then they can probably part amicably. Just as being right isn't always right, winning doesn't always mean you've won. In some situations, if you play that kind of game, you can win the battle and lose the war. This is especially true in relationships with family and friends. There will be people with whom you want to be close and maintain contact even when you have different ideologies and beliefs. Value the friendships you have with people who have different perspectives, because they provide you with a view you might not otherwise know about. And, as parents, you will want to be able to appreciate different perspectives in order to relate to your children.

Choose your battles wisely: If the past 10 times you walked into the lion's den you got chewed up, perhaps it is time to pick a new den. Some arguments aren't worth having, and there is no use arguing with some people. Some topics have no definite solution and may never be resolved. You have to enjoy debate if you want to discuss religion or politics. It may mean something about you if you continually enter conflictual situations knowing that there isn't any real possibility for resolution.

Realize that the other person has important reasons: No one does anything for no reason at all. If someone seems to be overreacting or blowing an event out of proportion, keep in mind that there must be some important reason. If someone seems to be really upset, you can bet there is something going on, even if he or she can't tell you what it is. Try to find out what is really upsetting someone if he or she seems to be overreacting to the situation.

Recognize the different levels of interaction: Recognize when you are discussing a topic on two different levels. If you borrow someone's stapler and she becomes extremely upset because of some traumatic event in her life that made her acutely aware of her boundaries, talking about staplers won't do much good. What may seem like a trivial thing to one person may have deep implications for another. Sometimes, it is important to notice the depth of the reaction and to assess whether you are arguing about the same thing and/or on the same level.

Negotiating Skills

An excellent source of information on improving negotiating skills is *Getting to Yes* (Fisher and Ury, 1981). The thesis of the book is "Don't bargain over positions." In other words, let go of the idea that there is only one solution to the problem. It is far more beneficial to determine what you want to accomplish than to take a position and defend it as the only answer.

There are a number of problems with positional bargaining because each party is more involved in defending a stance than in looking for options. Positional bargaining is inefficient and endangers relationships. In place of playing hardball or just giving in, Fisher and Ury offer an alternative they call *principled negotiation,* which is outlined in the following four points:

1. *Separate the people from the problem:* Human beings have complex emotions and mysterious motives at times. It is better to focus on the problem at hand than on the people involved. Looking at the task to be solved gives all the parties involved the opportunity to work side by side rather than going at it face to face.

2. *Discuss mutual interests rather than positions:* Focus on what the other person really wants and try to figure out the underlying need. Consider how your needs might also be met by assisting the other person in accomplishing his or her goals.

3. *Invent options for mutual gain:* Do some brainstorming and try to generate a variety of possibilities. The process for doing this is to assess the problem in the real world and analyze it in theory. Ask yourself what is wrong, and then sort the symptoms into categories. Generate broad ideas about what might be done and put them into action with specific steps.

4. *Have a set criterion:* Insist that the results be based on some objective standard.

These four tenets of principled negotiation are relevant from the beginning of the process to the point at which either an agreement has been reached or you decide to break off the effort. The process can be divided into three phases—analysis, planning, and discussion—and the same four points can be followed in each stage.

Whatever your assertiveness and conflict management skills are, there will be times when it seems that the other person just is not willing to bring things to a satisfactory conclusion. Besides being able to let go of the disagreement, there will be times when taking it to the next step could be beneficial. That means being able to forgive someone you have had problems with, even if he or she wants to continue creating conflict.

> **❝** *First keep peace within yourself, then you can also bring peace to others.* **❞**
>
> Thomas á Kempis

Staying Centered

Sometimes, the greatest skill you can possess in managing conflict is the ability to not "get got" when someone is trying to get you. Have you ever had to deal with someone you knew wanted to get you mad or wanted to get into an argument that had no possible solution? Even if you didn't react at first, once you got hooked, you got no credit for having tried to resist. What makes some people good at coping with conflict is their ability to go more than one or two rounds before getting hooked.

For example, Al and Bob are having an argument. Before they can begin to use conflict resolution, they may have to stop trying to antagonize each other. If Al makes a critical comment about Bob, Bob has a choice between responding in kind or trying to defuse the situation. Let's say that he makes an "I" statement asking for clarification. Maybe Al is in a bad mood and ignores this attempt at conciliation and makes another critical statement. Bob could respond in kind and be negative or critical, because he tried being nice once and feels justified. Or, he could hang in there and offer another neutral comment by paraphrasing what Al has said. Maybe, though, Al is in a really bad mood and just wants an excuse to blow up. He has been used to Bob taking the bait in the past, so he isn't about to give up easily, and this time he really gives Bob a "double zinger" to get the usual response!

At this point, as many people might do, Bob could retaliate and give Al a taste of his own medicine. After all, didn't Al start it? And hasn't Al been the one to escalate? Or, Bob could try once more to clearly express his intent not to get hooked into an old game that is unproductive for both of them. Let's say that Bob uses his best communication skills: he uses "I" statements, paraphrases, and asks for clarification. Perhaps, surprisingly, Al begins to express what he is really upset about and begins to talk about what he really wants. There are times when it is important not to repeat old patterns to convince someone that you really want to do things differently.

Sometimes, to manage conflict, you have to be able to manage your own tendencies to want to get back at someone who doesn't seem to be playing by the rules. It may take more than one or two attempts at engaging someone in a positive manner before the interaction can change. If your intent is to manage the conflict, though, it could be well worth the effort.

Guidelines for Getting Professional Help

The following article was published by the *Los Angeles Times–Washington Post Service*. It appeared in the newspaper under the heading "Mental Disorders Hit Third of Americans."

During the course of their lifetimes, every third American will experience at least one acute mental disorder, according to a health organization report. In 1988, more than 40 million people, including 9.5 million children, suffered some kind of major mental illness, be it anxiety, depression, schizophrenia or the effects of drug use. Combined with emotional disorders, these mental dislocations contribute to a wide range of problems across social systems, notably family violence, unemployment, homelessness, criminal violence, and suicide. So says *Prevention Report,* a monthly digest of the Public Health Service, in an analysis of mental health in America.

"The vast majority of these people have what would be called a psychiatric diagnosis," says Thomas Plaut, acting deputy director of biometrics at the National Institute of Mental Health. "Some are alcoholics, some abuse drugs, but virtually all have mental problems severe enough to require inpatient care," he said.

The good news is that leaves two-thirds of us employing our coping skills in dealing with daily life. While most of us may not need inpatient care, that doesn't preclude the possibility of benefiting from counseling during a particularly difficult period in life.

Where to Look for Help

Knowing how to get professional help for yourself or others is sometimes a difficult task. Should you ever have occasion to seek professional help, you might consider the following questions (Atwater, 1999):

1. *When should you seek professional help?* Whenever your personal problems begin to interfere with your health, work, relationships, or personal life, it's time to seek professional help. Another sign that it is time to seek the assistance of a professional occurs either when your present methods of coping are no longer effective or when you are engaged in old, self-defeating strategies that you know from experience do not work. Still another sign is when your family or friends are tired of being used as therapists and become openly concerned about you. Most important, whenever you feel overwhelmed and desperate and you don't know what to do, it's best to seek help. However, you don't have to have a

serious problem, much less a psychological disorder, to benefit from therapy. More and more people are seeking therapy as a means of personal growth, to improve their coping skills, and to get more out of life.

2. *Where do you find help?* Help is available in a variety of settings. Many therapists work in the comprehensive mental health centers now available in most communities. Staffed by a combination of psychiatrists (medical doctors with the ability to treat disorders requiring drugs and hospitalization), psychologists (people with clinical training in the methods of assessment and treatment), clinical social workers (people with supervised clinical training as part of their master's degree program in the field of social work), and counselors (people with training in personality theory and counseling skills, usually at a master's level), these centers offer a variety of services, including emergency help, all at a nominal fee that depends on income and ability to pay. Many therapists work in private practice, in either a group or an individual setting. They are usually listed in the Yellow Pages by their respective professions. Although they are relatively expensive, you may be reimbursed for part of the fee, depending on the type of insurance you have. If you have insurance such as an HMO, PPO, or other group plan, the company itself usually maintains a list of approved panel providers. A person who wishes to see a therapist can request a copy of this list, may have access to a Web site where he/she can search for a provider, or may ask a referral specialist at the insurance company about different providers, after a brief telephone interview, called an *intake*. Often a referral specialist can enter a set of demographics into a computer, requesting specifics such as gender, areas of specialization, type of therapist, location, and language fluency, so that a good match can be made. Other referral sources include the American Psychological Association, as well as state and local psychological associations, which often maintain a list of potential providers that have joined that particular association.

3. *What can you expect from therapy?* Most therapies provide benefits such as an empathic, caring, and trusting relationship; hope for the demoralized; and a new way of understanding yourself and the world. Beyond this, a lot depends on the goals and progress made in your particular therapy. People seeking relatively short-term therapy usually acquire a better understanding of their problems as well as the necessary skill to cope with a person or family crisis. Those undergoing relatively long-term therapy may aspire to more fundamental changes in their personality and may remain in therapy for a year or longer.

4. *How long must you go?* The recent trend toward short-term therapies and the increased concern for containing health care costs have made the length of therapy a major issue. Consequently, the appropriate length of treatment often becomes an empirical issue to be decided by clients and their therapists. According to Luborsky (1988), there are two key issues to consider

> **"** *Many individuals see counselors not because they are depressed but because they want an informed opinion about their situation. They want to see new possibilities and new ways of looking at old problems. And they want the wisdom of someone who has helped other people in similar circumstances.* **"**
>
> *Robert L. Veninga*

in deciding when to terminate therapy. First, is the crisis or problem that brought you to therapy under control? You need not have resolved all of your difficulties, but you should have more understanding and control over your life so that your difficulties do not interfere with your work and personal activities. Second, can you maintain the gains acquired in therapy on your own? It is best to discuss these two issues with your therapist before deciding to terminate therapy. At the same time, bear in mind that in therapy, as in all close relationships, there will be unsettling as well as gratifying occasions. Therapy can become so uncomfortable that you may want to quit. However, if you put yourself into it and keep going, you'll eventually find that it is a very rewarding experience.

What Makes a Good Therapist?

The following list is from the article "A Buyer's Guide to Psychotherapy," by Frank Pittman III (1994):

1. Good therapists have got to like doing therapy. They feel refreshed after an emotional workout.

2. Good therapists have got to be optimistic, believing that life is a comedy, not a tragedy, even if you can't get out of it alive. They can't be afraid of failures and embarrassment and pain, or even of tragedies. Good therapists aren't protective of their clients.

3. Good therapists have got to be eager detectives and explorers, people who like to solve mysteries and figure out how life works. They have a homing device that leads them quickly and directly to the aspects of the situation that don't make sense. Good therapists don't take things at face value, they don't assume they understand everything from the beginning, and they certainly don't assume that everyone is alike and that one solution fits all.

4. Good therapists certainly have to be warm—
they may not be especially loving or nurturing, but they delight in intimacy. They must be able to understand and share experiences: their own, those of their customers, and those of the people whose lives are touched by their customers.

5. Good therapists have got to have a sense of humor. Without it, they may try to protect their customers from the cruelties of life—those unpleasant but necessary experiences that give people chances to expand consciousness and build character.

6. Above all, good therapists have got to be fairly sane—not rigidly, anxiously, cautiously sane, but able to see fairly clearly how the world works. It also helps if therapists are

happy people, not stuck in happiness like manics or TV weather forecasters, but able to experience a full range of human emotions.

In conclusion, Pittman says:

Most important, if a therapist is gentle and soothing and makes you feel that your life is not your fault, run for your life. Choose the therapist who pisses you off by insisting that you take more than your share of the responsibility for your life and your relationships. Hire the one who cuts through your defenses, your projections, and your rationalizations, one who makes you feel like a fool for continuing to screw up your life in the same old way and offers optimism that he or she finds life worth living, so you can come to feel that way too.

CHAPTER REVIEW

Self-Defeating Behavior

We are our own worst enemy at times. It is important to understand the various components of self-defeating behavior in order to make changes. Limiting beliefs are frequently responsible for undermining our own efforts. Unless we address those limiting beliefs, we may develop a pattern of learned helplessness. It is essential to get involved in different settings with people who have a sense of control over their lives.

Coping Strategies

General types of coping are problem-focused coping and emotion-focused coping. Coping strategies can also be categorized as active-cognitive strategies, active-behavioral strategies, and avoidance strategies. Some coping skills are developing support systems, practicing self-relaxation, talking yourself through it, rewarding accomplishments, and keeping a sense of humor. All of these skills contribute to developing self-efficacy, which can lead to a heightened sense of competence.

Components of Change

There is a great deal of information about making changes in life. Specific guidelines on how to use such self-help information are sometimes needed as well. It is often important to explore the part of you that doesn't want to change as

well as the part that does. The formula for change addresses the various components that need to be clarified to accomplish behavior goals. It is often necessary to overcome objections to change while preserving the positive intention behind those objections.

A Model for Change

There are steps to follow that can lead to a decision-making process that will facilitate making a change in your behavior. There can be a logical, rational, systematic manner in which to address the illogic of certain behavior patterns.

Stress Management

Anxiety is not always negative; it depends on how much you have and when you create it. Some stress can provide motivation, if you know how to read your early warning signals and Stop at the Top. You can handle stress by remembering the difference between times you have handled stress well and times you haven't. Type A personality has some negative effects; it might be useful to adopt some of the strategies of Type B.

Conflict Management

Certain attitudes are more conducive to resolving disagreements. Sometimes, having the proper attitude is a prerequisite to conflict management. Some of the valuable points to consider are: Let go of the need to be right; don't offer resistance; acknowledge the other person's position; state your opinion as your point of view; agree to disagree when necessary; choose your battles wisely; realize that all people have important reasons for feeling the way they do; and know that some discussions become difficult because you are arguing on two different levels. Fisher and Ury (1981) list four concepts useful in constructive negotiations: separate the people from the problem; discuss mutual interests rather than positions; invent options for mutual gain; and have a set criterion for evaluation.

Guidelines for Getting Professional Help

It is possible that one-third of the U.S. population will utilize the services of some type of mental health organization during the course of their lifetime. If you feel overwhelmed and desperate, it may be useful to get help. You don't have to have a psychological disorder to benefit from therapy. Most therapies provide a caring and trusting relationship, hope for the future, and a new way of understanding yourself and the world. Most people in therapy acquire a better understanding of their problem and the necessary skills to cope with the situation.

SOURCES AND SUGGESTED READINGS

Fisher, Roger, and William Ury. *Getting to Yes: Negotiating Agreement Without Giving In.* Boston: Houghton Mifflin, 1981.

Kleinke, Chris L. *Coping with Life Challenges.* Belmont, CA: Wadsworth, 1999.

O'Grady, Dennis. *Taking the Fear out of Changing: Getting Through Tough Life Transitions.* Dayton, OH: New Insights Press, 1994.

Santrock, J. W., A. M. Minnett, and B. D. Campbell. *The Authoritative Guide to Self-Help Books.* New York: Guilford, 1994.

Sapolsky, Robert. *Why Zebras Don't Get Ulcers.* Revised edition. New York: Freeman, 1998.

Seaward, B. L. *Managing Stress: Principles and Strategies for Health and Well-Being.* Fourth edition. Boston: Jones and Barlett, 2004.

Seligman, M. E. P. *Helplessness: On Depression, Development, and Death.* San Francisco: W.H. Freeman, 1978.

Web Site Resources

Association for Conflict Resolution
http://www.mediate.com

The Effectiveness of Psychotherapy: The *Consumer Reports* Study
http://www.apa.org/jounals/seligman.html

Suicide ... Read This First
http://www.metanoia.org/suicide

Techniques and advice on conflict management
http://www.briefings.com/tm/ConflictMgmt.html

National Institute on Alcohol Abuse and Alcoholism
http://www.niaaa.nih.gov

Anxiety Disorders
http://www.adaa.org

Mood Disorders
http://www.drada.org

Stress and You: This site discusses the signs of chronic fatigue and makes suggestions about getting help for it
http://www.chronicfatigue.org/History.html

REACTION AND RESPONSE—WHAT DO YOU THINK?

Chapter Eight   Level I Assignments

In response to the information in the chapter:

1. In what areas do you most need greater coping skills? What is it that you need to change to improve your skills?

2. What strategies for coping do you usually employ, and what new strategies did you learn about in this chapter? What can you do to develop a better support system for yourself when you are dealing with difficult times in life? What will you do to improve your sense of confidence about your abilities to solve problems?

3. How is stress sometimes useful? What did you learn about how you create or reduce the amount of stress in your life? What did you learn about how to monitor your stress level so that you can "stop at the top" instead of going too far?

In response to the class activities, group discussions, and exercises:

1. What are your opinions and reactions?

2. What did you learn or rediscover?

3. How are you going to apply what you learned?

Chapter Eight   Level II Assignments

1. After completing the *formula for change* section, what did you learn about how to deal with your resistance to change? How is the goal you say you want sometimes different from the one you really want? How is having a *bigger* purpose important for motivation in making a change?

2. How do you stay centered and not "get got" when someone is trying to get you into an argument?

3. How do you manage conflict, and what did you learn about what you can do in the future?

Chapter Eight   Level III Assignments

1. Have you ever been in counseling or therapy? What did you find helpful? What did you learn about how to get help? What would you recommend to a friend who was in need of professional help?

2. Regarding self-defeating behavior, in what situations are you most likely to "shoot yourself in the foot"? What limiting beliefs undermine your own efforts at accomplishing what you want in life? What behavior and thought patterns do you need to change? How, specifically, will you start that process?

3. How can you apply the model for change? Where and when do you most need to apply that process?

CHAPTER 9

LIFE CHANGES

It had nothing to do with turning 50. No, really, nothing at all. I just suddenly knew that what I wanted most in life was a Harley. Each time a motorcycle roared past me in my minivan, which was equipped with the kids, dog, and rooftop carrier, every cell of my being yearned for the feeling of being young, wild, and free. I knew that I needed an opportunity to respond to the long-silenced voice of my youthful self that used to ride.

The universe heard my call and provided the opportunity to satisfy my longings. The department chair was going to India on sabbatical in search of another form of enlightenment than the two-wheeled variety. It wasn't exactly a hog, but the Honda Shadow VT 1100cc was a reasonable facsimile, and the price was right. I knew I had to have it. My wife didn't. At first, she was calm and calculating and proceeded as if there was a negotiation in progress. She listed numerous rational objections. Finally, she laid her cards on the table and went for the emotional ploy with a "What about the children?" move. In the end, she just said "NO!!!"

So I begged, borrowed, and sold everything I could, and then cleaned out *my* bank account. I rode off with my coconspirator, Earl, for the big transaction that was going to put me back in the fast lane of life. My wife's objections lingered longer in my mind than I wished.

Her words scattered like the breeze after I picked up the bike. It was July and nearly 90 degrees—definitely T-shirt weather. Helmet strapped down tight, I headed out through the country. The endorphins were kicking in with the exhilaration of accelerating down the road. I was in the wind . . . and this was near heaven.

The first thought that brought me back to earth came when I looked down at the asphalt and realized I was doing 85 . . . and I was still in third with a gear to go. Instead of feeling young, wild, and free, I felt old, vulnerable, and scared.

The next morning, full-blown buyer's remorse set in. I hated to admit it, but I began to wonder, "What was I thinking?" It was too late to take the thing back: the seller had cashed the check. I would have to find a buyer on my own. Fortunately, it took only a few weeks before a kindred soul responded to the ad in the paper and bought my fantasy.

Maybe it was a little crazy. Maybe it was a bit of midlife temporary insanity. I guess I've come to my senses. But I still get a little wistful when I'm driving along in my minivan with a carload of "When are we going to get there?" and a Harley roars by. But I'm older now and perhaps a bit more mature. I've been able to admit that maybe I should have listened to my wife.

Life Span Development

There appears to be a revolution in the life cycle. People are leaving childhood sooner but taking longer to grow up and much longer to die. In the 19th century, only 1 in 10 reached 65, yet in contemporary America, 8 in 10 reach 65. Puberty arrives earlier by several years than it did at the turn of the century. Adolescence is prolonged well into the 20s, though, as more young adults live at home longer. For many, true adulthood doesn't begin until 30. Most baby boomers—born after World War II—do not feel fully "grown up" until they are into their 40s.

Unlike members of the previous generation, most of whom had their children launched by middle age, many late-baby couples or stepfamily parents will still be battling with rebellious children while they themselves wrestle with the passage into middle life. For thousands of generations, one of our most basic instincts was to reproduce ourselves as soon as possible. In the space of one generation, though, middle- and upper-middle-class Americans have decided to postpone childbirth for 10 to 20 years. This radical voluntary alteration of the life cycle may be the most revolutionary change of all (Sheehy, 1995).

Middle age has been pushed far into the 50s and only reluctantly acknowledged then. Because of increased longevity, the time span of the 50s, 60s, and beyond is changing so radically that it now includes stages of life that are nothing like what our grandparents experienced. Everything seems to be off by at least a decade: 50 is now what 40 used to be.

Because of all the life span changes we are experiencing, it helps to further explore developmental theory, both past and present. Gail Sheehy (1995), in her book *New Passages,* says that we have a greater need than ever before to recognize the passages of our lives, not only because we are living longer but because the rapidity and complexity of changes taking place are reshaping the adult life cycle into something vastly different from what we knew before. Václav Havel, the philosopher and president of the Czech Republic, stated in his speech at Independence Hall, Philadelphia, on July 4, 1994: "Experts can explain anything in the objective world to us, yet we understand our own lives less and less. We live in the post-modern world, where anything is possible and almost nothing is certain" (Sheehy, 1995).

Human Development

For years, developmental researchers have debated whether human development occurs in an orderly progression or in a series of stages with abrupt changes from one stage to the next. Many people assume there is a continuous development and that human beings follow a linear course in life. According to that belief, each new development is built on all the developments that came before. But that isn't always the way that people develop. Some of the most important phenomena in human development are nonlinear in nature. Human development may occur rapidly or slowly, it may plateau or even appear to reverse,

all at the same time, depending on which developmental aspect you consider. Some behaviors appear to be acquired in an orderly progression; others may appear in an abrupt shift (Dworetsky, 1995).

Perhaps it would be useful to think of human development as occurring in movements similar to that of the common child's toy called a Slinky. There are loops within loops as the springy toy moves along. It can have ups and downs as it progresses. It can go up and down stairs as the end flips over and becomes the beginning, over and over again.

Even with the complexities of the tasks and events that we face in life, there are common themes and issues that all of us must contend with as we grow from childhood through old age. At one time, most developmental studies were concerned with childhood and adolescence, and they stopped at adulthood. The fact that there were also studies about aging and the waning years of life gave the erroneous impression that not much changed during the adult years. That notion has been increasingly challenged by the middle-aged adults who have many questions about how to contend with all of the societal and cultural changes that have come about in the late 20th century. Consider the following excerpt from *New Passages* regarding the book *Passages* (Sheehy, 1976), which addressed many of the concerns adults have had about the progression of their lives:

> The book *Passages* helped to popularize an entirely new concept: that adulthood continues to proceed by stages of development throughout the life cycle. Unlike childhood stages, the stages of adult life are characterized not by physical growth but by steps in psychological and social growth. Marriage, childbirth, first job, and empty nest are what we call marker events, the concrete happenings of our lives. A developmental stage, however, is not defined by marker events; it is defined by an underlying impulse toward change that signals us from the realm of mind or spirit. This inner realm is where we register the meaning of our participation in the external world: How do we feel about our job, family roles, social roles? In what ways are our values, goals, and aspirations being invigorated or violated by our present life structure? How many parts of our personality can we live out, and what parts are we leaving out?
>
> (Sheehy, 1995, p. 12)

It is internal discontent that often signals the necessity to change and move on to the next stage of development.

Adjustment in Old Age

Having entered the new millennium, we are bombarded by contradictory information about what it means to grow old. With increased medical knowledge and greater health, will longevity be a blessing or a cure? George E. Vaillant (2002), who has written extensively about adult development, has a new book on the Harvard Study of Adult Development entitled *Aging Well*. In this book, he describes what he has learned about successful adjustment in old age. What is special about the Study of Adult Development is that it consists of grandparents and great-grandparents who have been followed since adolescence. In surveying the people in the study, Vaillant has come to the conclusion that old age is not an oxymoron. Not only are those in old age less depressed than the general public, the majority of the elderly suffer fewer incapacitating illnesses than previously believed.

Although there are patterns that emerge in the study, Vaillant reminds us that the past often predicts but never determines our old age. Among the significant findings to emerge from the Study of Adult Development:

▶ It is not the bad things that happen to us that doom us; more important it is the good people who happen to us at any age that facilitates enjoyable old age.

▶ Healing relationships are facilitated by a capacity for gratitude, for forgiveness, and for letting people into your life.

▶ A good marriage at 50 predicted positive aging at 80.

▶ Alcohol abuse—unrelated to unhappy childhood—consistently predicted unsuccessful aging, in part because alcoholism damaged future social supports.

▶ Learning to play and create after retirement and learning to gain younger friends as we lose older ones add more to life's enjoyment than retirement income.

▶ Objective good physical health was less important to successful aging than subjective good health. It's all right to be ill as long as you don't feel sick.

All of the various cohort groups in the study repeatedly demonstrated that it was social aptitude—or emotional intelligence—that leads to adjustment in old age. Consistent with Reinhold Niebuhr's famous Serenity Prayer, adjustment in old age depends on the courage to change the things that you can and the serenity to accept the things you cannot.

Erikson's Stages of Development

It was Eric Erikson who revolutionized our view of human growth and development, introducing the theory that each stage of life, from infancy through to advanced age, is associated with a specific psychological crisis that shapes a major aspect of our personalities. A brief word about the term *crisis* is appropriate here. Although it is commonly used, it is important to note that it has a different meaning from the everyday use. Erikson used the term to indicate that there was a necessary struggle with the turning points that usher in a new stage. *Crisis* was used to indicate the crucial period of decision between progress and regression. It also indicated an involvement with the issues that needed to be resolved within each stage. With that in mind, let's look at Erikson's stages of development.

Erikson described human development over the entire life span in terms of eight stages, each marked by a particular crisis to be resolved. At these turning points, we can achieve successful resolution of our conflicts and move ahead, or we can fail to resolve the conflicts and regress. To a certain extent, our life is the result of the choices we make at each stage. By getting a picture of the challenges at each period of life, we will be able to understand how earlier stages of development influence choices that we make later in life. Our childhood experiences have a direct impact on how we deal with adolescence. The degree to which we master the tasks of adolescence and develop an identity has a bearing on our ability to cope with the significant issues of adulthood. As we progress from one stage to another, we will, at times, meet with roadblocks and detours. These barriers are often the result of having failed to master basic psychological competencies at an earlier period (Corey and Schneider-Corey, 2003).

The following are Erikson's eight developmental stages:

1. *Trust versus mistrust:* During infancy (the first year of life), it is important to develop a sense of trust. This requires physical comfort and a minimal amount of fear about the future. Infants' basic needs are met by responsive, sensitive caregivers.

2. *Autonomy versus self-doubt:* After gaining trust in caregivers, infants start to discover that they have a will of their own (early childhood, ages 1–3). They assert their independence. If infants are restrained too much or punished too harshly, they are likely to develop a sense of shame and doubt.

3. *Initiative versus guilt:* As preschool children (ages 3–6) enter a widening social world, they are challenged more and need to develop more purposeful behavior to cope with these challenges. Children are now asked to assume more responsibility. Uncomfortable guilt feelings may arise, though, if the children are made to feel too anxious.

4. *Industry versus inferiority:* As children move into the elementary school years, they direct their energy toward mastering knowledge and intellectual skills. The danger during this stage (middle childhood, ages 6–12) involves feeling incompetent and unproductive.

5. *Identity versus role confusion:* Individuals (adolescence, ages 10–20) are faced with finding out who they are, where they are going, and how they fit in. An important dimension now is the exploration of alternative solutions to roles. Career exploration is also important.

6. *Intimacy versus isolation:* Individuals (early adulthood, 20s–30s) face the developmental task of forming intimate relationships with others. Erikson described intimacy as finding oneself, yet losing oneself in another person.

7. *Generativity versus stagnation:* A chief concern of people in this stage (middle adulthood, 40s–50s) is to help the younger generation develop and lead useful lives. It is also a time of considering the gap between one's dreams and what one has achieved and what one still wants to accomplish.

8. *Integrity versus despair:* Individuals at this stage (late adulthood, 60s onward) look back and evaluate what they have done with their lives. Key tasks now are to adjust to retirement, losses, and the death of others.

Whereas Erikson emphasized the mastery of certain tasks in development, others have stressed the satisfaction of needs. Abraham Maslow postulated that there is a hierarchy of motives that determines our behavior. Both Maslow and Erikson are often discussed in the context of personality, yet each have contributed to developmental psychology as well. There is a connection between the two approaches in that how, when, and if someone goes through a particular stage has a great deal to do with the level of needs that are being met at any given time for that person.

Marcia's Identity States

James Marcia expanded on Erikson's stages work and divided the identity crisis into four states. These are not stages, but rather processes that adolescents go through. All adolescents will occupy one or more of these states, at least temporarily. But, because these are not stages, people do not progress from one step to the next in a fixed sequence, nor must everyone go through each and every state. Each state is determined by two factors:

Is the adolescent committed to an identity, and

Is the individual involved in searching for his or her true identity?

The states are:

Identity Foreclosure: The adolescent blindly accepts the identity and values that were given in childhood by families and significant others. The adolescent's identity is foreclosed until he or she determines his or her true identity. The adolescent in this state is committed to an identity but not as a result of his or her own searching or crisis.

Identity Moratorium: The adolescent has acquired vague or ill-formed ideological and occupational commitments; he or she is still undergoing the identity search (crisis). He or she is beginning to commit to an identity but is still developing it.

Diffusion: The state of having no clear idea of one's identity and making no attempt to find that identity. These adolescents may have struggled to find their identity, but they never resolved it, and they seem to have stopped trying. There is no commitment and no searching.

Identity Achievement: The state of having developed well-defined personal values and self-concepts. Their identities may be expanded and further defined in adulthood, but the basics are there. They are committed to an ideology and have a strong sense of ego identity.

Maslow's Hierarchy of Needs

Maslow was one of the most powerful forces behind the humanistic movement in psychology. He called the humanistic approach the *third force* in psychology because it was an important alternative to both the psychoanalytic and behavioral approaches. From Maslow's point of view, the psychoanalytic theories placed too little emphasis on the development and personality of normal and well-adjusted individuals, and the behavioral theorists often ignored the individual altogether. Humanists do not believe that behavior is governed either by unconscious drives and motives or by external stimuli and rewards in the environment. They argue that people have a free will and are born with an inner motivation to fulfill their potential. Maslow (1971) called the inner motivation to fulfill potential **self-actualization.** The humanists view self-actualization as a life-long process rather than as a goal that a person eventually reaches.

Maslow believed that people are motivated to fulfill their higher growth needs only when they have satisfied their basic needs. Before a person can be free to engage in self-actualization, fulfilling his or her potential, that person has to meet his or her physiological needs (food, water, air, sleep, sex, etc.) and the need for safety and security. Then he or she is free to fulfill the needs for love, belonging, self-esteem, and approval from others. Maslow placed self-actualization at the top of the **hierarchy of needs** and thus the attainment of that level can easily be interfered with by complications at lower levels.

Here is how Maslow's hierarchy might explain motives and behaviors: Imagine that you arrived in a strange town, hungry and broke. According to Maslow, you would be motivated, first of all, to ensure a supply of food and water to satisfy your physiological needs. Then perhaps you would look for a job to obtain money for shelter and security. Only after you had a secure base of operation would you begin to make connections in the community to develop a sense of belonging. Once you felt that you belonged and that you shared love with other people, your sense of self-esteem could develop as your loved ones and friends held you in high regard. At that point, as a fulfilled member of a community, you might begin to develop your full potential (Dworetzky, 1995).

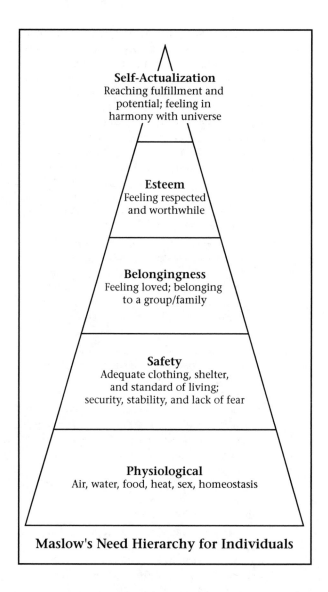

Maslow's Need Hierarchy for Individuals

Future Passages

There will be new stages in the life cycle to contend with in the future. During speaking engagements about life transitions, Gail Sheehy often recites the following figures to get people to think differently about longevity. A woman who reached age 50 in the 20th century—and remains free of cancer and heart disease—can expect to see her 92nd birthday, and the average healthy man who was 65 in the 20th century will live to be 81. Worldwide, people are living longer, and two-thirds of the total gains in life expectancy have been made in this century alone.

Given the fact that we will all be living longer, it is important to reevaluate some of our expectations about the life cycle. In her latest book, *New Passages*, Sheehy compiles information on how different generations have gone through the stages of development over the course of the 20th century.

She conducted personal discussion groups with people representing various populations in America, evaluated numerous surveys, and spent several years working with the Census Bureau. As a result of her work in updating her original book, *Passages*, she has come to the conclusion that we all need to stop and recalculate. She proposes a new concept of a "Second Adulthood" in middle age. Consider the day you turn 45 as the infancy of another life. Revising the various stages that people go through while growing up and encountering the different markers of life-changing events, Sheehy came up with the following titles:

Provisional Adulthood (18–30)
First Adulthood (30–45)
Second Adulthood (45–85)
Age of Mastery (45–65)
Age of Integrity (65–85)

The length of time in Provisional Adulthood addresses the fact that more people are living at home longer and spending more time on education and career preparation. Adolescence has been prolonged. Many people today start to take on the adult role only in their 30s. This is the period of the Tryout Twenties.

The First Adulthood is a time when commitments are made. This incorporates settling down, raising a family, and dedicating oneself to work and career. What was once thought of as a midlife crisis may now be thought of as the "little death" of First Adulthood. This is a time when changes are considered, with the realization that one could live perhaps another 50 years. This period incorporates the Turbulent Thirties and the Flourishing Forties.

The Second Adulthood is the time when people cope with sometimes being in the pits and other times reaching the peaks. All this is due, in part, to dealing with the birth of the Second Adulthood, coping with menopause (both male and female), and handling the crisis of finding meaning in life while confronting one's own mortality. This is the time of the Flaming Fifties and the Serene Sixties.

Each stage presents its own struggles and opportunities for a new dream. The age that someone enters or leaves a period will vary; it is the presence and possibilities of each of the three different territories that is important. Despite all the shifts in the life cycle that have been mentioned, there are still predictable passages that will occur between them. But the timetable is stretched out about 5 or 10 years. Age norms for major life events have become highly elastic. Sheehy describes a situation where we are all swimming around furiously in the fishbowl of life and we can't see the obvious: The bowl has gotten much bigger, and the water levels have all changed (Sheehy, 1995).

People in their 20s, 30s, and early 40s face the uncertainty presented by changes in the norm. Their private lives are no longer following a linear progression as they did for their parents. They may be leading cyclical lives that demand they start over again and again. Three lives in one may sound like a bargain, but it comes at a price! People in the Provisional Adulthood stage live at an accelerated pace, even though many of the responsibilities of full adulthood are delayed. The Age of Mastery can't be about coasting until retirement any more. It must be a preparation for stages that few people reached in the past. Most people in the Age of Integrity will continue to work in one way or another—part-time, consulting, or self-employed—not only because they

> **"***The gods have two ways of dealing harshly with us—the first is to deny us our dreams, and the second is to grant them.***"**
>
> *Oscar Wilde*

want to feel a sense of purpose and self-worth, but because they will have to be prepared to support themselves for greatly elongated lives.

Sheehy's impression from talking with people all over the United States is that the middle years do not mean descent. On the contrary, the middle years are often the stage of the greatest well-being in the lives of healthy people. That is a perspective that hasn't been fully realized yet for many Americans. She has also come to the conclusion that there may no longer be a standard life cycle. People are increasingly able to customize their life cycles—an interesting and challenging endeavor.

Life Passages

Although there are numerous theories of human development with various stages that people pass through, in this section we cover three broadly defined times in life: childhood, adulthood, and old age. There are endings associated with any transition, and this is especially true as we pass from one stage to another in the course of our lifetime.

In her book *Necessary Losses* (1986), Judith Viorst writes that for every transition we experience or every choice we make to do something new, we have to deal with the inevitable loss and need for letting go that come with the process of change. All too often, people focus solely on what they are anticipating for the future when considering a change in their life. It is good to think about the positive elements of embracing a new choice or transition, but it is also important to acknowledge the downside or the loss. It actually helps to facilitate the process of change when all aspects of a decision are considered.

There are issues inherent in each stage of life regarding what we must leave to move on. The child who can hardly wait to start school has to confront the reality of leaving the security of home. Many an adolescent has complained about parents' restrictiveness and expressed the need to experience freedom, but, as evidenced by the number of "boomerang children" returning home these days, there are many who realize after leaving that there are benefits to living at home.

The same holds true for the transition from being single to getting married, leaving school for the world of work, being childless to having children, and being employed to finally retiring. There truly are "necessary losses" for many of life's changes. To gain the benefits that come when entering a new phase in life, it is often necessary to make sacrifices in other areas. This holds true even when the change is one that is highly desired and a conscious choice. When a door opens to a new phase in life, some things must be left behind.

We avoid dealing with the losses incurred when moving through stages. Numerous changes occur while going through a stage, in addition to the changes that occur in the transition from one stage to another. And, paradoxically, we alternately embrace and resist those changes. We all know that we need to change as life progresses. We want to change and we don't. Our ambivalence is evident in that we think people who haven't changed in 20 years are stuck in a rut, but given the opportunity to make changes ourselves, we frequently decide that it can wait until later.

Many changes in life come with mixed emotions, and part of maturity involves the ability to handle ambiguity. Few decisions in life are made on the basis of being 100 percent sure about the right course of action. More often, we have to make decisions with limited information based on a 60/40 split. When the part of us that does want to do something reaches a majority, we usually go ahead and make the change. The part that didn't want the change, however, may demand acknowledgment and compensation. That is the nagging little voice that expresses reservations after the fact. It is also representative of the loss that occurs any time you commit to a particular course of action. Some part of you may be unhappy about not getting what it wanted and might have to learn to live with that.

Let's explore some life changes and the endings and losses necessary to continue through life's developmental stages. We will also see how changes during each stage affect subsequent life transitions. What happens during childhood affects passages in adulthood and how we cope with change in general. We will also learn how to go through transitions in a manner that is useful for personal growth. How we navigate through the changes of adult life affects how we confront old age and make peace with dying. Information is offered to help cope with loss and deal with the unavoidable issue of death. Let's start by looking at some of the events of childhood that affect later behavior during transitions.

Significant Childhood Events

Many events that occur during childhood can affect a person long into adulthood. Children do not have the same coping skills that adults do for dealing with difficulties, yet they are subjected to similar events. Some of those events, such as divorce, abuse, death of family members, and frequent moves, may influence how a child learns to deal with changes in general during his or her lifetime. To a certain degree, some trauma may actually have an inoculating effect in preparing a person to deal with later hardships. Many people, though, become oversensitized to any kind of transition or change in life that seems to be out of their control.

The End of Childhood   One way to consider the effect that childhood had on your ability to cope with change is to think about when childhood ended for you. A major developmental demarcation for many people was when they decided that it was time to grow up. How and when that occurred has significance for other decisions in life. The child who was forced at 8 to take over the role of man of the house, due to death or divorce, will handle subsequent changes differently from a child allowed to have a more normal childhood.

When did childhood end for you? Some people remember a specific event or time, others remember a particular year. For example, childhood's end is very vivid for me. I can remember almost the exact moment when I realized my childhood had ended. I was in the sixth grade. I had skipped a grade, so I was younger than most of the others, and I had just turned 11. I still wanted to play cowboys and Indians at that age, and I wanted a gun and holster set with all the extras for my birthday. My parents were really nice and gave me a whole cowboy outfit: hat and boots, the whole works. I remember thinking, "Gosh, this is great. Wow! I am going to look cool out in the street playing cowboys and Indians." I had my boots and hat on, and I went and stood in front of the mirror, doing a little quick-draw-and-shoot-yourself routine. As I was putting on the belt for the holster, I realized it was at the last notch and that I could barely get it buckled. I looked down at that belt and a voice in my head said, "Oh, no, I'm too big!" Suddenly, it was as if my whole world changed. Part of me said, "You're too old for this stuff. You're not a kid anymore."

I think I even went outside wearing the outfit and looked up and down the street. I was trying to see if I could still play kid games. As I stood there, though, I realized I was too old for that. Suddenly, I didn't want anybody to see me. I became embarrassed and went back in the house and took off all the stuff. I put it back in the box and put the box underneath my bed, and that was it. At that moment, I knew my childhood had ended.

Some people may relate more to a particular year as a transitional period than to a particular event. Although I remember the cowboy outfit incident, I also knew I had to grow up when I went from elementary school to junior high school. That was a big change and included emotional loss for me, but nobody ever really talked about the significance of what must be left behind to grow up. I don't think I even realized the impact of that transition until many years later, when I began to understand the concept of necessary losses.

Over the summer between sixth and seventh grade, a lot happened without my even knowing it. I could still play kickball on the playground in the sixth grade. I could walk home with my best buddy, Larry Cooper, with our arms over each other's shoulders. We could swap hats, share lunches, chase cats and girls, and throw rocks on the way home from school. He was my best friend and we hung out together. Three months later, after that summer, I could never touch him again. I could never again do some of the fun things we had done, and our friendship changed. We went off to junior high school, and we had to talk and walk differently. We learned to smoke cigarettes and act "bad," and be mean and surly because now we were in junior high. Guys were now in the locker room changing clothes for gym, so everybody was slightly homophobic. Because of

the new rules for behavior, we had to be scared about any physical contact with another guy.

In June, at the end of sixth grade, I could put my arm around my buddy because he was my best friend, but three months later, all that had changed. I think a number of people of junior high age experience a degree of isolation as a result of that change. We weren't supposed to hug our parents anymore, we couldn't touch our friends, and the opposite sex was a mystery. There are great opportunities that come from growing up, but there are also some things that we need to mourn about the end of childhood. The innocence of childhood friendships is one.

Moving Other childhood events that may affect your reaction to change have to do with moving and the meaning of *home*. Some people lived in the same house the whole time they were growing up, and some had to move every two years whether they liked it or not. Perhaps they grew up in a military family, or a parent worked for an organization that frequently required relocation. Census Bureau statistics indicate that we are a highly mobile society, with as much as 20 percent of the population moving every two years. The people who live in the same home the whole time they are growing up will probably have a reaction to life changes different from the person who moves a dozen times.

In *Necessary Losses*, Viorst (1986) points out that sometimes, parents just walk into a room and say, "Okay, pack your bags. We're moving, and you have two days to be ready to leave." The kids are left standing there, feeling confused, wondering "Well, don't I get to think about this? What about my friends? What am I going to do with my pets? And the school play is next week." Some parents may respond with "That's too bad. Pack your bags and hurry up." The family is in the car and gone before anyone knows it, and there is little time for reaction. Sometimes, the kids don't get to acknowledge their grief about the losses involved in moving. Even if it is positive for the family in the long run, it is important to deal with the process of transition. Some parents expect kids to be good little soldiers and just deal with whatever needs to be dealt with and simply go on from there. They forget that some adults don't handle life's surprises very well, let alone children.

After a number of such moves, some people decide that it isn't worth trying to make new friends because they're going to be gone soon anyway. Others get to the point where endings are no big deal, and they seem unaffected by them. They come into a new school and make new friends immediately because they have learned that if connections are going to be made, they had better be made quickly. Some people become isolated; others become more friendly. In either case, the early experience of continual change may have a later effect in life when other necessary transitions occur. Some learn to be superficial because they feel that nothing is ever going to last. Their method of coping may be to remain detached to avoid disappointment. That style may make it difficult to make connections with others later in life, even when connections are desired. Some people learn to handle frequent change by displaying disruptive behavior. They may continue that pattern into adulthood whenever there are life-altering changes that they feel unable to avoid.

Leaving Home   Another event that indicates the formal end of childhood is leaving home. How and when that happens has implications for a number of adult transitions. Leaving home is seldom a lightweight issue for anyone. The time of departure from the nest has implications for trust, commitment, risk, and support from the world. There is a big difference between the person who was kicked out of the house at 15 after an angry confrontation and the person who left home at 25 with his or her parents saying, "Please come back for dinner on Sunday and bring your laundry." Years later, those two people will have very different reactions to changes in their lives. They will also have different coping styles for dealing with the uncertainties of life's events, many of which are beyond our control. Some people look forward to new things in life with a positive attitude; they may see change as an opportunity for adventure. Others seem to avoid anything new at all costs; they view change and transition as something to dread, and they feel anxious about what may seem like an out-of-control situation.

Adult Transitions

People used to think that once you became an adult you magically became finished developmentally and remained that way the rest of your life. Nothing could be further from the truth. Many developmental psychologists believe that most of the developmental stages occur in adulthood. That will be even more true as life expectancy increases. The concept of middle age has been expanded as statistics support the notion that some people may spend 20 years in

> ## Questions for Critical Thinking
>
> *When did childhood end for you? What childhood events influenced your attitudes about change? How have those events affected your willingness or ability to deal with changes in your present circumstances?*
>
> _____
>
> _____
>
> _____
>
> _____
>
> _____
>
> _____
>
> _____
>
> _____
>
> _____

retirement. Personally, I subscribe to the theory "Old age is always 15 years older than I am at the present."

There are many changes—mental, physical, and emotional—that people go through as adults. As Erikson stated, people must grapple with the conflicts of one stage before they can move on to a higher one. Further evidence of the need to develop coping skills to deal with transition is the projected rate of change for the future. Many areas of life are changing at an accelerated rate. People who examine trends are already predicting that future generations will have three or four careers during the course of a lifetime. With all of the medical advances that are being made, today's 20-year-olds may routinely look forward to living well into their 90s.

How you learned to deal with transitions at an earlier stage in life has implications for how you cope with change in the future. Some people seem to go through life at top speed. Others accept change gracefully as it occurs in natural tempo. And some dig in their heels and avoid change at all costs. Whatever your style of coping, as an adult you will deal with a significant number of changes. Some of those are leaving school or college, starting a job or career, getting married, having children, changing physically, changing jobs or careers, and having a basic midlife crisis. Today's middle-aged adults are sometimes referred to as the "sandwich generation" because they are taking care of children and parents simultaneously. Is it any wonder that some people have midlife crises? As positive and enriching as some of those events just mentioned can be, there is also an aspect of loss in each. Inherent in each decision is an element of letting go of something from the past.

"For every door that closes, there is another one that opens somewhere." That expression is usually used to console someone who has experienced a loss or disappointment. Well, it is also useful to consider that for every door that opens, there are trade-offs and things that must be left behind. One reason for considering the losses involved with endings is to learn to be more open and receptive to whatever the future holds. Those who have truly considered what they are giving up are usually better able to incorporate the positive elements of moving on to the next stage.

In fact, weighing the trade-offs beforehand might make it easier to adjust to a new situation and to embrace its positive aspects. For example, let's consider the decision to get married. Many couples, once they become engaged, never explore any of the potential problem areas of the relationship. On a conscious level, they agree to look only at the bright side and think about what the future holds. On an unconscious level, both may be experiencing fears as the wedding date approaches. Threatening to cancel the wedding after an argument may be due to ignoring the unavoidable losses inherent in moving from single life to married life. The *wedding bell blues* is an indication that all the implications of a given decision may not have been considered, hence the reservations at the last minute.

You may think that because I suggest considering the loss involved in such a decision, I'm not supporting the institution of marriage. It is precisely because I am in favor of the nuclear family and the institution of marriage that I encourage people to talk about the endings related to new beginnings. Each partner will have to give up certain things in return for receiving the benefits of what marriage can provide. For instance, both men and women sacrifice a degree of freedom and autonomy. By considering what each is giving up, they can also enhance their ability to receive what is on the other side of the door that they open together. Relationships can actually be stronger when couples have explored what they are leaving behind. Perhaps the divorce rate

> **"When you can't change the wind, adjust your sails."**
>
> H. Jackson Browne

would go down if there were as much premarital counseling as there is premarital sex.

Here is a case study that exemplifies another aspect of dealing with adult transitions. A man I'll call "Jack" was having a great deal of difficulty after getting a promotion. He couldn't understand why getting the job he had wanted for years would leave him depressed. The problem was that he had spent so much time looking at all the things this new position would bring him that he didn't pay any attention to the price he would have to pay for getting it. He had been sure that the raise, the prestige, and the excitement of the new life for his family would be worth it. By concentrating solely on what was in store in opening the door ahead of him, he forgot to evaluate what he was closing the door on and leaving behind. The whole family had to move from one coast to the other, selling the home they had lived in for 15 years. His wife had to leave behind a friend she had known since childhood, and his children had to leave schools and friends they liked and enjoyed. And what had Jack gained? It's true he made more money, but he also worked longer hours, had more responsibilities, and felt more job pressure. He and his family might have been better off had he considered the losses before taking that new step. This does not mean "Don't take risks." It just means that for every "yes," there is a corresponding "no" in some other aspect of life.

Remember that all decisions are made on the basis of incomplete information. Seldom is anyone 100 percent sure that a decision is right. Even when you reach the point at which 90 percent of you wants that new car and thinks it is a great buy, the other 10 percent will still bring up some questions. However small the part being ignored, it will come back screaming, "What have you done?" Listening to and considering all parts—positive, negative, and ambivalent—will make you more comfortable with the final decision. When going through life's transitions, sometimes the smaller part that is reluctant to change simply needs time to grieve for the loss of what is ending. Acknowledging and dealing with that grief can enable a person to embrace the new order and move ahead with greater certainty.

Questions for Critical Thinking

What do you want to accomplish as an adult? What do you want to have done before you reach "old age"? What events have happened in you life that you think will influence your transitions through adulthood?

_____

_____

_____

_____

_____

_____

_____

_____

_____

Coming to Terms with Old Age

Most people look forward to the golden years when they can finally retire, and it can be a wonderful and relaxing time in life. Part of the American dream is living comfortably in retirement and enjoying leisure time. It is also a time of endings and letting go of former ways of life. Giving up a lifetime occupation can be unsettling. For many people, a major part of their identity is tied up in their work, and it is important to acknowledge that to move toward developing a new identity in old age.

One man who came to me for counseling was distraught about his impending retirement. He felt compelled to retire at a young enough age that he still had the physical capability to be active, but he was overwhelmed at the thought of quitting his job. He came to understand that being required to quit school and go to work at an early age had profoundly affected his life. From childhood on, he had believed that his worth as a human being was directly related to what he produced. As an adult, he felt that his main role in the family was to provide for everyone's welfare. It was, therefore, disconcerting to think of not having a job. He also realized that part of his fear of dying was based on his experience of friends who had passed away shortly after retiring. He was

afraid that if he retired, he too might die in a short time. It was a self-imposed double bind: If he didn't retire soon, he might not have the physical ability to do the things he wanted to do, but if he did retire, he might not live long enough to enjoy those things anyway. Giving himself permission to focus on some of his own needs and to develop a belief that he was more than a paycheck to his family helped him to resolve his problems. He also needed time to develop a new perspective and to separate retirement from the notion of death.

Regardless of whether one has had a specific career, the later stage of life is when people consider the meaning that their life has held. It is also the time to confront the issues of dying, as well as determine the focus of one's energy in the time remaining. Generativity may be the focus of middle age, but integrity is the key element in old age, according to Erikson. That means coming to terms with what one has done with one's life and giving it meaning.

There are many theories about life stages. The difficulty lies in trying to link those stages to any specific age. In other words, chronological age is an increasingly unreliable indicator of what people will be like at a given point in their life (Halonen and Santrock, 1997). A group of five-year-olds shows less variation than a group of 40-year-olds. That comparison is even more dramatic when considering a group of people in their 70s and 80s.

Some people are incapacitated mentally and physically by the time they are 65 years old. Others may live active lives and be productive in many ways well into their 80s. Regardless of the exact age when one approaches the end of one's life, there are some issues that are universal in dealing with the aging process. These include staying connected to family and community, evaluating and making sense of one's life, changing the emphasis and priorities of time and energy, and developing a sense of purpose in life.

The element of balance has gained importance in today's society. More and more people are complaining about the lack of leisure time in their lives. At the same time, that may be the very thing people have the most of in old age. While older people may be assessing their lives and putting things in perspective, it may be good for younger people to consider how to have more balance in life while still in a position to effect change.

A book by R. N. Boles (1978) entitled *The Three Boxes of Life* describes the areas in which we place importance and emphasis: the box of learning, the box of work, and the box of play. Boles's thesis is that we are out of balance in our society because emphasis is put on only one particular box during each stage in life. Generally, we focus on learning when young and on working when middle-aged, supposedly reserving play for old age. Boles points out the benefits of spending a more equal amount of time in each of the boxes during each of the different stages of life. Undoubtedly, work experience at an early age would help young people better understand the value of an education, but they also need time to enjoy their youth and take advantage of their physical abilities. The phrase "Youth is wasted on the young" probably comes from middle-aged people who spend too much time in the work box. It also means that by the time people have money and freedom to enjoy special interests, they must also deal with the limitations of aging.

Research on adjustment in old age supports the theory that good mental health comes from being involved in different activities (Dworetzky, 1995). Even very old people are happiest when still learning and acquiring new skills. A great deal of satisfaction is derived from volunteer work and its accompanying sense of accomplishment. Play is important, but it might be healthier for people of all ages to balance the three boxes in their lives.

The ultimate adjustment in old age is adjusting to the inevitability of death, the onset of which

> *"Life would be infinitely happier if we could only be born at the age of eighty and gradually approach eighteen."*
> *Mark Twain*

is declining health. In old age, people must learn to cope with the loss of physical strength and ability. And the longer we live, the more likely it is that we will have dealt with the deaths of friends and relatives. Perhaps that is part of the process of preparing for our own deaths. Even though death is an inevitable part of the life cycle, it is still a difficult subject to deal with in our society.

As medical advances create legal issues about life and death, this topic will have to be addressed further in the future. When we have the means to support life even when there is no sign of brain activity, the question arises of when someone is actually dead. Another issue currently being addressed concerns the right to die. When more people who are terminally ill begin to consider assisted suicide as an answer, society will need to discuss the issues of death and dying on deeper levels.

THOUGHTS TO LIVE BY

If I had my life to live over, I'd dare to make more mistakes next time. I'd relax; I would limber up. I would be sillier than I have been this trip. I would take fewer things seriously. I would take more chances. I would climb more mountains and swim more rivers. I would eat more ice cream and fewer beans. I might have more actual troubles, but I'd have fewer imaginary ones.

You see, I'm one of those people who live sensibly and sanely, hour after hour, day after day. Oh, I've had my moments, and if I had to do it over again, I'd have more of them. In fact, I'd try to have nothing else. Just moments—one after another—instead of living so many years ahead of each day. I've been one of those people who never goes anywhere without a thermometer, a hot water bottle, a raincoat, and a parachute. If I had to do it all over again, I would travel lighter.

If I had my life to live over, I would start barefoot earlier in the spring and stay that way later in the fall. I would go to more dances. I would ride more merry-go-rounds. I would pick more daisies.

Source: Eighty-five-year-old woman, Portland Adventist Hospital.

Transitional Times

Whether contending with the normal passages in life or with the necessary losses inherent in those passages, most people go through a similar process in dealing with transition. Just as there are similarities in dealing with significant loss, there is a common path toward coping with and resolving issues about significant life changes.

At any life stage, you can undergo change in many areas. You can have changes in close relationships or in your home life. You can experience change in your personal habits and lifestyle. Work- and job-related changes usually mean a change in your financial situation. You can even have major changes in something as abstract as your beliefs and values. Some people go through a transition when they lose their youthful identity and sense of idealism. It is important to understand the process of change and have information about how to make the transition as smooth as possible, given that it is a lifelong journey.

Bill Bridges (1980) discovered in his seminars that people going through changes in their lives, regardless of the type of change, have similar experiences. Each experiences (a) an ending, followed by (b) a period of confusion and distress, leading to (c) a new beginning, in the cases that go that far. These stages may seem obvious, but it is difficult for some people to let themselves go through all of them. Some people want to deny that an ending has even happened. Some try to avoid an ending by starting something new long before they are ready. In our society, it is difficult to allow time out, and few people take the time needed to be in the *neutral zone* necessary before entering a new phase in life. I've known people who couldn't tolerate a day of introspection following an ending in their life before they rushed off to start something new. The steps may be simple (dealing with the ending, neutral zone, and beginning), but we have much to learn about how to use them to the best advantage.

Each person in transition will deal with those steps in a different manner. People who have chosen their ending will have a different perspective than those who have not. According to Bridges, there are some basic rules that seem to apply in either case:

1. The first rule is that you will find yourself coming back in new ways to old activities when you are in transition. For example, we frequently take up old hobbies again as a source of comfort in times of change. When there are events in our lives that require dealing with the new and unknown, it is often comforting to return to activities that are a predictable source of pleasure.

2. The second rule is that every transition begins with an ending. We have to let go of the old thing, both outwardly and inwardly, before we can pick up the new. Many people make it difficult to proceed through a transitional time in life by refusing to acknowledge that an ending has happened. They cling to the belief that they can hold on to all the old elements of their life while simultaneously entering into a new phase.

3. Rule number three is that, although it is advantageous to understand your own style of dealing with endings, some part of you will resist that understanding as though your life depended on it! Some of the most useful information in the world is simple to understand yet difficult to put into practice. For example, some people resort to a particular pattern of behavior (avoidance, denial, or self-destructiveness) whenever they have to deal with change in their lives. The behavior pattern may not help them deal with the situation, yet they insist on doing it. Have you ever been in a cycle where what you did to cope with change and uncertainty made things even more unsettled? Sometimes, it is useful to pay attention to old patterns or listen to an old friend who might be able to point them out.

Part of the reluctance to deal with endings is that it often requires learning a whole new way of being. *It is hard enough to stop doing the things that don't work, let alone the things that do!* And that is often exactly what is required. What was valuable and successful at one stage may be the very thing causing difficulty in another. The following guidelines (Bridges, 1980) are important in searching for meaning and purpose in life, especially in life's second half:

- We must unlearn the style of mastering the world that we used to take us through the first half of life. Things that were useful at age 25 may not be at all helpful at age 50.
- We must resist the temptation to abandon the developmental journey and stay forever at some attractive stopping place. Perhaps you have heard the term *arrested development?* The person who was popular in college may have had a wonderful time during those years, but if he never grows beyond the behavior and

> *"What we call the beginning is often the end. And to make an end is to make a beginning. The end is where we start from."*
>
> T. S. Eliot

attitudes of those times, he will probably restrict his choices in later adult life.

▶ We must recognize that it will take effort to regain the inner home. Regaining a sense of well-being and comfort after a transitional period takes commitment. Finding a previous sense of peacefulness and contentment requires dealing with all aspects of change.

Endings

There are four aspects of dealing appropriately with endings. To move into the neutral zone and be able to address new beginnings, it is valuable to consider how each of the following concepts pertains to your situation:

Disengagement: Most changes start with a need to separate from the old ways. The process of transition begins with the clarification that comes from letting go, whether it is a physical or mental letting go.

Disidentification: In breaking the old connections, a person often loses ways of self-definition. Change requires that we define ourselves differently. In most cases, this disidentification process is really the inner side of the disengagement process. We need to loosen the bonds of who we think we are so we can move toward a new identity.

Disenchantment: To really change—not just switch positions—you must realize that part of your old reality was in your head and not out there in the real world. The world can still be a beautiful place even if you give up some of your fairy tales about life.

Disorientation: This is a necessary part of transition, yet some of our fears come from going into this emptiness. Most people understand the importance of not jumping right into another marriage after divorce, but it can be difficult to stay in that in-between phase and just be with yourself. Yet, out of the confusion can come clarification about future moves. Perhaps the prospect of staying with the unknown of the neutral zone awakens old fears about death and abandonment, but that is all the more reason why it is important to spend time there.

All of these aspects of dealing with endings are evident in a divorce situation, for example. The process of divorce means disengaging from someone; yet for some people, the psychological disengagement may occur before, during, or even long after the actual divorce decree. Before one is free to move on, there needs to be disengagement from the relationship. Disidentification takes place when one separates one's identity from the relationship and the view of oneself as a married person. It is reflected in the internal evaluation of who one is now that one isn't married, and who one wants to be as a single person. Disenchantment may mean giving up the belief that someone else is responsible for giving one meaning, purpose, approval, or happiness in life. Disorientation may be the confusion of "What's next?" Do you want to have another relationship, and if so, when? How long is long enough to heal and let go? Who might be a potential future partner, and what traits should that person have? Answering these questions is part of the work to be done in the disorientation of the neutral zone.

The Neutral Zone

After dealing with the ending phase of transition, it is time to be in the neutral zone. Bridges (1980) offers the following suggestions for how best to use that time to assess the past and the future.

▶ Find a regular time to be alone.

▶ Begin a log of neutral-zone experiences.

▶ Take this pause in the action of your life to write an autobiography.

▶ Take this opportunity to discover what you really want.

▶ Think of what would be unlived in your life if it ended today.

▶ Take a few days to go on your own version of a passage journey.

Mostly, the neutral zone provides time to do whatever you do as though it were part of an elaborate ritual, and to do it with your total attention. For once in your life, you don't have to produce results or accomplish anything. Whatever you are feeling is just you, and you are there to be alone with and really listen to yourself. "Treating ourselves like appliances that can be unplugged and plugged in again, at will, or cars that stop and start with the twist of a key, we have forgotten the importance of fallow time and winter and rests in music" (Bridges, 1980, p. 130).

> " Perhaps one has to be really old before one learns to be amused rather than shocked. "
>
> Pearl Buck

New Beginnings

After spending the needed time in the neutral zone, it is useful to decide on the best things to do to have a new beginning. One person's safety involves inactivity, whereas another's may be perpetual motion. In both cases, a new beginning upsets a long-standing arrangement. When you are ready to move on, there are two signs to look for. The first is the reaction of your friends: Do they see what you propose to do as something new or as simply an old pattern? The second is from the transition process itself: Have you really moved through endings into the neutral zone and found there the beginning you now want to follow, or is this beginning a way of avoiding an ending or of aborting the neutral-zone experience?

Once you have allowed the direction of your change to emerge, there are steps you can take to get the results you want. The first is to stop getting ready and act. Some people spend so much time waiting for a sign that they are doing the right thing that they never do anything. The second thing you can do is begin to identify yourself with the final results of the new beginning. There are many things that aren't very enjoyable to do, such as folding the laundry, but the end results can be satisfying and worthwhile: having the laundry done and being able to move on to other things. Imagining that you are through your transition and actively involved in the change in your life can bring good feelings.

Change seems inherently to cause some degree of stress, even when the change is a positive one. The previous information can be helpful, though, in going through life's inevitable changes. Even though life's transitions may not always be easy, much can be learned. And some experiences can help us through subsequent changes as we go through life's stages.

A final note: It is important to keep the need for developmental growth in perspective. When dealing with changes in life circumstances, it helps to have a sense of humor. Even if you are one of the people who considers becoming a better person the purpose of life, you still have to deal with the everyday tasks of life. Keep in mind that after enlightenment comes the laundry!

Health and Wellness

The single most important factor to consider when making changes or learning new coping skills is your level of energy. Perhaps that sounds a bit overstated, but consider the following situations: When are you most susceptible to getting hooked by others and ending up in negative interactions? When are you irritable, short-tempered, and dissatisfied with the world in general? For most of us, those situations are more likely to occur when we feel drained and low on energy. We don't want the world to require one more thing of us, and it seems to take an extra amount of effort just to accomplish ordinary daily tasks.

There are times when we all find ourselves saying and doing appalling things. What causes us to take a course of action that we know, even as we are doing it, isn't the right one? It may be many things, but lack of energy is usually a contributing factor. When our resources are depleted, even things that don't usually bother us will get to us. Conversely, when we have an abundance of energy, it seems that moving through life is effortless. Even the events, behaviors, and people who usually bother us don't have much impact. When we do have difficult situations to contend with when our energy level is normal or high, we are usually able to think clearly and take an appropriate course of action. Further, we are usually more patient when we are feeling that our life is in balance, and patience is a trait that contributes to the improvement of a number of situations.

Given that the amount of energy we have is central to so many different behaviors, it is valuable to explore the various methods for creating and maintaining energy. One of the primary methods for creating energy is to be aware of and take care of our bodies, called self-care. This comes more easily for some than others, oftentimes because of what an individual learned in childhood and their teens about caring for themselves. Some people simply do not know how. But wellness is a concept that means more than just taking care of your physical being.

Life Choices

There are a number of factors that contribute to a sense of well-being. Many people believe that it is important to have a holistic approach to health, one that incorporates many factors. Some of the areas to consider are the following:

- How and what we eat.
- How we maintain physical fitness.
- How we work and play.
- How we relax.
- How we develop relationships with others.
- How we address our spiritual needs.

Health and wellness are more than the absence of discomfort or disease. Good health means paying attention to and taking care of, or balancing, all the areas of your life. There are people who turn 50 and look like they are 40, while others of the same age may look 65. The difference probably has a lot to do with the choices they made throughout their lifetime. In their *Wellness Workbook,* Travis and Ryan (1988) offer a number of points that capture the essence of wellness:

- Wellness is a choice—a decision you make to move toward optimal health.
- Wellness is a way of life—a lifestyle you design to achieve your highest potential for well-being.
- Wellness is a process—a developing awareness that there is no endpoint, but that health and happiness are possible in each moment, here and now.
- Wellness is an efficient channeling of energy—energy received from the environment, transformed within you, and sent on to affect the world outside.
- Wellness is the integration of body, mind, and spirit—the appreciation that everything you do and think and feel and believe has an impact on your state of health.
- Wellness is the loving acceptance of yourself.

Taking Care of Your Body

Although the American public is becoming increasingly aware of the importance of exercise and good dietary habits, current research suggests that many of us are overweight, or even obese. People today are taking an active role in maintaining their health, which is positive, and there are prospects for increased longevity, but there is still work to be done! As people assume more responsibility for their health, in terms of diet, sleep, exercise, exposure to stressors, recreation and leisure, as well as intellectual stimulation, they become healthier.

Diet   One way to take care of your body is to pay attention to the kind of fuel you put into it.

Few of us would expect our cars to run on substandard gas, yet we insist on filling ourselves with food that results in poor performance. The next time you reach for something that you know isn't good for you, consider the following:

- How will this make me feel in an hour?
- How does this contribute to my energy level in the long run?
- How might this affect my weight or appearance?
- Am I really hungry?
- Am I trying to satisfy some other need?

Few of us really need more information on nutrition; many of us were introduced to the basic four food groups in elementary school. Although there have been advances in the field of nutrition with regard to the importance of certain foods, it might be more important to consider making the commitment to yourself to improve your overall eating habits. That can be accomplished by being more aware of what you are eating, as well as when and how you eat.

Suggestions for a Healthy Diet

- Eat a variety of foods, including plenty of fresh fruits and vegetables.
- Cut down on salt and caffeine.
- Cut down on animal fat.
- Cut down on sugar.
- Use alcohol in moderation.
- Take multiple vitamin supplements.
- Eat five small meals a day, rather than three major meals.

Exercise   Dozens of studies link regular physical exercise with lower levels of depression and anxiety. People who exercise regularly are less depressed, but could it also be that people who are more depressed exercise less? To demonstrate a causal link between exercise and depression, McCann and Holmes (1984) performed an experiment with women students at the University of Kansas. Students were randomly assigned either to an exercise group, involving running and aerobic exercise, or to a control group, which involved no exercise program. Before the experiment began, the women were tested to measure the degree of their depression. Later, they were retested, once after five weeks of the exercise program and again after 10 weeks. Results showed that only the students in the exercise group became markedly less depressed.

It is not clear how or why exercise affects depression. Some explanations focus on the changes in body and brain chemistry, resulting in rising levels of endorphins in the blood during exercise. Endorphins are naturally synthesized in the brain and are released in response to strenuous exercise or even pain. It is hypothesized that these endorphins, as well as the neurotransmitter serotonin, are responsible for the well-being and inner peace experienced by many after a hard workout. Other explanations suggest that the sense of mastery over one's body gained through exercise may contribute to a greater sense of personal control over other aspects of one's life as well, thereby alleviating the passivity and helplessness often found in depressed people (Peterson and Seligman, 1984).

Pyramid Building*

With much fanfare, the USDA recently retired the old Food Guide Pyramid and replaced it with MyPyramid, a new symbol and "interactive food guidance system." The new symbol is basically the old Pyramid turned on its side.

The good news is that this dismantles and buries the flawed Pyramid. The bad news is that the new symbol doesn't convey enough information to help you make informed choices about your diet and long-term health. And it continues to recommend foods that aren't essential to good health, and may even be detrimental in the quantities included in MyPyramid.

As an alternative to the USDA's flawed pyramid, faculty members in the Harvard School of Public Health built the Healthy Eating Pyramid. It resembles the USDA's in shape only. The Healthy Eating Pyramid takes into consideration, and puts into perspective, the wealth of research conducted during the past 10 years that has reshaped the definition of healthy eating.

Building a Better Pyramid

If the only goal of the Food Guide Pyramid is to give us the best possible advice for healthy eating, then it should be grounded in the evidence and be independent of business. Instead of waiting for this to happen, nutrition experts from the Harvard School of Public Health created the Healthy Eating Pyramid. It is based on the best available scientific evidence about the links between diet and health. This new pyramid fixes fundamental flaws in the USDA Pyramid and offers sound information to help people make better choices about what to eat.

The Healthy Eating Pyramid sits on a foundation of daily exercise and weight control. Why?

These two related elements strongly influence your chances of staying healthy. They also affect what and how you eat and how your food affects you. The other bricks of the Healthy Eating Pyramid include:

Whole grain foods: The body needs carbohydrates mainly for energy. The best sources of carbohydrates are whole grains such as oatmeal, whole-wheat bread, and brown rice. They deliver the outer (bran) and inner (germ) layers along with energy-rich starch. The body can't digest whole grains as quickly as it can highly processed carbohydrates such as white flour. This keeps blood sugar and insulin levels from rising, then falling, too quickly. Better control of blood sugar and insulin can keep hunger at bay and may prevent the development of type 2 diabetes.

Plant oils: Surprised that the Healthy Eating Pyramid puts some fats near the base, indicating they are okay to eat? Although this recommendation seems to go against conventional wisdom, it's exactly in line with the evidence and with common eating habits. The average American gets one third or more of his or her daily calories from fats, so placing them near the foundation of the pyramid makes sense. Note, though, that it specifically mentions plant oils, not all types of fat. Good sources of healthy unsaturated fats include olive, canola, soy, corn, sunflower, peanut, and other vegetable oils, as well as fatty fish such as salmon. These healthy fats not only improve cholesterol levels (when eaten in place of highly processed carbohydrates) but can also protect the heart from sudden and potentially deadly rhythm problems.

Vegetables (in abundance) and fruits (2 to 3 servings daily): A diet rich in fruits and vegetables can decrease the chances of having a heart attack or stroke; protect against a variety of cancers; lower blood pressure; help you avoid the painful intestinal ailment called diverticulitis; guard against cataract and macular degeneration, the major cause of vision loss among people over age 65; and add variety to your diet and wake up your palate.

Fish, poultry, and eggs (0 to 2 servings daily): These are important sources of protein. A wealth of research suggests that eating fish can reduce the risk of heart disease. Chicken and turkey are also good sources of protein and can be low in saturated fat. Eggs, which have long been demonized because they contain fairly high levels of cholesterol, aren't as bad as they're cracked up to be. In fact, an egg is a much better breakfast than a doughnut cooked in an oil rich in trans fats or a bagel made from refined flour.

Nuts and legumes (1 to 3 servings daily): Nuts and legumes are excellent sources of protein, fiber, vitamins, and minerals. Legumes include black beans, navy beans, garbanzos, and other beans that are usually sold dried. Many kinds of nuts contain healthy fats, and packages of some varieties (almonds, walnuts, pecans, peanuts, hazelnuts, and pistachios) can now even carry a label saying they're good for your heart.

Dairy or calcium supplement (1 to 2 servings daily): Building bone and keeping it strong takes calcium vitamin D, exercise, and a whole lot more. Dairy products have traditionally been Americans' main source of calcium. But there are other healthy ways to get calcium than from milk and cheese, which can contain a lot of saturated fat. Cumulatively, three glasses of whole milk, for example, contain as much saturated fat as 13 strips of cooked bacon. If you enjoy dairy foods, try to stick with no-fat or low-fat products. If you don't like dairy products, calcium supplements offer an easy and inexpensive way to get your daily calcium.

Red meat and butter (use sparingly): These sit at the top of the Healthy Eating Pyramid because they contain lots of saturated fat. If you eat red meat every day, switching to fish or chicken several times a week can improve cholesterol levels. So can switching from butter to olive oil.

White rice, white bread, potatoes, pasta, and sweets (use sparingly): Why are these all-American staples at the top, rather than the bottom, of the Healthy Eating Pyramid? They can cause fast and furious increases in blood sugar that can lead to weight gain, diabetes, heart disease, and other chronic disorders. Whole-grain carbohydrates cause slower, steadier increases in blood sugar that don't overwhelm the body's ability to handle this much needed but potentially dangerous nutrient.

Multiple vitamin: A daily multivitamin, multimineral supplement offers a kind of nutritional backup. Although it can't in any way replace healthy eating, or make up for unhealthy eating, it can fill in the nutrient holes that may sometimes affect even the most careful eaters. You don't need an expensive name-brand or designer vitamin. A standard, store-brand, RDA-level one is fine. Look for one that meets the requirements of the USP (U.S. Pharmacopeia), an organization that sets standards for drugs and supplements.

Alcohol (in moderation): Scores of studies suggest that having an alcoholic drink a day lowers the risk of heart disease. Moderation is clearly important, since alcohol has risks as well as benefits. For men, a good balance point is one to two drinks a day. For women, it's at most one drink a day.

The Healthy Eating Pyramid summarizes the best dietary information available today. It isn't set in stone, though, because nutrition researchers will undoubtedly turn up new information in the years ahead. The Healthy Eating Pyramid will change to reflect important new evidence. The Healthy Eating Pyramid is described in greater detail in *Eat, Drink, and Be Healthy: The Harvard Medical School Guide to Healthy Eating* is authored by Walter C. Millet, M.D., and is published by Simon and Schuster (2001) and Free Press (2005). The previous excerpt was reproduced from an article titled "Food Pyramids: What should You Really Eat?" from the Nutrition Source, a website maintained by the Dept. of Nutrition at the Harvard School of Public Health, http://www.hsph.harvard.edu/nutritionsource. The contents of this website are not intended to offer personal medical advice, which should be obtained from a health-care provider.

*Source: © 2005 President and Fellows of Harvard College.

Balanced Lifestyle

Consider how we divide the day. In a 24-hour period, most people spend about eight hours sleeping, eight hours at work, and eight hours involved in all other activities—including leisure pursuits. If you enjoy your work, at least half of your waking hours will be spent in meaningful activities. But if you dread getting up and hate going to work, those eight hours can have a negative impact on the rest of your day.

What can you do if you find your job meaningless? One method of dealing with dissatisfaction at work is to notice how you really spend your time. Which activities are draining and which are energizing? Make a list and keep track over time. Focus on the factors that you can change rather than the ones you can't. Or perhaps you can redefine your goals for the job you have. You might be able to find ways of advancing within your present job, of creating a more flexible job description or schedule, or of acquiring skills that could prepare you to move on.

If you are stuck in a dead-end job that is creating frustration, you might do well to consider a change in careers. The option of changing jobs as a way to create more meaning in life always exists, but it is also important to consider what price will be paid for making a change. Given the number of sources indicating that people will have two or three careers in the future, it might be advisable to consider each job as a potential step to another one (Corey and Schneider-Corey, 2003).

Assessing the potential that your work has for contributing to the meaning in your life could enhance your sense of wellness. Brugh Joy (1979) believes that people get sick for one of two reasons: either they are leading highly restricted lives that are too small for the person they could potentially become, or they are leading lives that are too expansive—they are trying to be and do more than is possible for them. *It is important to determine the right balance between those two approaches to life.*

Work alone does not provide fulfillment for most people, however. Even a job that is rewarding may take a great deal of energy. Most people need a break at some point. During leisure time, we can have more control over our activities. Many psychologists emphasize the importance of play and the ability to let go and be spontaneous. Leisure time is the time to rejuvenate the spirit and go with the flow rather than having to make something happen on a certain schedule. Leisure time can also provide that necessary balance for creating the energy required at work.

There should be a balance between work and leisure (more will be said on this in the next chapter), and that will be different for each individual. Some people schedule leisure activities in such a manner that they miss the point of recreation. You may have heard the term *workaholic*. Be cautious of activities that create more stress instead of less. Some people work too hard at having a good time or get involved in sports and activities that are too competitive. Remember that the point of leisure is to enhance a feeling of wellness and balance in life. Leisure activities should also provide some form of relaxation. In his book *The Guide to Stress Reduction* (2001), L. J. Mason suggests that we have a right to relax and feel good. He offers a number of activities that could increase relaxation during leisure time:

▶ Sitting in a quiet place for as long as 10 minutes a day and just letting your mind wander.

▶ Playing a sport that has a calming effect on you.

▶ Truly listening to music without any other background activity.

▶ Walking in the woods or on the beach.

▶ Getting a massage.

▶ Practicing some form of meditation.

▶ Practicing some form of muscle relaxation technique.

▶ Soaking in a hot tub.

▶ Allowing yourself to have fun with friends.

Finally, having a balance of work and leisure in life may help people adjust to retirement. If we do not learn how to pursue interests other than work, we may have difficulty when we retire. Some research indicates that many people die soon after retirement (Siegel, 1988). It appears that having a balance of work and leisure is as important for lifelong wellness as for developing meaning and purpose in life.

Lifestyle and Being Overweight

Changes in lifestyles, as well as higher consumption rates of foods rich in fat and carbohydrates, are contributing considerably to a more overweight population around the world. Obesity is a growing health concern for both developed and developing countries. World Health Organization (WHO) figures indicate that obesity is a "global epidemic." Obesity is a severe condition of overweight. There are more than one billion overweight adults, and at least 300 million of them are clinically obese. Overweight affects more people than malnutrition and hunger (WHO, 2004). However, economists still know very little about its causes, consequences, and potential remedies. In particular, economists wonder why obesity is more prevalent in Western industrialized countries, many developing countries, and new transitional economies.

Unfortunately, obesity is not a well-documented problem; thus, statistical data are hard to obtain. The United States has the highest percentage of obese and overweight population (64.5 percent); Mexico (62.3 percent), the United Kingdom (61 percent), and Australia (58.4 percent) follow close behind. The lowest percentages are recorded in Japan (25.8 percent) and Korea (30.6 percent).

Many speculate that this trend may go up, particularly when we consider the incidence of obesity among children and adolescents. According to the American Obesity Association (2004), the percentage of obese children grew from 7 percent in 1976–1980 to 15.3 percent in 1999–2000. A similar trend occurred among adolescents, rising from 5 percent in 1976–1980 to 15.5 percent in 1999–2000. Multiple studies have shown that obese children are likely to become obese adults.

Consequences of Weight-Related Problems

Obesity and overweight problems have serious social and economic consequences. Multiple studies have shown that obesity negatively affects earnings and wages, particularly for females (Cawley, 2004). In the Organization for Economic Co-operation and Development (OECD), obesity-related medical costs are rising, although the contribution of obesity to the total health bill is not easy to determine.

Obesity carries both direct and indirect costs. Direct costs include those for preventive, diagnostic, and treatment services. Indirect costs occur through losses in labor-force participation due to increases in health-related problems, including type 2 diabetes, heart disease, certain cancers, stroke, and depression. The data show that increased incidence of obesity is associated with increased observed health expenditures and decreased life expectancy.

Studies based in the United States reveal that health care costs for overweight and obese individuals average 37 percent more than for people of normal weight, adding an average of $732 to the annual medical bills of each American. Estimated medical costs connected to obesity and smoking each account for about 9.1 percent of all health expenditures in the United States (Finkelstein, Fiebelkorn, and Wang, 2003).

Exploring the Roots of the Problem

Leaving genetics aside, weight-related problems are caused by the difference between calories consumed and calories used. Cultural and socio-demographic factors contribute to this calorie imbalance. Some argue that obesity growth is mainly due to a higher intake of calories, but others state that it is mainly caused by a lower expenditure of calories in daily activities.

In connection with the higher-calorie-intake argument, a popular justification is the growth of fast-food and soft-drink consumption, associated with increases in dietary intake of saturated fats, sugars, and calories. In addition, increases in serving portions are also considered quite important. Other researchers argue that female labor participation is a contributing factor: Presumably, healthier home-cooked dinners have been widely replaced by TV dinners or restaurant dinners—which frequently take place in fast-food restaurants. Cutler, Glaeser, and Shapiro (2003) analyze changes in food consumption between the mid-1970s and mid-1990s and observe that the growth in calories is enough to explain the increase in weight. In the process, they partially invalidate the fast-food argument, pointing out that the main reason for increased dietary caloric intake was calories consumed outside the main meals (i.e., snacks). They also failed to find a strong interrelationship between obesity and the number of women working.

In terms of calories expended, other researchers emphasize the role of reduced physical activity and technological change—products of the transition from rural to urban societies—as well as a higher rate of passive entertainment. Lakdawalla and Philipson (2002) concluded that a worker who spends his/her career in a sedentary job will be heavier than someone in a highly active job. Further, they estimated that about 40 percent of the total growth in weight in the United States may be due to expansion in calories, potentially through increased food abundance (agricultural innovation), and about 60 percent

due to demand factors, such as a decrease in physical activity.

Other potential economic explanations that justify the imbalance of calories refer to the consequences of becoming a more industrialized society in which the value of time increases. As Chou, Grossman, and Saffer (2004) point out, in industrialized societies, workers sell more of their time to the labor market and have less disposable time for entertainment and other household activities (including food preparation). This lack of time is what may explain the growth of fast-food restaurants in the United States. Their results indicate that not only restaurant availability and restaurant food prices matter when explaining weight gain, but also a set of sociodemographic characteristics of the individuals. In particular, they conclude that wealthier and more educated individuals are less likely to have obesity problems, whereas black and Hispanic people are more likely to suffer from obesity or have higher weights. Thus, all evidence shows that obesity is a complex phenomenon, linked not only to the demand and supply conditions of food products, but also to economic transitions and cultural change of societies. This makes it harder to disentangle.

There are, however, some cultural differences that should be taken into consideration in order to understand the spread of obesity and weight-related problems around the world. For instance, the spirit of massive consumption and the idea of "getting a good value for your money" are more linked to some countries than others. In addition, the effects related to the imitation of Western lifestyles are also different, depending on the degree of reception and adoption of these new cultural habits, which include the consumption of fast food, sodas, and snacks.

Conclusions

Population and consumption data reveal that socioeconomic and cultural factors are affecting the spread of obesity around the world. Although economists have recently started exploring the economic causes and consequences of obesity, providing a solution to this problem may require a complex vision that incorporates more than economic incentives to help consumers eat healthier foods (such as providing mandatory nutritional food information, taxing food products with high levels of sugars, carbohydrates, and fats, or subsidizing certain fruits and vegetables for lower-income groups). Given that both consumption and expenditure of calories matter, new health policies promoting more active lifestyles should be put forward by countries affected by the obesity epidemic. This would alleviate the symptoms of new sedentary lifestyles common to all industrialized countries. The fight against weight problems may also require having an understanding of the sociological perspectives of cultural change and economic growth, reminding individuals that "they are what they eat."

Death and Dying Issues

We live in a "death-denying" society, according to Elisabeth Kübler-Ross (1975), whose book *On Death and Dying* is a standard in the field. For example, we have at least 50 euphemisms for the word *dead*. If language reflects what is important in a culture, then in ours, it must be important not to mention death. We avoid using the word *dead* with such phrases as "kicked the bucket," "six feet under," "crossed over," "gone to meet her maker," "peaceful slumber," "cashed in his chips," "croaked," "bit the dust," "beamed up," and "bought the farm." It would appear that we need to learn to confront the reality that we will all have to deal with the loss of someone close to us at some time.

The same forces that have influenced our language are apparent even in hospitals. Kübler-Ross started her work with terminally ill patients in hospitals, where she noticed that doctors and nurses often had a difficult time coping with someone who was dying. Logically, it seems that medical personnel would be more willing than anyone to discuss feelings about death with their patients. This didn't appear to be the case. She found that some doctors not only wouldn't talk to the patient about dying, but didn't even want family members to mention the possibility. That has changed considerably over the past 20 years, partially as a result of the work Kübler-Ross has done and the hospice program she started. There are places now where terminally ill people can go to get support in talking about and dealing with their situation. Increasingly, society may have a need and obligation to provide such care, especially with the increase of AIDS patients.

Why is it that we have such difficulty dealing with death? In part, it is due to the vast changes that have taken place in our society since the turn of the century. Factors that have influenced people's attitudes toward dealing with death and dying include the following:

Medical advances and the infant mortality rate: In the early 1900s, the majority of people lived in large families in rural settings. The infant mortality rate was much higher then. Nearly one child in 10 died before reaching the first year. The current rate is approximately one death for every 100 births during the first year. Back then, childhood diseases were far more likely to be fatal. Consequently, it was not uncommon for children in large families to experience the death of at least one sibling. Conditions today are different because of smaller families, a lower infant mortality rate, and the eradication of certain childhood diseases.

Death as part of the life cycle: Given that many people in rural settings had an agricultural lifestyle, they were much closer to the natural cycle of life. The passing of seasons, the raising of crops and livestock, and closeness to the earth helped them to see death as part of the natural order of things. A hundred years ago, death was not something to be conquered, but an event to be accepted. Today, death is fought in many ways. We have the pseudoscience of cryogenics, in which people pay to have their bodies frozen, hoping that someday a cure will be found for whatever killed them and they can be brought back to life. People seem preoccupied with beating the grim reaper rather than accepting death as inevitable.

Dealing with the reality of death: A century ago, when someone died, the immediate family was intimately involved in the burial process. If Uncle Joe fell off the barn roof and broke his neck, he was laid out on the kitchen table. The family built the coffin, dressed him, conducted the services, and more than likely buried him in the family cemetery out back. That process was beneficial because it gave people time to grieve for the loss they had suffered. Today, 90 percent of people die in hospitals, often under conditions that severely limit visitations. The hospital then takes them to the mortuary, the mortuary takes them to the funeral home, and the funeral home takes them to the cemetery, where a machine digs the grave. Then a minister, who might not even know the person, delivers the eulogy.

Limited exposure to death: At the turn of the century, death was real to people; when someone died, there was a significant connection because usually the person was known to them. However, people didn't have to deal with death constantly. Today, we hear about death every day, all day. The media bombard us with news about catastrophes and death tolls. People have had to learn to

> **"** *Do not go gently into that dark night. Old age should burn and rave at close of day; rage, rage against the dying of the light.* **"**
>
> *Dylan Thomas*

> **"** *When you were born, you cried and the world rejoiced. Live your life in such a manner that when you die, the world cries and you rejoice.* **"**
>
> *Native American saying*

numb themselves to such information. As a result, when a death occurs that has significance in their lives, many people aren't prepared to deal with it.

Stages of Dealing with Loss

Kübler-Ross introduced the stages that people go through in dealing with death—their own impending death or the death of others. These stages apply to more than just the loss experienced due to death. People often need to go through a period of mourning over the endings or losses resulting from changes in any number of areas of their lives. People who have lost a job or gone through a divorce know that there are stages to resolving the feelings about those events. The stages are as follows:

Denial: Most people first respond to a traumatic event with "No, no, it can't be happening." That can last from a day to a week or even longer in some cases.

Anger: Anger is a normal response to accepting the reality of an event. Life isn't fair, it isn't equal, and sometimes, bad things do happen to good people for no reason.

Bargaining: Once people realize that anger doesn't change the circumstances, they try all forms of bargaining: "I promise I'll never ever again. . . ." Unfortunately, during this stage, some people feel guilty even when they had absolutely nothing to do with what happened. They may have a distorted idea that by feeling bad, they can undo what happened.

Depression: This is much different from the sadness that some people feel without knowing the reason. People for whom depression is an ongoing process need to get help. People who are depressed as the result of a loss need to know that it is a normal response and part of the process of healing. I have known people who have actually wondered what was wrong with them when they were still having problems a few weeks after the death of a parent. Grief is a normal reaction.

Acceptance: When people have gone through all of the previous stages, they are likely to arrive at a

point of resolution. But if they have skipped any stage, they may prolong the process. A person doesn't go from denial to acceptance overnight, or reach acceptance by avoiding any of the stages. It is also important to note that people may not go through the stages in a neat, orderly fashion. Some people report cycling through all of the stages a number of times.

The Grieving Process

Kübler-Ross provides important background for dealing with loss, but there is also more current information on the grieving process. The early work that Kübler-Ross did focused on terminally ill patients coping with their own inevitable deaths. There are some areas of overlap with the grieving process that people go through after experiencing the death of someone close, but there is also specific information that is useful to the survivors. The following concepts are from *Grief Counseling and Grief Therapy: A Handbook for the Mental Health Practitioner,* by William Worden (1991). There is evidence that all humans grieve a loss to one degree or another (Bowlby, 1980). Attachments to others come from an early need for security and safety. If the goal of attachment behavior is to maintain an affectional bond, any disruption of that connection will be distressing. The greater the potential for loss, the more intense and varied the reactions.

The Four Tasks of Mourning

1. *To accept the reality of the loss:* Many people deny that a death has occurred; thus, the first task of grieving is to come to terms with the fact that the person is dead and will not be returning. Accepting the reality of the loss takes time because it is an emotional as well as a cognitive process. Belief and disbelief are intertwined in this phase.

2. *To work through the pain of grief:* It is necessary for the bereaved person to go through the pain of grief. This may be difficult for some because of the contradictory messages from our society. Although grief is expected to

CASE STUDIES AND STUDENT STORIES

Elizabeth looked in the mirror one morning and realized she was 80 years old. She could hardly believe that so many years had passed. As she peered into her special hand mirror, she could see every wrinkle and every flaw in her weathered face. Her image was a reminder of how much she had changed since the days of her youthful appearance.

Remembering her formerly radiant self, she began to recall memories of an earlier time in her life. It was 1945, and World War II was raging. Elizabeth had suffered a particularly bad day working as a welder, and she felt hot and tired. During this time period, many women were called to do the former tasks of their husbands, and welding was commonplace.

As Elizabeth rounded the corner to her rooming house, she saw two well-dressed Army officials. One of them was carrying a briefcase. Arriving at her door, she realized they were looking for her. They had come to give her the news that her husband was missing in action. With the final word spoken by the senior officer, Elizabeth collapsed to the floor and sobbed uncontrollably. She was just 19 years old, pregnant, worked at a job that she hated, and she had just received the dreadful news that her husband was missing in action, and was most likely dead.

For three days Elizabeth lay in bed crying continuously and refusing to eat. She longed for her husband, Andrew, whom she had loved for such a short time. She longed for their home in the country, and she longed for the family that she had hoped to create with him.

On the fourth day she was revived by the news that her mother, Anna, was coming to visit. Her mother had received word of her severe blow and was traveling 1200 miles to be with her daughter. Upon arriving, Elizabeth's mother held her in her arms and they both wept.

As they talked and shared feelings, Anna began to recount a very similar story. During World War I her husband had died of influenza. And, she, too, was pregnant with no where to go. She explained to her daughter that life events sometimes seem almost impossible to handle, but she learned that with help, support, and courage, things can eventually be dealt with. Anna told her daughter to take as much time as she needed, and promised that she would always be close by to see her through this time.

As Elizabeth continued to peer into her hand mirror, she remember how important those words had been for her. She grieved for the loss of her husband, but she began to pour her energy into planning the arrival of her new baby. She moved in with her sister and found a more suitable job. Following the birth of her little girl, she met a wonderful man who loved her and accepted her tiny daughter as though she were his own.

Elizabeth put down the mirror and simply sat and reflected on the transitions of her life. Her husband of 50 years had died the day before, and she was again at a time when change would be inevitable. She recalled their family, the arrival of three more children, her wonderful career, and a husband who had been a best friend until the day he died. She knew she would grieve and she knew there would be difficult days ahead. But, she also knew that losses are a part of life and that life can go on.

Elizabeth got up from her dressing table and took one last glimpse at herself. Then she made her way downstairs to console her four children who were waiting in the living room. Today was their Daddy's funeral. It was now her turn to help her children to deal with the transitions of loss, just as her mother had helped her so many years before. She gently kissed her husband's picture, whispered soft words of love to him, and asked for his support. She hoped that she could do as good a job as her mother had long ago.

Source: D. Juanita Woods

some degree, our society is uncomfortable with mourners' feelings and therefore may convey messages that imply mourners are "only feeling sorry for themselves." Remember, though, that those who avoid all conscious grieving usually experience some form of depression sooner or later.

3. *To adjust to an environment from which the deceased is missing:* The survivor usually is not aware of all the roles played by the deceased until he or she is gone. Not only do the bereaved have to adjust to the loss of the roles previously played by the deceased, but death confronts them with the

challenge of adjusting to their own sense of self. Adjustment to one's sense of the world may also be occurring. Loss through death can challenge one's fundamental life values and philosophical beliefs. It is not unusual for the bereaved to feel they have lost direction in life.

4. *To emotionally relocate the deceased and move on with life:* Some people have difficulty understanding the notion of emotional withdrawal. If we think of it as relocation, then the task for the bereaved is to evolve an ongoing relationship with the thoughts and memories they associate with the person who died, but to do it in a way that allows them to continue with their lives. The task for the bereaved, possibly with the help of a counselor, is not to give up the relationship with the deceased, but to find an appropriate place for the dead in their emotional lives. This needs to be a place that enables them to go on living effectively in the world.

Anyone interested in assisting the bereaved needs to be familiar with the broad range of behaviors that fall under the description of normal grief. Because the list of normal grief behaviors is so extensive and varied, these behaviors can be described under four general categories.

Normal Grief Reactions

1. *Feelings:* Many feelings may be experienced to varying degrees. These include, but are not limited to, sadness, anger, loneliness, fatigue, helplessness, shock, yearning, emancipation, numbness, and even relief.

2. *Physical sensations:* Some people experiencing acute grief are worried about physical sensations. The following are some of the most common sensations experienced by people who are going through the grieving process: hollowness in the stomach, tightness in the chest, tightness in the throat, oversensitivity to noise, breathlessness, weakness in the muscles, lack of energy, and dry mouth.

3. *Cognitions:* Many different thought patterns mark the experience of grief. Certain thoughts are common in the early stages of grieving and usually disappear after a short time. But sometimes, if such thoughts persist, they can trigger feelings that can lead to depression or anxiety. Common thought processes include disbelief, confusion, preoccupation, hallucinations, or a sense of the presence of the person who died.

4. *Behaviors:* The following behaviors are common after a loss and usually correct themselves over time: appetite and sleep disturbances, absent-minded behavior, crying and sighing, overactivity, dreams of the deceased, avoiding reminders of the deceased, and carrying or treasuring objects that belonged to the deceased.

The Time Frame for Grieving People who haven't experienced the death of a loved one may want to know how long it will take to get to the stage of acceptance. Healing is a very personal thing and depends greatly on the circumstances. The response to the death of someone who has been ill for some time will undoubtedly be very different from the response to a sudden and unexpected death. One benchmark of a completed grief reaction is when the survivor is able to think of the deceased without pain. Also, mourning is finished when a person can reinvest his or her emotions back into life and in the living. In general, though, here are some guidelines on what to expect:

The first two or three days: During this time, the impact of the trauma may be the strongest. This is the period when a person is most likely to be in shock and/or denial. Some people move into heavy grieving at this point; others are still numb from having to deal with all of the circumstances surrounding the loss.

The next two or three weeks: It is common for a person to have a loss of appetite, difficulty sleeping, inability to focus, and a tendency to cry every day during this period.

The following two or three months: This is the time when people often need the most support. Everyone wants to help for the first few days or weeks, but after a few months, people go back to their own lives, while the person suffering the loss may just be starting to recover. That is a very tenuous position, and people feel vulnerable during this period. It is during this time that it is possible to really help someone who has experienced a loss by reaching out and letting him or her know that the support is still there. For some people, it may take as long as eight months to a year to feel as though the healing process has begun to diminish in intensity.

The next two or three years: Holidays and special anniversary dates will have an impact on people who have experienced the death of someone close. There seems to be an important psychological turning point after the one-year mark, though. Some people report feeling that they not only were healed, but also could give themselves permission to start getting on with life. However, it is not uncommon for people to have emotional reactions for years after the event during special times that call up old memories.

Many things can be said to someone who has experienced a significant loss, but remembering to listen is the most important thing to do. People need to share the pain and know that someone will be there while they are going through it. We might not know where a person is in the process of grieving, so it can be difficult to know what to say. To be there for someone, it might be necessary to deal with anger, sadness, guilt, or sense of hope and acceptance.

How to Help Someone

In the book *Parting Is Not Goodbye* (1986), Kelly Osmont offers some excellent information on how to be helpful to someone who is going through the grieving process. (Osmont's book and pamphlets about the grieving process can be ordered from Nobility Press, 811 NW 20th, Suite 103, Portland, OR 97209.)

There are many ways in which families, friends, and professionals in the field of bereavement can be supportive of those who are grieving. When assessing the needs of a grieving person, it helps to understand the circumstances. Don't assume that the death of a 90-year-old grandmother will be mourned in the same way as the death of a 5-year-old child. Perhaps the most important aspect to consider is the level of attachment the person had to the deceased. It might be more difficult to lose a grandparent than a parent in some situations. That could be true if the grandparent was a significant source of love, care, and support. Many extended family members are called on these days to fulfill the parental role. There are enormous differences in the grief process that depend on attachment, the age of the person who died, how the person died, and the gender of the survivor. Also, in our society, it is usually more difficult for men than for women to express their grief openly. Please consider the following guidelines as suggestions only. Most important, trust your heart and your instincts:

1. *Don't try to lessen the loss with easy answers:* "She isn't hurting anymore," "It must have been his time," and "Things always work out for the best" are remarks that are seldom helpful. It is more important for the bereaved to feel your presence than to hear anything you might say. Remember, there are no ready phrases that take away the pain of loss. Phrases that usually don't help: "There must have been a reason" (not all things in life make sense); "I know how you feel" (none of us knows exactly how someone else feels); "It was God's will" (first, find out about the survivor's religious beliefs); "Time will heal" (time alone doesn't always heal; it also takes experiencing the grieving process). Phrases that do help: "This must be painful for you" (then the griever feels free to describe the pain); "You must have been very close to her" (the survivor can talk about the relationship); "It must be hard to accept" (listen to the difficulties); "I really miss him; he was a special person. But that can't compare to how much you must miss him. Tell me what it's like" (then just listen).

2. *Don't feel you must have something to say:* Your presence is enough. Especially with fresh grief, your embrace, your touch, and your sincere sorrow are all the mourner may need. Be sure to call or visit the survivor, no matter how much time has passed since the death. The griever still appreciates knowing you care.

3. *Take the initiative:* Don't merely say, "If there's anything I can do, give me a call." Make specific offers of help. Each thoughtful gesture keeps the survivor from having to continually reach out for assistance.

4. *Help with the children and everyday concerns:* You might run errands, answer the phone, prepare meals, or do the laundry. These seemingly minor tasks loom large to the survivor, for grief drastically depletes physical energy. Invite children on family outings. They shouldn't be shielded from grief, but occasionally, they need a break from the sadness at home.

5. *Listen:* A bereaved person desperately needs a listener who is accepting, supportive, and willing to listen patiently to often repetitive stories. The need to tell the story decreases as healing progresses. And each time the story is told, the finality of the death sinks in a little more. When feelings of anger, frustration, disappointment, fear, and sadness are expressed, accept those feelings. If the survivor keeps them bottled inside, it will slow the healing process.

6. *Allow the expression of guilt feelings:* A natural reaction to hearing someone express guilt is to respond with "You mustn't feel guilty. I'm sure you did everything you could." Don't try to rescue people from their guilt feelings, which are natural and normal during the grief process. What most people actually feel is regret. Guilt implies a purposeful act that intends injury; we feel regret when we wish we had somehow been able to change things. Ask nonleading questions: "What could you have done differently?" These help survivors conclude that they did the best that they could.

7. *Allow survivors to grieve in their own way:* Don't push mourners to get over the loss. If they need to rake leaves or chop wood to release energy and tension, let them. If they want to pore over old pictures or read every book on grief they can find, let them. We all grieve in our own way; avoid being judgmental.

8. *Accept mood swings:* Expect good days and bad days for some time. The highs and lows are part of the process. These feelings have been described as waves that sweep in uncontrollably. Gradually, the good days become more frequent, but bad ones will occur even a year or more after the death of a loved one.

9. *Remember special days and times:* Double your efforts to be sensitive to the mourner's needs during

difficult times of the day or on days with special meaning, such as holidays, the loved one's birthday or wedding anniversary, and the anniversary of the death. Mark your calendar so you'll remember to reach out to the person on or before those special days.

10. *Know that recovery takes time:* Don't expect the grieving person to be "over it" within a few weeks. Recovery doesn't happen the day after the funeral or even two months after it, as many people believe. Sometimes, the real grieving is just beginning by then. It may be more than a year before you see the results of your caring and support, but when your friend smiles again and feels less pain, the reward is there. If the mourner doesn't seem to be recovering at all despite your best efforts and the passage of time, suggest professional help to assist in learning new ways of coping. Find out which professionals in your region are experi-enced in working with the bereaved. Don't assume that all counselors and clergy are trained in this area.

11. *Write or verbally share your memories of the one who died:* During the first few months after a death, there is a tendency to focus on the survivors, while the survivors are focusing on the one who died. By relating your memories of the deceased, you are offering a precious memento to the grieving person. Your love and concern are shown not only in what you share, but in the fact that you took the time to do so.

12. *Know that your friend will always remember his or her loved one:* For the rest of the survivor's life, tears may be shed when a special memory is recalled. Your friend is who he or she is today because of having loved that person. Denying the deceased's past existence denies a part of your friend. Love your friend's past as well as his or her present, and you and your friend will be the richer for it.

CHAPTER REVIEW

Life Span Development

Many of the predictable transitions in life have been altered drastically during the course of the past generation. People are growing up faster but living longer at home. Life expectancy has increased, with the possibility that many people will experience a second adulthood rather than, or as part of, a midlife crisis. According to Erikson, even though the timing of major life events has changed, there are still developmental stages that everyone contends with. How a person resolves the conflicts of each stage has implications for the manner in which challenges of subsequent stages are met. Maslow's hierarchy of needs determines whether someone has the time, energy, or inclination to accept the challenges of life presented by the maturational process.

Life Passages

Many significant events that occur during childhood may influence how you go through subsequent transitions in life. These events include when childhood ended for you and how you left home. To enter a new phase in life, it is necessary to leave some things behind. There are necessary losses inherent in many of life's transitions, however beneficial the new choices you make. Growth and development continue through adulthood, and how you experience transitions at one stage of life has implications for later ones. Old age is a time of readjusting priorities and creating a balance that gives meaning and purpose to life.

Transitional Times

Many people have difficulty with transitions because they avoid going through the required stages or mix up the order in which they go through them. When a major life change occurs, you need to deal with the ending phase first. This is followed by time in the neutral zone to allow incorporation and integration of the events and their meaning. Only then is it time to address the options that represent a new beginning. Some of the issues that need to be addressed during a transitional stage in life are disengagement, disidentification, disenchantment, and disorientation. There are specific behaviors that can assist you on the journey through life's stages.

Health and Wellness

Our level of energy often determines whether or not we use our coping skills. Having a balanced life, particularly in the areas of work and leisure, is an important part of coping. Taking care of your body by eating right and getting exercise will contribute to your overall mental and physical health.

Pyramid Building

No sooner did the USDA offer an update on the traditional food pyramid than the Harvard School of Public Health came out with their critique. While the new pyramid which was widely published in the media was an improvement over the old one, there are still some misleading aspects to the new one. Nutritionists at Harvard offer suggestions to build a better pyramid.

Lifestyle and Being Overweight

Not only is it a problem in the United States, but obesity is becoming a global health problem. Numerous sources report the rapid increase in childhood obesity and diabetes. Nutrition is important for good health, and has implications for relationships and human behavior.

Death and Dying Issues

Many of our inhibitions about dealing with death and dying have to do with the significant changes in our society since the turn of the century. In the agricultural society of a hundred years ago, death usually had personal meaning for people. These days, we are exposed to death every day in the media while being insulated from the process of dealing with it when it does affect us personally. The stages of coping with death or loss are denial, anger, bargaining, depression, and acceptance. Although you may not go through the stages in an orderly fashion, it is usually necessary to have experienced each of the stages in order to heal. There is a somewhat predictable timetable that most people go through in coping with loss, and there are things one can do to help someone who is coping with the death of a loved one.

SOURCES AND SUGGESTED READINGS

Abboud, L. "Expect a Food Fight as U.S. Sets to Revise Diet Guidelines." *Wall Street Journal*, August 8, 2003, p. B1.

Albom, M. *Tuesdays With Morrie*. New York: Doubleday, 1997.

Boles, R. N. *The Three Boxes of Life*. Berkeley, CA: Ten Speed Press, 1978.

Bridges, William. *Transitions*. Philippines: Addison-Wesley, 1980.

Corr, C. A., C. M. Nabe, and D. M. Corr. *Death and Dying, Life and Living*. Fourth edition. Belmont, CA: Wadsworth, 2003.

Freeman, S. J. *Grief and Loss: Understanding the Journey*. Belmont, CA: Brooks/Cole, 2005.

Hooper, M., and R. Heighway-Bury. *Who Built the Pyramid?* Cambridge, MA: Candlewick Press, 2001.

Kübler-Ross, Elisabeth. *Death: The Final Stage of Growth*. Englewood Cliffs, NJ: Prentice Hall, 1975.

Kushner, Harold. *When Bad Things Happen to Good People*. New York: Avon, 1983.

Levine, Stephen. *Who Dies? An Investigation of Conscious Living and Dying*. Garden City, NY: Doubleday, 1982.

Osmont, Kelly. *Parting Is Not Goodbye*. Portland, OR: Nobility Press, 1986.

Viorst, Judith. *Necessary Losses*. New York: Fawcett Gold Medal, 1986.

Worden, William, J. *Grief Counseling and Grief Therapy: A Handbook for the Mental Health Practitioner*. New York: Springer, 1991.

Web Site Resources

Adult Develoment and Aging: APA Division 20
http://www.iog.wayne.edu/apadiv20/apadiv20.htm

Compassionate Friends (support for bereaved parents)
http://www.compassionatefriends.org

American Obesity Association (2004): childhood obesity
http://www.obesity.org/subs/childhood/prevalence.shtml

National medical spending attributable to obesity: how much, and who's paying?
http://content.healthaffairs.org/cgi/content/full/hlthaff.w3.219v1/DC1

World Health Organization (2004): obesity and overweight
http://www.who.int/dietphysicalactivity/publications/facts/obesity/en

Articles on Grief and Loss
http://www.aarp.org/griefandloss

REACTION AND RESPONSE—WHAT DO YOU THINK?

Chapter Nine   Level I Assignments

In response to the information in the chapter:

1. When you were young, did you get messages to "hurry up" in life or to "stay little"? Did you feel pushed to grow up fast, or were you held back? What are some of the beliefs that you developed about change during childhood? Are there beliefs that you would like to replace?

2. Did you live in the same house while growing up, or did your family move a lot? Did your parents divorce? If they did, what was it like when they remarried? When changes occurred in the family, how were they handled?

3. How do you take care of your health? Almost everyone knows what they should do, but how often do you make the right choices about taking care of yourself? What do you need to do more in order to have a healthier lifestyle? What gets in your way?

In response to the class activities, group discussions, and exercises:

1. What are your opinions and reactions?
2. What did you learn or rediscover?
3. How are you going to apply what you learned?

Chapter Nine   Level II Assignments

1. What transitions have you experienced in life? How did you handle the ending, neutral zone, and new beginning of the transition? What do the transitions of adulthood mean to you? How was the information in the chapter about going through transitions useful to you?

2. What do you think you will be doing in five years? In 10 years? What would you need to be doing in the next year if you were to be working toward those goals?

3. If 50 is the new 30, as some are saying, how do you think that will affect you?

Chapter Nine   Level III Assignments

1. What do you think happens when you die? How does that influence how you live? What kind of funeral do you want to have, and how do you want to be remembered?

2. What did you learn in this chapter about how to help people who have experienced the loss of someone close?

3. How do you deal with endings in general? Do you try to ignore them? Do you deny the necessity by hanging on when you should let go?

10

POSITIVE LIVING

Ah, the ignorance of youth! A friend and I (waxing wise in our 60s and 40s) were discussing recently all the things we didn't know in our teens, 20s, and 30s—and the frustrations of seeing young people we care about being equally ignorant. Unfortunately, wisdom isn't transferable. We seem to learn best the hard way, by causing unnecessary heartache for ourselves and others. But maybe someone younger will reconsider the following insights one gains with age:

The importance of funerals and sympathy cards: What a downer death is. If I didn't know the deceased, I didn't go to the funeral. When an older friend's mother died, I didn't attend. When she told me later that it would have meant a lot to her to have me there, I learned that we go to funerals not only to say goodbye, but to support those left behind. And when my mother died, the sympathy cards meant more than I could have realized.

When family and friends protest, listen: "But I love him!" and "This is my life, thank you" are frequent retorts when people who care about us offer advice or voice doubts about a current love interest or life decision. The more they protest our choice or voice concern, the more we dig in our heels. Yet, these are people who know us and love us best, so perhaps we should listen. Their view of reality may be sharper than our love blindness.

Learning family history from older relatives: Nothing bores the young like old folks talking about the past. But who doesn't reach an age when they wished they had listened? Especially after older relatives and parents die, we feel the gap of those missing memories—How old was I when I had the mumps? What's the real story about Grandpa being shot by a jealous husband? Now is the time to query older relatives about family history, to record interviews about the world when they were young. We can also write or record what we know to pass on to our children and grandchildren.

People's problems can't always wait: George Raveling, [former] head basketball coach at the University of Southern California, tells the story of a young boy asking to talk with him on the playground. Raveling had to leave, promising the youth he'd catch up with him the next day. That night, the boy killed himself. People are more important than work or schedules. The time we spend with someone now could make a difference in his or her life.

Honesty is the best policy: "Oh, what a tangled web we weave, when first we practice to deceive." Ever forget who you told what about whatever? Life gets pretty complicated (not to mention embarrassing and even painful) when we weave a web of lies. It's so much easier to tell the truth. Then we don't have to try to keep our stories straight. Not telling the truth simply breeds distrust.

The consequences of ignoring that little voice inside: Think about the dumbest thing you've ever done. Do you recall a persistent little voice warning you otherwise? It may say, "This guy is lying to you," "You know this isn't the right thing to do," or "You know this relationship is going nowhere." But we shush it up like we do a demanding child, so determined are we to pretend that everything is swell or will certainly get better. Call it intuition, conscience, or whatever. That little voice is usually looking out for us. If we'd learn to listen and to trust it, we'd save ourselves a lot of grief.

Ah, wisdom. It compensates for the ravages of gravity.

Source: Article by Jann Mitchell.

Values and Meaning

Whether you realize it or not, every time you make a choice about taking a particular action in life, you are making a value decision. What is it that matters to you most in your life? The answer is important because your priorities and personal values influence your everyday interactions. They affect your relationships with others in your world. Personal values relate to all parts of your life and actually form the basis of your decision making. Values can be about abstract ideas or specific people and situations. Examples of values are evident in the emphasis that you put on family, friends, helping others, honesty, security, creativity, financial achievement, material possessions, good health, and having a career.

Although a discussion of values can be frustrating because of the abstract nature of the subject, it is still a worthy topic because our values influence so much of our behavior. Three interrelated concepts might help to explain the impact that your value system has on your life. They are values, standards, and behavior. *Values* are the ultimate ideals and goals that people have for themselves that are often shared by the greater community at large. *Standards* represent the attempts of people and groups to make rules that will ensure that the values are preserved and expressed. *Behavior* represents the manner in which individuals interact with each other, frequently by conforming to the standards of society to preserve those values.

These general concepts may be more evident and concrete if you consider specific ideas. Think back on all the information that has been given in previous chapters. Often, you were asked to assess your reactions and consider your opinions regarding the material. Some of what was presented may have seemed controversial or contradictory to your beliefs. What you thought about, as well as what behavior you considered changing, was directly related to your value system and beliefs. Consider which concepts brought up strong reactions. More than likely, you will then be able to identify some of your personal values.

In this next section, we continue to explore how your values influence the goals you set for yourself. Clarifying your values will assist in life planning by helping you develop appropriate and consistent goals. A clear set of goals in life often makes decision making much easier. Having a more coherent strategy for making decisions can in turn enable you to develop and enjoy greater meaning in life. Congruence in all these areas may free up energy to focus on your greater purpose in

> " *This above all: to thine own self be true, and it must follow, as the night the day, thou canst not then be false to any man.* "
>
> William Shakespeare

the world and consider what truly brings you satisfaction in life.

Values Clarification

Why bother to clarify our values? Knowing our own values is a crucial part of learning about ourselves. What sorts of things are really meaningful to us? What are we striving for and working toward? What sort of world do we want to see come into being? To the extent that we can't answer these questions, we have failed to come to terms with ourselves. An immature person is one who still has a great deal to learn about himself or herself. An important part of life span development is creating, clarifying, and understanding our values.

Humans are the only creatures that can reflect on their own existence. Not only do we behave in certain ways, but we *think* about the things we do. Values represent the ultimate reasons people have for acting as they do—their basic aims, objectives, aspirations, ideals. Values also have to do with the rationalization of behavior. It is how we justify and explain our actions. Because we tend to prize authenticity in our fellow humans, it is important to have our values and behavior in line with each other. Nothing turns us off faster than a hypocrite: a person who verbally subscribes to a value but violates it in action.

Each of us has preconceived ideas about behavior. Consider the values involved in such questions as the right to own guns versus handgun control, bans on sexually explicit books versus freedom of literary expression, the public's right to know versus an individual's right to privacy, and "freedom of choice" versus "right to life." Our personal values related to these questions may influence the way we perceive and label behavior, our own and others'.

Perhaps another reason for being concerned with values is the change in emphasis on the needs of the individual as opposed to those of the community or society. Over the past two decades, college students have shown an increased concern for their own well-being and a decreased concern for the well-being of others, especially

> *"Values are the basis upon which people decide what they are for or against, or where they are going and why. In other words, they give direction to life."*
>
> D. Campbell

the disadvantaged. Today's college freshmen are more strongly motivated to be well off financially and less motivated to develop a meaningful philosophy of life than college students were 20 or even 10 years ago. There appears to have been an almost complete reversal in goals for college freshmen between 1968 and 1994. In the 1960s, students placed a great degree of importance on philosophy and very little importance on financial gain. Fortunately, some signs indicate that currently students are shifting again toward a stronger interest in the welfare of society. One recent study reported that students' participation in community service stimulated them to consider societies' moral order. More students are showing an active interest in the problems of homelessness, child abuse, hunger, and poverty (Halonen and Santrock, 1997).

Life Goals

Having considered your values and what is truly important in life, take a moment and think about what goals would most likely be a reflection of those values. What do you want to accomplish that would support, and be supported by, your beliefs? Many of us have high ideals about what kind of person we would like to be and what we would like to do with our lives, but fail to develop a specific plan of action that might realize those ideals. There is an old saying: "If you don't know where you are going, you will probably end up somewhere else." It is valuable to have a clear sense of where you want to go and what you want to accomplish to make the right decisions about how to get there.

One method for developing clearer goals is to consider the process itself. How do you go about deciding what is an appropriate and realistic goal to pursue? Some people solve that problem by just never setting any goals. They seem to have adopted the strategy "How can I fail, if I never had any objectives in the first place?" Often, that backfires, after years of wandering aimlessly, when they realize they can't get what they want by just

watching life happen. Many human potential seminars support the notion of making lists of things that you want to accomplish in life. Some even go so far as to suggest that successful people write down what they want and review the list frequently. What do you think would happen if you made a list of what you want to accomplish in the next 5, 10, and 20 years and read it daily?

As you begin to think about your goals, take a moment and review your past goal-setting behavior. Do you have a tendency to set your goals too high? Do you become unrealistic and set too many goals, or create ones that are so difficult or complex it would be almost impossible *not* to fall short? Some people set their sights too high as a form of self-sabotage. An aspect of this type of self-defeating behavior is that it creates a built-in excuse for not trying something in the future. People who are afraid of being outside their comfort zone may create reasons for why they have to stay there and avoid taking risks.

Another method for minimizing the effects of disappointment is to set goals that are too low. Some people decide to do something only after there is an almost iron-clad clause that guarantees they can't fail. Although they accomplish their objective of avoiding unpleasant feelings, the results of doing a "sure thing" are often disappointing. Goals, almost by definition, need to be a challenge that will bring a sense of satisfaction when you reach them.

It is certainly important to dream and have big plans in life, but perhaps it is best to develop goals

> Look to this day,
> For it is life, the very life of life.
> In its brief course lie all
> The realities and verities of existence,
> The bliss of growth,
> The splendor of action,
> The glory of power—
>
> For yesterday is but a dream,
> And tomorrow is only a vision,
> But today, well lived,
> Makes every yesterday a dream of happiness
> And every tomorrow a vision of hope.
> Look well, therefore, to this day.
> —Sanskrit proverb

that are clear, practical, and within the realm of possibility. Many people have discussed the value of having short-term goals and breaking down large accomplishments into smaller chunks. It is sometimes easier to make progress and have good solid goals when you think about each step necessary to accomplish the larger plan. Successful goals:

1. Must be your own, not what someone else thinks you should accomplish.
2. Must be realistic and attainable.
3. Don't conflict with your value system.
4. Can be written down, with specific interim steps.

Meaning and Purpose

It might be said that there are two main quests in life. The first quest is the pursuit for a means to live. The second pursues meaning to make life worth living. Victor Frankl, a European psychiatrist, stated, "Ever more people today have the means to live, but no meaning to live for." In Frankl's estimation, the minimum standard essential for survival is a "what for" or a "whom for."

Frankl dedicated his professional life to the study of meaning in life. He is widely known for his approach to therapy, *logotherapy,* which means "healing through meaning." What distinguishes us as humans is our search for a purpose. For many people, the search for meaning in life is a primary motivational force. Humans can choose to live and/or die for the sake of their ideals and values. In one of his books, *Man's Search for Meaning* (1984), Frankl shows that there is always an element of choice in any circumstance in life. Everything can be taken from a person except the ability to choose his or her attitude in a particular situation.

Drawing on his experiences in the death camps at Auschwitz, Frankl asserts that inmates who had a vision of some goal, purpose, or task in life had a much greater chance of surviving. We are constantly confronted with choices, and the decisions we make influence the meaning of our lives. Frankl was fond of quoting Nietzsche, who said, "He who has a *why* to live for can bear with almost any *how.*"

The Pursuit of Meaning

There are a number of ways by which people establish meaning in their lives. Whatever the method, there is a connection between having a sense of meaning and having a general sense of well-being and satisfaction. A number of studies indicate that many people who have religious faith are happier and cope with difficulty more readily. In one recent study, older adults' self-esteem was highest when they had a strong religious commitment and lowest when they had little religious commitment (Krause, 1995). But there are other ways in which people create meaning and purpose in life. For many, it is establishing priorities that transcend personal interests. For others, it is an intense focus on creating and having a feeling of accomplishment. The following are some of the ways people establish meaning in their lives (Arkoff, 1995).

Religious or spiritual: For many people, religious or spiritual pursuit makes life meaningful. Many turn to religion with new or renewed dedication when they find that their lives lack purpose, or when the purposes they have set themselves are threatened. Although religion has been

> ❝ For the weak, it is impossible. For the fainthearted, it is unknown. For the thoughtful and valiant, it is ideal. ❞
>
> *Victor Hugo*

SEARCH FOR MEANING IN LIFE

Our business in life is not to get ahead of other people but to get ahead of ourselves. To break our own record, to outstrip our yesterdays by todays, to bear our trials more beautifully than we ever dreamed we could, to whip that temper inside and out as we never whipped it before, to give as we have never given, to do our work with more force and a finer finish that ever—this is the true idea—to get ahead of ourselves.

Source: Author unknown.

reported to be on the wane or on the increase in the United States at various times during the past few decades, most surveys do not show a notable secularization or weakening of religion during the past half-century.

Dedication to a cause: A second important source of meaning is dedication to a cause that takes us beyond personal concerns and allows us to identify with something larger than ourselves. The particular cause one dedicates oneself to may not matter significantly. It is the courage of one's convictions, not the content, that counts. Bertrand Russell stated, "Those whose interest in any such cause is genuine are provided with an occupation for their leisure hours and a complete antidote to the feeling that life is empty."

Creativity: Many writers and artists have alluded to the importance of the creative process in establishing meaning in life. Even those fortunate enough to have acquired wealth and fame as a result of their work often say they will continue to create because it gives them a reason to get out of bed in the morning. Psychologists emphasize that the creative road to meaning is not limited to artists. A creative approach to cooking, studying, accounting, or gardening adds something valuable to life. Business ventures are a creative process for some people.

Service to others: Some psychologists believe that a sense of meaninglessness can be attributed to the rise in individualism and a weakening of commitment to society or the common good. To help, nurture, or serve others provides meaning for many individuals. Altruistic persons tend to be happier than those who are selfish. Helping others removes us from preoccupation with our own concerns. Helping attenuates feelings of separateness or isolation and gives us a sense of connection or belonging.

Self-actualization: Another source of meaning comes from actualizing ourselves or fulfilling our potential. We find meaning by making the most of ourselves and becoming what we can be. When we fail to make full use of our abilities, we feel stagnant and discontent. We humans appear to be impelled to grow and enhance ourselves. At times in our lives when we are becoming more competent at something, feeling ourselves fuller, becoming better persons, we seldom stop to ask about the meaning of life. When we are actively involved in personal growth, we inherently have more meaning in life.

Decision Making

Most major decisions involve value conflicts. If you get the job you want, you may have to move to another town; career values may then conflict with family and friendship values. When you have a decision that involves two or more conflicting values that are of major importance to you, the decision can be difficult to make. You can make these decisions more effectively if you have considered what your most important values are and the priority that you give to each. That was the purpose in exploring the concept of goals.

Even when you have a clear sense of your goal, though, it is not uncommon to play self-torture games when it comes to making difficult decisions. Before providing specific information about improving your decision-making process, it may be useful to consider some of your underlying beliefs. Many people think that they have to be 100 percent sure before making a decision. The reality is that most of us have to make decisions based on 70 percent certainty and 30 percent uncertainty. Even when we are getting what we want, there frequently is a part of our being that wants to play devil's advocate and express objections and reservations. It is valuable to learn and accept that in any difficult decision, there are merits to any number of solutions. As a result, some of the best decisions are made when the majority of thoughts, feelings, and issues support a particular course of action.

It is important to gather as much pertinent information as possible when considering making major decisions. Yet, one of the hardest things for most people to realize is that *all decisions are made on the basis of incomplete data*. There are very few circumstances in life where you have all the information available at the exact time that you need to make the decision. Some people agonize over every little detail or obsess over the possibility that there is something that they have forgotten to consider. It can be reassuring to know that often in life, you have to make decisions based on doing the best you can with what you know at the moment.

That said, let's explore the actual procedure for making good decisions. Psychologists have formulated a number of systems. Most often, they recommend that we proceed systematically through a number of steps. The acronym ACTION indicates some of the fundamental steps that could be taken to increase the probability of a successful decision (Halloran and Benton, 1987):

A: Analyze the situation and gather information. Accept the challenge of the situation.

C: Consider the alternative solutions. Be open to all possibilities and remain flexible.

T: Take action and select a solution after evaluating the possibilities.

I: Implement the solution and make a commitment to applying it.

O: Ongoing evaluation: Encourage and accept feedback on your solution.

N: Need for change: After you have tried the solution, consider the need for modification.

In reviewing this section, keep in mind that if you assess your most important personal values and have some idea of their priorities in your life, you will be better able to make decisions and will feel more in control of your life. You will also feel more comfortable with your decisions after you have made them. If you are not now living your life according to your values, it will be helpful to consider ways to change how you spend your time so that your lifestyle can become more consistent with your values. As you go through life, your values may change. Take time every so often to assess your lifestyle to see if it is in keeping with the personal values that are currently a priority in your life (Heplinger and Black, 1997).

Factors Influencing Decisions

The following information is designed to help you examine how you currently make decisions and offers several approaches to making future decisions.

Information Factors   To make sound decisions it is important to gather enough information to evaluate your options. You can research your options with objective sources, and also make connections and get experience to collect more direct information.

Decision-Making Experience   Confidence in decision-making abilities comes from having made successful decisions in the past. Think about the positive decisions you have made already. How did you make those decisions? What resources helped guide you through your decision-making process?

Personal Factors   Support and influence from family and friends can have a big effect on your decisions, especially significant ones that may affect the important people in your life.

Consider how your options are compatible with your values, interests, and abilities. An example could be: "My previous experience as a student teacher has confirmed my interests in becoming a teacher. Plus, having the summers off will allow me to spend more time with my family." You may need to evaluate yourself to clarify your interests, values, skills, and personality style.

The number of desirable options is often a factor. People with many interests and abilities find decision-making difficult because they believe they will have to sacrifice appealing options. Those with undefined interests find decision-making difficult as well because none of the options appear attractive.

Decision-Making Styles

There isn't necessarily one model or style that is always the right way to make decisions. And remember, different people are successful and satisfied using different styles. So what works well for your friend may not be the style that works best for you.

The method you use to make decisions will depend on your personal decision-making style and the weight of the decision. Each decision-making style has advantages and disadvantages; what is most important is that you use a style that is comfortable and effective for you. You can always use a different style depending on your situation.

It is often best to use a planned decision-making style when making important or complicated decisions. In other words, gather information and apply a systematic and deliberate approach that is a balance between logical reasoning and intuition. A planned approach takes time and energy but is worthwhile when you have to make important decisions. You will also be more confident with your decision if you know you have done your homework and it feels right intuitively.

Other decision-making styles can be used when you face time constraints, or when the decisions are not of great consequence. Sometimes it is easier or more comfortable to make a decision based on your emotions, to let other people influence you, or to leave the decision up to fate.

The Pros and Cons Model for Decision Making

On a piece of paper, write down the decision you are considering making. Write it as if you had already made the decision (for example, "Accept the XYZ Company job offer in Los Angeles").

Divide the piece of paper into two columns, with "Pros" at the top of one column. Write down the outcomes of the decision that you believe are positive. In the "Cons" column, write down the outcomes of the decision that are negative or less desirable.

In the course of writing down your pros and cons, you will probably notice that there are some outcomes that are uncertain or are too hard to predict. Write these outcomes down on a separate piece of paper.

Conduct research about the outcomes that you are unsure about, then add those to the Pro or Con column.

For the outcomes that are simply too hard to predict, you might want to talk with other people to get their input or opinions. If possible, evaluate whether the outcome is a pro or con and add that to your table.

As you begin to complete the table, it may become clearer whether the decision you are considering is advisable. Note that some outcomes carry more weight than others, though, so the number of pros and cons in each column is not necessarily indicative of whether or not you should move forward with the decision.

Source: Copyright 1998–2005 Counseling Center, University of California, Berkeley.

Questions for Critical Thinking

What influence do your values and beliefs have on your future goals? What do you want to accomplish in the next five years? What plan do you have for moving toward those goals in the next year? What steps will you take this month? What are you going to do this week?

_____

_____

_____

_____

_____

_____

_____

_____

_____

Work and Leisure

Work is more than a livelihood. It is a way we give to others as we take care of ourselves. It is a chance to exercise our initiative and creativity and develop our skills and abilities. It can be a statement of who we are, to ourselves and others. According to British economist E. F. Shumacher, "A person's work is undoubtedly one of the most decisive formative influences on character and personality. Business is not here simply to produce goods, it also produces people, so that the whole thing becomes a learning process."

Work is more than just the activities that take up the majority of your hours each week. If you feel good about the career you are in, it will improve the quality of your life. If you don't like your job and dread the hours spent there, it is bound to have an effect on how you feel about yourself. A well-known psychologist, Eric Fromm, studied the relationship between working conditions and the rest of a person's life during the 1950s. He and a number of other psychologists found that not only are the frustrations of a repressive workplace often brought home and dumped on the family, but so too is the authoritarian structure of the work environment. A man who is an obedient pawn at work may turn into a dictator at home (Daniels and Horowitz, 1998).

Stressful working conditions may also affect not only people's mental health, but their physical health as well. People who are ill suited for their jobs often experience more illness and take more time off from work. People who are satisfied with their jobs visit the doctor less frequently and live longer than those who are dissatisfied with their jobs (Atwater and Duffy, 1999). This further supports the notion that it is important to explore what career path is best for you.

In choosing a career, it is important to consider what you value most about your work. What do you consider an ideal workday? What must your work have to make it rewarding for you? Do you want to be your own boss? What kind of physical working conditions are important to you? What kind of responsibilities do you need? Do you want to work with people or work alone? Is the basic purpose of your work, such as public service, important to you? The answers to these questions depend on your work values and what motivates you.

Historically, workers have been motivated by two main concerns. One is economic necessity and the need to generate income to provide food, shelter, and clothing. The other is the so-called work ethic—the belief that a nonproductive lifestyle is unacceptable. Today's workers, however, grew up in relative affluence, and many seem to take financial security for granted. Although earning money is a necessity, it is no longer enough to guarantee job satisfaction. The emphasis on personal fulfillment that emerged in the 1970s and 1980s has extended to the workplace. Many people today have high expectations for their jobs; they want opportunities to learn, use their talents, and contribute something worthwhile.

With these trends in mind, let's examine work and motivation. A major shift in our belief about what motivates people in the workplace has occurred in the last half of the century. McGregor (1960) describes two basic theories of work motivation. Theory X assumes that people inherently dislike work and that they have little ambition. According to Theory X, workers need and prefer to be coerced, directed, and threatened to be productive. In contrast, Theory Y assumes that people find work as natural and satisfying as play or rest. According to Theory Y, workers can and will exercise self-direction and self-control

when they are committed to attaining organizational goals. This is especially true if they can simultaneously fulfill their personal needs for autonomy, achievement, and recognition.

A number of disciplines that study the work environment agree that one motivation to work is to avoid the unpleasant situation of not having basic *survival needs* met. Everyone is motivated to work to have enough money to provide food and shelter. But there is also considerable agreement that what motivates people is the uniquely human need for self-actualization. People also have *pleasure needs,* which are enjoyment and a sense of gratification. These needs are met through the intrinsic satisfaction gained from work activities. Finally, we are motivated by a need to contribute to the welfare of others, including family, our community, and our nation. Satisfying our *need to contribute* also helps us to derive a feeling of self-worth from our occupational endeavors.

Therefore, it would be valuable to explore and understand the process of deciding on an occupation and selecting a career. From the previous information, it should be obvious that one's selection of a life's work has significant implications for part of one's overall life satisfaction.

Theories of Career Development

Three major theories describe the manner in which individuals make choices about careers: Ginzberg's developmental theory, Super's self-concept theory, and Holland's personality type theory. Each of these theories has something to offer in understanding how and why we may choose a certain career path. A brief overview of the theories of Ginzberg and Super will be offered, with more emphasis on Holland's type theory because of our exploration of personality types in previous chapters.

Ginzberg's Developmental Theory Ginzberg's developmental theory of career choice subscribes to the view that people go through distinct stages while exploring and deciding on a career path: the *fantasy stage,* the *tentative stage,* and the *realistic stage.* Many children, when asked what they want to be when they grow up, have an unrealistic view of the world. They may answer "the president," "a movie star," "a superhero," or "a doctor," without much understanding of what those choices might actually entail. During adolescence, individuals go through different phases of the *tentative stage.* They often progress from evaluating their interests, to evaluating their

SELF-ASSESSMENT

First, as quickly as possible, list 20 things that you like to do. There are no right or wrong answers; just put down what interests you and what you really love doing. Next, use the following code for the 20 items listed:

1. Put an R by any item that involves some Risk. The risk might be physical, intellectual, or emotional.
2. Place the letter P next to items you prefer doing with People. Use the letter A for items you prefer doing Alone.
3. Place a 3 next to any item that would not have been on your list five years ago.
4. Indicate the date when you did it last.

Now look back over your list and the codes and ask yourself:

1. What does your list look like?
2. Can you identify any patterns in the things you love to do?
3. Are there some things you're pleased with?
4. Are there some things you like to do that you have not done lately? Why?
5. Is there anything that you would like to change? How might you go about it?

capacities, to evaluating their values while thinking about careers. In their late teens and early 20s, most people enter the *realistic stage* and begin to explore available careers and finally select a specific job.

Super's Self-Concept Theory   Donald Super's view, reflected in the career self-concept theory, is that an individual's self-concept plays a central role in career choice. He believes a number of changes occur during adolescence and young adulthood regarding vocation. First, between ages 14 and 18, adolescents develop ideas about work that correspond to their already existing global self-concept. This is called the *crystallization phase.* Between 18 and 22, during the *specification phase,* they narrow their career choices and initiate behavior that enables them to enter some type of career. Between 21 and 24, young adults complete their education and enter the work world; this is called the *implementation phase.* The decision on a specific career is often made between 25 and 35 during the *stabilization phase.* Finally, after reaching 35, individuals seek to advance their careers and reach higher-status positions; this is called the *consolidation phase.* The age ranges should be thought of as approximations (Santrock, 1999).

Holland's Personality Type Theory   John Holland believes it is important that one's personality type fit one's occupation. Often, personality and style affect the selection of a particular career. When individuals find careers that fit their personalities, they are more likely to enjoy their work and stay in their jobs longer than their counterparts who work at jobs not suited to their personalities. He has proposed six basic career-related personality types: realistic, investigative, artistic, social, enterprising, and conventional. I am indebted to John Santrock (Lifespan Development, 1999) for the following descriptions.

Realistic: People who have this type of vocational interest like the outdoors and working in manual activities. They sometimes are less social, may have difficulty in demanding situations, and prefer to work alone or with other realistic persons. This type shows a match with blue-collar occupations such as labor, farming, truck driving, and construction.

Investigative: This type is interested in ideas more than in people, is rather indifferent to social relationships, is troubled by emotional situations, and may be perceived by others as somewhat aloof. Most of the scientific, intellectually oriented professions fall into this category.

Artistic: Artistic types have a creative orientation and enjoy working with ideas and materials to express themselves in new ways. They often have a distaste for conformity, valuing freedom and ambiguity. Relatively few artistic occupations exist, and some artistic types choose careers in their second or third most typical career type and express their artistic tendencies in hobbies and leisure.

Social: Social types tend to have a helping orientation. They enjoy nurturing and developing others, often the less advantaged. Showing a much stronger interest in people than in intellectual pursuits and often having excellent interpersonal skill, they are likely to be best equipped to enter "people" professions such as teaching, social work, counseling, and the like.

Enterprising: Their skills include being able to persuade other people to do something and to adopt their own attitudes and choices. Therefore, enterprising types are good at coordinating the work of others to accomplish a task. They match up best with such careers as sales, management, and politics.

Conventional: This type usually functions best in well-structured circumstances and jobs and is skilled working with details. Conventional individuals like to work with numbers and perform clerical tasks, as opposed to working with ideas or people. They are best suited for structured jobs such as bank tellers, secretaries, and file clerks.

Holland agrees that people are seldom pure types, but the basic idea of matching the abilities and attitudes of individuals to particular careers is an important contribution to the career development field.

Work Satisfaction

People love to gripe about their jobs and having to go to work, but many of those same people say they would continue to work even if they didn't need the money. But that doesn't mean that the same people are happy with all aspects of their jobs. Job satisfaction is a multidimensional concept that is not easily measured. A job has many aspects. A person might be satisfied with one aspect, such as promotional opportunities, and dissatisfied with another, such as job security.

Job satisfaction is a highly personal matter that depends on more than just the nature of the work. Two people sharing the same job may have very different levels of satisfaction. Satisfaction also depends on the subjective perception of the working conditions. And, to some extent, the tendency to feel satisfied with work may be a personality trait that transcends specific job characteristics.

Even though there may be great individual differences when it comes to assessing job satisfaction, there are still some general findings that are useful in considering various occupations. There have been literally thousands of studies done on worker satisfaction. The findings are important insofar as some people have unrealistic expectations of the work world, and the information may serve to clarify matters. Unrealistic ideas about work may be due to the fact that colleges and universities create expectations that are not realistic. People just entering the workforce frequently make less money than coworkers. After five years on the job, satisfaction tends to rise steadily with age and years on the job. A major reason is greater job security as well as more realistic expectations (Atwater and Duffy, 1999).

In exploring the determinants of satisfaction, three main categories of factors contribute to whether individuals are satisfied with their jobs: organizational, group, and personal. Organizational factors include pay, opportunities for promotion, the nature of the work, policies and procedures of the organization, and working conditions. Individuals might feel different levels of satisfaction about each of these factors.

The job satisfaction of individuals in a work group may also be influenced by both their coworkers and their supervisors or managers. Workers want friendly, cooperative coworkers and considerate supervisors.

Individuals' needs and aspirations also can influence job satisfaction. If a person wants a high-status job, attaining that goal will likely enhance the person's job satisfaction. Another factor is the extent to which a job enables the worker to achieve other ends. The person attending college might take a job on a temporary basis because it allows flexibility in scheduling. The person may be satisfied as long as he or she is in college, but may become considerably less satisfied when considering the job on a permanent basis after graduation.

As a general rule, college-educated people have more job satisfaction than people with less education. But job satisfaction increases for all people as they grow older. The most common pattern is a steady increase in job satisfaction from the age of 20 to at least 60 for both college-educated and non-college-educated people. This pattern has been found for both men and women. Satisfaction probably increases because as we get older we get paid more, we are in a

WHAT IS MOST IMPORTANT IN A JOB?

1. Chances to do some thing that makes you feel good about yourself.
2. Chances to accomplish something worthwhile.
3. Chances to learn new things.
4. Opportunity to develop your skills and abilities.
5. The amount of freedom you have on your job.
6. Chances you have to do things you do best.
7. The resources you have to do your job.
8. The respect you receive from people you work with.
9. Amount of information you get about your job performance.
10. Your chances for taking part in making decisions.
11. The amount of job security you have.
12. Amount of pay you get.
13. The way you are treated by the people you work with.
14. The friendliness of people you work with.
15. Amount of praise you get for a job well done.
16. The number of fringe benefits you get.
17. Chances for getting a promotion.
18. Physical surroundings of your job.

Source: Sicard, *Individuals in Transitions,* 1994.

higher-status position, and we have more job security (Halonen and Santrock, 1997).

Leisure

Numerous psychology texts quote Freud regarding the importance of love and work in our overall adjustment in life. Yes, it is important to feel productive and have a meaningful career that enables you to contribute to the world. And having an intimate relationship with another person is an important part of life satisfaction. But there is another area of life that deserves equal attention. That is leisure time and the ability to play.

No matter how much you like your job, it's important to have enough time off to do the other things in life that you enjoy. Most Americans feel that they are working more and playing less—a perception that seems to be confirmed. In 1987, a Lou Harris poll found that in little more than a decade, the number of hours Americans work would increase from about 40 hours a week

to 48 hours. According to a survey by Day-Timers (*Parade,* 1994), the average American worker puts in 46 hours a week at the office and 6 more hours at home for a total of 52 hours of work. Although we often complain about having to go to work, it appears that adults view leisure as boring or unnecessary. Perhaps this condescending view of leisure is partly due to the country's strong founding work ethic.

One factor influencing this trend is the growing practice of business and other organizations to employ fewer workers and assign them additional responsibilities. This may increase productivity, but the average worker feels overworked. The growing commitment to work has heightened the nation's productivity, but by the same token, the precarious balance of work and play has become even more threatened. Many people are becoming so absorbed with work that they aren't giving the loving care needed to make marriage work or providing growing children with enough attention or taking part in community

LIFE

People are unreasonable, illogical, and self-centered. Love them anyway.
Honesty and frankness make you vulnerable. Be honest and frank anyway.
The good you do today will be forgotten tomorrow. Do good anyway.
What you spend years building may be destroyed overnight. Build anyway.

Give the world the best you have and you get kicked in the teeth. Give the world the best you've got anyway.
Life is not a hundred-yard dash, but more a cross-country race. If we sprint all the time, we not only fail to win the race, but never even last long enough to reach the finish line.

Source: Joseph Kennedy.

endeavors (Schor, 1992). We seem to be locked in a cycle of work and spend due to our need for more possessions. Meanwhile, time has become a premium in our society, making leisure time an even more precious commodity.

What is this precious commodity? Leisure refers to the pleasant times outside work when individuals are free to pursue activities and interests of their own choosing. Although the balance between work and play depends on the needs of the individual, it is important to have activities that refresh and renew you.

There are many things that need to be done during your "free time," when you are not at work, that don't qualify as leisure. Working around the home, doing the dishes, mowing the lawn, or running errands probably would not be considered leisure. These activities might be considered maintenance activities. Therefore, leisure may be defined as any activity we've chosen to do, excluding work and maintenance activities.

The objectives of planning for a career and planning for creative use of leisure time are basically the same: to help us develop feelings of self-esteem, reach our potential, and improve the quality of our lives. If we do not learn how to pursue interests apart from work, we may well face a crisis when we retire. In fact, there is some evidence that many people die soon after their retirement (Seigel, 1989). If we do plan for creative ways to use leisure, we can experience both joy and continued personal growth (Corey and Schneider-Corey, 2003).

Constructive Use of Leisure

It is important to learn how to use leisure in a positive manner. Some people become so obsessed with an activity that they miss the whole point of relaxation. Perhaps you have been around someone who was trying so hard to hurry up and have fun that you both became exhausted. This doesn't mean that a leisure time activity can't be strenuous; many people who engage in action sports or hobbies feel more energized. The difference is that they return from the activity refreshed and with more energy, not angry and more anxious.

On the other end of the continuum, it may not be a positive use of leisure just to be sitting in front of the television. Many adults spend the majority of their evening watching television. Although TV may be a source of entertainment some of the time, often it is used as time to recuperate and unwind. In that sense, television viewing could be considered more of a maintenance activity. The ease of pushing a button to be entertained is a temptation, but many who have curtailed their viewing habits have been amazed at how many other interesting things there are to do in life.

In contrast, the positive use of leisure requires a certain degree of choice and planning. Ideally, you should select activities that are compatible with your interests and lifestyle rather than just doing whatever is convenient at the time. To enjoy an activity to the fullest, you may have to acquire the necessary skills. You

CASE STUDIES AND STUDENT STORIES

Kelley grew up in a home with an extremely critical and demanding father. His dad was always calling him either stupid or lazy. His only way of handling the cruel words was to show his dad how hard he could work. By the time he was 21 he had earned his father's respect, but his work ethic had escalated into a compulsion.

When Kelley entered the work world he continued to be driven by a need to demonstrate his competence. He excelled at his job with a plumbing contractor and soon became a lead man. He would put more hours in than anyone in the company. His superiors greatly appreciated him, and he was promoted repeatedly.

After Kelley got married, he found that he expected his wife to have the same work ethic as he did. Together they rebuilt their house and yard, and even built a barn. Kelley kept thinking that the more he did, the more respect he would gain from his wife and his peers, if not his father.

Even his recreational activities tended to be overly competitive. He often felt as keyed up after a game as before—even after a round of golf. Family vacations and activities were just further opportunities to become anxious with planning, organizing, and trying to have everything go just right.

His long hours and intensity soon took a toll on him, though, and one day he collapsed in the middle of a commercial plumbing job. He just couldn't move, and he was confused and disoriented. When he went to the doctor he was diagnosed as being in a state of total exhaustion. His approach to both work and leisure time activities had caused him to completely use up his physical and mental reserves.

When Kelley arrived at his doctor's office, he was told that he had two choices: either get into counseling . . . or get into counseling. His doctor found him a group that was designed to help people who had a difficult time relaxing and doing activities just for the sake of enjoyment. It was there that he realized that he was *addicted* to work and could not relax unless he was busy doing something. The empathy that he found from the group not only helped him to make a plan to change but also gave him the means and the motivation to do so.

Today Kelley is a different man. Through exploration of his compulsion to be active and *producing* something constantly, he began to realize the price he paid. Slowly, he began to channel that intensity and drive into a determined will to change. He began to realize the importance of leisure time for himself and his family.

Kelley has taken up a hobby, carving. People come from miles around to buy one of his treasures because of the joy that he puts into his creations. His work is both leisure and relaxation for him. He says that when he creates a carving, his mind rests and his body rejuvenates. It took Kelley a long time to learn the value of leisure time as much as work time, but today he is healthier and happier for learning to find the balance.

Source: D. Juanita Woods

must also budget your time and money to keep up the activity. This is especially true for sports, where a certain level of proficiency enhances the enjoyment of the experience (Atwater and Duffy, 1999).

Ideally, constructive leisure activities provide a break in our usual routine while being interesting and absorbing enough to create energy and excitement. Just passing time and being away from work is not always refreshing. The most valuable leisure activities are those that you look forward to doing and that give you a sense of accomplishment and renewal afterward.

Life Satisfaction

There are many factors that pertain to overall satisfaction in life. One of these is civility. According to M. Scott Peck (1978), the great lack of civility in America is the major factor in the breakdown in family life, unethical practices in business, selfishness, and dishonesty in politics. Civility means much more than politeness. Civility is all-embracing, a general awareness that personal well-being cannot be separated from the well-being of the groups to which we belong: our families, our businesses, and our nation.

Lack of civility is tied to unreasonable expectations of constant happiness and constant comfort in recent decades. When life presents us with painful experiences, when something hurts us, when we feel unfulfilled—we feel cheated. And too many of us, too often, reach for instant happiness by illegitimate means that disregard the interests of other people.

Peck says that the route to improved civility begins with greater awareness of our shortcomings and our tendencies to manipulate others. Greater awareness leads to a willingness to accept pain in the short term, recognizing that it is an unavoidable part of any personal growth process. Learning how to handle pain realistically is a prerequisite for warmer, more meaningful relationships over the long term. Civility does not happen automatically. You have to train yourself to be aware of your true motives, to be honest with yourself and others, and to judge yourself first (*Bottom Line/Personal*, Vol. 14, July 30, 1993).

Understanding Happiness

Why talk about being happy? Doesn't everyone know how to enjoy life? Who needs to learn how to be happy? We just do it, right? It would be nice if that were true, but it isn't. Some people think that when things are going well in life, something must be wrong. For some people, being happy is outside their comfort zone. They may feel that they don't deserve to be happy, that happiness only happens to other people.

I once knew a women who thought she could only have three good days in a row before something bad happened, and I saw her make this belief come true. If life had been going smoothly for three days, she would make sure something bad happened on the fourth day. She was so sure that something was going to hit the fan that she took an extra big fan with her just to make sure it did. Then, when something did hit the fan, she would relax and feel happy because then she knew for sure that she had three good days ahead.

The first step in enjoying life is to examine your beliefs about how much happiness is available, what happens if you have it, and whether you deserve to have it. Many people believe that happiness is an unlimited commodity and that, although you can't have it continuously, your feeling happy doesn't deprive anyone else of an opportunity for happiness. Some people act as if there is only so much joy to go around and you have to be careful not to exhaust the supply.

> **❝***Happiness is easy. It is letting go of unhappiness that is hard. We are willing to give up everything but our misery.***❞**
>
> *Hugh Prather*

Many of the popular ideas about what makes people happy are wrong, according to David G. Myers (1992). Taking into consideration a number of variables such as age, race, gender, and economic status, studies by psychologists have measured little difference in levels of happiness. People are about as happy today as their parents were 30 years ago. In short, researchers have established that external circumstances have little effect on psychological well-being. However, in his book *The Pursuit of Happiness: Who Is Happy and Why*, Myers states that researchers have identified four inner traits that foster happiness: self-esteem, a sense of personal control, sociability, and optimism.

Self-esteem: Happy people like themselves, and they anticipate that others will like them, too. This tends to set up a positive self-fulfilling prophecy. Expecting to be liked makes it easier for others to respond to them in a positive manner. Also, some people have less anxiety and depression because they feel good about themselves. As long as their positive outlook is based on genuine achievement of realistic goals, that self-esteem is healthy.

Personal control: People who have a strong sense that they control their own lives and feel satisfied with themselves are twice as likely as the national average to be very happy. Those who have little control over their environment suffer greater stress and worse health. Effective time management is one method of gaining a sense of control. People who can't plan their time and fill it purposefully are left feeling empty; those who are happy tend to be punctual and efficient.

Sociability: People with sociable, outgoing personalities tend to be happier and more satisfied with their lives. People who like socializing tend to be cheerful and high-spirited; their friendliness makes it easier for them to find friends, mates, and jobs. The support they get from their large circle of friends then makes them even happier. The emphasis here is that it is important for most people to have social contacts, not that being introverted reduces the ability to be happy.

Optimism: Optimistic people are not only happier, they are also healthier. They suffer fewer illnesses and have stronger immune defenses. Those who think in positive terms get positive

OPTIMISM AND SUCCESS

According to Martin Seligman, a University of Pennsylvania psychologist, how people respond to setbacks—optimistically or pessimistically—is a good indicator of how well they will succeed in school, sports, and certain kinds of work. To test his theory, Seligman devised a questionnaire to screen insurance salespeople at MetLife. Job applicants were asked to imagine a hypothetical event and then choose the response (A or B) that most closely resembled their own. Some samples from his questionnaire:

You forget your spouse's (boyfriend's/girlfriend's) birthday.

A. I'm not good at remembering birthdays.
B. I was preoccupied with other things.

You owe the library $10 for an overdue book.

A. When I am really involved in what I am reading, I often forget when it's due.
B. I was so involved in writing the report I forgot to return the book.

You lose your temper with a friend.

A. He or she is always nagging me.
B. He or she was in a hostile mood.

You are penalized for returning your income tax forms late.

A. I always put off doing my taxes.
B. I was lazy about getting my taxes done this year.

You've been feeling run down.

A. I never get a chance to relax.
B. I was exceptionally busy this week.

A friend says something that hurts your feelings.

A. He or she always blurts things out without thinking of others.
B. My friend was in a bad mood and took it out on me.

You fall down a great deal while skiing.

A. Skiing is difficult.
B. The trails were icy.

You gain weight over the holidays and you can't lose it.

A. Diets don't work in the long run.
B. The diet I tried didn't work.

Seligman found that those insurance salespeople who answered with more Bs than As were better able to overcome bad sales days, recovered more easily from rejection, and were less likely to quit. People with an optimistic view of life tend to treat obstacles and setbacks as temporary (and therefore surmountable). Pessimists take them personally; what others see as fleeting, localized impediments, they view as pervasive and permanent.

Source: Martin Seligman.

results. Psychologist Martin Seligman (1991) found that new Metropolitan Life salespeople with an optimistic outlook sold more policies and were half as likely to quit during their first year. Optimism does have a flip side, though. Unrealistic optimism can make people believe they are invulnerable and stop them from taking sensible steps to avoid danger. The recipe for well-being includes optimism to provide hope, a dash of pessimism to prevent complacency, and enough realism to understand the difference between those things we can control and those we can't (Seligman, 1991).

Finding Flow

What activity so absorbs you that you lose all sense of time? For some fortunate people, it is their life's work that produces such a state. For others, it is a hobby or avocation. People have a number of ways of talking about the state of being "in the groove," but most descriptions have in common a feeling of being alive, focused, energized, and really one with what they are doing. They are fully in the present moment and experience increased satisfaction with life. In whatever situation it is that you experience that kind of feeling, being able to "go with the flow" adds value and meaning to life.

Researcher Mihaly Csikszentmihalyi (1995) interviewed 90 leading figures in the fields of art, business, government, education, and science to find out more about creativity. He then applied to creativity his concept of flow: the enjoyment we experience when we are engaged in mental and physical challenges that absorb us. He found common elements in the experiences of the people he interviewed that are helpful in learning to develop that state of flow. He says that the first step toward a more creative life and "finding flow" is to cultivate your curiosity and interests. He offered the following specific suggestions:

- Try to be surprised every day. Make the effort to become absorbed in something new.
- Try to surprise at least one person every day. Break out of your patterns with others, and do something they might consider unpredictable.
- Write down each day what surprised you and how you surprised others. Most creative people keep a journal of some kind. After a few weeks of keeping track of your experiences, you might notice new areas to explore.
- Wake up in the morning with a specific goal to look forward to, something you are excited about accomplishing.

Questions for Critical Thinking

What are your beliefs about happiness? Is there such a thing as too much happiness? Does your being happy deprive someone else? Is there only so much to go around? Do you have to do something to "deserve" it?

_____

_____

_____

_____

_____

_____

_____

_____

_____

- Take charge of your schedule. Carve out time for yourself when you are most likely to feel creative.
- Solve problems creatively. Look at things from as many viewpoints as possible. Experiment with different and alternative solutions.

(Santrock, 1997)

Trying these suggestions will help increase your creative energy. And exploring new things that you enjoy will increase the likelihood that you experience a sense of "flow" in your life.

Forgiveness and Love

Forgiveness is an important element in human relations because everyone experiences something negative in the course of a lifetime. We all have been hurt or unfairly treated at one time or another. Some people experience their feelings, deal with the situation, and then get on with life. Others who may have been truly victimized continue to make themselves victims by hanging on to the emotions, holding a grudge, or wanting revenge.

Elisabeth Kübler-Ross, who pioneered the work being done with the terminally ill, stated in an interview that she wanted to be known as the "life and living lady," and not the "death and dying lady" (*Parade*, August 11, 1991). In that same interview, she discussed the importance of forgiveness.

"The overall purpose of communication is—or should be—reconciliation."

M. Scott Peck

Questions for Critical Thinking

Is there anyone whom you need to forgive? What issues to you need to resolve? What do you need to do to let go?

_____

_____

_____

_____

_____

_____

_____

_____

_____

Her primary mission was to bring death out of the closet to show people the way to live. She believes that it is only when you understand that time on earth is truly limited—and you have no way of knowing when your time is up—that you begin to live each day to the fullest. In her workshops on "Life, Death, and Transitions," she deals with people who have been physically or emotionally wounded and who need to find a way through the pain. As a result of her work, she has learned a great deal about the power of forgiveness.

After World War II, Kübler-Ross was working for an organization called International Voluntary Service for Peace. While visiting a concentration camp in Poland, she met a young Jewish girl named Golda, who had lost her entire family in the gas chambers. She learned that Golda, after being liberated from the concentration camp, had gone to work in a hospital in Germany to help children who were victims of the war. She had been bitter and wanted revenge when she was first released from the camp, but had then realized that, if she acted on those feelings, she would be no better than Hitler himself. Her work in the hospital was to purge her bitterness toward the German people. She returned to the camp because she had decided she would stay there until she could forgive the German people. She knew that only then would she be free. And that led to her work in helping to heal the very people who had been her captors. This is what led Kübler-Ross to where she is today: working with healing, forgiving, and learning to live life to the fullest.

Letting Go

Most people harbor a hurtful memory—some injustice, some mistake that they vow they will not only never forget but also never allow to happen again. But to forgive doesn't mean to give in; it means to let go. Forgiveness is really about letting go of the pain. It is a way of releasing the tie to the person who hurt you.

If forgiveness is so good, why do people carry around so much blame, anger, and resentment? One reason is that forgiveness feels like weakness or capitulation to some people. They think forgiving means that they were wrong and someone else was right. Yet, according to Sidney and Suzanne Simon (1990), in their book *Forgiveness: How to Make Peace with Your Past and Get On with Your Life,* forgiving helps you compensate for the powerlessness you felt when you were hurt or victimized.

Forgiveness isn't about letting the other person off the hook; it's about pulling the knife out of your own heart. Forgiveness often takes time because it is a journey through various stages. At first you experience anger, sadness, shame, or other negative feelings. Later, you begin to reframe the event or make sense of it by taking into account mitigating circumstances. Finally, rather than thinking of the person who hurt you as bad, you may begin to see that person as someone who was weak, sick, needy, or ignorant. What is important is that you let go of your anger and open your heart to understanding. Forgiveness is the reward that comes from the process of healing, so work to heal yourself rather than focusing on forgiving the other person. Experts offer the following suggestions to start healing:

- Forgive the person, not the deed.
- Don't think that forgiving is forgetting.
- Find ways to let out the bad feelings.
- Write a letter to the person who hurt you.
- Look forward in time.
- Enjoy your growing sense of strength and serenity.

> ❝*It is a law of human life, as certain as gravity: to live fully we must learn to use things and love people—not use people and love things.*❞

Love

In his book *Teach Only Love* (1983), G. G. Jampolsky relates his experiences working with terminally ill children. He discusses the fact that the bottom-line common denominator in life-and-death situations is love. He expands that notion to include all human relations. He feels this is the most important part of the work he has done over the years. With as much medical healing as he has done, he still emphasizes the need for love in healing both physical and emotional wounds. It is just as important to put that in practice in everyday life.

Few of us are in danger of being too loving or too compassionate. For that reason, it might be useful to have an occasional reminder about the value of treating each other with more love and kindness. Both seem to be in short supply in the world, and a number of people have problems due to not having experienced enough love. Most of us, it would seem, are looking for more love in our lives.

You have to love yourself before you can love anyone else. To a large degree, that is what this book is about, and I hope that the information offered has helped teach you to care more about yourself and others. We could all benefit from more love in the world.

Closure

In this final section, it is appropriate to consider the themes that appear throughout this book. An emphasis has been placed on being more accepting of yourself because that will create inner peace and a sense of internal balance. People who have gained in self-awareness and acceptance have a more balanced approach to life, and an increase in self-esteem provides a greater appreciation for individual differences and cultural diversity.

Human behavior can seem complex at times, but the really important aspects of life we all share in common. We all want to be cared for and

needed at times. We all want to find meaning and purpose in our lives and to be able to give something back to the world. Mentally healthy and well-adjusted people have a greater capacity for doing just that. I hope your human relations course has given you an opportunity to gain a greater understanding of who you are and how you got that way. The topics in this book are important to consider because they affect your everyday life and your relationships with others. They also provide an opportunity to assess your own behavior and consider what beneficial changes you might want to work on.

On another level, though, the content of this book is just a smoke screen. While you have been reading about and discussing the various aspects of human behavior, a more important process has been taking place. You have been communicating, relating, and connecting on a personal level. In doing so, you have had the experience of seeing, hearing, and feeling the joy and hardships of your fellow travelers through this journey we call life. Consider how this text and your human relations course have affected the way you relate to others.

Now comes the real challenge: How do you deal with people outside the classroom who may have no idea what you have experienced? Even if the changes you have made are positive and in your best interests, there will probably be some people who are not excited or impressed. There is a greater degree of safety in a classroom, where everyone tacitly agrees to operate by slightly different rules for a short time each week. The real test begins now as you continue to live your life the way you want in a world that may not always approve. That is the challenge and the opportunity.

Being Yourself

To paraphrase an earlier quote: To be yourself in a world that is constantly trying to make you be like someone else is a very difficult task. As you continue to take the risks involved in being true to yourself, you will undoubtedly be greeted with mixed reactions. Stay strong and centered, but also be respectful, and don't try to change everyone else because you have made changes. If there are ways in which you are starting to exercise new choices, keep in mind that, even though some people will be supportive, others may feel threatened. If you truly change, they may have to change also. If one part of a system is changed, the whole system is affected eventually. By the

FORGIVENESS ENABLES A PERSON TO STOP BEING A PRISONER OF THE PAST

Do you want to stay depressed and resentful or take a stab at forgiveness and feel better? What else can be the answer to this question by psychologist Lewis Andrews, author of *To Thine Own Self Be True?* Andrews maintains that until you forgive, you carry your enemies around with you. Forgiveness enables you to stop being a prisoner of the past. After "why" is understood, the next question is "how?" Whichever method you choose, therapists and spiritual leaders stress the importance of two things:

1. It doesn't matter so much whether or not the person you've forgiven accepts it. The important thing is the fact you did it; it's your burden you're releasing.
2. Forgiving yourself is essential to becoming free of the past and to truly forgiving others. One way to do this is to make verbal or written amends to those you have wronged—not just apologizing but ensuring that you don't repeat that wrong. You'll feel better about yourself and less resentful toward others. Writing a letter or personally confronting the person you want to forgive are the most direct methods.

Anne-Sophie Walker, a Portland counselor, wrote a letter to her alcoholic mother.

I did it because I wanted to be happy; to hold a grievance was just holding myself in prison. It was really a love letter—and the easiest thing I have ever done. I let go of seeing the appearances, what she had said and done. I saw who she really was; I saw the light in her and in myself. She said it was the most beautiful letter she had ever received, and we cried in each other's arms—it was a holy instant. She recognized behind her guilt that she was lovable, and she was grateful. Forgive, and you see the love that was always there. And it's really important to see what you did to push the person away; it's what we haven't given that stands in the way.

Here are some other forgiveness methods used by therapists, ministers, and self-help programs:

1. Write a letter but don't send it. Put it in a bottle and toss it out to sea or stick it in a balloon and release it to the sky.
2. Symbolically release your resentments on paper and ceremonially burn it (a New Year's tradition with some people).
3. Write about it in your journal and read it to a trusted person.
4. Mentally direct good wishes toward the person who wronged you; pray for him or her. Substitute a negative thought about the person with a positive one.
5. Try affirmations, such as "I love you, I bless you, and I let you go."
6. Deal with the issue, then drop it. Thinking and talking about grievances keeps them alive.
7. Make a list of all your resentments—against whom and for what. Then go through the list again, noting what you could have done differently in each situation ("I could have taken the dispute between me and my boss to a higher supervisor instead of just feeling mistreated"; "I could have asked my neighbors to pay for the damage instead of banning their children from my yard").

As philosopher George Santayana said, "Those who cannot remember the past are condemned to repeat it." So look back—but don't stare.

Source: Article written by Jann Mitchell.

WHAT IS SUCCESS

To laugh often and much;
To win the respect of intelligent people and the affection of children;
To earn the appreciation of honest critics and endure the betrayal of false friends;
To appreciate beauty;
To find the best in others;

To leave the world a bit better, whether by a healthy child, a garden patch, or a redeemed social condition;
To know even one life has breathed easier because you have lived;
This is to have succeeded.

Source: Ralph Waldo Emerson.

same token, that may be the positive effect you have on others.

Rather than trying to explain to others about all of your experiences and the new information you have gained, remember that just your behaving differently will change the way others treat you. But people may not be pleased with your changes even if they are positive for you. It is important to know how to stand up for your rights without imposing your beliefs on others. It is also important to be forewarned that personal change and growth may lead to conflict in some cases.

Why the cautionary note about making positive changes in your behavior? Occasionally, I

GUIDE FOR CONSTRUCTIVE LIVING

1. Before you say anything to anyone, ask yourself three things: (a) Is it true? (b) Is it kind? (c) Is it necessary?
2. Make promises sparingly and keep them faithfully.
3. Never miss the opportunity to compliment or to say something encouraging to someone.
4. Refuse to talk negatively about others; don't gossip and don't listen to gossip.
5. Have a forgiving view of people. Believe that most people are doing the best they can.
6. Keep an open mind; discuss, but don't argue. (It is possible to disagree without being disagreeable.)
7. Forget about counting to 10. Count to 1000 before doing or saying anything that could make matters worse.
8. Let your virtues speak for themselves.
9. If someone criticizes you, see if there is any truth to what he or she is saying; if so, make changes. If there is no truth to the criticism, ignore it and live so that no one will believe the negative remark.
10. Cultivate your sense of humor; laughter is the shortest distance between two people.

hear younger students in my human relations courses say that now they are going to go home and "fix" their parents, or older people say that they are going to "use it on their kids." Some spouses want to go home and confront their partners with the changes that they think ought to be made—and now! Keep in mind that most people don't want to have something "done to them," regardless of how beneficial it might be.

Part of developing good human relations skills is knowing how and when to present information to someone. The most valuable message in the world probably will not be heard or will be heard inaccurately if it is delivered in anger. Caring and openly expressing those emotions is a prerequisite for improving communications in most situations. I hope you have detected that as one of the major themes throughout the book.

CHAPTER REVIEW

Values and Meaning

It is useful to clarify your values and become more aware of how they influence your behavior. Having a better understanding of your values will enable you to establish goals in life. Having clearer goals will, in turn, help you to make better decisions. When we have a sense, a purpose, and a meaning in life, we experience a greater degree of satisfaction in everyday living.

Decision Making

One of the factors for increasing life satisfaction is learning to make good decisions. Many people lack this skill. We often have to make a decision based on the best information at the time, and not making a decision is a decision. There are different types of conflicts, depending on the circumstances. Few decisions are made with 100 percent certainty. This section provides methods for approaching decisions when 60 percent of you wants one thing, and 40 percent wants another.

Work and Leisure

Finding satisfying work is an important part of life. There are a number of theories about career selection. The better you know yourself—your abilities and interests—the more likely it is that you will be able to find a career match. Leisure is also an important part of life. Leisure is more than just doing nothing or watching television. Activities that are beneficial create a sense of excitement, generate energy, and give meaning and purpose to one's life.

Life Satisfaction

There is an increasing lack of civility in this country. Becoming more concerned about others can increase one's satisfaction in life. People in general are about as happy today as they were 30 years ago. Some of the factors that influence happiness are self-esteem, personal control, sociability, and optimism.

Forgiveness and Love

We all experience unfortunate things and, at times, feel that people or the world has treated us unfairly. Holding grudges or hanging on to anger and resentment is debilitating. Learning to forgive and move on can free you to have a greater range of experiences in life. Hand in hand with that is allowing yourself to be more caring toward others in the world. Many psychologists talk about the importance of self-love as a means of being more loving with the significant people in your life. Being more empathic, and willing to express that, would contribute considerably to the alleviation of a vast number of problems in society.

Closure

The theme of how to have more choice and balance in life runs throughout this book. As important as the content of the book is, the process of interacting with others about your reactions and what you have learned is more important. The real challenge comes as you incorporate the significant lessons and apply them in your everyday life. Many people will be supportive of your positive changes, but some may feel threatened. It is beneficial to remember that staying centered and being true to yourself will go a long way in influencing others.

SOURCES AND SUGGESTED READINGS

Corey, Gerald. *I Never Knew I Had a Choice*. Monterey, CA: Brooks-Cole, 2006.

Frankl, V. E. *Man's Search for Meaning*. New York: Simon & Schuster, 1963.

Jampolsky, G. G. *Teach Only Love: The Seven Principles of Attitudinal Healing*. New York: Bantam, 1983.

Kushner, Harold. *When Bad Things Happen to Good People*. New York: Avon, 1981.

Myers, D. G. *The Pursuit of Happiness: Who Is Happy and Why*. New York: William Morrow, 1992.

Peck, M. Scott. *The Road Less Traveled*. New York: Simon & Schuster, 1978.

Seligman, M. E. P. *Learned Optimism*. New York: Knopf, 1991.

Carney, C. G., and C. F. Wells. *Working Well, Living Well: Discover The Career Within You*. Fifth edition. Pacific Grove, CA: Brooks/Cole, 1999.

Holland, J. L. *Making Vocational Choices: A Theory of Vocational Personalities and Work Environments*. Third edition. Odessa, FL: Psychological Assessment Resources, 1997.

Lock, R. D. *Job Search: Career Planning Guide, Book 2*. Fifth edition. Pacific Grove, CA: Brooks/Cole, 2005.

Schlossberg, N. K. *Retire Smart, Retire Happy*. Washington, DC: American Psychological Association, 2004.

Dalai Lama. *An Open Heart: Practicing Compassion in Everyday Life*. Boston: Little, Brown, 2001.

Dalai Lama and H. C. Cutler. *The Art of Happiness: A Handbook for Living*. New York: Riverhead, 1998.

Jampolsy, G. G. *Forgiveness: The Greatest Healer of All*. Hillsboro. OR: Beyond Words, 1999.

Hales, D. *An Invitation to Health*. Tenth edition. Belmont, CA: Wadsworth/Thomson Learning, 2005.

Web Site Resources

APA HelpCenter: Psychology at Work
http://helping.apa.org/work/index.html

John Holland's Self-Directed Search
http://www.self-directedsearch.com

The Occupational Outlook Handbook
http://www.stats.bls.gov/ocohome.htm

U.S. Department of Labor Online: service to explore wages, worker productivity, unsafe conditions, legal rights, and protection from sexual harassment
http://www.dol.gov

CAREERS.WSY.COM: updates of employment issues and more than 1000 job-seeking articles
http://www.careerjournal.com

The Riley Guide: Employment Opportunities and Job Resources on the Internet
http://www.rileyguide.com

Information on a healthy balance between optimism and pessimism
http://www.youmeworks.com/optimisminterview.html

Healthy People 2010
http://www.health.gov.healthypeople

A site designed by an expert who guides you through step-by-step decision making
http://www.mapnp.org/library/prsn_prd/decision.htm

REACTION RESPONSE—WHAT DO YOU THINK?

Chapter Ten   Level I Assignments

In response to the information in the chapter:

1. What did you learn about your core values and beliefs? How do those ideas influence you regarding human relations?

2. Having thought about goals and decision making, what would you like to accomplish in the course of your lifetime? What are some important things that you would like to be able to say you have done?

3. What did you learn about work and careers? What type of job would best suit your personality and lifestyle? How do you use your leisure time? Do you have too much, or too little? Is what you do actually rejuvenating?

In response to the class activities, group discussions, and exercises:

1. What are your opinions and reactions?
2. What did you learn or rediscover?
3. How are you going to apply what you learned?

Chapter Ten   Level II Assignments

1. What did you learn about the general concepts regarding life satisfaction? What contributes to life satisfaction for you? How can you make changes that will contribute to an increased sense of satisfaction in life?

2. How often do you have an optimistic outlook? What can you do when you feel pessimistic?

3. What are the important concepts that you have learned from this book? How are you going to use that information in your life? How have you increased "choice and balance" in your life? Has that helped to improve your human relations?

Chapter 10   Level III Assignments

1. Have you ever had a time when you needed forgiveness from someone else? What did you hope that the other person would think or do? How can that be useful in considering what you need to do to start forgiving someone you have hurt or wronged?

2. What would it take for you to be more forgiving with others? What could you do to contribute to an increase of caring and compassion in the world?

3. What gives you meaning and purpose in life? When do you feel the most alive? How can you begin to express that sense of well-being with others around you?

acculturation The various means that an ethnic group may use in adapting to a dominant culture.

affirmation Statement that enhances or supports positive self-regard.

aggressive behavior Achieving desired goals by hurting or disregarding others. Enhancing oneself at the expense of others.

assertive behavior Standing up for one's own rights without depriving others of theirs. Expressing views honestly and openly without hurting others.

assimilation Describes those that do not desire to maintain their cultural identity and seek sustained contact with a culture other than their own.

association Staying in the present; paying attention to and enhancing feelings.

attribute Personal trait or characteristic.

attribution theory The theory that people tend to overestimate the influence of a person's personality and underestimate the impact of a situation.

bidirectional The tendency for two people to exert mutual influence on each other.

blame shifting Finding fault in others rather than in oneself.

cognitive ability The intellectual capacity to think, reason, and comprehend.

cognitive perception Filter that influences how an individual understands communications or situations.

cognitive restructuring Modifying the thoughts, ideas, and beliefs that maintain an individual's problems.

conceptualization Dealing with abstract ideas and their application.

congruence When words, nonverbal expression, and actions all agree and overlap.

continuity Continuous progression in life span development.

conversion therapy Therapy that attempts to change a person's sexual orientation.

criteria Standards by which something is evaluated.

decoding Interpreting and attaching meaning to a message.

demarcation Significant event or transition that may indicate change in a person's life.

dichotomy Division into two contradictory parts.

differentiate To separate one's self or ideas from another's.

dissociation Decreasing feelings by distancing oneself from a situation. Thinking about a particular event as though it were in another time and place.

dominant culture The accepted norms of the group that comprises the majority of people of a particular race or ethnic group.

double bind A "no-win" situation in which any response results in pain or confusion.

double standard Attitude or belief that is not equitably applied; what is permissible for one person is not for another. Commonly used in reference to different treatment of or expectations for males and females.

dyad Two people in a discussion; a pair.

dysfunctional Displaying behaviors that seriously interfere with one's ability to maintain one's well-being.

encoding Putting thoughts into words and producing a message.

ethnicity The consciousness of a cultural heritage shared with other people.

euphemism Substitution of an inoffensive word or phrase for one thought to be offensive.

exemplary An example of a particular idea or behavior.

extrovert A person who discovers his or her identity and stability in life with and through others.

family of origin The family system in which an individual was raised; the people who had significant impact on a person's development.

family system therapy Therapy based on the assumption that psychological adjustment is related to patterns of interaction within the family unit.

fear of success The tendency to lower one's aspirations to avoid pressure or anxiety resulting from doing well.

flow Being in a totally absorbed state of mind. An activity, whether work or play, that engages all of the person's skills and abilities.

free will The idea that people are capable of making choices that affect their lives and are responsible for those choices.

gay relationship A homosexual relationship.

gender role The sociocultural definition of male and female; the set of expectations that prescribe how females and males should think, act, and feel.

genogram A diagram of a family tree developed by Murray Bowen that includes information about significant events, relationships, education and occupations, marriages and deaths, problems and addictions, and pervasive themes in the history of a family.

group think The motivation of group members to maintain harmony in decision making by downplaying differences of opinion.

hierarchy of needs Maslow's stage theory of motivation.

homophobia Fear of homosexuals, their behavior, or possible feelings of attraction for one's own sex.

ideal self The person one wishes to be.

"I" message A message that describes the speaker's position without evaluating the position of others.

inextricable Incapable of being untangled or separated.

innate Characteristic, trait, or behavior that one is born with.

inner child The aspects of a person that are related to the needs, ideas, and feelings that were experienced as a child.

intimacy Closeness and personal sharing that results from physical, intellectual, and/or emotional contact.

introvert A person who discovers his or her identity through introspection—the examination of one's thoughts and feelings.

irrational belief Private viewpoint, often incorrect, that leads to inappropriate emotions and behaviors.

learned helplessness Seligman's term for the tendency to give up when faced with adversity, usually based on the assumption from past failures that one is unable to do anything about a given situation.

listening Truly hearing what someone is saying; interpreting and understanding the significance of the communication.

locus of control The extent to which an individual feels that what happens to them and what they achieve in life is due to their own abilities and actions. For some that focus is internal, and for others that focus is external.

lose-lose situation An approach to conflict resolution in which each person tries to deprive the other of what he or she wants and neither is happy with the outcome.

message Information delivered from the sender to the receiver in an act of communication.

motive The need or desire that causes someone to act.

myth A story, fable, or epic that attempts to explain the natural and social history of the world.

need satisfaction The attempt to satisfy a need or desire.

nonverbal communication Message communicated by other than linguistic means.

paradox A statement that seems contradictory or unbelievable but may actually be true.

paraphrase A concise response to a speaker that states the essence of the speaker's message in the listener's own words.

passive behavior Avoiding or removing oneself from a conflictual situation; being unwilling or unable to stand up for one's needs.

personality type Classification based on distinctive thoughts, emotions, and behaviors that characterize the way an individual adapts to the world.

pluralism The process through which cultural differences are acknowledged and preserved.

presenting problem The problem that an individual presents as primary, when the real problem may be something else.

primary emotion Basic emotion such as anger, sadness, happiness, or fear.

projection Attributing one's own problems, fears, and faults to others.

psychobabble Self-improvement jargon that is often vague and ineffectual.

rational-emotive therapy Albert Ellis's form of therapy that focuses on behavioral changes, especially in eliminating irrational and self-defeating behaviors and beliefs.

reciprocity The tendency of people to like individuals who like them back.

repertoire The range and number of skills available to a person.

response Observable feedback.

risk The chance of injury or loss involved in trying something new and stretching one's abilities.

self-actualization The motivation to develop one's full potential as a human being.

self-concept The relatively stable set of perceptions that an individual has of himself or herself.

self-defeating behavior Behavior that sabotages one's own efforts.

self-disclosure Sharing intimate details about oneself with others.

self-efficacy An individual's beliefs about his or her ability to master situations and produce positive outcomes.

self-esteem How a person evaluates himself or herself in comparison to others.

self-fulfilling prophecy A prediction or expectation of an event that makes the outcome more likely to occur than would otherwise have been the case.

self-talk The internal dialogue that represents nonvocal thinking; stream of consciousness.

social clock The timetable according to which individuals are expected to accomplish life's significant tasks.

social comparison The process by which individuals evaluate their thoughts, feelings, behaviors, and abilities in relation to other people.

socialization The process of inculturating a person with the accepted norms of society.

stereotype A generalization about a group's characteristics.

stress management A program or procedure for appraising stressful events and developing coping skills.

tactile communication Nonverbal communication that focuses on the importance of touch.

thought stopping Concentrating on unwanted thoughts and becoming aware of when they occur; consciously stopping unwanted thought patterns.

Type A behavior A cluster of behaviors that are thought to be related to coronary problems.

Type B behavior The behavior pattern of individuals who live a more relaxed lifestyle.

Type C behavior The cancer-prone personality, which consists of being inhibited, uptight, lacking in emotional expression, and being otherwise constrained.

win-lose situation A one-up approach to conflict resolution in which one person gets what he or she wants at the expense of another person.

win-win situation A cooperative approach to conflict resolution in which both parties win with a solution that is acceptable to all concerned.

"you" message A message that describes another person or his or her behavior and attributes blame.

Abboud, L. (2003, August 8). "Expect a food fight as U.S. sets to revise diet guidelines." *Wall Street Journal*, p. B1.

Ackerman, Diane. (1991). *A natural history of the senses*. New York: Vintage Press.

Adler, A. (1927). *Practice and theory of individual psychology*. New York: Harcourt, Brace & World.

Adler, Ronald, & Towne, Neil. (2003). *Looking out/looking in*. Belmont CA: Thompson/Wadsworth.

Ainsworth, M. D. S., Blehar, M. C., Waters, E., & Wall, S. (1978). *Patterns of attachment: A psychological study of the strange situation*. Hillsdale, NJ: Erlbaum.

Alberti, R. E., & Emmons, M. L. (1986). *Your perfect right: A guide to assertive living*. San Luis Obispo, CA: Impact.

Altman, Irwin, & Taylor, Dalmas. (1973). *Social penetration*. New York: Holt, Rinehart and Winston.

Arkoff, Abe. (1995). *The illuminated life*. Needham Heights, MA: Allyn & Bacon.

Aronson, E. (1988). *The social animal* (4th ed). New York: W. H. Freeman.

Atwater, Eastwood. (1986). *Human relations*. Englewood Cliffs, NJ: Prentice Hall.

Atwater, Eastwood. (1993). *Psychology of adjustment*. Englewood Cliffs, NJ: Prentice Hall.

Atwater, Eastwood & Duffy, Karen. (1999). *Psychology for living*. Englewood Cliffs, NJ: Prentice Hall.

Bach, G. R., & Torbet, L. (1989). *The inner enemy*. New York: Berkeley Books.

Bandura, Albert. (1977). *Social learning theory*. Englewood Cliffs, NJ: Prentice Hall.

Bandura, Albert. (1997). "Self efficacy: Toward a unifying theory of behavioral change." *Psychological Review* 84.

Barber, B. K. (1996). Parental psychological control: revisiting a neglected construct. *Child Development, 67*, 6.

Baron, Robert A. (1990). *Understanding human relations: A practical guide to people at work*. Boston: Allyn & Bacon.

Bass, Ellen, & Davis, Laura. (1994). *The courage to heal*. (3rd ed). New York: HarperCollins.

Baumeister, Roy F., (Ed.). (1999). *The self in social psychology*. Philadelphia: Psychology Press.

Baumeister et al. (2000). Self-esteem, narcissism, and aggression. *Current Directions in Psychological Science, 9*, 26–29.

Baumrind, D. (1991). *Parenting styles and adolescent development*. In J. Brooks-Gunn, R. Lerner, and A. C. Petersen (Eds.), New York.

Beattie, Melody. (1987). *Codependent no more*. New York: Harper/Hazeldon.

Beck, A. (1993). *Cognitive therapy and the emotional disorders*. New York: New American Library.

Bennett, M. J. (1993). "Towards ethnorelativism: A developmental model of intercultural sensitivity." In R. M. Paige (Ed.), *Education for the intercultural experience* (pp. 21–71). Yarmouth, ME: Intercultural Press.

Benson, Herbert. (1984). *Beyond the relaxation response*. New York: Times Books.

Berglas, Stephen. (1991). *The success syndrome*. New York: Penguin.

Berry, J. W. & Sam, D. L. (1997). Acculturate and adaptation. In J. Berry, M. Segall, & C. Kogitcrbasi (Eds.), *Cross-cultured psychology* (Vol. 3, pp. 291–326). Boston: Allyn & Bacon.

Bernie, Eric. (1972). *What do you say after you say hello?* New York: Bantam.

Black, Claudia. (1982). *It will never happen to me*. Denver: M.A.C.

Blonna, R., & Levitan, J. (2000). *Healthy sexuality*. Englewood, CO: Morton.

Boles, R. N. (1978). *The three boxes of life*. Berkeley, CA: Ten Speed Press.

Bolton, Robert. (1979). *People skills*. New York: Simon & Schuster.

Borysenko, Joan. (1988). *Minding the body, mending the mind*. New York: Bantam.

Bowlby, J. (1980). *Attachment and loss: Loss, sadness, and depression*. (vol. 3) New York: Basic Books.

Bowen, Murray. (1978). *Family therapy in clinical practice*. New York: Jason Aronson.

Bower, S. A., & Bower, G. H. (1996). *Asserting yourself: A practical guide for positive change*. Reading, MA: Addison-Wesley.

Bradshaw, John. (1988a). *Bradshaw: On the family*. Deerfield Beach, FL: Health Communications.

Bradshaw, John. (1988b). *Healing the shame that binds you*. Pompano Beach, FL: Health Communications.

Brandon, Nathaniel. (1987). *How to raise your self-esteem*. New York: Bantam.

Brandon, Nathaniel. (1994). *The six pillars of self-esteem.* New York: Bantam Books.

Bridges, William. (1980). *Transitions.* Philippines: Addison-Wesley.

Brislin, R. (1993). *Understanding culture's influence on behavior.* Fort Worth, TX: Harcourt, Brace.

Bucher, R. (2000). *Diversity consciousness.* Upper Saddle River, NJ: Prentice Hall.

Burns, D. D. (1999). *Ten days to self-esteem.* New York: HarperCollins.

Burns, D. D. (1989). *The feeling good handbook.* New York: Penguin Books.

Buscaglia, Leo. (1982). *Living, loving, and learning.* New York: Holt, Rinehart and Winston.

Cameron-Bandler, Leslie. (1985). *Solutions.* San Rafael, CA: Future Pace.

Cawley, J. (2004). The impact of obesity on wages. *Journal of Human Resources, 39*(2), 451–474.

Cohen, S. (1998). *Types of stressors that increase susceptibility to the common cold in healthy adults. Health Psychology 17,* 214–223.

Chou, S.-Y., Grossman, M., & Saffer, H. (2004). An economic analysis of adult obesity: Results from the behavioral risk factor surveillance system. *Journal of Health Economics, 23,* 565–587.

Cline, Foster, & Fay, Jim. (1990). *Parenting with love and logic.* Denver, CO: Pinon Press.

Coontz, Stephanie. (1992). *The way we never were.* New York: HarperCollins.

Coontz, Stephanie. (1997). *The way we really are.* New York: HarperCollins.

Corey, G., & Schneider-Corey, M. (2006). *I never knew I had a choice.* Pacific Grove, CA: Brooks/Cole.

Corr, C. A., Nabe, C. M., & Corr, D. M. (2003). Death and dying, life and living (4th ed). Belmont, CA: Wadsworth.

Courtois, Christine. (1996). *Healing the incest wound.* New York: Norton.

Covey, Stephen. (1989). *The seven habits of highly effective people.* New York: Simon & Schuster.

Crooks, Robert, & Baur, Karla. (1997). *Our sexuality.* Menlo Park, CA: Benjamin-Cummings.

Csikszentmihalyi, M. (1990). *Finding flow.* New York: Harper & Row.

Csikszentmihalyi, M. (1995). *Creativity.* New York: HarperCollins.

Currier, Cecile. (1982). *Learning to step together.* Baltimore, MD: Stepfamily Association of America.

Cutler, D. M., Glaeser, E. L., & Shapiro, Jesse M. (2003). Why have Americans become more obese? *Journal of Economic Perspectives, 17*(3), 93–118.

Cyrus, V. (2000). *Experiencing race, class, and gender in the United States.* Mountain View, CA: Mayfield.

Dalenberg, C. J. (1996). Accuracy, timing, and circumstances of disclosure in therapy of recovered and continuous memories of abuse. *Journal of Psychiatry and Law, 24.*

Daniels, V., & Horowitz, L. (1998). *Being and caring.* Prospect Heights, IL: Waveland Press.

Davidson, J. Kenneth, Sr., & Moore, N. (2001). *Speaking of sexuality: Interdisciplinary readings.* Los Angeles, CA: Roxbury.

DeAngelis, Barbara. (1992). *Are you the right one for me?* New York: Delacorte.

Devito, Joseph A. (1990). *Messages: Building interpersonal communication skills.* New York: Harper & Row.

Dobrithc, W., & S. Dranoff. (2000). *The first line of defense: A guide to protecting yourself against sexual harassment.* New York: Wiley.

Dworetzsky, John. (1995). *Human development.* St. Paul, MN: West.

Dyer, Wayne W. (1977). *Your erroneous zones.* New York: Avon.

Dyer, Wayne. (1989). *You'll see it when you believe it.* New York: Avon.

Ellis, A. (1984). *Reason and emotion in psychotherapy.* Secaucus, NJ: Lyle Stuart.

Ellis, A., & Yeager, R. J. (1989). *Why some therapies don't work.* Buffalo, NY: Prometheus.

Emery, Gary, & Campbell, J. (1986). *Rapid relief from emotional distress.* New York: Ballantine.

Epstein, S. (1973). The self-concept revisited: Or a theory of a theory. *American Psychologist, 28.*

Erikson, E. H. (1950). *Childhood and society.* New York: Norton.

Ernst, Cecile, & Angst, J. (1983). *Birth order.* New York: Springer-Verlag.

Fast, Julius. (1970). *Body language.* New York: M. Evans.

Finkelstein, E. A., Fiebelkorn, I. C., & Wang, G. (2003). National medical spending attributable to overweight and obesity: How much, and who's paying? *Health Affairs, W3,* 219–226.

Fisher, Roger, & Ury, W. (1981). *Getting to yes: Negotiating agreement without giving in.* Boston: Houghton Mifflin.

Foward, Susan. (1990). *Toxic parents.* New York: Bantam.

Fox, B., & Joyce, C. (1991, January 12). "Americans compete for control over sex." *New Scientist.*

Frankl, Victor E. (1984). *Man's search for meaning.* New York: Simon & Schuster.

Franzoi, Stephen. (2003). *Social psychology.* New York: McGraw-Hill.

Freeman, S. J. (2005). *Grief and loss: Understanding the journey.* Belmont, CA: Brooks/Cole.

Friedman, M., & Rosenman, R. (1974). *Type A behavior and your heart.* New York: Knopf.

Furstenburg, Frank. (1994). Reconsidering the effects of marital disruption. *Journal of Family Issues, 15,* 173–190.

Gardiner, H., & Kosmitzki, C. (2002). *Lives across culture.* Boston: Pearson.

Gibran, Kahlil. (1923). *The prophet*. New York: Knopf.

Gil, Eleana. (1988). *Outgrowing the pain*. San Francisco: Launch Press.

Glasser, William. (1965). *Reality therapy*. New York: Harper & Row.

Goldberg, L. R. (1993). "The structure of phenotypic personality traits." *American Psychologist, 48*.

Goleman, Daniel. (1995). *Emotional intelligence*. New York: Bantam.

Goode, D. (1994). Perspectives in international psychology. Eds. Pervin and Lewis. *The encyclopedia of adolescence* (pp. 746–758). New York: Garland.

Goodman, Gerald. (1988). *The talk book: The intimate science of communicating in close relationships*. New York: Ballantine.

Gordon, Thomas. (1975). *Parent effectiveness*. New York: Peter H. Wyden.

Gottlieb, Daniel. (1991). *Family matters*. New York: Penguin.

Gottman, John. (1994). *Why marriages succeed or fail*. New York: Simon & Schuster.

Gottman, John, & Silver, N. (1999). *The seven principles for making marriage work*. New York: Crown.

Gray, John. (1992). *Men are from Mars, women are from Venus*. New York: HarperCollins.

Greene, B. (1993). Human diversity in clinical psychology. *The Clinical Psychologist, 46*(2).

Haffner, D.W. (1998). Sexuality education. *Social Policy, 28*.

Haffner, D. (1995). *Facing facts: Sexual health for adolescents*. New York: SEICUS.

Hall, Edward. (1969). *The hidden dimension*. Garden City, NY: Anchor.

Hall, Margaret C. (1991). *The Bowen family theory and its uses*. Northvale, NJ: Jason Aronson.

Halloran, J., & Benton, C. (1987). *Applied human relations: An organizational approach*. Englewood Cliffs, NJ: Prentice Hall.

Halloran, J., & Benton, C. (1997). *Applied human relations: An organizational approach*. Englewood Cliffs, NJ: Prentice Hall.

Halonen, J. S., & Santrock, J. W. (1997). *Human adjustment*. Dubuque, IA: Times Mirror Higher Education Group.

Hanna, Sharon L. (2003). *Person to persons: Positive relationships don't just happen*. Englewood Cliffs, NJ: Prentice Hall.

Harris, Thomas A. (1969). *I'm OK—you're OK*. New York: Harper & Row.

Harter, S. (1999). *The construction of the self*. New York: Guilford.

Hartman, Taylor Don. (1987). *The color code: A new way to see yourself, your relationships, and life*. Trabuco, CA: Taylor Don Hartman.

Hecklinger, F., & Black, B. (1996). *Training for life*. Dubuque, IA: Kendall Hunt.

Helsin, R., & Alper, T. (1991). Touch: A bonding gesture in *Nonverbal interaction*. J. M. Wiemann & R. P. Harrison (Eds.), Beverly Hills, CA: Sage.

Hazan, C., & Shaver, P. (1987). Romantic love conceptualized as an attachment process. *Journal of Personality and Social Psychology, 52*, 511–524.

Hendrix, Harville. (1990). *Getting the love you want: A guide for couples*. Holt & Company.

Herdt, G. ed. (1994). *Homosexuality and adolescents*. New York: Hawthorne Press.

Hooper, M., & Heighway-Bury R. (2001). *Who built the pyramid?* Cambridge, MA: Candlewick Press.

Hopper, J. (2002). The online games people play. Brandweek, vol. 43.

James, M., & Jongeward, D. *Born to win*. Reading, MA: Nass Addison-Wesley (1972).

Jampolsky, G. G. (1979). *Love is letting go of fear*. Millbrae, CA: Celestial Arts.

Jampolsky, G. G. (1983). *Teach only love: The seven principles of attitudinal healing*. New York: Bantam.

Jeffers, Susan. (1987). *Feel the fear and do it anyway*. New York: Fawcett Columbine.

Johnson, Earvin "Magic." (1992). *What you can do to avoid AIDS*. New York: Random House.

Jones, S. E. & Yarborough, A. E. (1985). A naturalistic study of the meaning of touch. Communications Monographs, 52, 19–56. Jourard, Sidney. (1971). *The transparent self* (rev. ed). New York: Van Nostrand Reinhold.

Joy, Brugh. (1979). *Joy's way: A transformational journey*. Los Angeles: Tarcher.

Jung, C. G. (1961). *Memories, dreams, and reflections*. New York: Vantage.

Kinsey, A., Pomeroy, W., & Martin, C. (1948). *Sexual behavior in the human male*. Philadelphia: Saunders.

Kleinke, Chris L. (1998). *Coping with life challenges*. Belmont, CA: Wadsworth.

Kolb, D. A. (1971). *Organizational psychology*. Englewood Cliffs, NJ: Prentice Hall.

Kolb, D. A. (1984). Experiential learning. Prentice Hall, Inc., Englewood Cliffs, NJ.

Krause, N. (1995). Religiosity and self-esteem. *Journal of Gerontology: Psychological Sciences:* 236.

Kroeger, Otto, & Thuiesen, J. (1988). *Type talk*. New York: Delacorte.

Kromkowski, J. A. (1995). *Race and ethnic relations* Annual eds., 95–96. Guilford, CT: Duskin.

Kübler-Ross, Elisabeth. (1975). *Death: The final stage of growth*. Englewood Cliffs, NJ: Prentice Hall.

Kushner, Harold. (1983). *When bad things happen to good people*. New York: Avon.

Lair, Jess. (1969). *I ain't much baby but I'm all I've got*. New York: Doubleday.

Lakadawalla, D. & Philipson, T. (2002). The growth of obesity and technological change: A theoretical and empirical analysis. NBER working paper series, 8946.

Lamb, M. E., Thompson, R. A., Gardner, W. P., Charnov, E. L, & Estes, D. (1984). Security of infantile attachment as assessed in the "strange situation": Its study and biological interpretation. *The Behavioral and Brain Sciences, 7*, 127–171.

Lazarus, R., & Folkman, S. (1984). *Stress appraisal and coping*. New York: Springer.

Leman, Kevin. (1985). *The birth order book*. New York: Dell.

Lerner, Harriet Goldhor. (1989). *The dance of intimacy*. New York: Harper & Row.

Levine, Stephen. (1982). *Who dies? An investigation of conscious living and dying*. Garden City, NY: Doubleday.

Levinson, D. J., et al. (1978). *The seasons of a man's life*. New York: Knopf.

Locke, D. C. (1998). *Increasing multicultural understanding: A comprehensive model*. Newbury Park, CA: Sage.

Luborsky, Lester. (1988). *Who will benefit from therapy?* New York: Basic Books.

Luft, Joseph. (1969). *Of human interaction*. Palo Alto, CA: Mayfield.

Lykken, D. T. (1997). Incompetent parenting: Its causes and cures. *Child Psychiatry and Human Development, 27*, 3.

Lyman, Lawrence. (1995). *Journal of Psychology—Interdisciplinary and Applied, 3*.

Maccoby & Martin, (1983). Socialization in the context of the family. *Handbook of Child Psychology*. New York: Wiley.

Maltz, Wendy. (1991). *The sexual healing journey*. New York: HarperCollins.

Maltz, W., & Holman, B. (1987). *Incest and sexuality: A guide to understanding and healing*. New York: Lexington.

Maslow, Abraham H. (1969). *The healthy personality*. New York: Reinhold.

Maslow, H. (1971). *The farthest reaches of human nature*. New York: Viking.

Mason, L. J. (2001). *Guide to stress reduction*. Berkeley, CA: Ten Speed Press.

Masters, W. H., & Johnson, V. E. (1986). *On sex and human loving*. Boston: Little, Brown.

Masters, W. H., Johnson, V. E., & Kolodny, R. C. (1992). *Human sexuality*. New York: HarperCollins.

May, Rollo. (1969a). *Love and will*. New York: Norton.

May, Rollo. (1969b). *Man's search for himself*. New York: Norton.

McCann, I. L., & Holmes, D. S. (1984). Influence of aerobic exercise on depression. *Journal of Personality and Social Psychology, 46*, 1142–1147.

McAnulty, R., & Burnette, M. (2003). *Fundamentals of human sexuality*. Boston: Pearson Education.

McGoldrick, M., & Carter, B. (2005). *Self in context: The individual life cycle in systemic perspective*. New York: Gardner Press Inc.

McGregor, Douglas. (1960). *The human side of enterprise*. New York: McGraw-Hill.

McKay, M., & Fanning, P. (2000). *Self-esteem*. Oakland, CA: New Harbinger.

McWilliams, John-Rodger, & McWilliams, Peter. (1990). *Life 101*. Los Angeles: Prelude Press.

Mehrabian, Albert. (1986, September). Communication without words. *Psychology Today*, pp. 48–54.

Mehrabian, A. (1993). *Differences in positive and negative connotations in nicknames and given names. Journal of Social Psychology, 133*, 737–739.

Montague, Ashley. (1971). *Touching*. New York: Harper & Row.

Myers, D. G. (1992). *The pursuit of happiness*. New York: Morrow.

Myers, P. B., & Myers, K. D. (1985). *Manual: A guide to the development and use of the Myers-Briggs Type Indicator*. Palo Alto, CA: Consulting Psychologists Press.

Myers-Briggs, Isabel. (1989). *Gifts differing*. Palo Alto, CA: Consulting Psychologists Press.

Nelson-Jones, Richard. (1998). *Human relationships: A skills approach*. Pacific Grove, CA: Brooks/Cole.

Nieto, S. (1992). *Affirming diversity: The sociopolitical context of multicultural education*. White Plains, NY: Longman.

Novak, M. A., & Harlow, H. F. (1975). Social recovery of monkeys isolated for the first years of life. *Developmental Psychology, 11*, 453–465.

O'Grady, Dennis. (1994). *Taking the fear out of changing: Getting through tough life transitions*. Dayton, OH: New Insights Press.

Orenstein, Peggy. (1994). *School girls: Young women and self-esteem*. New York: Doubleday.

Osmont, Kelly. (1986). *Parting is not goodbye*. Portland, OR: Nobility Press.

Peale, Norman Vincent. (1976). *You can if you think you can*. Guilford, CT: Fawcett.

Peck, M. Scott. (1978). *The road less traveled*. New York: Simon & Schuster.

Pervin, L. (1989). *Personality: Theory and research*. New York: Wiley.

Peterson, C. & Seligman, M. E. P. Causal explanations as a risk factor for depression. *Psychological Review, 91*.

Pittman, Frank. (1994, January–February). "A buyers guide to psychotherapy." *Psychology Today*.

Pittman, J. F., & Lloyd, S. A. (1988). Quality of family life, social support, and stress. *Journal of Marriage and the Family, 50*, 53–67.

Plutchnik, R. (1980). *Emotions: a psychoevolutionary hypothesis*. New York: Harper & Row.

Powell, John. (1969). *Why am I afraid to tell you who am?* Chicago: Argus Communications.

Prochaska, J. O. & Diclemente, C. C. (1995). Common problems: common solutions. *Clinical Psychology: Science and Practice, 2*, 101–105.

Rathus, A., Nevid, S., & Fichner-Rathus, L. (2000). *Human sexuality in a world of diversity*. Needham Heights, MA: Allyn & Bacon.

Robinson, T. L., & Howard-Hamilton, M. F. (2000). *The convergence of race, ethnicity, and gender.* Upper Saddle River, NJ: Prentice Hall.

Rogers, Carl. (1961). *On becoming a person.* Boston: Houghton Mifflin.

Rogers, C. and Freiberg, H. J. (1993). Freedom to learn. New York: Merrill.

Rosellini, G., & Worden, M. (1989). *Barriers to intimacy.* New York: Ballantine.

Rubin, L. B. (1985). *Just friends.* New York: Harper & Row.

Rubin, Z. (1973). *Liking and loving: An introduction to social psychology.* New York: Holt, Rinehart and Winston.

Sanders, Catherine. (1989). *Grief: The mourning after.* New York: Wiley.

Sandmaier, S. (1995, July/August). The gift of friendship. *Family Therapy Network.*

Santrock, J. W., Minnett, A. M., & Campbell, B. D. (1994). *The authoritative guide to self-help books.* New York: Guilford.

Santrock, John W. (1999). *Lifespan Human Development.* New York: McGraw-Hill.

Satir, Virginia. (1972). *Conjoint family therapy.* Palo Alto, CA: Science and Behavior Books.

Satir, Virginia. (1976). *Making contact.* Millbrae, CA: Celestial Art.

Satir, Virginia. (1986). *The new people making.* Palo Alto, CA: Science and Behavior Books.

Scarf, Maggie. (1987). *Intimate partners: Patterns in love and marriages.* New York: Random House.

Schachter, S., & Singer, J. (1962). Cognitive, social, and psychological determinants of emotional states. *Psychological Review, 60,* 379–399.

Schor, J. (1992). *The overworked American.* New York: Basic Books

Seligman, A. W., & Smith, T. W. (Eds.). (1994). *Anger, hostility, and the heart.* Mahwah, NJ: Erlbaum.

Seligman, M. E. P. (1975). *Helplessness: On depression, development, and death.* San Francisco: Freeman.

Seligman, M. E. P. (1991). *Optimism.* New York: Knopf.

Selye, Hans. (1974). *Stress without distress.* New York: J. B. Lippincott.

Sheehy, Gail. (1976). *Passages.* New York: Bantam.

Sheehy, Gail. (1995). *New passages.* New York: Random House.

Sheldon, W. H. (1954). *Atlas of man: A guide for somatotyping the adult male of all ages.* New York: Harper & Row.

Sidney, Simon. (1990). *Forgiveness: How to make peace with your past.* New York: Warner Books.

Siegman, A. W. & Smith, C. W. (Eds.). (1994). *Anger, hostility, and the heart.* Hillsdale, NJ: Erlbaum.

Siegler, R. S. (1989). Mechanisms of cognitive development. *Annual Review of Psychology, 40.*

Simons, J. A., Kalichman, S. & Santrock, J. W. (1997). *Human adjustment.* Dubuque, IA: Brown and Benchmark.

Simonton, O. C., Matthews-Simonton, S., & Creighton, J. L. (1978). *Getting well again.* New York: Bantam.

Smith, Manuel J. (1975). *When I say no I feel guilty.* New York: Bantam.

Singelis, T. M. (Ed.). (1998). *Teaching about culture, ethnicity, and diversity.* Thousand Oaks, CA: Sage.

Snarch, David. (1996). *Passionate marriage.* New York: Norton.

Sommers, Christina Hoff. (1994). *Who stole feminism?* New York: Simon & Schuster.

Spitz, R. A. (1945). Hospitalism: An inquiry into the genesis of psychiatric conditions in early childhood. *The psychoanalytic study of the child.* In A. Freud (Ed.), New York: International Universal.

Stacy, Judith. (1991). *Brave new families.* New York: Basic Books.

Sternberg, Robert J. (1986). A triangular theory of love. *Psychological Review, 93,* 119–135.

Stewart, John. (1990). *Bridges, not walls.* New York: McGraw-Hill.

Sue, D. W., & Sue, D. (1990). *Counseling the culturally different: Theory and practice.* New York: Wiley.

Sulloway, Frank. (1996). *Born to rebel.* New York: Pantheon.

Takaki, R. (1993). *A different mirror: A history of multicultural America.* Boston: Little & Brown.

Tannen, Deborah. (1990). *You just don't understand.* New York: Ballantine.

Tatelbaum, J. (1980). *The courage to grieve.* New York: Harper & Row.

Tavris, Carol. (1989). *Anger: The misunderstood emotion.* New York: Simon & Schuster.

Taylor, S. F. (1989). *Positive illusions: Creative self-deception and the healthy mind.* New York: Basic Books.

Temoshok, L., & Dresher, H. (1992). *Type C syndrome.* New York: Random House.

Travis, J. W., & Ryan, R. S. (1988). *Wellness workbook.* Berkeley, CA: Ten Speed Press.

Valliant, G. (2002). *Aging Well.* Little, Brown.

Viorst, Judith. (1986). *Necessary losses.* New York: Ballantine.

Viscott, David. (1983). *Risking.* New York: Pocket.

Visintainer, M. (1982). Tumor rejection in rats after inescapable or escapable shock. *Science, 216,* 437–439.

Wail, Mary Sykes. (1993, September/October). The shadow of doubt. *Family Therapy Networker,* pp. 18–30.

Waitley, Dennis. (1993). *The new dynamics of winning.* New York: Morrow.

Walker, V., & Brokaw, L. (1998). *Becoming aware.* Dubuque, IA: Kendall-Hunt.

Wallerstein, J. S., & S. Blakeslee. (1977). *Second chances: Men, women, and children a decade after divorce.* New York: Basic Books.

Walsh Slagle, Kate. (1982). *Living with loss.* Englewood Cliffs, NJ: Prentice Hall.

Wegner, Daniel. (1994). *White bears and other unwanted thoughts*. New York: Guilford.

Weiss, L. H. & Schwartz, J. C. (1996). *The relationship between parental type and older adolescents personality. Child Development, 67*.

Weiten, W., & Lloyd, M. (2006). *Psychology applied to modern life: Adjustment in the 21st century*. Belmont, CA: Thompson/Wadsworth.

Westheimer, R. K., & Lopater, S. (2002). *Human sexuality: A psychosocial perspective*. Philadelphia: Lippincott, Williams & Wilkins.

Westheimer, Ruth K. (1998). *Dr. Ruth talks to kids*. New York: Aladdin.

Whitfield, Charles L. (1988). *Healing the child within: Discovery and recovery for adult children of dysfunctional families*. New York: Ballantine.

Whitehead, B. (1994, October). The failure of sex education. *Atlantic Monthly*, pp. 55–58.

Wholey, Dennis. (1991). *Becoming your own parent*. New York: Doubleday.

Wlodkowski, J., & Ginsberg, M. (1995). *Diversity and motivation: Culturally responsive teaching*. San Francisco: Jossey-Bass.

Woititz, Janet G. (1983). *Adult children of alcoholics*. Deerfield Beach, FL: Health Communications.

Woititz, Janet G. (1985). *Struggle for intimacy*. Deerfield Beach, FL: Health Communications.

Worden, William J. (1991). *Grief counseling and grief therapy*. New York: Springer.

Ziglar, Zig. (1977). *See you at the top*. Gretna, LA: Pelican.

Zimbardo, P. G. (1987). *Shyness*. New York: Jove.

Zimbardo, P. G. (1990). *Shyness: What it is, what to do about it*. Reading, MA: Addison-Wesley.

Zweig, C., & Abrams, J. (1990). *Meeting the shadow*. New York: Tarcher.

The Healthy Eating Index. USDA Center For Nutrition Policy And Promotion.
http://warp.nal.usda.gov/fnic/HEI/hlthyeat.pdf
Assessed On December 13, 1999.

National medical spending attributable to overweight and obesity. How much, and who's paying?
http://content.healthaffairs.org/cgi/content/fullhlthaff.w3.219v1/DC1

World Health Organization. Obesity and Overweight. Geneva: WHO.
http://www.who.int/dietphysicalactivity/publications/facts/obesity/en/

Articles, discussions, and tools for coping with grief and the loss of a loved one.
www.aarp.org/griefandloss/

Articles On Grief And Loss
www.aarp.org/griefandloss/

American Obesity Association. Childhood Obesity. Available On The World Wide Web:
http://www.obesity.org/subs/childhood/prevalence.shtml

American Obesity Association. (2004). *Childhood obesity*.
http://www.obesity.org/subs/childhood/prevalence.shtml.

Abortion, 183, 184, 187
Abstinence-only sexuality education, 183, 184, 187
Acceptance, 15, 257
Accountability, 86–89
Acculturation, 10
Ackerman, Susan, 56
ACOA (Adult Children of Alcoholics), 117, 123
Acquaintance rape, 189–190
Action and results, 29–31
Action stage of change, 224
Active listening, 17, 167
Active-behavioral strategies, 213
Active-cognitive strategies, 213
Adler, Alfred, 101
Adolescence, 236, 237, 239, 241
Adrenaline, 141
Adult transitions, 244–246
Affirmations, 22, 158
African Americans. See Race and ethnicity
Age of Integrity, 240, 241
Age of Mastery, 240, 241
Aggressive behavior, 70, 71, 142
Aging, 237–238, 246–247
Aging Well (Vaillant), 238
Agreeableness, 73
Aguilar, Carlos, 9–10
AIDS (acquired immunodeficiency syndrome), 178–180, 183, 184, 202, 203, 256
  contracting, 204
  defined, 204
  incidence of, 205
  origins of, 204–205
  prevention of, 205–206
Alarm stage of stress, 227
Alcohol, 95, 118–124, 190, 253
All-or-nothing thinking, 43
Altman, Irwin, 45
Analytic/Precisive personality style (owls), 79, 81, 82
Andrews, Lewis, 282
Anger, 130, 131, 133, 138–146, 257
Angst, Jules, 101, 102
Anorexia nervosa, 216
Anxiety, 133, 139, 211, 225
Anxiety disorders, 216
Appollinaire, Guillaume, 61
Arousal, emotions and, 128
Arranged marriage, 171
Arrested development, 248
Artistic career-related personality type, 273
Assertiveness, 67–68, 228
  beliefs about, 68–69
  bill of rights of, 69
  defined, 70–71
  persistence and, 49
  personality and (see Personality)
  skills, 71–72
Assimilation, 10
Assisted suicide, 247
Associative feelings, 135–137, 226
Attachment styles, 158–159
Attention deficit disorder (ADD/ADHD), 216–217
Attention-seeking, 52, 54–55
Attentiveness, 15
Attitude, 85
Attractiveness, attraction and, 153
Attribution theory, 67
Authoritarian parents, 114–115

Authoritative parents, 114–115
Autonomy versus self-doubt developmental stage, 238
Avoidance strategies, 213
Avoidant attachment style, 159

Bach, Richard, 30
Bailey, Michael, 198, 200
Bambi-Godzilla type of relationship, 163–164
Bandura, Albert, 75
Bargaining, 257
Bass, Ellen, 191–192
Bates, John, 119
Bates, Marilyn, 82
Battered wife syndrome, 118
Baumrind, Diana, 114
Baur, K., 20–21
Bears, 78–83
Beattie, Melody, 123
Behavior, defined, 265
Being and Caring (Daniels and Horowitz), 31–32
Belief systems, 30, 87–89
Belongingness needs, 240
Berglas, Steve, 211
Bigger Hammer Theory, 5
Biological clock, 156
Biological perspective, 74, 76
Bipolar disorder, 216
Birth control, 179, 184, 185, 187, 202, 203, 205
Birth order, 101–108
Blame, 43
Blamers, 137
Blind self, 47, 48
Body language, 16, 18–19, 55, 166
Boles, R. N., 246–247
Born to Rebel (Sulloway), 101
Bowen, Murray, 99–100
Boylston, Karen, 132
Bradshaw, John, 108–109, 123
Brain, layers of, 128
Brandon, Nathaniel, 40–41
Brave New Families (Stacy), 98
Breadth of disclosure, 45–46
Brick-and-balloon combination, 154–156
Bridges, Bill, 248–249
Browne, H. Jackson, 38, 56, 245
Brunni, Frank, 193
Bucher, Richard, 12
Buck, Pearl, 250
Buel, Sarah, 118
Bulimia, 216
Burns, David, 44, 139
Burns, George, 98

Calcium, 253
Calories, 255
Cameron, Paul, 201
Campbell, D., 266
Cannon-Bard theory of emotions, 128
Captain-of-Your Ship Theory, 87
Career development, theories of, 271–273
Cascade AIDS Project, 178, 179
Catastrophic thinking, 226
Catch-22 (Heller), 6
Cause, dedication to, 268
Cerebral cortex, 128
Cervical cancer, 203

Change
  components of, 218–223
  fear of, 211–212
  model for, 223–224
Chapman, Gary, 158
Character development, 83–84
Chemical dependency, indicators of, 120–121
Chess, Stella, 108
Chief enabler role, 122
Child abuse, 36–37, 49, 53, 87, 98, 115, 120–122, 196
Childhood events, significant, 242–244
Chlamydia, 202
Choice and balance concept, 8, 137
Churchill, Sir Winston, 122
Civil unions, 170
Civility, lack of, 276
Classism, 13
Clichés, self-disclosure and, 46
Cline-Fay Institute, 112
Closing of the American Mind, The (Schlesinger), 10
Closure, 281, 283–284
Codependence, 27, 161–164
Cognitive psychology, 74, 75
Cognitive restructuring, 43–44, 143, 214–215
Collective unconscious, 49
Color Code, The (Hartman), 83
Comfort zones, expanding, 59–61
  assertiveness (see Assertiveness)
  attribution theory, 67
  fear of failure, 63–65
  fear of success, 61–63
  personality and (see Personality)
  thinking patterns, 65–66
Commitment, 27–28, 30, 157–158
Common sense approach, to emotions, 128
Communication (see also Emotions)
  barriers to, 15
  body language, 16, 18–19, 55, 166
  in functional families, 108
  gender and, 19–21
  listening, 16, 17, 85, 167, 260
  in marriage, 166–167, 172, 173
  methods to improve, 15, 19
  nonverbal, 16, 18–19, 55
  paralanguage, 16, 18
  process of, 15–16
  reasons for, 14–15
  responses to, 15–16
  self-talk, 20–23, 25, 41, 43, 44, 214–215
  shyness and, 23, 25
  space and distance and, 19
  touch and, 19, 55–57
Companionate love, 157
Compatibility, 155
Competencies, 75
Competition versus cooperation, 73
Competitive society, 23
Complementary needs theory, 154
Conclusions, jumping to, 43
Condom use, 184, 187, 203
Conflict management, 70, 228–231
Congruence, 38
Conscientiousness, 73
Consciousness raising groups, 11
Constructive guilt, 144
Consultant parents, 113

Contemplation stage of change, 224
Contraception, 179, 184, 185, 187, 202, 203, 205
Controlling/Directive personality style (bears), 78–83
Conventional career-related personality type, 273
Coolidge, Calvin, 31
Coontz, Stephanie, 95–97
Coping skills, 210–235
  components of change, 218–223
  conflict management, 228–231
  defined, 213
  model for change, 223–224
  professional help and, 231–233
  psychological disorders and, 216–218
  self-defeating behavior and, 210–213
  strategies, 213–216
  stress management and, 224–228
Cose, Ellis, 9
Costa, Paul, 73
Countershock, 227
Courage to Heal, The (Bass and Davis), 191–192
Courtois, Christine A., 195
Covey, Stephen R., 84–85
Creativity, 268, 279
Crewe, Onetin, 103
Critical thinking skills, guidelines for, 29
Criticism, 15, 133, 134, 166
Crooks, R., 20–21
Crying, 147
"Cultural Diversity: Towards a Whole Society" (Hurwitt), 12
Culture
  families and, 98–99
  personality and, 73–74
  sexual orientation and, 200
Curran, Dolores, 109
Currier, Cecile, 109–111
Curtis, Rebecca C., 211
Czikszentmihalyi, Mihaly, 279

Dairy products, 252, 253
Damon, William, 40
Dance of Intimacy, The (Lerner), 160
Darling, Nancy, 115
Date rape, 189–190
Davis, Laura, 191–192
DeAngelis, Barbara, 169
Death and dying, 246, 256–261, 264, 279–280
Decision making, 268–270
Decoding messages, 15
Defense mechanisms, 139–140
Deffenbacher, Jerry, 142
Democratic parents, 114
Denial, 257
Depression, 133, 139, 142, 210, 216, 251–252, 257
Depth of disclosure, 45–46
D.E.S.C. model of conflict resolution, 70
Desire, 30
Despair, as emotional reaction, 158
Destructive guilt, 144
Detachment, as emotional reaction, 158
Developmental theory of career choice, 271–272
Devil's advocate, 7–8

Diclemente, Carlo, 223
Diet and nutrition, 251–253, 255
Different Mirror, A: A History of Multicultural America (Takaki), 10
Diffusion, 239
Disclosing, 16, 17, 45–48
Discrimination, 13, 14
Disenchantment, 249
Disengagement, 249
Disidentification, 249
Disorientation, 249
Displacement, 139
Dissociative feelings, 135–137, 226
Distance and space, categories of, 19
Diversity, 8–10, 171
  acknowledging and overcoming barriers, 13–14
  consciousness, 12–13
  dimensions of, 11
  skills, 13
Diversity Consciousness (Bucher), 12
Divorce, 95, 97, 109, 166, 171–172, 245, 249
Dolphins, 78, 79, 81, 82
Domestic violence, 115, 117–119, 162
Dominant culture, 10
Donne, John, 14
Don't Count Your Chickens approach, 148–149
Double bind, 6, 54
Double standards, 4–5, 27
Drill sergeant parents, 113
Drug abuse, 95, 118–121
Dyads, communication and, 14
Dying, 246, 256–261, 264, 279–280
Dysfunctional families, 115, 117–124

Eating disorders, 216
Ectomorph, 76
Ego, 74
Ehrhardt, Anke, 183
Elephant-in-the-Bottle Technique, 86
Eliot, T. S., 249
Ellis, Albert, 140, 143–144
Emerson, Ralph Waldo, 18, 283
Emotion-focused coping, 213
Emotional Intelligence (Goleman), 132
Emotional cut-offs, 100
Emotional reasoning, 43
Emotional self, 37
Emotions, 127–151
  anger, 130, 131, 133, 138–146, 257
  Cannon-Bard theory of, 128
  classification of, 130
  components of, 129
  in context, 130
  controlling, 131–132, 134–137
  defense mechanisms, 139–140
  emotional intelligence, 132–134
  excitement and joy, 148–149
  family beliefs and, 130
  getting in and out of, 131
  guilt, 139, 144–146, 260
  James-Lange theory of, 128
  limiting, 130–131
  overcontrol of, 128
  range of, 131
  repressed, 130
  sadness, 130, 131, 146–148
  thought distortion, 138–139
  types of, 129–130
  undercontrol of, 128
  understanding, 127–130
Empathy, 85, 133, 137
Encoding messages, 15
Encoding strategies, 75
Endomorph, 76
Endorphins, 252
Enterprising career-related personality type, 273
Entropy, law of, 22
EQ (emotional quotient), 132
Equal Employment Opportunity Commission (EEOC), 188
Erikson, Eric, 238–239, 244, 246
Ernst, Cecile, 101, 102
Esteem needs, 240
Ethnic groups. *See* Race and ethnicity

Ethnicity, defined, 11
Ethnocentrism, 13
Excitement and joy, 148–149
Exercise, 251–252
Exhaustion stage of stress, 227
Expectancies, 75
Expressive behaviors, 129
External attributions, 67
External locus of control, 44–45
Extraversion, 73
Extroversion versus introversion, 77
Eye contact, 16, 18–19, 21

Facial expression, 16, 18
Facts, self-disclosure and, 46
Failure, fear of, 63–65, 211
Falbo, Toni, 101
False memory debate, 194–196
Familiarity, attraction and, 153
Family influences, 94–126
  birth order, 101–108
  dysfunctional families, 115, 117–124
  family history, 95–96, 264
  family of origin, 99–101
  family structures, 96–97
  functional families, 108–109
  on marriage, 157
  parenting, 111–115
  race and culture and, 98–99
  stepfamilies, 97, 98, 109–111, 116
Family protection process, 100
Family Service America, 98
Fast, Julius, 18
Faulkner, Nancy, 193
Fear, 130
  of change, 211–212
  of dying, 246
  of failure, 63–65, 211
  of looking foolish, 4
  overcoming, 24, 25–26
  of success, 61–63
Feel the Fear and Do It Anyway (Jeffers), 24, 65
Feelers, 137
Feeling Good Handbook, The (Burns), 139
Feelings. *See also* Emotions
  self-disclosure and, 46
  shyness and, 25
Feminine Mystique, The (Friedan), 11
Femininity, 11
Feminism, 11
Fertility rate, 98
Fight-or-flight response, 22
Filters, 43
  concept of, 15
  personality and, 72
Firpo, Ignatius Joseph, 45
First Adulthood, 240, 241
First-day morgue syndrome, 3–4
Fish, in diet, 252
Flexible thinking, 13
Flooding, 166
Ford, Henry, 10
Forgiveness, 279–280, 282
Forgiveness: How to Make Peace with Your Past and Get On with Your Life (Simon and Simon), 280
Four Horsemen concepts, 166
Frankl, Victor, 267
Franklin, Benjamin, 15
Franzoi, Stephen, 153, 154
Free will, 83, 239
Freedom to Learn for the 80s (Rogers), 31
Freud, Sigmund, 18, 39, 74, 101, 274
Friedan, Betty, 11
Friendship-warmth touch, 55
Friendships, 174–175
Fromm, Eric, 270
Fruits, in diet, 252
Functional families, 108–109
Functional-professional touch, 55
Fundamental attribution theory error, 67
Furstenberg, Frank, 171

Gaddy, Levone, 9
Gay households, 98
Gay marriage, 170–171, 183

Gender
  communication and, 19–21
  defined, 11
  identity, 199
  roles, 11, 106
General adaptation syndrome (GAS), 227
Generalizations, 15
Generalized anxiety disorder, 216
Generativity versus stagnation developmental stage, 239
Genetics
  personality and, 76
  psychological disorders and, 216, 217
  sexual orientation and, 198, 200
Genital herpes, 202
Genital warts, 201–202
Gestalt therapy, 16
Gestures, 16, 18, 19
Getting attention, 52, 54–55
Getting the Love You Want (Hendrix), 173
Getting to Yes (Fisher and Ury), 230
Gibran, Kahlil, 166
Gifts, 158
Gifts Differing (Myers-Briggs), 77
Ginzberg's developmental theory, 271
Glass ceiling, 62
Global labeling, 43
Go for the Gusto approach, 148–149
Goals
  change and, 218–219
  evaluating, 29
  learning, 31–32
  life, 266–267
  reasonable, 215
  setting effective, 28–29
Goethe, Johann Wolfgang von, 213
Goleman, Daniel, 132
Goodman, Gerald, 17
Goodman, Steve, 65
Gottlieb, David, 173–174
Gottman, John, 166–168
Gray, John, 19, 172
Grief, 256–261
Grief Counseling and Grief Therapy: A Handbook for the Mental Health Practitioner (Worden), 257–258
Groth, Nicholas, 201
Group think, 228
Groups, communication and, 14
Guilt, 139, 144–146, 260

Hall, Edward, 19
Hamlet (Shakespeare), 22
Happiness, understanding, 277, 279
Harlow's experiments, 158
Harter, Susan, 40
Hartman, Taylor, 73, 83
Harvard School of Public Health Nutrition Source, 252, 253
Harvard Study of Adult Development, 238
Harvard University, 23
Havel, Václav, 237
Healing the Child Within (Whitfield), 24
Health and wellness, 250–252
Healthy Eating Pyramid, 252–253
Healthy voice, 44
Heller, Joseph, 6
Helplessness, learned, 212–213
Hendrix, Harville, 173
Hermaphrodites, 199
Herpes simplex virus (HSV), 202
Hesler, Richard, 55
Heterosexuality, 197–198
Hidden agenda, 15
Hidden self, 47, 48
Hierarchy of needs, 52, 239–240
High-anxiety avoidance, 211
Hill, Anita, 188
Hippocrates, 76
HIV (human immunodeficiency virus), 178–179, 184, 187, 202, 204
Holland, John, 271, 272–273
Holmes, Oliver Wendell, 4

Homicide rate, 95
Homophobia, 196–197, 243
Homosexuality, 98, 170–171, 183, 196–198, 200–201
Honesty, 264
Hopper, Jim, 195
How to Raise Your Self-Esteem (Brandon), 41
Howitzer Mantras, 44
HPV (human papilloma virus), 202
Hugo, Victor, 267
Human behavior, basic principles of, 3–8
  choice and balance concept, 8, 137
  double standards, 4–5
  fear of looking foolish, 4
  first-day morgue syndrome, 3–4
  ninety-percent rule, 7
  paradox, 5–6
  playing devil's advocate, 7–8
  positive double bind, 6
  risk taking, 6
  self-observation, 6–7
Human development, 237–239
Human potential movement, 75–76
Humanistic perspective, 74, 75–76, 239
Humor, sense of, 215
Hurwitt, Mara, 12
Hypertension, 142
Hypothalamus, 128, 198

"I" statements, 16, 71–72, 231
Id, 74
Ideal self, 38
Identity achievement, 239
Identity foreclosure, 239
Identity moratorium, 239
Identity states, 239
Identity versus role confusion developmental stage, 239
Illusions (Bach), 30
Imagery, 20–21, 143
In vitro fertilization, 179
Incest, 190, 191
Incongruence, 76
Indulgent (permissive) parents, 114–115
Industry versus inferiority developmental stage, 239
Infant mortality rate, 256
Inflection, of speech, 18
Ingham, Harry, 47
Initiative versus guilt developmental stage, 239
Inner child, 122–124
Inner critic, 43, 44
Intake, 232
Integration, 10
Integrity versus despair developmental stage, 239
Intellectualization, 139–140
Intention, 29–31
  positive, 221–223
Internal attributions, 67
Internal dialogue, 128, 138
Internal locus of control, 44–45
Internal noise, 15
Interrupting, 15, 19
Intersexed people, 199
Intimacy, 157–160, 179
Intimacy versus isolation developmental stage, 239
Intimate distance, 19
Intimate Partners: Patterns in Love and Marriages (Scarf), 164
Investigative career-related personality type, 272
IQ (intelligence quotient), 132–133
Irrational beliefs, 140

James-Lange theory of emotions, 128
Jampolsky, Gerald, 4, 281
Jeffers, Susan, 24, 65
Jefferson, Thomas, 85
Job satisfaction, 253, 273–274
Johari Window model, 47–49
Joker mask, 53
Judgment versus perception, 77
Jung, C. G., 49, 77, 117

Just Friends: The Role of Friendship in Our Lives (Rubin), 174

Kafoury, Ann, 165
Keirsey, David, 82
Kempis, Thomas á 230
Kennedy, Joseph, 275
Kinesics, 18
Kinsey, Alfred, 197
Kitchen sink fighting, 229
Know-It-All mask, 53
Kolb, D. A., 76
Kübler-Ross, Elisabeth, 256, 257, 279–280
Kurtus, Ron, 224

Labor, division of, 11
LaForge, Ralph, 228
Laing, R. D., 54
Leaf-in-the-Wind Theory, 87
Learned helplessness, 212–213
Learning, personal, 31–32
Learning goals, 31–32
Learning theory, 74–75
Learning to Step Together (Currier), 109–111
Leaving home, 244
Lee, John, 146
Leisure time, 253–254, 274–276
Lerner, Harriet, 160
Levay, Simon, 198
Lewis, Rick, 160
Life 101 (McWilliams and McWilliams), 22
Life changes, 236–263
  adolescence, 236, 237, 239, 241
  adult transitions, 244–246
  death and dying, 256–261
  health and wellness, 250–252
  hierarchy of needs, 52, 239–240
  human development, 237–239
  identity states, 239
  life passages, 241–247
  life span development, 236–241
  obesity, 251, 254–256
  old age, 237–238, 246–247
  significant childhood events, 242–244
  transitional times, 248–250
Life expectancy, 98, 236–238, 240, 251
Life goals, 266–267
Life passages, 241–247
Life principles, positive, 83, 84
Life satisfaction, 276–279
Life span development, 236–241
Limited perceptions, 13
Limiting beliefs, 30, 211–212
Listening, 16, 17, 85, 167, 260
Lloyd, Sally, 165
Locus of control, 44
Loftus, Elizabeth, 195
Logotherapy, 267
Loneliness, 23
Longevity, 236–238, 240, 251
Lookin' Good mask, 53
Looks-for-status exchange, 154
Lost child role, 122
Love, 153, 281. *See also* Sexuality
  expressions of, 158
  types of, 157–158
Love-intimacy touch, 55
Love Is Letting Go of Fear (Jampolsky), 24
Love languages, 158
Luft, Joseph, 47, 48
Lyman, Lawrence, 101

Magnification, 43
Maintenance stage of change, 224
Major depressive disorder, 216
Maltz, Wendy, 191, 193
Man's Search for Meaning (Frankl), 267
Marcia, James, 239
Marginality, 10
Marital rape laws, 119
Marriage
  age and, 95, 156–157, 182
  arranged, 171
  counseling, 173, 245
  gay, 170–171, 183

lifelong, 171–173
  myths, 164–166
  and society, 156–157
  success or failure of, 166–168
Mascot or detractor role, 122
Masculinity, 11
Masks, 51–53
Maslow, Abraham, 52, 239–240
Mass Mutual American Family Values Study, 97
Masturbation, 183
Maugham, Somerset, 22
Mayer, John, 132
McCrea, Robert, 73
McMartin Day Care Center case, 180
McWilliams, John-Rodger, 22
McWilliams, Peter, 22
Mead, Margaret, 172
Meaning
  purpose and, 267
  pursuit of, 267–268
Meeting the Shadow (Zweig and Abrams), 49
Melting pot theory, 10, 42
Melton, James, 24
Memory, emotions and, 134–135
Men Are From Mars, Women Are From Venus (Gray), 19, 172
Menarche, 180
Menopause, 241
Mental self, 37
Mesomorph, 76
Mexican Americans. *See* Race and ethnicity
Middle age, 236, 237, 239, 244–245
Minimization, 43
Mirroring, 17
Mischel, Walter, 75
Mitchell, Jann, 17, 24, 50–51, 53, 116, 119, 146, 164, 169, 264, 282
Mood disorders, 216
Mood management, 133
Motivation, 133, 219–220, 225
  work and, 271
Moving, 243–244
Ms. or Mr. Efficiency mask, 53
Ms. or Mr. Superior mask, 53
Multiculturalism, 10
Multigenerational transmission process, 100
Myers, David G., 277
Myers-Briggs, Isabel, 77
Myers-Briggs Type Indicator (MBTI), 76–78

Narcissism, 42
Native Americans. *See* Race and ethnicity
Natural History of the Senses, A (Ackerman), 56
Nature/nurture debate, 11, 76
Necessary Losses (Viorst), 241, 243
Needlman, Robert, 108
Needs, hierarchy of, 52, 239–240
Negative attention, 54, 55
Negative thinking, 22, 30, 43, 44
Negotiating skills, 230
Nelson, Portia, 193
Networking, 13
Neuroticism, 73
Neutral zone, 248, 249
New beginnings, 250
New Dynamics of Winning, The (Waitley), 20
New Passages (Sheehy), 237, 240
New Year's resolutions, 27, 28
Niebuhr, Reinhold, 238
Nietzsche, Friedrich, 267
Ninety-percent rule, 7
Nondirective parents, 114
Nonverbal communication, 16, 18–19, 55
Noradrenaline, 141
Nuclear family emotional system, 100
Nuts and legumes, in diet, 252

Obesity, 251, 254–256
Objections, to change, 220
Objectives, clarity of, 30

Observational learning, 75
Obsessive-compulsive disorder (OCD), 216
Old age, 237–238, 246–247
On Death and Dying (Kübler-Ross), 256
Open self, 47, 48
Open-ended questions, 16
Openness to experience, 73
Opinions, self-disclosure and, 46
Optimism, 277–279
Orenstein, Peggy, 182
Organization, first principle of, 85
Our Sexuality (Crooks and Baur), 20–21
Overcompensation, 140
Overfunctioning, 164
Overgeneralization, 43
Overreacting, 15
Owls, 78, 79, 81, 82
Ozawa, Takao, 9

Panic disorder, 216
Paradigms, 84
Paradox, 5–6, 62, 168
Paralanguage, 16, 18
Parent-child interactions
  assertiveness and, 69
  self-concept and, 39
Parenting, 111
  birth order and, 107
  effective, 113
  ethnic groups and, 115
  ineffective, 112–113
  influences on sexuality, 181
  responsiveness and demandingness, 114
  styles, 114–115
Parenting with Love and Logic (Cline and Fay), 112
Parting Is Not Goodbye (Osmont), 260
Partner selection, 154
Passages (Sheehy), 237, 240
Passionate love, 157, 158
Passionate Marriage (Snarch), 168
Passive (nonassertive) behavior, 70–71
Passive self-defeat, 211
Passive-aggressive behavior, 142
Pauses, communication and, 17
Peale, Norman Vincent, 30
Peck, M. Scott, 30, 213, 276–277
Peer influences, 62
  marriage and, 157
  sexuality and, 180–184
Pelvic inflammatory disease (PID), 203
Perceptions, limited, 13
Perfectionism, 42–43
Persistence, assertiveness and, 49
Personal control, happiness and, 277
Personal distance, 19
Personal learning, 31–32
Personality, 72–89
  biological perspective, 74, 76
  birth order and, 108
  character development and, 83–84
  cultural studies and, 73–74
  defined, 72
  elements of, 72–73
  genetics and, 76
  humanistic perspective, 74, 75–76
  principle-centered lives and, 84–85
  psychodynamic perspective, 74
  self-assessment of, 78–82
  social-cognitive perspective, 74–75
  theories, 74–76
  trait theories, 73
  types, 76–85
Personality type theory of career choice, 271, 272–273
Perspective, assertiveness and, 72
Phobic disorder, 216
Physical contact, 55–57
Physical reactions, shyness and, 25
Physical self, 38
Physiological changes, 129
Physiological needs, 240

Pittman, Frank, III, 232
Plant oils, in diet, 252
Plaut, Thomas, 231
Playing devil's advocate, 7–8
Please Understand Me: Character and Temperament (Keirsey and Bates), 82
Pleasure principle, 74
Pluralism, 10
Plutchik, Robert, 129
Poor Little Me mask, 53
Population growth, 9, 97
Pornography, 183, 190
Positional bargaining, 230
Positive double bind, 6
Positive intention, 221–223
Positive living, 264–286
  closure, 281, 283–284
  decision making, 268–270
  forgiveness and love, 279–282
  guide for constructive living, 283
  life satisfaction, 276–279
  values and meaning, 265–268
  work and leisure, 270–276
Positives, discounting, 43
Poultry, in diet, 252
Powell, John, 27
Power differential, 163–164
Power victims, 54–55
Prather, Hugh, 277
Pre-contemplation stage of change, 223–224
Prejudice, 13
Premature infants, touch and, 56
Preoccupation with self, 23
Preparation stage of change, 224
Principle-centered lives, 84–85
Private self, 38
Proactive choices, 85
Problem solving, 214
Problem-focused coping, 213
Prochaska, James, 223
Procrastination, 43
Professional help, 231–233
Projection, 139
Promoting/Emotive personality style (squirrels), 78–80, 82
Pros and cons model for decision making, 270
Protest, as emotional reaction, 158
Provisional Adulthood, 240, 241
Proximity, attraction and, 153, 154
Psychobabble, 161
Psychodynamic perspective, 74
Psychological disorders, 216–218
Psychological types, 76–85
Puberty, 236
Public distance, 19
Public self, 38
Public speaking, 14
Purpose, meaning and, 267

Quality time, 158
Questioning, 17

Race and ethnicity, 8–10
  defined, 11
  families and, 98–99
  parenting and, 115
  self-esteem and, 42
Racism, 13
Randall, Teri, 118
Rape, 189–190, 194
Rapport talk, 19, 21
Rational-emotive therapy (RET), 143–144
Rationalization, 139
Raveling, George, 264
Reaction formation, 139
Realistic career-related personality type, 272
Reality testing, 211
Reciprocity, attraction and, 153
Reflective coping, 142
Regression, 139
Relationship Enhancement (RE), 173
Relationships, 152–177
  attachment styles, 158–159
  Bambi-Godzilla type of, 163–164
  brick-and-balloon combination, 154–156

Relationships (*continued*)
  codependent, 161–164
  friendships, 174–175
  gay marriage, 170–171
  intimacy, 157–160
  lifelong marriage, 171–173
  marriage myths, 164–166
  partner selection, 154
  success or failure of, 166–168
  theories of attraction, 153–157
  types of love, 157–158
Relaxation, 143, 214, 254
Religion, 267–268
Remarriage, 97, 98, 109–111, 116, 171
Repair attempts, 166–168
Report talk, 19
Repressed emotions, 130
Repressed memory/recovered
    memory debate, 194–196
Repression, 139
Rescripting, 85
Resistance stage of stress, 227
Resistant/ambivalent attachment
    style, 159
Resources, change and, 219
Responsibility, 86
Restraining orders, 119
Retirement, 246, 254
Rhythm, of speech, 18
Risk taking, 6, 60, 61, 64, 65, 212
Risky behaviors, 28
Rogers, Carl, 31, 38, 75–76
Rogers, Will, 30
Rohypnol, 190
Role models, 83, 215
Roosevelt, Eleanor, 25, 212
Rouce, Charles, 39
Rouche, John, 212
Rowley, Scott, 171
RU486, 183
Rubin, Lillian, 174
Russell, Bertrand, 26

Sadness, 130, 131, 146–148
Safety needs, 240
Saints and Sinners routine, 161
Salad bowl analogy, 10, 42
Salovey, Peter, 132
Same-sex harassment, 188
Same-sex marriage, 170–171, 183
Sandburg, Carl, 147
Sandwich generation, 245
Santayana, George, 282
Santrock, John, 272
Sarcasm, 15
Satir, Virginia, 41, 76, 108
Scapegoat role, 122
Scarf, Maggie, 164
Schacter, Stanley, 128
Scheduling, 85
Scheflin, Alan W., 196
Schizophrenic disorders, 216
Schlesinger, Arthur, Jr., 10
Schwartz, David, 70
Scotty Dog Tag, 160
Second Adulthood, 240, 241
*Second Chances: Men, Women, and
    Children a Decade After Divorce*
    (Wallerstein), 171
Secure attachment style, 159
Selective memory, 135
Selective perception, 13
Self
  differentiation of, 100, 168
  dimensions of, 38
Self-acceptance, 41
Self-actualization, 74, 240, 268, 271
Self-assertiveness, 41
Self-assessment, 272
Self-attributions, 67
Self-awareness, 36–58, 133
  getting attention and, 52, 54–55
  Johari Window model and, 47–48
  locus of control and, 44
  masks and, 51–53
  self-concept (*see* Self-concept)
  self-disclosure and, 45–48
  self-esteem (*see* Self-esteem)
  shadow self and, 48–50

touch and, 55–57
Self-care, 250
Self-concept
  aspects of, 37–38
  definition of, 37
  human potential movement and,
    75–76
  importance of, 38–40
  sources of, 39–40
Self-concept theory of career choice,
    271, 272
Self-consciousness, 23
Self-deceit, levels of, 27–28
Self-defeat, passive, 211
Self-defeating-behavior, 39,
    210–213, 220–221
Self-discipline, 30, 32
Self-disclosure, 16, 17, 45–48
Self-efficacy, 75
  development of, 215–216
Self-esteem
  assessment of, 40
  building, 25, 28, 41
  definition of, 37
  happiness and, 277
  high, 41–42
  improving, 40–44
  negative comments and, 23
  race and culture and, 42
  relationships and, 160
  risk taking and, 212–213
Self-fulfilling prophecies, 39, 45,
    214
Self-handicapping, 211
Self-observation, 6–7
Self-perception, 214
Self-regulatory systems, 75
Self-relaxation, 214
Self-talk, 20–23, 25, 41, 43, 44, 71,
    214–215
Seligman, Martin, 212, 278, 279
Selye, Hans, 227
Sensing versus intuition, 77
Service to others, 268
*Seven Habits of Highly Effective People,
    The* (Covey), 84–85
*Seven Principles for Making Marriage
    Work, The* (Gottman), 167–168
Sex education, 179–181, 183–188
Sexism, 11, 13, 62
Sexpot mask, 53
Sexual abuse, 118, 120, 178, 180,
    183, 190–196, 201
Sexual arousal, 55
Sexual harassment, 188–189
Sexual orientation, 183, 184, 187,
    196–198, 200–201
Sexuality, 178–208
  beliefs and values and, 180–181
  date rape, 189–190
  early sexual activity, 182–183,
    185–186, 188
  Freud on, 74
  high school culture and, 181–183
  homosexuality, 98, 170–171, 183,
    196–198, 200–201
  parental influences on, 181
  perspectives on, 179–181
  sex education, 179–181, 183–188
  sexual abuse, 178, 180, 183,
    190–196
  sexual harassment, 188–189
Sexually transmissible infections
    (STIs), 179, 183–185, 187,
    201–206. *See also* AIDS
  contraception and, 202, 203
  incidence of, 202
  information about, 202–203
  terminology, 201
Shadow self, 48–50
Shadow work, 49
Shakespeare, William, 22, 265
Shaw, George Bernard, 6
Sheehy, Gail, 237, 240–241
Sheldon, William, 76
Shilts, Randy, 198
Shrinking of America, The
    (Zilbergeld), 38
Shyness

components of, 25
consequences and causes of, 23
dealing with, 25
Sibling relationships, 100–101
  birth order and, 101–108
Silence, communication and, 17
Simon, Sidney, 280
Simon, Suzanne, 280
Single-parent households, 97, 98
Six Pillars of Self-Esteem, The
    (Brandon), 40
Skill development, 30
Skinner, B. F., 75
Skolnick, Arlene, 97
Snarch, David, 167, 168
Sociability, happiness and, 277
Social career-related personality
    type, 273
Social-cognitive perspective, 74–75
Social comparison, 39–40, 153
Social distance, 19
Social exchange, 153
Social learning theory, 75
Social penetration, 45–46
Social Psychology (Franzoi), 153
Social self, 37
Social skills, 133
Social-polite touch, 55
Socrates, 37, 73, 154
Somatotype theory, 76
Sommers, Christina Hoff, 117
Space and distance, categories of, 19
Spanking, 119, 141
Speed, of speech, 18
Spielberger, Charles, 141
Spiritual self, 38
Spocks, 137
Sponges, 137
Spouse abuse, 115, 117–119, 162,
    196
Squirrels, 78–80, 82
Stacy, Judith, 98
Standards, defined, 265
STDs. *See* Sexually transmissible
    infections (STIs)
Stepfamilies, 97, 98, 109–111, 116
Stereotypes, 13, 15
Sternberg's Triangle, 157, 158
Stimulus event, 21–22
Stone, Kathleen, 24
Stop at the Top concept, 225, 226
Stress management, 138, 224–228
Subjective cognitive states, 129
Success, fear of, 61–63
Suicide, 55
  assisted, 247
Sulloway, Frank, 101
Super, Donald, 271, 272
Super stud mask, 53
Superego, 74
Superhero role, 122
Superiority, sense of, 42
Superstitions, 44
Support systems, 214
Supportive/Responsive personality
    style (dolphins), 78, 79, 81, 82
Surrogate mothers, 179
Survival needs, 271
Synergy, 85

Takaki, Ronald, 10
Tannen, Deborah, 19–21
Tavris, Carol, 142
Taylor, Dalmas, 45
Teach Only Love (Jampolsky), 4, 281
Teenage pregnancy rate, 179, 183,
    187
Ten Days to Self-Esteem (Burns), 44
Termination stage of change, 224
Thalamus, 128
Therapy, 231–233
Thinking patterns, expanding
    comfort zones on, 65–66
Thinking versus feeling, 77
Third force, in psychology, 75, 239
Thomas, Alexander, 108
Thomas, Clarence, 188
Thomas, Dylan, 257
Thomas, Sandra, 140

Thought distortion, 43, 138–139
Thought-stopping, 44, 215
Three Boxes of Life, The (Boles),
    246–247
To Thine Own Self Be True (Andrews),
    282
Touch, 19, 55–57, 158
Toxic shame, 123
Traditionality, 10
Trait theories, 73
Transactional analysis, 74
Transgendered (TG) person, 199
Transitional times, 248–250
Transsexuals, 199
Transvestites, 199
Traumatic events, 87–89
Triangles, 100
Trust versus mistrust developmental
    stage, 238
Twain, Mark, 26, 247
Twin studies, 76
Two-career households, 97
Two-for-One Principle, 148
Two Spirited, 199
Type A personality, 227
Type B personality, 227–228
Type C personality, 228

Unassertiveness, 23
Unconscious, 74
Underfunctioning, 164
Uninvolved parents, 114–115
Unknown self, 47–49

Vaillant, George E., 238
Values
  clarification of, 265–266
  decision making and, 268–269
  defined, 265
Vegetables, in diet, 252
Veniga, Robert L., 232
Verbal communication, 14–16
Victim role, 86–87
Viorst, Judith, 101, 241, 243
Viscott, David, 147
Vitamins, 253
Volume, of speech, 18

Waitley, Dennis, 20, 21
Walker, Anne-Sophie, 282
Wallerstein, Judith, 171, 172
Way We Never Were, The (Coontz),
    95–97
Wedding bell blues, 245
Wegner, Daniel, 22
Wellness Workbook (Travis and
    Ryan), 251
Westermeyer, Robert, 224
*White Bears and Other Unwanted
    Thoughts* (Wegner), 22
Whitfield, Charles, 24
Whitman, Walt, 24
Who Stole Feminism? (Sommers), 117
Whole grain foods, 252
Why Marriages Succeed or Fail
    (Gottman), 166
Win-win attitude, 85
Woititz, Janet, 123
Woods, D. Juanita, 26, 50, 88, 138,
    162
Woods, Tiger, 9
Worden, William, 257–258
Work ethic, 271, 276
Work-leisure balance, 253–254
Work satisfaction, 253, 273–274
Workaholics, 254
Working conditions, 270–271
World Health Organization (WHO),
    254

Yale University, 23
Yerkes-Dodson law, 225
You Just Don't Understand (Tannen),
    19–21
Your Right to Fly (Melton), 24

Ziglar, Zig, 172–173
Zilbergeld, Bernie, 38
Zimbardo, Phillip, 23